Philippines

Jens Peters

Philippines

6th edition

Published by
Lonely Planet Publications
Head Office: PO Box 617, Hawthorn, Vic 3122, Australia
Branches: 150 Linden St, Oakland, CA 94607, USA
               10 Barley Mow Passage, Chiswick, London W4 4PH, UK
               71 bis rue du Cardinal Lemoine, 75005 Paris, France

Printed by
SNP Printing Pte Ltd., Singapore

Photographs by
Chris Miles (CM)   Paul Steel (PS)
Krzysztof Dydynski (KD)   Richard I'Anson (RI)
John Pennock (JPk)   Tony Wheeler (TW)
Jens Peters (JP)

Front cover: Islands of the Bacuit Archipelago off El Nido, Palawan (Jens Peters)

Illustrations by
Boy Diego Jr
David Andrew

First Published
February 1981

This Edition
June 1997

Although the authors and publisher have tried to make the information as accurate as possible, they accept no responsibility for any loss, injury or inconvenience sustained by any person using this book.

National Library of Australia Cataloguing in Publication Data

Peters, Jens 1949-
Philippines.

6th ed.
Includes index.
ISBN 0 86442 466 3

1. Philippines – Guidebooks. I. Title. (Series: Lonely Planet travel survival kit).

915.990448

text © Jens Peters 1997
maps © Lonely Planet 1997
photos © photographers as indicated 1997

Jens Peters

Jens, born in 1949 in Germany, studied advertising, communications and arts education in Berlin. Since 1970 he has travelled for several months each year in countries outside Europe. So far he has visited the Philippines (his favourite country in South-East Asia) more than 50 times and spent over eight years there. In 1977 he began travel writing and has since worked as a freelance journalist for various travel magazines and self-published several guidebooks about tropical countries.

From the Publisher

This book was edited at the Lonely Planet office in Australia by Mic Looby, Kristin Odijk and Peter Turner. Paul Piaia was responsible for design and layout, with additional maps by Sandra Smythe, Jenny Jones and Sally Gerdan. Thanks to Simon Bracken and Adam McCrow for front and back cover design. Many thanks also to Boy Diego Jr and David Andrew for the great illustrations, and Colin Hall for translating.

Warning & Request

Things change – prices go up, schedules change, good places go bad and bad places go bankrupt – nothing stays the same. So, if you find things better or worse, recently opened or long since closed, please tell us and help make the next edition even more accurate and useful.

We value all of the feedback we receive from travellers. Julie Young coordinates a small team who read and acknowledge every letter, postcard and email, and ensure that every morsel of information finds its way to the appropriate authors, editors and publishers.

Everyone who writes to us will find their name in the next edition of the appropriate guide and will also receive a free subscription to our quarterly newsletter, *Planet Talk*. The very best contributions will be rewarded with a free Lonely Planet guide.

Excerpts from your correspondence may appear in updates (which we add to the end pages of reprints); new editions of this guide; in *Planet Talk*; or in the Postcards section of

our internet Web site – so please let us know if you don't want your letter published or your name acknowledged.

Thanks

In addition to the many German-speaking travellers who contributed to the new German edition of Jens Peters' guide, we'd like to thank everyone who took the time to write in with their helpful hints, useful advice and interesting anecdotes for this guide and *South-East Asia on a shoestring*. So, to the following people we say a big *salámat*:

Dr B Abtmaier, Lolita Adaro, Bob Allen, Mark & Maria Anderson, S Andrea, Michael & Erlinda Astle, Toby Atkinson, Brenton Ian Bart, JD Bate, A Belevitch, Corrine Bell, AM Benner, Don & Theresa Benoit, Russell Benton, George Beraman, Keith Bland, Michael Blaxland, Erik Bloom, Martje Bloot, Michael Bolton, George Boraman, Andrew Borlace, Celine Bouchacourt, A Boutin, Steve Bovard, David Boyall, Martine Broeders, Nigel Brooks, Vincent Bruni, Michael Burden, Thom Burns, Harald Busch, Patrick Calabrese, George Campbell, Edmond Carew, Lucy & Bo Carlson, Jason Carmichael, Yenda Carson, John Carter, Matt Chabot, Jeffrey Chase, Jacques Choulli, W Chua, K Cloostermans, Michelle Cohen-Peak, Garry Cowley, Tania & Blain Crellin,

Christopher Cresp, Olga d'Ajello, Bob Denny, Shane Dobson, C Donaghy, SE Durnien, Todd Ebert, Matt Edmonds, Anders Elf, KH Evans, Robert Farrington, J Fellenios, Gary & Mika Fishman, Johan Forsberg, Peter Freeman, Patrick & Anne Gabet, Chautal Gallou, Jozef Gommeren, John Gore, Georgie Greene, Sammy Grieve, Dan Habb, Danny Hahn, MJ Haines, Debbie Hall, Glenn Hartell, Paul Harvey, Daniel Hebb, Leif Hein, Judy Hicks, Yiu-yin Ho, Julia Hobday, Harlan & Cristy Hoffas, Sue Holdham, Ray Hossinger, David & Greeba Hughes, KO Jacobsson, F Jenneskens, Ove Jensen, Kim & Graham Johnsons, Leo Joki, JS Kacskos, Iwakami Katsuhiko, Lisa King, Dr Thom Kleiss, Steve Knaggs, DL Knight, Paul Komarnicki, Gedelita Kruger, S Lane, J & P Lantela, Debbie & Kevin Leafe, Eileen Lee, Simon Levy, Dan Lindfield, Andreas Loew, Jose Lomas, Frank Luck, Eileen Lufgendorf, Itay Lusky, Malcolm MacKellar, Lydia Mapua, Steven Marlborough, Jean Pierre Marsac, Shaun Martin, Fiona McElroy, Des McKenna, Jan Mellaerts, Mathew Meyer, Vivi Mikkelsen, John Milne, Lindsay Milne, Patricia &

Tim Minor, R Moller, Harald Mueller, BW Munro, Donald Munro, Charles Nagel, Robert Navon, Bluey Newton, Preben Nielsen, Stuart Norgrove, J Nygren, Kevin O'Mara, Gal Oren, Ian Owen, Thomas Parker, Jeffrey Parrott, Colin Paskins, N Patterson, A Pometta, Brian Powell, John Pullinger, A Pulola, John & Jane Querifel, Doug Reynolds, Stu Richel, Kevin Robinson, Peter Ruark, Tom Sabel, Ronald Sakamoto, Frank Schmidt, W & M Schramme-Argyropoulous, Gerhard Schuetz, P Screach, Eric Seaman, Clyde Shoebridge, Carl Simon, John Soar, D Somera, Tiki Sonderhoff, Peter Sprenger, Russell & Lilian Stapleton, Julie Stapleton, Robert Stauder, Alan Stevens, Sam Talbert, Simon Taylor, David Thompson, Rupert Thompson, Mike Thomsen, AL Threadgill, Tierney Thys, Elizabeth Tomas, P Tripcony, Rob Turner, NJ Turner, B Vallet, Martijn van Olst, Jan van Zadelhoff, F van Hoyweghen, James Vann, P Vazquez, Fernando Vega, Kit G Vilano, Susan Voss-Rothmeier, Wilma Wagner, Deborah Walter, Simon Watson-Taylor, Andrew Watts, Alexander Winter, David Yu, Ansun Yu.

Contents

Map Legend

BOUNDARIES

.... International Boundary
.... Provincial Boundary

ROUTES

.... Freeway
.... Highway
.... Major Road
.... Unsealed Road or Track
.... City Road
.... City Street
.... Railway
.... Underground Railway
.... Tram
.... Walking Track
.... Walking Tour
.... Ferry Route
.... Cable Car or Chairlift

AREA FEATURES

.... Parks
.... Built-Up Area
.... Pedestrian Mall
.... Market
.... Christian Cemetery
.... Non-Christian Cemetery
.... Reef
.... Beach
.... Mountain Range

HYDROGRAPHIC FEATURES

.... Coastline
.... River, Creek
.... Rapids, Waterfalls
.... Lake, Intermittent Lake
.... Canal
.... Swamp

SYMBOLS

✪ CAPITAL	.... National Capital	
◉ Capital	.... Regional Capital	
CITY	.... Major City	
● City	.... City	
● Town	.... Town	
● Village	.... Village	
■ ▼	Place to Stay, Place to Eat	
☕ ☕	.... Cafe, Pub or Bar	
✉ ☎	.... Post Office, Telephone	
❶ ❸	.... Tourist Information, Bank	
◗ 🅿	.... Transport, Parking	
🏛 ⛫	.... Museum, Youth Hostel	
⚏ ⚑	Caravan Park, Camping Ground	
❘ ✚	.... Church, Cathedral	
◖ ✡	.... Mosque, Synagogue	
⚎ ⚏	Buddhist Temple, Hindu Temple	
✛ ★	.... Hospital, Police Station	

♉ 🅟	.... Embassy, Petrol Station	
✈ ✝	.... Airport, Airfield	
🛏 ✿	.... Swimming Pool, Gardens	
❖ 🐘	.... Shopping Centre, Zoo	
🍇 ⊓	... Winery or Vineyard, Picnic Site	
← A25	One Way Street, Route Number	
🏛 ⚑	.... Stately Home, Monument	
☗ ▣	.... Castle, Tomb	
⌒ ⌂	.... Cave, Hut or Chalet	
▲ ※	.... Mountain or Hill, Lookout	
⚲ ⚟	.... Lighthouse, Shipwreck	
)(◎	.... Pass, Spring	
⚘ 🏌	.... Beach, Golf Course	
∴	...... Archaeological Site or Ruins	
	...... Ancient or City Wall	
	...... Cliff or Escarpment, Tunnel	
	.... Railway Station	

Note: not all symbols displayed above appear in this book

Map Index

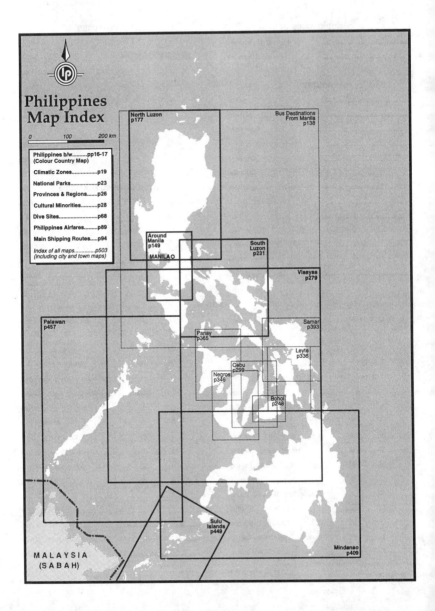

Philippines
Map Index

0   100   200 km

Philippines b/w..........pp16-17
(Colour Country Map)

Climatic Zones................p19

National Parks................p23

Provinces & Regions.......p26

Cultural Minorities.........p28

Dive Sites.......................p68

Philippines Airfares.........p89

Main Shipping Routes.....p94

Index of all maps.............p503
(including city and town maps)

North Luzon
p177

Bus Destinations
From Manila
p138

Around
Manila
p149

MANILA

South
Luzon
p231

Visayas
p279

Palawan
p457

Samar
p393

Panay
p365

Leyte
p336

Cebu
p299

Negros
p346

Bohol
p248

Sulu
Islands
p449

Mindanao
p409

MALAYSIA
(SABAH)

Introduction

'Few countries in the world are so little known and so seldom visited as the Philippines, and yet no other land is more pleasant to travel in than this richly endowed island kingdom. Hardly anywhere does the nature lover find a greater fill of boundless treasure.'

This was written about 100 years ago by Fedor Jagor, a German ethnographer. Today Jagor would be pleased to see little has changed. The Philippines still offers remarkable experiences: buried gold; unexplored caves; diving holes; sunken Spanish galleons; dense jungles with rare plants and animals; primeval people; active volcanoes; and uninhabited paradise islands.

Although travelling in the Philippine archipelago can tax your flexibility at times, you would have to go a long way to find people as friendly and helpful as the Filipinos. This place, as the locals like to remind you, is 'where Asia wears a smile'.

Compared with other countries of South-East Asia, the Philippines doesn't take up much room in the major travel catalogues. Because of this, there's no doubt that it loses out economically, but this country has recently been through enough natural and political upheavals for this to be a blessing in disguise. The Philippines simply isn't ready to withstand the stresses that mass tourism and its consequences would bring.

For the traveller, it is the variety the Philippines offers that is so interesting. The bustling capital of Manila contrasts with lonely islands fringed with superb beaches and gardens of coral. There are towns where you will find a thriving nightlife, but you can also visit mountain tribes who still live according to their own laws and traditions. There are huge rice terraces built eons ago with the most primitive of tools; wide sugarcane fields with subterranean rivers and lakes; or shadowy palm forest groves and dense jungle. If you can learn to be as laid back as the Filipinos amid all this natural beauty, you'll fit in just fine.

Facts about the Country

HISTORY

Philippine history is classified as beginning somewhere between 150,000 and 30,000 years ago. From this epoch stem the stone artefacts (palaeoliths) which have been found together with fossils of long-extinct mammals in Cagayan Province. These primitive stone tools were probably used by hunters who migrated over a land bridge from the Asiatic mainland. The oldest human bones which have so far been excavated have been dated at 50,000 years of age. However, many historians consider the Negrito or Aeta, who arrived about 25,000 years ago from the Asian continent, as the aboriginal inhabitants of the Philippines. They were later driven back by several waves of immigrants from Indonesia.

Immigration

In about 5000 BC the last land bridge sank into the ocean. Five immigration periods from Indochina between 1500 and 500 BC have been recorded. The last of these groups to arrive in their long canoes brought the first copper and bronze articles, and they are also credited with building the gigantic rice terraces at Banaue (Banawe), North Luzon. The immigration of Malayan peoples from 500 BC to 1500 AD brought further cultural changes, particularly in house construction (they built on piles), agriculture (they introduced plants and trees) and animal husbandry (they used water buffalo).

Indian influences came from the Buddhist-Hindu empire of Srivijaya (800-1377 AD) on Sumatra, and Majapahit (1293-1478 AD) on Java. During this period trade also began with Indochinese states. In particular, the merchants of the Sung Dynasty (960-1279 AD) visited the main island, Luzon, and the islands of the Visayas with their merchant ships. They mainly exchanged Chinese products like porcelain for native wood and gold. In 1380 the Arab-taught scholar Makdum arrived in the Sulu Islands in the south of the Philippines and began the 'Propagation of Islam'. His mission was most successful in Bwansa, the old Sulu capital, and Tapul Island. A powerful Islamic centre was finally established in 1475 by Sharif Mohammed Kabungsuwan, a Muslim leader from Johore. He married the very influential native princess Putri Tunoma, converted many tribes and was the first sultan of Mindanao.

The Spanish

The Muslims had already extended their power to a part of Luzon when Ferdinand Magellan, a Portuguese seafarer in the service of Spain, arrived on the scene on 16 March 1521. His first landfall was on Homonhon, an uninhabited island near Leyte, but it was on Mactan that he erected a cross and claimed the whole archipelago for Spain – with the blissful disregard typical of early European colonisers for the local inhabitants' claim to their country. Lapu-Lapu, a proud

Ferdinand Magellan

Filipino chief, opposed the Spanish authority and this led to a battle in which Magellan was killed.

Ruy Lopez de Villalobos was the next to try and claim the islands for Spain. He reached the island realm with an expedition in 1543 and named it 'Filipinas' after King Philip II of Spain. The permanent Spanish colonial occupation of the Philippines began in 1565. In November of that year Miguel Lopez de Legaspi landed with his fleet at Bohol. In Tagbilaran, Legaspi sealed a blood friendship with the island ruler Rajah Sikatuna. He went on to conquer Cebu a short time later and erect the first Spanish fort in the Philippines.

In 1571 Legaspi conquered Manila and a year later the whole country, with the exception of the strictly Islamic Sulu Islands and Mindanao, was under Spain's domination. With the zeal typical of the Spanish at the time, churches were built and the propagation of Catholicism began.

Push for Independence

Until 1821 the Philippines was administered from Mexico. Attempts by the Dutch, Portuguese and Chinese to set foot in the Philippines were successfully repelled by the Spanish, though the British managed to occupy Manila for a short time in 1762 during the Seven Years' War. They reluctantly handed it back to Spain under the conditions of the Treaty of Paris signed in 1763.

Dr Jose Rizal - Philippine National Hero

Jose Rizal was born on 19 June 1861 in Calamba, Laguna. Before moving to Manila in 1872 to study painting and sculpture, he was educated by his mother and private tutors. Once at the Santo Tomas University, he started his studies in medicine, philosophy and literary science. He continued at Madrid in 1882, where he graduated. To further his education, he spent the next few years in Paris, Heidelberg, London and Berlin. During this time he came into contact with European scholars and Philippine artists and patriots who shared his dream of independence and a sense of national dignity. In 1887 his book {Noli Mi Tangere} ('Do Not Touch Me') was published in Berlin. This socio-political work was written as a {roman à clef} and grappled with the issues of the Philippine reality and the suppressive policies of the Spanish colonial power. Although the Spanish censor banned the dissemination of the book, its stirring message achieved its aim. His second book, {El Filibusterismo}, as well as scores of inflammatory essays calling for an uprising against the Spanish were secretly distributed in the Philippines, finding a powerful resonance there.

In 1892 Rizal risked returning home and together with friends he founded the reform movement, Liga Filipina, on 3 July. He was arrested four days later and exiled for four years to Dapitan on Mindanao. He used the time in exile to develop his artistic and scientific skills, and he designed various pieces of technical apparatus and equipment. He also learnt several Philippine languages and worked as a teacher and doctor.

When the Philippine Revolution broke out in 1896, Rizal was condemned to death by a military tribunal in Manila for inciting people to revolt. On 30 December 1896, in front of the walls of Intramuros, now known as Rizal Park, he was executed by firing squad. ■

Dr Jose Rizal

After the opening of the Suez Canal in 1869, many young Filipinos left their country to study in Spain and other European countries. They brought back with them new ideas and thoughts of freedom. In 1872 there was a revolt in Cavite by about 200 Filipino soldiers against their Spanish masters. It was quickly put down, but it signalled the start of a determined struggle for freedom and independence.

The spiritual founders of the independence movement were the Filipino thinkers and patriots Marcelo H del Pilar, Graciano Lopez Jaena, Juan Luna and Dr Jose Rizal. The critical writings and poems of Rizal inspired many Filipinos in their fight for freedom. When Jose Rizal founded the 'Liga Filipina' in 1892, he was exiled as a revolutionary agitator to Dapitan, Mindanao. Andres Bonifacio then founded the secret organisation Katipunan. In August 1896 the armed struggle for independence broke out, first in Manila and later throughout the country. On 30 December 1896, after an absurd mockery of a trial, Rizal was executed by the Spanish authorities. He spent the last weeks of his life in the dungeon of Fort Santiago (see under Intramuros in the Manila chapter).

The USA

In 1898, as a result of a dispute over Cuba, a war between Spain and the USA broke out. Under Admiral Dewey the Spanish fleet was decisively beaten in Manila Bay. The Filipinos, seizing their chance to strike against the Spanish, fought on the side of the USA, and on 12 June 1898 General Aguinaldo declared the Philippines independent. The USA, however, ignored the role the Filipinos had played in the war and paid the Spanish US$20 million for the latter's ex-possession: this was ratified by the Paris Peace Treaty of 10 December 1898. General Aguinaldo was not recognised as president of the revolutionary government. The Filipinos had to begin the struggle against foreign domination again – this time against the formidable USA.

After President Roosevelt recognised the newly drawn-up Philippine constitution, Manuel L Quezon was sworn in as President of the Philippine Commonwealth.

WWII

Following the attack on Pearl Harbour, Japanese troops landed on Luzon and conquered Manila on 2 January 1942. The Filipino and US troops suffered defeats with high casualty rates in battles on Corregidor Island and the Bataan Peninsula. This brought about the brutal Japanese military rule which continued until 1944, when General Douglas MacArthur fulfilled his promise to return and liberate the Philippines from the Japanese. US troops landed at Leyte and, under their lead, the islands were recaptured from the Japanese forces.

On 4 July 1946 the Philippines received full independence as had been promised in 1935 by the USA. The first president of the republic was Manuel Roxas.

The Marcos Years

Ferdinand E Marcos was elected to power in 1965 and, unusually for the Philippines, was re-elected in 1969. The Marcos government found the country to be in a chaotic state. Corruption and crime had become the order of the day. People talked of the 'Wild East'.

In 1972 Marcos declared martial law and began to implement his concept of the 'New Society'. Within a short time some changes were apparent – guns disappeared from the streets, crime decreased and improvements in public health were made, but the land reform law of October 1972 only partly abolished land rents.

In foreign policy, the joining of international organisations like the Economic & Social Commission for Asia & the Pacific (ESCAP), Asian & Pacific Council (ASPAC), Association of South-East Asian Nations (ASEAN) and the Colombo Plan was successful. The Philippines was also a provisional member of the General Agreement on Tariffs & Trade (GATT).

Political peace, tax abatement and low wages were reasons for foreign companies to invest money again in the Philippines from the mid-1970s on. Not all Filipinos agreed with this political peace, and communist guerrillas of the New People's Army (NPA) and members of the Moro National Liberation Front (MNLF) tried to force change through violence. The opposition parties, the Democratic Socialist Party and the Philippine Democratic Party, had no influence on internal politics. The Communist Party of the Philippines was prohibited. Although martial law was abolished in January 1981, Marcos could continue his dictatorial form of government with so-called presidential decrees.

In the presidential election of June 1981 Marcos was confirmed as head of state for another six years, but the result was contested and allegations of vote-rigging were loud and many. Parliamentary elections were held in 1984 and the opposition United Nationalist Democratic Organisation (UNIDO, an amalgamation of 12 parties) won 63 of the 200 seats. The independent candidates won eight seats, and the government party, Kulisang Bagong Lipunan (KBL) – New Society Movement , won 125, including the mandate for 17 which were directly decided by Marcos.

Cory Aquino

A deciding factor in the surprise success of the opposition was not only the dissatisfaction of a large proportion of the population over the state of the economy, but also the response of many voters to the murder of the liberal opposition politician and popular former senator Benigno Aquino upon his return from exile on 21 August 1983. This, more than anything, sharpened the political awareness of all levels of society and moved hundreds of thousands of people to protest. The snap election planned for 7 February 1986 saw the opposition unite for the first time under Aquino's widow, Corazon 'Cory' Aquino of the Philippine Democratic Party (PDP-Laban), and her vice-presidential running mate Salvador Laurel, leader of UNIDO. They were pitted against the team of Marcos and Tolentino.

In the past Marcos had been in a position to decide more or less the outcome of the election, but this time events were being closely monitored by both internal and external sources. Cory Aquino rallied the people in a campaign of civil unrest and national protest of the non-violent Gandhian kind. Banks, newspapers and companies favoured by Marcos were boycotted, and 'People Power' began to make itself felt. The last straw for Marcos came when Defence Minister Juan Ponce Enrile and Armed Forces Vice-Chief of Staff Fidel Ramos joined the Aquino camp together with military units. Tens of thousands of unarmed civilians barricaded the streets, preventing loyalist soldiers from intervening and causing a major bloodbath.

Following the election both candidates claimed victory, and on 25 February both Ferdinand Marcos and Cory Aquino were sworn in as president in separate ceremonies. Later that same day Marcos fled into exile in Hawaii and Cory Aquino stood unopposed. She annulled the constitution and abrogated parliament.

This historic change of leadership was not really a revolution and it hardly touched the country's elite and the structures of power.

Through her ousting of the dictator, Cory Aquino became a national hero and an international celebrity. She restored democracy to the Philippines by re-establishing the political institutions of a democratic parliament and a supreme court.

Although she commanded considerable political power at the beginning of her presidency, Aquino did not manage to bring either the military or the feudal families under control. The president could only partly fulfil the Filipinos' hopes for well-being and democracy. The overwhelming majority of the population, living under conditions of appalling poverty, did not profit in any way from the period of economic expansion in 1987 and 1988. In fact, their economic misery became more pronounced from year to year. The much vaunted land reform, eagerly awaited by the numerous landless Filipinos, never really got off the ground.

During her period of office as president and commander-in-chief of the Armed Forces, Aquino survived seven attempted coups. However, it is clear she would not have survived the six year legislative period without the support of her defence minister, General Fidel Ramos. As a demonstration of her gratitude for his loyalty, she nominated Ramos to succeed her as president.

Fidel Ramos

As a Protestant, Fidel Ramos could not count on the support of the influential Catholic Church as he went into the election campaign which led to his narrow victory in mid-1992. The favoured candidate of the clergy, the lawyer Miriam Defensor Santiago, and the government spokesman Ramon Mitra failed to get elected, as did Imelda Marcos, the eccentric widow of the late president Marcos (who had died in exile).

President Ramos took office on 1 July 1992 and shortly after announced his cabinet. The goals announced by the government were ambitious. The main areas to be tackled were the creation of jobs, revitalisation of the economy, reduction of the enormous foreign debt of US$32 billion and the re-establishment of a political climate in which corrupt civil servants could no longer plunder state funds.

In addition, a reliable electricity service had to be established. In the early 1990s brownouts paralysed the country daily for several hours. The responsibility for this economically unacceptable state of affairs lay with the antiquated and badly serviced power stations. The failure of the Aquino administration to produce a far-sighted energy policy was one of the most serious negative points in the sobering catalogue of problems Ramos inherited.

Equipped with sweeping new powers, he moved to secure the ailing energy sector, encourage foreign investment and, in a surprise move, even lifted the ban on the Communist Party in an attempt to end the guerrilla war draining the resources of the country. In 1996 Ramos finally succeeded in securing a peace agreement with the Muslim freedom movement the Moro National Liberation Front (MNLF). The agreement foresaw the rebels being granted consider-able autonomy in most of the provinces on the island of Mindanao. A quarter century of underground fighting was ended in the southern Philippines with a stroke of the pen – formally, at least. Whether peace will in fact follow is uncertain. Both radical Christians and Muslim splinter groups, principally the extremist Moro Islamic Liberation Front (MILF), were against the agreement and promptly announced they would oppose it with violent means.

Ramos has pledged to reform the tax laws and break up the banking, telecommunications and transport cartels before his term ends in 1998, but many people doubt whether he has enough time or clout to carry out this ambitious programme.

GEOGRAPHY

The Philippines officially consists of 7107 islands of which only 2000 are inhabited. Only about 500 of the islands are larger than one sq km and 2500 aren't even named. The biggest islands are:

Luzon	104,683 sq km
Mindanao	94,596 sq km
Palawan	14,896 sq km
Panay	12,327 sq km
Mindoro	10,245 sq km
Samar	9,949 sq km
Negros	9,225 sq km
Leyte	6,268 sq km
Cebu	5,088 sq km
Bohol	4,117 sq km
Masbate	4,047 sq km

The total area of the Philippines is 307,055 sq km. From north to south the Philippines stretches for 1850 km and from east to west for 1100 km. The highest peak is Mt Apo, near Davao in Mindanao, at 2954m. Mt Pulog, north-east of Baguio in North Luzon, is the second at 2930m. There are 37 volcanoes, 18 of which are classed as active, including the Mt Mayon volcano near Legaspi in South Luzon and Mt Pinatubo north-west of Manila in Central Luzon. The longest rivers are the Cagayan, Pampanga

A (JP)
B (JP)
C (JP)
D (JP)
E (KD)
F (PS)

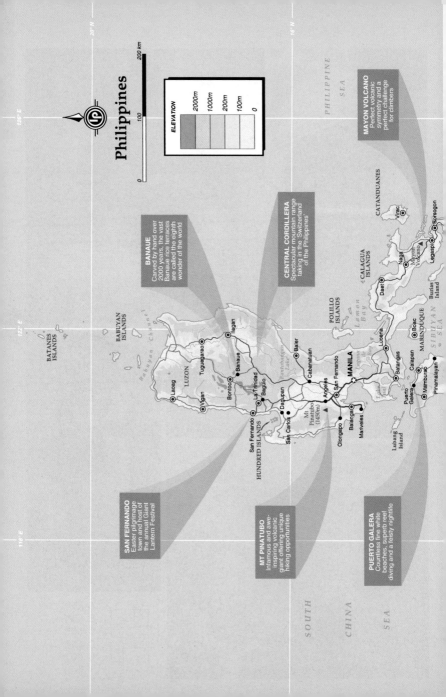

Philippines

ELEVATION
- 2000m
- 1000m
- 200m
- 100m
- 0

0   100   200 km

SAN FERNANDO
Easter pilgrimage town and host of the annual Giant Lantern Festival

MT PINATUBO
Infamous and awe-inspiring volcanic giant offering unique hiking opportunities

PUERTO GALERA
Countless fine white beaches, superb reef diving and a feisty nightlife

BANAUE
Carved by hand over 2000 years, the vast Banaue rice terraces are called the eighth wonder of the world

CENTRAL CORDILLERA
Spectacular mountain range taking in the 'Switzerland of the Philippines'

MAYON VOLCANO
Perfect volcanic symmetry and a perfect challenge for climbers

SOUTH

CHINA

SEA

PHILIPPINE

SEA

BATANES ISLANDS

BABUYAN ISLANDS

Bashuyan Channel

LUZON

Laoag
Vigan
Tuguegarao
Ilagan
Bontoc
Banaue
La Trinidad
Baigio
Dagupan
San Carlos
HUNDRED ISLANDS
San Fernando
Mt Pinatubo (1451m)
Angeles
Olongapo
Balanga
Mariveles
Baler
Cabanatuan
San Fernando
MANILA
Laguna de Bay
Batangas
Puerto Galera
Calapan
Mamburao
Pinamalayan
Lubang Island
Lubang Island

Candaba

Laguna
de Bay

Taal
Lake

Lamon
Bay

POLILLO ISLANDS

Luctena

Daet
Naga
Iriga
Legaspi
Mayon Volcano

CALAGUA ISLANDS

CATANDUANES
Virac

Boac
MARINDUQUE

SIBUYAN SEA

Burias Island

Sorsogon

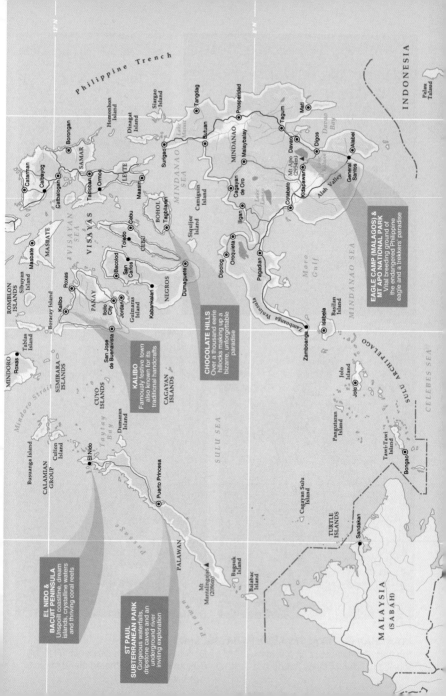

JOHN PENNOCK

CHRIS MILES

JOHN PENNOCK

JENS PETERS

ATI-ATIHAN FESTIVAL (KALIBO, PANAY ISLAND)
Top Left: Painted faces on parade.
Top Right: A fan of fancy headdress.
Bottom Left: A street dancer in full flight.
Bottom Right: A feathered friend takes a breather.

and Agno in Luzon, and Rio Grande de Mindanao and Agusan in Mindanao.

The islands of the Philippines can be divided conveniently into four groups. First there's Luzon, the largest and northernmost island and the site of the capital, Manila. The nearby islands of Marinduque and Mindoro are generally included with Luzon. At the other end of the archipelago is the second largest island, Mindanao. From Mindanao's south-western tip, the islands of the Sulu Archipelago form stepping stones south to Borneo. Third is the tightly packed island group known as the Visayas, which fills the space between Luzon and Mindanao. Seven major islands make up this group: Panay; Negros; Cebu; Bohol; Leyte; Samar; and Masbate. Cebu is the central island of the group and Cebu City is the shipping centre for the entire Philippines. Finally, to the west, there's the province of Palawan with more than 1700 islands.

Forces of Nature

The earth's crust is about 70 km thick and is composed of plates of varying size. Earthquakes occur depending on the amount of friction between these plates. Among the six largest plates, also called continental or tectonic plates, are the Eurasian and the Pacific plates and in between is squeezed the smaller Philippine plate. Strong earthquakes are fairly rare here, but there are light tremors from time to time.

One of the worst earthquakes to strike the Philippines this century hit on 16 July 1990. Measuring 7.7 on the Richter scale, the quake killed more than 1600 people and destroyed over 20,000 buildings, leaving more than 100,000 people homeless. Several strong aftershocks caused further damage to roads and houses. The worst affected cities were Baguio, Cabanatuan and Dagupan, all in northern Luzon.

The breaking points in the earth's crust are marked by deep trenches, high mountain ranges and volcanoes. The most prominent volcanic chain (the 'Ring of Fire') leads from Alaska and the Aleutian Islands, past the Siberian Kamchatka Peninsula, the Kuril

Islands and Japan to the Philippines. That the country's dormant volcanoes can suddenly turn dangerously active was proved by the massive eruptions of Mt Pinatubo in June 1991. After 600 years of peace the volcano erupted, ejecting up to 40 km into the stratosphere huge amounts of ash, mud and rocks, most of which rained down on the provinces of Pampanga, Tarlac and Zambales, causing widespread destruction. Nearly 900 people lost their lives as a result of the eruption, thousands more lost everything they owned. And there will be more victims in the future when the accumulated detritus from the eruption is loosened by monsoon rains and pours down the Zambales Mountains in an avalanche of mud to bury countless villages and whole tracts of the countryside.

Luzon and the northern Visayas also lie in the typhoon belt. Some of the whirlwinds wandering from the Pacific to the Chinese mainland also affect the Philippines. Violent storms can occur from June to January, although August to November are the peak months for typhoons. Typhoons nearly always cause power failures, and fires (often caused by candles being blown over) frequently follow. Overloaded electrical points, open fires and arson are other causes of the many fires in the Philippines.

GEOLOGY

Islands, islands, everywhere – the Philippine Archipelago has over seven thousand of them. Even if you only spent a day on each one, you would need 20 years to do it. Travelling in the Philippines means island hopping, covering a remarkable range of land formations; from the gigantic rice terraces of the Central Cordillera on Luzon to the majestic Mayon volcano in the south. The relatively small islands of Biliran and Camiguin are positively crowded with volcanic peaks, while mountainous Palawan shows no signs of volcanic activity. Instead, Palawan Province boasts chalk cliffs rising steeply out of crystal clear water near El Nido. Part of the Bacuit Archipelago, this area is just as popular a destination as the small dream islands of Boracay, North

Pandan and Malapascua. Then there are the Chocolate Hills on the island of Bohol, whose bizarre, bumpy landscape has piqued the curiosity of many an observer.

CLIMATE

The Philippines is typically tropical – hot and humid year-round. Although the weather pattern is fairly complex, it can be roughly divided into the dry season (January to June) and the wet season (July to December). January is usually the coolest month and May the hottest, but the average temperature is usually around 25°C throughout the year.

December to February is the 'cool dry' period, while March to May is the 'hot dry' period. You can expect rain every day in July, August and September. In May, Manila usually has daytime temperatures of 35°C to 40°C and at night it doesn't drop much below 27°C. This is the time of year when the rich citizens of Manila head for the perpetual spring of Baguio and the mountain provinces.

The best time to travel is from December to May. In December and January, however, you can expect rain on the east coast. March, April and May are the summer months. Normally, the rainy season starts in June; however, for a couple of years in the mid-1980s, the rainy season came considerably late. Typhoons usually come with the wet monsoon season from May to November. The south-west Visayas and Mindanao lie beneath the typhoon belt, but can occasionally be hit by a crosswind. Typhoons usually blow in from the south-east.

The Pacific Ocean coastline, comprising Luzon, Samar, Leyte and Mindanao, lies in the path of the north-east tradewinds, ensuring a mild oceanic climate. The monsoon season takes place from December/January to May and brings rain to the Pacific coast but primarily dry pleasant weather to the rest of the land. In North Luzon the Central Cordillera acts as a natural climate divider. During the first weeks of the north-east monsoons in December and January, it may rain on the eastern side of this mountain range in Banaue, while a little to the west it may be dry in Bontoc and Sagada.

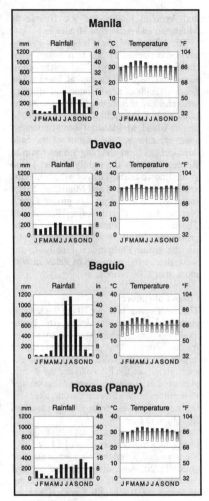

The south-west monsoon blows from June to December/January. The typhoons in the Pacific region are predominantly in the Marshall Islands and Caroline Islands. They travel in a north-westerly direction to the Chinese mainland between June and November but mainly in August/September.

ECOLOGY & ENVIRONMENT

As with many other areas of South-East Asia, the Philippines environment suffered heavily after WWII with the introduction of large-scale logging and mining operations. Some islands, notably Cebu, were so badly damaged that many of the more vulnerable species became extinct. Most of the larger islands retain their original forest cover only on the rugged mountain tops, which form havens for the plants and animals. Other islands, like Palawan, remain relatively untouched and visitors can still experience the original Philippines.

Tree felling and slash-and-burn clearing in the 1980s reduced vast wooded areas to shadows of their former splendour. Only the visible consequences of this selfish plundering of nature – erosion, soil degradation and climatic changes – managed to rouse the politicians from their torpor. At the beginning of 1989 deforestation was prohibited by law. Still, in the absence of an effective means of control, it remains to be seen whether this logging ban can bring a halt to the depredations caused by *kaingineros* (clearers so-called because they create farming land through the *kaingin*, or the slash-and-burn method). On the other hand, if there weren't so many timber orders from industrialised countries, fewer trees would be felled and whole forests could be saved.

Perhaps it was the catastrophe in Ormoc on Leyte in November 1991 that shook the Filipinos out of their traditional complacency concerning the environment. In the aftermath of a destructive typhoon, torrents of water thundered down to the plains from the mountains and caused havoc in the town of Ormoc, killing 5000 and leaving 50,000 homeless. Years of illegal tree felling in the hills above the town had left the slopes bare. There was nothing left to prevent the topsoil from being swept away by floods, a disaster waiting to happen in a country where massive amounts of rain can fall in short periods.

Although there is a long way to go, government agencies like the Department of Environment and Natural Resources (DENR) are trying to reverse the trend towards put-

Climatic Zones

0   100   200 km

1
2
3
4
5
Monsoon
Typhoon

There are five climatic zones:

1   Typical South-East Asian monsoon climate. Long dry season from November/December to May and intense rainy period from June to November/December.

2   Short dry season from March to May. Although the rainy season from June to February is long, it is not very intense.

3   No clear-cut dry season, with rain falling during most of the year. The heaviest showers are in the months of November, December and January.

4   No clearly defined dry season. The heaviest rainfall is in the months of April to September.

5   No clearly defined wet or dry season.

ting the economy before the environment. They have, for example, introduced schemes to re-employ people who lost their jobs after the woodcutting companies had moved on. The companies may have left behind barren forests, but fertile minds are helping to reshape this landscape by rehabilitating not only the devastated land but also the people who worked to make it that way.

Another serious problem, again made worse because large amounts of money are involved, are fishing methods using cyanide and dynamite. Cyanide is used to stun tropical fish living among coral reefs so they can be collected and shipped off – mostly to Japan. Apart from killing about half of the animals living around the reef, the poison gradually turns the coral into an algae-covered corpse. Dynamite is just as bad, and far more obvious to the observer. On Palawan, an attempt has been made to enforce the laws against this wanton destruction of the environment, partly as a result of continual warnings from the 'Green' newspaper *Bandillo ng Palawan*.

In Manila, no less a figure than First Lady Amelita Ramos kicked off a campaign to save the Pasig River. Large drums have been placed in department stores for people to donate money to help clean up the filthy river. The newspaper *Today* together with other sponsors has published full-page ads with photos of dead fish, appealing to people to stop polluting 'before toxic wastes lead our rivers and lakes to extinction'. The Department of Interior and Local Government (DILG), with the full support of President Ramos, publish a yearly list of the 'cleanest and greenest towns, cities and provinces'. And it is beginning to matter to people whether their town, city or province comes near the top of the list as clean and green, or at the bottom among the 'dirty dozen'. Palawan, at the top with its capital Puerto Princesa, is showing it can be done.

FLORA & FAUNA

According to the latest estimates, the Philippines has more than 200 species of mammals, 580 species of birds, 200 species of reptiles and 100 species of amphibious animals. Among these are species which can only be found on one or two islands. It is very likely that others are yet to be discovered.

In spite of this diversity, many of the plants and animals in the Philippines can be divided into three categories: the northern group, centred on Luzon; the southern group, from Mindanao to the Visayas; and the western group, centred on Palawan.

The northern group has links with southern China and Taiwan. Many of these species were blown in by monsoon winds or were washed in on the ocean tides.

The southern group includes species that originated in Australia and New Guinea. They came to the Philippines by using the islands of central Indonesia as stepping stones.

The western group, claiming a heritage from the Malay Peninsula and Borneo, arrived when these areas were connected by a land bridge to several of the Philippine islands.

Flora

The flora includes well over 10,000 species of trees, bushes and ferns, many of which are endemic to the Philippines. Most common

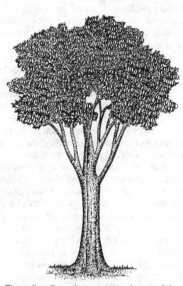

The yellow-flowering *narra* tree is one of the symbols of the Philippines.

are pines (in the mountains of North Luzon), palm trees and various kinds of bamboo (along the coasts and in the flat interior). In spite of uncontrolled tree felling in the 1980s, the Philippines remains 10% tropical rainforest. As well as gigantic vines and rare tree ferns, over 900 species of orchid make up the astounding variety of jungle flora.

There are also many vital cash crops, from the coconut palm to rice and sugar cane, as well as many different kinds of tropical fruit. The *narra* is the national tree of the Philippines and the sweet-scented *sampaguita*, which Filipinos like to wear around their necks, is the national flower.

Fauna

Countless species of animal are at home in the Philippines, many of them endemic. A noticeable number of them are smaller animals, like the rare mouse deer in south Palawan, the smallest species of red deer in the world. Lake Buhi, South Luzon, is home to the *sinarapan*, the smallest edible fish in the world – it's less than one cm long. The *tamaraw*, a short-horned wild dwarf buffalo, lives in the mountains of Mindoro. The fist-sized *tarsier*, the smallest primate in existence, and the *tabius*, the second smallest, are likewise native to the Philippines. Both are on the endangered list, and likely to remain on it, as they are also on the menu of the *haribon*, or Philippine eagle, the largest eagle in the world. It's their bad luck that the country's national bird – of which only 100 are left in the wild – is partial to small primates.

Parrots are mainly found in Palawan, and colourful butterflies abound in Cebu, Mindanao and Palawan. Also well represented in the Philippines are the ubiquitous cockroaches and mosquitoes. The latter are a favourite food of the little gecko, which is very popular as a household pet. The largest reptile of the lizard family found in the Philippines is the monitor. The cumbersome water buffalo, the *carabao*, is the most important domestic animal of the Filipinos and is not called the 'farmer's friend' for nothing.

Philippine crocodiles, the largest of the country's many reptiles, are rare. Although they still exist on Mindanao and Palawan, they are on the endangered list. As in all tropical ecosystems, there is a great variety of snakes: especially noteworthy is the metre long python and the poisonous sea snake.

For scuba diving enthusiasts, there's an

The Philippine monkey-eating eagle is one of the largest and most spectacular birds of prey in the world. Unfortunately, it is also one of the most endangered: it is estimated that only 100 birds remain in pristine forests on Mindanao and a few other islands. It feeds on mammals such as flying lemurs, squirrels, and as its name suggests, monkeys.

unbelievable array of fish, seashells and corals. Sea cows, whale sharks, dolphins and whales are also readily spotted in the Philippine waters.

Cruelty to Animals

Western animal lovers who spoil their little four legged darlings may be in for a shock, but Filipinos simply don't have enough spare money to spend on household pets. If they do look after animals, it's only because they serve a practical purpose. Pigs, chickens, fish and, in some regions, dogs, will all end up in the pot sooner or later. The lumbering water buffalo, the most popular beast of burden, is usually the only animal that people treat in a friendly fashion.

Endangered Species

Apart from those already mentioned under Fauna, the following animals are on the endangered list: scaly anteater; Palawan peacock-pheasant; Luzon bleeding-heart dove; Palawan bearcat; flying lemur; flying fox; hawksbill turtle; green sea turtle; and estuarine crocodile.

National Parks, Reserves & Sanctuaries

To visit one or more of the national parks is a must for any traveller. Mt Apo National Park on Mindanao and St Paul Subterranean National Park on Palawan are renowned for their pristine natural states. In Bicol National Park, on the other hand, illegal logging has left behind a totally denuded environment.

As with other parts of South-East Asia, many of the Philippine national parks were established only because the government yielded to local and tourist pressure to conserve these areas. Whether or not they will remain protected areas is uncertain. Just by going to a park and signing the visitors book will have helped to ensure that it will remain viable.

The protected areas range from mountain peaks to lowland rainforests and coral reefs. Unfortunately, several of these areas are too small to maintain their wildlife populations. Other areas have been drastically reduced from their recommended size, partly due to increasing pressure from human settlements on the perimeters of such areas.

Alternative conservation efforts such as captive breeding programmes have been established as emergency measures to prevent extinction of further species.

The Bureau of Forest Development (BFD) was established in 1973 to provide a central environmental authority to manage the remaining forested areas. This in turn has led to the recommendation or establishment of over 30 major protected areas, including 23 national parks (11 of which are classified as national recreation areas), six national wildlife sanctuaries and four strict nature reserves.

In Manila the main office of the BFD is in Diliman, Quezon City. It's here that you can get all the necessary permits for visiting national parks and other protected areas. The permits are a great help when you contact BFD representatives in the provinces, where arrangements can be made regarding camping supplies and, where necessary, local transport and a guide. The time spent getting the permit in Manila is well worth it.

In Manila it is also useful to visit the National Museum and the Ayala Museum, where you can enquire about meetings of the Haribon Society, a conservation group which can provide useful tips and contacts.

Camping equipment is essential in many parks and reserves, and it may also be necessary to hire local guides. The following list of parks provides a broad cross-section of the natural beauty of the Philippines.

Mt Makiling Forest Reserve (Laguna, Luzon) This former national park is close to the campus of the University of the Philippines at Los Baños and its Forest Research Institute. As a well-studied area, it offers a good introduction to the rainforest environment. It is often visited by organised groups. If you contact the Haribon Society or the Forest Research Institute, they may put you in touch with such a group.

Quezon National Recreation Area (Quezon, South Luzon) This park is in the narrow

NATIONAL PARKS
1 Balbalasang Balbalan NP
2 Fuyot NRA
3 Mt Pulog NP
4 Agoo-Damortis NRA
5 Hundred Islands NRA
6 Aurora Memorial NRA
7 Mt Arayat NRA
8 Minasawa Island SNR
9 Mt Banahaw-Cristobal NRA
10 Quezon NRA
11 Bicol NRA
12 Mt Isarog NP
13 Mayon Volcano NP
14 Bulusan Volcano NP
15 Calavite NWS
16 Mt Ilig-Mt Baco NWS
17 Apo Reef NP
18 Calauit SNR
19 Cuyo 'English Game' SNR
20 Cleopatra Needle NWS
21 St Paul Subterranean NP
22 Mt Bantalingahan NWS
23 Ursula Island SNR
24 Morenton Peak SNR
25 Turtle Island NP
26 Sohoton Natural Bridge NRA
27 Lake Danao NRA
28 Mahagnao Volcano NRA
29 Mt Kanlaon NP
30 Twin Lakes NP
31 Mt Malindang NP
32 Liguasan Marsh NWS
33 Mt Apo NP
34 Philippine Eagle NWS

NP - National Park
NRA - National Recreation Area
NWS - National Wildlife Santuary
SNR - Strict Nature Reserve

National Parks

isthmus of the Luzon Peninsula, east of Lucena. It is now an isolated patch of rainforest centred around a series of rugged limestone crags, with a trail leading to higher areas.

From this high vantage point, both sides of the peninsula can be seen. The old road that winds through the park has been bypassed, but a few buses and other vehicles still travel through the park every day.

A wide variety of wildlife can still be observed, including monkeys (macaques) and squirrels. Among the birdlife, the large hornbills are most conspicuous.

Mt Ilig-Mt Baco National Wildlife Sanctuary (Mindoro) This park is well known as the last refuge for the unique species of the Philippine dwarf buffalo, the tamaraw. After dropping to a very low level in the mid-1960s, its numbers are slowly increasing. Its rescue from extinction is a success story for Philippine conservationists. The tamaraw is best seen in the grassland areas, especially towards the end of the dry season.

The high forests of Mindoro cover six major vegetation types, from lowland rainforest to high-altitude pine forests, and contain a great diversity of wildlife. Visits to this park and other smaller protected areas on Mindoro can be organised from San Jose or Roxas.

Mt Kanlaon National Park (Negros Occidental) This large, rugged and well-forested park is centred around the Kanlaon volcano (2465m). It features two craters, one of which is still active with open barren areas at the higher elevations. The old crater is cylindrical and about a km wide, while the newer crater is more than 250m deep.

The extensive forests of the park are noted for their abundant wildlife, and also feature many waterfalls and small crater lakes fringed by trees. It's a major refuge for wildlife in the central Philippines and offers an exciting way for the more adventurous traveller to visit a rainforest.

The park's main attraction is the trek up the volcano, but facilities for visitors are limited. Access to the park can be organised from Bacolod and through several of the smaller towns closer to the park.

Mahagnao Volcano National Recreation Area (Leyte) This is a small park in central Leyte featuring a crater lake and diverse forest areas. It's part of the central mountain region of Leyte, extending north to the Lake Danao area, also proposed as a national park. In contrast to Negros, this region offers a relatively easy opportunity to visit a Philippine wilderness area. The main point of access is from Tacloban.

St Paul Subterranean National Park (Palawan) The focal point of this park, on the west coast of Palawan about 70 km from Puerto Princesa, is the Underground River, which is over eight km long and navigable by rubber dinghy or canoe.

The forested limestone peaks around the river area and St Paul Bay add to the park's remarkable beauty. The river cave is host to millions of bats and swiftlets, offering spectacular viewing at dawn and dusk. It is possible to camp on the beach not far from the main entrance of the river and it is well worth spending a few days in this beautiful area. The best access to the river area is by boat from the nearby town of Sabang.

Mt Apo National Park (Mindanao) This park was established in 1936 to protect the highest peak in the Philippines, Mt Apo (2954m), an active volcano near Davao. Its 'snow-capped' appearance is actually caused by a thick white sulphur crust.

The most famous inhabitant of the park is the haribon, or Philippine eagle. The numbers of this spectacular bird remain critically low, but experimental breeding programmes at nearby Calinan are helping to keep the eagle off the extinct list. Observing this splendid bird in the wild can be an unforgettable experience. As well as scanning the sky and tree tops to see an eagle, you should listen out for its piercing cry.

There are several walking tracks in the park, including three to the summit of Mt Apo. This park is characteristic of Mindanao's forested volcanic regions, and offers spectacular scenery and wildlife. Visits can be organised from nearby Davao.

GOVERNMENT & POLITICS

The Philippines has a constitutional form of government. The legislative power is vested in Congress, composed of the Senate (Upper House; 24 senators) and the House of Representatives (Lower House; 250 members). The president is elected directly by the voters for a six year term. President Fidel Ramos recently raised the possibility of scrapping the six year limit, but at the time of writing it remains.

Ramos often has to share the limelight with his erstwhile opponent (and would-be president), Miriam Santiago, who is known for her bluntness and determination to stamp out crime and corruption ('line them up and shoot them' is her approach). The former actor and present vice president, Joseph Estrada ('the poor man's Clint Eastwood'), is also skilled at getting good media coverage of his activities.

The administration of the Republic of the Philippines is divided into 12 regions (plus Metro Manila as the National Capital

Region) consisting of 76 provinces. Every province consists of a provincial capital and several municipalities, which in turn consist of village communities *(barangays)*. A barangay, with an elected 'barangay captain', is the smallest socio-political administration unit in the Philippines. The term 'barangay' originates from the time the archipelago was settled between 500 BC and 1500 AD. During that time, a barangay (or *balanghai*) was a large ocean-going outrigger boat which could carry up to 90 passengers. It was used by Malayan peoples to migrate to the Philippines.

National Flag & National Anthem

The national flag of the Philippines has a white triangle on the left. On either side tapering off to the left are two stripes, the top one blue, the bottom one red. The white triangle contains three five point stars and a sun with eight rays. The sun symbolises freedom and its eight rays represent the first eight provinces that revolted against Spanish colonial rule. The stars symbolise the three geographical divisions of the Philippines: Luzon; the Visayas; and Mindanao. The blue stripe stands for the equality and unity of the people. The red stripe (placed on top in wartime) symbolises the readiness of the Filipinos to fight to the death for their country.

On 12 June 1898, from the balcony of his house in Cavite, General Emilio Aguinaldo declared the independence of the Philippines. On this day the Philippine national flag was raised and the national anthem played for the first time. In the form of a march, the Marcha Nacional Filipina anthem was composed by Julian Felipe and the words were written by Jose Palma.

ECONOMY

About two-thirds of Filipinos live by fishing, agriculture and forestry. A significant contribution to their diet comes from ocean, coast and freshwater fishing. Rice is the most important agricultural product. The development of new varieties of rice at the International Rice Research Institute in Los Baños,

improvements in methods of cultivation and enlargement of the area of cultivation have brought the Philippines closer to self-sufficiency in food production.

The main products for export are coconuts (copra), abaca (Manila hemp), tobacco, bananas, pineapples and more recently cut flowers, including orchids.

Cattle farming is still relatively undeveloped. Poultry, pigs, sheep and goats are reared for meat, while buffaloes serve mainly as work animals.

The most important minerals are chrome, iron, copper, coal, nickel, gypsum, sulphur, mercury, asbestos, marble and salt. Test drillings for oil have been only partially successful.

The Philippines, like many Asian countries, is dependent on oil for its energy needs. Every year about US$2 billion has to be spent on crude oil imports. It is hoped that hydroelectric and geothermal power projects will go some way towards improving the energy situation. Around 20% of the total energy required is produced geothermally, which is equivalent to 8 million barrels of oil. The Philippines is second only to the USA in its use of geothermal energy sources.

Manufacturing occurs principally in and around Manila, and consists mainly of luxury goods, food, textile and leatherware industries. Vehicle components are also made domestically.

Economic analysts are worried that the Filipino passion for grand and impressive projects may limit the nation's ability to come to terms with its employment problems. There is a minimum wage set by the state but this often exists only on paper, and the country's large pool of skilled labour is often poorly utilised. At the time of writing, the nation's rate of inflation is 4.4%.

Tourism provides a significant source of income and from 1970 to 1980 the tourist flow increased from just 14,000 visitors to over a million. In the years of political unrest from 1983 to 1986 the figures declined, only to shoot up again in 1987. In 1995 more than 1.5 million tourists visited the country.

Manila saw a massive increase in hotel rooms in the 1970s, but this was not followed

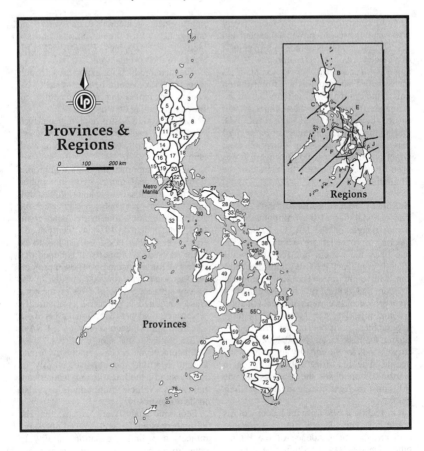

Provinces & Regions

Regions

Provinces

by a similar development in provincial areas. This lack of development outside Manila may eventually limit the growth of tourism, but it does make the Philippines more enjoyable for the budget traveller!

Income & Cost of Living

The basic level of income is fixed by the state. According to law, the lowest possible wage of a working person is 140 pesos per day, equivalent to about US$5.60. Tariff rates are numerous but few are in fact observed. There are also clear discrepancies in income between city and country. Here are some examples of average monthly wages in Manila (in the provinces the wages are on average 30% lower): restaurant staff (without tips) US$48; teachers or labourers US$100; office workers or policemen US$120; and engineers US$200. To cover the basic necessities of life in Manila a family of six needs at least 7000 pesos (US$280) per month.

In rural areas, a basic meal costs no more than US$2. A bottle of beer can be bought for the equivalent of US$0.35, and about US$0.25 is charged for soft drinks. Everything is a good deal dearer in exclusive

PROVINCES					
1	Batanes	31	Mindoro Oriental	62	Lanao del Norte
2	Ilocos Norte	32	Mindoro Occidental	63	Lanao del Sur
3	Cagayan	33	Albay	64	Bukidnon
4	Kalinga-Apayao	34	Sorsogon	65	Agusan del Sur
5	Abra	35	Romblon	66	Davao del Norte
6	Ilocos Sur	36	Masbate	67	Davao Oriental
7	Mountain	37	Northern Samar	68	Davao
8	Isabela	38	Western Samar	69	North Cotabato
9	Ifugao	39	Eastern Samar	70	Maguindanao
10	La Union	40	Biliran	71	Sultan Kudarat
11	Benguet	41	Aklan	72	South Cotabato
12	Nueva Vizcaya	42	Capiz	73	Davao del Sur
13	Quirino	43	Antique	74	Sarangani
14	Pangasinan	44	Iloilo	75	Basilan
15	Zambales	45	Guimaras	76	Sulu
16	Tarlac	46	Leyte	77	Tawi-Tawi
17	Nueva Ecija	47	Southern Leyte		
18	Aurora	48	Cebu	**REGIONS**	
19	Pampanga	49	Negros Occidental	A	Ilocos
20	Bulacan	50	Negros Oriental	B	Cagayan Valley
21	Bataan	51	Bohol	C	Central Luzon
22	Rizal	52	Palawan	D	Southern Luzon
23	Cavite	53	Surigao del Norte	E	Bicol
24	Laguna	54	Siquijorè	F	Western Visayas
25	Quezon	55	Camiguin	G	Central Visayas
26	Batangas	56	Surigao del Sur	H	Eastern Visayas
27	Camarines Norte	57	Agusan del Norte	I	Western Mindanao
28	Camarines Sur	58	Misamis Oriental	J	Northern Mindanao
29	Catanduanes	59	Misamis Occidental	K	Central Mindanao
30	Marinduque	60	Zamboanga del Norte	L	Southern Mindanao
		61	Zamboanga del Sur		

restaurants and bars. For instance, you'll pay about US$2 for a Coke at the swimming pool of a five star Manila hotel, while a beer in a Makati nightclub will cost around US$2.50.

POPULATION & PEOPLE

In 1996 the population stands at 70 million. The trend is for a growth rate of 2.3% a year. The Philippines' family planning programmes are hampered not only by the strong Catholicism of the Filipinos but also by the usual Asian wish for the 'insurance' of a large family in old age. Filipinos are inclined to be very fond of children and have on average six children to a family. Consequently, you will hear of 'family planting' rather than 'family planning', although the government is putting a great deal of effort into popularising the concept of birth control.

Nearly 40% of the population of the Philippines lives in the city. More than half of the total population is under 20 years of age, while those who are 65 or over account for only 7% of the population. The ratio of males to females is almost even, averaging out at 100 females to 99.7 males.

Manila is the largest city with two million people, but including the suburbs of Quezon, Caloocan and Pasay, the population of Metro Manila is over 10 million.

Cultural Minorities

Some six million Filipinos make up the so-called cultural minority groups or tribal Filipinos, which collectively comprise 12% of the total population. This figure includes the four million Muslims.

There are 60 ethnological groups all up, distributed mainly around North Luzon (Bontoc, Ibaloy, Ifugao, Ilokano, Kalinga, Tingguian), central Luzon (Negrito), Mindoro (Mangyan), and western Mindanao and the Sulu Islands (Muslim). Many of these groups are looked after by the Office for Northern Cultural Communities (ONCC) or

CULTURAL MINORITIES
1 Ita (Negrito)
2 Ilokano
3 Apayao, Tingguian
4 Kalinga
5 Bontoc
6 Ifugao
7 Ayta (Negrito)
8 Dumagat (Negrito)
9 Agta (Negrito)
10 Iraya (Mangyan)
11 Alangan (Mangyan)
12 Tadyawan (Mangyan)
13 Buhid (Mangyan)
14 Hanunoo (Mangyan)
15 Ati (Negrito)
16 Ata (Negrito)
17 Tagbanua
18 Batak
19 Pala'wan
20 Tau't Batu
21 Jama Mapun (Muslim)
22 Manobo
23 Bagobo
24 Mandaya, Mansaka
25 T'boli
26 Tasaday
27 Maranao (Muslim)
28 Subanon
29 Samal (Muslim)
30 Yakan (Muslim)
31 Badjao
32 Tausug (Muslim)

Cultural Minorities

the Office for Southern Cultural Communities (OSCC), which are responsible for protecting the cultural minorities' way of life, and assisting the government in bringing material and technical aid to these people. The minority groups themselves decide whether to use this service, and if so what type of aid they require.

It would be beyond the scope of this book to describe all the ethnological groups in the Philippines, but a selection of those which represent an important part of the population structure and are accessible to foreign travellers follows.

Warning Before you go into areas set aside for the indigenous people, please examine your motives carefully. If you just want to 'check out the natives' and take pictures for your slide night, you are very misguided. You won't be welcome, and will recognise this fact fairly promptly.

Most cultural minorities are quite friendly to strangers and foreigners. Should you be invited to eat with them, don't refuse without good (for example, religious) reasons, as it could be taken as an insult to the host. On the other hand, don't eat too much as the first invitation is usually followed by a second, then a third and so on. If they sing a song for you in the evening, you should have a song on hand to sing in return. Saying that you can't sing or don't know any songs will not get you off the hook as they won't believe you. A song book may be useful if you intend visiting many minorities.

Don't refer to Muslims as 'Moro'. The tag was first used by Spaniards who viewed the Muslims with contempt, probably because the Spaniards resented not being able to bring them under their yoke. Although many Muslims today proudly name themselves Moro, there are still some who feel discriminated against when a foreigner calls them by this name.

Badjao The Sulu Archipelago in the south of the Philippines, as well as the coast and waters of north-east Borneo and east Indonesia, are the domain of the Badjao (Bajau, or Badjaw). They are sea gypsies, many of whom still live in small boats as extended families. Today, however, most of them have given up the nomadic life and settled in houses built on stilts on coral reefs far out in the ocean or on sandbanks. No-one knows exactly how many Badjao there are but the figure is estimated at about 30,000, two-thirds of them living in Philippine waters. They are said in legend to have originated in Johor in Malaysia.

A Badjao boat, or *lipa* (pronounced 'leepa'), is made of wood, up to 12m long, and has a removable roof over its central section. The long, thin hull is fitted with a slatted floor to stand on when punting or spearing fish. The catch is then hung out to dry in the stern. There is a little oven over the stern where fish can be cooked. Apart from seafood, the mainstay of the Badjao diet is cassava, a nourishing tapioca plant used in stews.

Sea cucumbers are gathered to be sold for use in Chinese restaurants, but before they are sold they are cooked, cleaned and dried. In recent years seaweed has developed into a marketable crop. The Badjao, having adopted a settled lifestyle, have planted regular fields of seaweed on long stalks in the waters around their homes. After the harvest it is stretched out on the platform of the villages to dry, and is later sold to chemical and pharmaceutical companies.

The Badjao try to fit in with their Muslim neighbours who, in the Sulu Islands, are the Samal and the Tausug. On the sea, the Badjao consider themselves part of a mystical animist world ruled by the great god Tuhan, but many of them closer to land have adopted Islam. All Badjao revere *saitan*, the spirits of the winds, fish, trees, hills and so on, which are said to cause sickness if angered. Only the *jin*, a sort of medicine man, can make contact with these spirits.

A marriage celebration lasts for two days and only takes place when there is a full moon. The whole village joins in. After much clanging of *kulintangan* (xylophones), *tambol* (drums) and *agung* (gongs), men and women perform the *igal*, a traditional dance. Polygamy is allowed but is seldom practised. Couples rarely have more than five children.

The dead are buried on special islands which serve as graveyards and these are only visited for burials. Because contact with the spirits of the dead is maintained, the sea people are tied to the land. Before burial the corpse is washed and wrapped in a white sheet. As well as personal treasures, provisions are placed in the grave for the journey to the beyond.

Batak The Batak are semi-nomadic hunter-gatherers. They live in many small groups in the hills and coastal regions of north-east Palawan. During the rainy season, groups join together to form larger communities. The *kapitan* (leader) of each small group nominates one person, also known as a kapitan, to lead the larger community during this time. The kapitan makes all the important decisions, such as choice of settlement, sharing of work and organisation of gathering activities. During this settled period the Batak also plant crops.

Encroaching civilisation and disease have tragically decimated these shy indigenous people. One can only hope that international attempts to stop these people disappearing entirely are successful.

Bontoc The Bontoc live in thoroughly organised village communities in the Central Cordillera. Their houses are built close to the ground, and every *iti* (village) has two important accommodation arrangements – *ato* and *olog*. The village elders live in the ato, where social and political decisions are made and religious ceremonies prepared. An ato also serves as a guesthouse and sleeping quarters for young bachelors. Women are strictly prohibited from entering. About 10 women of marriageable age live in the olog, a flat house with an extraordinarily small entrance. This building is taboo to married men: only bachelors are allowed to enter an olog and spend the night with their intended wives. Before they get that far, both partners must fulfil certain rules of the game – the man must promise to marry his partner in the event of pregnancy; if he doesn't keep his promise, he will be socially isolated and not permitted to enter the olog again. The invitation and permission to spend the night together must be issued by the woman, and as a sign of her consent she 'steals' a small item of his property. Every Bontoc understands this hint, and when many tobacco pouches or pipes are purloined during the day in the village, you can bet the olog will be crowded that night.

Although the Bontoc are no longer feared as head-hunters, even today this act of revenge has not been completely wiped out. Justice in the mountains is strictly 'an eye for an eye, a tooth for a tooth', or more appropriately, 'a head for a head'. *Tuf-ay* (spear), *kalasag* (shield), *kaman* (head-axe) and *sangi* (satchel) comprise the equipment of a Bontoc warrior. The sangi serves as a carrier for the enemy's head. When a successful warrior returns from his expedition, there is a great celebration for two days in the village. As a sign of his heroic deed the hero is tattooed on the chest: this is known as *chak-lag* and is much coveted, as it symbolises strength and bravery. The tattooing on the arms of male and female Bontoc is called *pango*. *Fatek* simply means tattoo.

The Bontoc believe in a better life after death; their funerals are not sorrowful occasions and only the heads of the family are in mourning. The most important requisite of the ceremony, which lasts for several days, is a death seat, the *sungachil*. A short time after a person's death, the body is placed in an upright position in the death seat, bound fast and placed so as to be visible to all who pass in front of the house. The shroud is selected according to the status of the family. Old women sing the *anako*, the death song,

Bontoc houses

and a pig is sacrificed and eaten. After night-fall, a sort of recitation begins, called *achog*, in which the life history of the dead person is reflected upon. This ritual can be quite merry as it is very difficult to get a coherent, objective account of the deeds accomplished by the deceased during their lifetime. Day-break or exhaustion of the participants ends this part of the funeral ceremony.

Ifugao No other people of the Philippines apart from the Tasaday have attracted more attention than the Ifugao. They are the build-ers of the gigantic rice terraces of Banaue and the surrounding area. Over the last 2000 years they have shaped a technical and archi-tectural masterpiece with bare hands and primitive tools. The imposing terraced land-scape was constructed step by step from the bottoms of the valleys to heights of 1000m or more. These are productive rice fields with a perfectly functioning irrigation system on the steep mountain slopes. The boundary walls have a total length of about 20,000 km. From this measurement the rice terraces of the Ifugao exceed by far those of the Bontoc and Kalinga. They are often jus-tifiably referred to as the eighth wonder of the world.

The life of the Ifugao is full of ceremonies and celebrations at which *tapuy*, a rice wine, plays an important part, whether it's at a funeral or at the carving up of a wild pig brought in by the hunters. They originally learnt the rice wine manufacturing process from Chinese traders. Rice harvested under the full moon is preferred and in order to accelerate the process of fermentation, the rice is partly boiled in water. After adding sugar, the concoction is emptied into an earthenware vessel, sealed and left for one month to ripen (see the Drink section in the Facts for the Visitor chapter).

The Ifugao build their houses on piles; the windowless space under the pyramid-shaped roof is used as a bedroom, kitchen and store-room. In order to please the gods, the skull of a sacrificed pig is fixed on the outside of the house.

The Ifugao were feared head-hunters in their day. Even today, head-hunting is con-sidered a legitimate way of executing tribal judgements. Among the old laws which have survived through the centuries they also have one involving a kind of blood feud. This demands a life, or appropriate damages, in exchange for a wrong committed. For example, in the late 1980s, a bus driver caused a traffic accident which killed several Ifugao near Banaue. When the bus company refused to admit responsibility for the deaths and injuries, axes were sharpened in the vil-lages in question. After that no bus driver would drive into the Ifugao district for fear of being attacked, and until the last damages payment was made, the bus company had to hand over the last 50 km section of the Manila to Banaue route to local jeepneys.

The *bangibang* (war dance) is a compo-nent of this traditional vengeance. Equipped with spears, shields and axes, the warriors dance on the walls of the rice fields, their heads adorned with *katlagang*, a form of headdress made of leaves. The person who will carry out the act of vengeance is deter-mined by using a chicken. The warriors form a circle, kill a chicken and leave it to die in the circle. The one chosen is the one closest to the chicken when it finally comes to rest after its death throes.

Ifugao house

Ilokano The Ilokano are of Malay ancestry. About 200 to 300 BC they came through Borneo, Palawan and Mindoro to Luzon, where they settled. The majority of this group settled the coastal strips and adjoining mountain regions in northern and north-western Luzon.

Already settled ethnic groups like the Isneg and Tingguian could not stop the new wave of immigration, and were pushed into the hinterlands. Before the Ilokano were confronted with Christian beliefs, they had a multi-tiered and complicated religious system of gods and spirits. Only fragments of their superstitions have persisted and these are mainly ornamental – such as amulets and lucky charms generally only worn by the inhabitants of outlying Ilokano villages.

Isneg The Isneg (also known as the Apayao) live close to the rivers, particularly along the shores of the Apayao and Matalang rivers in the highlands of the Ilocos and Abra provinces in north-west Luzon. They are the descendants of the feared head-hunters in the Central Cordillera. Their leaders, named *mengal*, are celebrated, wealthy warriors. Positions of leadership are not inherited but bestowed on those with the greatest ability and charisma. The Isneg believe in ghosts which may take the form of people, animals, giants and monsters. They are protected by Anglabbang, the highest god of the head-hunters.

Isneg (Apayao) house

Kalinga The Kalinga live north of the Bontoc. They are also head-hunters. Wars and head-hunting expeditions have been largely restricted through the peace pact, *budong*, which they have worked out. This treaty declares above all that a Kalinga whose honour has been impugned does not lose the respect of the tribe if, instead of beheading the enemy, he accepts a water buffalo, for example, as payment.

Like the Bontoc, the Kalinga also have a house for the men and village elders. They call it the *dapay*. The *ebgan* is the place in which courtship takes place, initiation songs are sung, stories told and flutes played. Successful suitors spend the night with their women in the ebgan and both partners have the opportunity to consider a common future together. If they decide to separate, there are no disadvantages and any children will later be declared legitimate by the community.

A marriage is prepared over a long period by different ritual acts. Earthquakes, landslides and other bad omens can draw out the required ceremonies for months. When all the formalities have been accomplished, a house is built for the engaged couple. According to Kalinga tradition, marriages can only be celebrated in the Dadawak (the season for marriages) of March, September or October.

Mandaya & Mansaka The Mandaya live in the north-eastern and south-eastern part of Davao del Norte on Mindanao. Mandaya means 'inhabitant of the highlands'. The Mansaka are classified ethnologically with the Mandaya. They were originally highland people who settled in clearings deep in the mountains, though today many Mansaka live in the eastern coastal regions of Davao Bay.

Animism is practised by both groups, as demonstrated by the many idols carved out of wood which stand in their houses and fields. Also noteworthy are the numerous examples of silver work. Even more striking than the ear adornments and finger rings are the large round chain pendants which are worn by men and women and are frequently made from coins.

Kalinga houses

Mangyan Over 80,000 Mangyan live on Mindoro. The majority of them live in the dense jungles of the mountainous interior. The Mangyan are subdivided into the Iraya, Hanunoo, Alangan, Tadyawan, Batangan, Buhid and Ratagnon.

In earlier times the majority of the Mangyan lived and fished along the coast, but later retreated to the hills, changed their lifestyle and took up agriculture. They did not go there of their own free will but were driven back by new settlers. In their culture, land belongs to everyone. If someone approaches them with deeds of title, these peace-loving people simply withdraw.

Despite the inevitable influences of civilisation, the traditions and culture of the Mangyan have survived. Distances are measured in yells – the distance over which one scream is audible.

In the south of Mindoro there are settled Hanunoo who are often referred to as 'true Mangyan'. Hanunoo means 'real' or 'true'. As well as having their own form of writing (an elaborate syllabic script), they have their own postal system: if they want to send messages across great distances, they carve the text into a piece of bamboo and place it in a bamboo post. These 'post boxes' are spread over the entire area. If the Mangyan come across one of them they read all the letters and deliver those with destinations which are on their route, either personally or by placing them in a more advantageous 'post box'.

The *ambahan*, the stories told by the Mangyan, are also recorded by being carved in bamboo. A typical ambahan has each line made up of seven syllables. These poems are of a social nature. They may be read to children to discipline them, or they may be given to an adult to read in cases where speaking directly with the person may be embarrassing or painful.

Maranao The province of Lanao del Sur in the north of Mindanao is the homeland of the Maranao (or Maranaw). They are the 'people of the lake' – Lake Lanao. Of all the Philippine Muslim groups, the Maranao were the last to be converted to Islam. They successfully defended themselves against all colonisation attempts by the Spaniards and Americans, for which their natural environment provided considerable protection.

Today, the Maranao are concerned with preserving and maintaining their cultural identity. Marawi, lying on the northern tip of Lake Lanao, is an important spiritual centre for Muslims. Several Islamic schools and the

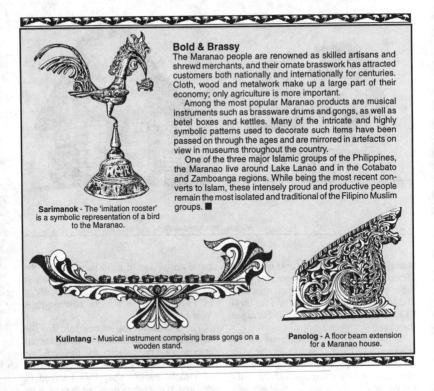

Bold & Brassy

The Maranao people are renowned as skilled artisans and shrewd merchants, and their ornate brasswork has attracted customers both nationally and internationally for centuries. Cloth, wood and metalwork make up a large part of their economy; only agriculture is more important.

Among the most popular Maranao products are musical instruments such as brassware drums and gongs, as well as betel boxes and kettles. Many of the intricate and highly symbolic patterns used to decorate such items have been passed on through the ages and are mirrored in artefacts on view in museums throughout the country.

One of the three major Islamic groups of the Philippines, the Maranao live around Lake Lanao and in the Cotabato and Zamboanga regions. While being the most recent converts to Islam, these intensely proud and productive people remain the most isolated and traditional of the Filipino Muslim groups. ∎

Sarimanok - The 'imitation rooster' is a symbolic representation of a bird to the Maranao.

Kulintang - Musical instrument comprising brass gongs on a wooden stand.

Panolog - A floor beam extension for a Maranao house.

Mindanao State University (MSU), a southern branch of the University of the Philippines, are here.

Negrito There are said to be 15,000 to 50,000 pure Negrito living in the Philippines; estimates vary wildly.

The various Negrito groups call themselves names like Agta, Ayta, Alta, Ita, Ati, Ata and Aeta, which are variations of 'man' or 'person'. They live dispersed over many islands but are principally found in eastern Luzon. They can be readily distinguished from all other Filipinos by their physical characteristics: they are darker and rarely taller than 1.5m. Their hair is cut short and crinkly, often decorated with a bamboo ornament. Their traditional clothing is made out of tree bark.

The Negrito are nomads and only a few of them have settled in one place. They often live in temporary huts built from twigs, branches, foliage and grass. Sometimes they work small fields in which they plant sweet potatoes, rice and vegetables. They also hunt animals, using bows and poison-tipped arrows.

Seafaring Negrito are called Dumagat. You meet them occasionally on secluded beaches on the Pacific coast of North Luzon, where they settle temporarily in hastily built huts.

The Negrito do not have laws as we know them, nor do they feel themselves bound to any authority. When decisions have to be made, the head of the family's word is final.

Pala'wan The Pala'wan live in the highlands of south Palawan. Their villages consist of three to 12 houses. They are led by a number of *panlima*, who are administrators and are also meant to help maintain the peace. The Pala'wan religion has Hindu and Islamic elements. The highest deity is Ampo, who is believed to pass on responsibility for the regulation of the affairs of humanity to his subordinate gods, the *diwats*. Religious celebrations include dancing, singing and drinking rice wine. A marriage is only agreed upon after lengthy negotiations between the two families concerned and is often arranged when the couple are still children.

Tasaday The Tasaday live in the mountains deep within the tropical rainforest of South Cotabato Province on Mindanao. The discovery of the Tasaday by the outside world has caused considerable controversy.

They were first discovered by the outside world in the early 1960s by a hunter named Dafal, but the first 'official' meeting didn't take place until June 1971. Their health was remarkable; from the dawn of time these semi-naked cave and forest dwellers lived on the fruit they gathered, and the fish, frogs, tadpoles and crabs they caught. They did not hunt or farm, and they used only primitive stone tools.

According to some reports, the 25 clan members had no contact with the outside world until they met Dafal. They did not even know of the existence of other tribal groups outside their forest. It's worth reading John Nance's book *The Gentle Tasaday*, which offers a fascinating, if controversial, account of the tribe.

The controversy arose in early 1986 with a report by Dr Oswald Iten of Switzerland and a *Stern* reporter Walter Unger, who suggested that the sensational discovery of the Tasaday was nothing but a publicity stunt staged by the Marcos government.

As the debate raged, scholars and journalists from all over the world demanded further proof and explanations. The Department of Anthropology convened an ultimately inconclusive symposium, and only a testimonial issued by the Filipino Congress, which had arranged for some Tasaday to be flown to Manila, could help clarify the situation. The authenticity of the Tasaday as an ethnic group was then confirmed by the highest government authorities. The most recent confirmation of the authenticity of the Tasaday was presented at the International Congress of Anthropological & Ethnological Sciences in early 1992 in Washington.

Tausug The majority of Tausug live on the island of Jolo in the Sulu Archipelago. They describe themselves as 'people in the current' and were the first in the Philippines to accept Islam. Nevertheless, traditional customs are still maintained. A Tausug wedding, or *pagtiaun*, is one of the richest, most colourful festivals celebrated anywhere on the Sulu Islands. The ceremonies and celebrations last a week. An important part of the activity is the *pangalag*, a wedding dance to the sound of gongs and drums.

The Tausug are renowned seafarers, diligent traders and excellent businesspeople. Prosperity and pride have helped make them the dominant tribe from Zamboanga to Sitangkai. Their cultural wealth is exhibited through their dress, the architecture of their houses, and in the style of their brass artefacts, jewellery and weapons.

Tau't Batu The Tau't Batu are referred to as 'people of the rock'. They live in caves in the Signapan Basin, north-west of Mt Mantalingajan, the highest peak in Palawan. They only leave their caves to hunt, gather fruit or harvest cassava and rice in unobtrusive fields. Other sources of nutrition, such as bats and birds, are found inside the caves. Their belief demands that nature be compensated for the death of any of the animals. Animals which have been killed will therefore be replaced by a representation in stone or wood.

A particular social custom is *bulun-bulun*, the communal living of several families brought about through the necessity to share nourishment. The Tau't Batu were not officially 'discovered' until 1978. To protect the lifestyle and habitat of this peaceful group, the Signapan Basin has been declared off limits to outsiders and is strictly enforced.

T'boli An estimated 60,000 T'boli live in about 2000 sq km in the south-west corner of Mindanao. The area is known as the Tiruray Highlands, and their culture is centred in the triangle formed by the villages of Surallah, Polomolok and Kiamba near Lake Sebu.

The T'boli do not have a village community structure. They live in houses set well apart from each other along the ridges of the highlands. In some cases, when there are close family ties, three or four houses are clustered together. Called long houses, or *gunu bong*, they stand on two-metre-high posts, and are about 15m long and 10m wide. The T'boli are monogamous people, but polygamy is allowed and is sometimes practised by the more prosperous as a status symbol.

T'boli women have a passion for decoration, and adorn themselves with ornamental combs, earrings, necklaces and chains, arm and foot bracelets, finger and toe rings and heavy, bell belts. You seldom see one without a head covering, either a *kayab*, originally a turban of abaca, more often today a simple towel; or a colourful *s'laong kinibang*, a large, round hat. The traditional clothing of both men and women consists of *t'nalak* – a material woven from abaca with a dark brown background lightened by red and beige designs. It takes several months to weave, but the weaving of the *kumo*, the wedding dress, takes even longer.

T'boli house

Yakan The Yakan mainly live on Basilan Island in the south of the Philippines, although some have settled near Zamboanga on Mindanao. They are peace-loving Muslims who live by agriculture and cattle breeding. The most important house in a village is the *langgal*, or prayer house, which is run by an imam. All larger annual ceremonies take place here, too. Absolutely essential elements to any festival are music and games, with water buffalo fights being particularly thrilling.

The Yakan are famous as exceptional weavers. A part of their unusual traditional clothing is the *kandit*, a red belt several metres long which is wrapped around the hips to hold up skin-tight trousers. Adornments men wear include a colourful turban known as a *pis*, or a helmet-shaped hat called a *saruk*. Old women can still be found with overlong artificial fingernails known as *suploh*.

EDUCATION

The Philippine education system is largely based on the North American model: primary education (elementary schools); secondary education (high schools); and higher education (colleges, universities). School attendance is compulsory for the first four years of the six year elementary school. With an illiteracy rate of only 12% of the population over fifteen, the standard of education is high compared with other developing countries, even if there is a noticeable drop in standards in non-urban areas.

ARTS
Dance

Filipinos have a boundless passion for dance, whether it be disco, cha-cha-cha, folk, modern or classical ballet. Traditional dance is derived from Malay, Spanish and Muslim influences. Among the most beautiful Malay dances are *tinikling* (bamboo or heron dance) and *pandanggo sa ilaw* ('dance of lights'); the best known Filipino-Muslim dance is *singkil* (court dance). You will also often see performances of the Philippine variations of the Spanish dances *habanera, jota* and *paypay* (the fan dance).

The good old folk dances, foremost among them the aforementioned national

---

Missed Opportunities

In no other country are there so many beauty contests. 'Miss' contests are a social event here, beauty queens are respected, admired and feted as celebrities wherever they go.

In the interest of getting to the top of the career ladder as quickly as possible, ambitious and beautiful young women of all social backgrounds match looks and wits by presenting themselves to the public and judges in beauty contests. The bigger contests at national level are attended by VIPs, who often sit on the jury as well. Apart from good looks, a candidate in the battle for the crown and a chance at the honour of being voted the 'fairest of them all' has to be over a minimum height and be able to produce at least a high school leaving certificate.

In the struggle for emancipation, Filipinas have not modelled themselves on men's behaviour, but have sensitively and skilfully retained their femininity, which by no means implies accepting men's claim to superiority. The Filipina not only rules the roost in the family and at home, but confidently wields power when in public office and has considerable influence in the workplace and the business world. ■

---

dance, tinikling, have become a great tourist attraction. Famed dance troupes such as Barangay, Bayanihan, Filipinescas or Karilagan have even found spots on popular TV shows.

Music

Until recently, traditional Philippine music was considered to be almost exclusively restricted to ethnic minorities. The 'civilised' Filipinos had fallen for US and British pop music and imitated it astonishingly well. In fact, the Filipino bands' ability to perform pop and folk music from the west has put them in great demand throughout South-East Asia. But now more and more musicians are rediscovering their cultural heritage and bringing old melodies back to life, using traditional instruments like bamboo flutes, gongs and wooden drums. Philippine folk songs sung in the original Tagalog have been enjoying a revival ever since *Bayan Ko* (My Country) was sung by the popular social critic Freddie Aguilar, eventually becoming an anthem of Marcos opponents during the uprising of 1986.

Film

Filipino films are produced in great numbers, dealing mainly with variations on the themes of violence and clichéd love stories. Productions like *Mababangong Bangungot* by Kidlat Tahimik are rare. This socially critical film was screened overseas under the title *The Perfumed Nightmare*.

In January 1981 the first film festival in Manila took place at the Philippines International Convention Center. Two more followed in 1982 and 1983, and organisers hoped the Manila International Film Festival (MIFF) would become an internationally recognised event. But further MIFFs, for economic and probably political reasons, have not taken place.

Painting

The most famous Philippine painters of the 19th century are Juan Luna and Felix Hidalgo. Luna's vast masterpiece *Spolarium* won a gold medal at the 1884 Madrid Exposition. In the mid-20th century Fernando Amorsolo, Vicente Dizon and Vicente Manansala were all internationally renowned. All three were graduates of the University of the Philippines School of Fine Arts.

The small gallery shops in Makati and the tourist belt of Ermita reflect the high level of Filipino painting; from primitive to realist, virtually all styles are represented.

SOCIETY & CONDUCT
Traditional Culture

The Philippines has developed a unique mixed culture of foreign influences and indigenous elements. Today, the Muslims and some of the isolated tribes are the only people whose culture remains unadulterated by Spanish and North American influences.

This foreign influence can be seen every day in the Philippines, as every afternoon even the smallest village square is converted into a basketball court. Ever since US colonial times the country has been crazy about this sport of giants – even though the Filipinos themselves tend to be a little under-tall.

Filipinos also love to gamble, and cockfighting gives them a great chance to indulge in this. It's also not unusual for sums of pesos to change hands after a game of jai-alai, the fast ball game from the Basque country also popular here. The average Filipinos are not great savers anyway; they live more to enjoy today and survive it if they can. Tomorrow will take care of itself.

The ability of the Filipinos to improvise and copy from their previous colonial masters is nowhere more apparent than in the jeepney. The army jeeps left behind by the Americans after WWII were converted into colourful, shining chrome taxis through painstaking detail work. Nowadays, these vehicles are produced locally.

Filipinos are strongly oriented towards the outside world. As a rule they don't place much store by anything produced in their own country. Imported wares are always in much greater demand than the best locally made products. They'll only make exceptions in the case of 'export quality' goods manufactured in the Philippines, which sometimes appear on the local market. Try telling Filipinos that we foreigners often keep our best quality products for ourselves and export cheaper stuff far and wide, and they'll stare at you in disbelief: what next!

Nevertheless, Filipino national pride is not to be underestimated. Of course, they are aware that there are serious problems in their country, but they are still not prepared to listen to foreign visitors pointing those problems out and attempting to voice their criticism. This is true above all for politics.

The ideas of the New Society propagated by Marcos really caught the national consciousness of the Philippines in the 1970s, just as People Power did in the 1980s. Perhaps as a reaction against the residual influence of occupying foreign powers, people began to rediscover their own cultural heritage and to care about their traditional arts and crafts. As a direct result of this, the national language began to find more and more favour and is strongly used today in theatre and literature, while *kundimans* (romantic and sentimental love songs) are also popular again.

One thing Filipinos and foreigners have in common is the discovery of the Philippines as a tourist centre. Most Filipinos know little about their own country. There are obvious financial and geographical reasons for this, but there's also the traditional lack of interest in one's neighbouring islands. When people have the money, they prefer to fly to Hong Kong, Europe or the USA for shopping and sightseeing. Until recently, the slogan 'See

Feather Weights

Sabong (cockfights) take place in a wooden arena known as a cockpit, and there is great activity as early as 8 am on most Sundays or public holidays. Before each fight, several *kristos* (bookkeepers) come into the ring to encourage the spectators to part with their money. They use a sign language for betting and, amazingly, nothing is noted down – it's all committed to memory. Four fingers raised means P40, horizontal fingers signify hundreds and fingers pointed downwards means thousands.

While bets are being taken, the expensive cocks are brought out and stirred up for the fight. Like boxers, they fight in different weight classes. Each cock is equipped with a razor-sharp spur fastened behind the leg. This deadly spur usually brings a fight to an end after a few seconds.

A 'non-pro', injured or sickly cock must be pecked twice by the winner. Only then is the fight officially over. Should the champion cock choose not to perform this concluding rite, the fight may be declared a draw. Wounded cocks are 'patched up' behind the cockpit; the dead ones end up in the pot. ■

the Philippines First' was hardly able to entice a single travel-happy Filipino. But now the situation has changed. With so many foreigners streaming into the country, travelling around and having a fine time, Filipinos are becoming curious about their homeland. After all, if outsiders are so attracted to the islands, there must be something worth seeing.

National Clothing

For men, there is no obligation to wear either a tie or a suit, even at official political receptions. The *barong tagalog* is the sensible alternative: it is a long-sleeved shirt which lets the air through and is worn untucked. Underneath, it is customary to wear a T-shirt. The short-sleeved style is known as a *polo barong*. These cool, semi-transparent shirts with their fine embroidery date from the Spanish era and have since become a symbol of national consciousness. Fine barongs are made from piña cloth, a fibre derived from pineapple leaf. The *terno* is the typical Philippine dress worn by women, recognisable by its stiff butterfly sleeves. It is only worn on formal occasions. The general fashion for women follows western trends.

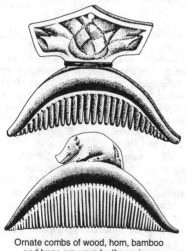

Ornate combs of wood, horn, bamboo and bone are worn by the various cultural minorities.

Dos & Don'ts

As history shows, foreigners have generally not come to the Philippines with friendly intentions. In spite of this, every visitor is heartily welcomed: the Filipinos are sociable and tolerant, and their natural openness charms many visitors.

But to say every visitor is welcome is not strictly true. There is one particular group of visitors the place can well do without: the paedophiles. The Philippines has the dubious distinction of being on the list of places where child abusers feel they can exploit the poverty of the people. Most of them are men from rich countries, whose foremost thought is to have pleasure at the expense of defenceless children. To call it decadence is to condemn it too lightly. The organisation End Child Prostitution in Asian Tourism (ECPAT) has been active for a considerable time in supporting the rights of children and youths. Investigators have arrested large numbers of foreigners for sexually molesting children.

On a lighter note, in the Philippines, as elsewhere, there are lots of toes you can tread on unless you're careful. Here are a few tips to help you avoid potentially embarrassing situations while you're travelling.

- Don't get annoyed if people stare at you. If they find you interesting – even exotic – then they'll want to get a good look at you.
- Do treat senior citizens with particular respect – always greet the elderly if there are any present.
- Do allow Filipinos a way out of an awkward situation. Especially, for example, when they may risk a possible 'loss of face' – a painful and embarrassing situation which the Filipino will try to avoid. Be mindful that they may give completely false information rather than admit they don't know – or they will just grin at you benignly pretending not to understand your question.
- Don't be punctual if you're invited to a social occasion! Turn up at least thirty minutes after the arranged time if you want to be a really polite guest. It is normal to remove your shoes before entering someone's home.
- Do take at least a taste of food if offered. If you like it, remember to leave some food on the plate to show you've had plenty.
- Don't remain silent in company, unless you want to imply that you are unhappy with the situation or don't like somebody present. Attempts to spend

time alone in a restaurant or pub are doomed to failure from the start. Chatty people ready to ask questions are always close at hand, especially if there is the possibility of alcohol. If you really need peace and quiet, go somewhere truly secluded.

- Don't be belligerent, even if an idiosyncrasy of the Filipinos is unpleasant or uncomfortable. You will achieve a lot more by being polite or sharing a joke. Foreigners who indulge in exaggerated reticence, arrogance or who take the opportunity to lord it over the locals financially or culturally, will never find a friend in the Philippines. They will have to make do with being ignored or mistreated.
- Do remember that there are black sheep among the Filipinos, just like everywhere else. For important information on this, see Dangers & Annoyances in the Facts for the Visitor chapter.

RELIGION

The Philippines is unique as the only Christian country in Asia – over 90% of the population claim to be Christian, 80% of these are Roman Catholic. The Spanish did a thorough job!

Largest of the minority religious groups are the Muslims (about 8%) who are found chiefly on the island of Mindanao and along the Sulu Archipelago. When the Spanish arrived toting their cross, the Muslims were just getting a toehold in the region. In the northern islands their influence was small and easily displaced, but in the south the people had been firmly converted and Christianity was never able to make a strong impression.

About 4% of Filipinos belong to the Philippine Independent Church, which was founded by Gregorio Aglipay in 1902 as a nationalist Catholic church. The Iglesia ni Kristo is the largest community of Protestant believers, to which 4% of the population belong. Baptists, Methodists, Mormons, Jehovah's Witnesses and members of other religious groups and sects make up about 2%. Except for a tiny percentage of Buddhist believers, the remainder of the population are animists.

LANGUAGE
History

The various waves of immigrants (Indonesians, Chinese, Malays etc) and the structure of the country (a series of islands) have brought about a multiplicity of languages and language groups. Today there are about 80 significantly different dialects spoken.

During the period of Spanish occupation, Spanish was taught in schools and, since education is mainly a prerogative of the wealthy, it developed as the language of politicians and the business community. Though small, the influence of Spanish on the local languages is still present today (for instance, in the numerical system and in the Zamboangan language in Chavacano). Spanish was abolished as a compulsory subject in 1968 in higher schools, but is still the mother tongue of a small percentage of the population, mainly the upper class.

Since in an occupied country the language of the colonial overlord often dominates, English became very important with the beginning of the US colonial era. Since the declaration of total independence from the USA in 1946, English has remained the language of commerce and politics in the Philippines. Newspapers, TV, radio announcements and even government statistics are evidence of this.

National Language The concept of a national language was formed after the Spanish-American War in 1898, but it wasn't until 1936, a year after the formation of the Philippines Commonwealth, that the Institute of National Language was established. President Manuel Quezon declared Tagalog the national language in that year, and a bill was incorporated into the Philippine constitution in 1946.

There were several other contenders for the role of the main language in this multilingual country – among them Cebuano, Hiligaynon and Ilocano. The compromises reached during the 70s still hold; the constitution of 1973 confirms Filipino as the main language. It is based on Tagalog but contains linguistic elements from the other Philippine languages. Since 1978 Filipino has been taught in schools and universities.

Gestures & Signs
As well as the spoken and written language, Filipinos use various gestures and signs. The hand movements which mean 'go away' to us signify 'come here' in the Philippines. The brief raising of the eyebrows is generally meant positively. One hisses to gain attention, for example, when calling to staff in a restaurant. The thumb is not used to indicate numbers – you indicate two beers, for example, with the ring finger and the little finger; using your middle finger could get you into trouble. Instead of pointing with your finger, you indicate discreetly by pointing pursed lips in the direction you want. Incidentally, in a *turo-turo* restaurant (turo means 'point') there is no menu: the food is displayed and customers point to what they would like to eat. When you want to pay the bill, look out for one of the waiters and draw a rectangle in the air with your index finger and thumb. Should the waiter be looking the other way, just hiss briefly. If Filipinos don't understand a question, they open their mouths.

Communicating
It is important to remember that English as spoken in the Philippines sometimes varies wildly from Standard English. For example, the correct answer to a negative question is 'yes'. So, if asked the question: 'You don't smoke, do you?' the answer 'yes' means 'yes, that's correct, I don't smoke'! It's not difficult to imagine a situation when offence could be given inadvertently, and you might never know. Imagine, for instance, what could happen if your host were to ask: 'You don't like Philippine food?'.

It is not vital to know the local language, as English will get you through most situations, but as in any country, locals will be pleased and surprised if you have learned even a few fragments of their language. The following may help.

Some Notes on the Language
In Filipino *p* and *f* are often interchanged (Filipino = Pilipino). This means that a written *p* can be pronounced as an *f*. This interchange is sometimes carried over into English by Filipinos (April = Afril) but it in no way impairs understanding.

Double vowels are pronounced separately (*paalam* = pa-alam). The combination *ng* is pronounced 'nang' and *mga* is pronounced 'manga'.

The syllable *po* underlines courtesy towards elders and persons of respect (eg, *Salámat po Ginang Santos*, Thank you Mrs Santos).

In the words and phrases following, an accent over the vowel of a syllable means that this syllable is stressed. There is sometimes more than one word given in Filipino.

Basics
Thank you.	*Salámat.*
Please.	*Pakí.*
Yes/No.	*Oó/Hindí.*
OK.	*Síge.*
Excuse me.	*Ipagpaumanhín.*
You're welcome.	*Waláng anumán.*
No problem.	*Waláng probléma.*
It's all right.	*Ayós ang lahát.*
Mr	*Ginoó*
Mrs	*Gínang*
Miss	*Binibíni*
man	*laláki/laláke*
woman	*babáe*
friend	*kaibígan*
I	*akó*
you	*ka/ikáw*
you (plural)	*kayó*

Hellos & Goodbyes
Hello/Greetings.	*Mabúhay.*
Good morning.	*Magandáng umága.*
Good day.	*Magandáng tanghalí.*
Good afternoon.	*Magandáng hápon.*
Good night.	*Magandáng gabií.*
Goodbye.	*Paálam/Adyós.*
Bye.	*Bay.*

Small Talk
How are you?
  Kumustá (ka)?
Well, thank you, and you?
  Mabúti salámat, at ikáw?
What is your name?
  Anóng pangálan mo?

How old are you?
Il ng taón ka na?
Where do you come from?
Tagásaáng bayán ka?
I don't know.
Áywan ko (hindí ko alam)

Getting Around

Where is the ...?	Saán ang ...
post office	koréyo
bus stop	hintáyanáng bus
petrol station	estasyón ng gas
police station	estasyón ng pulis
embassy	embassi
toilet	kubíta

boat	bangká
bus	bus
car	kótse
road	daán/kálye
ship	barkó
street corner	kanto
taxi	taksi
town/city	bayán/lungsód
tricycle	traysikel
village	báryo

How far is it?
Gaáno malayo?
Where does this bus go?
Saán papuntáang bus na itó?
What town is this?
Anóng bayán íto?
How many km to ...?
Ilán ang kilometro hanggáng ...?

left/right	kaliwá/kánan
straight on	dirétso
here/there	díto/diyán/doón
near/far	malápit/malayó
stop	pára

ENTRANCE	PASUKÁN
EXIT	LÁBASAN
NO ENTRY	BAWAL PUMASOK
OPEN	BUKÁS
CLOSED	SARÁDO
NO SMOKING	BAWAL MANINGARILYO

Accommodation

Do you have any rooms available?
May bakánte hó ba kayo?
Do you have air-con?
Mayroón bang air-conditión?
How much is a room?
Magkáno ang isáng kuwárto?
I'll take the room
Síge kukúnin ko ang kuwártong itó

hotel	otél
room	kuwárto
bathroom	bányo
mosquito net	kulambó
room with bath	kuwárto na may bányo

Food & Drink

food/meal	pagkaín
breakfast	almusál
lunch	panánghalían
dinner	hapúnan
restaurant	karindérya
bill	chit/kuwénta

beer	serbésa
black coffee	kapéng matápang
bread	tinápay
chicken	manók
coffee	kapé
egg	ítlog
fish	isdá
ice	yelo
meat	karné
milk	gátas
rice (cooked)	kánin
salad	insaláda
soup	sabáw
tea	tsa
vegetables	gúlay
water	túbig
wine	alak

Shopping

How many?
Ilán?
How much?
Gaáno/Magkáno?
What is this/that?
Ano itó?

Do you have anything cheaper?
Mayroón bang mas múra?

money	*péra*
expensive/cheap	*mahál/múra*
too expensive	*masyádong mahál*
big/small	*malakí/maliít*
more	*kauntí pa*
less	*tamá na*

Time & Dates

What time is it?	*Anóng óras na?*
today	*ngayón*
tomorrow	*búkas*
every day	*áraw-áraw*
tonight	*ngayóng gabí*
last night	*kahapong gabí*
yesterday	*kahápon*
day before yesterday	*noóng kamakalawá*
day after tomorrow	*sa makalawá*
week	*linggó*
month	*buwán*
year	*taón*

Days

Monday	*Lúnes*
Tuesday	*Martés*
Wednesday	*Miyérkoles*
Thursday	*Huwébes*
Friday	*Biyérnes*
Saturday	*Sábado*
Sunday	*Linggó*

Numbers

0	*walá*
1	*isá*
2	*dalawá*
3	*tatló*
4	*apát*
5	*limá*
6	*ánim*
7	*pitó*
8	*waló*
9	*siyám*
10	*sampú*
11	*labing-isá*
12	*labíndalawá*
13	*labíntatló*
20	*dalawampú*

21	*dalawampút isá*
22	*dalawampút dalawá*
30	*tatlumpú*
31	*tatlumpút isá*
40	*ápatnapú*
50	*limampú*
60	*ánimnapú*
70	*pitumpú*
80	*walampú*
90	*siyámnapú*
100	*isáng daán*
101	*isáng daán at isá*
200	*dalawáng daán*
201	*dalawáng daán at isá*
500	*limáng daán*
1000	*isáng libo*
5000	*limáng libo*

For a more complete selection of phrases, basic vocabulary and grammar for travel in the Philippines, see Lonely Planet's *Pilipino phrasebook* or *South-East Asia phrasebook*. A handy, easy-to-carry Filipino/English dictionary is *The New Dictionary* by Marie Odulio de Guzman.

CEBUANO
Cebuano is the second most widely spoken language in the Philippines. It's spoken in the Visayas and in many parts of Mindanao.

Basics

Thank you.	*Salámat.*
Please.	*Palihóg.*
Yes/No.	*Oó/Díli.*
OK.	*Síge/Síge taná.*
You're welcome.	*Waláy sapayán.*
Just a minute.	*Kadalí lang.*
What did you say?	*Unsa tó?*
Mr	*Ginoó*
Mrs	*Gínang*
Miss	*Dalága*
man	*laláki*
woman	*babáye*
friend	*amígo/a*
I	*akó*
you	*ikáw*
you (plural)	*kamó*

Greetings & Goodbyes

Hello/Greetings.	*Mabúhay.*
Good morning.	*Maáyong búntag.*
Good day.	*Maáyong udtó.*
Good afternoon.	*Maáyong hápon.*
Good night.	*Maáyong gabíi.*
Goodbye.	*Babáy/Síge.*

Small Talk

How are you?
Kumustá (na)?
How are you? (plural)
Kumustá (na) kamó?
Well, thank you, and you?
Maáyo man salámat, ug ikáw?
What is your name?
Unsay pangalan mo?
How old are you?
Píla na may ímong idad?
Where do you come from?
Tagá diíng lúgar ka?
I like (that)
Gustó ko (niána)
I don't like ...
Díli gustó ko ...

Getting Around

Where is the ...?	*Asáman ang ...?*
bus stop	*hulatán ug bus*
post office	*post office*
toilet	*kasílyas*
left/right	*walá/tuó*
straight on	*dirétso*
here/there	*dínhi/dínha, dídto*
near/far	*dúol/layó*
stop	*pára*

How far is it?
Unsa kaláyo (layo)?
Which bus for Cebu?
Únsang bus ang maodtong Cebu?
Where does this bus go?
Asa man moadto kíning bus?

boat	*sakayán*
bus	*track/bus*
car	*kótse/sakyanán*
island	*puló*

ocean/sea	*dágat*
road	*dálan*
town/city	*lungsód/siyudád*
village	*báryo*

Accommodation

Do you have air-con?
Nabáy air-condítion?
How much is a room?
Pilá ang usá ka kuwárto?
I'll take the room
Síge kuhaon ko ang kining kuwárto

hotel	*otél*
room	*kuwárto*
room with bath	*kuwárto nga anaáy bányo*
bed	*katré*
mosquito net	*muskitéro*

Food & Drink

food/meal	*pagkaón*
breakfast	*pamaháw*
lunch	*paniúdto*
dinner	*panihápon*
beef	*karnéng báka*
beer	*serbésa*
bread	*tinapáy (pan)*
chicken	*manók*
coffee	*kapé*
black coffee	*maisóg na kapé*
egg	*itlóg*
fish	*isdá*
ice	*ápa*
meat	*karné*
milk	*gátas*
pork	*karnéng báboy*
rice (cooked)	*kanú*
salad	*salad*
soup	*sabáw*
sugar	*asúkar*
tea	*tsaa*
vegetables	*utan*
water	*túbig*

The bill please.
Ang báyronon palíhog.

Shopping

How much?	*Tagpila, pila?*
What is this/that?	*Unsa ni?*
money	*kuwárta*
expensive/cheap	*mahál/baráto*
big/small	*dako/gamáy*
old/new (things)	*dáan/bágo*
less	*hustó na/diyutay*
more	*gamáy pa*

Time & Dates

What time is it?	*Unsang orása na?*
today	*karón*
tomorrow	*ugma*
last night	*kagabií*
yesterday	*gahápon*
day after tomorrow	*sunód ugma*
week	*semána/dominggó*
month	*bulán*
year	*tuíg*

Days

Monday	*Lunés*
Tuesday	*Martés*
Wednesday	*Miyérkoles (Miércules)*
Thursday	*Huwébes (Juéves)*
Friday	*Biyérnes (Viérnes)*
Saturday	*Sábado (Sábao)*
Sunday	*Dominggó*

Numbers

0	*walá*
1	*usá*
2	*duhá*
3	*tuló*
4	*upát*
5	*limá*
6	*únom*
7	*pitó*
8	*waló*
9	*siyám*
10	*napuló*
11	*únsi*
12	*dóse*
13	*tróse*
20	*báynte*
21	*báynte úno*
22	*báynte dos*
30	*tranta*
31	*tranta'y úno*
40	*kuwarénta*
50	*singkuwénta*
60	*sayesénta, sisénta*
70	*siténta, seténta*
80	*otsénta*
90	*nobénta*
100	*usá kagatós*
101	*usá kagatós ug usá*
200	*duhá kagatós*
201	*duhá kagatós ug usá*
500	*limá kagatós*
1000	*usá kalíbo*
5000	*limá kalíbo*

Facts for the Visitor

PLANNING
When to Go
Generally, the best time to travel is from the middle of December to the middle of May. That's off season for typhoons. However, you would be well advised not to travel more than necessary during the Christmas and Easter holiday periods – just find yourself a pleasant base and stay around there. The entire country is on the move at these times and you will hardly find a seat on any form of transport.

January and May are the months with the most colourful festivals. In the provinces along the Pacific coast, where vast amounts of rain can fall between November and January, the dry season usually begins in the second half of February at the latest. The rice terraces in North Luzon are at their best in March and April. Those are the pleasant, warm summer months, when island hopping is the most fun. It really heats up in May, when you'll be glad of the slightest breeze.

What Kind of Trip?
If you travel on your own in the Philippines, you'll often be asked solicitously: 'Don't you have a companion?'. In fact, it's a good way to meet the locals, so travelling alone doesn't mean actually being alone.

Among other things, the advantage of travelling in twos or threes is that the cost of taxis, boats and rooms can be shared. It's also handy to have someone there to look after baggage while the other gets tickets or looks at a hotel room.

Do-it-yourself travelling in the Philippines almost always means leisurely island hopping, and forgetting time while you're at it. That, after all, is what makes this country so special for tourists; however, if you have a specific interest in mind, you might want to spend time at one place with other like-minded people. Some visitors stay for months on Boracay because the windsurfing

conditions are ideal; others find wreck diving so fascinating they won't leave the Calamian Group in north Palawan until they have inspected every last sunken ship.

Charter tours are especially handy for people who have a limited amount of time. Although compared to other Asiatic countries, there is not a wide choice available.

Maps
The Nelles Verlag *Philippines* trilingual map is an excellent map of the islands at a scale of 1:1,500,000. For Manila, Metro Manila and environs within a radius of 50 km, Heinrich Engeler's city map of Manila, *Metro Manila*, is recommended. You'll find it at the National Book Store.

Detailed survey maps and nautical charts can be obtained from Namria (see under Maps in the Information section of the Manila chapter).

What to Bring
Bring as little as possible is the golden rule – you can usually get things you might need on arrival. A backpack is probably the best way of carrying your gear, but try to thief-proof it as much as possible and remember that backpacks are prone to damage, especially by airlines, where they easily get caught up on loading equipment. Travel packs are a relatively recent innovation that combine the advantages of a backpack and a soft carry bag. The shoulder straps either detach or can be hidden away under a zip-fastened flap so they don't catch on things.

The Philippines has enough climatic variations to require a fairly wide variety of clothing. At sea level you'll need lightweight gear, suitable for tropical temperatures. In Mountain Province or when scaling the odd volcano, you'll need warmer clothing – jumpers (sweaters) and a light jacket. Bring thongs (flip-flops) for use in hotel bathrooms and showers.

Soap, toothpaste and other general toiletries are readily available, but out in the sticks toilet paper can be difficult to find. It's almost impossible to buy tampons outside Manila and Cebu City. If you manage to find any, the price might be outrageous. Women travellers should stock up before they go. A first-aid kit is useful (see the Health section in this chapter).

The 3rd class on inter-island boats is equipped with bunks or camp beds. A big towel or a thin sleeping bag can really help you feel more comfortable on the thin rubber padding provided. Trips on outrigger boats can turn out to be quite splashy. A big plastic rubbish bag will save your bags from getting wet.

If you're a keen snorkeller, bring your mask and snorkel; there are superb diving areas around the islands.

Especially in country areas, electricity cannot be taken for granted, so don't forget to take along a torch (flashlight). A dynamo version will save taking batteries and avoid the problem of their disposal when flat.

A padlock is always worth carrying: you can often use it to make your hotel room more secure.

A pocket calculator can come in handy for checking the addition on dubious bills and working out exchange rates.

When it rains in the Philippines, it really rains, so bring an umbrella (it can double as a parasol if need be). Other possibilities include a sewing kit, Swiss army knife, travel alarm clock and a mosquito net.

You can bring a lot of happiness to children and adults in the Philippines through small tokens of appreciation, but don't overdo it. Filipinos are very inquisitive and interested in where the visitor comes from. To show them, or to offer a gift in return for hospitality or kindness, you can make good use of postcards from your country. People also like to look at pictures of your home, family, animals and plants. These things are good conversation starters.

You will be well liked if you're friendly – it doesn't cost anything. There's a fine local saying: 'A smile gives more light than electricity'.

SUGGESTED ITINERARIES

Anyone who wants to travel intensively around the Philippines needs plenty of time. Days and weeks pass very quickly, particularly if you want to go island hopping. You should plan a two or three week stay fairly well if you want to experience some of the country's more unusual aspects. If you only have a week or so, and don't particularly want to get to know Philippine airport architecture intimately, you would do well to restrict yourself to a round trip of North Luzon (eg, Manila-Banaue-Sagada-Baguio-Bauang-Manila).

There are all sorts of possible routes around the Philippines. From Manila you can head straight off to Mindanao or into the Visayas. You can travel south, via Legaspi and the Mayon Volcano, and go across from Matnog to Allen on Samar. From Allen, in northern Samar, you can head down through Samar and Leyte and go across to other Visayan islands.

See the Island Hopping section of the Visayas chapter later in this book for details of the interesting route from Puerto Galera to Boracay – it's one fantastic beach to another!

The following is a list of a few of the possibilities, but there are endless opportunities to discover the island world for yourself.

- From Manila to Mindoro via Batangas City (Puerto Galera-Calapan-Roxas), on to Tablas/Romblon, then to Panay via Boracay.
- From Kalibo back to Manila or from Iloilo City to Manila. Just to give you an idea, you should calculate about two weeks for this trip.
- From Panay to Cebu via Negros going south with a detour to Bohol, then back to Manila direct from Cebu City.
- From Panay (Iloilo City) or Cebu (Cebu City) to Palawan (Puerto Princesa), then travel to northern Palawan, returning to Manila from El Nido or Busuanga.
- From Cebu directly or via Bohol to Leyte and Samar, then through South Luzon to Manila.
- From Cebu to Mindanao (Zamboanga, Davao), then from northern Mindanao (Surigao) on to Leyte and Samar, returning to Manila via South Luzon.

HIGHLIGHTS
Top 10
One of the most magnificent pieces of scenery in the Philippines is the Central Cordillera in the north of the country. The journey through the mountains from Baguio via Sagada and Bontoc to Banaue, although not the easiest, is unforgettable. And then you have the absolute highlight, the magnificent rice terraces of Banaue.

The impressive countryside around Mt Pinatubo, on the other hand, was created by the forces of nature. Guided tours operate mostly from Angeles.

The active, cone-shaped Mayon Volcano at Legaspi in South Luzon is considered to be one of the most beautiful volcanoes in the world.

In spite of the first signs of its moving in the direction of upmarket tourism, the little island of Boracay still has that 'certain something'. Up till now, anyway. In another few years it'll just be one among many.

Perhaps not everyone's idea of a highlight, but unique at any rate, the Chocolate Hills on the island of Bohol are worth a visit. You can make a little detour there when island hopping through the Visayas.

Lake Sebu in the southern Tiruray Highlands, where the T'boli people live, must be the most beautiful lake in the Philippines. Unfortunately, this area, as well as others on Mindanao, is in conflict and not always safe.

On Palawan, St Paul Subterranean National Park and the Underground River, as well as El Nido and the Bacuit Archipelago, are two attractive places worth going to see.

The Philippines without fiestas would be unthinkable. The colourful Ati-Atihan Festival in Kalibo, Panay, is the most spectacular in the country. But each local fiesta has a fascination all its own.

Bottom 10
There are many Philippine towns without much in the way of flair or charm. San Jose on Mindoro, Tacloban on Leyte and Kalibo on Panay definitely belong to this group. These are staging posts for one night, if you have to go there at all.

Of all the tourist attractions in the country, Pagsanjan, south-east of Manila, gets the worst marks. This is not because of the waterfall and the raft ride up to it, but because of the high tips the boat operators demand on top of the fare. They can get quite aggressive, and people understandably take offence.

TOURIST OFFICES
The vast Department of Tourism (DOT) office in Manila could be more aptly called the Temple of Tourism. Computer print-outs with completely up-to-date information on various places are handed out. The regional DOT offices are smaller operations – but the staff are knowledgeable, have all the facts at their fingertips and can provide useful information sheets.

Several cities without DOT branches have opened tourist offices of their own. Usually, these offices can be found in the town hall.

Local Tourist Offices
DOT offices in the Philippines include:

Bacolod
    City Plaza (☎ (034) 29021)
Baguio
    DOT Complex, Governor Pack Rd
    (☎ (074) 442 7014, 442 6708)
Cagayan de Oro
    Pelaez Sports Complex, Velez St
    (☎ (08822) 723696, 726394)
Cebu City
    GMC Plaza building, Plaza Independencia
    (☎ (032) 254 2811, 254 6077)
Cotabato
    Elizabeth Tan building
    (☎ (064) 211110, 217868)
Davao
    Magsaysay Park Complex
    (☎ (082) 221 6798, 221 6955)
Iloilo City
    Bonifacio Drive (☎ (033) 337 5411, 337 8874)
Legaspi
    Meliton Dy building, Rizal St (☎ 243215)
Manila
    TM Kalaw St, Ermita (☎ (02) 523 8411)
San Fernando (La Union)
    Matanag Justice Hall, General Luna St, Town Plaza (☎ (072) 412098, 412411)
San Fernando (Pampanga)
    Paskuhan Village (☎ (045) 961 2665, 961 2612)

Tacloban
    Children's Park, Senator Enage St
    (☎ (053) 321 2048, 321 4333)
Tuguegarao
    2F Tuguegarao Supermarket (☎ (078) 844 1621)
Zamboanga
    Lantaka Hotel, Valderroza St (☎ (062) 991 0218)

Tourist Offices Abroad
Overseas Philippines DOT offices include:

Australia
    Highmount House, level 6, 122 Castlereagh St,
    Sydney, NSW 2000 (☎ (02) 9267 2695/2756)
Hong Kong
    Philippine Consulate, 6F United Centre, 95
    Queensway, Central (☎ (852) 866 6471/7859)
France
    Philippine Embassy, 3 Faubourg Saint Honore,
    75009 Paris (☎ (01) 42.65.02.34/0235)
Germany
    Kaiserstrasse 15, 60311 Frankfurt/M
    (☎ (069) 20893/20894)
Japan
    Philippine Embassy, 11-24 Nampeidai Machi,
    Shibuya-ku, Tokyo (☎ (03) 3464 3630/3635)
    Philippine Tourism Center, 2F Dainan building,
    2-19-23 Shinmachi, Nishi-Ku, Osaka 550
    (☎ (06) 535 5071/5072)
Korea
    1107 Renaissance building, 1598-3 Socho-dong,
    Socho-ku, Seoul (☎ (0822) 525 1707)
Singapore
    Philippine Embassy, 20 Nassim Rd
    (☎ 235 2184/2548)
UK
    Philippine Embassy, 17 Albemarle St, London
    WIX 7HA (☎ (0171) 499 5443/5652)
USA
    Suite 285, 3660 Wilshire Blvd, Los Angeles, CA
    90010 (☎ (213) 487 4527); Suite 507, 447 Sutter
    St, San Francisco, CA 94108 (☎ (415) 956 4050);
    Philippine Center, 556 Fifth Ave, New York, NY
    10036 (☎ (212) 575 7915)

VISAS & DOCUMENTS
Passport
It is necessary to have a valid passport; however, your passport has to be valid at least six months beyond the period you intend to stay.

Visas
Visa regulations vary with your intended length of stay. The easiest procedure is to simply arrive without a visa. The visa you are issued at the airport on arrival in Manila,

Cebu City, Davao, Laoag or Zamboanga, is valid for 21 days and free of charge.

If you get a visa overseas it will usually allow a 59 day stay. This will normally be granted for about US$35. If you arrive with a visa, make sure you let the immigration officer know, or risk having only the customary 21 days stamped in your passport.

Visa Extensions It is possible to get an extension from the Immigration Office (Commission on Immigration and Deportation; CID), Magallanes Drive, Intramuros, Manila, and its offices in Angeles, Cebu City and San Fernando (La Union).

When your visa expires, you present your extension application and passport to the various immigration officials, and these documents remain with the Immigration Office (Regular Service) for processing. You can get your extension in about one day if you pay an 'express service' fee of P250. Keep all receipts, as they are likely to be checked at the airport when you leave the country. Incidentally, anyone applying for a visa extension dressed in thongs (flip-flops) and shorts can expect to be refused service.

A number of travel agencies and restaurants run by foreigners will offer to take care of your extension application for a reasonable sum, normally between P150 and P200.

Don't overstay! If you don't extend your visa within the deadline you have one week to leave the country (there'll be a stamp in your passport confirming this!). All extensions must be submitted to the Immigration Office at least seven days in advance.

21 to 59 Day Visa You should request a 59 day visa from a Philippine embassy or consulate in your country. This will normally be granted for about US$35. If you're unable to make your application in person, you should send a letter of request asking for the application forms, and enclose a stamped, self-addressed envelope. Don't send in your passport straight away. You have to enter the Philippines within three months of the visa's issue, otherwise it automatically expires.

Anyone entering the Philippines without

a visa, or with only a 21 day visa, who wishes to stay for up to 59 days must pay P500 for a 38 day extension (Visa Waiver), plus a P10 'legal research fee'.

59 Day to Six Month Visa For this visa you must pay the following fees:

Application and Visa Fee (P450) – not applicable in the case of previously paid visa fees.
Alien Head Tax (P200) – applicable to persons over 16 years of age.
Alien Certificate of Registration (P400) – in the case of a second application within the same calendar year; this only costs P250.
Extension Fee (P200) – for each month of the extension period already begun.
Emigration Clearance Certificate (P500) – the fee can be paid at the airport on departure. You can also make the payment at the Immigration Office, though this must be done no sooner than 30 days before departure.
Legal Research Fee (P10) – additional to every other payable fee with the exception of the Alien Head Tax.

Six Months & Longer Visa For this privilege, you must pay – in addition to the extension fees listed above – a further P700 for a Certificate of Temporary Residence. When departing after a stay of one year or longer, there is a further travel tax to the tune of P1620.

The Immigration Office can order anyone applying for a visa extension of over six months to undergo an AIDS test, and can grant or refuse the application on the basis of the result.

Balikbayan After repeated alterations to the definitions of eligibility for Travel Tax Exemptions for Balikbayan (Filipinos living abroad and their foreign dependants), the following regulations are now in force: the Filipino Civil Registration Office, or the Philippine embassy or consulate in the new country of residence, will provide the applicant with a certificate affirming that no tax has been paid on any income. This can then be forwarded to the DOT for exemption from payment of the travel tax. The department's address is Room 117, Department of Tourism building, Agrifina Circle, Rizal Park, Manila (☎ 524 7734). The certificate of Travel Tax Exemption costs P20 at the DOT. It should be shown at the airport when leaving the country.

Photocopies
Make two copies of your documents and of the receipts of your travellers cheques and leave one copy at a permanent address so you can send for it if necessary. Exchange copies of your documents with your travelling companion or keep it in your luggage, quite separate from the originals. Identification problems and document replacement in the case of loss or theft will be a lot easier if you take these precautions.

If you take a personal address book containing important addresses and telephone numbers, you should make a copy of them and store them separately from the originals.

Onward Tickets
Officially, you must have an onward or return ticket before you're allowed to board a flight to the Philippines. This is even more necessary if you arrive without a visa. It has recently been reported that immigration officials in Manila have been denying entry to travellers who are unable to produce a departure ticket, especially when they don't have a visa stamped in their passport. If this happens, you can only hope to find some friendly person nearby who can quickly arrange the necessary ticket for you. You will find the airline offices upstairs in the airport building.

Travel Insurance
It is advisable to take out travel health insurance (including repatriation cover in case of serious illness) and baggage insurance (including belongings).

Driving Licence & Permits
If you want to hire a car, you will need a valid driver's licence from your country of origin – an International Driver's Permit may not be recognised.

Hostel Card

Card-carrying hostel members seeking discounts should note that there's only a handful of youth hostels and Y's in the Philippines. Facilities at a number of these places have been neglected and are well below acceptable standards.

Student & Youth Cards

Some bus and ship companies, as well as Philippine Airlines (PAL), have student discounts. You must be able to produce a student card when booking and when having tickets checked.

International Health Card

Vaccinations and immunisations are noted on the International Health Card. It is a document you may have to show at borders and should be as carefully looked after as your passport. Even if it has not been necessary to show the card in recent years, it wouldn't hurt to have it with you. Rules can be arbitrarily changed at any time without announcement.

EMBASSIES
Philippine Embassies Abroad

Australia
    1 Moonah Place, Yarralumla ACT 2600 Canberra
    (☎ (06) 273 2535)
Canada
    130 Albert St, Ottawa (☎ (0613) 233 1121)
France
    3 Faubourg Saint Honore, 75009 Paris
    (☎ (01) 42.65.02.34/0235)
Hong Kong
    United Centre, 95 Queensway, Central
    (☎ (852) 866 8738)
Indonesia
    Jalan Imam Bonjol 6-8, Menteng, Jakarta
    (☎ (6221) 315 5118)
Japan
    11-24 Nampeidai Machi, Shibuya-ku, Tokyo
    (☎ (03) 3496 6555)
Malaysia
    1 Changkat Kia Peng, Kuala Lumpur
    (☎ (03) 248 4233)
New Zealand
    50 Hobson St, Thorndon, Wellington
    (☎ (04) 472 9921)
Singapore
    20 Nassim Rd (☎ 737 3977)

South Africa
    Southern Life Plaza building, Schoeman St,
    Pretoria (☎ (02712) 342 6920)
Thailand
    760 Sukhumvit Rd, Bangkok 10110
    (☎ (02) 259 0140)
UK
    17 Albemarle St, London WIX 7HA
    (☎ (0171) 499 5443/5652)
USA
    1600 Massachusetts Ave NW, Washington D C
    20036 (☎ (202) 467 9300)
Vietnam
    27-B Tran Hung Dao St, Hanoi (☎ (084) 257873)

Foreign Embassies in the Philippines

Australian Embassy
    Doña Salustiana Ty Tower, 104 Paseo de Roxas,
    Makati, Manila (☎ (02) 817 7911)
Canadian Embassy
    Allied Bank building, 6754 Ayala Ave, Makati,
    Manila (☎ (02) 810 8861)
French Embassy
    Pacific Star building, Gil Puyat Ave, Makati,
    Manila (☎ (02) 810 1981)
Indonesian Embassy
    185 Salcedo St, Makati, Manila
    (☎ (02) 892 5961)
Japanese Embassy
    375 Gil Puyat Ave, Makati, Manila
    (☎ (02) 895 9050)
Malaysian Embassy
    107 Tordesillas St, Makati, Manila
    (☎ (02) 817 4581)
New Zealand Embassy
    Gammon Center building, Alfaro St, Makati,
    Manila (☎ (02) 818 0916)
Singapore Embassy
    ODC International building, 219 Salcedo St,
    Makati, Manila (☎ (02) 816 1767)
Thai Embassy
    Marie Cristine building, 107 Rada St, Makati,
    Manila (☎ (02) 815 4219)
UK Embassy
    LV Locsin building, 6752 Ayala Ave, Makati,
    Manila (☎ (02) 816 7116)
US Embassy
    1201 Roxas Blvd, Ermita, Manila
    (☎ (02) 521 7116)
Vietnamese Embassy
    554 Vito Cruz, Malate, Manila (☎ (02) 500364)

CUSTOMS

Personal effects, a reasonable amount of clothing, toiletries, jewellery for normal use and a small quantity of perfume are allowed in duty free. Visitors may also bring in 200 cigarettes, 50 cigars, or two tins of tobacco and two litres of alcohol free of duty. It is strictly prohibited to bring illegal drugs, firearms, or obscene and pornographic media into the country.

Visitors carrying more than US$3000 are requested to declare the amount at the Central Bank counter at the customs area. Foreign currency taken out upon departure must not exceed the amount brought in.

On entering the Philippines, visitors are allowed to have up to 5000 Philippine pesos in banknotes or other form with them. Departing passengers may not take out more than P1000 in local currency.

It is strictly forbidden to export drugs. In addition, coral, certain types of orchid, mussels and parts of animals, such as turtle shells and python skins, may not be exported.

MONEY
Costs
'Philippines 2000', the Ramos government's economic and political development programme, was designed to help the country catch up with the rest of Asia's economic 'tigers'; however, so far it has only brought steep price increases to most of the population. For travellers, accommodation and food have become more expensive (about 30% dearer than Thailand). You will get the best value for money in the mountains of North Luzon (Banaue, Batad, Sagada), while in the more popular tourist areas, such as the islands of Boracay and Cebu, you will have to dig deeper into your pocket. Some things seem amazingly cheap – local transport and beer are two good examples. Airfares within the Philippines are also good value but not as comparatively cheap as in past years. Some examples of approximate costs are:

Air travel (one hour domestic)	P1400
Apple (one)	P13
Aspirin	P20
Beer (one bottle)	P9
Big Mac	P40
Bus (ordinary) 100 km	P40
Bus (air-con) 100 km	P50
Cigarettes (one packet)	P14
Film (Ektachrome 100)	P170

Hotel room (bottom end)	P150
Meal (basic)	P80
Milk (one litre)	P30
Newspaper (daily)	P7
Orange (one)	P15
Petrol (gas; one litre)	P10
Pineapple (one)	P25
Potatoes (one kg)	P25
Rice (one kg)	P20
Shampoo (100ml)	P25
Soap (90g)	P10
Telephone call (local)	P3
Tomatoes (one kg)	P30
Toothpaste (25ml)	P10

Carrying Money
Money belts and secret pockets are sensible ways of protecting your money, tickets and documents.

Cash
In the Philippines, unlike many other countries, the rate of exchange is somewhat higher for cash than it is for travellers cheques. You'll get the best value for large US denominations like US$50 and US$100 bills. When selling currency, bear in mind that only clean banknotes are acceptable. Crumpled, torn or dirty ones will be rejected by moneychangers.

The US dollar is by far the most recognised foreign currency in the Philippines. Although the safety consideration with travellers cheques applies as much in the Philippines as anywhere else, cash does, as usual, have its advantages. You will often find it easier to change a small amount of cash rather than a cheque.

Travellers Cheques
If you want to keep on the safe side of the law and are prepared to accept an exchange rate about 5% lower, you should take travellers cheques rather than cash with you. Travellers cheques in US dollars issued by American Express (Amex), the Bank of America and Thomas Cook will be cashed by almost every Philippine bank, and certainly by the Philippine National Bank.

Hold on to your original purchase receipts, as most moneychangers and banks will not cash cheques unless you can produce this documentation.

The main problem is that changing travellers cheques can be slow, particularly away from Manila. Of the banks, the Philippines Commercial International Bank (PCI Bank) is said to offer the best rates for Amex travellers cheques. Another advantage of Amex travellers cheques is that they are more easily exchanged than other varieties.

Eurocheques

It is becoming increasingly difficult to use Eurocheques in the Philippines. Even in Manila you'll barely find a bank willing to accept this form of payment. Occasionally, resident foreigners will be willing to swap their pesos for Eurocheques. You can find out about current possibilities for deals of this sort in foreign-run restaurants and businesses.

ATMs

The age of electronic banking has reached the Philippines. If you intend to stay for an extended period in the Philippines it would be worth opening a bank account and applying for an ATM card.

The biggest accounting systems are BancNet (Allied Bank, Metrobank, PCI Bank) and MegaLink (Asian Bank, Bank of Commerce, Equitable Bank, Far East Bank, Philippine National Bank, Traders Royal Bank). Several hundred branch offices have been equipped with ATMs throughout the country.

Your MasterCard will allow you to withdraw as much as P20,000 in P4000 lots (debited from your account back home) per day from any PCI Bank ATM. Using a Visa card it is possible to get up to P4000 per withdrawal from any Philippine National Bank ATM.

It's a good idea to withdraw money only during regular banking hours, as the ATMs are connected to the central office in Manila. If your withdrawal isn't confirmed there, a 'response too late' message appears on the screen and you don't get any money.

Bank Account

If you're thinking of opening an account with a Philippine bank, you should be aware that only the first P100,000 are insured. By law, larger amounts do not have to be reimbursed should the bank suffer bankruptcy. Even two or more accounts at the same bank are not insured beyond a total amount of P100,000 when the holder of each account is the same person.

Credit Cards

International cards such as Amex, Diner's Club, MasterCard and Visa are accepted by many hotels, restaurants and businesses in the Philippines. With your Visa and MasterCard you can withdraw cash in pesos at any branch of the Equitable Bank (almost every big city has a branch). There are plenty of branches in Manila, for example, on the corner of United Nations Ave and Bocobo St (down from the Holiday Inn Manila Pavilion on the other side of the road), Ermita.

You can withdraw US dollars or travellers cheques on your Amex card in Manila at its office in the Ace building, Rada St, Makati.

Amex card holders can get US$1000 in travellers cheques every 21 days on their card account but you must have a personal cheque as well. Without a personal cheque for any 30 day period, card members may not exceed US$500 (US$1000 for Platinum Card members) or its equivalent in local currency.

The Equitable Bank has brought out its own national Visa card. Many of the hotels, restaurants and businesses displaying showy posters confirming that they accept 'Visa' are actually referring to this local version.

International Transfers

Having money forwarded can be time consuming. Even transfers by telex often take 10 days or longer. Presumably the banks make the money work for them first.

It's advantageous to have a safe-deposit account, as that way you can arrange for the desired sum of money to be sent by telex. Costs are in the vicinity of US$15 and the waiting time is two days.

In Manila, use Amex or the Philippine National Bank – the Bank of America tends to be slow. Payment will be made in pesos or

US dollar travellers cheques. Some banks are unwilling to pay in cash. If anything, they might offer you the amount in very small bills, which you're better off refusing.

Other Methods

If you wish to send money to the Philippines, do so by registered letter. To keep on the safe side, camouflage the valuable item with a piece of carbon paper and then fasten the contents to the envelope with a staple on the outside. Postal money orders present no problem. These take about 10 days.

Currency

The Philippine currency is technically spelt piso, but it's usually referred to as the peso (P). It's divided into 100 centavos (c). There are coins of 1, 5, 10, and 25 centavos, 1 and 5 pesos and, until 1998, 50 centavos and 2 pesos. From 1998, only coins inscribed 'Bangko Sentral ng Pilipinas' will be legal tender. Banknotes are available in denominations of 5, 10, 20, 50, 100, 500 and 1000 pesos.

Currency Exchange

Australia	A$1	=	P20.72
Canada	C$1	=	P19.39
Germany	DM1	=	P17.17
Hong Kong	HK$1	=	P3.41
Japan	¥100	=	P23.55
Malaysia	RM$1	=	P10.50
New Zealand	NZ$1	=	P18.18
Thailand	B1	=	P1.03
UK	£1	=	P41.09
USA	US$1	=	P26.27
Vietnam	D1	=	P2.38

Changing Money

In some towns there may be no bank at all and the only possibility of changing money may be at a hotel – at a poor exchange rate. Moneychangers are often faster and more efficient than banks, although it's wise to shop around since their rates vary. When you change money try to get a reasonable amount in smaller denominations: taxi drivers can almost never change big notes. In more remote areas it can be difficult to change even P100 notes.

As for foreign currency, it's no longer true to say that nothing other than US dollars exists, but it certainly exists more than most.

Banks You'll get the best exchange rate in Manila. In the provinces, you may lose as much as 20%. In remote districts only the peso and, possibly, the US dollar will be accepted; in those areas no other currency can be relied upon. Sometimes a bank will give you a better rate for your currency than a moneychanger, at other times the opposite will be the case. You could also be charged for a quick comparison of exchange rates.

Many provincial banks only exchange travellers cheques of US$100 or less. Cheques for larger amounts can only be cashed with the consent of the bank manager.

You are not permitted to take more than P1000 out of the country. Unused pesos can only be changed at the banking counter in the departure hall of Ninoy Aquino international airport (NAIA); you have to produce an official white (or yellow) exchange slip. These can be obtained from a bank or a licensed money exchange office.

Opening hours in Philippine banks are Monday to Friday from 9 am to 3 pm (a few banks stay open until 3.30 pm).

Moneychangers You'll get a fairly good exchange rate for cash from licensed moneychangers. In Manila, these will be found on Mabini St (between Padre Faura and Pedro Gil) in Ermita. The rate varies with the size of the bill – US$100 and US$50 bills are best, US$1 bills are hardly wanted at all. Some moneychangers will change travellers cheques. Besides your passport (a photocopy of which is taken on your first transaction), you will need to produce the receipts from your purchase of travellers cheques, showing the certified number of each cheque.

Black Market

There is said to be a small black market but the slightly better rate is not worth the risk. And the risk is real – there are a lot of money rip-off scams in Manila and any offer of a spectacular exchange rate is bound to be a setup. The scam artists have a wide variety of tricks involving sleight of hand and other subterfuges, and they usually approach you in a seemingly innocent way. For example, somebody comes up to you in the street in Ermita or Malate and shows you a card displaying an encitingly high exchange rate. Don't fall for it.

Illegal moneychangers often begin by offering you a perfectly correct exchange rate. You receive your pesos, the dealer takes the dollars. Then, all of a sudden, the dealer will apologise for having short changed you P50. The dealer takes the pesos back, counts them out again and ostentatiously places the allegedly missing P50 on top of the pile, while stealthily removing some other notes from the bottom.

Another favourite trick is to not pay out the agreed sum so as to provoke the customer into cancelling the deal. The customer then gets counterfeit dollars handed back while the dealer keeps the good dollars and pesos. There's no getting away from the fact that most black marketeers are consummate artists when it comes to fraud. This also goes for the young Filipinas who buttonhole male tourists before passing them on to their well-fed moneychanging 'brothers'.

Tipping & Bargaining

Just as in other countries, tipping is a personal decision. If you stay in the same hotel for a few days however, there is no doubt the hotel staff would appreciate a P20 tip.

Restaurant staff generally expect a tip (it is part of their wage), even if the menu states that a service charge is included. The money then goes into a kitty and is shared later with the cook and the cashier. If the service was particularly good, a tip of around 5% of the bill will show your appreciation.

Taxi drivers will often try to wangle a tip by claiming they have no change. If the charge on the meter appears to be accurate, the passenger should voluntarily round up the amount. For example, if the fare is P44, then P50 would be appropriate.

When shopping in markets or even shops,

Filipinos try to get a 10% discount. They almost always succeed. Foreign customers will automatically be quoted a price that is around 20% more than normal or, in places which deal mainly with tourists, up to 50% more. On the other hand, department stores and supermarkets offer set prices, and it is not customary to bargain.

Prayer For Tourists

Heavenly Father, look down on us your humble obedient tourist servants, who are doomed to travel this earth, taking photographs, mailing postcards, buying souvenirs and walking around in drip-dry underwear.

Give us this day divine guidance in the selection of our hotels, that we may find our reservations honoured, our rooms made up and hot water running from the faucets.

We pray that the telephones work, and the operators speak our tongue.

Lead us, dear Lord to good inexpensive restaurants where the food is superb, the waiters friendly and the wine included in the price.

Give us the wisdom to tip correctly in currencies we do not understand. Forgive us for undertipping out of ignorance and overtipping out of fear. Make the natives love us for what we are, and not for what we can contribute to their worldly goods.

Grant us the strength to visit the museums, the cathedrals, the palaces and the castles listed as a 'must' in the guidebooks.

And if by chance we skip a historic monument to take a nap after lunch, have mercy on us for our flesh is weak.

(Seen in the Shamrock Cafe, Sagada)

POST & COMMUNICATIONS
Postal Rates

Airmail letters (per 20g) within the Philippines cost P4 (ordinary/three weeks), P8 (special/one week) and P16 (speed/24 hours).

Airmail letters (per 10g) cost P6 to South-East Asia, P7 to Australia and the Middle East, P8 to Europe and North America, and P9 to Africa and South America.

Aerograms and postcards cost P5 regardless of the destination.

Sending Mail

So far all my letters have arrived home safely. If you are sending important items (such as film) by mail, it is best to send it by registered post. Registered express letters will be delivered – all going well – within five days. Around Christmas especially, you should make sure your letters are stamped immediately so that no-one can remove your postage stamps and use them again.

Receiving Mail

The Philippine postal system is generally efficient. You can get mail sent by poste restante at the GPO in all major towns. Ask people who are writing to you to print your surname clearly and underline it – most missing mail is simply misfiled under given names.

You can also have mail sent to an Amex office if you're using Amex travellers cheques or carrying an Amex card. Amex has offices in Manila and Cebu City. The Manila address is Clients' Mail, American Express, ACE building, Rada St, Makati. You can get information by calling ☎ 814 4777 (ask to be connected).

Parcels Depending on the country, only parcels weighing less than 10 or 20 kg will be dispatched by the Philippine postal service. They must also be wrapped in plain brown paper and fastened with string. Parcels sent to Europe by surface (sea) mail take from two to four months to reach their destination.

Parcel post rates are calculated in kilograms. There is a basic rate for the first kg, thereafter you are charged for every kg or part thereof. For example, this is the deal for the UK: maximum weight 20 kg (air), 10 kg (surface); rate for the first kg (air) P615, for each additional kg or part thereof P315; and rate for the first kg (surface) P426, for each additional kg or part thereof P166.

Opening Hours Opening hours in Philippine post offices are not the same everywhere. Many close at noon, and not all are open on Saturday. The following opening hours can usually be relied on: Monday to Friday from 8 am to noon and 1 to 5 pm. With few exceptions, post offices are closed on Sunday and public holidays, and at the end of the year there are at least three public holidays: Rizal Day (30 December); New Year's Eve; and New Year's Day. During the Christmas period, from mid-December to mid-January, mail is delayed by up to a month (see Public Holidays & Special Events later in this chapter).

Telephone

Phones are scarce in the Philippines. In an emergency try the nearest police station – which in many areas will have the only telephone (only four percent of Filipinos possess a phone). Phone numbers are always changing so get a local directory before calling.

It can take a ridiculously long time to be connected locally and the lines over long distances are bad. International calls are a breeze in comparison.

Long-distance overseas calls can be made from most hotels (operator or direct dialling; it depends on their equipment). A three minute station to station call to Europe costs about P300. It's a few pesos cheaper if you call from a Philippine Long Distance Telephone Company (PLDT) office.

Note that it is far cheaper to make station to station rather than person to person calls from the Philippines: the charges are about 25% less.

Try to call outside business hours (for the country you are ringing), the waiting time will be considerably shorter. On Sunday there is a 25% reduction in the charge.

Fax, Telegraph & Email

Many hotels and offices are equipped with fax machines, although sending an international fax from a hotel can be quite expensive (eg, P350 for one page to Europe). Private telecommunication companies, including Eastern Telecoms and PLDT, charge about P95 for the first minute (one page) and P85 for the following minutes.

Domestic fax transmissions are relatively cheap. From Manila to Cebu City the first minute costs P25 and the following minutes are P20.

The international telegram service is pretty prompt and reliable, but internal telegrams are likely to be delayed. There are two major domestic telegram companies: Radio Communications of the Philippines (RCPI); and Philippine Telegraph & Telephone Corporation (PT & T).

To Europe, 12 hour telegrams cost about P14 a word and to Australia they cost P15. Within the Philippines, a telegram to Cebu from Manila, for example, costs about P1.50 a word and takes five hours. To compare, a telex to Europe costs P85 per minute (four lines) through Eastern Telecoms.

If you're dying to send email, there are so-called Cyber Cafés opening up in many of the major cities. Manila, Baguio and Cebu City (see the individual listings) already have one or more compu-cafés, with or without drinks, and you can be sure more are on the way. Costs vary, but for about the cost of a short call home you can surf the Net or chat via keyboard for hours on end. See Online Services later in this section for more information.

BOOKS

Manila has a good selection of bookshops. There is a fairly active local publishing industry, mainly in English. Books on the Philippines tend to fall into either the coffee-table variety or the rather dry facts and history group. Unfortunately, most Philippine publications are sold out shortly after they have been published, and only rarely is a second edition printed. See Bookshops in the Information section of the Manila chapter.

Lonely Planet

Besides the book you hold in your hands, Lonely Planet publishes guides to the neighbouring countries of the Philippines. The *Tagalog (Pilipino) phrasebook* is also a handy pocket-size language companion.

For an overall guide to the region, look for *South-East Asia on a shoestring*. All guides are updated regularly, and are available in bookshops and hiking shops throughout the world.

For those with access to cyberspace, check out the award-winning Lonely Planet Web site at: http://www.lonelyplanet.com

Travel

New among travel books on the Philippines is *A Journey through the Enchanted Isles* by Amadis Guerrero, an interesting armchair tour of the Philippine islands.

Although published in the 80s, both *Luzon by Car* and *Philippine Vacations & Explorations* by Jill Gale de Villa still give useful information for your journey.

It is also tempting to read about treks undertaken by European travellers in the last century. Two of these are Fedor Jagor's *Travels in the Philippines* and Paul de la Gironnière's *Adventures of a Frenchman in the Philippines*.

History & Politics

Notable publications in the last few years have been *Who's Who in Philippine History* by Carlos Quirino, *In Our Image – America's Empire in the Philippines* by Stanley Karnow, *The Marcos Dynasty* by Sterling Seagrave and the excellently researched *Power from the Forest – The Politics of Logging* by Marites Dañguilan Vitug.

ONLINE SERVICES

At last count, there were 37 Internet Service Providers (ISPs) in the Philippines, and the numbers are growing rapidly. Information on the Philippines can be found on the Internet using the usual search engines. In late 1996 Yahoo listed well over 200 sites and more are sure to be added. Useful sites include Jake Taylor's Scuba Diving in the Philippines and Pete Gallo's Wreck Diving in the Philippines. Online access to Philippine newspapers such as the *Manila Bulletin* and *Inquirer* is also possible.

Major online providers are accessible in the Philippines and are adding lines all the time. Check before leaving for up-to-date numbers (on CompuServe, for example, at GOPHONES).

NEWSPAPERS & MAGAZINES

After 20 years of press censorship under Marcos, the change of government brought a flood of new national and local newspapers and magazines indulging in a journalistic free-for-all. Before, there was a group of four big government-friendly national dailies. Now about 20 publications, including the *Manila Bulletin*, *Inquirer*, *Malaya*, *The Manila Chronicle*, *Manila Standard*, *Newsday*, *Today*, *Daily Globe*, *The Philippine Star*, *The Journal* and *Evening Star* fight for a share of the market. All are in English. In contrast to the unilateral reporting during Marcos's time, the media today offers a fair and critical difference of opinion. *Tempo* and *Peoples* are vigorous tabloid papers, which appear in both English and Tagalog.

A lesser role is played by the Philippine papers *Balita*, *Taliba* and *Ang Pilipino Ngayon*, in keeping with their circulation and layout. In the Sunday editions of various newspapers a magazine is included. Newspapers printed in Manila but sold outside the capital are more expensive because of transport costs.

There are also a few magazines which appear weekly, among them *Free Press*, with its irreverent and critical articles, standing out.

International events are meagrely reported or analysed in the Philippine mass media. If you want more information, the following publications can be found on sale in the larger hotels: *Newsweek*, *Time*, *Asiaweek*, *Far Eastern Economic Review*, and the *International Herald Tribune*.

Both English-language newspapers, *Foreign Post* and *What's On & Expat*, appear weekly and are free in many hotels. As you might guess, both papers are aimed at expats and tourists.

Don't underestimate the power of the cartoon either – the number of comic books published and read each week is phenomenal.

RADIO & TV

Radio and TV operate on a commercial basis, and the programmes are continually interrupted by advertisements. There are 22 TV channels all up. Seven broadcast from Manila, sometimes in English and sometimes in Tagalog.

The development of satellite and cable TV has already made its mark in the Philippines. CNN, ESPN and BBC World are widely available, as well as local programming. Many hotels provide programmes from the Satellite Television Asian Region (STAR), which originates in Hong Kong, via AsiaSat 1. Several English-language channels, including one dedicated to movies, are available in addition to those in Chinese.

Sub-carriers on the satellite downlinks may also provide radio programming, including many international stations such as VOA, BBC World Service, Deutsche Welle etc. Consult your hotel for the availability of this service.

VIDEO SYSTEMS

Unlike the rest of the world, the Philippines was late in deciding that VHS should be the de facto standard for VCRs. Consequently, Betamax is still widespread, although gradually losing ground.

If you come from the USA, remember that the NTSC system is not compatible with PAL or SECAM. There is no point bringing NTSC videos from the USA as they will not be playable in the Philippines. Similarly, if buying videos here to take home, make sure it's an NTSC version before you buy it – converting it later costs a lot of money.

PHOTOGRAPHY & VIDEO
Film & Equipment

Take sufficient slide film with you as there is not a lot of choice in the Philippines. This is especially true of the provinces, where the use-by date on film has often expired. Kodak Ektachrome 100 costs about P170, a 200 costs P215 and a 400 costs about P250.

There's no problem with normal colour film, which is often preferred by Filipinos. Processing is fast and good value. High-gloss prints (nine cm by 13 cm) can be processed in an hour at a cost of P2.50 per print.

Officially you are only allowed to bring five cartridges of film in with you, but customs officials usually turn a blind eye to tourists.

Photography

The usual rules for tropical photography apply in the Philippines. Remember to allow for the intensity of the tropical light, try to keep your film as cool and dry as possible, and have it developed soon after exposure.

Video

The Philippines are full of colour and motion, providing an endless palette of themes for the amateur and professional camera buff. Remember to use your zoom sparingly – there's usually enough going on in front of the lens, it doesn't need any additional help.

Photographing People

Filipinos are fond of having their picture taken, but always remember that cameras can still be intrusive and unpleasant reminders of the impact of tourism – it's polite to ask before you photograph people. And a smile always helps. Under no circumstances should photographs be taken of soldiers or military installations.

Airport Security

Although airport X-ray equipment is said to be safe for film, it's certainly not *good* for film. If you're passing through airport security checks on a number of occasions, have your film inspected separately.

TIME

The Philippines is eight hours ahead of GMT/UTC, and two hours behind Australian Eastern Standard Time. When it's noon in the Philippines it's 8 pm the previous evening in San Francisco, 11 pm in New York, 3 am in London and 2 pm in Sydney.

Philippine time has a curious nature – it includes lack of punctuality. A rendezvous à-la-Philippine time is basically very loose. Either you are waited for, or you wait. Don't get upset – tomorrow is another day, and sunrise and sunset, at least, will be on time.

ELECTRICITY
Voltage & Cycle

The electric current is generally 220V, 60 cycles, although the voltage is often less. In some areas the standard current is the US-style 110V. Blackouts are common even in the tourist centres, so a torch (flashlight) might be handy.

Plugs & Sockets

An adapter may be needed for Philippine plugs, which are usually like the flat, two pin US type.

WEIGHTS & MEASURES

In general, the metric system is in use, although both metric and imperial are understood. Lengths are often given in feet and yards rather than centimetres and metres. Weight is normally expressed in grams and kilograms, and temperature in centigrade.

If you need to convert from one system to the other, use the Lonely Planet conversion chart inside the back cover of this book.

LAUNDRY

There are only a few laundries in the Philippines open to the public which are equipped with modern machinery. Self-service laundrettes with coin-operated machines are completely unknown.

If you don't want to wash your clothes yourself, hand them in to your hotel or guesthouse and you'll get them back within two to three days. They will not always be ironed. It costs about P15 to have a shirt or blouse washed and ironed.

HEALTH

See the Health chapter at the back of this book.

TOILETS

Philippine toilets are known as comfort rooms or CRs – *lalake* means 'gentlemen' and *babae* 'ladies' in Filipino. The toilets in restaurants and bars are usually dirty, and there is seldom toilet paper, but you will always find clean toilets in the lobbies of the larger hotels. Although Shakey's Pizza Parlours have expensive pizzas, they do have clean toilets!

Western-style sit-down toilets are the norm, although the Philippine variety is smaller.

WOMEN TRAVELLERS
Attitudes to Women
Many Filipino men think of themselves as irresistible macho types, but they can also turn out to be surprisingly considerate gentlemen. They are especially keen to show their best side to foreign women. They will address you respectfully as 'Ma'am', shower you with friendly compliments ('you are so beautiful' etc) and engage you in polite conversation.

But Filipinas too (for instance if travelling next to a foreign women on a bus) will not miss the chance to ask a few questions out of curiosity. You could be quizzed about your home country, your reason for travelling, and, of course, your husband, how many children you have etc. It is then not unusual for the Filipina to get out of the bus after a few km and be replaced by another one, who will then proceed to ask exactly the same questions all over again.

So it's a good idea to have a few answers ready. After a few days on the road you could be grateful for the conversation.

Safety Precautions
If drunken Filipinos pester you, it is best simply to ignore them. Simulated friendliness could easily be misunderstood as an invitation to get to know each other better. If a group of Filipinos starts a drinking session in a restaurant, it is not exactly recommended to sit down at a table next to them. In such cases, the best thing to do is just to change restaurants.

There have been cases of Filipinos sexually harassing foreign women, but they are very, very rare. In the absence of alcohol, frightening naivety and simple stupidity, probably the vast majority of cases could have been avoided.

Another word of advice: inspect hotel rooms with thin walls for strategic peepholes, and be wary of accepting cigarettes, food, drinks or sweets from friendly strangers as these gifts might be drugged. See also Dangers & Annoyances later in this chapter for more information.

What to Wear
Women are very fashion conscious in the Philippines, and they place a great deal of emphasis on being neat and tidy in their dress. Visiting foreign women should also pay attention to their outward appearance if they want to be treated with respect. Clothing can be still be practical, ie shorts and a blouse or T-shirt are quite acceptable while travelling. If you are swimming in a place where there are not many tourists, or you have Filipino friends with you, it is better to wear shorts and a T-shirt over your swimsuit. That way you will not draw unwanted attention to yourself or embarrass your friends on your behalf.

Particular care should be taken in Muslim areas, where wearing revealing clothing can cause real unpleasantness. Wear a knee-length skirt or pants, especially if you intend to visit a mosque.

Organisations
There are several international women's groups in Manila, such as the American Women's Club of the Philippines (☎ 817 7587) and the Australian Women's Association (☎ 816 3836). Check with your embassy also.

GAY & LESBIAN TRAVELLERS
Homosexuals are viewed tolerantly in the Philippines. Even if jokes are told about them (never meant in an insulting or prejudiced way), gay men ('bakla') and lesbians ('tomboy', 'binalaki' or 'binalalaki') are almost universally accepted as part of everyday Philippine society. An exception is made in the armed forces, where gays and lesbians are banned from military service.

Organisations
The Pink Triangle is a Philippine organisation for gays and lesbians which publishes an online magazine called Kabaklaan, where contact addresses, telephone numbers etc can be obtained. Also online is the Filipino Queer Directory Gay and Lesbian Organisation. Both can be found on the Internet, using Yahoo with the appropriate search criteria.

DISABLED TRAVELLERS

If you only look at what provisions have (or have not) been made in buildings, you'll see that the Philippines are really not suited for disabled people. Only a few hotels and guesthouses are equipped with wheelchair ramps, and only rarely has an architect thought of providing roomy toilets with big doors. On the other hand, these deficits are largely made up for by the sheer humanity of the people. When they see a disabled person, Filipinos are not stunned into inaction because they're so concerned, nor do they turn away helplessly. They behave perfectly naturally, without ingratiating themselves in an embarrassing way. And if needed, there's always someone there with a helping hand.

SENIOR TRAVELLERS

The older generation is treated with respect and deference in the Philippines, and this applies equally well to visitors. On the practical side, if you are a senior over 60 years of age, PAL will give you a 20% rebate on all inland flights, and you won't have to pay anything for the boat trip to the Underground River in St Paul Subterranean National Park.

TRAVEL WITH CHILDREN

A Philippine child is never alone, so an 'exotic' foreign child will definitely never spend a moment without someone to play with. Filipinos are simply crazy about children. If you travel with a child, people will often strike up a conversation with you.

It's a good idea when travelling with children to include as many specific activities for them as you feel comfortable with yourself. For instance, in Manila a visit to the Museum Pambuta will keep the kids occupied for quite some time. This can help make up for those 'boring adult places' you insist on visiting.

DANGERS & ANNOYANCES
Security

If you throw your money on the table in bars and restaurants, or flash large banknotes around, don't be surprised if you get mugged when you leave. Carelessness gets punished, and the crooks are waiting for opportunities,

just like their counterparts anywhere else in the world.

Look after your valuables and don't even let on that you have them. You will be taken for a wealthy foreigner regardless, even if you are not well off by western standards. Irresponsible behaviour will only provoke a challenge. This is particularly the case at Christmas, when the time of peace and goodwill mobilises a whole army of thieves and beggars to pay for their gifts with the help of money from tourists and locals alike.

Here are some hints on how to guard your possessions and look after your own safety:

- Money belongs in your front trouser pockets, in a pouch worn around your neck and under your clothes, or in a concealed money belt.
- Keep shoulder or camera bags in body contact; don't let them out of your sight. Develop the habit of keeping your hand underneath them.
- Don't pay your taxi fare until all of your luggage is unloaded.
- Deposit valuables in a hotel safe, or rent a safe-deposit box at a large bank: it will cost about P200 a year. This is recommended if you want to deposit tickets, documents, travellers cheques or souvenirs while travelling around the country. An important thing to remember when leaving is that all the banks are closed on public holidays. Unfortunately, it's very difficult to get a safe-deposit box: either they are all allocated or the bank will not accept short-term deposits.
- Don't reveal the name of your hotel or your room number to strangers. If necessary, give a false address.
- Look over your hotel room carefully before you check out: anything left behind becomes the property of whoever finds it.
- Wherever there are tourists there are thieves: for example, pickpockets on Ermita and thieves in the buses to Batangas and the Puerto Galera pier. Be particularly cautious around Ermita, especially on Mabini St and Rizal Park.
- If someone runs up to you, anxiously advising you that your money has been stolen, stay calm and don't immediately reach for the place where you keep your money. The pickpocket is just waiting for you to give your hiding place away.
- Pickpockets may masquerade as newspaper vendors, but they usually have only one newspaper, which they will hold up to your face while cleaning out your pockets with their free hand. Now and then these mostly youthful thieves will employ their tricks in restaurants, taking with them anything useful such as cigarettes and lighters.

- In Baguio and Banaue, tourists have been approached by one or two attractive young Filipinas (or two friendly Filipino men) and invited for coffee, which tastes a bit strange (not uncommon for native coffee in this area). After five or 10 minutes the visitors are out cold, and wake up 12 hours later in a park or field with their valuables gone.

- Beware the complete stranger who comes up to you, especially in the Ermita district (Mabini St, Rizal Park) or at the Nayong Pilipino near the airport, and spins you a line about remembering you. Don't accept any invitations to dinner, or tours of the town.

- Beware of westerners who either can't or won't go home and talk about 'extremely promising' ideas or having good connections. They will tell you that all they need is an investor and will assure you they're not in the least worried about how small or large the investment might be.

- *Calesas* (horse-drawn cabs) in the Ermita district, for example, along Roxas Blvd, are almost always on the lookout fur unsuspecting tourists. The favourite trick is to invite the tourists into the cab to take a picture. While this is happening, two Filipinos get in and tell the driver, who is in the know, to take them on a 'city tour'. After 200 to 300m the 'tour' is over, and the tourist has a tough time trying to get out of having to fork out P250 for the ride.

- Be wary of gambling card game with strangers. If the 'cousin' of your host allegedly works at the casino and offers to coach you in tricks, don't be taken in. I've met tourists who, after losing three games, still haven't realised the syndicate was working against them.

- Then there are the fake police who cruise the tourist quarters of Manila in twos or threes in a new limousine. They stop tourists, showing them a false police badge and, on the pretext of checking for counterfeit currency, ask them to step into the vehicle for a few minutes. These very experienced and terribly obliging gentlemen will then skilfully and swiftly help themselves to some of your cash, and on handing back the rest, will reassure you that the notes are perfectly good. Just to complete the trick, as you alight they'll helpfully draw your attention to the pickpockets and petty criminals allegedly waiting for you on every street corner.

- It is rare for Filipino police officers to show a badge as ID; usually their mark of authenticity is the neatly pressed uniform or the revolver hanging loosely from their belt. Plain-clothes officers are more likely to get about in a T-shirt, jeans and gym shoes, than in a suit. Number plates on police cars are, as on all government vehicles, white with red letters and numbers, and the first letter is usually 'S'. Number plates of licensed taxis are yellow with black lettering, and those of private vehicles are white with green lettering.

- As well as meeting fake police officers, you may come into contact with a related species: false immigration officials, whose favourite haunt is the Nayong Pilipino and the Intramuros/Rizal Park district. Their game is to demand to inspect passports, and then return them only on payment of a handsome sum. Genuine immigration officials make only occasional random checks of tourists' passports. In any case, they are normally satisfied with a photocopy – there's no need to have the original on you night and day.

- Finally, remember that crooks come up with new scams each year and Filipino thieves certainly don't lack ingenuity or imagination. Don't let them spoil your trip.

Drugs

According to the Drug Enforcement Agency (DEA) based in the USA, the Philippines is the second largest marijuana producing country in the world after Mexico. International drug syndicates also use the country as a transhipment hub for illegal drugs such as *shabu* (methamphetamine hydrochloride), which is a cheap version of crack reportedly manufactured in China.

The laws governing drug abuse have grown increasingly severe in the Philippines since the 80s. Unauthorised people are absolutely forbidden to handle, own or traffic in drugs.

So-called dangerous drugs are divided into two categories: prohibited drugs (opium, heroin, morphine, cocaine, LSD, marijuana); and regulated drugs (pharmaceutical drugs, sleeping pills, pain killers etc).

Penalties range from six to 12 years imprisonment plus a fine of P6000 to P12,000 for possession of marijuana, and up to P30,000 plus the death penalty for manufacture, trafficking, or import or export of any of the prohibited drugs.

Under Philippine law, people found in possession of over 750g of marijuana, 50g of hashish, 200g of shabu, or 40g of heroin, cocaine, opium and morphine will be given the death sentence.

The laws also impose these sorts of penalties for the abuse of regulated drugs, if possession and use is not certified by a doctor's prescription.

If a fine can't be paid in the time allowed,

the accused is free to bring in a lawyer, or to obtain the services of the Legal Assistance Office – if its staff can be motivated into action!

Other Problems

To avoid possible fire traps, see the Accommodation section later in this chapter. For problems sending and receiving mail see Post & Communications earlier in this chapter.

LEGAL MATTERS

If you are arrested, contact your nearest embassy or consulate immediately; however, they may not be able to do much more than provide you with a list of local lawyers and keep an eye on how you are being treated. Remember you are subject to Philippine law when in the Philippines.

BUSINESS HOURS

Businesses first open their doors in the morning between 8 and 10 am. Offices, banks and public authorities have a five day week. Some offices are also open on Saturday morning. Banks open at 9 am and close at 3 or 3.30 pm. Embassies and consulates are open to the public mainly from 9 am to 1 pm.

Offices and public authorities close at 5 pm. Large businesses like department stores and supermarkets continue until 7 pm, and smaller shops often stay open until 10 pm.

PUBLIC HOLIDAYS & SPECIAL EVENTS

Offices and banks are closed on public holidays; shops and department stores remain open. Good Friday is the only time in the year when the entire country closes down. Even public transport stops running, and PAL remains grounded on that day. The public holidays are: New Year's Day (1 January); People Power Day (25 February); Maundy Thursday, Good Friday and Easter Sunday (March/April); Bataan Day (9 April); Labour Day (1 May); Independence Day (12 June); All Saints' Day (1 November); Bonifacio (or National Heroes') Day (30 November); Christmas Day (25 December); and Rizal Day (30 December).

There are many town fiestas which take place on the numerous national holidays

over the year, and family festivals are held for two or three days in honour of the appropriate patron saint each year or so. It is hard to understand how some families shoulder this financial burden; the enormous expenses incurred bear no relation to the poverty and hardship of everyday life in the Philippines. Food and drink are offered with lavish generosity. and at the end of the fiesta some visitors even get the money for their journey home pressed into their hands. One or more bands are hired, and musicians and entertainers add to the atmosphere. There is also usually a beauty contest in which the contestants are heavily sponsored. Foreigners and visitors from distant towns get the same royal treatment as friends and relatives.

January
> *Appey* This is a three day thanksgiving festival of the Bontoc for a bounteous harvest. Countless chickens and pigs are slaughtered and sacrificed for this festival.

1 January
> *New Year's Day* As in western countries, the new year is colourfully and loudly welcomed. Families come together to celebrate the traditional *media noche*, the midnight meal. The streets are incredibly noisy and can be dangerous; fireworks are shot off for several days before New Year. Every year, accidental explosions of illegally produced fireworks result in chaotic scenes at the hospitals.

First Sunday in January
> *Holy Three Kings' Day* This is the official end of the Christmas season. The children receive their last Christmas presents on this day. In the towns of Santa Cruz and Gasan on Marinduque, the imitation kings are led on horseback through the town. Spectators throw coins and sweets to the children who run alongside the procession.

9 January
> *Black Nazarene Procession* What is probably the largest procession of the Philippines begins early in the afternoon in Quiapo at the Quiapo church. Thousands of Catholics crowd the streets in this part of Manila when the 'Black Nazarene', a life-size statue of Christ made of blackwood, is carried through the town.

Third Weekend in January
> *Ati-Atihan* This festival in Kalibo on Panay is the Rio de Janeiro or New Orleans Mardi Gras of the Philippines. It's an important and spectacular festival, when the town rages for three days. People dance, sing and play drums. Thousands of

people, outrageously costumed and cleverly masked, celebrate around the clock until the last evening, when a long procession of excited participants ends the intoxicating festivities.

This festival dates back to the middle of the 13th century, when 10 Datu families had to flee from Borneo. They sailed north-east to the island of Panay, where the resident Ati – small, dark Negrito people – gave them a piece of land on which to settle. A festival celebrated the event and the newly arrived people blackened their faces so they would look just like the local Ati.

Many years later the Spaniards used this ritual to counter attempts by Muslims to convert Kalibo. They got the inhabitants to dye their skin black, wear warlike clothing and pretend they were Ati. This victory against the Muslims was interpreted as being achieved through the intervention of Santo Niño, the child Jesus, and thus the festival started to take on a religious significance.

Third Sunday in January

Sinulog – Santo Niño de Cebu This is the climax of the week-long festival of Pasundayag sa Sinulog. Groups of people, all dressed in costume, gather in central Manila around the junction of Colon St and Osmeña Blvd until about 9.30 am when they make their way through the streets of Cebu City, sometimes marching, sometimes dancing the peculiar Sinulog steps and shouting 'Pit Señor' ('long live the child Jesus').

Sinulog is the traditional dance of the old women followers, who can also be seen dancing by themselves in front of the Basilica Minore del Santo Niño and Magellan's Cross any day of the week. Hotels are nearly always booked out on the holiday weekend.

Sinulog is also celebrated in Kabankalan on Negros during this weekend. As well as the actual Sinulog on the Sunday there are horse fights on the Saturday.

Fourth Weekend in January

Ati-Atihan in Ibajay One weekend after the festival in Kalibo, another festival takes place in Ibajay, 30 km to the north-west. The people of Ibajay say their Ati-Atihan is the original and only true one. Whatever the case, this festival is not fuelled by commercial interests or attended by hordes of tourists – but the locals, dressed in their simple but original costumes, celebrate with as much enthusiasm as the people in Kalibo.

Dinagyang This festival in Iloilo City includes parades, but the spectators are quiet and passive, unlike the crowds at the similar Ati-Atihan activities in Kalibo.

January/February

Chinese Lunar New Year Depending on the lunar calendar, Chinese New Year celebrations take place some time between 21 January and 19 February. There are ritual and traditional dragon dances in Manila's Chinatown.

February

Saranggolahan In many villages and towns this is the beginning of the kite-flying season. People of all ages take part in competitions with kites of the most varied forms, colours and sizes.

2 February

Feast of Our Lady of Candelaria This is a town festival with processions and parades in honour of Our Lady of Candelaria, the patron saint of Jaro, a district of the city of Iloilo. It's the biggest religious event in the western Visayas.

11 February

Feast of Our Lady of Lourdes This celebration is held in memory of the appearance of the 'Lady of Lourdes' in France. It takes place on Kanlaon St, Quezon City, and includes processions in the evening. The feast is also celebrated in San Jose del Monte, Bulacan Province.

14 February

St Valentine's Day This is a day for lovers – an important date for the romantic Filipinos. Small gifts and Valentine's cards are personally delivered or sent, and couples dress up to go to a nice restaurant, dancing or to the movies. Filipinos are deeply upset if they have to spend St Valentine's Day without a Valentine.

22 to 25 February

People Power Days These are thanksgiving days for the end of the Marcos era, peacefully brought about by the people. The Epifanio de los Santos Ave (Edsa) in Quezon City was the main scene of the so-called People Power revolution, and on this wide street the reinstalment of democracy is now celebrated every year. The 25th is an official holiday.

26 February

Dia de Zamboanga This is a festival held by and for Muslims and Christians, with cultural offerings, exhibits, regattas and religious ceremonies, in which the old Spanish and Muslim traditions of the city are given expression.

March/April

Moriones Festival Around Easter there are many passion plays. The most popular and colourful is the Moriones Festival in Marinduque. The Roman soldier Longinus is the focus of the week-long play, not Jesus. Longinus is blind in one eye and as he pierces the right side of the crucified Jesus with his spear, blood drops on his blind eye and suddenly he can see again with both eyes. The first thing he sees is Christ's passage to heaven; Longinus announces the incident and must flee. The Roman warriors want to stop this 'rumour' and capture him on Easter Sunday. His execution by beheading is the climax of the play.

Maundy Thursday (official holiday) Apart from Good Friday, Maundy Thursday is the most intensively celebrated day of the holy week. Deep in thought, people attend church, most of the traffic comes to a halt and a tangible silence reigns throughout the country.

On Maundy Thursday and Good Friday almost everything grinds to a halt – even Metrorail services in Manila and PAL flights. Things start again on Easter Saturday.

Good Friday (official holiday) The many crucifixions and scourges which take place throughout the country have grown into a real tourist attraction! The best known places are San Fernando (Pampanga Province), Antipolo (Rizal Province), Manila and Jordan (Guimaras Island).

Easter Sunday (official holiday) At daybreak throughout the land, church bells are rung to herald the resurrection of Christ. Also at dawn, mother and son processions begin – symbolising the risen Christ's meeting with his mother.

9 April

Bataan Day (official holiday) This is a national remembrance day at the Mt Samat Shrine recalling the disastrous battle against the Japanese in WWII and the degrading 'death march' on the Bataan Peninsula.

27 April

Bahug-Bahugan sa Mactan Magellan's landing and the battle which led to his death are acted out on the beach of Mactan, on Mactan Island, Cebu. There are fights in the water, but be early as some years the activities start at 8 am and are all over a couple of hours later.

April, May or June

Turumba Festival 'Turumba' means falling, leaping, jumping, skipping or dancing. This describes the behaviour of the participants in the procession in Pakil, Laguna Province.

1 to 30 May

Flores de Mayo – Santacruzan Throughout the whole country, processions in honour of the Virgin Mary take place in the afternoon and evening. Young girls in white dresses decorate the statues of Mary with flowers.

1 May

Labor Day This is a national holiday with no major activities attached.

3 May

Carabao Carroza Water buffalo races are held in Pavia, a few km north of Iloilo City on Panay Island. The fastest water buffalo from the surrounding 18 *barrios* (neighbourhoods) run against each other in a final deciding race. Beauty queens are also carried to the race track on festive sleds. Be there by 8 am. There is a town fiesta the following day.

14 & 15 May

Carabao Festival This is a two day celebration in honour of the farmers' patron saint, San Isidro. Farmers lead decorated water buffalo to the church square in a long procession on the afternoon of 14 May. There they kneel and are blessed. The next day the water buffalo races take place. Festivals are held in Pulilan (Bulacan Province), San Isidro (Nueva Ecija Province) and Angono (Rizal Province).

15 May

Pahiyas San Isidro is also honoured in Lucban and Sariaya, Quezon Province. On the day of the harvest festival, the house façades are decorated with agricultural products. There is a procession in the afternoon. The huge leaves and blooms, which look like coloured glass and shine in the sun, are particularly decorative on Lucban. They are made out of *kiping*, a rice dough, and eaten at the end of the festival, or given to the guests. The procession takes place in the afternoon.

12 June

Independence Day This is a national holiday with military parades.

24 June

Feast of San Juan Bautista The deeds of St John the Baptist are re-enacted on this day in San Juan, Manila. Friends, relatives and curious spectators are 'baptised'. Water is thrown from, and at, passing cars – keep your camera in a plastic bag!

Parada ng Lechon In Balayan, Batangas Province, St John's Day is celebrated with a 'suckling pig parade'.

First Sunday in July

Pagoda sa Wawa This is a river procession with the Holy Cross of Wawa in the pagoda boat. It takes place in Bocaue, Bulacan Province, 30 km north of Manila.

29 July

Pateros River Fiesta Pateros, a suburb of Manila, is the centre of duck breeding. From here, Manila is supplied with the Filipino delicacy *balut* (see Snacks in the Food & Drink section later in this chapter). The fiesta recalls the killing of a legendary crocodile which threatened the existence of the balut suppliers.

August

Kadayawan sa Dabaw For two weeks in August, Davao on Mindanao celebrates the Orchid Festival, the Fruit & Food Festival and the Tribal Festival.

Third Weekend in September

Peñafrancia Festival The ceremonious river festival in Naga, South Luzon, has become a great tourist attraction. The climax is the spectacular parade on the Naga River in honour of the Blessed Virgin of Peñafrancia.

10 to 12 October

Zamboanga Hermosa This is a festival with cultural performances, religious ceremonies, exhibitions, regattas and the choosing of Miss Zamboanga. The festival is dedicated to the patron saint of the city, Nuestra Señora del Pilar.

Second Weekend in October

La Naval de Manila This procession goes along the main streets of Quezon City to the Domingo Church. It commemorates the victorious sea battle against the Dutch plunderers in 1646. This festival is also celebrated in Angeles in Pampanga Province.

19 October

MassKara Festival On the weekend closest to 19 October, the largest festival on Negros takes place in Bacolod. There are street dances, and groups of people wearing costumes and smiling masks.

1 November

Undas (All Saints' Day) On this national holiday families meet at the cemetery and stay there the whole night. Numerous lights, candles and flowers on the graves make an impressive sight. There are booths and stalls in front of the cemetery.

23 November

Feast of San Clemente On this feast day a boat parade takes place in Angono, Rizal Province. It is a thanksgiving for the fishing people in honour of their patron saint, San Clemente.

30 November

Bonifacio Day This is a national holiday in honour of Filipino heroes, especially Andres Bonifacio, who headed the Katipunan, the revolutionary movement formed to fight the Spaniards.

Late November, early December

Grand Canao This is a festival of the hill clans in Baguio, North Luzon. There are dances and rituals in which, among other things, victorious warriors are honoured and water buffalo, pigs and chickens are sacrificed. There are also agricultural exhibitions and craft demonstrations.

8 or 9 December

Feast of Our Lady of the Immaculate Conception An impressive boat procession is held at night on the Malabon River and Manila Bay at the fishing community of Malabon in the north-west of Metro Manila. There are street processions in the afternoon.

16 to 25 December

Simbang Gabi You can hear Christmas carols practically all over the Philippines from about the beginning of November. Officially, however, the Christmas season begins on 16 December. Following the old traditions, religious Filipinos go to *simbang gabi* (night masses) which are held before dawn.

24 December

Giant Lantern Festival If 24 December is a Saturday, the most spectacular lantern parade and contest in the Philippines takes place on this date in San Fernando, Pampanga Province (otherwise on the Saturday before Christmas). Some of the *parol* (coloured paper lanterns) are so large they must be drawn by a tractor. For further

details see San Fernando (Pampanga) in the Around Manila chapter.

25 December

Christmas This family day, as in practically all Christian countries, is awaited with great excitement by children. However, grown-ups also seem to wait for a Christmas present impatiently, and ask repeatedly for a week beforehand, 'Where is my Christmas?'.

28 December

Holy Innocents' Day Just as people in the west play April Fools' Day tricks on 1 April, Filipinos try to catch one another out on this day.

30 December

Rizal Day This is a national holiday with street parades in memory of the Filipino national hero, Dr Jose Rizal, who on this day in 1896 was executed by the Spaniards. Statues of him are decorated with flowers, and national flags are lowered to half-mast.

Muslim Holidays

There are also some important dates associated with the Muslim calendar. As the Islamic calendar is lunar, it is 11 days shorter than the Gregorian one, so these dates change each year.

The Hari Raya Poasa, which marks the end of the four week fasting period of Ramadan, is the most important Muslim festival. In February the Hariraya Hajji is the time of pilgrimages to Mecca. Muslims spend most of the 10th day of the 12th month of their calendar in mosques. In March/April, Maulod-En-Nabi is the prophet Mohammed's birthday. It's a Muslim holiday with ceremonial readings from the Koran in all mosques.

ACTIVITIES
Caving

Compared with the number of caves in existence in the Philippines, only a handful have been explored. This is because very few Filipinos would willingly go into the unknown depths of the earth. In earlier times many caves served as burial grounds. It is not unusual to find bones and skulls, although you seldom find artefacts like vessels, tools, arms or jewellery – these have been gathered up during earlier explorations. If you shine a light in completely unknown caves you might find some war spoils left by the Japanese, which, according to the calculations of the American columnist Jack Anderson, are distributed over 172 hiding places in the Philippines and are worth close to US$100 billion.

Cycling

Regional mountain biking associations have sprung up all over, often with belligerent sounding names like COMBAT (Cagayan de Oro Mountain Bikers & Trekkers), M-BOMB (Mountain Bike Organisation of Metro Bacolod) and RAMBO (Road & Mountain Bikers Organisation of Cebu). They are all incredibly enthusiastic and genuinely glad to make contact with foreign bikers. They especially welcome fellow enthusiasts when there is a competition involved, such as the Guimaras International Mountain Bike Festival which was started as an annual event in February 1995, where international participation is actively encouraged.

Desert Islands

There are 7107 islands in the Philippines and more than 60% of them are uninhabited. One would think that this would be music to the ears of a modern-day Robinson Crusoe, but, unfortunately, most of these godforsaken islands are stark rocks or simply sandbanks sticking uninvitingly out of the sea. If you search, however, you will almost certainly find an idyllic spot with white sand and palm beaches. Try north of Bohol, or in Gutob Bay between Culion and Busuanga. I found 12 isolated islands there in one day!

Most budding Crusoes come to the conclusion that it is better to be isolated in pairs or groups. Of what use is the most beautiful place in the world if there is no-one to share it with?

Diving

Diving is a popular activity in the Philippines and not without reason. This country possesses a large selection of major diving areas, although many underwater sites have suffered violent ecological damage. You should use proven diving operators who know the remaining good diving sites.

Lots of diving businesses have grown over the last few years and an almost endless variety of programmes is available. During the high season (mid-March to mid-May) mobile dive bases are set up on various islands. You can hire diving boats at any time of the year and you can rent anything you need from Manila's diving shops, although it is better to bring some of your own equipment. PAL will raise your baggage limit to 30 kg to allow for this, but any oxygen tanks you bring must be empty. If you need to buy diving equipment, try Aquaventure Philippines or Scuba World on Pasong Tamo St and Vito Cruz Extension respectively in Makati, Manila. Besides locally made products they have imported gear from Japan and the USA.

In the Mindoro Strait, east of the little island of Apo, you will find the Apo Reef. At low tide this reef is partly exposed and is among the most spectacular diving areas in the Philippines.

Probably the best place for diving is in the Sulu Sea on the little-explored Tubbataha Reef. Because of the long distance from the port of departure – it's about 185 km from Puerto Princesa in Palawan – and because of the resultant high costs involved, very few companies offer expeditions to this area. The Quiniluban Group is also difficult to get to. It comprises the northern section of the Cuyo Islands and is a protected area for turtles. The island world of the Calamian Group (Busuanga, Culion, Coron), the Bacuit Archipelago (El Nido) and Honda Bay (Puerto Princesa) is relatively easy to get to and is one of the most popular diving areas. Sumilon Island off the south-east coast of Cebu is a year-round favourite.

Hundreds of years of maritime activity have ensured that the floor of the archipelago is littered with wrecks from typhoons, wars and collisions with reefs. Ideal conditions for exploration are found in the sound between the islands of Busuanga and Culion. It was here in 1944 that a fleet of 12 Japanese ships went down, seven of them in a small protected bay, where the wrecks now lie in 30 to 40m of crystal clear water. Subic Bay, which was a restricted military area for years, is a

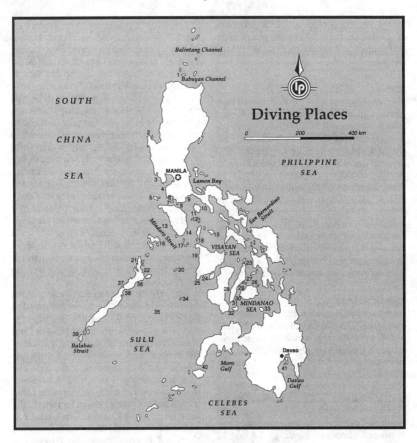

new, top class area for wreck divers. There are said to be at least 20 merchant marine and naval ships sunk in the bay.

For 250 years, Spanish galleons travelled between Manila and Acapulco in Mexico, laden with coins, gold, silk, porcelain, pearls and precious stones. Of the more than 30 trading vessels lost during this era, 21 sank in the coastal waters near the Philippines, mostly near Catanduanes, Samar and South Luzon. Fabulous treasures are said to be spread over the ocean floor and up to now the remains of only 14 of these wrecks have been located.

There is no law in the Philippines against searching for lost galleons. If you find one, however, you must inform the National Museum. If there is a recovery, the discoverer will get a share of the spoils. If you want to explore or photograph a known wreck, you should inform the National Museum of your intentions in writing. It is all too easy to be charged with illegal plunder of treasure.

Gold Hunting
There is so much that wasn't found by the gold-hungry Spaniards. For over 300 years they ruled these islands, yet compared to the

	Diving Place	Diving Season	Entry Point
1	Fuga Island	April – May	Fuga Island
2	Santiago Island	November – June	Bolinao
3	Bay	November – June	Barrio, Barretto, Olongapo
4	Nasugbu	November – June	Nasugbu
5	Lubang Islands	March – June	Catalagan (Batangas Province)
6	Balayan Bay	All Year	Anilao
7	Puerto Galera	All Year	Batangas City
8	Verde Island	All Year	Batangas City
9	Sigayan Bay	All Year	San Juan
10	Mopog Island	April – October	Lucena, Gasan
11	Tres Reyes Islands	April – October	Gasan
12	Dos Hermanas Islands	April – October	Gasan
13	Apo Reef	March – June	San Jose (Mindoro)
14	Buyallao	April – October	Mansalay
15	Cresta de Gallo	March – June	Romblon, Sibuyan
16	Calamian Islands	All Year	Coron
17	Semirara Island	March – June	San Jose (Mindoro)
18	Boracay Island	All Year	Kalibo
19	Batbatan Island	April – June	San Jose (Panay)
20	Cuyo Islands	March – June & October	Cuyo
21	Bacuit Bay	November – June	Liminangcong, El Nido
22	Taytay Bay	April – October	Taytay
23	Capitancillo Island	April – October	Sogod
24	Cresta de Gallo	All Year	San Joaquin
25	Nagas Island	All Year	San Joaquin
26	Danajon Island	All Year	Mactan
27	Mactan	All Year	Cebu City, Mactan
28	Pescador Island	All Year	Moalboal
29	Cabilao Island	All Year	Tagbilaran, Panglao Island
30	Panglao Island	All Year	Tagbilaran, Panglao Island
31	Sumilon Island	All Year	Dumaguete
32	Apo Island	All Year	Dumaguete
33	Mambajao	All Year	Balingoan, Camiguin
34	Cagayan Islands	March – June	Cagayancillo
35	Tubbataha Reef	March – June	Puerto Princesa
36	Green Island Bay	April – October	Roxas
37	Ulugan Bay	November – June	Bahile
38	Honda Bay	April – October	Puerto Princesa
39	Balabac Island	All Year	Balabac
40	Santa Cruz Island	All Year	Zamboanga
41	Talikud Island	All Year	Davao

pillage of South and Central America, their excesses here were humble indeed. Today the Philippines has an output of 30 tonnes of pure gold annually, placing it sixth on the world scale. Less than 10% of the land mass has been explored using the detailed methods of modern mineralogy, so there is still a lot of ground to be covered.

Visitors to the Philippines are allowed to search for gold, the only drawback being that they are not allowed to keep or take out of the country any gold that they might find, as all wealth belongs to the state.

The best way to go fossicking is to get in touch with small-claim holders and make yourself known to local gold panners. If you want to follow a hot tip absolutely legally, you must find a Filipino partner for the business and use their name to contract mining rights with the Bureau of Mines & Geo-Sciences.

Hiking & Trekking

There is always an alternative route available in the Philippines – not just on the freeways and asphalt-covered roads but along the paths which criss-cross the archipelago. It's possible to go from the far north to the deep south with minimum contact using motorised transport. On some islands, it is practically impossible to see a car. On Lubang Island,

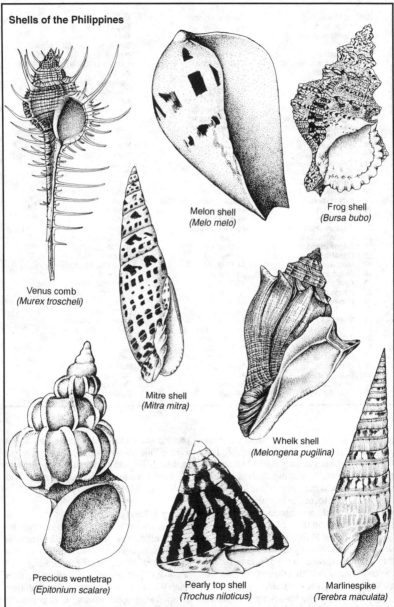

Shells of the Philippines

Venus comb
(*Murex troscheli*)

Melon shell
(*Melo melo*)

Frog shell
(*Bursa bubo*)

Mitre shell
(*Mitra mitra*)

Whelk shell
(*Melongena pugilina*)

Precious wentletrap
(*Epitonium scalare*)

Pearly top shell
(*Trochus niloticus*)

Marlinespike
(*Terebra maculata*)

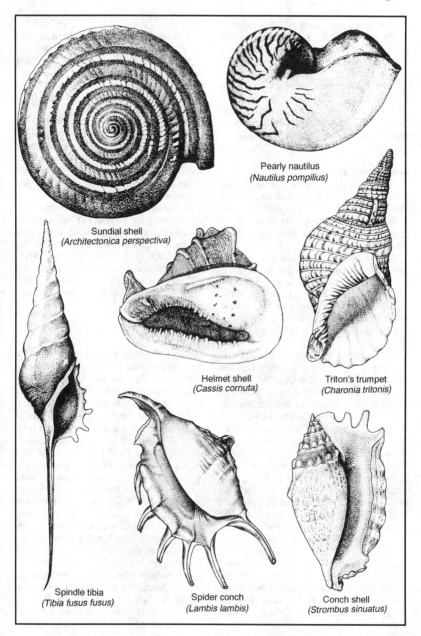

Sundial shell
(*Architectonica perspectiva*)

Pearly nautilus
(*Nautilus pompilius*)

Helmet shell
(*Cassis cornuta*)

Triton's trumpet
(*Charonia tritonis*)

Spindle tibia
(*Tibia fusus fusus*)

Spider conch
(*Lambis lambis*)

Conch shell
(*Strombus sinuatus*)

high-wheeled horse carts still dominate the traffic in spite of the introduction of a few jeeps. It is the same in Busuanga. There, once a day, a rattling old bus travels along the dirt road from Coron to Salvacion. The centre and the north of this island are practically free of cars.

There are wonderful opportunities for trekking along the Pacific coast in the Bicol region and Quezon Province in Luzon.

Mountaineering

There are no alpine summits in the Philippines, although there are volcanoes worth climbing. The official list records 37 volcanoes, 18 active and 19 dormant, but all unpredictable. The most dangerous include Mt Mayon and Mt Taal, which are both known to be explosive and consequently destructive. Other challenges for climbers are the volcanoes Mt Makiling (1144m) and Mt Banahaw (2177m) on Luzon; Mt Hibok-Hibok (1322m) on Camiguin; Mt Kanloan (2465m) on Negros; and Mt Apo (2954m – the highest mountain in the Philippines) on Mindanao.

All volcanoes are overseen by the Commission on Volcanology (Comvol), Hizon building, 29 Quezon Ave, Quezon City. This is where you can learn whether or not an eruption is predicted in the foreseeable future. Specific questions about climbs can be answered by the Philippine National Mountaineering Association in the Tours & Promotions section of PAL, 1500 Roxas Blvd, Ermita, Manila. The people at Lakay Kalikasan Mountaineers, a relatively new organisation, are committed and unfailingly helpful; they can be reached at Suite 401, Fil-Garcia Towers, 140 Kalayaan Ave on the corner of Mayaman St, Diliman, Quezon City, Manila (☎ 924 6421, 924 6411; fax 924 6419). They organise 'environmental outdoor programmes' and specialise in climbing destinations around Manila. Their favourite spot is without a doubt Mt Banahaw, but they also offer more distant places like Mt Kanlaon on Negros and Mt Pulog in North Luzon.

Sailing

Every two years Manila is the destination of the China Sea Race, a classic 1200 km regatta which starts in Hong Kong. This event not only serves to guide the participants through some exotic islands, but also brings with it thousands of spectators from the international yachting scene.

The monsoon which blows steadily from September to May in the north-east guarantees good sailing conditions, and many natural harbours invite sailors to rest. It is not uncommon for a crew to decide to spend the winter in one of the beautiful bays of Puerto Galera or Balanacan.

Favourite spots for yachts include the anchorages in the Visayas. For sailing enthusiasts there is also the opportunity to take part in a round trip. You can ask about this at the Manila Yacht Club (MYC) on Roxas Blvd. It is is helpful to foreign yachts as well, and will organise guides or an escort from the coastguard when sailing through pirate-infested waters.

Surfing

Surfing in the Philippines is still a relatively new phenomenon. Although American GIs stationed in Angeles and Olongapo were already looking for big waves in the 80s, it wasn't until the 90s that it really became widely popular. Enticing photos in glossy international surf magazines gave the final push, until finally the Surfers Association of the Philippines (SAP) was founded and surfing competitions were organised.

The best known surf beaches can be found at places like San Juan on the north-west coast of Luzon; Baler and Daet (Bagasbas Beach) on the Pacific east coast of Luzon; Puraran on Catanduanes; and, most important of all, on Siargao Island in the north-east of Mindanao. The south-east coast of Samar also has a few interesting places to offer. Surf season on the beaches of the South China Sea is from November until March, while the Pacific beaches have their best conditions from May until November when the wind blows steadily from the south-west.

Windsurfing

Some time in the mid-80s the first colourful sails could be seen darting about at White Beach on Boracay. Nowadays you couldn't imagine Boracay without windsurfers. From November until March, the time when the north-east monsoon *(amihan)* blows, the island is the unchallenged spot for windsurfing in the Philippines. The highlight of every season is the annual Boracay International Funboard Cup, held in January. It is Asia's most important windsurfing competition, which is reflected in the number of international entries.

A favourite destination for the boardsailing community is also Lake Caliraya, home of the Caliraya Windsurfing Fleet (CWF), about 80 km south-east of Manila in the rolling foothills of the Sierra Madre mountains. Non-members pay P30 per day to use the so-called Surfkamp here, a loose conglomeration of tents, storage facilities, boards and sails on a small peninsula sticking out into the lake. The windsurf fanatics here give everyone a warm welcome, whether beginner or ace.

WORK

Non-resident aliens may not be employed at all, nor (theoretically) even look for work, without a valid work permit. Foreign residents need the necessary work registration. For details, contact the Department of Labor and Employment (DOLE), Palacio del Gobernador, General Luna St, Intramuros, Manila (☎ 527 3577).

ACCOMMODATION

Prices for good inexpensive accommodation start at around P200.

The cheapest are the guesthouses in the mountains of North Luzon, although some will be pretty basic – with no electricity, for example. The best selection of well-equipped, medium-priced hotels can be found in Angeles, near Mt Pinatubo. On the popular little island of Boracay, during the high season from December until May, only a handful of resorts offer cottages for less than P500; however, during the off season all sorts of

attractive discounts are available. Reasonably priced accommodation from P150 up to P500 can be found on Palawan, the 'last frontier' of the Philippines.

Throughout the Philippines you will find that prices for single and double rooms are sometimes the same. This is because single rooms sometimes have a double bed and can therefore be used by two people; to the Filipinos this is the same as a double room. Double rooms usually have two beds.

The term 'bath' has generally been used throughout the book to mean a bathroom that is equipped with a toilet and shower. It is only in 1st class international hotels that you can expect a bathtub. Filipino homes normally have a shower and not a bathtub.

Should you have accommodation difficulties in smaller towns, go to the mayor or barrio captain. He will quickly arrange some shelter for you and may even find a place for you in the government resthouse.

In the provinces you may often be invited into private homes. It is the custom in the Philippines to offer guests the best food and lodging, but this can be very expensive for the family. By all means accept their hospitality, but don't offer money directly for your board and keep either – say it's to educate their children, for example.

Camping

As a general rule, you can pitch a tent anywhere you want in the Philippines. Needless to say, it is customary to ask politely for permission if your place for the night is obviously on private land. You will seldom get 'no' for an answer.

The ideal site is under the shade of a big, leafy tree. Never put your tent under a coconut palm, because a falling nut can cause serious problems. On a beach you can orient yourself by looking for the high water line, which is marked by flotsam and jetsam. If you are in the mountains, don't camp underneath a steep rock face, where things that go bump in the night could be loose stones and rocks. The middle of a dry river bed is also not as good a place as it might look – one heavy rain shower upstream and you could find yourself waking up in the middle of a raging torrent.

Ants can be a real pain if they decide to share your tent, so put all your provisions into tightly sealed containers, and keep them outside. Ash spread from a wood fire in a ring around your campsite should ward off the little pests for a while.

Rental Accommodation

If you intend staying anywhere for some time, ask about weekly and monthly rents. For a long stay it's worth taking a furnished apartment.

Homestays

There are several Homestay Associations in the Philippines. If you prefer to stay with private families, one of the presidents below will get you a list of members.

Antique Homestay Association
　Reylena E Rodriguez, Cerdena St, 5700 San Jose, Antique
Catanduanes Homestay Association
　Jose R Jacobo, 4810 San Andres, Catanduanes
Dapitan Homestay Association
　Rodolfo A Gallemit, Noli me Tangere St, 7101 Dapitan, Zamboanga del Norte
Ivatan Homestay Association
　Napoleon A Villegas, 3900 Basco, Batanes
Kalibo Ati-Atihan Homestay Association
　Pette R Candido, 101 C Laserna St, 5600 Kalibo, Aklan
Kalibo Homestay Association
　Remedios T Mapeso, 194 Roxas Ave, 5600 Kalibo, Aklan
Malaybalay Homestay Association
　Corazon Liwanag, Magsaysay St, 8700 Malaybalay, Bukidnon
Marinduque Homestay Association
　Dindo Asuncion, Murallon St, 4900 Boac, Marinduque

Cottages

On beach after beach, cottages are the only available accommodation. The price depends on the size and furnishings, and is usually meant for two people. An inexpensive cottage is nothing more than a simple hut made of bamboo and leaves, furnished with a crudely constructed bed, mosquito net and petroleum lamp. More expensive cottages will have a fan and bath, better

furniture and a veranda. The most expensive are stone-built, comfortably furnished with one or two beds, air-con and bath.

Hotels

Hotels in the top category charge around 25% for service and tax on top of the price of the room. It's often worth asking for a discount, or bargaining a little on prices as they'll often come down. Also keep in mind that there are often cheaper rooms without windows in the inner part of the building.

Maintenance in many hotels is a little lackadaisical, so it's a good idea to check if the electricity and water (shower and toilets) are working before you sign in. Beware of fire hazards in hotels – Philippine hotels don't close down, they burn down. Check fire escapes and make sure windows will open.

The lighting in hotel rooms is often rather dim. If you want to read or write in the evenings you should get a light bulb of at least 60 watts beforehand.

It might be advisable to deposit any valuables in the hotel safe. If a simple drawer is used as a locker, don't entrust your things to the hotel. It is also inadvisable to leave large amounts of cash with the hotel reception.

If you deposit your valuables in the hotel safe, get a receipt with an exact account of the details. Also ask whether there are certain times when you can't get them back – the night shift is not always entrusted with a key. When you do get your valuables back, check your cash and travellers cheques carefully.

FOOD

Filipino cuisine – with its Chinese, Malay and Spanish influences – is a mixture of eastern and western cuisine. It's usually referred to locally as 'native' food and can be really delicious, although it's not always the cheapest choice. Dishes are served all at once, with the result that certain dishes end up being eaten cold, something Filipinos don't seem to mind. It's not unusual to be offered cold fried eggs for breakfast, which is enough to turn most westerners off.

Westernised Filipinos usually eat with a spoon and fork; knives are not often used.

However, the original *kamayan* mode, namely eating with the fingers off a banana leaf, has come back into fashion, so there's no cutlery laid on the table in a kamayan restaurant. Such restaurants are flourishing throughout the Philippines.

When travelling around, go ahead and ask for the speciality of the province, which can be surprisingly good. As a rule of thumb, it is cheap and worthwhile eating where the locals eat, but even western food is not that expensive. In some restaurants you can get a complete western meal for around P100.

Snacks

In the mornings and afternoons a kind of tea break, called *merienda*, is taken. Besides this, *pulutan* (small morsels) appear on the table whenever alcoholic drinks are served.

At the eateries in the larger towns, grills are very popular in the evenings. You can get pork, chicken and seafood in the form of barbecue sticks. In the warm summer months of April and May, check with your nose first when selecting your choice of fresh meat for grilling.

The Filipinos have taken to US fast foods wholeheartedly, so there are plenty of hamburgers and hot dogs.

Snack favourites include:

bagoong – although not a snack itself, this pungent, fermented, salty sauce or paste made of fish or shrimp is often served with snack food. It is frequently prepared according to traditional folk recipes and eaten with snacks like green mango.

balut – a popular Filipino snack said to make you fit. Before a male suitor invites a woman up to see his stamp collection, he'll usually partake of a couple of baluts washed down with beer. Baluts can be purchased from street sellers and markets. A balut is a half-boiled, ready-to-hatch duck egg. You can distinguish the beak and feathers! Some baluts still contain some liquid so don't break open the whole egg: make a small hole first.

kilawin – small cuts of raw meat lightly roasted, then marinated in vinegar and other spices (ginger, onion, salt)

kinilaw – small cuts of raw fish or cuttlefish marinated with spices (ginger, onion, chilli) in vinegar or lemon

siopao – steamed dough ball with a filling such as chicken or pork; a quick snack

tapa – Baked dried beef served with raw onion rings. Available as a vacuum-packed preserved food but this tastes dreadful – remarkably like plastic.

Main Dishes

Rice is the staple food and will be served with most meals. Whatever the dishes are called that make up the meal, there are generic expressions to describe how the dish is cooked. Dishes with *ginataan* after them are cooked in coconut milk, while *inihaw* refers to grilled fish or meat.

adobo – a national standard dish made from chicken, pork, squid (*pusit*) and/or vegetables cooked with vinegar, pepper, garlic and salt

adobong pusit – squid or cuttlefish prepared with coconut milk, vinegar and garlic. The ink is used as a special seasoning.

ampalaya con carne – beef with bitter melon, prepared with onions, garlic, soy sauce and some sesame oil; served with rice

arroz caldo – thick rice soup with chicken cooked with onions, garlic and ginger, with black pepper added afterwards

asado – seasonal smoked meat, served with sour papaya strips (*atsara*)

aso – dog! Stray mongrel in a piquant sauce. This is (or was) a special dish in central and North Luzon. Because of many protests from dog-loving countries, this practice is now forbidden. The Ifugao have lodged an appeal with the government for exemption, stating that aso is a fundamental part of their culture and tradition.

atsara – Philippine sauerkraut; a very healthy and vitamin-rich dish of unripe papayas

bangus (milkfish) – herring-size fish that is lightly grilled, stuffed and baked

batchoy – beef, pork and liver in noodle soup; a speciality of the western Visayas

bulalo – substantial soup of boiled beef (kneecap), marrow and vegetables

calamares fritos – fried squid

caldereta – stew of goat's meat or beef, peas and paprika

crispy pata – pork rind or crackling seasoned with garlic, salt, pepper and vinegar, then baked in oil till crispy. There are many ways of seasoning and preparing it. It's often served cut into small pieces. There is usually more crackling than meat – which is how the Filipinos like it!

dinuguan – finely chopped offal (pork or chicken) roasted in fresh blood and usually seasoned with whole green pepper corns. This dish is also called chocolate meat on account of its dark colour.

gambas al ajillo – shelled raw shrimp prepared with olive oil, pepper, salt, paprika and a lot of garlic; served with white bread

kare-kare – stew of oxtail, beef shank, vegetables, onions and garlic. The stock can be enriched with peanuts and lightly fried rice, both finely ground.

lapu-lapu inihaw – grilled grouper, seasoned with salt, pepper, garlic and soy sauce. Lapu-lapu is the most popular eating fish in the country, but it's expensive. It was named after the Filipino chief who killed Ferdinand Magellan in battle.

lechon – suckling pig served with a thick liver sauce. Lechon *(litson)* is an important dish at fiestas.

lechon kawali – pork leg, baked and seasoned with green papaya, ginger, vinegar and sugar

lumpia – spring rolls filled with vegetables or meat; served with soy sauce, vinegar or a slightly sweet sauce

lumpia shangai – fried spring rolls filled with meat, whereas the bigger *lumpia sariwa* are filled with vegetables and served uncooked

mami – noodle soup; when made with chicken it's chicken mami, with beef it's beef mami etc

menudo – stew made from either small liver pieces or chopped pork, with diced potatoes, tomatoes, paprika and onions

misua soup – soup made from rice noodles, beef, garlic and onions

nilaga – soup with cabbage, potatoes and meat; with beef its *nilaga baka*

pancit Canton – a noodle dish made with thick noodles which are baked, then combined with pork, shrimps and vegetables. The pork is cooked in soy sauce beforehand.

pancit guisado – a noodle dish like pancit canton but thin Chinese noodles are used

pork apritada – pork is cut into small pieces and baked. The sauce includes tomato, onions, potatoes, pepperoni and garlic.

shrimp rebosado – shrimp baked in butter then cooked in a roux

sinigang – sour vegetable soup with fish *(sinigang na isda)* or pork *(sinigang na baboy)*; it can be served with rice

sisig – hearty stew made with pork cheek, which is first boiled then grilled until crispy. It's then diced and sauteed in oil with onions and pieces of liver seasoned with chilli, salt and pepper, and served on a cast-iron platter. This is a speciality of Pampanga Province.

tahong – large green mussels cooked or baked in sauce

talaba – raw oysters soaked in vinegar and garlic

tinola – stew of chicken, vegetables, ginger, onions and garlic

Desserts

ice cream – I would advise against ice cream in open containers from a travelling vendor. It would be better to buy the packaged Dairy Bars or cartons of excellent ice cream from Magnolia or Selecta.

halo-halo – dessert made from crushed ice mixed with coloured sweets and fruit, smothered in evaporated milk (halo-halo means 'mixed together'). It tastes noticeably better with a little rum.

Fruit

In a tropical country like the Philippines you would expect to find many colourful fruit stalls, but you would be looking in vain. Naturally, fruit like pineapple, bananas, papaya and mangoes are available, but not on every street corner.

abukado (avocado) – a pear shaped fruit, with a green skin which turns maroon then purple as it ripens. The soft, oily flesh has a taste reminiscent of nuts and surrounds a big, smooth stone in the middle. Avocados are in season from May until July.

atis (custard apple) – also known as 'sugar apple' or 'cinnamon apple', this fruit has a scaly, grey-green skin and looks rather like a hand grenade. To get at its soft white flesh it's best to cut the custard apple in half and remove its kernel with a knife. The skin is not palatable. The fruit is in season from August to October.

Atis (Custard Apple)

balimbing (carambola or star fruit) – an egg-shaped fruit with five segments which form a star shape in cross-section. The skin is yellow and has a shiny, polished appearance. The flesh is crisp, juicy and tart. It's in season from March until June.

bayabas (guava) – an apple-size fruit with light, crispy, faintly acidic flesh and numerous small, hard seeds. Rich in Vitamin C, it's in season from July to January.

Bayabas (Guava)

chico (sapodilla) – this roughly egg-shaped fruit has a brown skin and soft, sweet flesh that looks like wet sand. The skin is normally peeled off but you can eat it. It's in season from November to February.

Chico (Sapodilla)

durian – a large prickly fruit about which opinions are sharply divided: either you're crazy about it or you can't stand it. There's no in-between. Cutting open the outer shell reveals four segments with several large seeds surrounded by the flesh of the fruit. Depending on your tastes, the creamy yellow flesh either has a very pleasant aroma or stinks terribly. This fruit, with its 'hellish stench and heavenly taste', is in season from August to October.

Durian

granada (pomegranate) – a thick-skinned, brownish-red fruit about the size of an orange. The numerous fleshy seeds inside are crimson in colour and can be eaten fresh by spooning them out, or used to make jam or grenadine syrup.

Granada (Pomegranate)

guayabano (sour sop) – the fibrous, juicy flesh of this thorny fruit, which can weigh up to two kg, has a tart, tangy taste and is ideal for making tasty juices and mixed drinks. It's in season from August to November.

Guayabano (Sour Sop)

kaimito (star apple) – slicing a star apple reveals an arrangement of several star-shaped segments. Soft and juicy, it is best eaten with a spoon. There are green and violet kinds of kaimito, both of which are ripe and edible. The violet ones are sweeter. It's in season from January to March.

Kaimito (Star Apple)

kalamansi – this juicy, green lemon-like fruit is about the size of a pinball. It goes beautifully with black tea and is indispensable in the Filipino kitchen for the preparation of 'happy hour' drinks at sunset or whenever. Kalamansi are available year-round.

Kalamansi

langka (jackfruit) – this is a colossus among fruit. Greenish yellow with coarse skin, it can weigh up to 20 kg. The pale yellow flesh is split into portions and eaten in salads. The seeds should be cooked before being eaten. Jackfruit season is from February to July.

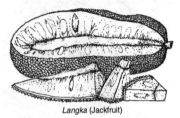

Langka (Jackfruit)

lanzones (lanson) – this looks like a little potato. Under its easily peeled, yellow-brown skin is a delicious, translucent flesh. But be careful, occasionally one of the flesh segments will contain small, bitter inedible seeds. It's in season from August to November.

Lanzones (Lanson)

makopa (roseapple) – this small, pear-shaped fruit has an appetising appearance and can be eaten whole, including the skin. Depending on ripeness, its taste ranges from sweet (green, white, light pink) to sour (dark pink, reddish). Best eaten between March and July.

Makopa (Roseapple)

mangga (mango) – this fruit can be up to 20 cm long with a large, flat stone. When the skin is green it is unripe, hard and very sour, but tastes marvellous with salt or a bitter, salty shrimp-paste called *bagoong*. The flesh of a ripe mango is yellow, juicy and vaguely reminiscent of the peach in taste. The mango is split into three by cutting the fruit lengthwise along the flat stone. The two side sections are eaten with a spoon, the centre piece should be speared with a pointed knife and the flesh gnawed off. The skin is inedible. The mango is in season between April and June.

mangostan (mangosteen) – this dark purple fruit is about the size of an apple and has a tough skin. To get to the sweet-sour, white flesh you break it open or use a knife. It's in season from May to October.

Mangostan (Mangosteen)

niyog (coconut) – a versatile fruit. While the hard flesh of older coconuts is dried in the sun and processed as copra, the young, green ones *(bukó)*, with their refreshing milk and soft flesh, are sold to be eaten. Here's one way to enjoy them: pour out a little of the milk, fill the nut up with small pieces of papaya, pineapple or maybe mango, together with half a bottle of rum, and leave it in the refrigerator for about twelve hours to soak in! Coconuts are available year-round.

pakwan (watermelon) – the size of a football, the flesh of this dark-green melon is red and watery. For a wonderfully refreshing dessert, pour a small glass of Cointreau over a chilled slice of watermelon. They are available year-round, but especially from April to November.

papaya – this is a species of melon which, when ripe, has a delicious, orange-red flesh and shiny green skin. It's best to cut one lengthways, remove the black seeds, sprinkle a little kalamansi juice over the halves and spoon out the pulp. The Papaya is in season right through the year.

piña (pineapple) – pineapples can be bought year-round. They're at their juiciest and sweetest during the main season from March to May.

rambutan – this is a funny-looking fruit, shaped rather like an egg with a reddish, hairy skin. Under the cute packaging you'll find a delicious translucent sweet pulp. Rambutans are sold in bunches and are picked from August to October.

Rambutan

saging (banana) – there are over 20 known varieties. You can eat them not only as freshly picked fruit, but also cooked, grilled, baked or roasted. Bananas are available year-round.

Saging (Banana)

suha (giant orange) – this fruit also goes by the name of *pomelo* and resembles a huge grapefruit. It tastes rather like a grapefruit too, except that it's somewhat sweeter. You'll have to peel away a very thick skin to get at the flesh, which is usually fairly dry. You can get giant oranges right through the year.

Suha (Giant Orange)

DRINKS

Perspiration and thirst are part and parcel of a stay in the tropics. Especially during the hot Philippine summer from March until May, you can be drenched with sweat in no time at all. Your body needs to replace all the fluid it has lost. After you've taken care of that basic need, your thoughts might turn to drinks that do more than just quench a tropical thirst. And you imagine them, of course, ice cold or on the rocks. Just what your stomach doesn't need, say the doctors. And they're probably right. But can you think of a drink that tastes good lukewarm? At any rate, ice cubes are generally harmless in the Philippines as they are usually produced in ice factories; however, the big ice blocks which are also produced in these factories often get dirty in transit.

Nonalcoholic Drinks

Most of the drinks in the Philippines are safe as they are in bottles or cartons, including milk and chocolate drinks.

Water In the Philippines, tap water is generally clean and safe to drink. In the towns, it is adequately chlorinated. In the country, it pays to be a bit more careful, as the water could come out of a well, or otherwise be of dubious origin. More and more businesses and restaurants are offering quite expensive mineral water packaged in plastic bottles filled with safe, uncarbonated drinking water. On the other hand, bottled soda water is only available in a handful of tourist resorts.

Tea & Coffee Unlike in other Asiatic countries, people seldom drink tea in the Philippines. About the only way you will see it made is with a teabag. However, real Chinese restaurants do serve proper tea.

Instead of tea, you will usually be served instant coffee in the Philippines. First class hotels provide good coffee made from top name brands of imported beans. Batangas coffee, also called Barako, is made from locally grown beans. This is good enough coffee, but the multinationals are forcing it off the market.

Coconut Juice If you want to enjoy the delicious, refreshing juice of a young coconut (bukó), get the fruit seller to open it for you to drink. A nut will contain up to a litre of bukó juice, which is pure and easy to digest.

Kalamansi Juice The tiny lemons known as kalamansi provide a sour extract when squeezed, which can be made into a healthy drink with the addition of a little sugar. Kalamansi juice can be drunk hot or cold.

Soft Drinks Internationally known drinks like Coke, Sprite, 7-Up and a few Philippine products, such as Royal and Tru Orange, are available on every corner.

Alcoholic Drinks

Basi This is made from fermented sugar cane juice, and is an ice-cold variation of sherry or port.

Beer Apart from the strong Red Horse beer, local beers are all light and, with a few exceptions, very drinkable. San Miguel is the best known beer and, with a 90% share of the market, is also the most successful. Competition is provided by Beer na Beer from the Asia Brewery. It's cheaper than San Miguel and is gradually building up its market share. Relatively new on the market from Denmark is Carlsberg, which is brewed in the Philippines, but whether it is 'probably the best beer in the world' or not is a matter of taste.

Hard Drinks Rum, whisky, gin and brandy of local manufacture are very good value. The well-aged rums of particularly fine quality are Tanduay, Anejo and Tondeña.

Palm Wine *Tuba* is a palm wine made from the juice of coconut palms. It is tapped from the crown of the tree. Tuba is drunk fresh or after a fermentation process. When distilled it is called *lambanog*.

Rice Wine *Tapuy (tapey)* is a rice wine and the end of its six month fermentation process is eagerly anticipated. Only after this period can you discover whether the intended taste has been achieved, or if the wine has become sour and undrinkable.

Wine Spirits are often called wine in the Philippines. If it is literally red or white wine you want, then you might have to try ordering 'grapes wine' if all else fails.

ENTERTAINMENT
Cinemas
Cinemas are good value – for a few pesos (P15 and up) you frequently get a double feature. There are particular starting times but no fixed entry times, which means there is a constant coming and going during the programmes. Disaster movies, murders and vampires are the preferred themes. Watch out for the national anthem – sometimes it is played at the end, sometimes at the beginning. If it is played, all the Filipinos will stand up. It's best to join them. Cameras are not allowed in cinemas.

Nightclubs
There is scarcely a town in the Philippines without at least one disco. Even in the depths of the provinces far from the nearest power station the Filipinos don't have to do without their dearly loved pleasure. Once a month, or even once a week, travelling discos drop in, to the immense pleasure of young and old, who can then boogie to their hearts' content on the village square under the stars.

The Filipinos are very keen on their nightlife – it certainly does not depend solely on tourists. Although they are more enticing after dark, you can, of course, frequent the bars during the day. However, serious drinkers will hang on to their money until happy hour when the price of drinks is reduced. Most nightclubs demand a cover charge and/or a table charge. It's justifiable if there's a good programme, but it's also advisable to enquire beforehand how much you are likely to be up for in the end. The bars and clubs in the big hotels can be excellent places for meeting people.

There are many bars with 'hospitality girls' always ready for a 'chat' and happy to let men buy them a 'lady's drink' – which is usually little more than cola and two to three times more expensive than beer! The bar and the girls both profit from this. In an expensive club, conversation with one of the hostesses can cost P200 an hour. Women from overseas should not be misled by notices saying 'unescorted ladies not allowed', as this only refers to the local professionals.

SPECTATOR SPORT
The Filipinos are sports enthusiasts. Basketball is their favourite sport and there has been a professional league since 1975. On the popularity scale, chess and boxing are near the top. Consequently, a lot of money was wagered on the outcome of the world heavyweight boxing championship in 1975 (when Mohammed Ali fought Joe Frazier in the 'thriller in Manila'), the World Basketball Championships in 1978 and the chess championship in 1978 (between Korshnoi and Karpov).

Tennis, golf, horse racing, bicycle races and motor racing have plenty of followers, but they're not in the national sport category. As a team sport in schools, volleyball is second in popularity to basketball.

Only rarely will you see a game of the once popular *sipa* being played. It's played with a plaited rattan ball which is kicked over a net using feet, knees, elbows or head (a similar idea to volleyball). It is now only played in a few areas in Mindanao and occasionally in Rizal Park in Manila.

Many pesos are risked at Jai-alai (pronounced 'high-aligh'), the frantically fast ball game of Basque origin. It is played in a court rather like a squash court. The players have a shovel-like holder called a *cesta*, with which they hurl a small, hard ball called a *pelota* against the wall. Their opponent must try to catch the rebounding ball and then hurl it back. The winner is decided by a knock-out competition and bets are placed on the outcome.

THINGS TO BUY
There are many souvenirs you can buy in the Philippines, particularly in the handcrafts line. Cane work, woodcarving, clothes and

articles made of shells are all popular. You can find many items in Manila, particularly around Ermita, in the Ilalim ng Tulay Market at the Quezon Bridge in Quiapo or the SM department store in the Makati Commercial Center, but there is also a wide variety in Cebu City, Davao and Zamboanga.

Cane Work & Basketry
In South Luzon *abaca* products are the main craft. Abaca is a fibre produced from a relative of the banana tree. Its best-known end product was the rope known as Manila hemp, but today it's made into bags, placemats and other woven products. There is some interesting basket work from Mountain Province and the island of Bohol. Mats and cane furniture are also good buys.

Clothing
The Philippines has become a major manufacturing centre for cheap western-style clothing, but many men come away from the Philippines with the shirt which is the Filipino national dress – the long-sleeved barong tagalog or its short-sleeved version, the polo barong.

Woodwork
Much of the woodcarving is of the tourist-kitsch variety but you can find some useful articles such as salad bowls. The Ifugao people in North Luzon's Ifugao Province also produce some high-quality woodcarving.

Other Items
Shell jewellery, wind chimes and plain shells are all popular purchases. Zamboanga and Cebu City are shell centres. The usual caveat applies to Philippine antiques. Brass ware is a speciality in Mindanao. Hand-woven cottons from Mountain Province are produced in such limited quantities they don't even reach Manila – they're much cheaper in Bontoc or Banaue than they are in Baguio.

Marble eggs and other marble items come from Romblon. Apart from the *piña* (pineapple-fibre) fabrics, Iloilo is also noted for *santos* (statues of saints).

Cebu is the guitar centre of the Philippines,

but note that cheap guitars are unlikely to be able to withstand drier, non-tropical climates. Lilang's Guitar Factory on Mactan Island is a good place to buy one – you'll find the people pleasant there, and guitars cost between P250 and P3000.

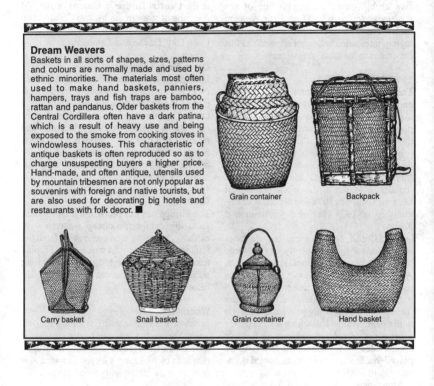

Dream Weavers
Baskets in all sorts of shapes, sizes, patterns and colours are normally made and used by ethnic minorities. The materials most often used to make hand baskets, panniers, hampers, trays and fish traps are bamboo, rattan and pandanus. Older baskets from the Central Cordillera often have a dark patina, which is a result of heavy use and being exposed to the smoke from cooking stoves in windowless houses. This characteristic of antique baskets is often reproduced so as to charge unsuspecting buyers a higher price. Hand-made, and often antique, utensils used by mountain tribesmen are not only popular as souvenirs with foreign and native tourists, but are also used for decorating big hotels and restaurants with folk decor. ∎

Grain container

Backpack

Carry basket

Snail basket

Grain container

Hand basket

Getting There & Away

AIR

Airports & Airlines

The best way to get to the Philippines is to fly. Although Cebu City, Davao and Laoag now have international airports, Manila's Ninoy Aquino international airport (NAIA) is virtually the only international gateway, so for most visitors the capital is their first experience of the country.

There are flights to Manila from most of the Philippines' Asian neighbours, including Japan, Hong Kong, Malaysia, Singapore and Thailand, as well as Australia, the USA and Europe.

There are flights to Cebu City from Hong Kong, Malaysia (Kota Kinabalu) and Singapore.

You can also fly to Davao in the south of Mindanao from Malaysia (Kuala Lumpur), and there are regular flights operating twice a week with Indonesia's Bouraq Airlines between Davao and Manado in the north of Sulawesi.

Make sure you confirm your onward flight with the airline at least 72 hours before departure. It's even better to confirm your outward flight when you arrive; that way you can be fairly certain that your booking has been registered on the computer. Don't check in at the last minute; flights are often overbooked and, in spite of a confirmed ticket, you can find yourself bumped from the flight! If you have excess baggage, it's worth giving the baggage handlers a generous tip and letting them take care of the problem.

You can take up to P1000 out with you and have unused pesos reconverted, but only if you have receipts from official money-changers or banks. The bank counter is in the exit hall.

Don't rely on the bank, however. In at least one instance, when a Philippine Airlines (PAL) and a Qantas flight both left for Australia on a Sunday night, the bank didn't have enough Australian dollars to meet demand.

In that situation, it's probably better to change your money into US dollars or another hard currency, rather than try changing pesos overseas at a bad rate.

Buying Tickets

The Philippines is no place to look for cheap airline tickets. Although Manila has over 300 travel agents, the lack of competition is astounding. Discounts are available but you have to be persistent and shop around. There are lots of agents around the Ermita area, particularly off Roxas Blvd and on TM Kalaw St, by Rizal Park. Check out these agents: Mr Ticket (☎ 521 2371; fax 521 2393), Park Hotel (Lobby), 1030 Belen St, Paco; Interisland Travel & Tours (☎ 522 1405; fax 522 4795), suite No 6, Midtown Arcade, Adriatico St, Ermita; and Blue Horizons Travel & Tours (☎ 893 6071; fax 892 6635), Shangri-La Hotel Manila, Ayala Ave, Makati.

Round the World Tickets RTW fares, as Round the World tickets are known, have become all the rage of late. Basically, two or more airlines get together and offer a ticket which gets you around the world using only their services. You're allowed stopovers (sometimes unlimited) and you have to complete the circuit within a certain period of time.

PAL offers RTW tickets in combination with Canadian Airlines and Varig Brazilian Airlines, which will take you from Australia to the Philippines, Asia, Europe, the USA and back to Australia for A$3200. The usual Apex booking conditions apply and you have 120 days to complete the circuit. From London, RTW tickets typically cost around UK£1000 to UK£1400, depending on the airlines and routes used.

Circle Pacific Tickets These are a variation on the RTW idea, and once again there's an option that includes the Philippines. PAL, American Airlines and Qantas have a ticket

Air Travel Glossary

Apex *A*-dvance *P*-urchase *Ex*-cursion is a discounted ticket which must be paid for in advance. You pay big penalties for changes or cancellations. Insurance can sometimes be taken out against these penalties.

Baggage Allowance This is written on your ticket: usually one or two items totalling 20 kg per person to go in the hold, plus one item of hand luggage.

Bucket Shop An unbonded travel agency specialising in discounted airline tickets. Not all are honest.

Bumped Just because you have a confirmed seat doesn't mean you're going to get on the plane; see Overbooking.

Cancellation Penalties If you have to cancel or change an Apex ticket there are often heavy penalties involved, insurance can sometimes be taken out against these penalties. Some airlines impose penalties on regular tickets as well, particularly against 'no show' passengers.

Charter Flights Group-tour charters can be cheaper than scheduled flights in the low season. Some tour operators will book you on a seat-only basis, though usually not very far in advance. Prices for unfilled seats may plummet as departure day nears, and 'bucket shops' do a thriving business in these last-minute bargains (though you may not have a wide choice of flight dates).

Check In Airlines ask you to check in a certain time ahead of the flight departure, typically 1-1/2 to 2-1/2 hours for international flights. If you fail to do so and the flight is overbooked, the airline may cancel your booking and give your seat to somebody else.

Confirmation Having a ticket written out with the flight and date you want doesn't mean you have a seat until the agent has checked with the airline that your status is 'OK' or confirmed. Meanwhile you could just be 'on request'.

Discounted Tickets There are two types of discounted fares - officially discounted (see Promotional Fares) and unofficially discounted. The lowest prices often impose drawbacks like flying with unpopular airlines, inconvenient schedules, or unpleasant routes and connections. A discounted ticket can save you other things than money - you may be able to pay Apex prices without the associated Apex advance booking and other requirements. Discounted tickets only exist where there is fierce competition.

Full Fares Airlines traditionally offer first class (coded F), business class (J) and economy class (Y) tickets. Thanks to discounts, few passengers pay full economy fare nowadays.

Lost Tickets If you lose your ticket an airline will usually treat it like a travellers cheque and, after enquiries, issue you with another one. Legally, however, an airline is entitled to treat it like cash and if you lose it then it's gone forever. Take good care of your tickets.

No Shows Passengers who fail to show up for their flight, sometimes due to unexpected delays or disasters, sometimes due to simply forgetting, sometimes because they made more than one booking and didn't bother to cancel the one they didn't want. Full fare passengers who fail to turn up are sometimes entitled to travel on a later flight. The rest of us are penalised (see Cancellation Penalties).

---

that lets you combine the USA, New Zealand, Australia, Asia and the Philippines in a loop around the Pacific. You can make as many stopovers as the three airlines' routes will permit and you have up to six months to complete the loop. The ticket must be purchased at least 30 days before departure, after which the usual cancellation penalties apply.

Although you must make all reservations before the 30 day cut-off point, you can alter flight dates after departure at no cost as long as you have a revalidation sticker on your ticket. If you want to change your route, requiring your ticket to be rewritten, there's a US$50 charge. Economy class Circle Pacific fares are US$2450 from the USA, A$3000 from Australia or NZ$3900 from New Zealand.

The USA From Los Angeles or San Francisco, the economy fare for direct flights is US$590/980 one way/return with Northwest

On Request An unconfirmed booking for a flight, see Confirmation.

Open Jaws A return ticket where you fly out to one place but return from somewhere else; if available this can save you backtracking to your arrival point.

Overbooking Airlines hate to fly empty seats and since every flight has some passengers who fail to show up, airlines often book more passengers than they have seats. Usually the excess passengers balance those who fail to show up but occasionally somebody gets bumped - most likely those who fail to reconfirm and/or who check in late.

Promotional Fares Officially discounted fares like Apex fares which are available from travel agents or direct from the airline.

Reconfirmation At least 72 hours prior of an onward or return flight you must contact the airline and reconfirm your intention to be on the flight. If you don't, you could lose your seat. You don't have to reconfirm the first flight on your itinerary or if your stopover is less than 72 hours, but it can't hurt. It also doesn't hurt to reconfirm more than once.

Restrictions Discounted tickets often have restrictions attached to them. Advance purchase is the most usual one (see Apex). Another is the minimum and/or maximum period between departure and return.

Standby A discounted ticket where you only fly if there is a seat free at the last moment. Standby fares are normally available only on domestic routes.

Tickets Out An entry requirement for many countries is that you have an onward or return ticket, in other words, a ticket out of the country. If you're not sure what you intend to do next, the easiest solution is to buy the cheapest onward ticket to a neighbouring country or a ticket from a reliable airline which can later be refunded if you do not use it.

Transferred Tickets Tickets cannot legally be transferred from one person to another. Travellers sometimes try to sell the return half of a ticket, but officials can ask you to prove that you're the person named on the ticket. This is rare with domestic flights, but on international flights tickets may be compared with passports.

Travel Agencies These vary widely and you should pick one that suits your needs. Full-service agencies do everything from tours and tickets to car rental and hotel bookings and some simply handle tours. A good one can save you a lot of money and headaches, but if all you want is the cheapest possible ticket, then find an agency specialising in this.

Travel Periods (Seasons) Some discounts - on Apex fares in particular - vary with the time of year and sometimes the direction of travel. Certain journeys have a high or peak season (when everyone wants to fly) and a low or off-peak season, and sometimes an intermediate or 'shoulder' season as well. At peak times official and unofficial discounts will be lower or nonexistent. Usually the fare depends on when your outward flight is - ie, if you depart in the high season but return in the low season, you pay the high-season fare. ■

Airlines and PAL, and you can tag two stopovers on to this fare at US$50 a time.

You can fly with United Airlines and Northwest Airlines from Tampa, Florida, for about US$784/1280 one way/return, and from Hawaii with PAL for about US$524/874 one way/return.

Northwest, PAL, Korean Airlines and China Airlines have budget fares from Manila to the USA. To go to the US west coast it costs US$400/450 in the low/high season.

Canada From Vancouver, the cost of an Asiana flight to Manila is C$900 return.

Australia You can fly from Australia to the Philippines with PAL or Qantas. There are two fare seasons – high and low – the high season is during the school summer break in December and January.

On PAL, the one way economy fares are A$810/880 (low/high season); return fares are A$1050/1300 (low/high season). These fares are valid for a stay of 28 days only. Qantas offers one way economy fares to Manila from Sydney, Melbourne, Adelaide or Brisbane for A\$810/950 (low/high season). Return fares are A\$1150/1350 (low/high season).

From Manila, costs are US\$350 if you fly to Darwin, US\$320 to Perth and US\$320 to Sydney.

New Zealand There are no direct flights between New Zealand and Manila so there are no real bargains. The cheapest fare available is on PAL via Sydney for around NZ\$1655.

The UK PAL, Malaysia Airlines and a number of European airlines, including British Airways, connect London and other European capitals with Manila. The regular economy one way/return fare from London to Manila is UK£467/823 with Malaysia Airlines.

You can get to Manila from London for much less by shopping around London's numerous bucket shops (travel agents who specialise in discount airline tickets). To find out what fares are available, scan the weekly 'what's on' magazine *Time Out* or *TNT*. Two excellent places to look for cheap tickets are Trailfinders on Earls Court Rd, or STA Travel on Old Brompton Rd. Typical discount fares between London and Manila are around UK£580 return.

Another way to get to the Philippines cheaply from London is to fly to Hong Kong and continue from there. Competition on the London to Hong Kong route is cut-throat. There are also attractively priced tickets available from London to Australia, with the Philippines as a stopover.

Continental Europe A one way/return fare with PAL from Frankfurt to Manila is DM1000/1600 (US\$665/1065), and from Zurich the cost is Sfr910/1500 (US\$742/1222) with Singapore Airlines. You can also find good ticket deals to the Philippines in Belgium and the Netherlands.

From Manila, you can fly to Amsterdam, Frankfurt or London for around US\$535, Paris for US\$545, Rome for US\$525 and Zurich for US\$550.

Asia Cheap deals within Asia tend to vary these days – one day one country is cheaper, the next day another. Currently it appears that Bangkok is no longer the bargain basement and that Hong Kong is the place for good deals.

From Hong Kong, the regular economy one way/return fare to Manila is HK\$1300/2480 with Air France or Cathay Pacific. From Japan, the one way/return fare is ¥71,000/86,500 with Japan Airlines. From South Korea, it costs US\$417/610 one way/return with Korean Airlines, and from Taipei, Taiwan, flights with Eva Air and PAL cost US\$215/430 one way/return.

From Malaysia, the fare from Kuala Lumpur is US\$260/\$470 one way/return, and from Kota Kinabalu it's US\$180/\$355 one way/return. In Thailand, the regular one way/return fare from Bangkok is US\$225/280. You can fly to Manila from Singapore for US\$270/410 one way/return, and from Ho Chi Minh City (Saigon), Vietnam, for US\$240/\$480 one way/return. From Jakarta, Java, it's US\$250/\$440 one way/return, and from Denpasar, Bali, it's US\$275/\$540 one way/return.

To Cebu City, flights from Singapore cost S\$874/1748 one way/return. From Kota Kinabalu, the one way/return flight costs M\$567/1078; from Hong Kong it costs HK\$1740/\$3320 one way/return.

To Davao, flights from Kuala Lumpur cost M\$1207/2321 one way/return; the one way/return fare from Manado, Sulawesi, Indonesia, is US\$150/262.

From Manila, one way fares include Bangkok US\$180, Hong Kong US\$120, Jakarta US\$220, Singapore US\$220, Taipei US\$125 and Tokyo US\$220.

SEA

Although there are many excellent connections by ship around the Philippine islands, the options from overseas are limited. You might find a passenger-carrying freight ship out of Hong Kong or Singapore, but it is increasingly unlikely in these containerised days.

There are several sea connections between Borneo and Mindanao, but since smugglers and pirates operate there, you're unlikely to be too popular on arrival.

The Aleson Shipping Lines' MV *Lady Mary Joy* regularly serves the Philippine cities of Zamboanga, Mindanao and Malaysia's Sandakan and Sabah once a week (US$34; 17 hours).

Once a week, the MV *Surya* of PT Pelajaran Fajar Lines makes the trip between General Santos, Mindanao, Philippines and Bitung (the port of Manado), Sulawesi, Indonesia (US$45; 36 hours).

The Pelni Lines' MV *Tilongkabila* provides a fortnightly service from Davao, Mindanao, Philippines to several ports in Indonesia (eg, Bitung/Manado), Sulawesi (US$65; 36 hours), Ujing Pandang, Sulawesi and Benoa/Denpasar, Bali. In Davao, contact Morning Star Mindanao Travel & Tours (☎ 221 1346; fax 221 8348), Unit 3 ATU Plaza, Duterte St.

DEPARTURE TAXES

When you depart from NAIA you have to pay a P500 airport tax. In Cebu City, it's P400 and in Davao P220.

WARNING

The information in this chapter is especially vulnerable to change – prices for international air travel are volatile, routes are introduced and cancelled, schedules change, rules are amended and special deals come and go. Airlines and governments seem to take a perverse pleasure in making price structures and regulations as complicated as possible; you should check directly with the airline or a travel agent to make sure you understand how a fare works. In addition, the travel industry is highly competitive and there are many lurks and perks. The upshot of this is that you should get opinions, quotes and advice from as many airlines and travel agents as possible.

The details given in this chapter should be regarded as pointers and not as a substitute for your own up-to-the-minute research.

Getting Around

AIR
Domestic Air Services

After monopolising the airline scene for many years, Philippine Airlines (PAL) is now facing competition from smaller companies, like Air Ads, Air Philippines, Asian Spirit, Cebu Pacific, Grand Air and Pacific Airways. Though modest enterprises, these other airlines offer worthy alternatives. There has been a dramatic increase in the use of domestic airlines ever since the catastrophic shipping disasters of the 1980s (the worst being the infamous collision between the MV *Doña Paz* and a petrol tanker, which claimed an estimated 4000 lives). The packed-out local commuter planes are proof enough of this.

A word of warning: you may be asked for proof of identity at check-in. It pays to have your passport, or a copy of it, with you.

Philippine Airlines (PAL) PAL flies to nearly all the larger cities. Over the Christmas period, between 15 December and 4 January, flights are usually fully booked, although it might be worth trying your luck on the waiting list.

The flight schedule changes two to four times a year but only in minor details, so you'll have a reasonable idea of what's available in local flights by consulting the Getting There & Away section in the Manila chapter and allowing for slight variations.

A current domestic flight schedule can be obtained at the PAL office on Roxas Blvd, Manila. (If there are none printed, you can make your own copy of the schedule displayed on the 1st floor.) The PAL fleet contains jets (A-300, Boeing 737) and turboprops (Fokker 50). Smoking is not permitted on board.

Be aware that flights may be cancelled, especially during the rainy season. Take this into account when planning linking international flights. It might be handy to have written confirmation from PAL if the flight is cancelled – this could save you having to pay a fee to have your ticket changed.

PAL customers are attended to in numerical order in the city offices. You have to take a number and wait your turn, even to obtain a small piece of information. It's always best to telephone if you want quick information. The Manila office has a round-the-clock Info-Service on ☎ 816 6691.

Students under 26 years of age taking round-trip flights (eg, Manila-Cebu-Manila or Manila-Zamboanga-Davao-Cebu-Manila) are entitled to a 15% reduction. Note: as well as your student card, you may be required to produce your passport (and a photocopy, including the photo) when purchasing the ticket.

PAL also offers a Golden Age Discount of 20% for passengers over 60 years of age. To be eligible for this, you have to pay P50 for an application form which you hand in to the discount counter, together with two photocopies of your passport. You will then receive an identification card which must be produced when you buy a ticket.

Bookings can be changed free of charge if made before noon on the day before the flight. After that, you'll have to pay a processing fee of about P50.

Airport tax payable on domestic flights is often included in the price of the ticket. The airport tax for international flights is P500 at present.

Passengers on domestic flights are officially allowed only 18 kg of luggage free of charge. This limit is not strictly enforced in the case of tourists, so it's handy to be able to produce your passport or a copy of it as proof. Extra baggage costs about P15 per kg (depending on the route).

The Philippines Airfares map in this chapter shows regular PAL airfares on some of the main routes. PAL flight frequencies vary considerably. On some main sectors there are several flights daily (around 10 from Manila to Cebu City), while on lesser

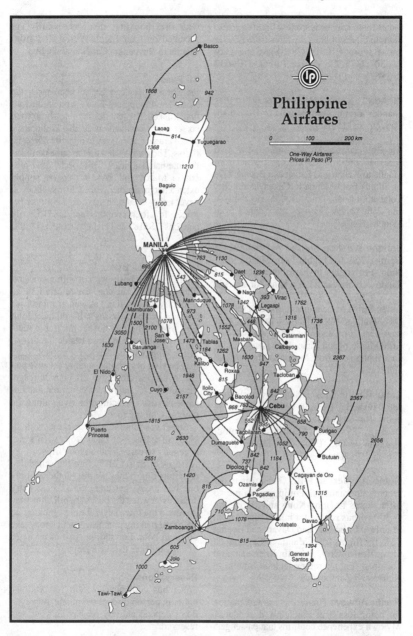

routes there may be just a few flights a week. Sample prices of one way fares from Manila are: Baguio P1000 (US$38); Cebu City P1630 (US$62); Puerto Princesa P1630 (US$62); and Davao P2656 (US$100).

Air Ads This well-run commuter airline flies Islander aircraft from Manila to Busuanga, Caticlan and Lubang.

Air Philippines Air Philippines has two types of aircraft: YS-11s for flights from Manila to Kalibo and Subic; and Boeing 737s for flights from Manila to Cagyayan de Oro, Cotabato, Davao, Iloilo City, Puerto Princesa and Zamboanga. Services are planned from Manila to Tacloban.

Soriano Aviation Soriano Aviation uses a Dornier 228 for flights from Manila to El Nido. For flights to Pamalican Island and Sandoval/Palawan it has a King Air aircraft.

Asian Spirit At the moment, Asian Spirit flies Dash 7 aircraft from Manila to Baguio, Catarman, Caticlan, Canuayan, Daet, Masbate, San Jose (Mindoro) and Virac. They plans to introduce flights soon from Manila to Marinduque and Naga.

Cebu Pacific This airline obviously had solid financial backing before opening its doors for business. They fly DC 9s and Boeing 737s from Manila to Bacolod, Cagayan de Oro, Cebu City, Davao, Iloilo City and Tacloban.

Grand Air Next to PAL, Grand Air is the second international Philippine airline to offer flights to Hong Kong and Taipei. An A-300 Airbus is used for inland flights from Manila to Cebu City and Davao, and Boeing 737s for flights from Manila to Cagayan de Oro, Iloilo City, Puerto Princesa and Tacloban. Future routes include Manila to Kaliba and Zamboanga.

Pacific Airways This airline has a reputation for being less than absolutely dependable. My own experience confirms that passengers with firm bookings don't necessarily get accepted on their flight. Pacific flies from Manila to Busuanga, Caticlan and Cuyo.

Air Pass
PAL passengers can get a cheap pass (the 'Visit-The-Philippines-Fare') with an international ticket. This entitles them to fly to four, six or eight destinations in the Philippines, which is an excellent way to organise domestic flights. The pass is valid for the same period as the international ticket. This special offer runs out in March and PAL has so far simply extended it for another year each time – but you never know what their next decision may be. Prices for four coupons are US$155, six coupons US$182 and eight coupons US$198.

BUS
Long Distance Bus
There are large buses with or without air-con (those without air-con are referred to as 'ordinary' or 'regular') as well as minibuses (also called 'baby buses'). If you have long legs, you'll find the most comfortable seats in the minibuses are those beside the driver. In the large overland buses, the back seats may be your best choice, mainly because you get to keep a close eye on your luggage. Beware: travel sickness is common, and not helped by drivers racing their rivals along the bumpy, winding roads.

Street vendors flock to the buses with all kinds of edibles at each stop, so it's not necessary to carry food on long trips.

Buses often set off before the scheduled departure time if they are full – if there is only one bus a day, get there early! In country areas, even when the buses are full, they may go round the town several times, picking up freight or making purchases, which may take up to an hour. For shorter trips of up to 20 km, it's quicker to take a jeepney.

Reservations
Some bus companies accept reservations, either in person or over the phone; however, don't depend entirely on having your seat reserved.

Costs

The fare is based on the number of km travelled, but it costs more to travel on unsealed roads. On long stretches, fares are always collected fairly late. First, conductors ask passengers their destinations then dispense the tickets; these will be inspected several times by different inspectors. If you have an international student card, show it when you state your destination. Discounts are not available during school holidays or on Sunday and public holidays.

One hundred km by ordinary bus should cost around P50 (US$1.90), by air-con bus around P60 (US$2.30).

Ordinary air-con bus fares from Manila are: Alaminos (237 km) P110/140; Baguio (250 km) P115/155; Batangas (110 km) P50/60; Olongapo (126 km) P60/80; and Legaspi (544 km) P240/295.

See Getting There & Away in the Manila chapter for details of where the bus terminals are and information about local buses.

TRAIN

The railway line from Manila (Tayuman railway station) to Ragay (about 60 km before Naga) in South Luzon is now the only one operating. The railway line does extend beyond Ragay but it's presently under repair. Typhoons damage bridges almost every year so train journeys can either be frequently interrupted or only partly completed. The trains are slow (it takes 9½ hours from Manila to Ragay) and cost about the same as buses.

JEEPNEY

These are the most popular form of transport for short journeys. They were originally reconstructed Jeeps left behind by the US army after WWII. Few of these old models are left. The new jeepneys, which may be Ford Fieras, are brightly painted in traditional designs, and the bonnets are decorated with mirrors and figures of horses.

In the provinces, it is important to negotiate a price before setting out on a long trip over unfamiliar territory. Before you start, ask other passengers about the price or check in a nearby shop, and then confirm the price with the driver. This may save you an unpleasant situation when you reach your destination. Jeepneys usually only leave when full (or overflowing) with passengers, so you must allow for long waiting periods. If you're prepared to pay for the empty 'seats', you can get the driver to leave immediately.

If you climb into an empty jeepney and the driver takes off straight away, it usually means you'll be charged for a 'Special Ride'. If you don't want this, you must make it clear that you're only prepared to pay for a regular ride. You might need to get the driver to stop straight away, especially if no more passengers are getting on. It costs about P1200 to rent a jeepney for a day and more if the roads are in bad condition; petrol (gas) is extra

Safety Tip If several men get into the jeepney straight after you and try to sit near you or get you to change seats under some pretext, they may be intent on relieving you of your valuables. Don't be fooled..

CAR & MOTORCYCLE
Road Rules

Traffic travels on the right in the Philippines, and there are as many unwritten laws as there are written ones. While traffic signs conform to international standards, Filipinos pay scant attention to them. Within town boundaries, it seems anything that gets you nearer your destination is allowed. On country roads, survival of the fittest is the maxim: buses and trucks have right of way. Know your road rules and make sure your vehicle is roadworthy. The locals don't call traffic police *buwaya* ('crocodiles') for nothing.

Whatever happens, don't allow yourself to be influenced by the overtaking antics of local drivers. Drive defensively, and avoid driving at night – the combination of unfamiliar roads, darkness and the absence of reflective road markers could prove painful.

If you drive to Manila, remember restrictions are in force from Monday to Friday. If your licence plate ends in a 1 or 2 you can't drive on Mondays, 3 and 4 are banned on Tuesdays, 5 and 6 on Wednesdays, 7 and 8 on Thursdays, and 9 and 0 on Fridays.

Rental

Apart from various local firms, the internationally known companies such as Avis, Budget and Hertz have good, reliable vehicles. You can rent cars by the day, week or month. The cheaper cars are usually booked, so it's worth reserving one if you want a particular model. A Toyota Corolla XL 1.3 with air-con and radio costs P1930 a day, or P11,580 a week, with unlimited km. Petrol (gas) costs about P10 a litre. Avis has several offices in Metro Manila (eg, in the Peninsula Manila Hotel in Makati), Angeles, Baguio, Cagayan de Oro, Cebu City, Davao, Iloilo City and Olongapo.

Unlike Thailand or Indonesia, there's no organised system for hiring motorcycles – you just have to ask around. For a 125 cc Honda, expect to pay P350 to P650 a day.

Purchase

You'll find cars and motorcycles for sale under 'Classified Ads – For Sale' in the *Manila Bulletin*, especially in the Sunday edition. The most common bikes are 125 cc. It's better (though dearer) to buy a 350 cc, as you can overtake faster and more safely. However, outside Manila, parts are hard to come by. A new 125 cc Honda costs about P65,000.

If possible, make sure you obtain the originals of the following documents:

* Contract of sale – have it drawn up by a lawyer.
* Registration certificate – pink paper, endorsed by the Land Transportation Office (LTO). A plate marked 'Ready for Registration' will do.
* Official receipt – you need this for the finance office. Get it at the LTO.

If you want to sell your car or motorcycle before leaving the country, you'll be paid in pesos. You can only exchange these (with difficulty) for foreign currency on the black market. It is recommended that you change dollars into pesos before you buy. You can do this officially at the Central Bank, which will give you a receipt for the transaction. You can change the pesos back into dollars without problems with this receipt.

It's useful to have the owner's manual

with you. A tool set – including screwdrivers and a spark plug key – is essential for all cars and motorcycles. For a 350 cc motorbike, it's imperative that you have a spare tube, patching kit, spark plugs and chain outside Manila. The highway police insist on a helmet for all motorbike riders.

If you are island hopping, you'll need a vehicle shipment clearance, which you can get from the police before you leave each island. You'll also need a photocopy of the sale contract or registration certificate.

BICYCLE

Although it's dangerous on busy roads, travelling by bicycle can be an interesting way to explore the Philippines. Just don't expect to go unnoticed – a German couple who rode from Davao in the south of Mindanao via the islands to Manila in four weeks caused quite a stir.

Buses and jeepneys will transport bikes for a small fee. Inland flights with PAL should also present no problem, apart from you having to remove the front wheel of your bike.

Rental

A few hotel and resort owners rent mountain bikes, for example, on Boracay, Camiguin and Cebu (Moalboal). Depending on the quality of the bike, it should cost around P150 to P300 a day.

Purchase

A good mountain bike costs about P7000 to P9000 in the Philippines. There are several bike shops in Manila at the Cartimar Market in Pasay City. There you will find a good selection of bikes in all price categories at fair prices. The shops in Cebu City are a bit more expensive.

HITCHING

As transport costs are so low, it's hardly worth anyone's while to hitchhike. Filipinos wouldn't dream of thumbing a lift, even if they were penniless. If you do hitch a ride, the driver might appreciate a few pesos to help pay for petrol (gas).

WALKING
This is a great way to meet people and enjoy nature close up. The entire archipelago is criss-crossed with walking trails, and with the right planning a hiker can avoid practically all contact with asphalt and exhaust fumes.

BOAT
Wherever you go, there's a boat ready to take you to the next island. For short trips, outrig-ger boats or 'pumpboats' are used. The motor is at the back – a very noisy arrangement. A 16 hp pumpboat uses about five litres of fuel for an hour's speedy motoring, so you can work out the cost of chartering from there.

The recent introduction of fast ferries has vastly improved the inter-island service, mainly in the Visayas region. They are air-con ships, mostly catamarans, with names like *Supercat, Island Jet, Water Jet* and *Bullet Xpress*. They are fitted with aircraft seats, a small bar and video screens, which makes them a real alternative to flying. The fares are also reasonable. Beware: the air-conditioning is fierce, so it might be an idea to wear a jacket or take a blanket – especially if you've got a sweat up dragging your baggage to the pier.

The quality of passenger ships varies greatly. The flagships of several companies run on the prestigious Manila-Cebu-Zam-boanga-Davao route. They are punctual and fast, and the service is relatively good.

Third class (deck class or sun deck) is quite acceptable, with bunks or camp beds under cover, whereas the air-con cabins and dormitories below deck are often cramped and grungy.

In early 1996 the three biggest Philippine shipping companies, William Lines, Go-thong Lines and Aboitiz Lines, amalgamated to become WG & A. Their inter-island ships were refitted and renamed *Superferry 1, Superferry 2* etc. WG & A's service is well above average, the quality of the ships has been markedly improved and, to top it all off, the ships are relatively punctual. If possible, buy tickets a few days before sailing as the ships are quickly booked out, especially around Christmas. It's a good idea to be on

board an hour before the scheduled departure time. Most of the time, meals and drinks (fish and rice, coffee and water) are included in the fare.

If you're travelling long distances by freighter, you must count on long, unsched-uled stops at various ports.

On the small passenger boats, which usually run over medium distances, tickets are available on board. Drinks are almost always for sale, but you must bring your own food. In contrast to the large ships, places on the upper deck are the most expensive.

The major shipping lines include WG & A, Sulpicio Lines, Negros Navigation, Viva Shipping Lines, Cebu Ferries and George & Peter Lines. You will find others listed in the *Yellow Pages* under 'Shipping'. First class fares are about twice that of the deck class fares.

Details of ships, departure times, travel-ling times and so on can be found in the Getting There & Away sections of the various island chapters. Remember that departure times are often not adhered to, so it makes sense to go down to the wharf even if you think you've missed the boat.

Examples of average 3rd class (deck class) prices from Manila are as follows: Bacolod (Negros) P480; Cebu City (Cebu) P520; Davao (Mindanao) P990; and Zam-boanga (Mindanao) P635.

LOCAL TRANSPORT
Bus
Only Manila has buses operating within the town (see the Getting There & Away section in the Manila chapter). Jeepneys supply public transport in all other Philippine towns and cities.

Jeepney
These colourful vehicles are part of any Phil-ippine street scene, and much to the relief of many, their cassette players have now been banned. The jeepneys' route is indicated, and the official charge is P1.50 centavos for the first four km and 25 centavos for each extra km. When you want to get out, just bang on the roof, hiss or yell *'pára'* ('stop').

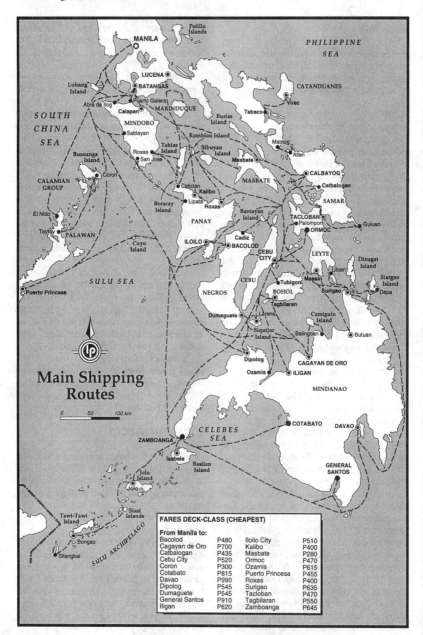

PHILIPPINE SEA

SOUTH CHINA SEA

MANILA

Polillo Islands

LUCENA

BATANGAS

Lubang Island

Abra de Ilog

Calapan

Puerto Galera

MARINDUQUE

CATANDUANES

Virac

Tabaco

Burias Island

MINDORO

Sablayan

Roxas

San Jose

Tablas Island

Romblon Island

Sibuyan Island

Matnog

Allen

Masbate

CALAMIAN GROUP

Busuanga Island

Coron

Caticlan

Kalibo

Lipata

Roxas

Boracay Island

Bantayan Island

MASBATE

CALBAYOG

Catbalogan

SAMAR

TACLOBAN

Palompon

ORMOC

Guiuan

El Nido

Taytay

PALAWAN

Cuyo Island

PANAY

ILOILO

Cadiz

BACOLOD

CEBU CITY

LEYTE

Dinagat Island

Siargao Island

SULU SEA

Puerto Princesa

CEBU

NEGROS

Tubigon

BOHOL

Tagbilaran

Maasin

Liloan

Surigao

Dapa

Dumaguete

Larena

Siquijor Island

Camiguin Island

Balingoan

Butuan

Dipolog

Ozamis

CAGAYAN DE ORO

ILIGAN

MINDANAO

Main Shipping Routes

0   50   100 km

CELEBES SEA

ZAMBOANGA

Isabela

Basilan Island

COTABATO

DAVAO

GENERAL SANTOS

Jolo Island

Jolo

Tawi-Tawi Island

Siasi Islands

Bongao

Sitangkai

SULU ARCHIPELAGO

FARES DECK-CLASS (CHEAPEST)			
From Manila to:			
Bacolod	P480	Iloilo City	P510
Cagayan de Oro	P700	Kalibo	P400
Catbalogan	P435	Masbate	P280
Cebu City	P520	Ormoc	P470
Coron	P300	Ozamis	P615
Cotabato	P815	Puerto Princesa	P455
Davao	P990	Roxas	P400
Dipolog	P545	Surigao	P635
Dumaguete	P545	Tacloban	P470
General Santos	P910	Tagbilaran	P550
Iligan	P620	Zamboanga	P645

Taxi

Under no circumstances should meters be switched off. Flat fare arrangements always favour the driver. It doesn't hurt to show taxi drivers that you know more than they think, so that they won't take roundabout routes. Air-con taxis begin at P20 (the old flag-down charge of P3.50 plus P16.50 surcharge). If possible, have small change handy as it is difficult to get change for anything over P20. If a meter has obviously been rigged and is running too fast, the only sensible thing is to stop and take another taxi.

In spite of fines of up to P5000, countless taxis still have rigged meters. Pay particular attention to the price display – sometimes horn and meter are linked, and units are added every time the horn is sounded! Make sure the meter is turned on when you start. The taxis that wait outside the big hotels, bus stations, wharves and air terminals almost always have meters that run fast. It usually pays to walk to the next street. New taxis are fitted with a digital indicator that cannot (yet!) be interfered with.

Safety note: as only a few taxis are equipped with central locking, you should make sure all doors are locked after you get in. You should also make it clear to the driver that you do not want other passengers getting in with you, even if they are 'friends' of the driver.

PU-cab

These are small 'Public Utilities' taxis without meters; their minimum price is P10 for a short town journey of about three km.

For longer journeys you pay more and need to negotiate the fee beforehand. You will find PU-cabs in Cagayan de Oro, Bacolod, Davao, Zamboanga and some other places but not Manila.

Tricycle

These are small motorcycles or mopeds with sidecars for passengers and they go much better than you might think. The fare must be negotiated, and is usually around P2 for a short ride.

Calesa

These two wheeled horse-cabs are found in Manila's Chinatown, in Vigan, where they fit the local scene very well, and in Cebu City, where they are called *tartanillas*. In Manila, Filipinos pay about P10 for short trips; tourists are usually charged more. Establish beforehand if the price is per person or per calesa.

Trishaw

These are bicycles with sidecars. As transport becomes increasingly motorised, trishaws are becoming rarer, even in the provinces. Prices start at about P2 per person for a short trip.

ORGANISED TOURS

For package tours, contact Blue Horizons Travel & Tours (☎ 893 6071; fax 892 6635), Shangri-La Hotel Manila, Ayala Ave, Makati, and Interisland Travel & Tours (☎ 522 1405; fax 522 4795), Suite No 6, Midtown Arcade, Adriatico St, Ermita.

Manila

In 1975, 17 towns and communities were combined to form Metropolitan Manila. Known as Metro Manila, this conglomeration had at last count a population of 10 million. San Nicolas, Binondo, Santa Cruz, Quiapo and San Miguel form the nucleus of the city, and boast markets (Divisoria Market, Quinta Market), churches (Quiapo Church, Santa Cruz Church), shopping streets ('Avenida' Rizal Ave, Escolta St), Chinatown (Binondo, Ongpin St), the official home of the president (Malacañang Palace in San Miguel) and many, many people.

The name Manila was originally two words: *may* ('there is') and *nilad* (a mangrove plant which grew on the banks of the Pasig River). Early inhabitants used the bark of the nilad to make soap.

Three years after founding the colony, King Philip II of Spain called the town Isigne y Siempre Leal Ciudad (Distinguished and Ever Loyal City). This grand title could not, however, replace the name Maynilad. If you want to know what Maynilad was like in the middle of the last century, read Fedor Jagor's classic book *Travels in the Philippines*, published in 1873.

Rizal Park, also known as Luneta Park, is the centre of Manila and is one of the city's main meeting places. The two most popular areas for tourists flank the park. To the north is Intramuros, the Spanish walled city badly damaged during fierce fighting in WWII. To the south are the tourist areas of Ermita and Malate, where the more peaceful modern invaders are drawn. Here you will find most of Manila's hotels and international restaurants. It's known as the 'tourist belt', and its main street is the waterfront Roxas Blvd. Ermita is about seven km north-west of Ninoy Aquino international airport (NAIA).

Manila's business centre is Makati, where the banks, insurance companies and other businesses have their head offices. Many embassies and airline offices are also here. At the edge of Makati, along E de los Santos Ave (almost always called Edsa), lies Forbes Park, a millionaires' ghetto with palatial mansions and its own police force.

At the other extreme is Tondo, Manila's main slum near Tayuman railway station. It's estimated that 1.5 million people live in slums in Metro Manila, and Tondo is home to about 180,000 of them – 17,000 huts in just 1.5 sq km. Other areas of Manila which may be of interest to the incurably curious traveller include Quezon City, the government centre, where you'll also find the Philippine Heart Center for Asia, the 25,000 seat Araneta Coliseum and the four-sq km campus of the University of the Philippines (UP), and Caloocan City, a light industrial engineering and foodstuff preparation centre.

Orientation

Manila is a sprawling city. Like Bangkok, it has a number of 'centres'. Makati, for example, is the business centre, while Ermita is where tourists tend to go. The area of most interest to visitors is roughly bounded by the Pasig River, Manila Bay and Taft Ave (ie, Intramuros, Ermita and Malate).

Intramuros is where you'll find most of the places of historic interest. The General Post Office (GPO) and the Immigration Office are also in this area. Further south is Rizal Park (Luneta Park), which extends from Taft Ave to the bayside Roxas Blvd. This is the central meeting and wandering place in Manila.

South of the park is the tourist centre of Ermita, which has a good range of accommodation, restaurants, airline offices and pretty much everything else you'll need. Further south again you'll find Malate and Pasay City, where there are a lot of upmarket hotels, particularly along the bay on Roxas Blvd. Nearby is the modern Cultural Center, built on reclaimed land jutting into the bay. Continue down Taft Ave and you'll reach the airport. To the south-east is Makati, and north of the river is the crowded and interesting Chinatown area.

Maps The Nelles Verlag *Manila* map is an accurate map of the capital, with a scale of 1:17,500.

Bookmark has two illustrated maps (*Metro Manila Landmarks* and *Makati*) which include noteworthy buildings.

The light-hearted *Survival Map of Manila* gives full details on entertainment, restaurants and shopping. Although an amusing read, much of the information is out of date.

Namria (formerly the Bureau of Coast & Geodetic Survey) on Barraca St, San Nicolas, is an excellently stocked shop which sells nautical charts and detailed maps. It is open Monday to Friday from 8 am until noon and 1 to 5 pm. There is a Namria branch in Fort Bonifacio in Makati.

Information
Tourist Offices There are two Department of Tourism (DOT) information centres in Manila: a reception unit at NAIA; and the main Tourist Information Center (☎ 523 8411) on the ground floor of the DOT building, TM Kalaw St, Rizal Park. It's open daily from 8 am to 5 pm. An information service is available around the clock on ☎ 524 1728 or ☎ 524 1660.

Visas The Immigration Office (Commission on Immigration and Deportation – CID; ☎ 407651) on Magallanes Drive, Intramuros, is open Monday to Friday from 8.30 am to noon and 1.30 to 5.30 pm.

Foreign Consulates The following is a list of foreign embassies and consulates in Metro Manila:

Australia
Doña Salustiana Ty Tower, 1104 Paseo de Roxas, Makati (☎ 817 7911)
Austria
Prince building, 117 Rada St, Makati (☎ 817 9191)
Belgium
Don Jacinto building, Dela Rosa St, Makati (☎ 892 6571)
Canada
Allied Bank building, Ayala Ave, Makati (☎ 810 8861)

Denmark
Doña Salustiana Ty Tower, 1104 Paseo de Roxas, Makati (☎ 894 0086)
France
Pacific Star building, Gil Puyat Ave, Makati (☎ 810 1981)
Germany
Solid Bank building, 777 Paseo de Roxas, Makati (☎ 892 4906)
India
2190 Paraiso St, Makati (☎ 892 5061)
Indonesia
Indonesia building, Salcedo St, Makati (☎ 856061)
Israel
PS Bank building, Ayala Ave, Makati (☎ 892 5329)
Italy
Zeta building, 191 Salcedo St, Makati (☎ 892 4531)
Japan
Gil Puyat Ave, Makati (☎ 895 9050)
Korea (South)
Alpap building, Alfaro St, Makati (☎ 817 5705)
Malaysia
107 Tordesillas St, Makati (☎ 817 4581)
Netherlands
King's Court building, Pasong Tamo St, Makati (☎ 812 5981)
New Zealand
Gammon Center building, 126 Alfaro St, Makati (☎ 818 0916)
Norway
69 Paseo de Roxas, Makati (☎ 893 9866)
Papua New Guinea
2280 Magnolia St, Makati (☎ 810 8456)
Singapore
ODC International Plaza building, 219 Salcedo St, Makati (☎ 816 1764)
Sweden
PCI Bank Tower II, on the corner of Makati Ave and Dela Rosa St, Makati (☎ 819 1951)
Switzerland
Solid Bank building, 777 Paseo de Roxas, Makati (☎ 819 0202)
Taiwan
Taipei Economic & Cultural Office (TECO), Pacific Star building, on the corner of Makati and Gil Puyat Aves, Makati (☎ 892 1318)
Thailand
Marie Cristine building, 107 Rada St, Legaspi Village, Makati (☎ 815 4219)
UK
LV Locsin building, 6752 Ayala Ave, corner of Makati Ave, Makati (☎ 816 7116)
USA
1201 Roxas Blvd, Ermita (☎ 521 7116)
Vietnam
554 Vito Cruz, Malate (☎ 500364)

MANILA

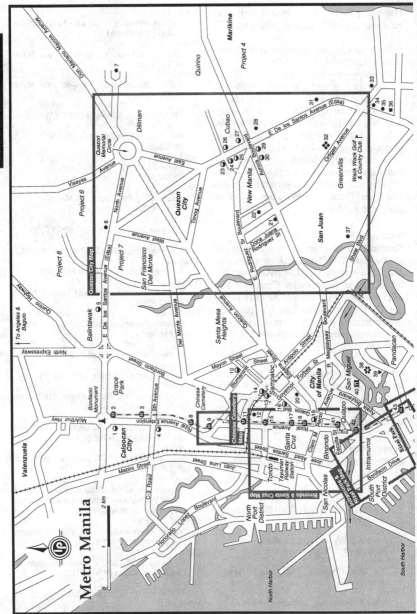

Metro Manila

MANILA

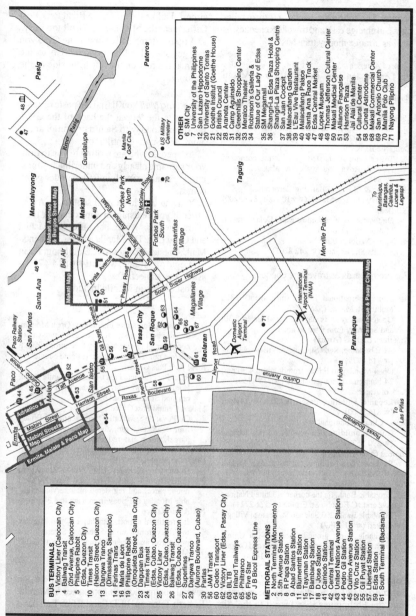

OTHER
6 SM City
7 University of the Philippines
12 San Lazaro Hippodrome
20 University of Santo Tomas
21 Goethe Institut (Goethe House)
22 British Council
28 Araneta Center
31 Camp Aguinaldo
32 Greenhills Shopping Center
33 Meralco Theater
34 Robinson's Galleria &
   Statue of Our Lady of Edsa
35 SM Megamall
36 Shangri-La Edsa Plaza Hotel &
   Shangri-La Plaza Shopping Centre
37 San Juan Cockpit
38 Malacañang Garden
39 L'Eau Vive Restaurant
40 Malacañang Palace
46 Santa Ana Race Track
47 Edsa Central Market
48 Lopez Museum
49 Thomas Jefferson Cultural Center
50 Makati Medical Center
51 Alliance Française
53 Harrison Plaza
   Jai Alai de Manila
54 Cuneta Astrodome
58 Makati Commercial Center
69 San Antonio Church
70 Manila Polo Club
71 Nayong Pilipino

BUS TERMINALS
2 Victory Liner (Caloocan City)
4 Baliwag Transit
5 Philippine Rabbit
   (2nd Avenue, Caloocan City)
   Philippine Rabbit
   (Edsa, Quezon City)
10 Times Transit
   Times Transit
   (Halcon Street, Quezon City)
13 Dangwa Tranco
   (Dimasalang, Sampaloc)
   Farinas Trans
14 Maria de Leon
16 Philippine Rabbit
19 Philippine Rabbit
   (Oroquieta Street, Santa Cruz)
23 Dagupan Bus
24 Times Transit
25 Victory Liner
   (Edsa, Cubao, Quezon City)
   Victory Liner
   (Edsa, Cubao, Quezon City)
26 Baliwag Transit
   (Edsa, Cubao, Quezon City)
27 Superlines
29 Dangwa Tranco
   (Aurora Boulevard, Cubao)
30 JAM Transit
56 Cedec Transport
60 Partas
62 Victory Liner (Edsa, Pasay City)
64 BLTB
65 Philtranco
66 Five Star
67 J B Bicol Express Line

METRORAIL STATIONS
2 North Terminal (Monumento)
3 5th Avenue Station
8 R Papa Station
9 Abad Santos Station
11 Blumentritt Station
15 Tayuman Station
17 Bambang Station
18 D Jose Station
41 Carriedo Station
42 Central Terminal
43 United Nations Avenue Station
44 Pedro Gil Station
45 Quirino Avenue Station
52 Vito Cruz Station
55 Lui Puyat Station
57 Buendia Station
59 Libertad Station
61 South Terminal (Baclaran)

Money The following banks and their branches can change cash and travellers cheques, as well as arrange money transfers:

Bank of America
    Lepanto building, Paseo de Roxas, Makati
    (☎ 815 5000)
Bank of the Philippine Islands
    BPI building, Ayala Ave, Makati (☎ 818 5541)
Citibank
    Citibank Center, Paseo de Roxas, Makati
    (☎ 817 2122, 813 9333)
Deutsche Bank
    Tower One, Ayala Triangle, on the corner of
    Paseo de Roxas and Ayala Ave, Makati
    (☎ 894 6900)
Hongkong & Shanghai Banking Corporation
    6740 Ayala Ave, Makati (☎ 810 1661, 814 5200)
PCI Bank
    On the corner of Makati Ave and Dela Costa St,
    Makati (☎ 817 1021)
Philippine National Bank
    Escolta St, Binondo (☎ 242 8501)

For credit cards & travellers cheques:

Adventure International Tours (Amex agent), 1810
    Mabini St, Malate (526 8406)
    Open Monday to Friday from 8:30 am to 5:30,
    and Saturday from 9 am to noon.
American Express (Amex)
    ACE building, Rada St, Legaspi Village, Makati
    (☎ 814 4777)
    Open Monday to Friday from 9 am to 4.30 pm;
    24-hour emergency assistance (☎ 815 4159).
Bank of America
    Lepanto building, Paseo de Roxas, Makati
    (☎ 815 5000)
Diners Club International
    Cougar building, Pasong Tamo St, Makati
    (☎ 890 5528)
Thomas Cook Travel
    Skyland Plaza building, Gil Puyat Ave, Makati
    (☎ 816 3701)
Visa Card & MasterCard
    Equitable Bank, on the corner of United Nations
    Ave and JC Bocobo St, Ermita (☎ 521 2721)
    Equitable Bank, 203 Salcedo St, Legaspi Village,
    Makati (☎ 812 5871)
    Equitable Bank, ground floor, Lai-Lai China-
    town Hotel, on the corner of Gandara and Ongpin
    Sts, Chinatown, Santa Cruz (☎ 733 1454)

Post & Communications

Sending Mail The quickest way to send mail from the Philippines is to take it to the Air Mail Distribution Center near the domestic airport. Unlike the GPO, the Rizal Park Post Office near the Manila Hotel isn't too busy.

A tip for stamp collectors: at the GPO you can get special release stamps. Go to the room at the rear on the left-hand side of the building.

Receiving Mail You'll find the poste restante counter to the left, at the back of the GPO. It's open Monday to Saturday from 8 am to 5 pm, and Sunday until noon.

Ask people who are writing to you to print your surname clearly and underline it – most missing mail is simply misfiled under given names.

You can also have mail sent to an Amex office if you're using an Amex card or travellers cheques. Amex has offices in Manila and Cebu City. The Manila address is Clients' Mail, American Express, ACE building, Rada St, Legaspi Village, Makati (☎ 814 4777 – ask to be connected).

Post offices in Manila include:

GPO
    Liwasang Bonifacio, Intramuros. Open Monday
    to Saturday from 8 am to 5 pm, and Sunday until
    noon; parcel service Monday to Saturday from 8
    am to 4 pm. There is a poste restante counter.
Rizal Park Post Office
    Rizal Park (Luneta Park), near the Manila Hotel,
    Ermita. Open Monday to Friday from 8 am to 6
    pm, and Saturday until noon.
Makati Central Post Office
    Gil Puyat Ave, Makati. Open Monday to Friday
    from 8 am to 5 pm, and Saturday until noon;
    parcel and registered mail service available
    Monday to Friday from 8 am to 4.30 pm.
Domestic Airport Post Office
    Domestic Rd, Pasay City. Open Monday to
    Friday from 8 am to 5 pm, and Saturday until
    noon; parcel and registered mail service avail-
    able Monday to Friday from 8 am to 4.30 pm.
NAIA Post Office
    International airport, Parañaque. Open Monday
    to Friday from 8 am to 5 pm, and Saturday to 4
    pm; parcel and registered mail service available
    Monday to Friday from 8 am to noon.

Fax, Telegraph & Telephone There are several communication companies in Manila. Eastern Telecom, PLDT and PT & T all have several branches where telegraph, telephone and fax services are available. There is a PLDT office on Escolta St in Manila, as well as at other central locations.

The area code for Manila is 02.

Email At the Mail Station Net, Park Square One, Ayala Center, Makati, you'll pay P50 for half an hour online and P90 for an hour, on a 'walk in' basis.

Travel Agencies For domestic and international air tickets check out:

Mr Ticket (☎ 521 2371; fax 521 2393), Park Hotel (lobby), 1030 Belen St, Paco
Interisland Travel & Tours (☎ 522 1405; fax 522 4795), suite No 6, Midtown Arcade, Adriatico St, Ermita
Blue Horizons Travel & Tours (☎ 893 6071; fax 892 6635), Shangri-La Hotel Manila, Ayala Ave, Makati

The last two companies can also be recommended for organised tours.

Scenic View Travel (☎ 522 3495; fax 521 8773) on the corner of Mabini and Soldado Sts, near the Ermita Tourist Inn, Ermita, sells WG & A inter-island boat tickets.

Bookshops The biggest and best assortment of books is in the National Book Store at 701 Rizal Ave, Santa Cruz, with branches in several parts of Metro Manila. The National Book Store in the Araneta Center in Cubao is very good.

The Bookmark on the corner of Greenbelt Drive and Makati Ave, Makati, specialises in scientific works and books about the Philippines. It also stocks magazines and stationery.

On Padre Faura St, between Mabini and JC Bocobo Sts, Ermita, is the Solidaridad Book Shop – 'an intellectual's delight' – with excellent sections on religion, philosophy, politics, poetry and fiction. Small and well stocked, it specialises in Asia and the Philippines.

The Tradewinds Bookshop in the El Amenecer building, General Luna St, Intramuros, specialises in Philippine literature, history, art, culture, as well as maps both old and new.

Libraries Libraries in Manila include:

Ayala Museum Library, Makati Ave, Makati (☎ 817 1191)
National Library, TM Kalaw St, Ermita (☎ 599177)

Campuses Manila's university campuses include:

University of the Philippines (UP), Diliman, Quezon City
University of Santo Tomas (UST), España St, Sampaloc

Cultural Centres The addresses of cultural centres in Manila include:

Alliance Française, Keystone building, Gil Puyat Ave, Makati (☎ 893 1967)
British Council, 7, 3rd St, New Manila, Quezon City (☎ 721 1981)
Goethe Institut Manila, 687 Aurora Blvd, Quezon City (☎ 722 4671)
Thomas Jefferson Cultural Center, Accelerando building, Gil Puyat Ave, Makati (☎ 818 4908)

Laundry There's a laundromat on R Salas St, Ermita, between Mabini and Adriatico Sts. Washing handed in before 11 am will be washed, ironed and ready by 8 pm the same day. The Minimum charge is P70 (for up to three kg), thereafter it's P20 per kg. The Laundryette Britania on Santa Monica St, Ermita, between Mabini and MH del Pilar Sts, is also recommended. It charges P25 per kg, and is open daily from 7.30 am until 10 pm.

Medical Services The addresses of reliable doctors and hospitals in Metro Manila include:

Makati Medical Center, 2 Amorsolo St, on the corner of Dela Rosa St, Makati (☎ 815 9911)
Manila Doctors Hospital, 667 United Nations Ave, Ermita (☎ 503011)
Manila Medical Center, 1122 General Luna St, Ermita (☎ 591661)

MANILA

General Practitioner (GP): Dr Heinz Varwig, Royal Match building (Hongkong & Shanghai Bank building), 6780 Ayala Ave, Makati (☎ 819 0820, 817 2632), speaks German and English, and consults Monday to Friday from 8 am to noon. Two English-speaking doctors consult in the afternoons from 2 to 4 pm, charging P300 for a consultation.

Emergency The Tourist Assistance Unit (TAU; ☎ 501728, 501660) in the DOT building, TM Kalaw St, Rizal Park, Ermita, is available around the clock. Other useful phone numbers include Emergency police ☎ 166 and Information ☎ 114.

Rizal Park

Popularly known as Luneta Park, this is an oasis in the centre of the city. Flowers, fountains, wide lawns and, of course, plenty of music attract thousands of strolling Filipinos every day in the late afternoon and evening. If you're there at 5 am, you can see the first eager Chinese doing their *t'ai chi*. Sunday is family day, with a chance to listen to the free concert at 5 pm. On New Year's Day there are great celebrations here.

It's interesting to watch the changing of the guard at the Rizal Memorial, which is close to where the national hero Dr Jose Rizal was executed by the Spaniards on 30 December 1896. The dramatic scene of the execution squad taking aim is the theme of a group of statues near the Rizal Memorial and forms the centrepiece of a light show. It can be seen at 6.30 pm (in Tagalog) and 7.30 pm (in English), except on rainy days, during power outages and sometimes for no apparent reason at all. Admission is P30, and the statues can also be viewed during the day for P5. Rizal's farewell poem, *Ultimo Adios* (Last Farewell), is inscribed on a brass plaque in different languages.

Tucked between the monument and the fish pond (towards TM Kalaw St) is Rizal's Fountain – a well from Wilhelmsfeld in Germany. They say Rizal used to drink from this well during his Heidelberg student days.

At the side of the park nearest the water is a playground where you can enjoy the Manila Bay sunsets. On the opposite side, near the Tourism building and the roller-skating rink, there's another playground with wonderful statues of dinosaurs and monsters.

On either side of the open-air auditorium are the Chinese and Japanese gardens, which are popular meeting places for couples.

Intramuros

Literally the city 'in walls', Intramuros is the Manila of the past. This is where Spaniard Miguel Lopez de Legaspi erected a fortress

PLACES TO STAY		10	Manila Cathedral	30	Rizal Park Post Office
29	Manila Hotel	11	Letran College	31	Rizal's Execution Spot
47	Holiday Inn Manila	12	Bastion de San Gabriel	32	Planetarium
	Pavilion	13	Revellin del Parian	33	Concerts in the Park &
		14	Puerta del Parian		Open-Air Stage
PLACES TO EAT		15	Bastion de Santa Lucia	34	Artificial Waterfall
44	Harbor View	16	Puerta de Santa Lucia	35	National Museum
	Restaurant &	17	San Agustin Church	36	Department of Finance
	Harbour Trips	18	Casa Manila Museum	37	Philippines Model
			& San Luis Complex	38	Agrifina Circle &
OTHER		19	Bastion de Dilao		Skating Rink
1	Rizal Shrine	20	Fortin San Pedro	39	Department of Tourism
2	Revellin de San	21	El Amanecer Building		(DOT), Tourist
	Francisco		& Tradewinds		Office & Tourist
3	Seamen's Club		Bookshop		Police
4	Immigration Office	22	Revellin de Recoletos	40	National Library
5	General Post Office	23	Manila City Hall	41	Rizal Memorial
6	Puerta Isabel II	24	Bastion de San Andres	42	Rizal's Fountain
7	Plaza Roma	25	Puerta Real	43	Quirino Grandstand
8	Palacio del	26	Aquarium	45	Army & Navy Club
	Gobernador	27	Bastion de San Diego	46	Museo Pambata
9	Puerta del Postigo	28	Bureau of Quarantine	48	US Embassy

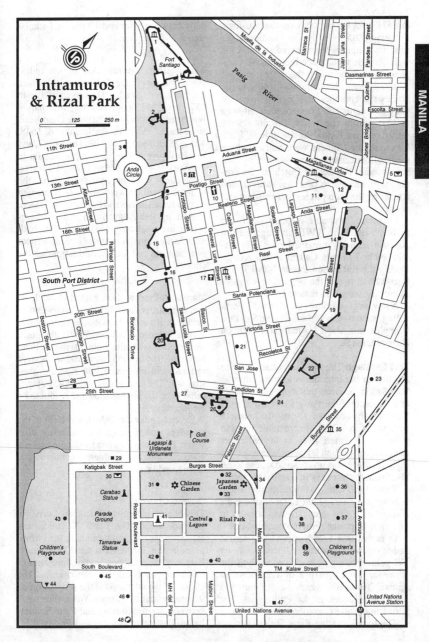

Intramuros & Rizal Park

0   125   250 m

in 1571 after his victory over the Muslims. Following attacks by the Chinese fleet and a fire, the Filipinos were forced to build the wall. A wide moat made the bulwark complete. Within the walls, the most important buildings were the numerous feudal lords' houses, 12 churches and several hospitals. Only Spaniards and Mestizos were allowed to live within the walls; Filipinos were settled on what is now the site of Rizal Park. Likewise, the Chinese were housed within range of the cannon, about where City Hall stands today. Neither the Dutch nor the Portuguese managed to take this fortress, and attacks by the Sulu pirates were also unsuccessful.

Intramuros was almost totally destroyed by bomb attacks in WWII, although the San Agustin Church remained relatively untouched and Manila Cathedral was rebuilt. During the restoration Puerta Isabel II and Puerta Real, two of the original seven gates of the city, were also restored.

A few original houses are also well worth seeing, such as Casa Manila in the San Luis Complex and the El Amanecer, both on General Luna St.

Fort Santiago The most important defence location of the Intramuros fortress-city was Fort Santiago. From this strategic location, at the mouth of the Pasig River, all Manila Bay could be observed. During the Japanese occupation in WWII, innumerable Filipino prisoners lost their lives in the infamous dungeon cells which lay below sea level – at high tide there was no escape. Dr Jose Rizal also spent his last days in a cell at this fort.

Today Fort Santiago is a memorial. There is an open-air theatre, the Rizal Shrine and a display of a few old cars which used to belong to important Filipino personalities.

In early 1988 Fort Santiago was turned inside out, with government permission, by US goldseekers who hoped to unearth the legendary war treasure of the Japanese general Yamashita, which was rumoured to have been hidden in the Philippines. Not surprisingly, all excavations were in vain.

The fort (including Rizal Shrine) is open daily between 8 am and 10 pm, and admission is P15, children P5.

San Agustin Church One of the oldest stone churches in the Philippines, this place has been through a lot. Destroyed by fire in 1574 and 1583, its present day incarnation was begun in 1599. The massive church has since had to endure the earthquakes of 1645, 1754, 1852, 1863, 1880, 1968 and 1970, and bombardment during fighting in Manila in February 1945. In 1879 and 1880 the crystal chandeliers were brought from Paris, the walls and ceilings were masterfully painted by two Italian artists and the choir stalls were carved by the Augustinian monks themselves. In a small chapel to the left of the high altar lie the mortal remains of Legaspi. There is a museum and a courtyard adjoining the church.

Manila Cathedral This cathedral, with its great cupola, is the Philippines' main Catholic church. It's in the Plaza Roma in Intramuros. Virtually destroyed during WWII, the place was rebuilt with the help of the Vatican between 1954 to 1958. Some old walls were restored and integrated into the new construction. The large organ with its 4500 pipes came from the Netherlands and is said to be the largest in Asia.

Every Sunday the cathedral echoes to the sound of young couples exchanging their vows. The doors are open to all, and this is a good opportunity to witness a genuine Philippine wedding.

Quiapo Church
This church is famous for its large crucifix of black wood. The Black Nazarene was carved in Mexico and brought to the Philippines by the Spaniards in the 17th century. Each day, especially on Friday, thousands of Catholics pay homage to the crucifix. The climax of the adoration is the procession on 9 January and in Passion Week (the week between Passion Sunday and Palm Sunday, before Easter) on Monday and Friday.

Chinese Cemetery

It may seem irreverent to recommend a cemetery as a tourist attraction but this one should not be missed. It contains some of the most ostentatious tombs in the world: virtual houses with mailboxes and toilets – some even have air-conditioners.

Things get lively on All Saints' Day (1 November), when the local Chinese come to honour their ancestors, just as Catholic Filipinos do. Most Sundays, in fact, it's a fascinating place to visit. Attendants, who also live in the cemetery, have started to offer guided tours. They charge a hefty P200 for a one hour tour, but they show the visitor the most impressive buildings and crypts. If asked, they will also open some of them up – and tell the most amazing stories while they're at it.

The Chinese Cemetery is in the north of the suburb of Santa Cruz, where Rizal Ave becomes Rizal Ave Extension. It has two entrances: the North Gate, which is almost always closed; and the South Gate, which is tucked away and can be reached from Aurora Ave via Pampanga and F Huertas Sts. Apart from taxis, the best way to get there from Ermita is by Metrorail to Abad Santos station.

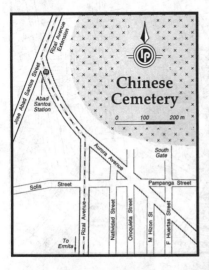

From there, it's about 600m to the South Gate. Otherwise, you can get a jeepney at Mabini St or Taft Ave going towards Caloocan City; they carry the sign 'Monumento'. Get off on the corner of Rizal and Aurora Aves. There's a P50 charge if you want to take your car inside the cemetery.

Chinatown

Chinatown is not a clearly defined suburb but a cultural and business district that takes in parts of Santa Cruz and Binondo, roughly the area between the three Chinese-Philippine friendship arches called the Welcome Gates. From Ermita you cross the Pasig River over the Jones Bridge, between the Immigration Office and the GPO, to the first gate, also known as the Arch of Goodwill. The southern part of Chinatown begins here. From Quintin Paredes St, which runs through the gate, several little streets wind crazily towards the big east-west curve of Ongpin St that stretches between the other two Welcome Gates.

Ongpin St is the main business street of Chinatown, but in the nearby streets you can also find exotic shops like herbal drug stalls, well-stocked Chinese grocers, small teahouses and spacious restaurants. Unlike the Chinatowns of other Asian cities, this one is very busy on Sunday.

Malacañang Palace

Malacañang Palace is the single most noteworthy attraction in the suburb of San Miguel. It's on Jose P Laurel St, on the banks of the Pasig River. Malacañang is a derivation of the old Filipino phrase '*may lakan diyan*', meaning 'here lives a nobleman'. The nobleman was originally Spanish aristocrat Luis Rocha, who built the palace. In 1802 he sold it to a high-ranking Spanish soldier and it then became the domicile of the Spanish heads of government. Later, the Americans used the palace as their residence.

The first Philippine head of state, Manuel Quezon, occupied the palace. A few years later it was used as the seat of office by Ferdinand Marcos until his reign ended in February 1986. It has since been renovated,

MANILA

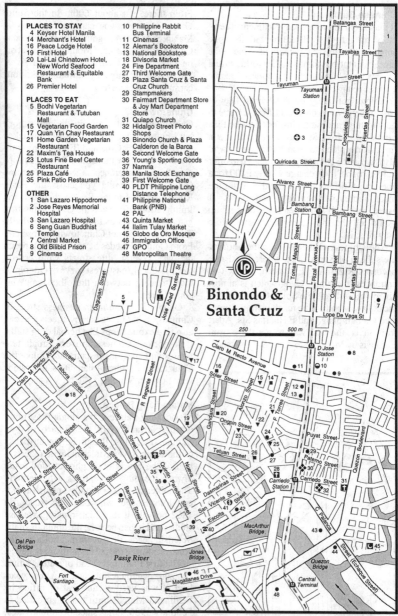

PLACES TO STAY
4 Keyser Hotel Manila
14 Merchant's Hotel
16 Peace Lodge Hotel
19 First Hotel
20 Lai-Lai Chinatown Hotel,
   New World Seafood
   Restaurant & Equitable
   Bank
26 Premier Hotel

PLACES TO EAT
5 Bodhi Vegetarian
   Restaurant & Tutuban
   Mall
15 Vegetarian Food Garden
17 Quan Yin Chay Restaurant
21 Home Garden Vegetarian
   Restaurant
22 Maxim's Tea House
23 Lotus Fine Beef Center
   Restaurant
25 Plaza Café
35 Pink Patio Restaurant

OTHER
1 San Lazaro Hippodrome
2 Jose Reyes Memorial
   Hospital
3 San Lazaro Hospital
6 Seng Guan Buddhist
   Temple
7 Central Market
8 Old Bilibid Prison
9 Cinemas

10 Philippine Rabbit
   Bus Terminal
11 Cinemas
12 Alemar's Bookstore
13 National Bookstore
18 Divisoria Market
24 Fire Department
27 Third Welcome Gate
28 Plaza Santa Cruz & Santa
   Cruz Church
29 Stampmakers
30 Fairmart Department Store
   & Joy Mart Department
   Store
31 Quiapo Church
32 Hidalgo Street Photo
   Shops
33 Binondo Church & Plaza
   Calderon de la Barca
34 Second Welcome Gate
36 Young's Sporting Goods
37 Namria
38 Manila Stock Exchange
39 First Welcome Gate
40 PLDT Philippine Long
   Distance Telephone
41 Philippine National
   Bank (PNB)
42 PAL
43 Quinta Market
44 Ilalim Tulay Market
45 Globo de Oro Mosque
46 Immigration Office
47 GPO
48 Metropolitan Theatre

Binondo & Santa Cruz

0   250   500 m

redecorated and partly reopened as a 'museum of historical, art and heritage values' (see the Museums section later in this chapter).

Cultural Center

The Cultural Center of the Philippines (CCP) was built under the umbrella administration of the ex-first lady Imelda Marcos. The P40 million project was opened in September 1969. Designed by Leandro Locsin, a leading Filipino architect, the CCP includes a theatre, art gallery and museum. It's open for public viewing daily between 9 am and 5 pm.

In the vicinity of the CCP is the Folk Arts Theater, Philippine International Convention Center, Film Theater, Coconut Palace and Westin Philippine Plaza Hotel. The Folk Arts Theater was built in the record time of only 70 days. Anyone interested in seeing the conference rooms of the Convention Center can take a tour. It's also worth popping in to the splendid Westin Philippine Plaza Hotel to see the elaborate modern interior decoration. It has what is probably one of the finest swimming pools in all of South-East Asia.

Nayong Pilipino

The Nayong Pilipino (Philippine Village) is a miniature version of the whole country – a concept which has become popular in a number of countries in the region. Typical houses and distinctive landscapes have been built on the 45 hectare site. Unfortunately, most of the houses are souvenir shops and are not traditionally furnished as you might expect. Jeepneys take you through the sites for free. There is the Museum of Philippine Dolls, Nayong Pilipino Aquarium, Aviary of Philippine Birds, Garden of Philippine Plants and more. A visit to the Philippine Museum of Ethnology is highly recommended (see the Museums section later in this chapter).

On Sunday afternoon, between 3 and 4 pm, you can watch folk dancing in the Mindanao section. The Nayong Pilipino is open Monday to Friday from 7 am to 6 pm (weekends to 7 pm). Admission is P25, children P15. Buses go from Taft Ave to the NAIA, which is right beside the Nayong Pilipino.

Jeepneys run between Nayong Pilipino and Baclaran, and from there you can carry on to Ermita by jeepney or Metrorail.

Zoo

You will find the Manila Zoological & Botanical Gardens at the southern end of Mabini St, at the beginning of Harrison St, in Malate. Of great interest here is the Philippine eagle and the dwarf buffalo from Mindoro. But the miserable accommodation (small enclosures, no shade, no plants) and the obvious neglect suffered by most of the creatures mean that animal lovers should give it a miss. It's open daily from 7 am to 6 pm. Admission is P6.

Forbes Park

Such a cluster of opulent mansions as you can see in Forbes Park and its neighbouring Dasmariñas Village seems more suited to Beverly Hills than Manila. This luxury walled neighbourhood even has its own police unit.

Forbes Park is in the south-east part of Makati. Buses marked 'Ayala (Ave)' go from Taft Ave in Ermita to the Makati Commercial Center. You then do the remaining one km by taxi, as visitors on foot wouldn't stand much chance of getting in; however, even taxis can be turned away if their passengers fail to give a known address. No photos are allowed and you may have to hand in your camera as you go in.

US Military Cemetery

The trim US Military Cemetery is directly east of Forbes Park. Here, in rank and file, are the remains of 17,000 US soldiers who died in the Philippines during WWII. In the circular memorial built on a rise are mosaics depicting the battles of the Pacific. It's worth seeing.

The cemetary is about two km from where Ayala Ave meets Edsa. The extension of Ayala Ave is called McKinley Rd and this leads to the cemetery via Forbes Park, San Antonio Church, the Manila Golf Club and the Manila Polo Club.

Faith Healers

The controversial methods of Filipino faith healers have achieved world notoriety through mass media coverage. Clearly, some of these 'doctors' are no more than dilettantes and charlatans out to make a buck, but others are so fast and skilful that even sceptics are astounded in spite of themselves.

Many patients travel to Baguio, some to Pangasinan Province, but there are also healers in Metro Manila. Anyone can watch after obtaining the consent of the patient.

For further information, get in touch with the Philippine Spiritual Help Foundation (☎ 521 6690). The founder of this organisation is the famous faith healer Alex Orbito, who also owns the travel bureau Orbit Tours.

Museums

You will find many interesting museums in Manila; here they are listed here in alphabetical order.

The **Ayala Museum** on Makati Ave, Makati, specialises in high points of Philippine history, chronologically presented in over 60 dioramas. There is also an ethnographic section which features artefacts, weapons and ships. Behind the museum is an aviary and tropical garden under a gigantic net. The museum is open from 9 am to 5 pm Tuesday to Sunday, and the charge is P30 (P10 for students).

The **Casa Manila Museum** on General Luna St, Intramuros, is one of the first examples of the restoration which Intramuros is undergoing. With its beautiful courtyards and antique furnishings, it's a faithful reproduction of a typical Spanish residence. Downstairs is a model of Fort Santiago and the bulwarks of Intramuros, as well as a photographic display. Attached to the museum is the Restaurant Muralla. The museum is open daily from 9 am to noon and 1 to 6 pm, except Monday, and admission is P15 (P5 for students).

The **Coconut Palace** is in the Cultural Center Complex, Roxas Blvd, Malate. This former guesthouse of the Marcos regime, made of the best tropical timbers, was built in 1981 for the first visit of Pope John Paul

II. It's open daily, except Monday, from 9 am to 4 pm. Admission is P100, including a guided tour which takes just under an hour.

The **Cultural Center Museum** is in the Cultural Center, Roxas Blvd, Malate. It has Oriental and Islamic art on permanent display on the 4th floor. The exhibits in the main gallery are changed from time to time. It's open Tuesday to Sunday from 9 am to 6 pm. Admission is P20 (P10 for students).

The **Lopez Museum** is in the Chronicle building (ground floor), Neralco Ave, Pasig. This is a private museum with a valuable collection of more than 13,000 Filipino books. The collection of historical travel literature is remarkable and includes one of three existing copies of *De Moluccis Insulis* (The Moluccan Islands) by Maximillianus Transylvanus. The work dates back to 1524 and contains the first printed account of Magellan's voyage to the Philippines. Also on display are some oil paintings by the well-known classical Filipino artists Felix Resurreccion Hidalgo and Juan Luna. It is open Monday to Friday from 8.30 am to noon and 1 to 4.30 pm. Admission is P20.

The **Metropolitan Museum of Manila** is on Roxas Blvd, Malate, near the Cultural Center. It has changing displays of various art forms, including work by old masters, and related documents. There's a small souvenir shop and the pleasant Met Café. It's open Tuesday to Sunday from 9 am to 6 pm. Admission is P20 (students P10).

The **Museo ng Malacañang** is on Jose P Laurel St, San Miguel. Here you used to be able to see examples of the extravagant lifestyle of the Marcos family (Imelda's famous shoes etc) which had been put on display by the indignant Cory Aquino. That's all been removed, however, and what's left are photos of former presidents. Disappointing, really. It's open Monday and Tuesday from 9 am to noon and 1 to 3 pm, and Thursday and Friday until noon for guided groups. Admission is P200. There's a public viewing on Wednesday from 9 am to noon and 1 to 3 pm, and on Thursday and Friday from 1 to 3 pm, at a cost of P20. Tickets can be bought at gate 3 of the palace, where you also have

MANILA

Chopping List

Single and double-edged swords of various designs are an integral part of the arts and crafts of the Muslims in the south of the Philippines. In Mindanao and the Sulu Islands in particular, the art of forging blades and shaping handles remains important. In Sulu, the classical type is the *kris*, called *kalis seko*, and the *kampilan*. Although they are rarely used in battle these days, swords are still of social and symbolic significance to the wearer.

1 Barong: a leaf-shaped, single-edged blade
2 Kampilan: the handle is supposed to represent the open mouth of a crocodile
3 Kris: a wavy-shaped blade
4 T'boli-bolo: the handle is decorated with brass curls
5 Dagger-kris: a weapon preferred by women
6 Talibong: a sabre with a single-edged, curved blade

to go through a security check. On certain official occasions the palace and museum are closed to the public. For information call ☎ 521 2307. There are jeepneys from Quiapo Market at Quezon Bridge to the palace.

The **Museo ng Sining** is in the GSIS building, Cultural Center Complex, Malate. This is the biggest museum of contemporary art in the country, and well worth a visit. Among the objects on display are tapestries and, in separate rooms, paintings by the famous Philippine artists Fernando Amorsolo and Hernando Ocampo. The museum is open Tuesday to Saturday from 8.45 to 11 am and 1 to 4 pm. Admission is free.

Just the thing for kids is the hands-on **Museo Pambata** on Roxas Blvd, Ermita. Children can go on their own voyage of discovery here, and there's not a 'Do Not Touch' sign to be seen. The friendly staff are also on hand to explain things if needed. Among the many attractions is a reproduction of a rain forest, a tram (streetcar) and a fire engine from old Manila. This museum is simply charming. It's open Tuesday to Saturday from 9 am to 5 pm, and Sunday afternoon from 1 to 6 pm. Admission is P50, children P30

The University of Santo Tomas (UST) on España St, Sampaloc, the oldest university in the Philippines, houses the **Museum of Arts & Sciences**. It has an extensive collection of historic documents and a library with more than 180,000 volumes. It's open Tuesday to Saturday from 9 am to 11.30 am and 2 to 4.30 pm. Admission is free.

The **National Museum** on Burgos St, Rizal Park, has many prehistoric finds, including a piece of the skull of 'Tabon Man' found in Tabon Cave, Palawan. There are also displays of pottery, weapons, costumes and ornaments. It's open Tuesday to Saturday from 9 am to noon and 1 to 5 pm. Admission is free.

The **Philippine Museum of Ethnology**, Nayong Pilipino, Pasay City, offers comprehensive information about the country's cultural minorities. Tools, weapons, musical instruments and everyday utensils are on display. Written explanations and photos illustrate the differences between the various

tribes. It's open Tuesday to Sunday from 9 am to 6 pm. Admission is P20, P10 for students.

Puerta Isabel II on Magallanes Drive, Intramuros, displays liturgical objects, *carrosas* (processional carriages) and antique bells. It's open daily from 9 am to noon and 1 to 6 pm, except Monday. Admission is free.

Ripley's 'Believe It Or Not' Museum in the Shangri-La Plaza Shopping Center (5th level) on Edsa, Mandaluyong, is an interesting cabinet of monstrosities. Here you'll find all sorts of curiosities: the tallest, fattest and shortest humans in the world; a shrunken head; and a man with four eyes. It also has a piece of the Berlin Wall, and you can have the moving experience of crossing a bridge during a simulated earthquake on the way out. Opening hours are daily from 10 am to 7 pm, and admission is P100.

The **Rizal Shrine** at Fort Santiago, Intramuros, is a memorial to the national hero Dr Jose Rizal. On display are some personal effects and his death cell. The shrine is open Tuesday to Sunday from 9 am to noon and 1 to 5 pm, but closed on public holidays. Admission is free.

The **San Agustin Museum**, San Agustin Church on General Luna St, Intramuros, has been established since 1973 in the Augustinian monastery. You can see frescoes, oil paintings, antique choir stalls, robes and other liturgical items. It's open daily from 9 am to noon and 1 to 5 pm. Admission is P30.

Markets

The **Baclaran Flea Market**, one of the biggest markets in Manila, is on Roxas Blvd, Baclaran, near the Baclaran Church. Every day, from Roxas Blvd up as far as Harrison St, good-value clothing, food, flowers and household goods are on sale. The busiest day is Wednesday, when crowds of churchgoers come looking for bargains after mass.

The **Cartimar Market** on the corner of Gil Puyat and Taft Aves, Pasay City, is the place for you if you're looking for a pet. The **Central Market** on Quezon Blvd, Santa Cruz, is a big market hall full of clothing and accessories, such as T-shirts, bags and shoes.

The **Divisoria Market**, San Nicolas, is on Santo Cristo St and the side streets nearby. It's a bright, lively market, where examples of almost everything produced in the Philippines (except handcrafts) are sold at reasonable prices. There's a good fruit and vegetable section. Watch out for pickpockets.

The **Quinta Market** on Carlos Palanca St, Quiapo, is also called the Santa Cruz or Quiapo Market. It's by Quezon Bridge, near Quiapo Church, and sells textiles, household goods and many other things. A broad selection of handcrafts are sold in the **Ilalim ng Tulay Market** under the bridge.

The **San Andres Market**, San Andres St, Malate, has a wide range of top-quality tropical fruit. Perhaps the best and certainly the most expensive fruit market in Manila, it is also open at night.

Swimming

Several 1st class hotels allow non-residents to use their swimming pools for an admission fee. Most of them are open from about 8 am to 7 pm.

Century Park Sheraton Hotel, Vito Cruz, Malate. Admission is P150, or P200 on weekends.
Manila Midtown Hotel, on the corner of Adriatico St and Pedro Gil, Ermita. Admission is P120.
Park Hotel, Belen St, Paco. Admission is P50.
Pool Bar, Guerrero St, Ermita. Admission is P60.
Seamen's Club, Bonifacio Drive, South Port District, South Harbour. The official name for this complex, which comprises a large swimming pool, table tennis tables, billiards, a library and restaurant, is the Manila International Seamen's Center. Admission is P75, free for sailors on shore leave. A monthly ticket costs P300, or P100 for sailors on shore leave.
Westin Philippine Plaza Hotel, Cultural Center, Roxas Blvd, Malate. Admission is P310.

Harbour Cruises

Golden Horizon Cruise Services (☎ 525 5698) organises one hour trips around the harbour and Manila Bay. The most impressive is the daily sunset cruise from 5.30 to 6.30 pm; price P60. On the weekend and public holidays it has extra trips all day, including morning cruises for P30.

Places to Stay

Manila has a wide range of accommodation. The tourist centre is in Ermita, where you'll find most of the government offices, while the business centre is in Makati. Most of the cheaper places to stay are in and around Ermita. There are a few top-end hotels in Ermita, but most upmarket hotels are strung out along the bay in nearby Malate and Pasay City. Some top-end places can also be found in Makati.

Places to Stay – bottom end

Binondo & Santa Cruz There are few good cheap hotels just north of the Pasig River.

The *First Hotel* (☎ 243 1855) on Ongpin St, Binondo, has fairly clean rooms with air-con and bath for P460/580 for singles/doubles, and there is a coffee shop. TV is P60 extra.

The *Merchants Hotel* (☎ 733 8111; fax 733 2717) at 711 San Bernardo St, on the corner of Soler St, Santa Cruz, provides reasonable rooms with air-con and bath for P550/660, and there's a restaurant and disco.

Rooms at the *Peace Lodge Hotel* (☎ 215521; fax 215520), 1285 Soler St, Binondo, are passable and clean, and cost P580 to P800 with air-con and bath, which is good value. The more expensive rooms have TVs, and there is a restaurant.

Ermita, Malate & Paco The 'tourist belt' area is where a good selection of inexpensive hotels and pension houses can be found. The Remedios Circle area of Adriatico St in Malate is a good place to start looking.

Probably the most popular travellers' centre in Manila is the *Malate Pensionne* (☎ 523 8304; fax 522 2383) at 1771 Adriatico St, Malate. This friendly and remarkably clean place is just off the main road which means it is quiet. Many travellers have praised it for its helpful staff and pleasant rooms. A dorm bed costs P130 with fan and P150 with air-con. Rooms cost P350 and P395 with fan, P580 with fan and bath, P800 and P880 with air-con and bath, and P990 with air-con, TV, kitchen and bath. Lockers can be rented and luggage left without charge

MANILA

Ermita, Malate & Paco

0   100   200 m

MANILA

PLACES TO STAY	44	Manila Diamond	37	Grand Café Juri's &
4	Mabini Mansion		Hotel		Guernica's
5	San Carlos	45	Pension Natividad	39	Geosphere Café
	Mansion	46	Tropicana Apartment	47	Sala Thai
9	Holiday Inn Manila		Hotel	49	Shakey's Pizza
	Pavilion & Avis	48	New Solanie Hotel	50	Chin Yuen Seafood
17	Hotel Soriente &	53	Winner Lodge		Palace
	International	54	Hotel Sofitel Grand	51	Aristocrat
	Supermarket		Boulevard Manila	59	My Father's
18	Swagman Hotel	55	Euro-Nippon Mansion		Moustache
19	Bayview Park Hotel	56	Marabella Apartments		
22	PM Apartelle	57	Admiral Hotel	OTHER	
26	Hotel La Corona	58	Aloha Hotel	1	Museo Pumbata
27	Birdwatcher's Inn &	60	Ambassador Hotel	6	National Library
	Birdwatcher's Bar	61	Hotel Royal Co-Co	10	Tourist Office
28	City Garden Hotel	63	True Home	11	Manila Doctors
29	Richmond Pension	64	Victoria Court Motel		Hospital
31	Pension Filipina &			12	Tabacalera Cigar
	Ralph Anthony	PLACES TO EAT			Factory
	Suites	2	Hong Kong Tea	13	Manila Medical
32	Sandico Apartel		House		Center
34	Aurelio Hotel	3	Maxim's Tea House	14	Western Police
35	Iseya Hotel, Iseya	7	KFC		Station
	Restaurant &	8	McDonald's	16	Equitable Bank
	Rooftop Restaurant	15	Max's & Hertz	20	US Embassy
38	The Garden Plaza	21	Emerald Garden	25	Ermita Church
	Hotel, Park Hotel,		Restaurant	42	Philippine Airlines
	Old Swiss Inn	23	Hang's 'N'	43	Gold Line Tours
	Restaurant & Mr.	24	Myrna's	52	WG & A
	Ticket	30	Barrio Fiesta	62	San Andres Market
40	Hotel Roma	33	The Pool Bar	65	Manila Zoo
41	Boulevard Mansion	36	Lili Marleen	66	Jai-alai de Manila

for up to one week, thereafter it costs P5 per day per piece. Not surprisingly, reservations are recommended. Airport service costs P120.

Only a few metres down the alley at No 1767, there's the *Shoshana Pension House* (☎ 524 6512), which has cramped, none-too-inviting rooms with fan for P200 and P250. There's also a cell-like dorm with four beds going for P100 per person.

Around the corner in the next alleyway leading back to Adriatico St, the unassuming little *Juan's Place* is an extremely friendly, family-run guesthouse, where you literally live with the family. The atmosphere is decidedly warm-hearted, and they provide cooking facilities. Double rooms go for P110 for one person, or P180 for two – easily the cheapest in Manila.

Joward's Pension House (☎ 521 4845) at 1726 Adriatico St, Malate, has relatively inexpensive rooms which are basic and small, but nevertheless OK for the money.

Singles with fan cost P280, with air-con P450. The entrance is next to Joward's Hot Pot Restaurant.

The *Pension Natividad* (☎ 521 0524; fax 522 3759) at 1690 MH del Pilar St, Malate, has maintained a high standard for years and is a sort of oasis in this hectic city. And, unlike most other pension houses, you can sit outside. It has dorm beds with fan for P150, rooms with fan for P430 and P480, doubles with fan and bath for P580, and with air-con and bath for P800 and P990. Staff will look after your luggage, and there's also a coffee shop.

In the central Ermita area, the *Santos Pension House* (☎ 523 4896) is at 1540 Mabini St, Ermita. It has rooms with fan for P295, with fan and bath for P370, and with air-con and bath for P500. The rooms vary in quality, with some starting to show their age.

The long-established *Mabini Pension* (☎ 524 5404; fax 595219) at 1337 Mabini St has rooms with fan for P380/450, with fan and bath for P400/550, and with air-con and bath for P650 and P700. The rooms are not the most attractive, but the people are friendly and will take care of visa extensions and look after luggage. Swiss travellers seem to prefer staying here.

On R Salas St, the Austrian-run *Si-Kat Inn* (☎ /fax 521 5955) has small but excellent rooms with air-con and bath for P500. It has a pub/restaurant.

There are a few self-styled apartelles, or little pension houses, in central Ermita. The *Tadel Apartelle* (☎ 521 9766) at 453 Arquiza St, Ermita, has small rooms with fan for P350, and good rooms with air-con and bath for P550 and P750. Next door, the *Yasmin Apartelle* (☎ 524 5134; fax 521 7225) is a more pleasant option. It has quiet, comfortable rooms with air-con for P500, and with air-con and bath for P600 and P700.

The *Sandico Apartel* (☎ 523 8180) on MH del Pilar St, Ermita, has passable, but ageing, rooms with air-con and bath for P495/530. They all have TVs, but most rooms are windowless.

The *Birdwatchers Apartelle* (☎ 525 1403; fax 258 5471) is a pleasant, comfortable place above the pub of the same name on A Flores St, a few metres off Mabini St, Ermita. It has really good rooms with air-con, bath and cooking facilities for P900.

The *Midtown Inn* (☎ 582882) at 551 Padre Faura, Ermita, has clean rooms with fan and bath from P425/500 and with TV, air-con and bath for P650/750. It's a bit pricey for what you get.

The *Ermita Tourist Inn* (☎ 521 8770-72; fax 521 8773) is at 1549 Mabini St, on the corner of Soldado St. Good value rooms with air-con and bath cost P540 to P600. It's a pleasant and fairly clean place, but rooms overlooking Mabini St are more than a little loud.

The *Manila Tourist Inn* (☎ 597721, 523 6634) at 487 Santa Monica St, Ermita, has quiet and fairly clean rooms with air-con and bath for P650.

The accommodation is quite comfortable at the *Iseya Hotel* (☎ 523 8166; fax 526 2778), 1241 MH del Pilar St, on the corner

of Padre Faura, Ermita, and there's also a rooftop restaurant. Singles/doubles with TV, fridge, air-con and bath go for P825. Note: rooms facing MH del Pilar St are quite noisy.

Parañaque & Pasay City In the area between the 'tourist belt' and the airport are a couple of hostel-style places.

The *Manila International Youth Hostel* (☎ 832 0680; fax 818 7948) at 4227 Tomas Claudio St, Parañaque, provides dorm beds for P100 (YHA members P75). A fridge and cooking facilities are available. The staff have been described as 'somewhat distant'. This is the headquarters of the Youth & Student Travel Association of the Philippines (YSTAPHIL). It's next to the Excelsior building on the corner of Roxas Blvd.

The *Townhouse* (☎ 833 1939; fax 804 0161) at the Villa Carolina Townhouse, Unit 31, 201 Roxas Blvd, Parañaque, has dorm beds with fan for P80, rooms with fan for P200/250, with fan and bath for P300/350, and with air-con and bath for P500/600. Weekly rates can be arranged. There's also a good and inexpensive restaurant. It's a pleasant place, with a friendly atmosphere created by Bill and Laura, who are keen travellers themselves. It's on a small side street called Sunset Drive, about five minutes by taxi from the domestic airport and NAIA. Airport service can be arranged for P50 (one or two persons).

Places to Stay – middle

Binondo & Santa Cruz

In this area, a couple of mid-range hotels can be recommended. The *Premier Hotel* (☎ 733 8301) on the corner of T Mapua and Tetuan Sts, Santa Cruz, has fairly comfortable rooms with air-con and bath for P770/890.

The best hotel in Chinatown is the *Lai-Lai Chinatown Hotel* (☎ 733 8001; fax 733 9552) on the corner of Gandara and Ongpin Sts, Santa Cruz. Comfortable rooms with TV, air-con and bath go for P940/1050. Suites are P1880. There is also a restaurant and coffee shop.

Ermita, Malate & Paco The majority of the hotels in this area are in the middle price

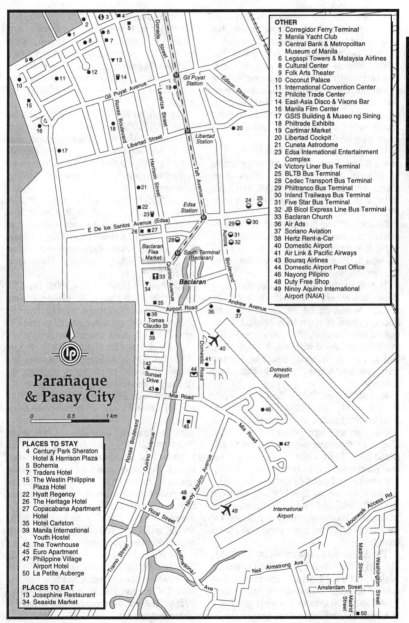

MANILA

OTHER
1 Corregidor Ferry Terminal
2 Manila Yacht Club
3 Central Bank & Metropolitan
  Museum of Manila
6 Legaspi Towers & Malaysia Airlines
8 Cultural Center
9 Folk Arts Theater
10 Coconut Palace
11 International Convention Center
12 Philcite Trade Center
14 East-Asia Disco & Vixons Bar
16 Manila Film Center
17 GSIS Building & Museo ng Sining
18 Philtrade Exhibits
19 Cartimar Market
20 Libertad Cockpit
21 Cuneta Astrodome
23 Edsa International Entertainment
   Complex
24 Victory Liner Bus Terminal
25 BLTB Bus Terminal
28 Cedec Transport Bus Terminal
29 Philtranco Bus Terminal
30 Inland Trailways Bus Terminal
31 Five Star Bus Terminal
32 JB Bicol Express Line Bus Terminal
33 Baclaran Church
36 Air Ads
37 Soriano Aviation
38 Hertz Rent-a-Car
40 Domestic Airport
41 Air Link & Pacific Airways
43 Bouraq Airlines
44 Domestic Airport Post Office
46 Nayong Pilipino
48 Duty Free Shop
49 Ninoy Aquino International
   Airport (NAIA)

Parañaque & Pasay City

0   0.5   1 km

PLACES TO STAY
4 Century Park Sheraton
  Hotel & Harrison Plaza
5 Bohemia
7 Traders Hotel
15 The Westin Philippine
   Plaza Hotel
22 Hyatt Regency
26 The Heritage Hotel
27 Copacabana Apartment
   Hotel
35 Hotel Carlston
39 Manila International
   Youth Hostel
42 The Townhouse
45 Euro Apartment
47 Philippine Village
   Airport Hotel
50 La Petite Auberge

PLACES TO EAT
13 Josephine Restaurant
34 Seaside Market

range. Some are only slightly more expensive than the pension houses and guesthouses, but most cost at least twice as much.

The *True Home* (☎ & fax 526 0351) at 2139 Adriatico St, Malate, is an unexpectedly beautiful building in this poorer looking part of Adriatico. Tastefully furnished rooms with fan and bath are P580, and with TV, air-con and bath from P1000 to P1300. All rooms have a different decor, and there is a swimming pool.

The *Hotel Roma* (☎ 521 9431; fax 521 5843) at 1407 Santa Monica St, on the corner of MH del Pilar St, Ermita, offers clean rooms with fan and bath for P600, and comfortable rooms with air-con and bath from P825 to P1045.

Directly above the International Supermarket, the *Hotel Soriente* (☎ 599133, 523 9456) is at 595 A Flores, on the corner of JC Bocobo St, Ermita, and has well-kept rooms with air-con and bath for P795.

The clean, friendly and accommodating *Royal Palm Hotel* (☎ 522 1515; fax 522 0768) at 1227 Mabini St, on the corner of Padre Faura, Ermita, is often fully booked. Well-maintained, comfortable rooms cost P1100 to P1750, and come with fridge, TV, air-con, bath and a complimentary breakfast. The new rooms on the Mabini St side are fairly loud however.

Rooms at the *Cherry Lodge Apartelle* (☎ 524 7631; fax 522 4172) at 550 JC Bocobo St, Ermita, are comfortable, with TV, air-con and bath from P840 to P1400. The more expensive rooms have fridges and round beds. There's also a coffee shop. This is a 'short-time' hotel (six hour rate is P360), and weekly and monthly rates are available.

The *Rothman Inn Hotel* (☎ 521 9251-60; fax 522 2606) at 1633-35 Adriatico St, Malate, has rooms with air-con, bath and TV for P1000/1200; the more expensive rooms have fridges.

The *Kanumayan Tourist Inn* (☎ 521 1161; fax 521 7323) is at 2317 Leon Guinto St, Malate, but there is also an entrance on Taft Ave. The most comfortable rooms cost P1000 to P1500 with air-con and bath. There is a beautiful swimming pool here.

The *Swagman Hotel* (☎ 599881-85; fax 521 9731) at 411 A Flores St, Ermita, is a clean and well-kept place. Rooms with fridge, TV, air-con and bath start at P1300. There's a 24 hour restaurant, airport service, and its own bus leaves three times a day for Angeles. This hotel is a favourite of the Aussies.

The *Garden Plaza* (☎ 522 4835; fax 522 4840) at 1030 Belen St, Paco (near Paco Park), has comfortable, spacious rooms with TV, air-con and bath from P1550 to P1900. Suites are from P2900 to P5500. The more expensive rooms have fridges and cooking facilities.

The friendly *New Solanie Hotel* (☎ 524 8641) at 1811 Leon Guinto St, Malate, is a quiet place, where good rooms with air-con and bath cost P1300 to P1600. They all have TVs, and the more expensive ones have fridges and cooking facilities. There is a coffee shop.

Las Palmas Hotel (☎ 524 5602; fax 522 1699) is at 1616 Mabini St, Malate. It's an old favourite with pleasant, recently redecorated rooms with air-con, bath, fridge and TV from P1600. There's also a swimming pool.

The well-run *City Garden Hotel* (☎ 536 1451; fax 524 4844) at 1158 Mabini St, Ermita, is owned by the same company as the Royal Palm Hotel, 150m away. Immaculate rooms with TV, fridge, air-con and bath cost P1350 to P2000. They are often fully booked.

The central and convenient *Centrepoint Hotel* (☎ 521 2751-61; fax 521 5331) at 1430 Mabini St, Malate, has a newspaper stand with international papers and a popular restaurant in the lobby. The hotel is a departure point for tour buses to various locations around Manila, including Puerto Galera. The rooms, which all have TV, air-con and bath, are OK and cost P1760 and P2100. The more expensive ones have fridges.

The *Hotel Royal Co-Co* (☎ 521 3911-18; fax 521 3919) at 2120 Mabini St, Malate, is an attractive place offering furnished rooms with TV, air-con and bath from P1300 to P2500. The more expensive rooms have a fridge and jacuzzi.

The *Palm Plaza Hotel* (☎ 521 3502-10; fax 508384) on the corner of Pedro Gil and Adriatico St has spotlessly clean and comfortable rooms with TV, fridge, air-con and bath from P2100/2400. It has a pool, and weekly and monthly room rates are available.

The *Aloha Hotel* (☎ 526 8088; fax 521 5328) at 2150 Roxas Blvd, Malate, has cosy rooms with air-con and bath for P1400. Suites with terraces overlooking the bay cost P2500.

The *Park Hotel* (☎ 521 2371-75; fax 521 2393) at 1032-34 Belen St, Paco, has rooms with air-con and bath for P1200/2100, and suites with jacuzzis for P3415. Rooms are quiet and comfortable, and have a TV and fridge. This place has a pleasant restaurant, a swimming pool and a handy airport service.

The *Ambassador Hotel* (☎ 524 6011-19; fax 521 5557) at 2021 Mabini St, Malate, is a big hotel, with quite good rooms with air-con and bath for P1850/2150 and suites for P3900. It has a nightclub and a swimming pool.

The *Hotel La Corona* (☎ 524 2631; fax 521 3909) at 1166 MH del Pilar St, on the corner of Arquiza St, Ermita, has well-maintained rooms with TV, fridge, air-con and bath from P1600/1900, including breakfast. Suites with a jacuzzi cost from P3500. The MH del Pilar St side is pretty noisy.

The *Admiral Hotel* (☎ 526 7061; fax 522 2018) at 2138 Roxas Blvd, Malate, has rooms with air-con and bath from P2600/2700. Suites are available for about P5800. The rooms are comfortable and come with a fridge and TV. There is also a swimming pool. This hotel is rich in tradition and has real character.

Makati In this area, some attractive mid-range hotels can be found around the 'food streets' of Pasay Rd and Makati Ave.

The *El Cielito Tourist Inn* (☎ 815 8951-54; fax 817 9610) at 804 Pasay Rd, Makati, is a pleasant, clean place with a restaurant and coffee shop. Rooms with air-con and

bath go for P980/1480, and suites from P1900. Staff are friendly.

The *Makati International Inn* (☎ 829 5989; fax 819 5722) at 2178 Pasong Tamo Ave, Makati, has nicely furnished rooms with TV, air-con and bath for P1190/1390. Some rooms have fridges and cooking facilities. This place is next door to the clean Health Spa, which offers good shiatsu massage.

The *Vacation Hotel* (☎ 843 7936) at 914 Pasay Rd, Makati, provides quiet and comfortable rooms with air-con and bath from P1500/1860, including breakfast. The standard rooms are a bit small.

The *Robelle House* (☎ 899 8209; fax 899 8064) offers some of the best accommodation in this category in all Manila. It's at 4402 Valdez St, opposite the International School. Rooms with air-con and bath cost from P1100/1225, and suites cost P1500. There's a charming restaurant and a swimming pool in a pleasant local atmosphere. Service is very friendly.

The Korean-run *Oka Hotel* (☎ 890 2014; fax 890 2077) at 8459 Kalayaan Ave, Makati, has pleasant rooms with TV, fridge, air-con and bath from P1200 to P2100 (includes breakfast). It's conveniently near Burgos St.

The pleasant *Inn Suites* (☎ 897 2053; fax 897 1965), with its posters of late, great stars like Marilyn Monroe, James Dean and Elvis in the stairway, is at 5012 Burgos St, Makati. The rooms are comfortable and tastefully furnished. They go for P1300 and P1500 with air-con and bath, apartments for P1700. Its delightful restaurant-bar, the Filling Station, is open 24 hours.

The *Century Citadel Inn Makati* (☎ 897 2370; fax 897 2666) is across the road and down a bit at 5007 Burgos St, Makati. Friendly rooms with TV, fridge, small kitchen, air-con and bath cost from P1700. It has a pool.

Only a few steps away from Makati Ave, the *Sunette Tower Hotel* (☎ 896 6407; fax 897 2096) is on Durban St, Makati. It has comfortable rooms with TV, fridge, small kitchen, air-con and bath for P1700 to P2900.

MANILA

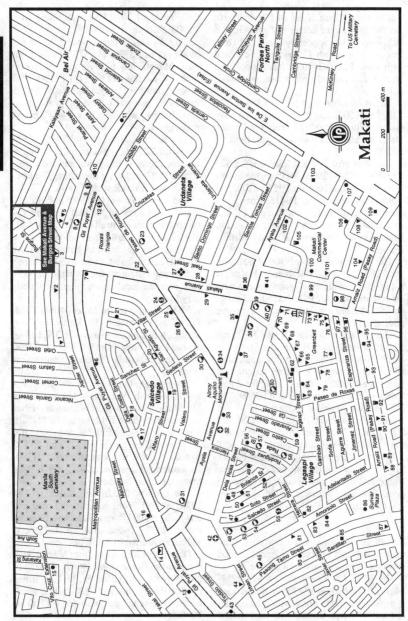

PLACES TO STAY
22 Mandarin Oriental Hotel
36 The Peninsula Manila
41 The Shangri-La Hotel Manila & Blue Horizons Travel & Tours
62 Charter House Apartelle & Asian Spirit Airlines
82 Amorsolo Mansion
85 Makati International Inn
89 El Cielito Tourist Inn & Proinsiya Restaurant
90 Pensionne Virginia & Goldilocks Bake Shop & Kashmir Restaurant
94 Vacation Hotel
96 New World Hotel
103 Hotel Inter-Continental
109 Hotel Nikko Manila Garden & Japan Airlines

PLACES TO EAT
1 Treffpunkt Jedermann Restaurant
2 Kusia Ni Maria Restaurant
3 Baan Thai Restaurant
4 Paper Moon Restaurant
5 San Francisco Steak House
28 Bistro RJ & Old Swiss Inn Restaurant
29 Nielson Tower Club & Restaurant
44 Maxim's Tea House
63 Café Rizal
65 Flavours & Spices Restaurant & New Garden Square
66 Boccalino Pizza Restaurant
67 La Tasca Restaurant & San Mig Pub
68 New Orleans Restaurant
69 Nandau Restaurant & Truffles Restaurant
70 Mario's & Itallianis Restaurant
71 Schwarzwälder Restaurant
73 Tia Maria's Restaurant
74 Shakey's Pizza
75 Le Soufflé Restaurant
76 Josephine Restaurant

78 Aling Asiang Restaurant, Aristocrat Restaurant & Prince of Wales Pub & Restaurant
79 Via Mare Restaurant & Greenbelt Square
81 Taste of Thailand Restaurant & Mile Long Arcade
83 Thai Room Restaurant & Creekside Building
87 Kamayan Restaurant
88 Racks Bistro
91 The Gold Ranch Restaurant
93 Angelino's Pizza
95 Foo Yiu Chinese Restaurant, Pep's Mexican Restaurant & National Book Store
97 Pizza Hut & Bookmark
101 Kimpura Restaurant & Makati Supermarket
104 Kowloon House
108 Jollibee, Pizza Hut & Wendy's

OTHER
6 Emirates Airlines & Thai Airways International
7 Garuda Indonesian Airlines, French Embassy, Taiwanese Embassy (Teco Office) & United Airlines
8 Japanese Embassy
9 Equitable Bank
10 Royal Brunei Airlines
11 Thomas Jefferson Cultural Center
12 Philippine National Bank (PNB)
13 Thomas Cook Travel
14 Makati Central Post Office
15 Scuba World
16 Swiss Air & Zuellig Wine & Spirits
17 Air France
18 Singapore Airlines
19 Air India, Cathay Pacific & Korean Air
20 Korean Embassy
21 KLM Royal Dutch Airlines & Northwest Airlines
23 Norwegian Embassy
24 Citibank
25 Qantas

26 Bank of America
27 Atrium of Makati (Atrium Shopping Mall) & Air Mauritius
30 German Embassy & Swiss Embassy
31 Israeli Embassy
32 Dr Varwig, GP & Hongkong & Shanghai Banking Corp
33 Finnair
34 Deutsche Bank
35 Makati Stock Exchange
37 Continental Air Micronesia
38 Canadian Embassy & Gulf Air
39 UK Embassy
40 Swedish Embassy
42 Makati Medical Center
43 Alliance Française
45 Dutch Embassy
46 Belgian Embassy
47 Royal Jordanian Airlines
48 British Airways
49 Air Canada
50 Egypt Airlines
51 Air Nuigini
52 Scandinavian Airlines System (SAS)
53 Indonesian Embassy
54 Italian Embassy
55 Equitable Bank
56 American Express
57 Thai Embassy
58 Austrian Embassy
59 Lufthansa German Airlines
60 Australian Embassy & Danish Embassy
61 PAL
64 Greenbelt Mall
72 Ayala Museum
77 United Supermarket
80 Aquaventure Philippines
84 Alitalia & Gallery Building
86 Makati Cinema Square
92 Equinox Disco & Gecko's Bar
98 Ayala Center Terminal & Park Square II
99 The Landmark Department Store
100 Fairmart Department Store
102 Rustan's Department Store
105 Hard Rock Cafe
106 National Book Store
107 SM Department Store

Parañaque & Pasay City *La Petite Auberge* (☎/fax 828 6311) is at 77 Madrid St, Parañaque. This pleasant little place is hidden away in the Merville Park Subdivision south of the airport. There are only five singles/doubles here, with air-con and bath for P1050, including breakfast. It has a good restaurant and swimming pool. A free airport service is available for international flights. As it is often fully booked, call first and arrange for staff to pick you up.

The Belgian lady who owns the immaculate *Euro Apartment* (☎ /fax 551 0723) on Lockheed St, Concorde Subdivision, Parañaque runs a tight ship. Rooms with air-con and bath go for P1150 and P1450 (for up to four people). The staff will look after left luggage. Phone and they'll pick you up from the airport.

Quezon City Several medium-sized hotels in this category can be found in Quezon City.

The *Villa Estela Hometel* (☎ 922 9136, 961160) at 33 Scout Santiago St, on the corner of Scout Dr Lazcano St, Quezon City, has clean, comfortable rooms with TV, fridge, air-con and bath for P920. It has a disco and a swimming pool.

The *Metropolitan Apartment Hotel* (☎ 921 4241; fax 921 4642) at 131 Malakas St, Diliman, is in a quiet area in Quezon City near the Philippine Heart Center for Asia. Spacious rooms with TV, air-con and bath go for P1265/1320. Two room apartments cost P2640.

The *Hotel Danarra & Resort* (☎ 927 5161; fax 924 2503) at 121 Mother Ignacia Ave, Diliman, Quezon City, offers good rooms with air-con and bath from P1400 to P2300. There's also a swimming pool within the trim hotel grounds.

The attractive *Sulo Hotel* (☎ 924 5051; fax 922 2030) on Matalino Rd, Diliman, Quezon City has comfortable rooms with air-con and bath from P2100/2460, and suites from P4000. It has a swimming pool.

Places to Stay – top end
Manila has plenty of 1st class hotels. Many like the Westin Philippine Plaza and Century

Park Sheraton offer reductions of 40% in the low season from June to September. Others, like the Manila Midtown Hotel, may cut their price by 50% for a stay of four weeks. The elegant Manila Hotel can be ranked with the Raffles in Singapore, Oriental in Bangkok and Peninsula in Hong Kong as among the oldest and most reputable hotels in South-East Asia. For a real extravagance, the hotel's 'imperial suite' is available – a penthouse with 10 rooms and your own butler for US$2000 a night. For those willing to settle for a mere five rooms (with butler, swimming pool and garden), there's the 'Mandarin suite' at the Mandarin Oriental in Makati. It only costs US$1800 per night.

Eighteen of the best luxury hotels in Manila are listed below. Prices are given in US dollars, and you should add a 10% service charge and a 13.7% government tax. Discounts are possible by booking through a travel agent. For example, a double room at the Philippine Village Airport Hotel normally costs US$160, but if you book through the World Class Travel office in the hotel itself, you only pay US$80.

Ermita, Malate & Paco The *Bayview Park Hotel* (☎ 526 1555; fax 521 2674) on Roxas Blvd has singles/doubles with air-con and bath for US$120/145, suites from US$240.

The *Century Park Sheraton* (☎ 522 1011; fax 521 3413) is on Vito Cruz in Malate. Rooms cost from US$210/240 and suites from US$380.

The *Holiday Inn Manila Pavilion* (☎ 522 2911; fax 522 3531) on United Nations Ave, Ermita, has singles/doubles from US$90 and suites from US$285.

The *Hotel Sofitel Grand Boulevard Manila* (☎ 526 8588; fax 526 0111) on Roxas Blvd, Malate, has rooms from US$140/200.

The *Manila Diamond Hotel* (☎ 536 2211; fax 536 2255), on the corner of Roxas Blvd and J Quintos St, Malate, has rooms from US$180/200 and suites from US$500.

The *Manila Hotel* (☎ 527 0011; fax 527 0022) at Rizal Park, Ermita, has rooms from US$236/265, suites from US$353 and a penthouse for US$2350.

The *Manila Midtown Hotel* (☎ 526 7001; fax 522 2629) on Pedro Gil, Ermita, has rooms from US$130/140. Suites start at US$200.

The *Westin Philippine Plaza Hotel* (☎ 551 5555; fax 551 5601) at the Cultural Center Complex, Malate, has rooms from US$185/220 and suites from US$390.

Makati The *Hotel Inter-Continental* (☎ 815 9711; fax 817 1330) on Ayala Ave has rooms from US$270 and suites from US$500.

The *Mandarin Oriental* (☎ 816 3601; fax 817 2472) on Makati Ave, has rooms from US$230/270 and suites from US$360.

The *Hotel Nikko Manila Garden* (☎ 810 4101; fax 817 1862) is on Fourth Quadrant, Makati Commercial Center. It has rooms from US$200/280 and suites from US$300.

The Peninsula Manila (☎ 819 3456; fax 815 4825) on the corner of Makati and Ayala Aves has rooms from US$200/210 and suites from US$400.

The *New World Hotel* (☎ 811 6888; fax 811 6777) on the corner of Esperanza St and Makati Ave has rooms from US$165.

The Shangri-La Hotel Manila (☎ 813 8888; fax 813 5499) on the corner of Ayala and Makati Aves has rooms from US$260/280 and suites from US$435.

Parañaque & Pasay City The *Traders Hotel* (☎ 523 7011; fax 522 3985) at 3001 Roxas Blvd, Pasay City, has rooms from US$140/160 and suites from US$250.

The *Hyatt Regency* (☎ 833 1234, 831 2611; fax 833 5913) at 2702 Roxas Blvd, Pasay City, has rooms from US$115.

Nearby, *The Heritage Hotel* (☎ 891 8888; fax 891 8833) has rooms from US$180/200. Suites are from US$380.

The *Philippine Village Airport Hotel* (☎ 831 4484; fax 833 8248) on Mia Rd, near the airport, Pasay City, has rooms from US$130/160 and suites from US$220.

Apartments

If you're staying for a while, it may be worth considering apartments instead of hotel rooms. It's possible to find apartments with cooking facilities, air-con, fridge, TV and so on for a monthly rent of P10,000 to P30,000. One month's rent must be paid in advance, and a deposit is required for the electricity. Rentals are available on a monthly, weekly and sometimes even daily basis. Daily rates include electricity and are around P400 to P1000. Apartments in Makati are often expensive, while those in Ermita and Malate are often unavailable, especially the cheaper ones – book early.

Ermita, Malate & Paco The *Victoria Mansion* (☎ 575851; fax 521 0193), 600 JM Nakpil St, Malate, has one room apartments for P400 daily and P11,400 monthly.

The *Casa Blanca I* (☎ 523 8251) at 1447 Adriatico St, Ermita, has one room apartments for P800 daily and P10,000 monthly. Two room apartments cost P1350 daily and P15,000 monthly.

The *San Carlos Mansion* (☎ 523 8110; fax 521 3768) at 777 San Carlos St, Ermita, has one room apartments for P780 daily and P14,850 monthly. Two room apartments cost P880 daily and P19,000 monthly.

The *Mabini Mansion* (☎ 521 4776) is at 1011 Mabini St, Ermita. A one room apartment costs P1300 daily and P18,100 monthly. A two room apartment costs P2260 daily and P28,250 monthly. It has a coffee shop.

The *Dakota Mansion* (☎ 521 0701; fax 521 8841) on the corner of Adriatico and General Miguel Malvar Sts, Malate, has one room apartments for P1300 daily and P18,100 monthly. Two room apartments cost P2300 daily and P28,500 monthly, and there's a restaurant and swimming pool.

The *Boulevard Mansion* (☎ 521 8888; fax 521 5829), 1440 Roxas Blvd, Ermita, has studios for P1300 daily and P18,000 monthly; standard one room apartments for P1300 daily and P18,000 monthly; suites for P2000 daily and P28,000 monthly; and a penthouse for P5000 daily and P70,000 monthly. It also has a coffee shop.

The *Pearl Garden Apartel* (☎ 525 9461) at 1700 Adriatico St, Malate, has one room apartments for P990 daily and P24,000 monthly. Two room apartments cost P1900 daily and P45,600 monthly. There's also a restaurant.

Robinson's Apartelle (☎ 522 05581; fax 521 9152) on Maria Orosa St, Ermita, has studios for P1450 daily, P8200 weekly and P25,500 monthly; one room apartments for P2000 daily, P12,000 weekly and P38,500 monthly; and two room apartments for P2690 daily, P27,000 weekly and P50,000 monthly.

The *Tropicana Apartment Hotel* (☎ 523 8031; fax 522 3208) at 1630 Luis M Guerrero St, Malate, has standard one room apartments for P1400 daily, P8500 weekly and P30,200 monthly. Deluxe one room apartments are P1520 daily, P9700 weekly and P35,000 monthly. Standard two room apartments are P3300 daily, P14,200 weekly and P48,500 monthly. Deluxe two room apartments are P2500 daily, P15,200 weekly and P55,000 monthly. It has a restaurant and a swimming pool.

Makati The *Amorsolo Mansion* (☎ 818 6811; fax 817 2620) at 130 Amorsolo St, on the corner of Herrera St, has one room apartments for P1300 daily and P18,500 monthly, and two room apartments for P2200 daily and P26,000 monthly.

The *Charter House I* (☎ 817 6001-16; fax 817 7071) at 114 Legaspi St, has one room apartments for P1750 daily and P45,000 monthly. There is a coffee shop and a small swimming pool.

Regine's Apartelle (☎ 812 6509; fax 812 6778) at 8429 Kalayaan Ave, near Makati Ave, has studios for P1700 daily and P42,000 monthly; one room apartments for P2400 daily and P59,000 monthly; and two room apartments for P3400 daily and P83,000 monthly.

The *Robelle Mansion* (☎ 899 7388; fax 899 7390) at 877 JP Rizal St, Makati, has one room apartments from P880 to P1100 daily and for P17,000 monthly.

The *Traveler's Inn* (☎ 895 7061; fax 896 2144) at 7880 Makati Ave, Makati, has one room apartments from P1210 daily and P22,000 monthly.

Parañaque & Pasay City The *Copacabana Apartment Hotel* (☎ 831 8711; fax 831 4344) at 264 Edsa Extension, Pasay City, has one room apartments for P1720 daily and P35,200 monthly; two room apartments for P3000 daily and P45,000 monthly; and three room apartments for P5000 daily and P54,500 monthly. There's a restaurant, coffee shop, sauna and swimming pool.

Quezon City The *Broadway Court* (☎ 722 7411; fax 721 7795) is at 16 Doña Juana Rodriguez St, New Manila (Quezon City). It has one room apartments costing P950 daily and P16,000 monthly. There's also a coffee shop and tennis court.

Places to Eat

Manila's restaurants have an impressive diversity of cuisines and prices. In most restaurants in Ermita you can get a decent meal for roughly P100. On Adriatico St, prices are higher. For a meal of several courses you can expect to pay P150 to P300.

The top restaurants in Makati are expensive, but a real gourmet would probably be prepared to pay the P300 to P500 or more for the excellent food, service and atmosphere. Sometimes, these meals are accompanied by cultural entertainment or a fashion show. A lunch buffet costs about P200 to P350.

Good wine will cost at least P500 a bottle. Wine is imported, and transport costs and import duties make it expensive. Maybe San Miguel beer is a better choice.

Only a few restaurants insist on formal dress. Otherwise, casual clothes are quite alright; however, even in a mid-range restaurant, thongs (flip-flops), shorts or singlets would be pushing tolerance a bit far.

Prices given for the following restaurants are for dinner for one person. Drinks are not included, nor are extra helpings or expensive items like lobster tails or caviar. For buffets in top hotels, about 25% is added for government tax and the service charge.

Filipino Ermita is a good place to explore Filipino cuisine, especially along MH del

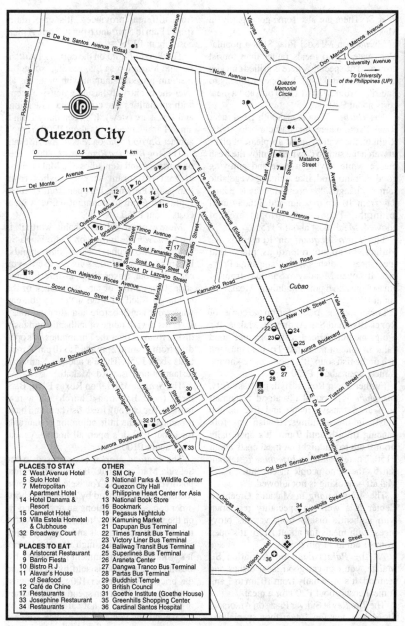

Quezon City

0   0.5   1 km

MANILA

To University
of the Philippines (UP)

Quezon
Memorial
Circle

PLACES TO STAY
2 West Avenue Hotel
5 Sulo Hotel
7 Metropolitan
  Apartment Hotel
14 Hotel Danarra &
   Resort
15 Camelot Hotel
18 Villa Estela Hometel
   & Clubhouse
32 Broadway Court

PLACES TO EAT
8 Aristocrat Restaurant
9 Barrio Fiesta
10 Bistro R J
11 Alavar's House
   of Seafood
12 Café de Chine
13 Restaurants
33 Josephine Restaurant
34 Restaurants

OTHER
1 SM City
3 National Parks & Wildlife Center
4 Quezon City Hall
6 Philippine Heart Center for Asia
13 National Book Store
16 Bookmark
19 Pegasus Nightclub
20 Kamuning Market
21 Dapupan Bus Terminal
22 Times Transit Bus Terminal
23 Victory Liner Bus Terminal
24 Baliwag Transit Bus Terminal
25 Superlines Bus Terminal
26 Araneta Center
27 Dangwa Tranco Bus Terminal
28 Partas Bus Terminal
29 Buddhist Temple
30 British Council
31 Goethe Institute (Goethe House)
35 Greenhills Shopping Center
36 Cardinal Santos Hospital

Pilar St. There are also some good places in Makati.

Myrna's on MH del Pilar St is a popular place catering to locals rather than tourist crowds. The speciality here is grilled chicken and bangus (milkfish). It's open Monday to Saturday from 7 am to 11.30 pm, and a meal costs about P80.

The *Harbor View* is at South Blvd, near Rizal Park, where the harbour trip starts. Right on the waterfront, it's a pleasant place to watch the sun go down and enjoy the fresh breeze while having a beer and enjoying good Filipino food, like sinigang (vegetable soup) or bangus. It's open Monday to Saturday from 10 am to 2 am and Sunday until midnight. Thongs (flip-flops) are not allowed. Meals cost about P175.

The *Patio Mequeni* on Remedios St, Malate, is an unpretentious place that specialises in dishes from Pampanga Province. It's open Monday to Saturday from 11 am to 3 pm and 6 pm to midnight. Meals cost about P175.

Locals like the *Aristocrat*, on the corner of Roxas Blvd and San Andres St, Malate. It's a big, medium-priced restaurant and good value in spite of the name. Try the lapu-lapu fish or the fish soup. It's open daily 24 hours. A meal costs about P150.

Further down Roxas Blvd, in Pasay City, *Josephine* is a popular seafood restaurant with an extensive menu and live combo music in the evenings. It also has folk dancing from 8 until 9 pm. It's open daily from 9 am to midnight. A meal costs about P150. There's another *Josephine* restaurant run by the same people in Greenbelt Park, Makati – smoking is not allowed.

The *Aling Asiang* in Makati's Greenbelt Center is a well-run speciality restaurant with authentic dishes from various provinces, with meals for about P175. It's open from 11 am to 11 pm daily.

At the *Palais daan* on Adriatico St, Malate, you can get good local dishes and seafood. It's open daily from 10 am to 1 am. A meal costs about P200 for a meal.

The *Tito Rey* at Sunvar Plaza on Amorsolo St, Makati, features finger-food specialities from different provinces. It's open daily from 11 am to 5 pm and 6 pm to 2 am. A meal costs about P175.

The *Barrio Fiesta* on the corner of Arkansas and Maria Orosa Sts, Ermita, is a good, medium-priced restaurant with branches all over the country. It has an extensive menu with specialities like crispy pata (crackling) and kare-kare (stew). It's open daily from 8 am to 1 am. A meal costs about P200. There's another *Barrio Fiesta* on Makati Ave, Makati.

The *Ang Bistro sa Remedios*, on the corner of Adriatico and Remedios Sts, Malate, is an elegant restaurant serving dishes from Pampanga Province. It's open from 11 am to 2 pm and 6 pm to midnight daily. A meal costs about P250.

More expensive, but probably worth it, is the *Kamayan Restaurant* on Padre Faura St, Ermita. The name means 'bare hands' because knives and forks are not used – you eat with your fingers here in true Filipino style. It has a line of jars at the back of the restaurant filled with tap water, so you can wash your hands before and after the meal. It serves a wide range of authentic and tasty dishes from all over the Philippines. It's open daily from 11 am to 2 pm and 5 to 10 pm. A meal costs about P250. There's another Kamayan restaurant on Pasay Rd, Makati.

The *Seaside Market* on Roxas Blvd, Baclaran (near Baclaran Church), is a real market. You can buy fresh fish here and have it prepared at the little adjoining restaurants for about P50. It's open all hours. A meal costs about P100.

The *Seafood Market* (as opposed to the Seaside Market) on JC Bocobo St, Ermita, positively bounces. You select your own seafood and it's cooked by a squad of short-order cooks lined up along an open window on the street side. They're all frantically stirring woks, scooping pots and juggling frying pans, while flames leap high all around them. It's wonderful entertainment for passers-by. Beware: the seafood is sold by weight and the prices given are per 100g. As one customer warned: 'You can spend a lot of money in that place if you're not careful, as it's by the weight and you may not realise. You are also given wet towels, that seem to be complimentary (you are not told otherwise) and they are later on the bill'. You can round off the menu with coffee and cakes at the *Café Alps* next door. It's open daily from 10 am to midnight. A meal costs about P300.

At *The Islands Fisherman* on Arquiza St, Ermita, guests select their own seafood, which can be cooked in Chinese, Japanese, Filipino or Thai style, or according to their own recipes. Unlike the ever-popular Seafood Market, it doesn't charge extra for the preparation of the seafood and side orders, or for service. It's open daily from 10 am to midnight. A meal costs about P250.

Chinese Manila has a great number of Chinese restaurants. For simple and economical Chinese food, try *Mrs Wong Tea House* on a little street between Padre Faura St and Robinson's shopping centre, Ermita. It's open daily 24 hours. A meal costs P75 to P100.

The *Hong Kong Tea House* on MH del Pilar St, Ermita, is a long-established, Cantonese-style Chinese restaurant with good noodle soup. It's open daily from 10 am to 4 am. A meal costs P75 to P100.

If you cross to the other side of MH del Pilar St and walk to the corner of United Nations Ave you'll find *Maxim's Tea House*, which offers good, inexpensive food. There's also a *Maxim's Tea House* on the corner of Pasong Tamo and Urban Sts, Makati, and on Ongpin St, Chinatown. They're open daily all hours. Meals cost from P75 to P100.

The *Sea Palace* on Mabini St, Malate, is a good and relatively cheap Chinese restaurant which also serves Filipino food. It's open from 11 am to 2.30 pm and 6 to 11.30 pm daily, with meals for about P150. There's another *Sea Palace* on Adriatico St, Malate.

Eva's Garden on Adriatico St, Ermita, is pleasant and reasonably priced. It's open Monday to Saturday from 11.30 am to 2 pm and 5 to 10 pm, and Sunday from 5 to 10 pm. A meal costs about P175.

Indian & Middle Eastern A good Indian restaurant next to the Kamayan Restaurant on Padre Faura, Ermita, is the *Kashmir*, which serves mainly north Indian and Pakistani dishes. It's open from 10 am to 11 pm daily, and meals cost about P200. There's another *Kashmir* restaurant on General Luna St, Makati.

Japanese The *Iseya Restaurant* on Padre Faura, Ermita, serves a good-value business lunch for around P120. It's open daily from 11 am to 2 pm and 5 to 11 pm, and meals are about P175.

The *Yamato* on Adriatico St, Ermita, is good for sushi and tempura. It's open daily from 11 am to 2 pm and 5.30 to 10.30 pm. Meals cost about P150.

The *Kimpura* on West Drive, Makati, in the Makati Supermarket building, is a popular, inexpensive and 1st class Japanese restaurant. It's open daily from 10.30 am to 3 pm and 5.30 to 11 pm. Meals cost about P300.

The *Tempura-Misono* is a popular Japanese restaurant in the Hyatt Regency Hotel, Roxas Blvd, Pasay City. It's open daily from noon to 5 pm and 6 to 11 pm. Meals cost about P500.

Korean The *Korean Village* on Adriatico St, Malate, is said to be the biggest Korean restaurant in Manila. Its specialities are spare ribs and beef stew. It's open Monday to Saturday from 11 am to 2 pm and 5 to 10 pm. Meals cost about P200.

The *Korean Palace* is also on Adriatico St, Malate. It's open from 11 am to 2 pm and 5 to 10 pm daily, and meals cost about P200.

The *Korean Garden* on Burgos St, Makati, is one of about 10 roughly comparable Korean restaurants in Makati. It's open daily from 11.30 am to 2.30 pm and 5.30 to 10.30 pm. Meals cost about P250.

Thai The *Sala Thai* on JM Nakpil St, Malate, is a popular, inexpensive restaurant. Among the dishes most ordered here are Thai curries, tom yum (a spicy, sour soup) and egg rolls. It's open daily from 10 am to 10 pm. A meal costs about P150.

Flavours & Spices on New Garden Square, on the corner of Legaspi St and Greenbelt

Drive, Makati, is a good restaurant where you can also buy Thai spices. It's open from 10 am to 10 pm. Meals cost about P175.

Another good restaurant is *Taste of Thailand* in the Mile Long Arcade, Amorsolo St, Makati, which is open daily from 11.30 am to 2 pm and 6.30 to 10 pm. Meals cost about P175.

The *Baan Thai* is on the corner of Makati Ave and Jupiter St, Makati. It looks authentic, and serves the typical Thai salads and soups, as well as fish dishes. It's open from 11.30 am to 2 pm and 3.30 to 10 pm. A meal costs around P200.

Australian & UK From the *Rooftop Restaurant* on the corner of Padre Faura and MH del Pilar St, Ermita, you can enjoy a good view over Manila Bay in this Australian restaurant and beer garden on top of the Iseya Hotel. It's open daily all hours. On Sunday there's an Aussie barbecue for P160.

The *Prince of Wales* in the Greenbelt Center, Makati, is a pub and restaurant serving typically British food like roast beef and Yorkshire pudding. It's popular with expats. There's a lunchtime buffet from Monday to Saturday. It's open Monday to Saturday from 11 am to midnight, and meals are about P175.

Dutch The *Holandia* on Arquiza St, Ermita, is a small restaurant with Dutch specialities. It's open Monday to Saturday from 10 am to 1 am and Sunday from 4 pm to 1 am. Meals cost about P175.

French The *L'Eau Vive* on Paz Mendoza Guazon Ave, Paco, is an out-of-the-ordinary restaurant, run by nuns and missionaries, which serves international and French cuisine. It's open Monday to Saturday from noon to 3 pm and 7 to 11 pm. Meals cost about P300.

German, Austrian & Swiss The *München Grill Pub* on Mabini St, Ermita, has Bavarian dishes and good-value meals of the day, with several courses for about P150. It's open Monday to Saturday from 10 am to 2 am. Meals cost about P100.

You could almost miss the little *Si-Kat Inn* on R Salas St, Ermita. It has a small selection of German and Austrian cuisine daily from 8 am until 10.30 pm. Meals cost around P150.

The *Schwarzwälder* on Makati Ave, Makati, has dishes like eisbein (knuckle of pork) with sauerkraut. It's open daily from 11.30 am to 2.30 pm and 5.30 pm to 3 am. Meals cost about P250.

The *Treffpunkt Jedermann* on Jupiter St, Makati, has found its own niche, offering Austrian cooking in a warm and friendly alpine atmosphere. It's open daily from 7 am to 2 am. A meal costs about P175.

The more expensive *Old Swiss Inn Restaurant* is in the Garden Plaza Hotel on Belen St, Paco. This restaurant serves excellent Swiss food such as fondue. It's open 24 hours daily, and a meal costs about P250. There's another *Old Swiss Inn Restaurant* in the Olympia Towers, Makati Ave, Makati.

Italian *Alda's Pizza Kitchen* on Adriatico St, Ermita, is a friendly restaurant, with a wide selection of good, inexpensive pizzas for about P100. It's open Monday to Saturday from 11 am to midnight, and Sunday from 3 pm to midnight.

La Gondola Italian Restaurant on Makati Ave, Makati, serves good pasta. Apart from making any pizza you could think of, staff offer Italian ham and home-made ice cream. It's open Monday to Saturday from noon to 2 pm and 7 to 11 pm daily. Meals cost about P400.

Mexican *Tia Maria's* on Remedios St, Malate, serves cocktails and good Mexican food. It's open Monday to Saturday from 11 am to midnight, and Sunday from 5 pm to midnight. Meals cost about P200. There's another *Tia Maria's* on Makati Ave, near Greenbelt Park, Makati.

Spanish *Guernica's* on MH del Pilar St, Ermita, offers dishes like paella but also serves steaks. Guitar music adds to the atmosphere. It's open Monday to Saturday from 11 am to 2 pm and 6 pm to midnight, and Sunday from 6 pm to midnight. Meals cost about P250.

The *Patio Guernica* on JC Bocobo St, near Remedios Circle, Malate, serves typically Spanish dishes, as well as steaks. It's open Monday to Saturday from 11 am to 2 pm and 6 pm to midnight, and Sunday from 6 pm to midnight. Meals cost about P250.

The *Muralla* in the San Luis Complex, General Luna St, Intramuros, serves Spanish and Filipino food. It's open daily from 11 am to 2 pm and 6 to 11 pm. Meals cost about P300.

US The *Steak Town* on Adriatico St, Malate, has good steaks and seafood, soup, salad, bread, dessert and coffee. Meals cost about P250. It's open from 11.30 am to 11.30 pm daily. There's another *Steak Town* on Makati Ave, Makati.

The Gold Ranch on Pasay Rd, Makati, serves excellent barbecued steaks. It's open daily (except holidays) from 11.30 am to 2.30 pm and 6.30 to 10.30 pm. Meals cost about P350.

The *New Orleans* on Legaspi St, Makati, specialises in US and Creole dishes, especially steaks and barbecued ribs, along with pretty good New Orleans jazz. It's open from 11 am to 2 pm and 6 pm to midnight daily. Meals cost about P400.

The *Café Adriatico* on the corner of Adriatico St and Remedios Circle, Malate, is a good place for a drink and/or meal. The menu features steaks, salads, seafood and fondue, topped off with various kinds of coffee and a good choice of cocktails. There are tables outside as well as upstairs overlooking the Remedios Circle street scene. It's open Monday to Friday from 10 am to 6 am and Sunday from 2.30 pm to 6 am. Meals cost about P250.

Mario's is a long-established place on the corner of Legaspi and Dela Rosa Sts, Makati. The steaks and salads are good, and it serves seafood, French and Spanish soups, and Californian wines.

Max's on Maria Orosa St, Ermita, is one of 10 branches of Max's in Manila. It serves chicken roasted in various ways, as well as Filipino dishes. It's open daily from 8 am to 11 pm, and meals cost about P150.

Vegetarian Vegetarian restaurants are pretty thin on the ground in Manila; however, there are a number of places which have vegetarian fare as well as fish and meat dishes. You have to watch out though, as some restaurants have a fairly loose definition of the word 'vegetarian'. This isn't the only place in the world where the word 'meat' is presumed to mean 'beef' – a 'meatless' dish may well include pork, chicken or some other flesh other than beef.

Bodhi in the Tutuban Mall, Claro M Recto Ave, Tondo, is a small restaurant with a wide selection of exclusively vegetarian food. The Tutuban Mall is the long building behind the somewhat larger Tutuban Center. It is open from 9 am to 8 pm daily. There's another *Bodhi* in the SM Megamall, Edsa, Mandaluyong.

The *Quan Yin Chay* on Soler St, Chinatown, is a small restaurant with good-value vegetarian dishes and fruit juices. It's open daily from 8 am to 9 pm. Meals cost about P75.

The *Kim Wan Garden* on General Miguel Malvar St, Malate, serves Chinese and vegetarian food with separate menus for both. The staff are friendly and give helpful advice on what to order. It's open daily all hours. Meals cost about P75.

Tia Maria's on Remedios St, Malate, features good Mexican food with vegetarian options. There's another *Tia Maria's* on Makati Ave, near Greenbelt Park, Makati. Opening times are Monday to Saturday from 11 am to midnight, and Sunday from 5 pm to midnight. Meals cost about P200.

Patio Guernica on JC Bocobo St, near Remedios Circle, Malate, is an excellent restaurant serving mainly Spanish food, as well as some vegetarian dishes. It's open Monday to Saturday from 11 am to 2 pm and 6 pm to midnight, and Sunday from 6 pm to midnight. A meal costs about P250.

The *Kashmir* on Padre Faura, Ermita, serves mainly north Indian and Pakistani dishes, many of which are vegetarian. It's open from 10 am to 11 pm daily. Meals cost about P200. There's another *Kashmir* restaurant on General Luna St, Makati.

The *Sala Thai* on JM Nakpil St, Malate, is a popular Thai restaurant which also serves

MANILA

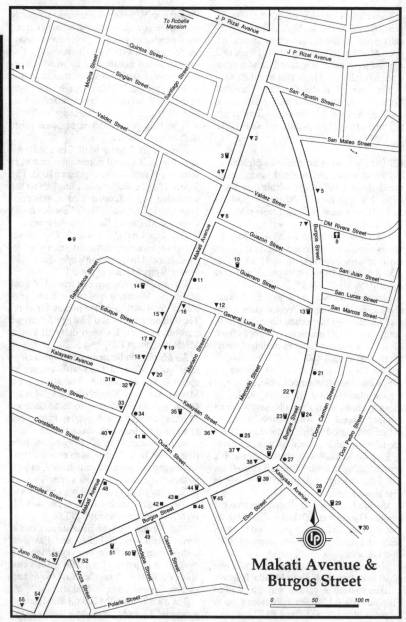

Makati Avenue &
Burgos Street

0   50   100 m

MANILA

vegetarian dishes. It's open daily from 10 am until 10 pm. Meals cost around P150.

If you prefer organic food, the inviting *Geosphere Café* is the place for you (for the uninitiated, organic foods are grown without synthetic fertilisers, pesticides or herbicides). In a relaxed atmosphere, you'll be served meals prepared with ingredients from the owners' garden. A meal costs about P100. Occasionally, it has traditional music concerts. The café is on Josefa L Escoda St, Paco, and is open from 10 am to 10 pm or later, depending on the atmosphere and the customers.

Fast Food There are lots of reasonably priced small Filipino food stalls on JC Bocobo St, between Padre Faura and Robinson's shopping centre. The average cost of a meal for one, with rice and one vegetable or meat serving, is around P50. It opens daily from 8 am to 10 pm.

Manila has many fast-food places, including *McDonald's*, *Wendy's*, *KFC*, *Pizza Hut* and *Shakey's Pizzas*. Shakey's is a Philippine institution – you'll find one on the corner of Mabini and Arquiza Sts, and another on Remedios St near Roxas Blvd. The Harrison Plaza shopping centre, beside the Century Park Sheraton Hotel, has a *Pizza Hut*, *McDonald's* and *KFC*. Jollibee is a local burger chain with numerous branches; there's one on Padre Faura, Ermita.

Mister Donut on Mabini St, Ermita, has excellent doughnuts and good coffee – not a bad breakfast alternative. It's open 24 hours a day. Meals cost about P25.

Buffets You can get breakfast buffets for about P200 to P250 daily from 6 to 10 am at *The Brasserie* in the Mandarin Oriental Hotel, Makati Ave, Makati; the *Café Ilang-Ilang* and *Lobby Lounge* in the Manila Hotel, Rizal Park, Ermita; and the *Centrepoint Hotel* on Mabini St, Ermita.

The *Concourse* in the Hotel Nikko Manila Garden, Fourth Quadrant, Makati Commercial Center, Makati, serves an international breakfast buffet daily from 6 to 10 am for P220, and a lunch buffet daily from 11.30 am to 2 pm for P350.

The *1930's Banquet Hall*, Admiral Hotel, Roxas Blvd, Malate, has a Filipino lunch buffet on Monday to Saturday from 11.30 am to 2 pm for about P280. The *Champagne Room* in the Manila Hotel, Rizal Park, Ermita, has a lunch buffet with international cuisine on Monday to Friday from noon to 3 pm for about P320, and on Sunday at the same times for about P380. For Italian food, the *Roma* in the same hotel has a lunch buffet on Monday to Friday from noon to 3 pm for P300.

Pier 7 in the Philippine Plaza Hotel, Cultural Center Complex, Malate, has a daily lunch buffet from 11.30 am to 2.30 pm serving steaks and seafood (a speciality) for P350.

The *Sabungan Coffee Shop* in the Manila Midtown Hotel on the corner of Adriatico St and Pedro Gil, Ermita, has breakfast buffets daily from 8 to 10 am for P250, and dinner buffets daily from 7 to 10 pm for P350. It serves Filipino and international cuisines.

Self Catering The *7-Eleven* on the corner of Padre Faura and Adriatico St, Ermita, is one of many branches found all over Manila which offer quick shopping 24 hours a day. There are three branches in Ermita alone.

La Tienda Supermarket on Burgos St, Makati, is the place for Spanish specialities like olives, sardines, brandy and wine.

The *Saentis Delicatessen* at 7431 Yakal St, Makati, offers a wide range of European delicacies, such as cheeses, cold meats, smoked goods, olives and much more.

At the *Sheraton Delicatessen Shop*, Vito Cruz, Malate, you can buy European specialities like bread and sausages among other things. The entrance is on the Harrison Plaza side of the hotel.

The *Treffpunkt Jedermann* at 140 Jupiter St, Makati, has all sorts of Austrian specialities from bakery items and meat to red and white wines.

Adriatico & Mabini Streets

PLACES TO STAY
1 Tadel Pension House
2 Yasmin Pension
7 Tropical Mansion Hotel
8 Royal Palm Hotel
11 Midtown Inn
13 Mabini Pension
14 Manila Tourist Inn
22 The Midland Plaza
25 Cherry Lodge Apartelle
26 Robinson's Apartelle
29 Centrepoint Hotel & Si-Kat Ferry Office
30 Si-Kat Inn & Si-Kat Pub & Restaurant
31 Casa Blanca I
33 La Soledad Pension House
34 Ermita Tourist Inn & Scenic View Travel
36 Santos Pension House
40 Manila Midtown Hotel
41 Las Palmas Hotel & Sensation Apartelle
42 Palm Plaza Hotel
44 Rothman Inn Hotel
45 Dakota Mansion
47 Manila Manor Hotel
49 Pearl Garden Apartel
52 Joward's Pension House & Joward's Hot Pot Restaurant
54 APP Mayfair Hotel
58 Shoshana Pension House
59 Juan's Place
60 Malate Pensionne & Chateau 1771 Restaurant
67 Victoria Mansion
69 Remedios Pension House & Café Nilad
78 Circle Pension & Penguin Café Gallery

79 Clé D'or Tourist Inn Hotel & Casa Pasta Ristorante
80 Royal Plaza Condominium

PLACES TO EAT
3 Shakey's Pizza
4 Holandia
5 The Islands Fisherman
6 Café Alps & Seafood Market
9 Jollibee, Kamayan Restaurant & Kashmir Restaurant
15 Mister Donut
16 München Grill Pub
19 Alda's Pizza Kitchen
20 Top Brass Restaurant & Zebrina Restaurant
21 Eva's Garden Restaurant
23 Food Stalls
24 Mrs Wong Tea House
28 Yamato Japanese Restaurant
39 Lotus Garden Restaurant
43 Zamboanga Restaurant
46 Kim Wan Garden Restaurant
48 Seoul Plaza Restaurant
50 Kopa Restaurant
51 Palais daan Restaurant
53 Steak Town Restaurant & The Chronicle Café
56 Sea Palace Restaurant
57 Dunkin Donuts & American Express
61 Korean Village Restaurant & Canadian Airlines, Saudi Arabian Airlines & TWA

62 Korean Palace Restaurant
63 Sea Palace Restaurant
65 Café Adriatico
66 Racks Bistro
68 Patio Guernica
70 Empress Garden Restaurant
71 Camp Gourmet Café & Restaurant
73 Korean Village Restaurant
74 Tia Maria's Mexican Restaurant
75 Patio Mequeni
76 Ang Bistro sa Remedios & Jazz Box & Larry's Café Bar
77 Café Adriatico 1900 s & Café Nikolai & In The Mood Dance Bar
81 Ducky's Restaurant
82 Cosa Nostra Café

OTHER
10 Solidaridad Book Shop
12 Philippine National Bank (PNB)
17 T'Boli Arts & Crafts
18 7-Eleven
27 Laundryette Britania
32 Robinson's Shopping Centre
35 Laundromat
37 Cathay Pacific
38 China Airlines, Interisland Travel & Tours & Midtown Arcade
55 Hobbit House & Remember When?
64 Ten Years After
72 Malate Church

Zuellig Wine & Spirits on Gil Puyat St, Makati, carries European wines and gallons of upmarket spirits.

Entertainment

There's plenty to do after hours in Manila. Although the hardline clean-up campaign of Mayor Lim has meant that most of the lights go out early in Ermita, elsewhere around town the nightlife scene is buzzing.

Cinemas Many cinemas are in the large shopping centres such as the Araneta Center, Harrison Plaza, Makati Commercial Center and Robinson's shopping centre, as well as on Rizal Ave and Claro M Recto Ave, in Santa Cruz. Films are advertised in the daily papers. Cameras aren't allowed in cinemas and have to be handed in for safekeeping. Less trusting types simply make sure their camera is not on view when entering the cinema.

Theatre Performances are irregular, so check the arts section of the daily papers or enquire at the tourist office (☎ 523 8411), or at the theatre itself. Manila's theatres include:

Cultural Center of the Philippines (CCP), Roxas Blvd, Malate (☎ 832 1125)
Folk Arts Theater, Cultural Center, Roxas Blvd, Malate (☎ 832 1120)
Meralco Theater, Meralco building, Ortigas Ave, Pasig (☎ 721 9777)
Metropolitan Theater, Lawisang Bonifacio, Lawton Plaza, Ermita (☎ 528 1490)
Rajah Sulayman Theater, an open-air theatre in Fort Santiago, Intramuros
William Shaw Theater, 5th level, Shangri-La Plaza Shopping Center, Edsa, Mandaluyong (☎ 633 4821). The performances are a pleasure to watch, covering musicals, comedies, classics and children's plays. The ticket office is open Monday to Friday from 10 am to 6 pm, Saturday until 1 pm.

Classical Music In idyllic Paco Park, San Marcelino St, Paco Park Presents puts on free chamber music at 6 pm on Friday.

The Puerta Real Evenings, which take place every Saturday night at 6 pm, offer free music in the greenery at the old fortress wall near the Puerta Real, Intramuros.

The free Concert at the Park takes place every Sunday at 5 pm in Rizal Park.

Jazz You can hear jazz nightly from 6 to 11 pm in the *Lobby Court* of the Philippine Plaza Hotel, Cultural Center Complex, Malate. There are also regular Sunday evening performances in the *Clipper Lounge* of the Mandarin Oriental Hotel, Makati Ave, Makati, and in the *Concourse Lounge* of the Hotel Nikko Manila Garden, Makati Commercial Center, Makati. Every Sunday from 10 am to 1 pm well-known musicians play at the Jazz Brunch in *The Lobby*, in the Peninsula Hotel Manila on the corner of Ayala and Makati Aves, Makati.

Folk Dance There's folk dancing on Sunday afternoon between 3 and 4 pm in the Mindanao section of *Nayong Pilipino* (Philippine Village) near the NAIA on Mia Rd, Pasay City. See the Nayong Pilipino entry earlier in this chapter.

The *Josephine* restaurant *on Roxas Blvd,*

Pasay City, features Philippine folk dances with dinner daily from 8 to 9 pm.

The *Zamboanga Restaurant* on Adriatico St, Malate, has Filipino and Polynesian dancing with dinner from 7 to 8.30 pm. It's open daily from 8 am to midnight, and costs about P200.

Folk Clubs The folk clubs here often have amazing 'sound-alikes' of Bob Dylan, Simon and Garfunkel and other big names in western music. Try the *Hobbit House* at 1801 Mabini St, Malate, which has a good international atmosphere and the dubious attraction of waiters who are all dwarfs. The minimum order after 8.30 pm is P60. Mexican dishes are a speciality. It's open nightly from 7 pm to 2 am. Admission is P50.

The popular *Galleon Club & Restaurant* on Kalayaan Ave, Makati, features what must be the best country & western music in Manila from Monday to Saturday. *My Father's Moustache* at 2144 MH del Pilar St, Malate, is a small rustic folk pub with a relaxed atmosphere. It has a special Mongolian barbecue, and is open nightly from 5 pm to 2 am.

Bistros & Music Lounges The classic watering holes are constantly being joined by new ones, others disappear after a short interval from the scene, leaving the stage for others to strut on. The ones given here are well established.

Bistro RJ in the Olympia building, Makati Ave, Makati, has live 50s and 60s music, including Beatles and Beach Boys' covers. It's open nightly from 6 pm to 3 am. Admission varies between P75 and P100, depending on the night. There's another *Bistro RJ* on Quezon Ave in Quezon City.

Café Adriatico on Adriatico St near Remedios Circle, Malate, started Manila's craze for bistros and is still a favourite. It's open Monday to Saturday from 10 am to 6 am and Sunday from 2 am to 6 am. Next door, the *Ten Years After* has half a plane sticking out of the building as if it had crashed; inside you can watch rock videos. It's open Monday to Saturday from 5 pm to

3 or 4 am. In the same area, *Moviola*, on Remedios Circle, Malate, is a piano bar and restaurant. It's open Monday to Saturday from 11 am to 4 am and Sunday from 6 pm to 4 am.

The *Penguin Café* on Remedios St near Remedios Circle, Malate, can be quite a lively place. It's open Tuesday to Sunday from noon to 2 pm and 6 pm to 2 am.

The *Remember When?* on Mabini St, Malate, is a pleasant, nostalgic bistro which plays popular oldies. It's next to Hobbit House, and is open daily from 4 pm to 3 am.

Pubs There used to be loads of pubs and bars in Ermita, but now there are only a few. Popular tourist and expat venues are *Grand Café Juri's* on MH del Pilar St, *Holandia* and *Hang's 'N'* on Arquiza St, the *Birdwatchers Bar* on A Flores St, and the *Si-Kat Inn* on Salas St.

Among the best-known pubs in Makati are the *Playhouse* on Burgos St, *San Mig Pub* on Legaspi St and the *Prince of Wales* in the Greenbelt Center.

You can also spend some pleasant afternoons and evenings in the restaurant bars with swimming pools. Among these open-air oases is the *Pool Bar*, tucked away on Guerrero St, and *Treasure Island*, a nice little place among the lagoon-like swimming pools of the Westin Philippine Plaza Hotel, where you can have a tropical cocktail while enjoying the magnificent sunset over Manila Bay.

Nightclubs Manila's nightlife is concentrated mainly in Makati, Pasay City and Quezon City. Makati and the Burgos area are especially lively. In Pasay City, a few nightclubs have opened in and around the Edsa International Entertainment Complex on Edsa.

The hottest address is *Zu*, in the Shangri-La Hotel Manila on the corner of Ayala and Makati Aves, Makati.

Other popular places include *Lost Horizon* in the Westin Philippine Plaza Hotel, Cultural Center Complex, Malate; *Equinox* on Pasay Rd, Makati; and *Euphoria* in the Hotel Inter-Continental, Ayala Ave, Makati. All the bigger hotels have their own bars and night-clubs, and the south end of Roxas Blvd is home to exclusive nightclubs featuring 1st class live music. The so-called disco-theatres are mainly in Quezon City – *Bigwig* on Quezon Ave, for example.

Casinos The Casino Filipina company runs gambling houses all over the country and simply rakes in the money. In Manila you can play at their *Hotel Sofitel Grand Boulevard Manila*, Roxas Blvd, Malati; the *Holiday Inn Manila Pavilion*, United Nations Ave, Ermita; and at *The Heritage Hotel* Edsa, Pasay City. Admission is P100, and visitors in casual clothes or beachwear will not be admitted.

Spectator Sport

Basketball Games of the professional basketball league, the Philippine Basketball Association (PBA), are played in Manila at the Cuneta Astrodome on Roxas Blvd, Pasay City, on Tuesday, Friday and Sunday at 5 and 7.30 pm. Admission is from P15 to P150. To find out which teams are playing call ☎ 833 7313 or ☎ 833 7323.

Jai-alai If not interrupted because of game-rigging and betting irregularities, super-speed jai-alai games take place seven days a week from 5 pm to 1 am at the Jai-alai de Manila stadium, next to Harrison Plaza on Adriatico St, Malate. Admission is P10.

Cockfights There are several cockpits in Manila: the Philippine Cockers Club in Santa Ana; Olympic Stadium at Grace Park, Caloocan City; Libertad on Dolores St, Pasay City; Elorde on Santos Ave, Parañaque; and La Loma on Calavite St, Quezon City. Fights are staged on Sunday and feast days. Admission is P20 to P200.

Horse Racing Races are held on weekend afternoons and Wednesday evening. Check the daily papers for more information, or contact the Philippine Racing Club or the Manila Jockey Club (☎ 711 1251). The race courses are at the Santa Ana race track, AP

Reyes Ave, Santa Ana, and in the San Lazaro Hippodrome, Felix Huertas St, Santa Cruz.

Things to Buy

Cigars At the La Flor de la Isabela cigar factory (☎ 524 8026), Tabacalera, on Romualdez St, Paco, single visitors or groups can be shown how the world-famous Coronas are made. You can also buy cigars and, if you like, have the boxes engraved with your initials. Staff prefer you to book.

Diving Equipment Two of the best diving equipment shops in Manila are Aquaventure Philippines, 2150 Pasong Tamo St, Makati (☎ 844 1996; fax 890 1967), and Scuba World, 1181 Vito Cruz Extension, Makati (☎ 895 3551; 890 8982). Both sell mainly US products, but also some Japanese-made equipment.

Handcrafts The Philippines is a great handcraft centre – check out the Ilalim ng Tulay Market next to Quinta Market on Carlo Palanca St, Quiapo, and the variety of handcraft places at Nayong Pilipino (Philippine Village). Good buys include canework, carvings, clothes, and hanging lamps made of shell.

The SM department store at the Makati Commercial Center and Landmark on Makati Ave are good for souvenirs if you can't get around the country. Prices are fixed and competitive.

In Intramuros, the El Amanecer building, 744 General Luna St, has Silahis for art and crafts, Chang Rong for antiques and Galeria de las Islas for paintings and sculpture. Further up General Luna, opposite San Agustin, is the Casa Manila in the San Luis Complex.

T'boli Arts & Crafts on Mabini St, Ermita, sells the handcrafts of the ethnic minorities on Mindanao. This small shop is up some steps, between Santa Monica and Padre Faura Sts.

Bargaining is not done as much in the Philippines as in other South-East Asian countries, but you should still haggle a little.

Stamps On the corner of Roquillo St and Rizal Ave, Santa Cruz, stampmakers will create personalised rubber stamps with the skill of surgeons for P30 in 15 minutes.

Shopping Centres The Araneta Center on the corner of Edsa and Aurora Blvd, Cubao, is a moderately priced shopping centre with nearly 2000 stores.

The Greenhills Shopping Center on Ortigas Ave, San Juan, has a large selection of restaurants ranging from the Aristocrat to Shakey's Pizza, a supermarket, several cinemas and banks, as well as spotless arcades with small, elegant boutiques.

The Harrison Plaza on Harrison St, Malate, has many different shops under one roof. It's air-conditioned, and has theatres and restaurants. Robinson's shopping centre, in Ermita, is similar but smaller, with three cinemas.

The Makati Commercial Center (MCC), Makati, is a modern shopping district between Ayala Ave, Makati Ave, Pasay Rd and Edsa. There is plenty to choose from, including imported goods, and some good bookshops. Restaurants and rest areas are interspersed among the shops, the best of which are probably SM Shoemart, Landmark and Rustan's. Other shopping centres in Makati are the Atrium of Makati (Atrium shopping mall) on Makati Ave, Makati Cinema Square between Pasong Tamo and Amorsolo Sts, and Greenbelt Square between Makati Ave and Paseo de Roxas.

Robinson's Galleria on the corner of Ortigas Ave and Edsa, Mandaluyong, features several fully air-conditioned floors of shops and a wide selection of restaurants.

SM City on the corner of Edsa and North Ave, Quezon City, is a big, air-conditioned shopping centre – a popular place to 'see and be seen'. Shoemart will change travellers cheques if you have your passport. Right next door is the SM City Annex. The SM group of companies also includes the SM Centrepoint on Aurora Blvd, Santa Mesa, and the more extensive SM Megamall, Edsa, Mandaluyong, which offers a wide variety of shops and facilities, including an ice-skating rink (rental skates are available).

Getting There & Away

Air Manila has two airports. For flights within the Philippines you use the domestic airport and for international flights the nearby Ninoy Aquino international airport (NAIA). Small airlines like Air Ads, Pacific Airways and Soriano Aviation have a small terminal building each, while Air Philippines, Cebu Pacific and PAL use the main building; PAL flights to Cebu, Davao and Puerto Princesa go from the Cebu Terminal (Terminal 2), which is slightly to the side. Passengers flying with Grand Air check in at the Philippine Village Airport Hotel. Make sure you tell your driver well in advance which terminal you want, as well as the name of the airline and the destination.

When you depart from NAIA, you'll have to pay a departure tax of P500 (see the Getting There & Away chapter earlier in this book).

The PAL offices are, with few exceptions, open Monday to Saturday from 8.30 am to 5 pm. It has a 24 hour telephone information and reservation service (☎ 816 6691). Destinations, flight times, and arrival and departure times of Air Ads, Air Philippines, Asian Spirit, Cebu Pacific, Grand Air, Pacific Airways and PAL are given in the previous Getting Around chapter.

Airline Offices Airline offices in Manila include:

Aeroflot Russian International Airlines
    United Life building, 835 Pasay Rd, Makati
    (☎ 893 7756)
Air Ads
    Andrews Ave, Pasay City (☎ 833 3264)
Air Canada
    Cityland Condominium II, on the corner of Esteban and Herrera Sts, Makati (☎ 810 4461)
Air France
    Century Tower building, 100 Tordesillas St, Makati (☎ 813 1160)
Air India
    Gammon Center building, Alfaro St, Makati (☎ 815 1280, 815 2441)
Air Mauritius
    Atrium of Makati, on the corner of Makati and Gil Puyat Aves, Makati (☎ 817 8680)
Air Nauru
    Pacific Star building, on the corner of Makati and Gil Puyat Aves, Makati (☎ 818 3580)

Air Nuigini
    Fortune building, Legaspi St, Legaspi Village, Makati (☎ 891 3339, 891 3342)
Air Philippines
    Ramon Magsaysay building, Roxas Blvd (☎ 526 4741)
    Sunlink Travel & Tours, 1666 Adriatico St, Malate (☎ 524 0812)
Alitalia
    Gallery building, Amorsolo St, Makati (☎ 892 5681)
American Airlines
    Olympia Condominium, on the corner of Makati Ave and Santo Tomas St, Makati (☎ 817 8645, 810 3228)
Asian Spirit
    LPL Tower, Legaspi St, Legaspi Village, Makati (☎ 840 3811)
Bouraq Airlines
    On the corner of Quirino Ave and Mia Rd, Parañaque (☎ 833 2902)
British Airways
    Filipino Merchants building, on the corner of Legaspi and Dela Rosa Sts, Legaspi Village, Makati (☎ 817 0361, 815 6556)
Canadian Airlines International
    Metro House, 345 Gil Puyat Ave, Makati (☎ 818 7866)
    Adriatico St, Malate (☎ 536 0105)
Cathay Pacific
    Gammon Center building, Alfaro St, Makati (☎ 815 9417)
    1555 Adriatico St, Ermita (☎ 525 9367)
China Airlines
    Midtown Arcade, Adriatico St, Ermita (☎ 590086, 523 8021)
Continental Air Micronesia
    SGV building, Ayala Ave, Makati (☎ 818 8701)
Egyptair
    Windsor Tower building, Legaspi St, Makati (☎ 815 8476)
Emirates Airlines
    Country Space I building, Gil Puyat Ave, Salcedo Village, Makati (☎ 816 0744)
Eva Air
    Don Tim building, South Superhighway, Makati (☎ 894 5671)
Finnair
    Pacific Bank building, Ayala Ave, Makati (☎ 818 2601, 818 2621)
Garuda Indonesian Airlines
    Pacific Star building, on the corner of Makati and Gil Puyat Aves, Makati (☎ 811 5612)
Grand Air
    APMC building, on the corner of Amorsolo and Gamboa Sts, Legaspi Village, Makati (☎ 893 9767)

Gulf Air
6750 Ayala Ave, Makati (☎ 817 9063)
Japan Airlines
Hotel Nikko Manila Garden, on the corner of Edsa and Pasay Rd, Makati
(☎ 812 1591, 810 9352)
KLM Royal Dutch Airlines
Athenaeum building, Alfaro St, Makati
(☎ 815 4790)
Korean Air
LPL Plaza, Alfaro St, Makati
(☎ 815 8911, 815 9261)
Kuwait Airways
Jaka II building, Legaspi St, Makati
(☎ 817 2778)
Lufthansa German Airlines
Legaspi Park View Condominium, Legaspi St, Makati (☎ 810 5018, 810 4596)
Malaysia Airlines
Legaspi Towers, on the corner of Vito Cruz and Roxas Blvd, Malate (☎ 575761, 525 9404)
Northwest Airlines
Athenaeum building, Alfaro St, Makati
(☎ 819 7341)
Gedisco building, Roxas Blvd, Ermita
(☎ 521 1911)
Pacific Airways
Domestic Airport Rd, Pasay City
(☎ 832 2731-32, 833 2390-91)
Pakistan International Airways (PIA)
Glass Tower building, Palanca St, Legaspi Village, Makati (☎ 818 0502, 894 1361)
PAL
PAL building, Legaspi St, Makati (☎ 817 1509, domestic 817 1479). Open Monday to Saturday from 8.30 am to 5 pm.
NAIA, Pasay City (☎ 831 0622). Open daily from 6 am to the time of the last PAL flight.
Domestic Airport, Pasay City (☎ 832 0991). Open daily from 4 am to 8 pm.
Botica Boie building, Escolta St, Binondo (☎ 241 5463). Open Monday to Saturday from 8.30 am to 5 pm.
S & L building, 1500 Roxas Blvd, Ermita (☎ 521 8821, 525 9217). Open Monday to Friday from 8.30 am to 5 pm, Saturday and holidays until noon.
PWU building, Taft Ave, Malate (☎ 598401, 524 6120). Open Monday to Saturday from 8.30 am to 5 pm.
Central Bank building, Mabini St, Malate (☎ 598422, 523 7046). Open Monday to Saturday from 8.30 am to 5 pm.
BPI Arcade, Aurora Blvd, Cubao, Quezon City (☎ 911 1327). Open Monday to Saturday from 8.30 am to 5 pm.
Quezon City Office, on the corner of Quezon Ave and Borromeo St (☎ 922 5334). Open Monday to Saturday from 8.30 am to 5 pm.

Qantas
China Bank building, Paseo de Roxas, Makati
(☎ 812 3734, 812 0607)
Royal Brunei Airlines
Saville building, on the corner of Gil Puyat Ave and Paseo de Roxas, Makati (☎ 897 3309)
Adriatico St, Malate (☎ 536 0105)
Royal Jordanian Airlines
Golden Rock building, Salcedo St, Legaspi Village, Makati (☎ 818 5901)
Sabena Belgian Airlines
Ralph Anthony suites, on the corner of Arkansas and Maria Orosa Sts, Ermita
(☎ 508636, 524 8636)
Saudi Arabian Airlines
Metro House, 345 Gil Puyat Ave, Makati
(☎ 818 7866)
Adriatico St, Malate (☎ 536 0105)
Scandinavian Airlines System
F&M Lopez building, Legaspi St, Makati
(☎ 810 5050)
Singapore Airlines
138 Dela Costa St, Makati (☎ 810 4951, 810 4960)
Swiss Air
Zuelig building, Gil Puyat Ave, Salcedo Village, Makati (☎ 818 8351)
Thai Airways International
Country Space I building, Gil Puyat Ave, Salcedo Village, Makati (☎ 815 8421)
United Airlines
Pacific Star building, on the corner of Makati and Gil Puyat Aves, Makati (☎ 818 7321)

Batanes PAL flies on Monday and Wednesday from Manila to Basco, and on Wednesday from Tuguegarao to Basco.

Bohol PAL flies daily from Manila to Tagbilaran.

Catanduanes PAL and Asian Spirit fly daily from Manila to Virac. On Monday, Wednesday and Friday PAL does Legaspi to Virac.

Cebu Cebu Pacific, Grand Air and PAL fly daily from Manila to Cebu City; PAL flies on Monday, Wednesday, Thursday and Sunday from Legaspi to Cebu City.

Leyte Cebu Pacific, Grand Air and PAL fly daily from Manila to Tacloban.

Lubang Air Ads flies on Tuesday, Thursday, Saturday and Sunday from Manila to Lubang.

Marinduque PAL flies daily from Manila to Boac.

Masbate PAL and Asian Spirit fly daily from Manila to Masbate. On Monday and Wednesday PAL does Legaspi to Masbate.

Mindanao Air Philippines flies daily from Manila to Cagayan de Oro, Cotabato, Davao and Zamboanga. Cebu Pacific and Grand Air fly daily from Manila to Cagayan de Oro and Davao.

From Manila, PAL flies daily to Cagayan de Oro, Cotabato, Davao and Zamboanga; on Monday, Wednesday, Friday and Sunday to Butuan; and on Monday, Thursday, Friday and Sunday to Dipolog.

Mindoro PAL has flights on Wednesday and Saturday from Manila to Mamburao, and on Monday, Wednesday, Thursday and Saturday from Manila to San Jose. Asian Spirit flies daily from Manila to San Jose. Pacific Airways plans to do flights on Monday, Wednesday and Friday from Manila to Sablayan.

Negros Cebu Pacific flies daily from Manila to Bacolod. PAL flies daily from Manila to Bacolod and Dumaguete.

Palawan Air Philippines and PAL fly daily from Manila to Puerto Princesa. Grand Air flies daily except Sunday.

Air Ads and Pacific Airways fly daily from Manila to Busuanga.

Soriano Aviation flies daily from Manila to El Nido.

Pacific Airways has flights from Manila to Cuyo on Monday, Wednesday and Friday.

Panay Asian Spirit and Pacific Airways fly daily from Manila to Caticlan; Air Ads flies on Monday, Friday and Saturday.

Air Philippines flies daily from Manila to Kalibo.

PAL flies daily from Manila to Iloilo City, Kalibo and Roxas. Grand Air flies daily except Sunday from Manila to Iloilo City.

Romblon PAL has flights on Tuesday, Thursday and Saturday from Manila to Tugdan on Tablas. Asian Spirit flies on Tuesday, Thursday and Sunday.

Samar PAL flies daily, except Wednesday and Saturday, from Manila to Calbayog, and daily, except Monday and Wednesday, from Manila to Catarman. Asian Spirit flies on Tuesday, Thursday, Friday and Saturday from Manila to Catarman.

Bus Bus companies use a combination of ordinary and air-con buses, but there aren't many of the latter. You can ring to get exact departure times, and possibly reserve a seat.

There is no central bus terminal in Manila. The terminals of the individual companies are scattered all over the city. Most of them are easy to reach by Metrorail.

Below is a list of addresses and major routes of bus companies (the number beside the bus company refers to its number in the Bus Destinations From Manila map key). Some of these bus routes are to islands beyond Luzon, and thus include ferry connections.

1 Baliwag Transit (☎ 364 0778), 199 Rizal Ave Extension, corner of 2nd Ave, Grace Park, Caloocan City. It has buses going north to Baliwag, Cabanatuan (Nueva Ecija Province) and San Jose del Monte (Bulacan Province). Get to its terminal by Monumento jeepney from Mabini St. The nearest Metrorail station is R Papa Station.

2 Baliwag Transit (☎ 912 3343), 33 Edsa, Cubao. It has buses going to Baliwag and San Jose del Monte (Bulacan Province), and further north to Aparri and Tuguegarao (Cagayan Province). Get to its terminal by Cubao jeepney from Taft Ave.

3 BLTB (☎ 833 5501), Edsa, Pasay City. It has buses going south to Batangas Province, Calamba (Laguna Province), Legaspi (Albay Province), Lucena (Quezon Province), Naga (Camarines Sur Province), Nasugbu (Batangas Province) and Sorsogon (Sorsogon Province). Get to its terminal by Baclaran jeepney or bus from Taft Ave or MH del Pilar St and change in Baclaran. The nearest Metrorail station is Edsa.

4 Cedec Transport, Cuneta Ave, Pasay City. It has buses going south to Naga (Camarine Sur Province), Legaspi (Albay Province), Catarman (Samar Island), Tacloban (Leyte Island) and Naval (Biliran Island). Get to its terminal by

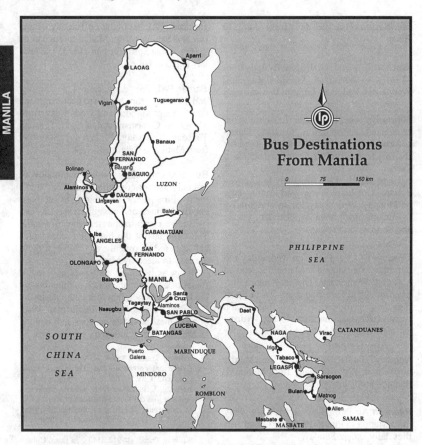

Bus Destinations
From Manila

0   75   150 km

Baclaran jeepney or bus from Taft Ave or MH del Pilar St. The nearest Metrorail station is Edsa.

5 Dagupan Bus (☎ 928 1694), New York St, Cubao, Quezon City. Buses go north to Dagupan, Alaminos and Lingayen (Pangasinan Province), and Baguio (Benguet Province). Get to its terminal by taking a Cubao jeepney from Taft Ave.

6 Dangwa Tranco (☎ 705718), 832 Aurora Blvd, on the corner of Driod St, Cubao. It has buses going north to Baguio (Benguet Province) and Banaue (Ifugao Province). Get to its terminal by taking a Cubao jeepney from Taft Ave.

7 Dangwa Tranco (☎ 731 2859), 1600 Dimasalang St, Sampaloc. It has buses going north to Baguio (Benguet Province). Get to its terminal by Blumentritt jeepney from Taft Ave. The nearest Metrorail station is Tayuman station.

8 Farinas Trans (☎ 731 4507, 731 4375), on the corner of M dela Fuente St and Laong Laan, Sampaloc. It has buses going north to Vigan (Ilocos Sur Province) and Laoag (Ilocos Norte Province). Get to its terminal by Blumentritt jeepney from Taft Ave. The nearest Metrorail station is Tayuman station.

9 Five Star (☎ 833 3009), Aurora Blvd (Tramo), Pasay City. It has buses going north to Dagupan and Bolinao (Pangasinan Province), and Cabanatuan (Nueva Ecija Province). Get to its terminal by Baclaran jeepney or bus from Taft Ave or MH del Pilar St. The nearest Metrorail station is Edsa station.

10 Inland Trailways (☎ 833 6280), Edsa, Pasay City. Buses go south to Legaspi (Albay Province), Lucena (Quezon Province), Naga (Camarine Sur

Destination (Town)	Km	Duration of Journey (Hours)	Bus Company Number
Alaminos (Laguna)	78	1.30	3,17,18
Alaminos (Pangasinan)	254	6.00	5,9,15,16,22
Angeles/Dau	83	1.30	5,9,14,15,16,19,20,21,22,23
Aparri	596	13.00	2,22
Baguio	246	6.00	5,6,7,14,16,21,22,23
Balanga	123	2.30	16
Banaue	348	10.00	6
Bangued	400	8.00	14,15,19,20
Batangas	111	2.30	3,11
Bauang	259	6.30	8,13,14,15,16,19,20
Bolinao	283	6.00	9,21
Bulan	653	16.00	3,12
Cabanatuan	115	2.30	1,2,9
Daet	350	7.00	3,4,10,12,17,18
Dagupan	216	5.00	5,9,21,23
Iba	210	5.30	21
Iriga	487	10.00	3,4,10,12,17
Laoag	487	10.00	8,13,14,15,16,19,20
Lingayen	227	4.30	5,9,22
Legaspi	550	12.00	3,4,10,12,17
Lucena	136	2.30	3,4,10,12,17,18
Matnog	670	17.00	3,4,10,12,17
Naga	449	8.30	3,4,10,12,17
Nasugbu	102	2.00	3
Olongapo	126	3.00	21,22,23
San Fernando (La Union)	269	7.00	8,13,14,15,16,19,20
San Fernando (Pampanga)	66	1.00	16,21,22,23
San Pablo	87	2.00	3,17,18
Santa Cruz/Pagsanjan	101	2.00	3,11
Sorsogon	604	14.00	3,4,10,17
Tabaco	580	12.00	17
Tagaytay	56	1.30	3
Tuguegarao	483	9.00	2,22
Vigan	407	8.00	8,13,14,15,16,19,20

Province) and Sorsogon (Sorsogon Province). Get to its terminal by Baclaran jeepney or bus from Taft Ave or MH del Pilar St and change in or before Baclaran. The nearest Metrorail station is Edsa station.

11 JAM Transit, Taft Ave, Pasay City. It has buses going south to Batangas and Laguna provinces. Get to its terminal by Baclaran jeepney or bus from Taft Ave. The nearest Metrorail station is Gil Puyat.

12 JB Bicol Express Line (☎ 833 2949), Aurora Blvd (Tramo), Pasay City. It has buses going south to Legaspi (Albay Province), Lucena (Quezon Province) and Naga (Camarine Sur Province). Get to its terminal by Baclaran jeepney or bus from Taft Ave or MH del Pilar St and change in or before Baclaran. The nearest Metrorail station is Edsa station.

13 Maria de Leon (☎ 731 4907), on the corner of Gelinos and Dapitan Sts, Sampaloc. It has buses going north to San Fernando (La Union Province), Vigan (Ilocos Sur Province) and Laoag (Ilocos Norte Province). Get to its terminal by Blumentritt jeepney from Taft Ave. The nearest Metrorail station is Bambang station.

14 Partas (☎ 709820), Aurora Blvd, Cubao. It has buses going north to Baguio (Benguet Province), Bangued (Abra Province), Laoag (Ilocos Norte Province), San Fernando (La Union Province) and Vigan (Ilocos Sur Province). Get to its terminal by Cubao jeepney from Taft Ave.

15 Philippine Rabbit (☎ 361 4821), Edsa, Quezon City. It has buses going north to Bangued (Abra Province), Laoag (Ilocos Norte Province), San Fernando (La Union Province), Tarlac (Tarlac Province) and Vigan (Ilocos Sur Province). Get to its terminal by Monumento jeepney from Mabini St; then catch another jeepney or bus heading for Cubao. The nearest Metrorail station is North terminal (Monumento).

16 Philippine Rabbit (☎ 711 5819), 819 Oroquieta St, Santa Cruz, with another entrance on Rizal Ave. It has buses going north to Angeles (Pampanga Province), Baguio (Benguet Province), Laoag (Ilocos Norte Province), Balanga

and Mariveles (Bataan Province), San Fernando (La Union Province), Tarlac (Tarlac Province) and Vigan (Ilocos Sur Province). Get to its terminal by Monumento jeepney from Mabini St. The nearest Metrorail station is D Jose station.

17 Philtranco (☎ 833 5061), Edsa, Pasay City. It has buses going south to Calbayog and Catbalogan (Samar Island), Daet (Camarines Norte Province), Davao (Mindanao Island), Legaspi (Albay Province), Lucena (Quezon Province), Naga (Camarines Sur Province), Tacloban (Leyte Island), Sorsogon (Sorsogon Province) and Surigao (Surigao del Norte Province). Get to its terminal by Baclaran jeepney or bus from Taft Ave or MH del Pilar St and change in or before Baclaran. The nearest Metrorail station is Edsa station.

18 Superlines (☎ 912 3447), 670 Edsa, Quezon City. It has buses going south to Daet (Camarines Norte Province) and Lucena (Quezon Province). Get to its terminal by Cubao jeepney from Taft Ave.

19 Times Transit (☎ 741 4146), 79 Halcon St, Quezon City. It has buses going north to Bangued (Abra Province), Laoag (Ilocos Norte Province), San Fernando (La Union Province) and Vigan (Ilocos Sur Province). Get to its terminal by Blumentritt jeepney from Taft Ave. The nearest Metrorail station is Tayuman station.

20 Times Transit (☎ 924 0828), Edsa, Cubao. It has buses going north to Bangued (Abra Province), Laoag (Ilocos Norte Province), San Fernando (La Union Province) and Vigan (Ilocos Sur Province). Get to its terminal by Cubao jeepney from Taft Ave.

21 Victory Liner (☎ 361 1506, 361 1514), 713 Rizal Ave Extension, Caloocan City. It has buses going north to Baguio (Benguet Province), Dagupan (Pangasinan Province), Iba and Olongapo (Zambales Province). Get to its terminal by Monumento jeepney from Mabini St. The nearest Metrorail station is North terminal (Monumento).

22 Victory Liner (☎ 977460, 928 9290), Edsa, Cubao. It has buses going north to Alaminos, Bolinao and Dagupan (Pangasinan Province), Baguio (Benguet Province), Olongapo (Zambales Province), and Tuguegarao and Aparri (Cagayan Province). Get to its terminal by Cubao jeepney from Taft Ave.

23 Victory Liner (☎ 833 5019), Edsa, Pasay City. It has buses going north to Baguio (Benguet Province), Dagupan (Pangasinan Province) and Olongapo (Zambales Province). Get to its terminal by Baclaran jeepney or bus from Taft Ave or MH del Pilar St and change in or before Baclaran. The nearest Metrorail station is Edsa station.

Leyte Air-con Philtranco buses leave Manila daily at 10 am and 2 pm for Tacloban. Trav-

elling time, including the ferry trip from Matnog to San Isidro, is 28 hours.

Mindanao Air-con Philtranco buses leave daily from Manila to Davao at 2 pm. Travel time, including the ferry from Matnog to San Isidro and Liloan to Surigao, is 45 hours.

Mindoro A daily through trip from Manila to Puerto Galera starts at the Centrepoint Hotel in Mabini St, Ermita, at 9 am. The air-con bus goes to Batangas and the MB *Si-Kat II* leaves at noon and arrives in Puerto Galera at around 2.30 pm. Bookings and tickets (P300) are arranged at the Centrepoint Hotel. Buses from Manila to Batangas leave the BLTB bus terminal regularly (see the Batangas section of the Around Manila chapter).

Samar Air-con Philtranco buses leave Manila daily at 10 am and 2 pm for Calbayog and Catbalogan, taking 25 and 26 hours respectively, including the ferry from Matnog to San Isidro.

Air-con Philtranco buses and Inland Trailways buses (the better of the two, because they have less stops) go from Manila to Catarman. This trip takes about 24 hours.

Train See Getting Around later in this chapter.

Boat Nearly all inter-island boats leave Manila from North Harbor. If you have trouble finding it, ask a coastguard opposite Pier 8.

Next to the North Harbor piers are the docking facilities of the Del Pan Bridge (coming from the sea it's the first bridge over the Pasig River). Various small vessels to neighbouring islands depart from here, but there is no schedule.

A taxi from Ermita to North Harbor costs about P40. It's difficult to get a taxi with a properly adjusted meter when travelling from North Harbor to Ermita, or other suburbs. The 'fixed price' is between P70 and P100. There's a roundabout way of getting to North Harbor by jeepney, but it involves heavy traffic and can take up to an hour: from Mabini St or Taft Ave get a jeepney to Divisoria; from there you change for a jeepney to North Harbor.

Shipping companies generally advertise departures in the Manila English-language dailies. There are plenty of departures from Manila. Although William, Gothong and Aboitiz Lines have formed the new company WG & A, their ships still leave from their respective piers. All the shipping companies sell their own tickets in their harbour offices. WG & A also has an office on the corner of MH del Pilar and San Andres Sts in Malate

Scenic View Travel (☎ 522 3495, 521 8770; fax 521 8773), near the Ermita Tourist Inn on the corner of Mabini and Soldado Sts, Ermita, also sells WG & A tickets.

Asuncion Shipping Lines (☎ 204024)
    Pier 2, North Harbor
    Destinations: Lubang/Mindoro; Palawan (Coron, Culion)
MBRS Lines (☎ 921 6716)
    Pier 8, North Harbor
    Destinations: Panay; Romblon
Negros Navigation (☎ 251 1103)
    Pier 2, North Harbor
    Destinations: Negros; Panay
Sulpicio Lines (☎ 252 6281)
    Pier 12, North Harbor
    Destinations: Cebu; Bohol; Leyte; Masbate; Mindanao; Negros; Palawan; and Panay
WG & A
    Aboitiz Lines (☎ 202726, 894 3211),
    Pier 4, North Harbor
    Gothong Lines (☎ 214121),
    Pier 10, North Harbor
    William Lines (☎ 219821),
    Pier 14, North Harbor
    Destinations: Cebu; Leyte; Mindanao; Negros; Palawan; Panay; Romblon; and Samar

Bohol From Manila to Tagbilaran, WG & A's MV *Superferry 5* leaves on Tuesday at 7 am, while its MV *Superferry 7* leaves on Saturday at 7 am (P550; 36 hours).

The Sulpicio Lines' MV *Dipolog Princess* leaves Manila for Tagbilaran on Wednesday at noon (28 hours).

Catanduanes The Regina Shipping Lines' MV *Regina Calixta* leaves Tabaco daily for San Andres at 8 am (2½ hours).

The Bicolano Lines' MV *Eugenia* leaves

Tabaco daily for Virac at 8 am (four hours). An additional small boat leaves daily at 9 am.

Cebu Several vessels run between Manila and Cebu City (P520; 20 to 22 hours). WG & A's MV *Superferry 8* leaves on Monday at 9 am, Wednesday at 3 pm and Friday at 7 pm. Its MV *Superferry 6* leaves on Saturday at 3 pm, and the MV *Superferry 10* leaves on Sunday at 9 am, Tuesday at 3 pm and Thursday at 7 pm.

The Sulpicio Lines' MV *Princess of the Orient* leaves on Tuesday at 10 am and Friday at 8 pm. Its MV *Princess of Paradise* leaves on Wednesday at 10 am, and the MV *Filipina Princess* leaves on Sunday at 10 am.

Leyte From Manila to Calubian, the Sulpicio Lines' MV *Palawan Princess* leaves on Wednesday at 10 pm (32 hours, via Masbate). It goes on to Baybay and Maasin.

From Manila to Palompon, WG & A's MV *Sacred Heart* leaves on Monday at 9 pm (33 hours, via Masbate). It goes on to Ormoc.

From Manila to Ormoc, the Sulpicio Lines' MV *Cebu Princess* leaves on Friday at 10 am (50 hours, via Masbate).

From Manila to Tacloban, WG & A's MV *Masbate Uno* leaves Manila on Monday at 10 am (29 hours, via Catbalogan on Samar) and on Friday at 7 am (P470; 25 hours direct). The Sulpicio Lines' MV *Tacloban Princess* leaves Manila for Tacloban on Wednesday at 10 am and Sunday at 9 am (24 hours).

Lubang From Manila to Tilik, the Asuncion Shipping Lines' MV *Catalyn B* leaves on Monday, Thursday and Saturday at 9 pm (eight hours). From Nasugbu to Tilik, a big outrigger boat of Montenegro Shipping Lines leaves on Monday, Wednesday and Friday, taking 2½ hours.

Marinduque From Lucena (Dalahican Pier) to Balanacan, the Viva Shipping Lines' MV *San Agustin Reyes* leaves daily at 8 am and 2 pm (2½ hours).

Two ferries leave Lucena (Cotto Pier) daily between 8 and 10 am for Buyabod, the port for Santa Cruz (4½ hours).

MANILA

Masbate From Manila to Masbate, WG & A's MV *Sacred Heart* leaves on Monday at 9 pm (P280; 18 hours). The Sulpicio Lines' MV *Palawan Princess* leaves Manila for Masbate on Wednesday at 10 pm (19 hours), while its MV *Cebu Princess* leaves on Friday at 10 am (24 hours).

From Lucena (Dalahican Pier) to Masbate, the Viva Shipping Lines' MV *Viva Peñafrancia V* leaves on Monday, Thursday and Saturday at 7 pm (12 hours). Its MV *Santa Maria* leaves on Tuesday, Friday and Sunday at 7 pm (12 hours).

From Bulan the MV *Matea I* leaves daily at noon (3½ hours). There may be a second boat.

Mindanao From Manila to Butuan, WG & A's MV *Superferry 2* leaves on Monday at 4 pm (P720; 40 hours, via Iloilo City on Panay). Its MV *Medjugorje* leaves on Thursday at 10 pm for Butuan direct (32 hours).

From Manila to Cagayan de Oro there are several ships each week. WG & A's MV *Superferry 5* leaves on Tuesday at 7 am (P620; 35 hours, via Tagbilaran on Bohol). Its MV *Superferry 9* leaves on Wednesday at 8 pm (38 hours, via Iloilo City on Panay) and Sunday at 11 am (32 hours direct), the MV *Superferry 2* leaves on Friday at noon (31 hours) and the MV *Superferry 7* leaves on Saturday at 7 am (35 hours, via Tagbilaran on Bohol). Negros Navigation's MV *Santa Ana* leaves on Friday at 2 pm (45 hours, via Iloilo City on Panay). The Sulpicio Lines' MV *Princess of Paradise* leaves on Saturday at 8 pm (25 hours).

From Manila to Cotabato, WG & A's MV *Superferry 3* leaves on Friday at 8 pm (P815; 44 hours, via Zamboanga). Its MV *Maynilad* leaves on Sunday at 7 pm (65 hours, via Dumaguete on Negros and Dipolog).

From Manila to Davao, WG & A's MV *Superferry 6* leaves on Tuesday at 8 am (P990; 46 hours, via Surigao). Its MV *Superferry 1* leaves on Saturday at 3 pm (52 hours, via Iloilo City on Panay). The Sulpicio Lines' MV *Filipina Princess* leaves on Sunday at 10 am (52 hours, via Cebu City and Surigao).

From Manila to Dipolog, WG & A's MV *Maynilad* leaves on Sunday at 7 pm (P545; 38 hours, via Dumaguete on Negros). It goes on to Cotabato.

From Manila to General Santos, WG & A's MV *Doña Virginia* leaves on Tuesday at noon (P910; 43 hours, via Zamboanga). Its MV *Superferry 1* leaves on Saturday at 3 pm (43 hours, via Iloilo City on Panay). It goes on to Davao.

From Manila to Iligan, WG & A's MV *Superferry 7* leaves on Tuesday at 5 am (P620; 34 hours, via Dumaguete on Negros). Its MV *Superferry 5* leaves on Friday at 3 pm (36 hours, via Iloilo City on Panay).

From Manila to Ozamis, WG & A's MV *Medjugorje* leaves on Monday at 9 am (P615; 32 hours).

From Manila to Surigao, WG & A's MV *Superferry 6* leaves on Tuesday at 8 am (P635; 26 hours). It goes on to Davao. The Sulpicio Lines' MV *Palawan Princess* leaves on Wednesday at 10 pm (53 hours, via Masbate and Calubian, Baybay and Maasin on Leyte). Its MV *Filipina Princess* leaves on Sunday at 10 am (45 hours, via Cebu City). It goes on to Davao.

From Manila to Zamboanga, WG & A's MV *Doña Virginia* leaves on Tuesday at noon (P645; 28 hours). It goes on to General Santos. Its MV *Superferry 3* leaves on Friday at 8 pm (32 hours). It goes on to Cotabato. The Sulpicio Lines' MV *Cotabato Princess* leaves on Saturday at 3 pm (45 hours, via Estancia and Iloilo City on Panay). It goes on to Cotabato.

Mindoro From Batangas to Puerto Galera, the Santo Domingo Shipping Lines' MV *Santa Peñafrancia VI* (car ferry) leaves daily at 8.30 am, 12.30 and 5 pm (P45; 1½ hours). Arrival is at Balatero, 2.5 km west of Puerto Galera. Si-Kat Ferry Inc's MV *Si-Kat II* leaves at noon (P150; 2 hours). The ferry can be booked in Manila at the Centrepoint Hotel, Mabini St, Ermita, in combination with an air-con bus ticket.

A big outrigger leaves daily at 9.30 and 10.30 am, noon and 1.30 pm (P60; 1½ hours) for Sabang. The 1.30 pm boat, the *Sabang Princess*, is the biggest and most comfortable. A Special Ride with an outrigger should not cost more than P800.

From Batangas to Calapan, Universal Aboitiz's fast MV *Supercat* leaves daily at 7.30 and 11.00 am and 2.30 and 7.30 pm (P150; 45 minutes). The fast ferries MV *Lourdes* and MV *Fatima* make the crossing eight times a day from 5.15 am until about 5.30 pm. Between 4.30 am and 5.30 pm there are about 12 regular ferries (two hours). You can catch a jeepney from Calapan to Puerto Galera, but only until about 4 pm (P30; two hours).

From Batangas to Abra de Ilog, a car ferry of Montenegro Shipping Lines or Viva Shipping Lines leaves daily at 3, 9 and 11 am and 3 pm (P60; 2½ hours). After the boat has docked, a bus leaves about 200m from the wharf in Wawa, heading for San Jose via Maburao and Sablayan. A big outrigger also leaves at 8 am.

From Batangas to Sablayan, the Viva Shipping Lines' MV *Peñafrancia* or MV *St Christopher* sails on Tuesday, Friday and Sunday (P150; nine hours).

From Batangas to San Jose, the Viva Shipping Lines' MV *Marian Queen* leaves on Monday, Wednesday and Saturday at 7 am (12 hours). Its MV *Santo Niño* sails on Tuesday, Friday and Sunday at 7 am (11 hours).

Negros From Manila to Bacolod, Negros Navigation's MV *Princess of Negros* leaves on Tuesday at 9 am and Friday at noon (P480; 22 hours). Its MV *San Paolo* leaves on Sunday at 2 pm and Wednesday at 4 pm (20 hours).

From Manila to Dumaguete, WG & A's MV *Superferry 7* leaves on Tuesday at 5 pm (P545; 26 hours). Its MV *Maynilad* leaves on Sunday at 7 pm (32 hours). The Sulpicio Lines' MV *Philippine Princess* leaves on Wednesday at noon (25 hours).

Palawan WG & A's MV *Superferry 3* leaves Manila for Puerto Princesa on Wednesday at 10 am (P455; 23 hours). The Sulpicio Lines' MV *Iloilo Princess* leaves on Thursday at 10 am and Sunday at 2 pm (24 hours).

From Manila to Coron, the Asuncion

Shipping Lines' MV *Catalyn A* leaves on Wednesday at 4 pm (22 hours). Its MV *Asuncion VII* leaves on Thursday at 4 pm, and the MV *Asuncion XI* leaves on Saturday at 4 pm.

The Asuncion Shipping Lines' MV *Asuncion IV* leaves Manila for El Nido on Wednesday at 7 pm (28 hours).

Note: the Asuncion Shipping Lines' boats are not in the best condition. If you want to travel by boat to Coron, it would be better to take a bus from Manila to Batangas and carry on with a Viva Shipping Lines boat (18 hours) from there.

From Batangas to Coron, the Viva Shipping Lines' MV *Viva Santa Ana* leaves on Monday at 6 pm. Its MV *Viva Peñafrancia IX* leaves on Thursday at 6 pm, and the MV *Maria Socorro* leaves on Saturday at 6 pm. All three of them carry on from Coron to Culion.

Panay From Manila to Caticlan (near Boracay), the MBRS Lines' MV *Romblon Bay* leaves on Tuesday at 1 pm and Friday at 2 pm (22 hours).

WG & A's *Superferry 1* will make the trip once a week (11 hours) in March and April, subject to demand. Telephone ☎ 216951 for information.

From Manila to Dumaguit (near Kalibo), Negros Navigation's MV *Don Julio* leaves on Wednesday at 3 pm (P400; 16 hours). WG & A's MV *Our Lady of Naju* leaves Monday, Wednesday and Sunday at 2 pm (15 hours). On Monday the ship may go to Batan (near Dumaguit).

From Manila to Estancia, the Sulpicio Lines' MV *Cotabato Princess* leaves on Saturday at 3 pm (17 hours). It goes on to Iloilo City.

There are several ships from Manila to Iloilo City (P510; 18 to 25 hours). Negros Navigation's MV *Saint Francis of Assisi* leaves on Monday, Thursday and Saturday at noon (18 hours). Its MV *Santa Ana* leaves on Tuesday and Friday at 2 pm (20 hours). WG & A's MV *Superferry 2* leaves on Monday at 4 pm (22 hours). Its MV *Superferry 9* leaves on Wednesday at 8 pm (22 hours), the MV *Superferry 1* leaves on Thursday at 5 pm and Saturday at 3 pm (18 hours), and the MV

Superferry 5 leaves on Friday at 3 pm (21 hours). The Sulpicio Lines' MV *Princess of the Pacific* leaves on Tuesday at 10 am (19 hours). Its MV *Cotabato Princess* leaves on Saturday at 3 pm (25 hours, via Estancia).

From Manila to Roxas, Negros Navigation's MV *Don Claudio* leaves on Monday at 1 pm and Thursday at 5 pm (P400; 16 hours). Its MV *Don Julio* leaves on Saturday at 5 pm (16 hours).

Romblon From Manila to Romblon on Romblon Island, MBRS Lines' MV *Salve Juliana* leaves on Tuesday at 1 pm and Friday at 3 pm (15 hours).

From Batangas to San Agustin on Tablas Island, the Viva Shipping Lines' MV *Viva Peñafrancia VIII* leaves on Monday, Thursday and Saturday at 7 pm (10 hours). It goes on to Romblon on Romblon Island and Magdiwang on Sibuyan Island.

From Batangas to Odiongan on Tablas Island, the Viva Shipping Lines' MV *Viva Peñafrancia IV* leaves on Tuesday, Thursday and Saturday at 6 pm (seven hours). Its MV *St Kristopher* leaves on Wednesday, Friday and Sunday at 6 pm (eight hours). The RN Hi Speed Ferries' MV *Florida I* leaves on Monday and Saturday at 4pm (4½ hours).

There are also several boats weekly from Lucena which go to Romblon on Romblon Island or to Magdiwang on Sibuyan Island.

Samar From Manila to Catbalogan, WG & A's MV *Masbate Uno* leaves on Monday at 10 am (P435; 23 hours).

The ferries MV *Michelangelo* and MV *Northern Samar* sail daily at 10 am and 4 pm from Matnog to Allen. The crossing takes 1½ hours. The ferry MV *Marhalika I* of St Bernard Services leaves Matnog for San Isidro daily at 6 am and 12.30 pm (two hours). The Matnog terminal fee is P12 per passenger.

Getting Around
International Airport You'll find free telephones near the luggage collection point, which you can use to make local (Manila) calls. These allow you to book a hotel room while you wait for your luggage. It costs P30 or US$1 to use a luggage trolley; the charge includes the service of a porter but, unlike the trolleys, porters can be hard to locate.

After going through the arrival procedure you have a chance to change money. Unlike the banks in town, the Philippine Commercial International Bank (PCI) and the Philippine National Bank (PNB) offer roughly the same rate, not quite as good as the one offered by moneychangers. Don't forget that you will also need some smaller notes as well as big ones; taxi drivers hardly ever have change. If you want to avoid the lines at the foreign exchange counter you could always get money with your Visa card from the ATM to the right of the right-hand exit.

Just behind the baggage check you'll find a DOT counter. Its nice staff will be glad to make enquiries at hotels for you.

If you want to confirm a connecting flight, the counters of the major airlines are two floors up; take the staircase in front of the arrival hall exit.

International Airport to the Domestic Airport Travellers landing in Manila and flying to another destination within the Philippines have to transfer to the nearby domestic airport. PAL passengers ride the bus provided for free. Others have to pay P250, or US$10 – and the bus only departs when it has at least one PAL passenger on board. The shuttle bus counter is at the arrival platform exit.

It's possible the bus will be delayed, so if you're in a hurry it would be better to take a taxi. A taxi ride to the domestic airport generally costs no more than P30, but you can be charged up to P150.

International Airport to the City Unfortunately, Filipinos don't seem to have heard of the saying 'You never get a second chance to make a first impression' in Manila. Since 1975 I've been arriving at the international airport at least twice a year, and nearly every time my arrival has been marred by some inconvenience. Comparing Manila with other Asian cities, like Bangkok or Hong

Kong, you can't help wondering why this place seems unable to provide a smooth arrival for visitors. And why on earth can't airport staff manage to arrange efficient transport to a hotel for visitors who are tired and worn out after many hours in a plane? For years, the airport managers have been experimenting with various ideas, none of which ever seem to benefit incoming travellers.

Bus Turn right when you leave the NAIA exit, go down the ramp about 200m and wait on the road for the appropriate bus to come along, for example, 'Cubao', 'Quezon City' and 'Monumento' for destinations along Edsa, as well as various bus terminals and areas such as Makati and Mandaluyong (P1.50 to P10, depending on distance). These buses (some of which are air-con) normally pass the domestic airport first.

Taxi At present, only air-con 'coupon' taxis with set fares are allowed to service the airport (eg, P250 to Pasay, P300 to Ermita, Malate and Makati, and P400 to Quezon City). If you don't want to put up with the hassle, then take the stairs up to the departure level. You'll find the nearest staircase before you come to the main exit from the arrival level, and there's another one outside about 50m to the left of the main exit. You can wait for a taxi to unload passengers at the departure level. Mind you, lots of sneaky taxi drivers have hit on this trick and now wait for victims at the departure level with special 'deals'. Normally, a taxi ride from NAIA to Ermita/Malate would cost around P70, but there's scarcely a driver who will do it for less than P100.

The meter should be switched on just before the taxi starts off. If the driver tells you the meter is out of order, you're quite entitled to get out; however, ordering the driver to stop and let you out after you've gone 500m can be awkward, especially at night. If you agree on a fixed price with the taxi driver, don't forget to specify the currency. It wouldn't be the first time a fare of '100' turns out to be US$100 instead of P100!

Some drivers nimbly put the meter forward P20 or so at the end of the journey. Others will proudly hand you 'official' fare lists, often impressively set in a leather binder with gold lettering. These have no legal validity whatsoever.

Keep your cool if you encounter problems with a driver on the way to the hotel. You're in a much better position once your luggage is out of the taxi and you can call on the hotel staff for support. For standard taxi fares, see the general Taxi section later in this chapter.

Metrorail A taxi from NAIA to the Metrorail South Terminal in Baclaran is unlikely to cost you more than P30 (providing a taxi will take you this short distance). From here, it's P10 to Pedro Gil station or United Nations Ave station in Ermita.

Jeepney This is the cheapest way to get from NAIA to Mabini St in Ermita. Turn right at the NAIA exit, go down the ramp about 200m and from there catch a jeepney with the sign 'Baclaran' until you reach Baclaran itself (P1.50). Change there into a jeepney with the sign 'Harrison-Mabini', which will take you to Mabini St (P1.50).

Coming back, catch a 'Baclaran' jeepney on MH del Pilar St, Ermita, get out in Baclaran and change into a jeepney with the sign 'Sucat-Highway' for the NAIA.

Domestic Airport The domestic airport is about two km away from NAIA. See also Getting There & Away earlier in this chapter.

Domestic Airport to the City Almost all of the taxi drivers waiting at the domestic airport refuse to switch their meters on and stubbornly demand a ridiculously inflated price for the journey. Rather than give in to these latter-day highwaymen, go through the carpark to Domestic Terminal Drive and flag down a passing taxi there. A normal fare to Ermita is around P60.

Bus Around Manila, city buses display their final destination on the front. A destination can be a large complex like NAIA, a street name like Ayala (for Ayala Ave in Makati) or a whole suburb like Quiapo (north of Pasig River). The fare is P1.50 for the first four km and 25 centavos for every km after that. At the end of Rizal Ave Extension there is a statue of Andres Bonifacio, known as the 'Monumento', a popular destination and stop for jeepneys and buses.

Train The Metrorail Light Rail Transit (LRT) is an overhead railway which runs on concrete pylons several metres high, linking the suburbs of Caloocan City and Pasay City. The line runs from North Terminal (Monumento) in Caloocan City, via Rizal Ave to Central Terminal near the Manila City Hall and via Taft Ave to South Terminal in Baclaran, Pasay City. A second Metrorail is being built at the moment. It will run from Taft Ave in Baclaran /Pasay City along Edsa to North Ave in Quezon City and should be completed by 2000. There are plans to have a section of the line open by mid-1988.

The Metrorail runs from 5.30 am until 10.30 pm daily, except Good Friday. During rush hour the trains can be badly overcrowded. The fare is a flat P10, irrespective of the distance you travel. Instead of tickets, you buy tokens that open the barriers to the platforms. Smoking, eating and drinking is banned on platforms and trains.

The following are the railway stations from north to south, and some of the prominent city features nearby:

North Terminal (Monumento)
    Andres Bonifacio Monument, Philippine Rabbit bus terminal (Edsa), Victory Liner bus terminal (Caloocan City)
Fifth Ave Station
    Caloocan City
R Papa Station
    Baliwag Transit bus terminal (2nd Ave)
Abad Santos Station
    Chinese Cemetery
Blumentritt Station
    Chinese Hospital, San Lazaro Hippodrome
Tayuman Station
    Dangwa Tranco bus terminal (Dimasalang St), Farinas Trans bus terminal, San Lazaro Hippodrome

Bambang Station
    Maria de Leon bus terminal, Times Transit bus terminal (Halcon St), University of Santo Tomas
D Jose Station
    Claro M Recto St (cinemas), Philippine Rabbit bus terminal (Santa Cruz)
Carriedo Station
    Chinatown, Escolta, Ilalim ng Tulay Market, Quinta Market, Quiapo Church, Santa Cruz Church, Central Terminal
    GPO, immigration office, Intramuros, Manila City Hall, Metropolitan Theater, United Nations Ave Station
    Manila Doctor's Hospital, Manila Medical Center, Holiday Inn Manila Pavilion, Paco Park, Rizal Park, tourist office, Western Police District
Pedro Gil Station
    Manila Midtown Hotel, Philippine General Hospital
Quirino Ave Station
    Malate Church, San Andres Market
Vito Cruz Station
    Central Bank, Cultural Center, De la Salle University, Harrison Plaza, Century Park Sheraton Hotel
Gil Puyat Station
    Cartimar Market, Philtrade Exhibits
Libertad Station
    Libertad Cockpit, Pasay Market
Edsa Station
    BLTB bus terminal, Philtranco bus terminal, Victory Liner bus terminal, Inland Trailways bus terminal, JB Bicol Express Line bus terminal, Five Star bus terminal
South Terminal (Baclaran)
    Baclaran Church, Baclaran Flea Market, Seaside Market

Jeepney You need to get to know Manila before you can travel through the city by jeepney without problems. Crowding and a limited view make it hard to see where you are going, so a seat by the driver is desirable. Jeepney routes are fixed; its main streets and stops are shown on the side of the vehicle, and often on the windscreen as well. For example, jeepneys with the sign 'Baclaran, Harrison, Santa Cruz, Rizal, Monumento' will go from Baclaran in Pasay City, through Harrison St to Harrison Plaza, down Mabini St, back down MH del Pilar St – both one way streets – past the City Hall (Lawton) to Santa Cruz, then down Rizal Ave and Rizal Ave Extension to Monumento in Caloocan City.

Jeepneys on the north-south route are almost always marked 'Baclaran' or 'Libertad' to show the southern end of their route, both in Pasay City. The northern end could be Monumento (Caloocan City, at the end of the Rizal Ave Extension); Blumentritt (a street in northern Santa Cruz, by the Chinese Hospital and near the Chinese Cemetery); or Divisoria (the Divisoria Market in the suburb of San Nicolas). Jeepneys in Ermita run along MH del Pilar and Mabini Sts (those marked 'Harrison') or Taft Ave (those marked 'Taft'). Jeepneys whose north-eastern destination is shown as 'Project 2', 'Project 3' or 'Project 4' go to Cubao, while those marked 'Project 6' and 'Project 8' head for Quezon City. The fare is P1.50 for the first four km.

For further information see also the Jeepney section of the Getting Around chapter earlier in this book.

Taxi Manila is crawling with taxis, unless you want one that is, in which case there are none around or they all have passengers. It's not unusual to find taxi meters which have been tampered with, so it's best to check the speed of the counter now and again. Make sure you have some change, as there's no guarantee the driver will have any. Taxis begin with P20 (the old flag-down charge of P3.50 plus P16.50 surcharge).

For further information see the Taxi section of the Getting Around chapter earlier in this book.

Car

Ace Car Rentals
   140 Valero St, Salcedo Village, Makati
   (☎ 812 3386)
Avis Rent-a-Car
   NAIA, Arrival Area (☎ 832 2088)
   Bayview Park Hotel, Ermita (☎ 526 1555)
   Holiday Inn Manila Pavilion, Ermita
   (☎ 522 2911, ext 2339)
   Manila Peninsula Hotel, Makati (☎ 844 8498)
   Century Citadel Inn Makati, Burgos St, Makati
   (☎ 897 2370)
Budget Rent-a-Car
   NAIA, Arrival Area (☎ 831 8247)
   Hotel Inter-Continental, Makati (☎ 815 8316)
   Peninsula Hotel Manila, Makati (☎ 818 7363)
   Hotel Nikko Manila Garden, Makati
   (☎ 816 7261)
Thrifty Car Rental
   Centrepoint Hotel, 1430 Mabini St, Ermita
   (☎ 521 0731)

Further companies can be found in the *Yellow Pages* under 'Automobile'.

Driving Traffic in Manila is chaotic and noisy, especially to someone who is used to fairly strict traffic controls. There are few bus stops and they are not always used. Buses and jeepneys stop wherever they see potential passengers, and then taxis of various companies try to get in ahead of them. Horns and hand signals are used most often, brake lights and blinkers rarely, and traffic-lane markings seem to be thought of as a waste of paint. However, the battered vehicles usually last longer than their appearance would lead you to believe, and there are few accidents.

Around Manila

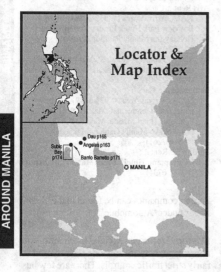

Locator &
Map Index

Dau p165
Angeles p163
Subic
Bay
p174
Barrio Barretto p171
◉ MANILA

All the trips described in this chapter can be done as day trips from Manila. The map shows towns that can be reached by bus within three hours. Olongapo, Pagsanjan and Matabungkay, however, deserve an overnight stay.

Some destinations can be combined (the volcano at Tagaytay and the beach at Matabungkay, for example). And some towns can be visited on the way to other destinations: Olongapo and Subic Bay are on the way to the Hundred Islands and San Pablo is on the way to South Luzon.

There's an expressway from Metro Manila north to Dau and Mabalacat, a little beyond Angeles, and another south to about Calamba. Buses using expressways rather than the ordinary roads carry the sign 'Expressway'.

Mt Pinatubo, the country's most infamous natural landmark, lies 80 km north-west of Manila in the eastern Zambales Mountains. In July 1981, this volcano erupted after six centuries of slumber. Violent eruptions continued for several weeks after, making it the worst volcanic outburst the world has seen this century. Pinatubo lost 300m in height as a result of the eruption and volcanologists say it could be quite some time before the mountain finally settles down at its new height of roughly 1450m.

CAVITE & TERNATE

Cavite is on a narrow, scythe-shaped peninsula around 35 km south-west of Manila. It has an excellent protected harbour that has been valued since Spanish times. The Philippine navy is stationed there today. The city itself offers no real attractions to the tourist, and this goes for its beaches too. But for those who just want to get out of Manila, it makes a pleasant day trip. The popular **theme park** known as Covelandia is located just outside the city. The **Aguinaldo House Museum** in the suburb of Kawit, Cavite, is worth seeing.

About 40 km south-west of Cavite at the entrance to Manila Bay, there are two exclusive, expansive resort-hotels. The better-heeled representatives of business, politics and show business like to spend their weekends here.

Places to Stay

The *Caylabne Bay Resort* (☎ 815 8385) in Ternate, has rooms with air-con and bath from P2000/2600 and upwards. It is attractive and comfortable, with a tennis court, golf course and swimming pool. Also on offer are Hobie Cats and windsurfing. Reservations can be made in Manila (☎ 814 8800).

The spacious and well-run *Novotel Puerto Azul Resort* (☎ 574731; fax 536 1584), also in Ternate, has rooms with air-con and bath from P3000 and suites from P5000. They have a swimming pool, tennis court, squash courts, golf course, Hobie Cats and windsurfing.

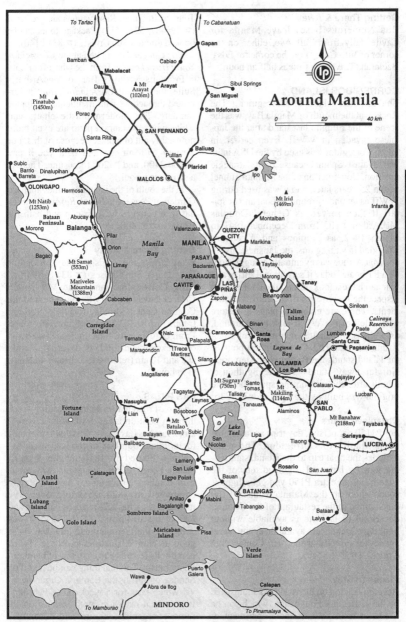

Around Manila

0   20   40 km

AROUND MANILA

Getting There & Away

Bus Numerous buses leave Manila for Cavite daily from Taft Ave, either on the corner of Vito Cruz or on the corner of Edsa, Baclaran. Travelling time is half an hour.

CORREGIDOR ISLAND

The fortified island of Corregidor ('The Rock'), at the mouth of Manila Bay, was the scene of the Filipino last stand after the Japanese invaded in WWII. Even earlier, in 1898, Corregidor was used by the USA in its war against Spain because of its strategic position. Construction of the Malinta Tunnel began 25 years later, and it was used during WWII as an underground arsenal and hospital. It then served as General Douglas MacArthur's HQ from December 1941 to March 1942, as Filipinos and Americans struggled in vain against the Japanese invaders. MacArthur was eventually smuggled out on a PT boat. Today it's a national shrine and you can have a look around the bunkers and inspect the rusty relics of the fortress armaments. There are elaborate plans to restore what's left of the WWII junk lying around, as well as the shattered remains of MacArthur's former HQ. On the highest point of the island stands the Pacific War Memorial. Not far away stands a white lighthouse, rebuilt after the war on the spot where the original was built by the Spaniards in 1836.

Organised Tours

For P1150 per person, day trips are available from Manila to Corregidor. The price includes the boat trip to the island, sightseeing tour by bus, and a guided tour of the island. For an extra P150 you get a light & sound show in the Malinta Tunnel. P160 buys lunch in the restaurant of the Corregidor Hotel (á la carte is available without booking). Tickets are available at any travel agency or directly at the pier. Contact Sun Cruises (☎ 831 8140).

Places to Stay

Accommodation on the island is administered by the Corregidor Foundation, which can be found in room 212 of the Department of Tourism Building. Reservations are preferred (☎ 596487, 523 8411). Package tours can be booked through Sun Cruises (☎ 831 8140).

You can get a dorm bed at the *Corregidor Youth Hostel* not far from the wharf for P250.

From its Visitor's Bar to MacArthur's Suite, the elegant *Corregidor Hotel* is furnished throughout with traditional Philippine furniture. The modern plastic chairs and tables on the restaurant patio are even more noticeably out of a place because of this. For a room with air-con and bath you'll pay P2100/2400, and P4200 for a suite. There is a swimming pool.

In the south of the island near the Japanese Garden of Peace, the *Beach Resort Complex* has neat cottages with air-con and bath for P2100 and P2400.

Getting There & Away

Boat Under the aegis of the Corregidor Foundation, Sun Cruises (☎ 831 8140) runs daily Corregidor tours. The MV *Island Cruiser* leaves the ferry terminal next to the Cultural Center Monday to Friday at 8 am (return trip at 2.30 pm), taking 1½ hours. From October until June, there are two boats on weekends and holidays, departing Manila at 8 and 10 am (return trip 2.30 and 4.30 pm) (1½ hours).

LAS PIÑAS

The coast road leaves Manila heading south through built-up areas until, after about 20 km, it reaches Las Piñas. This town is famous for its unique **bamboo organ** in the San Jose Church. Started in 1816 by the Spanish Father Diego Cerra, the organ was made from bamboo to save money and was finally completed in 1824. Standing over five metres high, it has 832 pipes of bamboo and 122 of metal. From 1973 to 1975 it was overhauled in Germany and now sounds as good as new. A small shop on the church porch sells records and cassettes of bamboo-organ music. The real thing can be heard on Sunday or during the Bamboo Organ Festival which lasts for a week every February. It's a social occasion, with internationally famous organists, choirs and ensembles taking part. On normal weekdays the organ can be seen from 2 to 4 pm only.

By the way, Las Piñas is the place where the jeepneys are built, piece by piece in painstaking individual production. The people in the workshops have no objection to visitors watching them at work. They finish work for the day at 4 pm, and they have Sundays off. As you leave the church, the Sarao Motors **jeepney factory** is about three km farther south on the main street.

Getting There & Away
Bus In Manila there are plenty of buses to Las Piñas that you can stop in Taft Ave. Destinations shown will be either Zapote or Cavite. The trip takes half an hour.

If you want to continue from Las Piñas to Tagaytay or Matabungkay, you can go to the main street and board any of the many buses coming through from Manila on the way to Nasugbu.

Jeepney Another possibility is to get a jeepney to Baclaran (you can get one from MH del Pilar St in Ermita), then go on with a Zapote jeepney to Las Piñas.

TAGAYTAY (TAAL VOLCANO)
Tagaytay is located about 70 km south of Manila and was once intended to become an alternative to the summer town of Baguio. Its high altitude (600m) and cool climate would seem to make it ideal to take over this role. However, in the end nothing came of it, although the idea was brought up again after a serious earthquake rattled Baguio in mid-1990, and shares in the exclusive apartment buildings which had been built in the meantime were offered.

The sprawling town offers visitors superb views of the volcanic island with its crater lake, but only if the weather is clear. The volcano is one of the smallest and most dangerous in the world. Anyone who wants to climb it can arrange to be taken over to the volcanic island from Talisay, 17 km east of Tagaytay. An attractive alternative route is to go on to Batangas and then to San Nicolas.

About 10 km east of Tagaytay, on Mt Sungay (750m) a lookout complex was built. From here you have a marvellous view of Lake Taal to the south, Laguna de Bay to the east and almost as far as Manila to the north. Jeepneys go up there regularly from the Skyline Junction in Tagaytay, stopping on the way at the turn-off down to Talisay.

Telephone
The area code for Tagaytay is 046.

Places to Stay
The accommodation is pleasant, although varying in quality, at the *Villa Adelaida* (☎ 413 1267), Foggy Heights. Rooms with fan and bath cost P1200. At weekends it can cost 20% more. They also have a swimming pool here. Coming from Manila, you turn to the left instead of the right at the traffic circle before Tagaytay. The Villa is by the road that runs down to the lake. You can make reservations in Manila (☎ 813 4613).

On National Rd (Aguinaldo Highway) the *Taal Vista Hotel* (☎ 413 1223; fax 413 1225) provides tidy and comfortable accommodation, although a touch too expensive maybe. It has rooms with air-con and bath for P2500. Folk dances with native music are often performed at the lookout in front of the hotel at noon. In their Kamayan Restaurant (where you can eat with your fingers in traditional Filipino style) they offer a sumptuous buffet and dancing. You can make reservations in Manila (☎ 817 2710).

Places to Eat
There are several restaurants in the Grandview Complex at the Aquino Monument, including the *Café Adriatico* and the *Ang Hang Restaurant* with spicy food. The main reason to visit the *Freddie Aguilar Music Lounge & Restaurant* is not so much the food, but the chance to catch the most popular singer and social critic in the Philippines live on stage. When available, Freddie Aguilar performs his melodic songs every Friday and Saturday evening in a two-hour show. The place is normally closed during the week.

AROUND MANILA

Getting There & Away

Bus Several BLTB buses run daily from Manila to Tagaytay, marked 'Nasugbu'. There are also others that pass through (1½ hours).

To get to Tagaytay from Pagsanjan you go by jeepney to Santa Cruz. There you get a Manila bus and get out at the junction at Calamba. From Calamba you go by jeepney through Binan to Palapala and from there you get a bus to Tagaytay. It takes about three hours. As an alternative, instead of getting out at Calamba, you can continue to Alabang and there change to a jeepney to Zapote, where you can catch a bus from Manila heading for Tagaytay.

Jeepney From Talisay to Tagaytay there are several jeepneys a day on the 17 km of dusty, narrow road (P12). A Special Ride costs P200.

TALISAY

Talisay is right on Lake Taal and a good starting point for trips to the volcanic island. These trips are on offer from various local lodging houses in the Banga and Leynes districts. A boat to the volcano and back costs around P500, including guide; without guide P400. It makes sense to have a guide if you go to the lake in the old crater (last eruption 1911), whereas you don't really need one for the new crater (last eruption 1965). You should allow for at least half a day's stay on the island. Warnings made by basically lazy guides about hordes of dangerous snakes at the crater lake should be dismissed with a benign smile. You might have to cope with heavy swells and occasionally get sopping wet, so a plastic bag for your camera is a good precaution. See also the San Nicolas section below in this chapter.

About five km west of Talisay in Buco, on the edge of Lake Taal, is an old seismological station of the Philippine Institute of Volcanology & Seismology (PHIVOLC). Its scope has been extended to that of a 'Science House', with staff always on duty and information available on the work of volcanologists, the instruments and the geology of Lake Taal.

Places to Stay

Just outside Talisay, and handily located for a trip to Taal Volcano, *Rosalina's Place* (cellular ☎ 0973-738 094) at Banga has singles/doubles with fan and bath for P200/250, a little overpriced considering the condition of the rooms. Facing Rosalina's, the *International Resort* charges P500 for rooms with fan and bath.

In Leynes (half-way between Tagaytay and Talisay), the *Taal Lake Guest House* (cellular ☎ 0973-736066) will give you a basic, comfortable room with fan and bath for P300/400. The place is actually the former Natalia's Guest House.

Also in Leynes, *Gloria de Castro's Store* is a friendly little place with rooms with fan and bath from P300 to P500, which is slightly high for what you get.

A little more expensive, but an alternative to be recommended, is *Milo's Paradise* (☎ 720318) in Balas, near the turn-off for Tagaytay. Run by a German-Philippine couple, this is a relatively new resort with swimming pool; the cottages are roomy (good for four) and quiet, costing P600 to P800. There is a beautiful view of the volcanic lake from here.

Getting There & Away

Bus From Manila the trip to Talisay is in two stages. First you get one of the numerous daily BLTB buses marked 'Lemery' or 'Batangas' and go as far as Tanauan. From there you can get a jeepney at the public market going to Talisay. Total travelling time is two hours.

From Batangas, it's best to use the many daily Manila buses to get to Tanauan. This route is also served by jeepneys, but buses are more comfortable. In the public market in Tanauan you can get a jeepney to Talisay. The total travelling time is two hours.

Jeepney A few km east of Tagaytay a dusty road takes you the 17 km down to the lake and Talisay. Jeepneys wait at the turn-off and leave when they are full. The fare is P12, and a Special Ride costs P200. The last one leaves at 5 pm. Jeepneys also cover the route from the Aquino Monument to the turn-off (P2).

To reach Talisay from Pagsanjan you begin by catching a jeepney to Santa Cruz. Then catch a Manila bus and get out at the junction at Calamba. From there, catch a jeepney to Tanauan, where you can pick up a jeepney to Talisay. Total travelling time is about 2½ hours. Instead of going through Calamba, you can use jeepneys from Pagsanjan and Santa Cruz via San Pablo to Tanauan and Talisay.

NASUGBU

The beaches at Nasugbu are worth noting. The one at White Sands is three to four km to the north and can be reached by outrigger boat (P300). Out of Nasugbu in the direction of the beach, there is a good seafood restaurant, the Dalam Pasigan.

Places to Stay

Enjoy the romance of having no electricity at the *White Sands Beach Resort* in Munting-buhangin Cove, Natipuan, where cottages with bath go for P750 and P1000. The accommodation is pleasant and they have a restaurant. Reservations can be made in Manila (☎ 833 5608).

At the *Maryland Resort* rooms with fan and bath cost P600 and P1420 with air-con and bath. It has a restaurant and a swimming pool.

The popular *Maya-Maya Reef Club* (cellular ☎ 0912-322 8550; fax 322 8554) has cottages with air-con and bath for P1960/2130 set in attractive grounds. You can cool off in the swimming pool after a game of tennis, and there is also a dive shop. Reservations can be made in Manila (☎ 810 8118; fax 815 9288).

Getting There & Away

Bus BLTB buses leave Manila for Nasugbu hourly from 5.30 am (two hours).

MATABUNGKAY

Matabungkay has the most popular beach in the neighbourhood of Manila, so on weekends there are lots of day trippers. Although the sand is not dazzlingly white, it's not bad

and the water is clean. Among the main attractions are thatched-roof rafts with tables and chairs which can be hired for around P400 per day and anchored over the reef to act as platforms from which to swim and snorkel. The hirer also brings out food and ice-cold drinks to order. Day trips to nearby Fortune Island can be arranged for P600 to P800.

Places to Stay

You probably know what colour scheme to expect at *The Greendoors Cottages*, where adequate rooms with fan will cost you P300, P500/700 with fan and bath, and P700/900 with air-con and bath.

Rooms at the *Swiss House Hotel* (cellular ☎ 0912-322 4631) are in good condition and pleasantly furnished throughout. With fan and bath they cost P650, and with air-con, bath and fridge P950.

Under German management, the *Twins Beach Club* (cellular ☎ 0912-322 8163), Ligtasin, offers good quality and a comfortable place to stay. Rooms with fan and bath cost P650 and P850 with air-con and bath. They have a sea water swimming pool and also offer windsurfing.

Australian management is in charge at the *Coral Beach Club* (cellular ☎ 0912-318 4868; fax 324 3183). Well-maintained rooms with fan and bath go for P1200 and P1760 with air-con and bath. The attractive cottages are pleasant to stay in, and there is a pool in the grounds. Reservations can be made at Swagman Travel (☎ 526 1295; fax 522 3663).

In Calatagan, about 20 km south of Matabungkay, the up-market *Punta Baluarte Inter-Continental Resort*, (☎ 892 4202; fax 892 4211) provides its distinguished guests with rooms with air-con and bath from P2500 to P3300. It has a restaurant, swimming pool, golf course, riding and tennis courts. You can make reservations in Manila (☎ 894 1466, 893 4491).

Getting There & Away

Bus From Manila to Matabungkay take a bus with the destination Nasugbu, then get out at Lian and do the last few km by jeepney. BLTB buses leave hourly from 5.30 am. These leave about 100m from the bus stop in the direction of the town centre. Special Rides in a tricycle cost about P50.

At 12.30 pm a BLTB bus goes from Manila to Matabungkay and on to Calatagan, which saves changing at Lian. A tricycle from the highway to Matabungkay (two km) costs P10.

From Matabungkay to Manila, take a jeepney to Nasugbu bus terminal and carry on by bus.

Jeepney There are jeepneys that run from Nasugbu to Matabungkay via Lian.

From Batangas to Matabungkay and Nasugbu is a three- or four-stage trip by jeepney: one from Batangas to Lemery, another from Lemery to Balayan, and a third from Balayan to Nasugbu, or from Balayan to Balibago and jeepney or tricycle (P30) from Balibago.

LEMERY & TAAL

From Lemery, not too inviting a place, you can get to Ligpo Point, eight km to the south, via San Luis. The small island of Ligpo is just offshore. It is a popular place with divers, even though the underwater setting is fairly ordinary. The beach here is better than the one at nearby Anilao.

Taal is about one km east of Lemery. It's a peaceful small town with a few old buildings in colonial style and the impressive Basilica Minore of Saint Martin of Tours, built between 1858 and 1878.

Places to Stay

The only possible accommodation in Lemery seems to be at the *Vila Lobos Lodge*, which is a basic, rather noisy place with small rooms and a disco. Rooms with fan and bath are P180, with air-con and bath P350.

In San Luis, the rooms at *Ligpo Beach Resort* cost P500/750 with fan and bath, and the *Ligpo Island Hotel & Resort* (on Ligpo Island, of course) will let you have a room with fan and bath for P600/1000. Both offer diving.

Getting There & Away

Bus Several BLTB buses do the three-hour trip to and from Manila daily.

Jeepney From Batangas, several jeepneys run daily (1½ hours).

SAN NICOLAS

You can cross from San Nicolas to the volcanic island in Lake Taal. The round trip is a bit expensive at between P700 to P800. If you set out very early, you may see a magnificent sunrise. For a few pesos extra the boatman may take his passengers up to the old crater with the lake inside it. However, some of them insist on an extra P200 for this little detour! It is easy to get lost on the way down to the lake, so it is advisable to have a guide. On the edge of the old crater a few shepherds live who know the island well and can act as guides. As protection against sharp, high grass and pointed lava stones, you should wear long trousers and suitable shoes.

There are four craters on the island. If you are climbing to the new crater, which last erupted in 1965, you don't need a guide. It doesn't take long and there is no need to stay overnight in San Nicolas.

Boats also go to the island from Subic (not to be confused with the former US naval town to the north-west), a little north of San Nicolas. The road along the lake's edge between Subic and San Nicolas is practically impassable for ordinary vehicles.

Places to Stay

You can ask for a room at the store, where you can sit outside on the corner of the plaza. It is also where you arrange boat trips.

The *Lake View Park & Resort* has basic cottages with bath from P400 to P600.

Getting There & Away

Jeepney Several jeepneys run daily from Lemery to San Nicolas (30 minutes). The last jeepney from San Nicolas to Lemery leaves at 5 pm. See also details for getting to and from Batangas later in this chapter.

ANILAO
In Anilao there are various diving centres where you can arrange trips to diving spots in Balayan Bay near Cape Bagalangit and near Sombrero and Maricaban Islands. Boat hire for a day trip to Sombrero Island is around P800.

The beach at Anilao is not to be recommended. You can, however, hire thatched bamboo rafts with tables and benches for P300 at places like the Anilao Beach Resort. These are anchored some distance out from the beach and are good platforms for swimming and snorkelling.

Places to Stay
Anilao is a tourist haunt, so accommodation is relatively expensive. The *San Jose Lodge* on the edge of town has rooms for P150/200. The pleasant *Anilao Seasport Centre*, about two km out of town, has well appointed rooms with fan and bath for P800. You can also arrange full board for P1500 per person. They have Hobie Cats, and windsurfing and diving are offered. You can make reservations in Manila (☎ 801 1850; fax 805 4660).

The *Aqua Tropical Resort* has a Manila address: c/o Aqua Tropical Sports (☎ 587908, 521 6407; fax 818 9720), Manila Midtown Hotel, Pedro Gil, Ermita. Attractive and comfortable rooms with fan go for P750, with fan and bath for P1100 and with air-con and bath for P1900 and P2500. They have a swimming pool and provide diving equipment for diving trips they organise. The resort is near Bagalangit, a few km southwest of Anilao. You can also reach it from Anilao by boat.

Getting There & Away
Bus & Jeepney From Batangas, there are several buses and jeepneys daily, although it may be necessary to change at Mabini. The trip takes 1½ hours.

BATANGAS
Batangas is the capital of the province of the same name. There is talk of developing an industrial zone in and around the city, which would provide a convenient location for foreign investors. The South Super Highway is to be extended to Batangas and the possible reopening of the old Manila to Batangas railway is being considered. The depth of Batangas Bay and the ease with which harbour facilities could be constructed are also being put forward as advantages Batangas has over other regions.

Tourists mainly use Batangas as a transit point on the way to Puerto Galera on Mindoro. However, it is also a good point from which to make day trips to Lake Taal, to the hot springs at Calamba and Los Baños, to Bauan Beach and to Tabangao, further out on the rocky coast seven km from Batangas, which is good for diving and snorkelling.

Telephone
The area code for Batangas is 043.

Places to Stay
Most of the inexpensive hotels in town are in a bad condition. The relatively centrally located *Avenue Pension House I* (☎ 725 3720) at 30 JP Rizal Ave is acceptable. Quite decent doubles with fan and bath cost P300, with air-con and bath P350. If you only stay for 12 hours or less there is a reduction of one third in the bill. Considering where it is, it's not too loud.

The *Guesthaus* (☎ & fax 723 1155), 224 Diego Silan St, on the corner of MH del Pilar St, has basic, clean rooms with fan and bath for P350/450 and with air-con and bath for P600.

Located on the outskirts of town in the direction of Manila, the *Alpa Hotel* at Kumintang Ibana has gone up-market; rooms with air-con and bath now cost from P850 to P2000. Oh well, at least there's a swimming pool.

Getting There & Away
Bus Always ask for Batangas City when enquiring about transport, otherwise there will be confusion as to where in Batangas Province you wish to go.

Several BLTB and JAM transit buses leave Manila daily for Batangas (P50; 2½ hours). If you want the harbour in Batangas, look for the buses for Batangas Pier. The trip takes three hours or more. Beware of pickpockets on these buses – they often operate in teams of three.

If you arrive in Batangas from Mindoro, you can take one of the Manila buses waiting at the pier and go directly to Manila, or go into town by jeepney and get a bus there – either the regular bus or a BLTB air-con bus to Pasay City/Manila.

If you are going from Manila to Batangas and on towards Puerto Galera, there is a daily combined bus and ship service from the Centrepoint Hotel on Mabini St, Ermita, leaving at 9 am sharp.

Jeepney There is an interesting back-roads route from Batangas to Manila via Lemery which allows for a detour to Lake Taal. Go by jeepney from Batangas to Lemery, then take a jeepney to San Nicolas on the southwestern edge of the lake. The trip takes 1½ hours. The last jeepney back to Lemery leaves at 5 pm, which gives you ample time to catch the last BLTB bus in Lemery for Pasay City/Manila. If instead of Manila you are heading for Santa Cruz or Pagsanjan, then change at Calamba.

To go to Batangas from Pagsanjan quickly, take a jeepney to Santa Cruz; from there, catch a Manila-bound bus as far as Calamba. From Calamba, either take a jeepney directly to Batangas or take a jeepney to Tanauan and then can catch a Batangas-bound bus travelling from Manila.

CALAMBA

The national hero Jose Rizal was born in Calamba, a small town on the south-west shore of the inland lake Laguna de Bay. **Rizal House**, with its garden, is now a memorial and museum. It's across from the town hall and is open Tuesday to Sunday from 8 am to noon and 1 to 5 pm.

There is a whole row of resorts along the highway in the Los Baños direction, a few km south of Calamba. These resorts take advantage of the local **hot springs** and are a popular source of relaxation for stressed-out inhabitants of Metro Manila. Almost all

of them offer overnight accommodation, although the facilities can be used by non-residents for an admission fee.

In 1995, an **amusement park**, The Enchanted Kingdom, was opened 10 km north of Calamba at Santa Rosa. With its claim to be 'the country's first and only world-class theme park', it's open every day, all year round. Rides such as the Space Shuttle, Jungle Log Jam, Wheel of Fate, and the 30m-high Ferris wheel are complemented by interactive displays, an archaeological dig and much more. Admission is P380 for adults with the usual discounts.

Telephone
The area code for Calamba is 049.

Places to Stay
At the *Coco Villa* (☎ 545 1277), Bagong Kalsaga, acceptable rooms with fan cost P250/350 and with fan and bath P300/450. The swimming pool is set in peaceful grounds with a garden. It's opposite *Crystal Springs* (☎ 545 2496), which has roomy singles/doubles with air-con and bath for P1300, each with its own private mini-pool. This is a generously laid-out establishment with eight differently sized swimming pools.

Getting There & Away
Bus In Manila, the buses marked 'Santa Cruz' leave the BLTB bus terminal daily and frequently go through Calamba (one hour).

In Batangas, the buses marked 'Manila' leave the pier and market daily and frequently go through Calamba (1½ hours).

Similarly, in Santa Cruz and Pagsanjan, numerous Manila-bound buses go through Calamba daily, taking an hour.

LOS BAÑOS
Just south of Calamba, the University of the Philippines (UP) has a forestry institute with botanical gardens in Los Baños. The garden is not overly botanical but it has a big swimming pool. Not far from the UP is the International Rice Research Institute (IRRI). Look for the sign 'UP Los Baños' on the main road.

Los Baños is noted for its **hot springs** which you can bathe in. Most resorts are outside the town, along the highways as far as Calamba. About two km along the road to Calamba, between the highway and Laguna de Bay, you will find Alligator Lake, a deep crater lake which has none of the reptiles you would expect to find in it.

Not far from Los Baños is the **Philippine Art Center**, from where you get a good view over Laguna de Bay. A Special Ride there in a jeepney costs P30. At nearby Mt Makiling there is a nice park with a zoo and pool, and good views. Jeepneys to Scout Jamboree Park go there. Mt Makiling is a 1144m-high volcanic massif, the upper slopes of which are covered in jungle with a vast variety of flora.

Telephone

The area code for Los Baños is 049.

Places to Stay

The *Lakeview Resort Hotel* (☎ 536 0101) at 728 Lopez St has adequate rooms with fan and bath for P385 and with air-con and bath from P715 to P1500. It is a pleasant place, with four swimming pools.

The attractive rooms at the *City of Springs Resort Hotel* (☎ 536 0731; fax 536 0137) at 147 N Villegas St cost between P660 and P1350 with air-con and bath. Some of them are equipped with a Roman bath and whirlpool. This resort has several swimming pools.

About 100m from the City of Springs Resort, the *Los Baños Lodge & Hot Springs* (☎ 536 0498) at 145 N Villegas St offers rooms with fan for P455 and with air-con and bath for P560/875, and there is a swimming pool. Check-out time at the weekends is 9 am! Take a jeepney in Los Baños towards the City of Springs.

Getting There & Away

Bus In Manila, BLTB buses marked 'Santa Cruz' leave daily, frequently going via Los Baños (1½ hours).

From Santa Cruz and Pagsanjan, the numerous buses marked 'Manila' go through Los Baños (one hour).

There is no direct route from Batangas to

Los Baños. Best take a bus to Calamba through to the bus terminal, then carry on by bus or jeepney.

ALAMINOS

Alaminos is known for **Hidden Valley**, a fascinating private property and resort with lush tropical vegetation and several springs. This wonderful natural area is a paradise for botanists and a popular subject for film makers and photographers. Like Los Baños, there are **hot springs** all around here. It's five km from the town centre. Tricycles firmly demand P100 for the short stretch from Alaminos to the gates. Here visitors are again hit hard. The admission fee seems to go up each year – at the moment it's a whopping P1200. This includes a drink on arrival, buffet lunch, snacks in the afternoon and use of facilities such as the swimming pool, showers, changing rooms etc.

Places to Stay

Hidden Valley Springs has singles with air-con and bath for P2565 and doubles with air-con and bath for P4700 and P5000, including a breakfast buffet. The rooms are pleasant enough, although they would cost quite a bit less in other surroundings. The price for overnight accommodation includes the admission fee for the resort. Reservations can be made in Manila (☎ 818 4034).

Getting There & Away

Bus Several BLTB, Philtranco and Superlines buses leave Manila daily and go through Alaminos, for example, those marked 'San Pablo', 'Lucena', 'Daet', 'Naga' and 'Legaspi' (1½ hours).

Jeepney Mt Makiling lies between Los Baños and Alaminos, so the route from Los Baños is a bit roundabout. Go by jeepney from Los Baños to San Pablo, then take either a Manila-bound bus or a Tanauan-bound jeepney to Alaminos. The trip takes an hour.

SAN PABLO

San Pablo is known as the City of the Seven Lakes. It's a good centre for walks. There's one around Sampaloc Lake, which has restaurants built on stilts along the lakeside, and others to Pandin and Yambo Lakes. The remaining four lakes are Calibato, Mohicap, Palakpakin and Bunot.

Climbers may like to tackle nearby **Mt Makiling**, a volcanic mass of 1144m with three peaks. This is best reached from Alaminos or Los Baños. However, if you are starting from San Pablo, the best climb is the 2188m-high **Mt Banahaw**. This dormant volcano, with its springs and waterfalls, is credited with mystical powers. Especially at Easter, many Filipinos come to meditate and pray in the ravines and drink or bathe in the 'holy water' of the splashing streams. The climb usually begins at Kinabuhayan, which is reached by jeepney from San Pablo. Three days are needed for the climb.

About 10 km south of San Pablo, just before Tiaong, is Villa Escudero, a **coconut plantation** and resort combined. Admission is P555 (Friday, Saturday and Sunday P635), including guided tour, lunch buffet, trip on a raft and use of the facilities such as swimming pool and billiards etc. In this complex, reminiscent of the Spanish colonial era, it is worth paying a visit to the museum, which has many valuable historical and cultural artefacts.

Telephone

The area code for San Pablo is 093.

Places to Stay

You can experience a beautiful view of Sampaloc Lake from the friendly *Sampaloc Lake Youth Hostel* (☎ 4448) at Efarca Village, Schetelig Ave, a pleasant place to stay on the outskirts of town. It has dorm beds for P120 and doubles with fan and bath for P150. A tricycle from the church or plaza in San Pablo will only cost a few pesos.

Comfortable cottages at the *Villa Escudero*, (☎ 3676) Tiaong, cost between P1875 and P5140 with fan and bath, and include three meals. They have a swimming pool. Reservations can be made in Manila (☎ 523 2944; fax 521 8698).

Getting There & Away

Bus Several BLTB, Philtranco and Superlines buses leave Manila daily marked 'Lucena', 'Daet', 'Naga' and 'Legaspi'. All of these go through San Pablo (two hours).

Jeepney From Pagsanjan you get to San Pablo in two stages. First take a jeepney from Pagsanjan to Santa Cruz, then catch another jeepney to San Pablo (1½ hours).

Numerous jeepneys run daily from Los Baños to San Pablo (30 minutes).

PAGSANJAN

A trip to Pagsanjan (pronounced pag-san-han) – where the final scenes of Francis Ford Coppola's Vietnam War film *Apocalypse Now* was filmed – is a must. The **Magdapio Waterfalls** are only part of Pagsanjan's attractions; it's the river trip through the picturesque tropical gorge which is the real drawing card.

Two *banqueros* will paddle you upstream against the strong current in a *banca* (canoe). It's a feat of strength which taxes even two men paddling together. At the last major waterfall you can ride on a bamboo raft for an extra P30. You come downstream at a thrilling speed. Shooting the rapids is at its most exciting in August and September, when the river is high. Don't hold on too tightly to the sides of the boat and keep your hands inside or your fingers may get crushed. Use a plastic bag to keep your camera dry.

All inclusive, the officially fixed price of this harmless bit of fun is P250 plus P7 admission to the falls. (Up to three people can ride in a banca; if you go alone, it costs P450.) However, tips may be requested, even demanded vehemently. Readers' letters have told of boat operators making most aggressive demands at times – sums of from P500 to P1000 have been mentioned. According to most reports, anyone who is not prepared to give in to a demand for extra payment made halfway up to the waterfall, is not going to enjoy the rest of the trip. So pay up or suffer. You can, of course, skip the trip, save your money and let others be annoyed. The banqueros, who are arranged through the

Pagsanjan Youth Hostel, Pagsanjan Falls Lodge and Willy Flores Lodge, apparently will not cause an unpleasant scene if challenged. However, there is no guarantee against unpleasant surprises.

If you feel like trying your luck on your own, don't go on weekends, when there are so many tourists it resembles an anthill. If you stay overnight in Pagsanjan and leave for the falls at sunrise, you'll be on the river long before the hordes arrive. As sunlight comes late in the deep valleys, photographers will have difficulty taking pictures with normal equipment in the very early morning.

Organised day tours from Manila can be arranged for about US$45 at the various travel agencies and tourist offices.

Telephone

The area code for Pagsanjan is 049.

Places to Stay

A good rule for most places in Pagsanjan is to find your own way there. The area is not too big and you don't really need a guide, especially since you're expected to pay them a commission, plus the room will end up costing more! An overnight stay in nearby Santa Cruz can provide temporary respite from the tourist traps in Pagsanjan.

Staying at the *Asian Philippine Traveller's Inn* (☎ 645 1845) in Pagsawitan, Santa Cruz, would be a real alternative to finding accommodation in Pagsanjan. Tidy rooms with fan and bath cost P200 and with air-con and bath P300/350 (with TV and fridge). They can also be rented for only 12 hours, in which case they cost 30% less. The hotel is fairly big, set in large grounds.

In Pagsanjan, the *Pagsanjan Youth Hostel* (☎ 645 2347), 237 General Luna St, has no-frill dorm beds with fan for P80 and singles/doubles with fan for P150/180. Go through the city gate to the end of Rizal St, turn right over the river, then right again. The hostel is a fair way down on the left. Look for the sign.

The atmosphere is friendly and homely at the *Willy Flores Guesthouse*, 821 Garcia St, where basic but pleasant rooms with fan go for P150/200 and with fan and bath for P250/300. The staff will help organise boat trips.

Miss Estella y Umale's *Riverside Bungalow* (☎ 645 2465) at 792 Garcia St has two bungalows with fan-cooled rooms and bath for P400 and with air-con and bath for P1200. The cooking is good.

If you want a larger room, try the *Camino Real Hotel* (☎ 645 2086), 39 Rizal St. They'll charge you P500 for a comfortable room with fan, and P750 for one with air-con and bath.

The *Pagsanjan Falls Lodge* (☎ 645 1251) is a relatively good hotel, but a bit pricey at P880 for a room with fan and bath, and P1100 with air-con and bath. There is also a disco here and a beautiful pool.

The *Pagsanjan Village Hotel* (☎ 645 2116), Garcia St, will let you have a pleasant single/double with fan for P550, a single/double with air-con for P600, and with air-con and bath for P1000.

Covering a big area with room for three swimming pools, the *La Corona de Pagsanjan Resort* (cellular ☎ 0912-306 9766; fax 322 3198) has excellent rooms with air-con and bath for P1440 and P1800 (with fridge and TV).

Places to Eat

There are plenty of good eating places in Pagsanjan, such as the *Dura-Fe Restaurant* on General Jaina St which has very good food. It closes early at night. Also recommended is the *D & C Luncheonette* on National Rd near Pagsanjan Falls Lodge.

The *Me-Lin Restaurant* in Mabini St near the plaza has good food, nice staff and genuine home-made pizza for P50. People find the *Hidden Café* in Garcia St a pleasant garden restaurant. It is right alongside the river and serves inexpensive Filipino and European food.

Getting There & Away

Bus BLTB and JAM Transit buses leave Manila daily for Santa Cruz (P50; two hours). The last few km are done by jeepney (P2). Special Rides by tricycle aren't necessary, even when the driver tries to persuade the innocent foreigner to the contrary.

To get to Pagsanjan from Batangas, it's quickest to get a Manila-bound bus as far as Calamba. There, get a bus coming from Manila to Santa Cruz and go on to Pagsanjan by jeepney.

There are two shortcuts when travelling from Tagaytay to Pagsanjan which save you going right back to Manila. One involves travelling by bus to Zapote, then by jeepney to Alabang, by bus to Santa Cruz and by jeepney to Pagsanjan. Alternatively, take a bus from Tagaytay to Palapala, then a jeepney through Binan to Calamba, then a bus to Santa Cruz and a jeepney to Pagsanjan.

If you are going to South Luzon from Pagsanjan, there are several Supreme Lines buses running daily from Santa Cruz to Lucena (three hours). If you don't want to wait for a bus, you can go by jeepney from Santa Cruz to Lucban and then get another jeepney to Lucena. All buses from Manila marked 'Daet', 'Naga', 'Legaspi' etc, go through Lucena, so you don't have to go right back to Manila.

AROUND PAGSANJAN

Visits to the following destinations make good day trips from Pagsanjan. Paete is the best known Philippine centre for **woodcarving** in ebony. The **Japanese Garden** is a memorial to the Japanese soldiers who died in WWII in and around Pagsanjan. **Caliraya Reservoir** is a massive artificial lake with resorts like Sierra Lakes and Lake Caliraya Country Club. The village of **Lucban**, halfway along the road to Lucena, is a good example of what villages must have looked like during the era of Spanish rule. Lucban has its harvest festival on 15 May (see Public Holidays & Special Events in the earlier Facts for the Visitor chapter).

LUCENA

Depending on the tide, boats leave either from Dalahican or from the river harbour of Cotta Port, six km south-east and south of Lucena respectively, to Marinduque and Romblon.

If you don't get to Dalahican Beach, you won't have missed anything – it's dirty and swampy. On the other hand, a trip to **Quezon National Park** between Lucena and Atimonan would be worth the trouble, especially if you are the kind of birdwatcher who likes adventure. This is not a reference to the numerous birds who are at home in the park, but the fact the military have set up a camp here.

The Maharlika Highway crosses the park and is used by all the large buses, so it is better to take a minibus. These take the old zigzag road and stop at the picnic ground in the middle of the park. There are interesting walks through the vegetation with its beautiful flowers, monkeys and so on. If you want to continue south, you can take a minibus to Atimonan and change to a larger bus there.

Telephone
The area code for Lucena is 042.

Places to Stay
In Iyam District the *Tourist Hotel* (☎ 714456) has rooms with fan for P100/120, with fan and bath for P160/180 and with air-con and bath for P300/400. It is basic but fairly clean and has a small restaurant.

The *Hotel Halina* (☎ 712902) at 104 P Gomez St charges P180/250 for rooms with fan and bath, and P350/420 if they have air-con and bath. Suites are P680. Accommodation facing the back yard is quiet.

In the Isabang District, just outside town on the left-hand side coming from Manila, *The Lucena Fresh Air Hotel & Resort* (☎ 712424) is set in generous grounds. They have pretty good rooms with fan for P145/175, with fan and bath for P220 to P280 and with air-con and bath for P440/755. This place is clean and comfortable; right on the button at these prices. The rooms at the back are large and quiet, and there is also a nice swimming pool and a restaurant with good meals for about P60.

Also in the Isabang District, the *Travel Lodge Chain Motel* (☎ 714489) will give you a single/double with fan and bath for P200/260, with air-con for P420/500 and a suite for P725. It has a swimming pool.

JOHN PENNOCK

JENS PETERS

JENS PETERS

MANILA
Top: A harbour tour at sunset, Manila Bay.
Bottom Left: Warriors on the march.
Bottom Right: A colonial balcony in Intramuros, Manila.

JOHN PENNOCK

CHRIS MILES

JOHN PENNOCK

AROUND MANILA
Top: Dawn breaks over Lake Taal, Batangas Province.
Bottom Left: Day's end, Manila Bay.
Bottom Right: Corn fields of Ilocos Norte Province.

Getting There & Away

Bus Plenty of Philtranco, Superlines and BLTB buses go from Manila to Lucena every day (three hours). They may be going only as far as Lucena or be on their way to Daet, Naga, Legaspi or Matnog.

Several Supreme Lines buses go from Santa Cruz/Pagsanjan to Lucena daily and take three hours. To save waiting, you can take a jeepney from Santa Cruz to Lucban and change there for another to Lucena. The other more complicated way is to take a bus from Santa Cruz to Los Baños, then a jeepney to San Pablo, and from there another bus to Lucena.

There are also several Supreme Lines buses that make the run from Batangas to Lucena every day (three hours).

SAN FERNANDO (PAMPANGA)

Don't confuse San Fernando (Pampanga), the capital of Pampanga Province 50 km north of Manila, with the San Fernando that is the capital of La Union Province, northwest of Baguio on the coast. This town is notorious at Easter. On Good Friday at noon you can see at least one fanatical 'believer' being nailed to a cross in a rice field in the barangay San Pedro Cutud. In 1996 there were 14 such 'believers'. These imitators of Christ are accompanied on their 'Via Crusis' (way of the cross) to 'Golgotha' by hordes of flagellants, who whip their backs until they bleed, watched by a crowd of curious onlookers.

On 24 December – if it's a Saturday, or on the Saturday before if not – several oversized lanterns that would not be out of place in a huge disco are put on show on the square at Paskuhan Village. At about 8 pm the ceremony begins, and at about midnight the lanterns are paraded through the town to the town centre accompanied by a lot of hullabaloo. The 'Giant Lanterns' are taken back to Paskuhan Village the next day, where they remain on view until January. As it is possible the schedule of the lantern festival may be altered at short notice, it would be best to check times and dates with the tourist office in about mid-December. (See also Public Holidays & Special Events in the earlier Facts for the Visitor chapter.)

Paskuhan Village, the 'Christmas Village', is on the Expressway just outside San Fernando. It is not really a village, but a small amusement park (admission P13). Built in the shape of an oversize Christmas star, it houses a tourist office, the Pinatubo Museum (admission P10), the Pinatubo House constructed from material ejected during the eruption, a swimming pool (admission P40) and several little souvenir shops.

In September 1995, San Fernando narrowly escaped catastrophe when heavy rain around Mt Pinatubo sent enormous mudslides south-east down the Pasig-Potrero River system, causing tremendous flooding. Wide areas of San Fernando and the province were submerged under for days. But much worse, low-lying areas were completely filled with mud, and whole communities disappeared under the slimy mess. Bacolor, right before the gates of San Fernando, was especially badly hit. Since then, even the big church has remained submerged under the grey mass, with little more than the roof sticking out. A hastily erected dike is now supposed to prevent San Fernando from being next in line.

Information

Tourist Office The tourist office (☎ 961 2665; fax 961 2612) is at the Paskuhan Village on the Expressway.

Telephone The area code for San Fernando is 045.

Places to Stay

Opposite the church, you'll find pleasant accommodation at the basic *Pampanga Lodge*, where singles/doubles with fan cost P100/180 and doubles with fan and bath P200. You can also get 12-hour rates.

In the Juliana subdivision on the outskirts of town, the *Boliseum Motel* (☎ 961 2040), has good rooms with air-con, bath and TV for P450. It's a bit out of the way, but quiet.

Getting There & Away
Bus Only a few buses go direct from Manila to San Fernando along the old MacArthur Highway. Most use the quicker Expressway. There are several Philippine Rabbit and Victory Liner buses every day. Buses from Manila to Olongapo almost always go into San Fernando; if necessary, you can get a jeepney from the nearest cross-roads into the town. The buses take about an hour.

Numerous Victory Liner buses go from Olongapo through San Fernando daily, almost all on the way to Manila or Baguio. Travelling time is an hour or more.

Victory Liner buses from Baguio to Olongapo go through Angeles and San Fernando, and it is possible to get on them.

Jeepney There are several jeepneys from Angeles to San Fernando daily (30 minutes). Most come from Mabalacat or Dau, north of Angeles.

ANGELES
Until 1991, Angeles was home to Clark Air Base, run by and for the US Air Force. In that year, the Americans had to respect the wishes of the Philippine senate that they leave the country. The withdrawal was accelerated a little by the eruption of Pinatubo, which didn't just destroy the air base, but made a total mess of Angeles itself and the surrounding area. Even considering how much has already been cleaned up and how well life has returned to normal here, it will still take a few years for the area to fully recover.

The sudden withdrawal of the Americans had serious repercussions on the economy of the town at first. However, the efforts put into converting the huge area of the former base into an industrial, airport and tourism complex have already shown considerable results. In the meantime, more than 100 national and international companies are conducting business in the Clark Special Economic Zone (CSEZ), development of the Clark International Airport is well under way, the Holiday Inn Resort Clark Field Hotel has been opened, as has the Mimosa Golf & Country Club, and sporting/tourist

events such as the International Hot Air Balloon Festival, go-kart rides, and drag races are taking place.

Various local hotels now offer Pinatubo tours, which has led to surprisingly high occupation rates. The tourists have also meant more business for the bars, restaurants and nightclubs that did manage to survive the fateful year of 1991 or have been rebuilt in the meantime.

Information
Visas The Immigration Office is on 7th St in Dau. You can get your visa extended here, but your application and passport will probably be sent to Manila for processing and will not be available for a few days. Some travel agencies and hotels run by foreigners will also offer to take care of your extension application for a reasonable sum.

Money The Philippine National Bank (PNB) in Dau changes travellers cheques. Money-changers at the checkpoint, and the Norma Money Changer in a side street near the Folk House Restaurant, will all change cash.

Post & Communications International calls can be made and faxes sent at reasonable rates from the Faxtel Center at the hotel Marlim Mansions and the Angeles Business Center behind the Manhattan Transfer Restaurant, both on MacArthur Highway; the Bluestar Communication Center on Don Juico Ave near the Oasis Hotel and on Malabañas Rd in the Premiere Hotel; Checkmark Consulting Services on Santol Rd, Clarkview (24 hour service); and Margaritaville Business Center, Fields Ave.

Telephone There are two area codes for Angeles: 045 and 0455.

Travel Agencies Bookings and reconfirmations of national and international tickets as well as visa extensions can be made at Swagman Travel on Fields Ave, and Mr Ticket, which can be found on Tuesday, Thursday and Saturday afternoon in the restaurant of the Sunset Garden Inn.

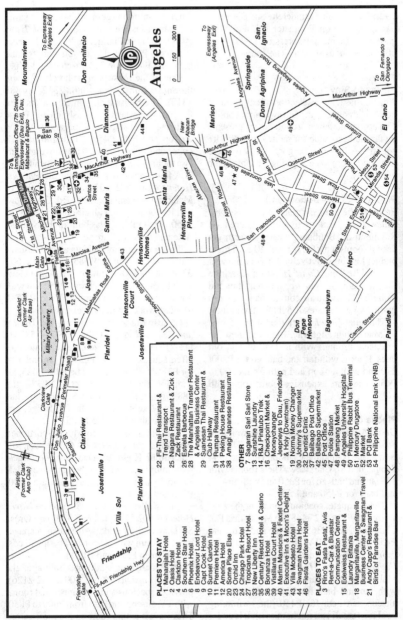

Angeles

PLACES TO STAY
1 Maharajah Hotel
2 Oasis Hotel
4 Clarkton Hotel
5 Southern Star Hotel
6 Phoenix Hotel
8 Endeavour Lord Hotel
9 Capt Cook Hotel
10 Sunset Garden Inn
11 Premiere Hotel
17 Americana Hotel
20 Some Place Else
23 Orchid Inn
24 Chicago Park Hotel
27 Tropicana Resort Hotel
33 New Liberty Inn
35 Century Resort Hotel & Casino
36 Bonanza Hotel
39 Vistilana Court Hotel
40 Marlim Mansions & Faxtel Center
41 Executive Inn & Moon's Delight
44 Swagman Narra Hotel
46 Fiesta Gardens Hotel

PLACES TO EAT
3 Rino's Fasta Pasta, Avis
   Rent-a-Car & Bluestar
   Communication Centre
15 Edelweiss Restaurant &
   Laundry Britania
18 Margaritaville, Margaritaville
   Business Center & Swagman Travel
21 Andi Capp's Restaurant &
   Birds of Paradise Bar

22 Fil-Thai Restaurant &
   Trend Transport
25 Niagara Restaurant & Zick &
   Zack Restaurant
26 Estrella Barbecue
28 The Manhattan Transfer Restaurant
   & Angeles Business Center
29 Suanesan Thai Restaurant &
   Club Halfway
31 Rnnpa Restaurant
34 Peking House Restaurant
38 Amagi Japanese Restaurant

OTHER
7 Sagaran San Sari Store
13 Sunshine Laundry
14 R&J Pinatubo Trek
16 Checkpoint Market &
   Moneychanger
17 Jeepneys to Dau, Friendship
   & Nepo (Downtown)
19 Norma Money Changer
30 Johnny's Supermarket
32 Dentist Clinic
37 Bailbago Post Office
42 Bailbago Supermarket
45 Post Office
47 Police Station
48 Pampang Market
49 Angeles University Hospital
50 Philippine Rabbit Bus Terminal
51 Mercury Drugstore
52 PCI Bank
53 PCI Bank
54 Philippine National Bank (PNB)

Laundry Britania Launderette and Sunshine Laundry, both on Perimeter Rd, and Margaritaville Laundry Express on Fields Ave, offer a two-hour service. The charge is P22 to P25 per kg.

Places to Stay

Angeles has a large selection of comfortable hotels with restaurants and swimming pools. The accommodation around here represents by far the best value for money in the entire country. All rooms are good for two; there just don't seem to be any single rooms in the whole city.

Places to Stay – bottom end

Probably the cheapest place in town is *Some Place Else*, next to the little church on Raymond St, Balibago, where you can get decent rooms with fan for only P125. This is budget lodgings, but value for your money.

The *Vistillana Court Hotel* on Charlotte St, Balibago, has good rooms with fan and bath for P170, with air-con and bath for P270 (with TV) which are all right for the money.

The quiet *New Liberty Inn* (☎ 602 5896) on MacArthur Highway, Balibago, is set in extensive grounds with a stand of big, old trees. Rooms with fan and bath go for P200/270 and with air-con and bath from P300 to P450. The more expensive rooms come with a TV.

Places to Stay – middle

Under Australian management, the well-kept *Southern Star Hotel* (cellular ☎ 0973-714911) is in a lane behind the Clarkton Hotel at 1934 Sampaguita St, Clarkview. Their rooms with TV, fan and bath go for P350 and with air-con and bath for P450 and P500.

The adequate, spacious rooms at the *Premiere Hotel* (☎ 602 3448) on Malabañas Rd, Clarkview, cost P365 with fan and bath, and P450 if you want TV, air-con and bath.

Just across the road and along a bit, the *Endeavour Lord Hotel* (☎ 785 1210) on Malabañas Rd, Plaridel I, has tidy rooms with fan and bath for P350, and with TV, air-con and bath for P450 (the swimming pool is so small you might miss it). It is under

Australian management and the same company runs the nearby *Capt Cook Hotel* (☎ 6024021) on Plaridel St, Plaridel I, where you'll pay P325 for a nice room with fan and bath, and P425 with TV, air-con and bath.

One of the most popular hotels in town, the *Sunset Garden Inn* (☎ 888 2312; fax 888 2310). The Swiss management makes sure the rooms are kept spotlessly clean. Those with fan and bath cost P365 and with TV, air-con and bath P450. Accommodation is quite comfortable here, and they have an exercise room. Reservations are recommended.

A few steps down the road, the *Phoenix Hotel* (☎/fax 602 2074) on the corner of Malabañas Rd and Perimeter Rd, Clarkview, will let you a room with air-con and bath for P550. The building was built in the Spanish style and is in good shape.

The rooms are immaculate at the German-run *Clarkton Hotel* (☎ 785 1231; fax 602 0784) at 620 Don Juico Ave, Clarkview. With fan and bath they charge P250 and with TV, air-con and bath from P475 to P1200. You can work out in their exercise room.

Close to MacArthur Highway, the *Tropicana Resort Hotel* (cellular ☎ 0973-758731; fax 713116) at 151 Fields Ave, Balibago, offers squeaky clean rooms with fan and bath for P375, with air-con and bath for P425, all with TV. The *Orchid Inn* (☎ 602 0370; fax 888 2708) at 109 Raymond St, Balibago, has nice, well-kept rooms with TV, fridge, air-con and bath from P475 to P525.

The pleasant, generously proportioned *Woodland Park Hotel* (☎ 602 3529), off MacArthur Highway, Dau, has the largest swimming pool of any hotel in Angeles. Rooms with TV, air-con and bath are P520, P620 and P800.

The well-maintained *Swagman Narra Hotel* (☎ 602 5133; fax 602 5231) on Orosa St, Diamond, is under Australian management. A room with air-con and bath will cost you between P575 and P1200.

On MacArthur Highway, Balibago, the *Marlim Mansions* (☎ 602 2002, 602 2126), provides spacious and well appointed rooms with TV, air-con and bath from P600 to P850. They have a tennis court on the roof.

Past the Oasis Hotel on the north-west edge of town, the *Maharajah Hotel* (☎ 602 2372) on Texas St, Villa Sol, is a biggish place with fairly good rooms with air-con and bath for P600/660.

Places to Stay – top end

On Don Juico Ave, Clarkview, the *America Hotel* (☎ 785 1023; fax 785 1022), will put you up in a comfortable room with TV, air-con and bath for P675, with TV and fridge for P895 and in a suite for P1320 and P1875 with jacuzzi, fridge and TV.

Enjoy peace and quiet at the pleasant *Oasis Hotel* (☎ 602 3301; fax 602 3164) at Clarkville Compound, where comfortable and tastefully furnished singles with air-con and bath go for P800, doubles with air-con and bath for P960, and suites for P1150.

Places to Eat

Thanks to the former American air base, Angeles not only has a large selection of comfortable hotels but also a wide range of international restaurants. Almost all the restaurants listed below offer an inexpensive menu of the day and serve Filipino dishes in addition to their individual specialities.

A first-class place to go for outstanding steaks is the *Maranao Grill Restaurant* in the Oasis Hotel, a well-run establishment also frequented by up-market Filipinos. The *Swiss Steak House*, one floor above the Black Jack Bar near the basketball court, is also known for its steaks. You can sit outside on the balcony here and watch the world go by. The *Manhattan Transfer Restaurant* on MacArthur Highway near Fields Ave specialises in American cooking. Several hotel restaurants, including the *Swagman Narra Hotel Restaurant*, feature Australian food.

Austrian, German and Swiss food can be found at the *Edelweiss* near the checkpoint, *Zick & Zack* on Santos St, the rough and ready *Estrella Barbecue* on Fields Ave, the *Panorama Restaurant* at the Clarkton Hotel and the *Sunset Garden Inn Restaurant*, while *Rino's Fasta Pasta* on Don Juico Ave offers Italian cuisine.

AROUND MANILA

Dau

PLACES TO STAY		
17	Woodland Park Hotel	

PLACES TO EAT	
1	Jollibee
2	Dunkin Donuts
4	Michael's Fast Food & Coffee Shop
8	Shakey's Pizza & KFC
10	Barrio Fiesta Restaurant
13	McDonald's
14	Nangking Chinese Restaurant & Philippine National Bank (PNB)

16	Rosie's Diner
19	American Legion Restaurant

OTHER	
3	Buses to North Luzon
5	Partas Bus Stop
6	Philippine Rabbit Bus Stop
7	Victory Liner Bus Stop
9	Buses to Manila
11	Caltex Petrol Station
12	Northwest Airlines
15	Nita's Handcraft
18	Immigration Office

Those who are partial to Japanese cooking will appreciate the *Amagi Restaurant* on MacArthur Highway. Just across the road and along a bit, the *Peking House Restaurant* serves inexpensive Chinese food. *Andy Capp's*, one floor above the Birds of Paradise Bar on Fields Ave, specialises in Indian curries. Just across the road, the *Fil-Thai Restaurant* provides good, standard Thai fare as does the *Suanesan Thai Restaurant* not far from there.

Definitely to be recommended is the popular *Margaritaville* which is open and busy round the clock. The menu offers a wide choice of fare, with excellent Thai dishes from P50 in addition to American and Filipino food. The inexpensive snack stands at the basketball court next to the Chicago Park Hotel (such as *Heidi's*, with outstanding chicken curry for P25) are becoming more and more popular.

The standard temples of fast food, such as *McDonald's*, *KFC*, *Shakey's Pizza*, *Jollibee* and *Rosie's Diner* can be found around the Expressway junction in Dau, just north of Angeles..

Entertainment

There are countless bars along Fields Ave and Santos St. Some of them are fairly basic but you will find a few elaborately decorated karaoke clubs which have opened up since the American withdrawal and are mostly frequented by Filipinos. On the other hand, the number of discos has been cut drastically. Of the few left, the *Music Box* next to the Chicago Park Hotel is probably the most popular.

You can enjoy oldies and country & western music every night in the *Midnight Rodeo* on Santos St, and the *Club Halfway* in Fields Ave has excellent entertainment, with first-class showbands for P100 admission.

For a very late (or early) drink, *Margaritaville* on Fields Ave, is the place to go. It's open 24 hours and is busy all the time.

Getting There & Away

Bus From Manila, several Philippine Rabbit buses run daily to Angeles (P50; 1½ hours). Be careful about buses which are not marked 'Expressway/Dau', as these follow side streets and make lots of stops. You can also take a bus from any of the companies – Philippine Rabbit, Victory Liner, Partas, Fariñas or Maria de Leon Trans – to Baguio, Laoag, Vigan, San Fernando (La Union), Dagupan or Alaminos, get out at Dau and go the short way back to Angeles by jeepney or tricycle. To go from Angeles to Manila you can get a Philippine Rabbit bus at its terminal in Angeles or catch a bus in Dau coming from North Luzon.

Convenient air-con buses are also operated by various hotels from Manila to Angeles (two hours) and return (P200, to Ninoy Aquino International Airport P300).

The Blue Bus leaves Manila daily at 10.30 am and 5.30 pm (except Monday and Sunday when it's 7.30 pm; this bus leaves the airport at 6.30 pm) from the Centrepoint Hotel, Mabini St, Ermita, for the Sunset Garden Inn, returning at 8 am and 1.30 pm (except Monday and Sunday, when it's 3 pm; this bus carries on to the airport).

Another air-con bus leaves Manila daily at 11.30 am, 3.30 and 8 pm (Wednesday 9 pm) from the Swagman Hotel, A Flores St, Ermita, for the Swagman Narra Hotel, returning at 8 am, noon and 3 pm. An airport service is offered after arrival at the Swagman Hotel in Manila for P100.

Another air-con bus leaves Manila daily at noon and 7 pm from the Birdwatchers Bar, A Flores St, Ermita for the Southern Star Hotel, returning from Angeles at 9 am and 3 pm (at 6 pm from the Birdwatchers Bar to the airport).

From Subic to Angeles, an air-con bus leaves daily at 9 am for the Endeavour Lord Hotel and Southern Star Hotel, returning at noon (P200; two hours). Another air-con bus leaves Subic daily at 12.30 pm for the Swagman Narra Hotel, returning at 10 am.

Hourly Victory Liner buses run from Olongapo to Angeles daily (two hours). In Olongapo you can also get a Manila bus; get off before San Fernando (Pampanga) and wait for a bus or jeepney to Angeles.

Victory Liner buses run from Baguio to Angeles hourly every day from 5.30 am to 5 pm

(P103; 4½ hours). They are the ones marked 'Olongapo'. Buses from other companies such as Philippine Rabbit and Victory Liner travel from Baguio to Manila via Dau; it is just a short way from Dau to Angeles by jeepney or tricycle. Similarly, to go from Angeles to Baguio it's best to go to Dau and get on one of the buses from Manila.

Numerous buses of various companies travel daily from Laoag, Vigan and San Fernando (La Union) to Dau on the way to Manila. If you get out in Dau, it's only a short way by jeepney or tricycle to Angeles. To go from Angeles to San Fernando (La Union), Vigan or Laoag, it's best to go to Dau and get on the buses coming through from Manila.

Car & Motorcycle An air-con taxi from Manila to Angeles costs around P600 if the meter is running correctly. Set prices of between P800 and P1000 are normal and quite acceptable. An air-con limousine, eg from Nissan Car Lease, costs US$60 or P1500 from the international airport to Angeles (plus a P100 tip that the driver expects). The ticket counter is before the exit at the arrivals level.

Avis Rent-a-Car (cellular ☎ 300 9477) has an office on Don Juico Ave, Clarkview, between Clarkton and Oasis Hotels.

Trend Transport (☎ 785 1712) on Fields Ave will rent motorcycles for P500 to P600 a day.

Getting Around

Bus Apart from hotel buses, all buses stop in Dau, roughly two km north of Angeles where you can catch a jeepney (P2) back to town. A tricycle from Dau to one of the Angeles hotels listed here will cost P20 to P30, depending on the distance.

Jeepneys & Tricycles It's a waste of time looking for taxis in Angeles. Jeepneys charge normal fares, but beware of Special Rides: they can turn out costly! Tricycles are comparatively expensive: P10 to P30. Filipinos do pay less than this.

MT PINATUBO

For many of those involved, the violent eruption of Mt Pinatubo on 15 June 1991 was like a bad dream.

The clouds of steam and detritus produced by the eruption shot up to 40 km into the stratosphere, darkening the sky. Brilliant flashes of lightning rent the daytime darkness eerily, accompanied by rolling thunder and frightening, seemingly endless, earthquakes. Unbelievable amounts of ash and sand settled in wide areas around the volcano, stones the size of fists flew through the air and, to top it all off, a powerful typhoon chose this of all times to lash North Luzon violently. As a result of the heavy rainfall, awe-inspiring avalanches of *lahar* (mud) raced down the hillsides, demolishing bridges, shoving houses aside like toys, and burying entire villages. Most of the Aeta people living on Pinatubo managed to flee down the slopes of the mountain in time to save themselves from being suffocated by the ash falling relentlessly all around them. Many people fled to Manila, unsure whether the volcano would also start to exude deadly, red-hot poisonous gases.

And it had all started so innocently. In April 1991, exactly two months before the big bang, the mountain had quietly rumbled awake, after 600 years of peace nestled into the Zambales Mountains, sending out white clouds of steam which rose gently from a small opening at the side of the actual crater.

Yet only one week later the seismometers which had been hurriedly installed by the volcanologists delivered convincing evidence that pressure was building up in a magma chamber deep inside the volcano, and that slowly but surely magma was rising up through a chimney from the underground reservoir, heading for the crater. As the first major eruptions shook the area on 9 June, no-one could have guessed the inferno that was to follow in the next few days.

It wasn't until the beginning of September that the volcano finally settled down again, allowing the full extent of this natural catastrophe to be estimated: more than 1000 hectares of fertile farmland laid to waste, more than 40,000 houses destroyed, nearly 250,000 people left homeless and nearly 900 fatalities.

Pinatubo Tours

Filipinos, however, don't give up so easily. Although the eruption of Pinatubo had seemed like the end of the world at first, the local population took a quick breather then rolled up their shirt sleeves and got down to making the best of the situation. The idea was to turn the negative event into something positive, and so the concept of having tours to Pinatubo was born. Some said the idea was absurd, but they had to eat their words later. For, as far as tourism is concerned, the eruption of the volcano has not just brought calamity to the Philippines, but has provided the island state with a new attraction. The ash and sand deposited by the eruption in a wide area around Pinatubo has created a magnificent landscape. To the west of Angeles the grey mass of coagulated material can reach heights of up to 20m. The impressive terrain is criss-crossed with bizarre ravines, through which you can wander for hours. Other areas can be better explored with a vehicle, and for those who want to have the big picture, an aircraft will provide the perfect vantage point – it can all be arranged.

Half-Day Hikes It's a good idea to start early, for the heat starts to build up in the ravines from about midday onwards. Ideally you should do this in a small group. Under no circumstances should you set out on your own, as there are innocent looking places with treacherous hot quicksand where a helping hand and a rope would be needed to pull you out.

Several hotels in Angeles offer interesting hikes with experienced guides, eg the Sunset Garden Inn on Malabañas Rd. Tours lasting several hours are also organised by Trend Transport (next to Rick's Café) on Fields Ave and R & J Pinatubo Trek (next to the Park Inn), Perimeter Rd, for about P500 per person.

If you want to hike under your own steam, take a jeepney to Friendship Gate ('F Gate')

and carry on with another jeepney to the village of Sapang Bato (a Special Ride will not be necessary). In Sapang Bato you have to register at the small Information & Registration Office (P50 per group), then you can get going. If you don't use a guide be careful as there are no signposts.

Four hours in the area should be enough to get a first-hand impression of the immense power of nature. Only the most adventurous with mountaineering experience should attempt the eight-km trek to the volcano itself.

It is not possible to give a reliable description of a stable route, as parts of the terrain change out of all recognition during the rainy season due to shifts in the mass of ashes and sand.

Whole-Day Tours The following round trip is no problem with a normal car during the dry season; you can hire a car from Avis. Heading south-west from Angeles towards Porac the first section is a drive of 75 km in all. This stretch takes you through a broad plain once covered by productive sugar cane plantations and now an uneconomic desert, stretching as far as the eye can see. The sight of half-submerged communities can only begin to convey an understanding of what unbelievable quantities of material were spewed out by Pinatubo. From Porac, carry on via Santa Rita to the road for San Fernando. On the right is Bacolor, the half-submerged suburb of San Fernando; you can make a short detour to have a look at it. The exhibition of photographs in Paskuhan Village near San Fernando, the next stop, gives a good visual impression of what happened. You can then take the Expressway or the road back to Angeles. Basic round trips are available at Trend Transport, Fields Ave.

Sightseeing Flights The airstrip of the former Clark Aero Club has been reopened for small aircraft. Omni Aviation offers flights from here with a two-seater Cessna for P2000 per hour. A four-seater aircraft is available for P3500 an hour, but it may have to be ordered from Manila. There are two ultra-lights available for P1500 per hour. It's better to make a reservation (☎ 961 4574; fax 961 4655). Ultra-light aircraft belonging to the Angeles City Flying Club (ACFC), c/o Woodland Park Resort, Lizares St, Dau (☎ 602 3529), all fly directly from the Flight Park of the club itself at MacArthur Highway, Mabiga, Mabalacat (north of Dau). An unhurried short flight usually lasts about 25 minutes and costs P600. One-hour flights that take you further afield are also available. For solo flights a pilot's licence and health certificate are necessary, both of which can be obtained from the ACFC.

When to Go For safety reasons, car tours and hikes should only be attempted in the dry season, the best months being February, March and April. Theoretically, sightseeing flights are possible year-round, except during a typhoon. However, rainy days with lots of low clouds could also ruin any plans you may have had.

Equipment Those sensitive to the sun should wear long-sleeved clothing and preferably some head protection. When hiking, water is absolutely essential (two litres per person for four hours). Please do not leave empty bottles and rubbish in the area.

If going by car, take a tow rope and shovel, as well as a board for supporting the jack in case of a flat tyre.

BATAAN PENINSULA
It's not possible to do a round trip of the Bataan Peninsula. The stretch from Bagac to Olongapo is blocked for military reasons by the Philippines Navy.

On Mt Samat, a little to the south of Balanga, the provincial capital, is Dambana ng Kagitingan, a national monument to the victims of the Battle of Bataan. There is a cross over 90m high from which you get a good view over the former battlefield and Manila Bay.

A large part of the south of the peninsula is industrialised. Most of the almost 650 manufacturing plants in the province, including the biggest, are in the Export Processing Zone in Mariveles, where textiles,

clocks, electrical appliances and car parts are made. Logging will also become important in the future: Tree Resources and Environmental Enterprises (TREE) has already planted half a million trees on Bataan.

Getting There & Away
Bus Lots of Philippine Rabbit buses leave Manila daily for Balanga, Mariveles and Morong. Most go to Balanga. The travelling time to Mariveles is three hours.

Several Victory Liner buses run daily from Olongapo to Balanga (1½ hours).

Note: During the rainy season the trip can take longer, as parts of the road from San Fernando to Olongapo are often blocked by mudslides from Mt Pinatubo.

OLONGAPO
Olongapo used to be where the 7th Fleet of the US Navy was stationed. In 1991 the Philippine senate made the momentous decision not to extend the Military Bases Agreement (MBA) which had regulated the lease of the bases since the end of WWII. In the meantime, the first steps have been taken to turn part of the former military area into a busy industrial zone. Other areas have been earmarked for the development of tourism, among them what's left of the rainforest, in fact an area where Ayta tribesmen used to train US marines in jungle survival. It is specifically being set aside for eco-tourists and adventure seekers. This is not a bad idea, considering it would put an end to the total deforestation being planned by the gentlemen with chainsaws. A tour through the Jungle Environmental Survival Training Camp (JEST) costs P250.

The economic forecast for Olongapo and Subic Bay has been efficiently promoted, not least by Richard Gordon, the ambitious former mayor of Olongapo and present chairman of the Subic Bay Metropolitan Authority (SBMA). He even speaks of creating a new Singapore and has had a model constructed of his vision for the area.

The former base itself was turned into Subic Bay Freeport after the US Navy withdrew. Hotels, restaurants, swimming pools, tennis courts, casino, duty-free shops and such like are among the attractions. Just like the old days when the Americans were still here, access is over the river bridge at the end of Magsaysay Drive. Visitors must show ID and sign in.

From Olongapo you can easily do a day trip to Mt Samat on the Bataan Peninsula. Take a Victory Liner bus from Olongapo to Balanga and from there go on by jeepney or minibus to the Mt Samat turn-off. The last seven km you have to hike uphill. A hat is recommended.

Olongapo is also a good starting point for trips with a rented car, to the Mt Pinatubo area for instance, or along the Zambales coastline.

Information
Tourist Office There is a tourist office in Building 29, Subic Bay Freeport Zone (☎ 222 3503).

Telephone The area code for Olongapo is 047.

Places to Stay
The *Ram's Inn* at 765 Rizal Ave has reasonable rooms with fan for P150 and with air-con for P200.

The *Moonstone Apartments* (☎ 222 5301) at Rizal Ave has seen better days. It has doubles with air-con and bath from P770 to P840. TV costs P40 extra. Apartments cost P900 and P1250. It is near the big market, a few minutes on foot from the Victory Liner bus terminal in the direction of Manila.

South of the centre, on land belonging to the former base, *Subic Bay International Hotel* (☎ 888 2288) Santa Rita Rd, Subic Bay Freeport Zone is probably the best accommodation in Olongapo. They charge P2000 to P4700 for rooms with air-con and bath.

Getting There & Away
Air Air Philippines flies daily from Manila to Olongapo and back (P450; 30 minutes).

Bus From Manila, several Victory Liner buses leave the bus terminal in Caloocan City (the Rizal Ave Extension) for Olongapo

daily, and also from Pasay City (Edsa) (P60; two to three hours). There are also several Victory Liner buses from Alaminos to Olongapo daily (five hours).

Victory Liner buses run roughly every hour from 5.30 am to 5.30 pm daily between Baguio and Olongapo, and it is possible to board them at Angeles. In Angeles you can also catch a San Fernando jeepney, get out at the turn-off to Olongapo and wait for the next bus. Travelling time from Baguio is six hours (P110); from Angeles, it takes two hours. Victory Liner buses run several times a day from San Fernando to Olongapo (1½ hours).

Car Avis Rent-a-Car has an office at the Subic Sports Plaza, Perimeter Rd (☎ 222 3873) and at the Subic Bay International Hotel, Santa Rita Rd, Subic Bay Freeport Zone (☎ 252 3152).

Budget Rent-a-Car (☎ 233 2609, 233 4122) can be found at 38 Magsaysay Drive.

Boat The Grand Seaway Ferries' MV *Eagle Ferry* leaves Manila for Olongapo daily at 10 am and 3.30 pm from the Cultural Center Complex on Roxas Blvd (2 hours; P130). The boat departs from Olongapo daily at 7 am and 1pm from Subic Bay Freeport Zone.

Getting Around
The Airport The Subic international airport (Cubi airport) is on a peninsula five km south of Olongapo. Jeepneys and shuttle buses do the run between the main gate to Subic Bay Freeport and the airport.

BARRIO BARRETTO & SUBIC
The withdrawal of the US Navy didn't just mean the end of an era in Olongapo, but also in Barrio Barretto and Subic, both of which were almost completely economically dependent on the American base. Attempts are now being made to attract tourists and investors to the facilities left behind on the former base. Both places have an assortment of hotels and entertainment facilities. Apart from Olongapo, Barrio Barretto and Subic will probably have a future as centres for wreck diving: see also Subic Bay below.

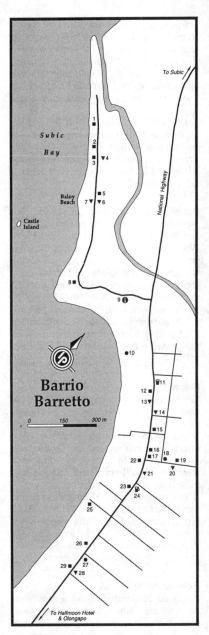

PLACES TO STAY
1 The Set
2 Sandy's Place
3 Pynes Inn & Restaurant
5 El Peso Inn & El Peso Café
8 Heaven Too
12 Bart's Resort Hotel
15 Samori Hotel
16 Dryden Hotel
17 Subic Bay Garden Inn & Subic Bay
   Garden Coffee Shop
19 Marmont Resort Hotel
22 By the Sea Inn, By the Sea Restaurant,
   By the Sea Travel & Tours & Buses to
   Angeles
23 Mariott Hotel
25 Suzuki Beach Hotel
26 Casa Monte Hotel
29 Hotel California

PLACES TO EAT
4 La Casa Verde Restaurant
6 Mr Pumpernickel
7 Beach Boulevard Café
13 Mango's Beach Bar & Restaurant
14 Swiss Tavern
20 VFW
21 Vives Pizza Restaurant
28 Coffee Shop

OTHER
9 Tourist Information
10 Palladium Beach Resort
11 Midnight Rambler
18 Marmont Fitness Center
24 Caltex Petrol Station
27 Swagman Travel

AROUND MANILA

Telephone
Overseas calls can be made from the travel agents By the Sea Travel & Tours.

The area code for Barrio Barretto and Subic is 047.

Travel Agency Reservations and confirmations of national and international flights can be made at Swagman Travel, 30 National Highway (☎ 222 4610). They also take care of visa extensions.

Diving
Information on diving courses and wreck diving in Subic Bay is available at Capt'n Gregg's Dive Shop, National Highway and at Subic Bay Aqua Sports, Building 249, Waterfront Rd, Subic Bay Freeport Zone, Olongapo (☎ 252 7343; fax 813 5677).

Places to Stay

Barrio Barretto At Baloy Beach, *Heaven Too* is a bit rough and ready. Rooms with fan cost P200. The *Pynes Inn* (☎ 222 5755) has well-appointed rooms with fan and bath for P250. They all have beautiful balconies overlooking the bay.

At 61 National Highway, *Casa Monte Hotel* (☎ 222 4628) provides rooms with fan, bath and TV for P250, and with air-con and bath for P300. Refrigerators cost P50 extra. A 20% discount is given on the weekly rate which is payable in advance. The accommodation is OK, but a bit tired looking.

Actually a motel with rooms of varying standard, the *Mariott Hotel* at 85 National Highway (☎ 222 4580) has cottages for P350, and rooms with air-con and bath for P600 and P650. The cottages are fine, if a bit small and without baths.

On the corner of National Highway and Montelibano St, the *Subic Bay Garden Inn* (☎ 222 4550) has good rooms with air-con, bath and TV for P400, some have a refrigerator. The eponymous garden is a bit on the small side.

Bart's Resort Hotel (☎ 223 4148; fax 223 4149) at 117 National Highway has pleasant rooms with fan and bath (and sea view) for P400 and with air-con, bath and TV for P490 and 650. The grounds are small but in good condition, as is the swimming pool.

At 99 National Highway, the *By the Sea Inn* (☎ 222 4560; fax 222 2718), offers a whole selection of comfortable rooms with air-con, bath, refrigerator and TV from P400 to P1300. Accommodation in the new wing is better than in the older one. It has a good restaurant which is open round the clock.

Next to the Subic Bay Garden Inn, the *Dryden Hotel* (☎ 222 4547) at 58 National Highway is a quiet, clean place where rooms with air-con and bath cost P600.

The *Halfmoon Hotel* (☎ 222 4987; fax 222 4918) on National Highway has rooms with TV, air-con and bath from P750 to P1350 set in beautiful grounds. The rooms looking down on the pool are the quietest. There is a P30 charge for non-residents to use the pool.

In Montelibano St, the *Marmont Resort Hotel* (☎ 222 3791; fax 222 5571) has rooms with air-con, bath and TV from P900 and suites from P2600. It also has monthly rates. The accommodation is comfortable, although parts of the building could use redecorating. They have a swimming pool; non-residents pay P50 admission.

Directly on the water a bit off the road, the *Suzuki Beach Hotel* on National Highway is the best hotel in Barrio Barretto. They have immaculate rooms with air-con and bath for P1500 and P2000, the better ones looking down on Subic Bay.

Subic The *Bamboo Inn*, Calapacuan, provides good rooms with fan and bath for P500 and with TV, air-con and bath for P800. Weekly and monthly rates are available. The attraction here is the Bambooza Floating Bar, and they also have a good restaurant.

Set in pleasant, well-maintained grounds, the *White Rock Resort Hotel* (☎ 222 2398, 222 2398) has singles with air-con and bath for P2650 and doubles with air-con and bath for P3350. They have a restaurant and swimming pool, and admission for day visitors is P30.

Places to Eat

The *By the Sea Restaurant* in the hotel of the same name on the National Highway has excellent food.

The *Swiss Tavern* predictably enough offers Swiss cuisine, and the *Coffee Shop* gives you value for your peso with a wide selection of Philippine and international dishes (try the crispy tacos).

Just over from the Marmont Hotel, the pub-restaurant *VFW* (The Veterans Bar) serves American food. There are more restaurants at Baloy Beach, including *Mr. Pumpernickel* with good German food, the *Beach Boulevard Café* and *El Peso Café*.

Entertainment

Along the National Highway a handful of bars has survived the withdrawal of the Americans, fortunately including the *Midnight*

Rambler, where super music, great sound and good drinks add up to a fantastic atmosphere.

Getting There & Away
Bus From Olongapo to Barrio Barretto, you can take the Victory Liner buses which go to Iba, Santa Cruz and Alaminos.

Jeepney Several Blue Jeepneys run daily from Olongapo to Barrio Barretto (five km) and Subic (12 km). But look out – this is a happy hunting ground for pickpockets. The trip takes 15 minutes.

AROUND OLONGAPO, BARRIO BARRETTO & SUBIC
Subic Bay
Three hundred years after they conquered Manila, the Spaniards decided to build an arsenal in Olongapo. Until that time they had simply not taken any notice of the strategic importance of the deep bay at Subic and had anchored their ships near Cavite, where they were also repaired and fitted out. With the outbreak of the Spanish-American War at the end of the 19th century, Subic Bay was planned to be extended and built into the most important naval base in the Philippines. But the idea never got past the planning stage. Before the defensive cannon positioned on Grande Island at the narrow inlet to Manila Bay could be readied to fire, the Americans attacked the Spanish fleet in the bay and totally destroyed it.

In 1900 the Americans began to build Subic Bay into a naval station. They towed in an enormous floating dry dock and a support base for the navy was constructed. During WWII the Japanese occupied Olongapo and Grande Island but had to retreat at the beginning of 1944 after suffering heavy losses. The victorious Americans consolidated their claim to various bases on the Philippines in the 1947 Military Bases Agreement with the Philippine government which granted them rights to use Subic Bay and the surrounding coastal waters for 99 years.

In the 1950s, Cubi airport was built on an artificial peninsula. A gigantic undertaking for its time, this required not only piling up enormous quantities of earth, but hauling away an entire mountain.

The Vietnam War set new standards for Subic Bay. On average, 30 warships anchored daily in the bay, several thousand American military personnel were stationed there, and the number of Philippine support staff rose to 15,000.

In 1979 the 1947 agreement was amended: the Americans transferred the sovereign right to the bases to the Filipinos, and their usage rights were codified in a lease agreement which was set to expire in 1991. The use of Subic Bay was to bring in US$500 million a year to the Philippine state.

Although the eruption of Mt Pinatubo in June 1991 resulted in the destruction of numerous facilities in the Subic Bay Naval Station, the Americans wanted to continue using the military base. However, the Philippine government turned down an extension of the agreement in September 1991 but, as a compromise, granted the Americans three years to withdraw from Subic Bay.

Since the lifting of military restrictions, Subic Bay has become a top-class diving area for wreck divers. There are at least 20 wrecks on the ocean floor, among them the battle cruiser USS *New York*, built in 1891 (sunk in 1941; depth 27m), the Japanese passenger ship *Oryoku Maru* (sunk in 1944; depth 20m), and the Japanese freighter *Seian Maru* (sunk in 1945; depth 27m).

Subic Bay Tours By The Sea Travel & Tours in Barrio Barretto (☎ 222 4558) organises boat trips (four hours; P400 per person, minimum of three passengers).

Grande Island
Grande Island is at the entrance to Subic Bay, about 40 minutes by boat from Olongapo. Up until the withdrawal of the US Navy, only Americans were allowed to visit the island, which was used as an R & R resort. It is now open to the public, although it is used almost exclusively by locals.

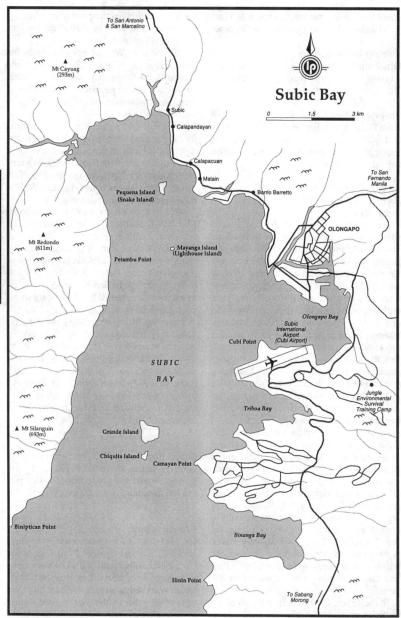

Getting There & Away

A day tour from Olongapo to Grande Island costs P875, including the trip there and back, a complimentary drink on arrival, lunch buffet and use of the facilities. Departure from SBMA in Olongapo, Fleet Landing. Reservations can be made in Olongapo (☎ 223 3401).

Mt Pinatubo

Just as in Angeles, Barrio Barretto and Olongapo are good starting points for tours of Pinatubo.

Sightseeing Flights Flights with a Cessna 180 to Pinatubo can be booked at Subic Bay Aqua Sports, Building 249, Waterfront Rd, Subic Bay Freeport Zone, Olongapo (☎ 252 3005, 252 7343).

Pinatubo Lake

The so-called Pinatubo Lake, or New Lake, at Buhawen was created by damming caused by lava flowing unchecked into the valley. All that remains of the little town of Buhawen is a bell tower, the school and the rooftops of various houses sticking forlornly out of the waters. Above the lake a dam can be made out which was constructed by the local Benguet-Dizon Mining Company. If it were to burst, it would probably mean the destruction of all the towns and villages in the valley right down to the coast. An employee of the company accompanies visitors from the checkpoint to the lake and gives them a little tour when there.

Getting There & Away Occasionally, By the Sea Travel & Tours, Barrio Barretto (☎ 222 4558) organises trips to the Pinatubo Lake for P450 per person. It is possible to make the trip by hire car, for example from Avis in Olongapo. From Barrio Barretto, head for San Marcelino via Subic. When there, turn right for San Rafael then go up the road towards Buhawen along the wide riverbed of the Marbella River to the lake. The road from San Marcelino to Buhawen is quite dusty, so it would be better to drive in an enclosed vehicle rather than an open jeep. Remember: Mudslides on Pinatubo caused by heavy rainfall can change the entire landscape, including the way up to the lake.

North Luzon

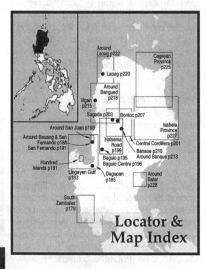

Around Laoag p222
Cagayan Province p225
Laoag p220
Around Bangued p218
Vigan p215
Sagada p203   Bontoc p207
Around San Juan p193   Isabela Province p227
Around Beuang & San Fernando p188   Halsema Road p199   Central Cordillera p201
San Fernando p191   Banaue p210
Baguio p195   Around Banaue p213
Hundred Islands p181   Baguio Centre p196
Lingayen Gulf p183   Dagupan p185   Around Baler p228
South Zambales p179

Locator & Map Index

At over 100,000 sq km, Luzon is the largest island in the Philippines and is home to about half of the country's population. Luzon dominates economic and cultural affairs in the country and has many tourist attractions.

Most impressive are the Mountain and Ifugao Provinces, with their rice terraces and numerous ethnic minorities, but many travellers are attracted to the Hundred Islands National Park and the beaches on Lingayen Gulf. The cultivated provinces of Ilocos Norte and Ilocos Sur with old Spanish churches, sand dunes and the historic town of Vigan are less frequently visited.

The West Coast

THE ZAMBALES COAST

The mountainous province of Zambales borders on the South China Sea to the west. The coast between San Antonio and Iba has a number of beaches, some of which are over several km long and some have accommodation. Dasol Bay, about 80 km north of Iba, has fine beaches that have not been visited much, such as Tambobong White Beach, 15 km outside Dasol. Also remarkable are the extensive salt works north of Santa Cruz.

From Manila you can take the direct route to Alaminos and the Hundred Islands National Park, or you can make an interesting detour along the coast road, passing through Olongapo on the way. The catastrophic effects of the Pinatubo eruption are very much in evidence here and will be for years to come.

Getting There & Away
Every day, a number of Victory Liner buses make the trip from Olongapo to Alaminos (five hours), via San Antonio (45 minutes), Botolan (two hours) and Iba (2½ hours). If you want to start from Manila, first of all take a Victory Liner bus, or a ferry, to Olongapo and change there.

San Antonio, Pundaquit & San Miguel
After about an hour's travel from Olongapo, you come to San Antonio, a pleasant little town with a clean market. At least twice a day a jeepney runs the five km from the San Antonio plaza south-west to Pundaquit.

Pundaquit is a small fishing village on an attractive bay with a long beach. Using Pundaquit as a base, you can hire a boat for about P600 to P800 a day to explore the bays that cut deeply into the south coast of Zambales, or day trip to **Camera Island** or **Capones Island**. Both islands have white beaches and are rocky, but parts of Capones Island are covered with palms and bushes. There is a lighthouse at the western end of the island which juts out from the sea like a cathedral. Occasionally a few tourists come here to go diving.

From Pundaquit you can walk along the wide beach to San Miguel and beyond, after crossing a fairly shallow river.

NORTH LUZON

Places to Stay There is no accommodation directly on the beach at San Antonio; the following two places are in nearby San Miguel. Basic rooms with fan and bath at the *San Miguel Hotel* in San Miguel go for P150 and with air-con and bath for P250. The intriguingly named *Big Foot Resthouse* also in San Miguel is a pleasant place to stay and a lot better than the San Miguel. They will provide you with a room with fan and bath for P170 and with air-con and bath for P300 (with TV P320).

The quiet little *Capones Beach Resort* on Pundaquit beach (☎ 632 7495; fax 631 7989) offers adequate, practically furnished rooms with fan and bath for P500, and with fridge, air-con and bath for P700. Prices are subject to a 40% discount from July until October. The restaurant is one of these places where you end up spending more than you wanted to. Billiards and diving are available.

Places to Eat The *Meathouse Carlsberg Garden Restaurant* in San Miguel serves both Filipino and German dishes. You may be lucky and get live music with your meal at the *San Miguel Restaurant* which prepares good Filipino food.

In San Antonio you can eat cheaply at the market.

Botolan
Until the last eruption of Pinatubo, Botolan was a good base to visit the Negrito of the Zambales Mountains. Former weapon carriers (old lorries) used to leave this little place about seven km south of Iba to go inland to Maguisguis or Villar – maybe they have started doing that again. However, the Ayta-Negrito have lost their ancestral living area, some of them having been evacuated to other islands, like Mindoro.

Places to Stay The pleasant, tidy *Fil-Aussie Lodge* at Binoclutan is about seven km south of Botolan. It has dorm beds for P75, rooms with fan for P500 and fan and bath for P600, but the price is reduced for longer stays.

Iba
Iba is the capital of Zambales Province. There are several beach resorts a little outside the town but some of these, unfortunately, have gone a bit downhill – except for the prices. Probably the best beach around Iba is the one slightly north of the centre, just behind the airstrip.

The Kalighawan Festival is celebrated here in March of each year with parades, games, beauty contests and agricultural exhibitions.

Telephone The area code for Iba is 047.

Places to Stay Attractively located on a palm-lined, gently curving bay, the cottages at the *Vicar Beach Resort* (☎ 711 4252) cost P450/600 with fan and bath.

About one km north of Iba, the *Sand Valley Beach Resort* (☎ 911 1739) will give you a room with fan and bath for P450 and with air-con and bath for P800. This place is past its peak.

The accommodation is very good at the *Rama International Beach Resort* in Bangantalinga, about four km north of Iba, on National Rd. A fan room costs P350, with fan and bath costs P500/750, and with air-con and bath costs P750/1065. The resort is well maintained, has a restaurant, and diving trips are offered.

LUCAP & ALAMINOS
Lucap is a relatively small place on the Gulf of Lingayen. It is the starting point for the **Hundred Islands National Park**. Lots of local tourists come here during Easter week when hotels may be booked out. There is not much happening here for night owls, as the few restaurants close at 10 pm.

Entertainment in nearby Alaminos is limited to bowling and discos. On Sunday there are cockfights a little outside of town. You can do trips from Alaminos to Agno, Sabangan Beach, with its Umbrella Rocks, or Colaya, where there is a subterranean river in the **Nalsoc Caves**. To get there, take a jeepney to Bani, then go on to Tiep and continue by tricycle (for about P30) to Colaya.

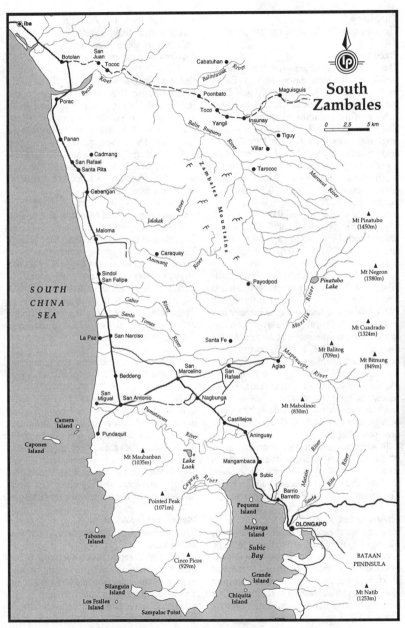

Telephone
The area code for Alaminos is 075.

Places to Stay
The following prices are valid during the off season. For the high season, which is Easter week and the weekends in April and May, some hotels raise their tariffs 50% to 100%.

Most of the accommodation is in Lucap. The *Kilometre One Tourist Lodge* has basic singles/doubles with fan for P150/250. It also serves as a youth hostel. *Gloria's Cottages* is longer in the best condition, but is acceptable for the money. Clean and spacious rooms with fan cost P150/200 and with fan and bath P200/300. Right opposite, the *Ocean View Lodge* (cellular ☎ 0912-320 5579) has rooms with fan for P200/225, with fan and bath for P250/300 and with air-con and bath for P700. It is well kept and has a restaurant.

At the *Hundred Islands View Lodge* (cellular ☎ 0912-3146180) rooms with fan and bath are P350/550 and with air-con and bath P450/750; it has a restaurant and karaoke bar.

There is a beautiful roofed-over patio restaurant right on the water at *Maxine by the Sea* (cellular ☎ 0912-304 9461), where neat, down-to-earth rooms with fan cost P250 and with air-con and bath P550. Don't be misled by the name, because *The Last Resort* needn't be your last resort. Rooms with fan and bath are fairly good value at P350, and with air-con and bath P450. Boating facilities are available.

In Alaminos, the pleasant *Alaminos Hotel* (☎ 552 7241) on Quezon Ave has singles with fan for P120, doubles with fan and bath for P180 and with air-con and bath for P450. The rooms are in fairly good condition.

Places to Eat
You can eat cheaply in Lucap at the small *Canteens* by the wharf, but some of the lodge restaurants, such as the *Ocean View Restaurant* and the airy *Maxine by the Sea Restaurant* also have good, inexpensive food. Apart from *The Last Resort Restaurant*, restaurants close quite early on most days, sometimes even by 8 pm.

At Alaminos, the *Plaza Restaurant* is worth a visit; they also sometimes feature folk singers there. You could also try the *Imperial Restaurant*.

Getting There & Away
Bus Dagupan Bus, Five Star, Philippine Rabbit and Victory Liner buses go hourly every day from Manila to Alaminos (P110; six hours). You may have to change at Lingayen. These buses go via Dau/Angeles (P80; 3½ hours). It is also possible to take a bus from Manila to Dagupan and change there. The advantages are frequent departures and air-conditioning.

Several Victory Liner buses travel daily between Olongapo and Alaminos (five hours).

A few Philippine Rabbit buses travel daily from Baguio to Alaminos (P90; four hours). The last bus will probably leave at about noon. You can also go to Dagupan with the Dagupan Bus company and change there.

To travel from Banaue to Alaminos you will have to take the first Baguio bus early in the morning then get off at Rosario and board a Dagupan, Lingayen or Alaminos bus coming from Baguio.

Tricycle Tricycles between Alaminos and Lucap cost P20 to P25 for up to four people.

HUNDRED ISLANDS
The Hundred Islands are not palm-fringed dream islands, but coral formations of varying sizes with scrub and occasionally small, white beaches. They're of limited appeal for snorkelling as the water is not always crystal clear, often obscuring the reputedly colourful underwater world, which has been damaged by the use of dynamite for fishing.

Places to Stay & Eat
Take adequate food supplies with you if you want to spend a night or several days on an island. The cheapest place for food is the market at Alaminos and you should be able to get a can of water from the hotel at Lucap. The fee for putting up your own tent is P10 a day on Quezon, Governor's and Children's islands. You can rent a so-called pavilion on

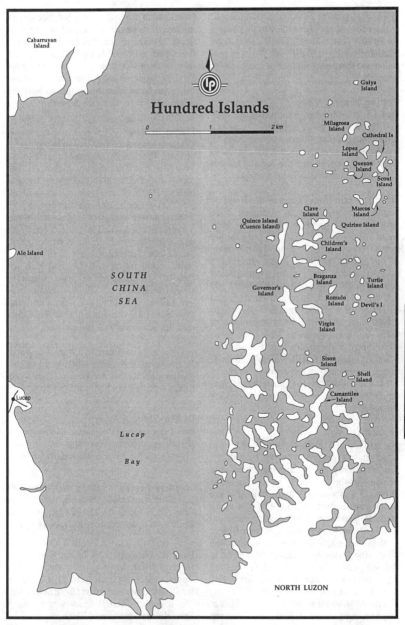

Hundred Islands

0   1   2 km

Cabarruyan
Island

Guiya
Island

Milagrosa
Island

Cathedral Is

Lopez
Island

Quezon
Island

Scout
Island

Marcos
Island

Clave
Island

Quinco Island
(Cuenco Island)

Quirino Island

Children's
Island

Alo Island

SOUTH
CHINA
SEA

Braganza
Island

Turtle
Island

Governor's
Island

Romulo
Island

Devil's I

Virgin
Island

Sison
Island

Shell
Island

Lucap

Camantiles
Island

Lucap

Bay

NORTH LUZON

NORTH LUZON

Quezon Island for P600 or a two-roomed cottage for six people on Governor's Island for P1000. On Children's Island cottages are available for P350 and P900. Water is provided and there are toilets. You can cook for yourself.

Getting There & Away
Bus To get to Hundred Islands National Park you first have to go to Alaminos. There is a direct connection to Alaminos from Manila, but the alternative route along the Zambales coast via Olongapo (see the Around Manila chapter) should also be kept in mind.

Boat The fare from Lucap to the Hundred Islands National Park by outrigger boat, which can take up to six persons, has been fixed officially at P275 plus P5 entry fee per person. It is wise to agree upon the duration of the trip or the driver might return after only 30 minutes. You can also go on an island round trip which will cost you between P100 and P200, depending on the duration and extent of the trip. This makes it possible to choose your 'own' island and be dropped off there, but don't forget to fix a time to be picked up for the return trip. Four or five hours of island life will probably be quite enough, especially when there is no shade. Most day trippers go to Quezon Island, particularly on weekends. You can get drinks at the kiosk there.

BOLINAO
Bolinao is a little town north-west of Lucap, which hasn't yet been overrun by tourists. Unfortunately, there are no acceptable beaches in the area, so you have to drive about 15 km south-west to Patar if it's a beach you're after. Of course, if you really want to get away from it all, you could arrange to cross over to one of the offshore islands, although the woodland near the shore slopes steeply for about 10m down to the sea there. Take your own snorkelling equipment as it is next to impossible to find even a pair of goggles in Bolinao.

The **Bolinao Museum** on the outskirts of town has a collection of Philippine flora and

fauna which is worth a look, but, because of the lack of money, it has only a few historical items. In the town centre is the church, which dates back to 1609. It used to double as a fortress during attacks by pirates and by the English, Japanese and Americans. If you can catch the priest when he is not too busy, he might tell you more about those times.

Places to Stay
Offering basic accommodation in the centre of town, the *A & E Garden Inn*, next to the Five Star Bus Terminal on Mabini St, has rooms with fan for P150/200, with fan and bath for P200/300 and with air-con and bath for P500. A tree house with bath costs P300. The tree-house restaurant here is interesting.

Attractively located on the ocean front only a few metres from the centre of town, the *Celeste Seabreeze Inn* will give you a basic, small room with fan and bath for P250/300. Their pleasant patio restaurant specialises in seafood. They also rent outrigger sailing boats. Right next door, the *Piscador Village Inn* has a big garden restaurant. Basic rooms with air-con and bath go for P500.

Outside of Bolinao in Patar, the *Dutch Beach Resort* is a modern little building in a garden directly on the beach. They have rooms with fan and bath for P600/800.

Getting There & Away
Bus From Manila to Bolinao via Alaminos (P160; six hours), Five Star and Victory Liner buses run several times daily.

Jeepney Several jeepneys and minibuses leave the market at Alaminos for Bolinao daily (P15; one hour). The last jeepney from Bolinao to Alaminos leaves at about 5 pm.

Boat An outrigger boat leaves Bauang for Bolinao (P100; two hours) daily at 4 am. Information can be obtained from the Gatchalian family at the entrance to the China Sea Resort. The departure from Bolinao is at 9 am. A Special Ride costs around P500.

LINGAYEN

Lingayen, which dates back to about 1611, is the capital of Pangasinan Province. It is a mixture of old and new - the church, town plaza and the group of spruce buildings around them date back to Spanish colonial times, while its modern face is provided by the Capitol Building and other rather boring buildings. The old town is on the road leading from Alaminos to Dagupan; the new town is about a km north of it towards the coast.

Lingayen Beach is outside the town. As on other well-known but not particularly impressive beaches at the southern end of the Lingayen Gulf, you will find many Filipinos from smog-plagued Manila here in search of recreation.

Not quite five km east of Lingayen, the little town of Binmaley is home to an impressive church and many little workshops where furniture in colonial style is manufactured.

Telephone

The area code for Lingayen is 075.

Places to Stay

Although the building has suffered considerable earthquake damage, the *Viscount Hotel*

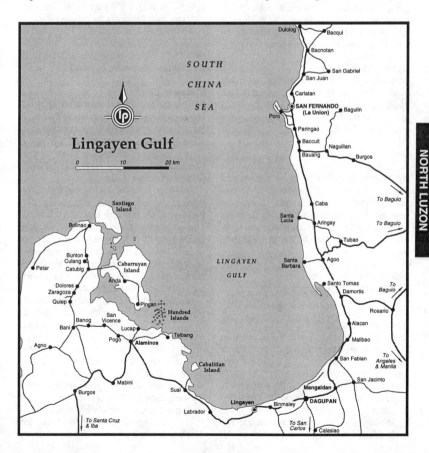

on Alvear St has acceptable rooms with fan and bath for P250 and with air-con and bath for P350.

The rooms are a bit small at the clean *Lion's Den Resort* on Lingayen Beach; with fan and bath they cost P350. It has a restaurant, but if you want to buy fresh fish and vegetables in the nearby market, where you can go by tricycle for P2, the hotel restaurant staff will prepare them for about P20. *Letty & Betty Cottages*, also on Lingayen Beach, has rooms or cottages for P200/300.

The pleasant *Lingayen Gulf Resort Hotel* (☎ 542 6304), on the Provincial Capitol ground near the beach, provides comfortable rooms with fan and bath for P500/625, with air-con and bath for P675/900, all with sea views. You can also swim in their pool.

Getting There & Away
Bus Dagupan Bus and Five Star run many buses daily from Manila to Lingayen (P100; 4½ hours) via Dau/Angeles, where you can also board the bus. Alaminos bound buses also stop in Lingayen.

DAGUPAN
In 1590, Augustinian monks declared the community of Bacnotan to be a town and named it Dagupan. It became an important trading and educational centre, eclipsing the provincial capital, Lingayen. Only three km north in Bonuan is Bonuan Beach and adjacent Tondaligan Beach; the trip there by jeepney costs P3.

Telephone
The area code for Dagupan is 075.

Places to Stay
The only decent inexpensive hotel in Dagupan is the *Vicar Hotel* (☎ 522 2616) on AB Fernandez Ave, within walking distance of the various bus terminals. Basic but adequate rooms with fan and bath cost P150/200. The hotel is on the 1st floor of a fairly large building, but the entrance in a passageway can be hard to find.

Slightly more up-market, the central *Victoria Hotel* (☎ 2081) on the corner of AB

Fernandez Ave and Nable St near the bridge over the San Pedro River has attentive staff, recently decorated rooms and acceptable prices. Rooms in the old wing with fan and bath cost P285/325, and with air-con and bath P345/395. Bigger and more comfortable air-con rooms in the new wing cost P500/580.

The trim and friendly *Floren Hotel* (☎ 522 0666) on Rizal St is a pleasant little place. Inviting rooms with air-con, bath and TV cost P650.

The best hotel in the centre of town is the *Star Plaza Hotel* on AB Fernandez Ave (☎ 523 4888; fax 523 4777). Comfortable rooms with air-con, bath and TV cost P650 and from P850 to 2600 for suites facing the river.

About three km outside of Dagupan, on the beach in Bonuan the *Snow White Inn* (☎ 523 4236) has rooms that befit its name for P600, with air-con, bath and TV.

Places to Eat
Pangasinan Province is known for its excellent bangus (milkfish) – said to be the best in the country. They are bred in countless fish ponds between Dagupan and Lingayen. Nearly all the restaurants in town prepare bangus in a variety of ways, eg stuffed or filleted (boneless bangus).

D'Original Dawel is a big, basic, but very popular seafood restaurant at the bridge over the river at the northern end of Arellano St. The menu has no prices, so check the price and weight of fish, shrimps etc when you order. The beach in Bonuan has more seafood restaurants, including *Siapno's Restaurant* and *D'Executives Restaurant*, which are mostly patronised after dark.

In town itself the *Dagupeña Restaurant* on AB Fernandez Ave (near the Vicar Hotel) can be highly recommended. They offer a large selection of Philippine dishes; the house speciality is sizzling boneless bangus for P80. *Aljas Fastfood* has ice-cold beer in addition to standard Philippine fare like adobo (P25) and menudo (P30). If you prefer Chinese cooking, then *Mr Lim* in Arellano St won't disappoint you. It's a very big restaurant.

If you have an appetite for fast-food, then *McDonald's* and *Shakey's Pizza* are in the

CSI Market Square Shopping Center on AB Fernandez Ave, as is the popular *Goldilocks Bake Shop* for coffee and cakes. *Pedro's* in the Floren Hotel, Rizal St, is similar.

Entertainment

Arellano St has restaurants and a row of discos for nightlife. Some offer shows after 10 pm, eg the *Base Disco*, while others, like the *Big Box Disco*, let the guests do the dancing. Admission is around P50.

Getting There & Away

Bus Frequent Dagupan Bus, Five Star and

Victory Liner buses run from Manila to Dagupan (P100; five hours) via Dau/Angeles.

From Bolinao to Dagupan, there are also numerous Dagupan Bus buses available. They take approximately two hours and go via Alaminos.

Minibuses leave Alaminos for Dagupan (one hour) practically every hour.

From Baguio to Dagupan a fleet of buses makes the trip daily, including Byron Bus vehicles leaving every half hour between 6 am and 4 pm, and Dagupan Bus and Philippine Rabbit buses, the last one of which leaves around noon (two hours).

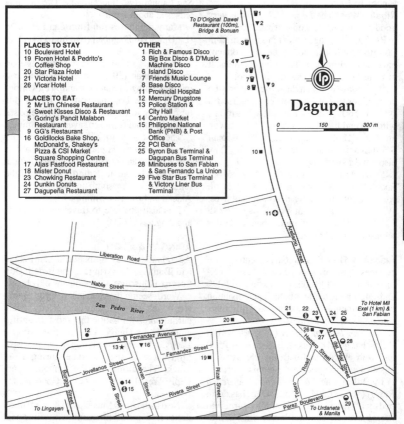

PLACES TO STAY
10 Boulevard Hotel
19 Floren Hotel & Pedrito's Coffee Shop
20 Star Plaza Hotel
21 Victoria Hotel
26 Vicar Hotel

PLACES TO EAT
2 Mr Lim Chinese Restaurant
4 Sweet Kisses Disco & Restaurant
5 Goring's Pancit Malabon Restaurant
9 GG's Restaurant
16 Goldilocks Bake Shop, McDonald's, Shakey's Pizza & CSI Market Square Shopping Centre
17 Aljas Fastfood Restaurant
18 Mister Donut
23 Chowking Restaurant
24 Dunkin Donuts
27 Dagupeña Restaurant

OTHER
1 Rich & Famous Disco
3 Big Box Disco & D'Music Machine Disco
6 Island Disco
7 Friends Music Lounge
8 Base Disco
11 Provincial Hospital
12 Mercury Drugstore
13 Police Station & City Hall
14 Centro Market
15 Philippine National Bank (PNB) & Post Office
22 PCI Bank
25 Byron Bus Terminal & Dagupan Bus Terminal
28 Minibuses to San Fabian & San Fernando La Union
29 Five Star Bus Terminal & Victory Liner Bus Terminal

Dagupan

NORTH LUZON

SAN FABIAN

San Fabian is a friendly little place, a few km north-east of Dagupan. Just outside town, **White Beach** stretches from Nibaliw West to Bolasi. The old name of Center Beach was more accurate. Like almost all beaches in the Lingayen Gulf, the sand is not dazzling white but brownish-grey. A few more resorts are four or five km north-east of San Fabian, on the beach at Bolasi and Alacan, but they have not been developed much for tourism yet.

Telephone

The area code for Dagupan is 075.

Places to Stay

Nibaliw West The *Lazy 'A' Resort* has very good rooms with air-con and bath from P700 to P1650 and cottages with fan and bath from P600 to P2800. The more expensive cottages have two bedrooms and cooking facilities. It has a restaurant and a swimming pool.

If you stay for seven days you will only be charged for five at *Charissa's Beach Houses* (☎ 523 6860). This friendly place lets rooms with fan and bath for P850 and with air-con and bath P1200. An additional 50% discount is offered from June to mid-March. They also have a swimming pool.

Sierra Vista Beach Resort (☎ 523 6843; fax 522 3366) is a small, attractive hotel with solidly built, pleasantly decorated cottages. With air-con and bath you'll pay P1000/1300. They have a swimming pool and offer windsurfing and diving.

Alacan & Bolasi Spacious, slightly worn cottages at the *Windsurf Beach Resort* (cellular ☎ 0918-380 1666) in Alacan cost P390 and P460 with fan and bath. The cuisine in the restaurant is European and Philippine. The manager, Frederic, is Swiss.

The *San Fabian Resort* (☎ 523 6758) in Bolasi has good rooms with air-con for P500 and with air-con and bath for P550/650. It has a swimming pool and a tennis court.

In Bolasi, the *San Fabian PTA Beach Resort* (☎ 523 6504; fax 523 4115) has dorm beds with fan for P225, tastefully furnished rooms with air-con and bath from P670 to

P1550, or the Presidential Suite costs P2900. The last-named is the former San Fabian Presidential Resthouse, where the late President Marcos used to stay when he was travelling through northern Luzon. A swimming pool is one of the pleasures awaiting guests at the resort.

Places to Eat

Miss Saigon in Nibaliw is a novel place, built around a Vietnamese junk. Well worth a visit.

Getting There & Away

Bus Several Dagupan Bus and Byron Bus buses go south from Baguio to Dagupan via San Fabian (two hours) daily. The last one leaves at about 2 pm.

Many minibuses run from San Fernando (La Union) to Dagupan (two hours) via San Fabian.

Many buses also run daily from Dagupan to San Fabian (30 minutes). Take either a minibus going to San Fernando (La Union) or one of the Dagupan Bus or Byron Bus buses going to Baguio. Some of these buses may be coming from Lingayen or Alaminos.

The best way to get from Manila and Angeles to San Fabian is to take a bus heading for San Fernando (La Union), Vigan or Laoag. Get out at Damortis and cover the remaining 15 km south to San Fabian via Alacan and Bolasi by minibus.

It is also possible to travel from Manila and Angeles via Dagupan.

ARINGAY & AGOO

Agoo and Aringay lie between San Fabian and Bauang. In Aringay, the small **Don Lorenzo Museum** is opposite the old church.

Worth seeing in Agoo is the **Agoo Basilica**, which was rebuilt in 1892 after a severe earthquake. Probably the most beautiful church in La Union, it has a Shrine of Our Lady and is the most important place of pilgrimage in the province during Holy Week. The climax of the Semana Santa (Holy Week) activities is the Good Friday procession.

Next to the Agoo Municipal Hall, the **Museo Iloko** is a small museum with liturgical objects, antique furniture and china. Next door, in **Imelda Park**, visitors can pass the time in a beautiful tree house. On the northern outskirts of Agoo a large stone statue of an eagle marks the start of the Marcos Highway, which leads to Baguio. On the way there, near Pugo, is the former **Marcos Park** with golf course, swimming pool, hostel and cottages. Towering over it all is a huge bust of Marcos partly carved into the rock.

Several hundred thousand Filipinos congregated on **Apparition Hill** near Agoo at the beginning of March 1993, to witness the appearance of the Blessed Virgin Mother which had been prophesied. The miracle didn't happen, but even serious newspapers reported that the air was filled with a miraculous fragrance and that thousands of pilgrims had seen the sun dancing.

Places to Stay
The *Agoo Playa Resort* (cellular ☎ 0912-308 2614) has rooms with air-con and bath from P1200/1500. It is attractive, comfortable and beautifully laid out. It has a swimming pool.

Getting There & Away
Bus Numerous Philippine Rabbit, Times Transit, Fariñas Trans and Maria de Leon buses run from San Fernando to Manila via Agoo (one hour).

From Manila, take any bus heading for San Fernando, Vigan or Laoag (five hours).

AROUND BAUANG
Bauang has developed into the most popular beach resort in North Luzon, but nearly all the places to stay are on the long beach between Baccuit and Paringao, a little to the north of Bauang proper and about five km south of San Fernando. You can't see much from the road except a few signposts. If arriving by bus or jeepney, ask the driver or conductor in advance to drop you off at your hotel. If it is full, walk along the beach and you will find plenty of alternative accommodation.

The small White Beach near Poro Point offers snorkelling and is a good alternative to the beach at Bauang.

In **Naguilian**, 10 km east of Bauang, *basi*

(an alcoholic drink made from fermented sugarcane juice) is manufactured, which is reputed to be the best in the country and is especially popular with Ilokanos. The sweet variant of basi tastes a bit like sherry or port.

Information
Travel Agencies Swagman Travel (☎ 415512) on the National Highway handles reservations and confirmation of inland and international flights and visa extensions. It is also the agent for a few resorts.

Telephone The area code for Bauang is 072.

Places to Stay
The following prices apply during the high season from December to May. They are about 25% cheaper in the off season from June to November, so it is worth haggling a bit. The following are only a small cross section, and there are many others.

At the southern end of the beach at Baccuit, the pleasant *Hideaway Beach Resort* (cellular ☎ 0912-311 2421) is a large house with rooms with fan and bath for P280 and with air-con for P400.

Leo Mar Beach Resort at Baccuit has plain but cosy rooms with fan and bath for P350/400. Next door, the *Jac Corpuz Cottages* has rooms with bath from P200 to P300 in basic cottages.

The *Penthouse Resort* (☎ 413708) at Paringao has rooms with fan and bath for P250/350. Good monthly rates are offered.

Near the highway, the *Koala Motel* (☎ 242 0865; fax 415448) at Pagdalagan Sur has OK rooms with fan and bath for P250/395, with air-con and bath for P395/ 450.

Also on the highway, the *Mark Teresa Apartel* (☎ 412084) at Paringao has two-bedroom apartments for P500. It has favourable monthly rates (P3000) but is often booked out. About 700m further north, the *Eastside Hotel & Resort* (☎ 242 0531; fax 242 0528) has pleasant rooms with air-con and bath for P600 and with air-con, bath, TV and fridge for P600.

Built in Mediterranean style, but unfortunately situated in a residential area near the beach, the *Umay Kay Homes* at Pagdalagan Norte is a pleasant place to stay. Spacious, comfortable and tastefully furnished rooms with fan and bath cost P500. Rooms with kitchen cost P750. Monthly rates are possible.

Heading back to the beach, the *Cesmin Beach Cottages* (☎ 412884) at Pagdalagan Sur has cottages with fridge, cooking facilities, air-con and bath from P600 to P800. The monthly rates are favourable. The *Southern Palms Beach Resort* (☎ 415384; fax 415529) also at Pagdalagan Sur has comfortable rooms with air-con and bath from P675 to P1075. The rooms of different sizes have TV, and

some have kitchens. There is also a nightclub on the premises, and a pool.

Further along the beach, the *Fisherman's Wharf Beach Club* (☎ 415384; fax 242 1641) offers rooms with TV, fridge, air-con and bath

PLACES TO STAY
1	Shalom Beach Cottages
2	Oceana Apartments
7	Miramonte Beach Resort
8	Driftwood Resort & Shipside Housing Area
9	Acapulco Beach Resort
10	Ocean Deep
11	Blue Lagoon Resort
12	Sunset Bay Swiss Beach Resort
13	Coral Point Beach Resort
14	Lorenza Beach House
15	Meridian Beach Cottages
16	Natalna Beach Home & Patio del Sol Restaurant
17	California Resort & Rosalia Beach Resort
18	Umay Kay Homes
20	Southern Palms Beach Resort & Stilletto's Nightclub
21	Koala Motel & Tramps Nightclub
22	Cesmin Beach Cottages & Fisherman's Wharf Beach Resort
24	Bali Hai Beach Resort, South Pacific Resort & Sea Breeze
25	Cabaña Beach Resort
26	Eastside Hotel & Resort & Cogon Hut Restaurant
27	China Sea Beach Resort & Coconut Grove Resort
28	Villa Estrella Beach Resort
29	Cresta del Mar Hotel & The Penthouse Resort
30	Mark Teresa Apartel
31	Long Beach Hotel & North Palm Beach Resort
33	Nalinac Beach Resort
35	Jac Corpuz Cottages & Leo Mar Beach Resort
36	Lourdes Beach Homes
37	Bauang Beach Resort & Mendoza Beach Resort
38	Hideaway Beach Resort

PLACES TO EAT
19	Tunuan Ti Bauang Restaurant
32	Jasmine Restaurant

OTHER
3	La Lorma Medical Center
4	Philippine Rabbit Bus Terminal
5	Mascotte Disco
6	Nightclub District
23	Swagman Travel Office
34	Bayside Disco

NORTH LUZON

To Vigan & San Juan

Lingsat
Carlatan
Poro Point
San Fernando Bay
SAN FERNANDO
Poro
White Beach
San Francisco
Airport
SOUTH
Canaoay
San Vicente
CHINA
Pagudpud
Pagdalagan Norte
SEA
Pagdalagan Sur
Paringao

Around Bauang & San Fernando

0   1   2 km

To Bauang (1km) & Manila

Bacuit

To Naguilian & Baguio

for P650 and P750. The rooms, which are in attractive stone-built bungalows built a bit too close together, are pleasant and spacious.

In Paringao, the *China Sea Beach Resort* (☎ 414821; fax 242 0822) will give you a room with fan and bath for P650 and with air-con and bath for P750. The accommodation is pleasant, and the resort has a restaurant, swimming pool and dive shop. Also in Paringao, the sophisticated *Coconut Grove Resort* (☎ 414276; fax 415381) provides comfortable and spacious rooms with air-con and bath from P850 to P1200. They offer a 25% discount from June until November. An interesting feature here is the large outdoor lawn bowling complex, in addition to the swimming pool.

The attractive *Bali Hai Beach Resort* (☎ 412504; fax 415480) in Paringao has nice duplex cottages in well-groomed grounds. Comfortable rooms with fan and bath go for P790 and with air-con and bath for P890. Monthly rates can be arranged. It has a relatively large swimming pool. At the *Cabaña Beach Resort* (☎ 412824; fax 414496) also in Paringao, rooms with air-con and bath cost P850. The resort has a swimming pool with a bar, and you can also use the gym.

Built in the Spanish colonial style, the well-run *Villa Estrella Beach Resort* (☎ 413794; fax 413793) in Paringao provides very comfortable rooms with TV, air-con and bath for P1400.

Places to Eat
Try one of the resort restaurants along the beach for a change, though their prices are decidedly higher. The cuisine at the *Villa Estrella* is good, as it is at the *Fisherman's Wharf* and *Bali Hai*. Also worth trying is the Mongolian barbecue at the *Cabaña* on Saturday night. At the highway you could always go to the inexpensive little *Jasmine Restaurant* and the pleasant *Tunuan Ti Bauang Restaurant* for typical Philippine food.

Entertainment
Although it was true until recently that the only entertainment available at Bauang was billiards, videos and a few resort restaurants, there is now some sign of nightlife at the *Captain's Club* at Fisherman's Wharf and *Stiletto's* at Southern Palms. Not far from these two resorts, right on the National Highway, *Tramps* nightclub starts opening for business in the afternoon. The *Tradewinds Disco Club* at the Villa Estrella Beach Resort is usually patronised by better-off Philippine nationals. There are more discos and a few bars in Poro Point junction near San Fernando. You can get there by tricycle from Bauang Beach for P30.

Getting There & Away
Air PAL flies at irregular intervals from Manila to San Fernando and back. They usually fly when the highway is blocked because of typhoon damage or suchlike, or the flight connection between Manila and Baguio has been temporarily discontinued. The airport is between San Fernando and Bauang.

Bus There are plenty of Partas, Philippine Rabbit, Times Transit, Fariñas Trans and Maria de Leon buses travelling between Manila and Bauang (P120; 6½ hours). Take any one going to San Fernando, Vigan and Laoag. These buses go via Dau/Angeles and you can board them there.

The best way to catch a bus on the highway from Bauang to Manila is to stop every bus until you get one that suits you. At Christmas time, when a lot of buses are full, the best idea is to take a jeepney to the bus company terminals in San Fernando and try to get a decent seat there.

To go from Baguio to Bauang, you have a choice of several Philippine Rabbit and Eso-Nice Transport buses bound for San Fernando (P30; 1½ hours). The trip along the winding Naguilian Rd down to the coast is especially attractive in the late afternoon. For the best view, sit on the same side as the driver. You can also go by jeepney, which is a bit faster than the bus (P25).

There are many jeepneys daily from San Fernando to Bauang (30 minutes). You can get off on the highway near the beach resorts.

From Laoag and Vigan there are several Partas, Philippine Rabbit, Times Transit, Fariñas Trans and Maria de Leon buses daily, all going to Manila. The trip to Bauang takes five hours from Laoag and three hours from Vigan.

Boat An outrigger boat leaves Bolinao for Bauang daily at 9 am. The trip takes two hours and costs P100. Information can be obtained at the TV-repair shop The Islander, Arosan St, Bolinao. Departure from Bauang is at 4 am. A Special Ride costs around P500.

SAN FERNANDO (LA UNION)

Also called the city of the seven hills, San Fernando is the capital of La Union Province. There is a good view over the South China Sea from **Freedom Park**, also known as Heroes Hill. The **Museo de La Union**, next to the Provincial Capitol Building, provides an even better view from its terrace, as well as giving a cultural overview of the province. It's closed on weekends. The little **Fil-Chinese Pagoda** on Gapuz Zigzag Rd and the big **Ma-Cho Temple** on Quezon Ave, which is really worth seeing, bear witness to the Chinese influence in San Fernando. From 12 to 16 September, the Chinese-Filipino religious community holds an annual celebration of the Virgin of Caysasay at the Ma-Cho Temple.

About three km south-west of San Fernando, on the bay south of Poro, there is a reasonable stretch of beach near the Acapulco Beach Resort. The rest of the beach is fairly stony and not really suitable for swimming. Most of the hotels are isolated and inconveniently located, except for getting to the airport.

Information

Tourist Office The tourist office (☎ 412411; fax 412098) is in the Mabanag Justice Hall on General Luna St, Town Plaza.

Money The rate of exchange at the Central Bank (☎ 412631) is sometimes better than at the Philippine National Bank (☎ 412561), both on Quezon Ave.

Telephone The area code for San Fernando is 072.

Places to Stay

San Fernando Centrally located on a through road, the *Plaza Hotel* (☎ 412996; fax 414938) on Quezon Ave offers good singles/doubles with fan and bath for P330/395, and rooms with air-con and bath for P540. Suites are P760.

On the northern edge of town, the *Sea & Sky Hotel* (☎ 415279) on Quezon Ave has immaculate rooms with air-con and bath from P500 to P700; a suite with fridge and TV costs P1000. The quiet rooms have a balcony and a beautiful view of the sea, and there is a good restaurant and a small swimming pool.

Also on Quezon Ave, the *Hotel Mikka* (☎ 415737) on the first floor is conveniently near the Partas bus terminal. Spotless rooms cost P440/500 with air-con and bath.

San Francisco & Poro See the Around San Fernando & Bauang map for the location of these hotels.

About two km south-west of San Fernando, the *Ocean Deep* (☎/fax 414440) in San Francisco is a small place with passable rooms with fan and bath for P250/350. They offer scuba diving and instructor courses.

The quiet little *Sunset Bay Swiss Beach Resort* (☎/fax 414843) in Canaoay has pleasant, clean rooms with air-con and bath for P550/650. It also has a restaurant.

In Canaoay, the *Acapulco Beach Resort* (☎ 412696) is the biggest hotel on the bay at Poro. Rooms with air-con and bath go for P650 and P800. The *Blue Lagoon Resort* (☎ 412531) also in Canaoay is attractively decorated. Comfortable rooms with air-con and bath cost P750 and P850. Some rooms have a small living room attached.

North of San Fernando The *Oceana Apartments* (☎ 413611) at Carlatan, two km north of San Fernando, has indifferently furnished apartments with air-con and cooking facilities from P600 to P1200, depending on size. This place offers fairly favourable monthly rates.

NORTH LUZON

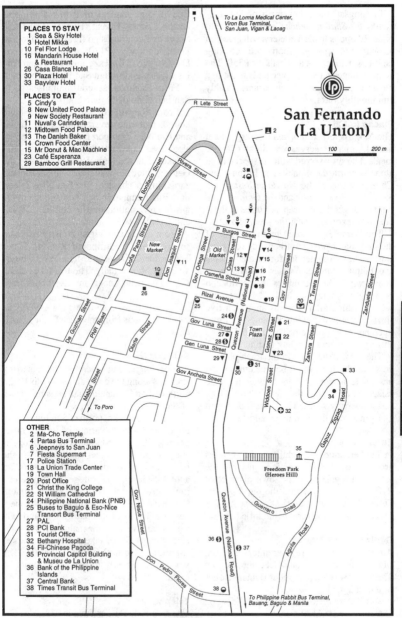

PLACES TO STAY
1 Sea & Sky Hotel
3 Hotel Mikka
10 Fel Flor Lodge
16 Mandarin House Hotel
   & Restaurant
26 Casa Blanca Hotel
30 Plaza Hotel
33 Bayview Hotel

PLACES TO EAT
5 Cindy's
8 New United Food Palace
9 New Society Restaurant
11 Nuval's Carinderia
12 Midtown Food Palace
13 The Danish Baker
14 Crown Food Center
15 Mr Donut & Mac Machine
23 Café Esperanza
29 Bamboo Grill Restaurant

OTHER
2 Ma-Cho Temple
4 Partas Bus Terminal
6 Jeepneys to San Juan
7 Fiesta Supermart
17 Police Station
18 La Union Trade Center
19 Town Hall
20 Post Office
21 Christ the King College
22 St William Cathedral
24 Philippine National Bank (PNB)
25 Buses to Baguio & Eso-Nice
   Transort Bus Terminal
27 PAL
28 PCI Bank
31 Tourist Office
32 Bethany Hospital
34 Fil-Chinese Pagoda
35 Provincial Capitol Building
   & Museu de La Union
36 Bank of the Philippine
   Islands
37 Central Bank
38 Times Transit Bus Terminal

To La Lorma Medical Center,
Viron Bus Terminal,
San Juan, Vigan & Laoag

San Fernando (La Union)

0   100   200 m

R Lete Street

Rivera Street

A Bonifacio Street

Doña Paza Street

Don Joaquin Street

New Market

Old Market

Gov Ortega Street

Osias Street

P Burgos Street

Osmeña Street

Rizal Avenue

Gov Luna Street

Gen Luna Street

Gov Ancheta Street

Quezon Avenue (National Road)

Gov Lucero Street

P Tavera Street

Zandueta Street

Town Plaza

Gomez Street

Zamora Street

Widdoes Street

Freedom Park
(Heroes Hill)

Capuz Zigzag Road

Guerrero Road

Aguila Road

De Guzman Street

PNR Road

Mabini Street

Olarte Street

Gov Ninoz Street

Don Pedro Flores Street

To Poro

To Philippine Rabbit Bus Terminal,
Bauang, Baguio & Manila

NORTH LUZON

In Lingsat, three km north of San Fernando, the *Shalom Beach Cottages* on Santo Niño Rd opposite the cemetery, will give you a clean and spacious room with cooking facilities, fridge, fan and bath for P350. The stone cottages have a terrace and are set in a pleasant garden. It has favourable weekly and monthly rates.

Places to Eat
The *New Society Restaurant* on Burgos St at the old market serves excellent Chinese meals. The soup served with the special meal alone is worth the money. The Filipino and Chinese meals at the *Mandarin Restaurant*, the *Crown Food Center* and the *Garden Food Center* are good and cheap. All three of these are on Quezon Ave near the town plaza.

The *Sea & Sky Restaurant* in the hotel of the same name on the northern edge of town, can also be recommended for its international and Filipino cuisine. *Nuval's Carinderia* on Don Joaquin St specialises in the Ilokano cooking of the region. It also has 'jumping salad', named after the way in which live shrimp react to having kalamansi (lime) juice poured over them. This place, like the shrimp, is always jumping at dinner time.

The *Café Esperanza* in the town plaza is very popular for a snack between meals and has made a name for itself with its large selection of cakes (they even have black forest cherry gateau). The *Danish Baker* on Quezon Ave sells good bread and cakes.

Entertainment
In San Fernando, the nightlife mainly centres around Poro Point junction, just outside town. A tricycle from the town plaza costs P10. There you will find the big *Mascotte Disco*, the smaller *Mama's Disco* and *Annie's Disco* as well as several rustic little bars.

Getting There & Away
Air PAL flies at irregular intervals from Manila to San Fernando (see the Getting There & Away section under Bauang earlier in this chapter).

PAL has an office in the CAP Building on Quezon Ave (☎ 412909).

Bus A large number of Partas, Philippine Rabbit, Times Transit, Fariñas Trans and Maria de Leon buses go from Manila to San Fernando daily (P120; seven hours) via Dau/Angeles. Buses going to Vigan and Laoag also go through San Fernando.

From Dagupan, several minibuses go to San Fernando daily (two hours).

From Baguio to San Fernando (two hours), there are several Philippine Rabbit and Eso-Nice Transport buses daily. Jeepneys also cover this route and they are slightly quicker than the large buses. (See also the Getting There & Away section under Bauang earlier in this chapter.) The Eso-Nice Transport Bus terminal in San Fernando is at the gas (petrol) station on the corner of Rizal and Ortega Sts.

From Laoag and Vigan to San Fernando, several Partas, Philippine Rabbit, Times Transit, Fariñas Trans and Maria de Leon buses go on to Manila daily. The trip takes about 4½ hours from Laoag and 2½ hours from Vigan.

To San Fabian and Dagupan, you can catch a minibus from the Casa Blanca Hotel on Rizal St.

SAN JUAN
A wide, long, clean beach with good surfing stretches along the coast about five to 10 km north of San Fernando near the small town of San Juan.

At Tabok, two km north of San Juan, street traders sell a wide variety of locally made pottery. The Don Mariano State College is about eight km further north-east, off the main road in wooded mountains at 600m above sea level. The college has an interesting Agricultural Training Development Center (ATDC) where students study beekeeping. The local dark narra honey and light sunflower honey are the main varieties gathered. To get there, take a jeepney marked 'Sapilang' from Bacnotan (P2.50). The whole way directly to the ATDC costs P5 extra.

Telephone
The area code for San Juan is 072.

RICHARD I'ANSON

JENS PETERS

JENS PETERS

NORTH LUZON
Top Left: A woman in traditional headwear, Banaue.
Top Right: Catholic grandeur, Spanish style.
Bottom: Rice terraces near Mayoyao, Ifugao Province.

JOHN PENNOCK

JOHN PENNOCK

JENS PETERS

JOHN PENNOCK

NORTH LUZON
Top: Rice terraces at Banaue.
Left: Fidelisan Waterfall near Sagada,
   Mountain Province.

Middle Right: Malegcong rice terraces
   near Bontoc, Mountain Province.
Bottom Right: Hundred Islands

Surfing

Surfing season is from July until September and from November until March.

It costs P100 to hire a surfboard for two hours, eg in the Monaliza Resort and in the Surf Camp.

Places to Stay & Eat

In Urbiztondo, about two km south of San Juan, the *Hacienda Beach Resort* is a rustic building with basic rooms with fan for P160/230 and rooms with fan and bath for P300 and P450. Right next door, flash your enigmatic smile at the *Monaliza Resort* (☎ 414892), where doubles with fan cost P250 and P400 and with fan and bath P380 and P500. The rooms are of different sizes; the more expensive have refrigerator and cooking facilities.

Just south of the Hacienda, the *Surf Camp* (fax only 413708) is a pleasant little establishment, with dormitory bunks for P100 and cottages with fan and bath for P500. The cottages come complete with refrigerator and cooking facilities.

On the wide beach in Montemar Village at Ili Norte, between 700m and one km north of San Juan, there are a few good accommodation possibilities. The *Sunset German Beach Resort* (☎/fax 414719) has rugged little stone cottages where rooms with fan and bath cost P400. This is a small, well-tended place with plenty of greenery. The very good restaurant serves excellent Filipino and international cuisine. Right next door is the *Scenic View Tourist Inn* (☎ 413901). Dorm beds with fan cost P100, good rooms with veranda, fan and bath cost P250/300 and rooms with air-con and bath cost P450/500. Suites are P750. It has a roof-top restaurant and a swimming pool. There is no direct access to the beach, so you have to go the long way round.

Between Las Villas and the Scenic View Tourist Inn, the *Casa del Mar* (☎ 415678) has rooms with fan and bath for P400. They are in good condition and have a big bath. The European cuisine in the restaurant is good.

On the beach at Ili Norte, 700m outside San Juan, the attractive, Spanish-style *Las Villas Resort* (☎/fax 412267) has pleasant and well-maintained rooms with air-con and bath from P600 to P1500. A good restaurant and a small swimming pool round off the attractions.

Getting There & Away

Bus All buses between Manila and Vigan and Laoag go through San Juan. It takes 7½ hours from Manila, four hours from Laoag and two hours from Vigan.

Jeepney Several jeepneys travel every day from San Fernando to San Juan (P5; 30 minutes), leaving from the corner of P Burgos St and Quezon Ave. Their signs may say 'Bacnotan' or 'Sapilang'. If you want to go to a resort in Montemar Village, get out at the turn-off in Ili Norte and walk the rest of the way.

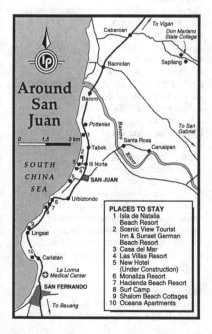

Around San Juan

0   1.5   3 km

SOUTH
CHINA
SEA

To Vigan
Cabaroan
Don Mariano
State College
Bacnotan
Sapilang
Baroro
Potteries
To San
Gabriel
Tabok   Santa Rosa
Carusipan
Ili Norte
SAN JUAN
Urbiztondo
Lingsat
Carlatan
La Loma
Medical Center
SAN FERNANDO
To Bauang

PLACES TO STAY
1 Isla de Natalia
   Beach Resort
2 Scenic View Tourist
   Inn & Sunset German
   Beach Resort
3 Casa del Mar
4 Las Villas Resort
5 New Hotel
   (Under Construction)
6 Monaliza Resort
7 Hacienda Beach Resort
8 Surf Camp
9 Shalom Beach Cottages
10 Oceana Apartments

Central Cordillera

BAGUIO

Baguio (pronounced Bag-ee-o with a hard 'g') is the summer capital of the Philippines. This City of Pines, City of Flowers or City of Lovers, as it is also known, is certainly the most popular place for Filipinos to travel. In the hot summer months, Filipinos who can afford it move to this cool mountain town, which is at an altitude of 1500m. Easter is the busiest time by a long chalk, when hotels raise their prices and 300,000 visitors flock to the town, but it's a mystery where they all stay. They rave about the zigzag road (Kennon Rd) and the cooler climate.

From March until May, Baguio shows its best side and displays all the flair of a typical holiday resort. But in the cold months, like December and January, there's not much to hang around for. The frothy Philippine atmosphere with the relaxed jollity of the lowland Filipinos is missing. The people you meet in the streets at night are a cheerless lot in their woolly jackets, in contrast to the usual laughing faces and colourful T-shirts with cheeky slogans.

Baguio is still remembered for the destruction of the massive earthquake that shook the north of Luzon on 16 July 1990 – the pictures went around the world. Baguio suffered serious damage but most places have now either been repaired or rebuilt.

Orientation

Maps Bookmark has published the illustrated map *Baguio Landmarks* which offers a bird's-eye view of the city's most important streets and noteworthy buildings.

Information

Tourist Office The tourist office (☎ 442 6708) is on Governor Pack Rd. It is open daily from 8 am to noon and 1 to 5 pm.

Money The Equitable Bank (☎ 443 5028), Golden Court Building, Magsaysay Ave will give a cash advance on Visa or MasterCard.

Various textile traders at the market will change US-dollars (cash) at a good rate (shop around though).

Post & Communications You can access the internet and take care of your email in the Cyberspace Café in the Mount Crest Hotel at the corner of Legarda Rd and Urbano St.

The area code for Baguio is 074.

Bookshops There is a well-stocked branch of Bookmark in Session Road.

Dangers & Annoyances Keep in mind that Baguio is a favourite hunting ground of various tricksters who will claim acquaintance with you at the airport or immigration office for ulterior motives. They will engage you in small talk or pretend that their sister is working in the same country you come from and invite you for a drink (to drug and rob you). Don't go!

City Market

The things on sale at this wonderful market are mostly local products made or grown in surrounding Benguet Province. You will find basketware, textiles, silver jewellery and woodcarvings as well as vegetables, fruit, honey and so on. Look out for the strawberries and the sweet, heavy strawberry wine. In the meat section, the grinning dog heads are no longer sold. After strong international criticism, this highland delicacy was forbidden by the government, so dog meat is no longer prominently displayed at markets where Westerners go.

The traditional arts & crafts of the mountain dwellers are sold in the adjoining Maharlika Livelihood Center, a large complex with numerous shops. You can buy woodcarvings at more reasonable prices there, direct from the makers in the so-called Woodcarver's Village. You will find it on Asin Rd, about four or five km west of Baguio.

Burnham Park

Burnham Park is a green belt with a small artificial lake in the middle of town. It is

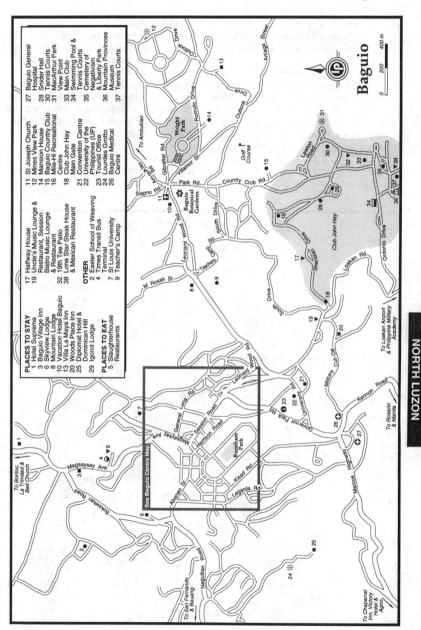

Baguio

0   200   400 m

PLACES TO STAY
1   Hotel Supreme
3   Baguio Village Inn
6   Skyview Lodge
8   Mountain Lodge
    Vacation Hotel
13 Villa La Maya Inn
20 Woods Place Inn
25 Diplomat Hotel &
    Dominican Hill
29 Igorot Lodge

PLACES TO EAT
5   Slaughterhouse
    Restaurants

17 Halfway House
19 Uncle's Music Lounge &
    Restaurant, Session
    Bistro Music Lounge
    & Restaurant
32 19th Street Patio
38 Lone Star Steak House
    & Mexican Restaurant

OTHER
2   Easter School of Weaving
4   Times Transit Bus
    Terminal
7   St Louis University
9   Teacher's Camp

11 St Joseph Church
12 Mines View Park
14 Mansion House
15 Baguio Country Club
16 Mile-Hi Recreational
    Centre
18 Club John Hay
    Main Gate
21 Convention Centre
22 University of the
    Philippines (UP)
23 Tourist Office
24 Lourdes Grotto
26 Baguio Medical
    Centre

27 Baguio General
    Hospital
28 Snider Hall
30 Tennis Courts
31 MacArthur Park
    View Point
33 Main Club
    Swimming Pool &
    Tennis Courts
35 Cemetery of
    Negativism
    & Liberty Park
36 Mountain Provinces
    Museum
37 Tennis Courts

named after Daniel Burnham, the town planner of Baguio. There are boats for hire, a children's playground and other attractions.

Mountain Provinces Museum

This small museum at Club John Hay gives a vivid picture of the life of the cultural minorities in the Central Cordillera mountains. Artefacts like baskets, jewellery and pottery are on display here. The opening hours are Tuesday to Sunday from 9 am to noon and 1.30 to 5 pm. Admission costs P10.

A jeepney from the main gate of Club John Hay to the museum costs P2.

St Louis Filigree

Young silversmiths are trained at the St Louis University trade school. It's here that you can watch them make the finest filigree. Their work is on sale in the St Louis Filigree Shop at fixed prices, but not all have a hallmark. If you want one, arrange to get it while you are there. The opening hours for both the workshop and the shop are Monday to Saturday from 8 am to noon and 1 to 5 pm.

Easter School of Weaving

The Easter School of Weaving is on the north-western outskirts of Baguio. The

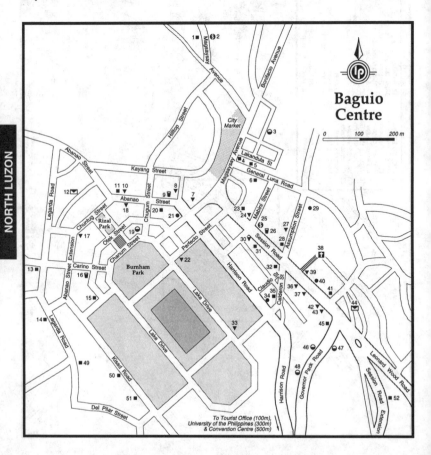

Baguio
Centre

0   100   200 m

weavers make tablecloths and clothing, and you can watch them at work. It's expensive to buy here.

Jeepneys leave from Kayang St or from Chugum St, on the corner of Otek St.

Club John Hay

Club John Hay, in the south-east suburbs of town, was formerly called Camp John Hay and was a recreation base of the US Army. It has been run by the Bases Conversion Development Authority (BCDA) as a 'Resort & Recreation Area' since it was given back to the Philippines in July 1991. Open to the public are a golf course, swimming pools and tennis courts, as well as the restaurants: the Half Way House, the 19th Tee Patio and the Lone Star Steak House. The Americans also left behind the unique 'Cemetery of Negativism', where bad habits are buried under humorous gravestones. This glimpse into homespun American philosophy is well worth seeing.

Club John Hay can be reached from the city centre by jeepney from Kayang St or by taxi to the main gate. Jeepneys and taxis also drive around the camp grounds themselves.

Baguio Botanical Gardens, Wright Park & Mines View Park

Unfortunately, all that is left of the different types of houses of the Central Cordillera, which used to be on view in the botanical gardens one km out of town, is a broken-down Ifugao hut. There is also a handcraft centre with a souvenir shop. You can combine a trip to the botanical gardens with an excursion to Wright Park, where you can go horseback riding for P80 per hour for the horse plus P80 for the guide, and to the Mines View Park, 2½ km out of town, behind the Baguio Botanical Gardens, where you can get a beautiful panoramic view of the valley and the mountains. (You do have to work your way through crowds of souvenir stalls before you get to the viewpoint.)

PLACES TO STAY		
1	Leisure Lodge	
4	Villa Rosal Hotel	
5	New Belfranlt Hotel & Fast Food Shopping Arcade	
6	Highland Lodge	
11	Swagman Attic Inn	
13	Mount Crest Hotel & Cyberspace Café	
14	Holiday Villa Court & Joey's Place	
15	Benguet Pine Tourist Inn	
20	Cypress Inn	
23	Mido Hotel & Sunshine Restaurant	
28	New Plaza Hotel	
31	Baguio Goodwill Lodge & 456 Restaurant	
32	Benguet Prime Hotel, Jollibee & Benguet Supermarket	
35	Burnham Hotel & Cook's Inn Restaurant	
41	Patrio de Baguio & Songs Music Gallery	
45	Baden Powell Inn	

49	Baguio Palace Hotel & Mr Ching Cuisine Restaurant	
50	Venus Parkview Hotel	
51	Kisad Hotel	
52	Casa Vallejo	

PLACES TO EAT		
7	Café Teria & Fast Food Center & Maharlika Livelihood Center	
8	Music Box Pizza House	
10	50 Diner	
17	Café by the Ruins	
18	Manila Café	
21	Sunshine Department Store	
22	The New Ganza Steak & Chicken House	
24	Star Café	
27	Cozy Nook Restaurant	
30	McDonald's	
33	The Solibao Restaurant	
36	Sizzling Plate Restaurant	
37	Shakey's Pizza	
39	Mister Donut & Swiss Baker	
42	Kowloon House & Mario's	
43	Barrio Fiesta	

OTHER		
2	Equitable Bank	
3	Dangwa Tranco Bus Terminal & Lizardo Trans Bus Terminal	
9	Peak a Boo Disco	
12	City Hall & Post Office	
16	Alberto's Music Lounge & Spirits Disco	
19	Eso-Nice Transport Bus Terminal	
21	Maharlika Livelihood Center	
25	Philippine National Bank (PNB)	
26	Rumours Disco	
29	St Louis Filigree Shop	
34	Avis Rent-a-Car & PAL	
38	Cathedral	
40	Bookmark	
44	Post Office	
46	Byron Bus Terminal Dagupan Bus Terminal & Partas Bus Terminal	
47	Victory Liner Bus Terminal	
48	Philippine Rabbit Bus Terminal	

To get all these attractions, take a jeepney from Magsaysay Ave, opposite the city market, or from Harrison Rd, on the corner of Perfecto St.

Bell Church
There is a Chinese temple a little to the north of town in the direction of La Trinidad. This place is run by the Bell Church Sect, which believes in a mixture of Buddhist, Taoist, Confucian and Christian doctrines. You can, on request, get your fortune told by one of the priests.

To get to Bell Church, catch a jeepney from Magsaysay Ave, on the corner of Bonifacio St.

Faith Healers
The mass media have given much coverage to the practices of the Filipino faith healers, who 'open' the skin of the patient with their fingers and 'operate' with their bare hands – a dubious business. But as faith can move mountains, there are always sufferers who come from all over the world to Baguio to be saved. If you aren't put off by blood or bad smells, you can always watch one of these miracles. According to critical reports in some Western mass media, however, most of these healers don't like to be watched too closely. If they do let you, then it is only for a hefty fee. Taxi drivers can usually organise a visit.

Places to Stay – bottom end
Apart from the small rooms and thin walls, the *Highland Lodge* (☎ 442 7086) on General Luna Rd is low-end accommodation by any standard. Rooms cost P150/220 and with bath P250/350. There is no restaurant, but there is room service. For a few pesos more, you'd be better off at one of the next two places. The *Baguio Goodwill Lodge* (☎ 442 6634), 58 Session Rd, has good value rooms at P200/280 and with bath for P350/420.

A popular place in this price category, the *Benguet Pine Tourist Inn* (☎ 442 7325) at 82 Chanum St on the corner of Otek St, is also good value, with dorm beds for P150, rooms

for P250 and P350 and with bath for P500. The rooms are quiet and cosy.

The atmosphere is friendly at the rustic *Casa Vallejo* (☎ 442 3045),111 Session Rd Extension, where fairly good rooms go for P220/350 and with bath for P380/550.

The accommodation is OK at the *Cypress Inn* at 29 Abanao St (☎ 442 2416) – but only if you are a sound sleeper (there are karaoke bars right next door). Rooms for three to five people, with bath, cost P350 to P500.

Places to Stay – middle
East of the town centre, the *Mountain Lodge* (☎ 442 4544) at 27 Leonard Wood Rd has rooms with bath for P600 and doubles with bath and fireplace for P900. This pleasant hotel is good value, offering quiet and comfortable accommodation in a friendly atmosphere.

Convenient for most of the bus terminals, the *Baden Powell Inn* (☎ 442 5836) at 26 Governor Pack Rd has dorm beds for P140 and rooms with bath from P800. It also has spacious, comfortable suites with two bedrooms, kitchen and open fireplace for P2500. The rooms are quiet, as they are at the back looking downhill and away from the noise of the street.

The *Burnham Hotel* (☎ 442 2331; fax 442 8415) at 20 Calderon St will accommodate you in a room with bath for P875 and P985, the more expensive rooms have TV. This is a fine, tastefully decorated building which also has a good Chinese restaurant.

Spacious, comfortable rooms at the *New Belfranlt Hotel* (☎ 442 4298) on General Luna St cost P800 upwards, with TV and bath.

Run by Australians, the *Swagman Attic Inn* (☎ 442 5139; fax 442 9859), 90 Abanao St, is a pleasant place to stay near the town hall. Nicely furnished rooms with TV and bath go for P765 and P1055.

On the corner of Calderon St and Session Rd, the *Benguet Prime Hotel* (☎ 442 7066; fax 442 8132) offers comfortable rooms with TV, fridge and bath for P1500 and P1850, although those facing the street are on the loud side.

Places to Stay – top end

At the corner of Legarda Rd and Urbano St, the *Mount Crest Hotel* (☎ 442 3324; fax 442 6900) has comfortable rooms with bath for P1200/1300.

The rooms at the *Baguio Palace Hotel* (☎ 442 7734) on Legarda Rd are a little bit expensive, at P1200 with bath, and suites for P2200. However, it's clean and comfortable and has a Chinese restaurant.

Halsema Road

What a road! And what a misleading official name: Halsema Mountain Highway. It runs between Baguio and Bontoc and used to be called the Mountain Trail, which gives you a better idea of what kind of surface to expect. In the 1920s, the civil engineer EJ Halsema supervised the widening of the trail, and in 1931 a more-or-less acceptable road was opened to traffic. This enormous undertaking provided access to the mineral resources (gold, silver and copper) of the Central Cordillera mountain range. To this day however, the roadwork has not been completed. Although there is a short stretch of surfaced road in the south, the majority of the route remains a bumpy, dusty track, winding through steep passes.

Actually, Halsema Road doesn't begin in Baguio but a few km further east of La Trinidad, the capital of the province of Benguet. From here it twists through 130 km or so of breathtaking mountain scenery in a north-easterly direction until it reaches Bontoc, the capital of Mountain Province.

About seven km east of La Trinidad at Acop's Place, a winding road breaks off heading for Kibungan, a small town in a mountain area which is also called the 'Switzerland of Benguet'. Apparently the temperature here can drop below freezing in December and January. Around Kibungan the area is known as Madaymen, and is famous for its market gardens. North of here are the Palina rice terraces.

Shortly after Acop's Place the Halsema Road leads over a pass known as 'Guerrilla Saddle'. From here you can see the Ambuklao reservoir on the right, which is fed by the Agno River. A little further on, a road turns off which takes you there. This road also takes you to Kabayan and, from Ellet Bridge, to Mt Pulog, the second highest mountain in the Philippines.

Further north of Acop's Place, around Atok, the 'Salad Bowl of Benguet' begins: vegetable fields as far as the eye can see. The road really starts to climb here, until just before Catubo where the height of 2255m is reached.

A trail leads from Catubo to Kabayan, crossing the foothills of Mt Singakalsa, also known as Mt Timbac, where the famous Kabayan mummies can be found in the Timbac Caves.

In Sinipsip, the Dangwa Tranco Bus Company runs a big restaurant. The beautiful Natubleng vegetable terraces stretch into the distance on both sides of the road. The slopes south of Sinipsip are particularly impressive, with their terraces filling every last inch of ground.

Abatan is exactly 90 km from Baguio. It's a busy little place at a road crossing, with a big market, loads of shops and stalls. If you take the road that turns off to the north-west you end up in Mankayan (where two companies run copper mines) and Cervantes. The road that runs south-east goes to Loo and through the Loo Valley along the Agno River to Kabayan.

About 10 km north-east of Abatan, Halsema Road reaches the border to Mountain Province and Mt Data with the comfortable hotel of the same name. It's about another 30 km from here to Bontoc. The rest of the way the road is accompanied on the right by the Chico River in a wide valley. Seven km before Bontoc you come to the last fork in the road. If you want to go to Sagada, then turn off to the left here. ■

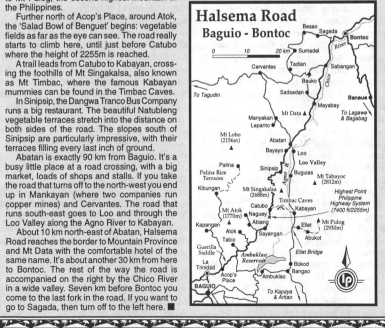

Halsema Road
Baguio - Bontoc

The cosy little *Woods Place Inn* (☎ 442 4641), 38 Military Cut-Off Rd, on the corner of Wagner Rd, has tidy, comfortable rooms for P1000 and pleasantly furnished rooms with balcony, TV and bath for P1500. A suite with a jacuzzi will cost you P1950.

Just outside town, the *Hotel Supreme* (☎ 443 2011; fax 442 2855) at 113 Magsaysay Ave, has rooms with bath for P1195, and suites with cooking facilities are P2250. It is quiet and has a swimming pool.

Opposite the Baguio Botanical Gardens, the *Vacation Hotel Baguio* (☎ 442 3144) at 45 Leonard Wood Rd has comfortable rooms with TV and bath from P1220 to P1900. It's a well-looked after hotel, and they also have a disco.

Places to Eat
The simple restaurant in the Dangwa Tranco Bus Terminal serves good and cheap Filipino cuisine. The so-called *Slaughterhouse Restaurants*, next to the slaughterhouse near the Times Transit Bus Terminal on Balajadia St, are also simply furnished. However, they offer excellent meat dishes at reasonable prices, and are very popular with locals.

The *Cook's Inn* at the Burnham Hotel, Calderon St, and *Mr Ching Cuisine* at the Baguio Palace Hotel, Legarda Rd, are two of the best Chinese restaurants in town.

Both *The Solibao* and the *New Ganza Steak & Chicken House* are at Burnham Park and have tables outside. There are other restaurants of varying quality and price on Session Rd. One of these is the *Sizzling Plate*, where you can have a proper breakfast. The *Swiss Baker* is the place for a good breakfast and tasty cakes, while *Mario's*, which has been around for a long time, is well known for its steaks (from P150) and wines. The *Kowloon House* right next door serves Chinese dim sum 24 hours a day.

The *Swagman Attic Inn Restaurant* on Abanao St serves passable international cuisine and is open 24 hours. Friends of fast food can choose between *McDonald's, Jollibee* and *Shakey's Pizza*, all on Session Rd.

If you would like to try traditional Cordillera cooking and drinks, then *Café by the Ruins* opposite the town hall is the place to go. This bamboo restaurant is tastefully decorated with plants and traditional artwork, and its menu consists mainly of seasonal specialities, served with tapuy (rice wine), basi or salabat (ginger tea) – a request for San Miguel beer will only get you raised eyebrows here.

Entertainment
For years folk pubs were all the rage in Baguio, but with the demand for a more modern sound, sing-along and karaoke have established themselves here in the mountains, with *Joey's Place* on Legarda Rd and the *Cosy Nook* on Assumption Rd the most popular venues. The *Music Box Pizza House* on Zandueta St has a 'different' atmosphere, if you're not turned off by plastic chairs and large pitchers of beer (too large for some of the patrons it would seem); the music here is more raw and passionate. The atmosphere is more pleasant at *Alberto's Music Lounge* in Carino St.

Jazz freaks meet in the evening at the *Songs Music Gallery*, next to the Patria de Baguio, located appropriately enough on Session Rd, although classical music is sometimes played. The *Café Legarda* in the Mount Crest Hotel, at the corner Legarda Rd and Urbano St, is a chic and trendy bar always filled with students; solo singers and bands take turns every night. The guests in the *Café Teria* at the Maharlika Livelihood Center are entertained with jazz and oldies.

By far the most popular disco is *Spirits*, in a magnificent building on Otek St. *Rumours* on Session Rd and the *Crystal Den* at the Victory Hotel, Marcos Highway, are also popular.

Things to Buy
In Baguio look for Ifugao woodcarvings and hand-woven fabrics. The cottons, produced in such limited quantities that they rarely reach Manila, are cheaper in Bontoc or Banaue than in Baguio. The baskets and salad bowls are very cheap, but a bit bulky to carry home.

Getting There & Away
Air PAL has return flights daily between Manila and Baguio (P1000; 35 minutes). Asian Spirit flies on Monday, Wednesday, Friday and Saturday (P765).

PAL has an office at Loakan Email (☎ 442 2734, 442 6753) and on Harrison St (☎ 442 2628, 442 2695).

Bus From Manila to Baguio (P115; six hours), there are plenty of Dagupan Bus, Dangwa Tranco, Philippine Rabbit and Victory Liner buses daily. Buses go via Dau/Angeles, where you can also board the bus.

From Olongapo, you can get to Baguio by Victory Liner bus. These leave hourly and take six hours. They go via Angeles.

From Dagupan to Baguio (two hours), there are plenty of Byron Bus buses every day, leaving every half hour from 6 am to 4 pm, and Dagupan Bus and Philippine Rabbit.

From San Fernando, several Philippine Rabbit and Eso-Nice Transport buses travel daily to Baguio (P30; two hours) via Bauang. You can also go by jeepney.

From Banaue, the Dangwa Tranco buses run a daily service to Baguio, leaving between 6.45 and 7.30 am, and sometimes at 4 pm. They follow the southern route via Bayombong, San Jose and Villasis (P130; nine hours).

From Bontoc, Dangwa Tranco buses run daily to Baguio (P130; eight hours), leaving at 6, 7, 8 and 9.15 am.

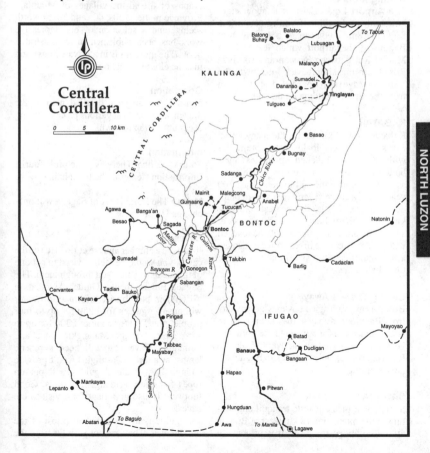

NORTH LUZON

From Sagada, there are Dangwa Tranco and Lizardo Trans buses which run daily to Baguio, leaving at 6, 6.30, 7, 8 and 9 am (P135; seven hours).

Look out for buses from Sagada and other places in Mountain Province, which have sometimes been stopped by military and Narcotic Commission (NARCOM) officials searching passenger luggage for marijuana.

Car Avis Rent-a-Car (☎ 442 4018) can be found in the Padilla Building on Harrison Rd.

Getting Around
The Airport Loakan airport is about eight km south of Baguio. If you're catching a flight to Manila, you can get a jeepney from Baguio to the airport which leaves from Mabini Rd, between Session and Harrison Rds. From the airport back into town, the jeepneys leave from Loakan Rd, about 100m from the airport building on the right.

KABAYAN
Kabayan is well known for the many burial caves of the local Ibaloy tribe. Mummies with their legs hunched up against their bodies lie in hollow tree trunks which serve as coffins. Some are said to be at least 500 years old. Because several caves were plundered in the 1970s, the nearest and best known of them have since been sealed. Those that are still open can only be reached with guides after long hikes. You can also see a few mummies in a small museum in the town hall.

Getting There & Away
Bus A Dangwa Tranco bus may go any day from Baguio to Kabayan (6½ hours). There is no connection for Abatan to the north. To get there, you have to walk over to Halsema Road or take the daily bus back to Baguio the next morning.

SAGADA
Sagada is a pleasant little tranquil community in the mountains 18 km west of Bontoc at 1480m above sea level. It is principally known for its caves and the so-called 'hanging coffins'.

St Mary's School next to the church of the same name was established in 1912. The event is celebrated every year from 5 to 10 December, including a procession on 7 December with a dancing competition in traditional costumes afterwards. On 9 December there is a competition involving theatre groups, singing and music.

A little further towards Bontoc, near the turn-off to Banga'an, try a visit to the informal **Masferré Gallery**, dedicated to the late Eduardo Masferré. The display of his photographs of life in the villages of Mountain Province in the 1930s, 40s and 50s is worth seeing, and a selection of his impressive work has been published in an illustrated book. The museum is in a private house and may be closed to visitors.

Orientation
Maps You can get a detailed map of the Sagada area for P6 at various places offering accommodation in town.

Information
Tourist Office There is a helpful Tourist Information Center at the town hall.

Money The Rural Bank of Sagada will only change US dollars.

Caves
If you are a climber and are curious to see the caves, you would be well advised to get one of the locals to guide you through them. The Sagada Environmental Guides Association (SEGA) in the Tourist Information Center will arrange guides for P250 for up to four people, plus P80 for a lamp; P300 for up to six people. For the Matangkib Cave and Sumaging Cave you will need kerosene lamps, as a torch (flashlight) won't provide enough light. Careful guides will put up ropes for safety at dangerous spots. Good footwear is also important for a visit to the caves.

A guide is not essential for most of the burial caves. They are not very far from the centre of town – at most a 30-minute walk away. Among these are the **Matangkib**, **Sugong** and **Lumiang** caves. **Sumaging Cave** (Big Cave) does not contain any coffins. You need a guide to go into this cave, as a thorough exploration can take up to six hours. The water is almost waist high in places and there are a few narrow places to negotiate. There is a beautiful view of a vast valley with rice terraces from the path near the Sumaging Cave. A guide is also advisable to visit the **Crystal Cave**, as it is narrow and involves a difficult climb and descent. However, the Crystal Cave was closed to the public in 1995

due to visitors breaking off and taking mineral deposits. It is doubtful it will be open to tourists again in the foreseeable future.

Hiking

It's an interesting two-hour hike to **Echo Valley**. Starting off at St Mary's School behind the church, take the trail up to the cemetery, then go through the cemetery and take the path down into the valley. You can catch your first view down into the valley from the hill next to the cemetery, which has a cross on it. From Echo Valley, where coffins can be seen hanging from the rock

NORTH LUZON

Sagada

0   50   100 m

To Besao &
Lake Danum

Bokong
Waterfall

To Banga'an

To Mount Ampacao,
Bagnen & Mount Polis

Ambasing

To Sumaging
Cave (800m),
Crystal Cave,
Balangacan Cave
& Suyo

Lumiang
Cave

600m
approx.

Cemetery

Lookout

Echo Valley

Sugong

Matangkib
Cave

Underground
River

Kiltepan Peak
(1636m)

To
Bontoc

◆ Coffins
◇ Hanging Coffins

PLACES TO STAY	26 A-Seven House	7 Jeepneys to Bontoc
1 Daoa's Guesthouse	27 Mapiyaaw Sagada	8 Tourist Information,
3 Sagada Guesthouse	Pensione	Rural Bank,
6 Country Inn & Café		Town Hall, Police
12 Masferré Inn & Café	**PLACES TO EAT**	Station & Post Office
& Sagada Bakery	2 Log Cabin	10 Market
13 Green House	9 Café Bilig	16 St Mary's School
14 New Hotel (Under	11 Shamrock Café	17 St Mary's Church
Construction)	22 Rock Café	19 St Theodore's
15 Olahbinan Resthouse	28 Village Bistro	Hospital
18 St Joseph's Resthouse		20 Sagada Weaving &
21 Rocky Valley Inn	**OTHER**	Souvenir Shop
& Restaurant	4 Ganduyan Museum	23 Josephine's Store
25 Pines View Inn	5 Buses to Baguio	24 Masferré Gallery

face, you go upriver until you come to a cave opening where the Underground River flows out. To the right a path leads to the Matangkib Cave, and from there it's only a few steps to the road. You can also go into the Underground River cave where in a short time you will reach the path that passes by outside.

Although the flow is reduced almost to a trickle in April and May, a visit to **Bokong Waterfall** with its natural swimming pool is worthwhile and very refreshing after touring the caves in Sagada. It's a little hard to find, so you may have to ask for directions. It takes about 30 minutes to get there on foot from Sagada. To get there from the centre of the township first walk 300m in the direction of Bontoc, then after Sagada Weaving turn left up the stairs.

About 1½ km east of the centre of Sagada a bumpy trail turns off the road to Bontoc and leads up to **Kiltepan Peak** which is 1636m high. It has a transmitting tower on the top and the view down on the rice terraces at Kilong and Tetep-an is magnificent.

You can walk from Sagada to **Banga'an** in not quite two hours through a beautiful landscape with rice terraces. There is also supposed to be a connection by jeepney now. About another two hours on the other side of Banga'an there is an impressive waterfall, the Bomod-ok ('Big Waterfall'). There is only enough light for sunbathing from morning until noon, so make sure you don't leave Sagada too late. Turn off right after the school in Banga'an and carry on to the village of Fedilsan. For a few pesos one of the children in the village will take you to the waterfall.

The hike to the top of **Mt Ampacao** (1889m) is more than worth the effort (two hours). The view of Sagada and its surrounding area from up there is magnificent. You can avoid going back down the same route through Ambasing by taking the path to the little Lake Danum (2½ hours) and hiking from there back to Sagada (one hour).

The beautiful hike to **Mt Polis** (1829m) south of Sagada takes a bit longer. You need about three to four hours if you take the

so-called Old Spanish Trail that begins just outside of Ambasing and leads to Bagnen and Mt Polis. Steps that have been hewn into the hillside lead up to the summit.

Places to Stay

The places to stay in this popular little town are all of the basic variety, but inexpensive. If you don't want a cold shower in the morning, then order a bucket of warm water for P10 the night before. And when we say cold water, in Sagada it really means cold!

The *Sagada Guesthouse* is a cosy place to stay, with rooms for P75/150. The *St Joseph's Resthouse* is across from the hospital where the bus stops and has comfortable, spacious rooms for P75/150. You can even get a massage there for P50. The *Masferré Inn* is very popular – 'quaint, charming, cosy and rustic' was how one traveller described it. The spacious rooms there go for P75/150.

The *Green House* is a quiet, older private house with a newer building next to it. Both have their own kitchens, and guests may use them for a small fee. Rooms are P75/150

Also very quiet is the cosy *Pines View Inn* with its family atmosphere. There are only two rooms for P65/130 as well as a big living room and kitchen. The nearby friendly *A-Seven House* also has rooms for P65/130.

The *Rocky Valley Inn* near Matangkib Cave has rooms with balcony for P55/110. The accommodation here is pleasant and they have a good restaurant.

The *Mapiyaaw Sagada Pensione* is idyllically located in a natural rock garden 600m from the town centre heading towards Bontoc. It's a three-storey building, but somehow manages to be cosy, with a fireplace and big balcony on each floor. It has dorm beds for P60, singles/doubles for P75/150 and doubles with bath for P200 (one bathroom is shared between two rooms).

The *Olahbinan Resthouse* has comfortable rooms from P100 to P250, with bath for P500, and also has a suite (two rooms with bath) for P1000. If you want more 'upmarket' accommodation in Sagada, this will fit the bill perfectly.

NORTH LUZON

Places to Eat

You can eat well and cheaply (P50) at the *Café Bilig* and the *Shamrock Café*, where excellent yoghurt and several Mountain Province specialities are available. The *Village Bistro* in the south of Sagada can also be recommended, not least because you can sit outside. At the *Log Cabin* the food is extremely good, but an early reservation is recommended as it is limited in the number of guests is can serve for dinner. It's small, but cosily furnished and a popular place to eat. Several of the guesthouses serve large evening meals and breakfasts, but you should book ahead, say by 4 pm. Most restaurants in Sagada close at 9 pm, and there is a curfew in force at the moment.

Things to Buy

Weavers make beautiful materials at Sagada Weaving, and you can buy traditional woven goods, but at fairly stiff prices. Josephine's Store sells handcrafts made by local highlanders, such as jewellery, baskets and woodcarvings.

Getting There & Away

Bus Several Dangwa Tranco and Lizardo Trans buses leave Baguio daily for Sagada (P135; seven hours). The departure times are 7.30, 8, 9 and 9.30 am. Sit next to the driver or on the right side of the bus for the best view. It gets fairly cool, so take a jacket or jumper out of your luggage before it gets stowed away.

Buses leave Sagada for Baguio at 5.30, 6, 7 and 9 am.

Jeepney From Bontoc to Sagada (P20; one hour), there are at least four jeepneys daily, usually leaving at 6, 7, 8.30 and 10.30 am from the Caltex petrol station.

If you want to go from Sagada to Banaue via Bontoc on the same day, then the best thing is to take the first jeepney at 6 am from Sagada to Bontoc, and catch the jeepney to Banaue there, which leaves at about 7.30 am from the Mountain Hotel.

Getting Around

Bicycle The area around Sagada is not just good for hiking, mountain biking is also fun here. You can rent a mountain bike for P80 a day from the place next to the Rock Café.

BONTOC

At an altitude of about 900m, Bontoc is the capital of Mountain Province and is right in the middle of Central Cordillera.

Woven materials are made on old looms in and around Bontoc, for example, in the All Saints Elementary School and in Barangay Samoki, a village on the other side of the river. As well as woven materials, locals also make simple utensils. It takes about 30 minutes to walk from Bontoc to Samoki.

Information

Tourist Office A small tourist information centre is just along from the Chico Terraces Inn.

Money The branch of the Philippine National Bank in Bontoc changes travellers cheques.

Telephone The area code for Bontoc is 074.

Bontoc Museum

You can get a good overview of the differences and similarities between the mountain tribes in the small but excellent Bontoc Museum. The friendly staff are always happy to give detailed information about life in Mountain Province. The opening hours are from 1 to 5 pm, although they may be open in the morning from 8 am to noon. Admission is P20.

Trekking

The guides Jessie and Kinad will arrange three-day or longer treks (they prefer four-day treks) to Kalinga villages.

Juliet Soria also offers one-day and longer treks and charges P500 per day for up to four people. For five people and more, the cost is P100 each. She can be contacted through hotels in Bontoc, eg the Pines Kitchenette & Inn.

Filipinos used shields made of engraved buffalo leather or carved timber to protect themselves in battle.

Massage

If you feel like a soothing massage after your strenuous walks up and down the mountains, go to the Massage Centre in Bontoc (it's a small building). There are two blind masseurs who will give you a professional massage lasting one hour for P150.

Places to Stay

Let's put it this way: accommodation in Bontoc was obviously at its best a long time ago. If, for example, you've come up Halsema Road from Baguio by car and are looking forward to a cosy little hotel room in Bontoc, you're out of luck. Your best bet would be to stop between Abatan and Bontoc at the *Mt Data Hotel* about 10 km north of Abatan, you can't miss the signs. It's a decent hotel, with comfortable rooms with bath for P800/1100. In Bontoc itself you have the following choices.

The *Mountain Hotel* (☎ 3018) has small, basic rooms for P75/150. The basic and slightly run-down *Bontoc Hotel* also charges P75/150. The *Chico Terrace* (☎ 3099) has rooms for P70 and doubles with bath for P200. It is basic but fairly good accommodation and has some rooms with three or five beds.

The basic *Happy Home Inn* (☎ 3021) is all right for the money at P75/150 for singles/doubles, and P200 for double rooms with bath. A hot shower costs an extra P10.

Breakfast can be arranged on request at the *Village Inn* where singles go for P75 and doubles for P140. The rooms are basic and tiny; two doubles share a small bath.

The *Pines Kitchenette & Inn* near the museum has rooms for P75/150 and with bath for P250/300. This is relatively good accommodation, the best in Bontoc at least.

The *Vista Pensione*, behind the town hall, has only a few basic and small rooms. Singles cost P150 and doubles with bath cost P300.

Places to Eat

Food is pretty good in Bontoc – try the great cinnamon rolls at the local baker's. Almost all of Bontoc's restaurants close at 9 pm. You can eat well at the spacious *Pines Kitchenette & Inn* where you can also get a good-sized breakfast. The food in the pleasant *New Double Eatery* across from the All Saints Mission Elementary School is good and inexpensive, which is also true of the *Bontoc Diner's Restaurant*, on the southern edge of town, which has beautiful views of the valley and the river.

Getting There & Away

Bus There are six Dangwa Tranco buses from Baguio to Bontoc every day, leaving hourly between 5 and 10 am. The 150 km trip takes about eight hours (P130). There is also a daily bus from Banaue to Bontoc, except on Sunday, which leaves between 10 and 11 am and takes 2½ hours.

Jeepney From Banaue to Bontoc (P60; 2½ hours), jeepneys leave at 7 and 10 am and noon, sometimes earlier.

There are at least five jeepneys a day from Sagada to Bontoc (P20; one hour). They leave at 6, 7, 8.30, 10.30 and noon.

There are two jeepneys which travel daily

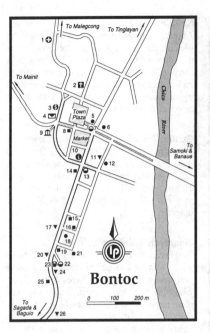

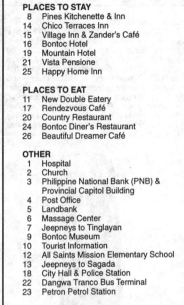

PLACES TO STAY
8 Pines Kitchenette & Inn
14 Chico Terraces Inn
15 Village Inn & Zander's Café
16 Bontoc Hotel
19 Mountain Hotel
21 Vista Pensione
25 Happy Home Inn

PLACES TO EAT
11 New Double Eatery
17 Rendezvous Café
20 Country Restaurant
24 Bontoc Diner's Restaurant
26 Beautiful Dreamer Café

OTHER
1 Hospital
2 Church
3 Philippine National Bank (PNB) &
   Provincial Capitol Building
4 Post Office
5 Landbank
6 Massage Center
7 Jeepneys to Tinglayan
9 Bontoc Museum
10 Tourist Information
12 All Saints Mission Elementary School
13 Jeepneys to Sagada
18 City Hall & Police Station
22 Dangwa Tranco Bus Terminal
23 Petron Petrol Station

between Bontoc and Tabuk via Tinglayan. They leave at 6 am and 1.30 pm.

AROUND BONTOC
Malegcong
The rice terraces at Malegcong are beautifully laid out, some of them even more so than at Banaue. In contrast to the Ifugao, who built their rice terraces with earthen walls, the Bontoc preferred stone walls to separate their fields.

Getting There & Away A jeepney leaves Bontoc early in the morning in the direction of Malegcong (P40). It stops at the end of the track at a little shelter where people wait for the jeepney. From there you can make it on foot through the rice terraces to Malegcong. A second jeepney may make the trip in the late afternoon.

As there is little chance of a connection by jeepney the whole way from Bontoc to

Malegcong any more, the trip will take two hours on foot, which is quite a walk. It can get very hot; take some kind of headcover as well as provisions, including water.

From Bontoc, a track goes north past the Provincial Capitol Building and the hospital as far as the valley with the rice terraces below Malegcong. It's a bit of a short-cut if you take the roughly cut, steep stone stairs just outside of town, which lead off right from the track and meet up with it again later. A narrow stone staircase leads off from the end of the track down to the rice terraces. You can then take a path through the rice terraces to the village of Malegcong.

Mainit
Mainit means hot – probably a reference to the hot springs in this little place where people pan for gold. It leaves most other people cold, so it's no great loss to miss it.

Esteemed Rice

The Ifugao people, who live in North Luzon's Central Cordillera mountain range, have a unique way of safeguarding their annual rice harvest. Skilled woodcarvers, they sculpt sacred figures – the most famous being the male and female deities called the Bulul – and place them at the entrance of the village storehouse to keep an eye on the rice. It is said that these other-worldly figures not only guarantee that the grains last until the next harvest, they also miraculously increase the amount of rice in the storehouse. ■

Ifugao god Bulul, the protector of rice.

Getting There & Away There may be a jeepney which leaves Bontoc daily for Guinaang at about 6.30 to 7 am. From there it is about 45 minutes on foot downhill to Mainit.

There may be a jeepney in the afternoon from Guinaang back to Bontoc. There is also a track from Mainit to Malegcong. It is hard to find, so a guide may be useful. The track starts before you get into Mainit, at a sulphur spring, which you can smell a long way off. If you are coming from Guinaang, you have to turn right at the sulphur spring and follow the track past the rice terraces to Malegcong.

Natonin

About 35 km east of Bontoc as the crow flies, well off the beaten track in other words, lies the little mountain village of Natonin. It is surrounded by rice terraces that seem to go on for ever in all directions. They were built by the Balangao, a minority group who make this area their home.

Getting There & Away Once a day, a jeepney goes from Bontoc to Natonin via Barlig. It may only go as far as Barlig or Cadaclan, where another jeepney takes over. It's about 15 km from Cadaclan to Natonin, and you may have to cover them by foot if you're unlucky.

Tinglayan & Kalinga Villages

Tinglayan is a good starting point from which to visit Kalinga villages. From there you can try to get to the villages with Kalinga who have been to see their relatives in hospital. However, the area must be regarded as risky because of ambushes and numerous fights between the politically distinct units of the Armed Forces of the Philippines (AFP), the New People's Army (NPA) and the Cordillera People's Liberation Army (CPLA). You should check the situation before you go there.

The following round trip will take at least three days on foot, including stopovers in the villages. You can count on three hours from Tinglayan to Tulgueo, one hour or more from Tulgueo to Dananao, two hours from Dananao to Sumadel and one hour from Sumadel to Malango. From Malango you get on to the main road and go back to Tinglayan.

Always get a guide to take you from one village to the next to reduce the likelihood of an attack. Women are normally honoured and treated with respect by the Kalinga, as a Kalinga who attacks a woman loses face for good, but women should also have a guide. Unfortunately, generous travellers have caused expectations of handouts. There have been reports of emphatic demands for hundreds of pesos for the construction of a (non-existent) school.

Getting There & Away From Bontoc to Tinglayan there is a daily jeepney, which leaves after the arrival of the bus from Baguio between 1 and 2 pm. There are several checkpoints on this stretch and the soldiers may check baggage thoroughly. They might also want to see identity documents.

The jeepney returning from Tinglayan to Bontoc does not leave until 6 am the following morning.

Lubuagan & Chico Valley Dam
In and around Lubuagan, the former government of president Marcos came into direct conflict with the Kalinga because of the Chico Valley dam project, which was to comprise four single dams and produce 1000 megawatts of electricity.

The Chico Valley dam would have been the largest in South-East Asia and would have flooded the Kalinga's valleys, forcing them to resettle. The Kalinga were opposed to the move as it would have meant the end of their centuries-old culture, which has developed in isolation from the colonised lowlands. The Kalinga's religion was another reason for their opposition to the move. They live in a world of gods and spirits and show great respect to the dead, so their ancestors' resting places must be left undisturbed.

At first there was only scattered fighting against the surveying of the dam. In 1980, however, following the murder of Bugnay's Chief Macliing Dulag, who had been sabotaging the works of the national energy company, the 20 or so groups of Kalinga, comprising about 100,000 members, formed a united front. Macliing was shot by several volleys of machine-gun fire through the thin walls of his hut and it is said that the murderers were wearing military uniforms. The conflict widened and soldiers and construction workers were beheaded and rebellious Kalinga shot. Members of the NPA (New People's Army) joined the Kalinga and instructed them in the use of modern M-16 rifles.

Today, relations between the mountain dwellers and the NPA, as well as the government, are anything but harmonious. The Kalinga now distrust any power which tries to intrude on them. They continue to be vigilant and regard any stranger as a threat – do not venture into the mountains alone.

BANAUE
Banaue is at an altitude of about 1200m. The rice terraces around Banaue have been called the eighth wonder of the world. It took the Ifugao tribespeople, with their primitive implements, over 2000 years to create this imposing landscape. Unfortunately, the younger generation no longer feels the call to be rice farmers and carry on the labour-intensive tending of the fields, so the preservation of the rice terraces is in danger. UNESCO could provide the necessary financial support to save the terraces, as they have been nominated for inclusion in the UNESCO World Heritage list.

The Ifugao normally plant rice according to the following timetable: in the second half of December, they begin to sow the seed; from the beginning of February to the middle of March, they transplant the first seedlings; from the middle of April until the middle of June, they weed the fields; in July, the harvest takes place; and from the beginning of August until the middle of December, they work on improvements to the rice terraces and preparing the fields for the next seeding.

Orientation
Maps You can buy a useful map of Banaue's surroundings at the Tourist Information Center for P10. It shows the way to various interesting sights and describes them in detail on the back. However, the times given for hikes are at best vague.

Information
Tourist Office A small Tourist Information Center can be found next to the Sanafe Lodge. Among other things, they have lists pinned up with information on Special Rides by jeepney.

Money There is an authorised foreign exchange counter at the Banaue Hotel. However, the exchange rate is poor and there is a fee of P50 for each travellers' cheque.

The RSR Store across from the Sanafe Lodge will change cash.

Telephone The area code for Banaue is 074.

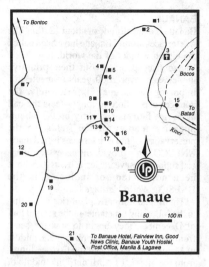

PLACES TO STAY
1   Traveler's Inn
2   Brookside Inn
4   Cozy Nook Inn
5   Halfway Lodge & Restaurant
6   Stairway Lodge & Restaurant
7   Terrace Ville Inn
8   Wonder Lodge & Restaurant
9   Green View Lodge
10 People's Lodge, Bakery & Restaurant &
    Las Vegas Restaurant
12 Banaue View Inn
14 Valgreg Lodge
16 Sanafe Lodge & Tourist Information
    Centre
19 Jericho Guest House
20 Spring Village Inn
21 J & L Pension

PLACES TO EAT
11 Cool Winds Restaurant

OTHER
3   Church
13 Market
15 School
17 RSR Store
18 Town Hall

Museum

In the same building as the Banaue View Inn there is a small museum which has traditional Ifugao household objects, jewellery, clothing etc on display. There are also a few interesting books on exhibition. Admission is P20 and don't be afraid to ask them to let you in; they're not actually open on a regular basis. It's worth seeing this museum if you missed the one in Bontoc.

Things to See & Do

There are a number of things to do around Banaue. You can visit several Ifugao villages, take some of the paths through the rice terraces, enjoy the panorama from **Banaue View Point** or take a refreshing dip in the water of the **Guihon Natural Pool**. On the way there you can make a detour to the bronzesmiths of **Matanglag**, or visit Josef Blas, who makes artistic woodcarvings, as do the friendly villagers in **Poi-tan**. Set in beautiful surroundings, the village has kept alive its tradition of woodcarving and weaving. In contrast, the neighbouring village of Tam-an has obviously specialised in selling souvenirs to tourists.

A tricycle to **Banaue View Point** costs P80; jeepneys to Bontoc also use this route. Colourfully dressed Ifugao wait at the view point for photographers, and expect a few pesos for a photo.

Trekking Guides are more than happy to guide small groups through the mountains and can be contacted via jeepney drivers at the market.

The following tour is beginning to get popular, although you have to be fit to do it (the terrain is tough at times) and only experienced trekkers should attempt it on their own. It starts in Banaue and takes you to the View Point (two hours), then to Pula (eight hours) and via Cambulo (two hours) to Batad (two hours). From there you go back to the road (two hours) which takes you back to Banaue (five hours).

Places to Stay

There are plenty of small places to stay, all within walking distance of the market where the buses arrive.

The *Brookside Inn, Jericho Guest House* and *Traveler's Inn* (☎ 386 4020) all have simple but clean rooms for P60/120. The *Wonder Lodge* (☎ 386 4017) has simple but good quality rooms for P75/150.

The *Cosy Nook Inn* (☎ 386 4003) is under family management and lives up to its name, with cosy beds ('fluffy' one satisfied customer called them) for P75/150. It is located across from the Halfway Lodge, up some stone steps on the hillside.

The rooms at the *Halfway Lodge* (☎ 386 4082) are basic, but clean and cosy, and cost P75/150 and with bath for P200/300.

Accommodation is basic but good at the *Stairway Lodge* (☎ 386 4053) where pleasant singles/doubles cost P75/150 and double rooms with bath P250.

The *People's Lodge* (☎ 386 4014) is a wonderful, friendly place with a bakery and restaurant. The rooms are basic, clean and comfortable, and cost P75/100 and with bath P350. If your room doesn't have en-suite facilities, the view of the rice terraces from the shared toilets will more than make up for it!

Just outside Banaue, on the way to the Banaue Hotel, the cosily furnished *J & L Pension* (☎ 386 4035) offers rooms for P150/250. An Ifugao house costs P300.

As you would expect, there is a beautiful view of Banaue from the pleasant and quiet *Banaue View Inn* (☎ 386 4078), where dorm beds go for P100 and rooms with bath for P400/450.

Really good rooms at the *Spring Village Inn* (☎ 386 4037) cost P200/300, with bath P500.

The *Terrace Ville Inn* (☎ 386 4069) has passable rooms with bath for P350.

Enjoy the beautiful view of the town from the quiet and attractive *Fairview Inn* (☎ 386 4002) where cosy rooms with bath go for P250/350.

You can get a gorgeous view of the terraces from the *Green View Lodge* (☎ 386 4021), which is a good place with tastefully decorated rooms for P100/200, with bath for P350/400. The single rooms are OK for two people.

The *Sanafe Lodge* (☎ 386 4085) has dorm beds for P120, singles with bath for P450 and doubles with bath for P650. The rooms are quite comfortable, if a little overpriced.

The *Banaue Youth Hostel* provides dorm beds for P150. It is administered by the Banaue Hotel, whose swimming pool is available for use.

The exclusive *Banaue Hotel* (☎ 386 4087; fax 386 4048) is tastefully decorated throughout and is the best place to stay in Banaue. Their singles with bath go for P1360 and doubles with bath for P1550. Non-residents can use the swimming pool for P15.

Places to Eat

Most hotels have a small restaurant or else the staff will cook meals for guests. The *Cool Winds Restaurant* next to the market provides large helpings of good food and local musicians sometimes have a jam session here. The *People's Restaurant*, *Halfway Restaurant*, *Stairway Restaurant* and the *Las Vegas Restaurant* are good and cheap, although they all close at 9 pm, as do almost all the restaurants in Banaue. If it's getting late, there's nothing for it but to go to the *County Folkhouse* next to the Town Hall.

The restaurant at the up-market *Banaue Hotel* is excellent. In the evening, if there are enough guests by say 8.30 pm, then a performance of Ifugao dances will be held. Although these performances are in contrast to the world of international hotels and seem perhaps a little out of place in this setting, they are at least relatively authentic. Admission is P20. On the way back to the village at night it is likely to be very dark, so don't forget to take a flashlight.

Getting There & Away

Bus From Manila to Banaue (P160; 10 hours), a Dangwa Tranco bus leaves daily at 7 am. Tickets are on sale from 6.30 am prompt, and can be sold out by 6.45 am. No reservations can be made. You can also take a Baliwag Transit bus from Manila which goes almost as far as Banaue. Take one bound for Ilagan, Tuguegarao and Aparri. Get off in Solano, just before the turn-off to Banaue, take a jeepney to Lagawe and then go on by jeepney to Banaue. The last jeepney leaves Lagawe for Banaue at 5.30 pm, so make sure you don't arrive too late as there is no accommodation in Lagawe.

There are only a few daily Dangwa Tranco buses from Baguio to Banaue (P130; nine hours), taking the southern route via Villasis, San Jose and Bayombong. They leave at 6.45 and 7.30 am and between 6 and 8 pm. You have to be at the bus terminal early, as the bus will leave up to an hour early if it is full, especially at Easter. The departure times are often altered, so it's a good idea to check the day before leaving.

If you want to go from Baguio to Banaue via Bontoc, you will have to stay the night in Bontoc, as there is no direct connection.

To go from San Fernando and Bauang to Banaue, take a bus at about 5 or 6 am headed for Manila and get off at the turn-off to Rosario. From there catch the bus from Baguio to Banaue (see above), which gets there about an hour after leaving Baguio. The bus is likely to be full to bursting, but some passengers may get off there.

It's best to travel from Angeles to Banaue in three stages. With waiting, the trip lasts about ten hours in all, so start as early as possible. Start off with a bus from Dau to Tarlac (every bus heading towards Baguio, La Union, Vigan and Laoag goes through there), which takes one hour. In Tarlac, take a tricycle to the Baliwag Transit Bus Terminal (P5) and from there the next bus to Cabanatuan (1½ hours). In Cabanatuan, don't carry on to the bus terminal but get out beforehand at the McDonald's at the highway and stop a bus heading north, eg to Roxas, Tuguegarao or Aparri, which you then take to Solano (four hours). Carry on from the Mountain Lodge & Restaurant in Solano by jeepney to Banaue (two hours). The last departure from Solano to Banaue is around 4 pm. You can also take a jeepney from Solano to Lagawe and change there into a jeepney heading for Banaue. The last departure from Lagawe to Banaue is around 5.30 pm.

From Banaue to Tuguegarao and Aparri take one of the buses mentioned from Banaue to Manila or Baguio, and get off at Bagabag, Solano or Bayombong. Then wait for the Manila to Tuguegarao or Aparri bus. The trip takes four or six hours respectively.

From Banaue to Baguio, the Dangwa Tranco buses leave at 6.45 and 7.30 am, and sometimes even at 5 am.

From Banaue to Manila, a Dangwa Tranco bus leaves daily at 7 am (10 hours).

Jeepney From Bontoc to Banaue, a jeepney leaves from the Mountain Hotel every day at 7.30 am (P60; 2½ hours). Apparently another jeepney makes the trip around noon or in the early afternoon. From Banaue to Bontoc, jeepneys leave at 7 and 10 am, and 1 pm.

Getting Around
Tricycle You can hire a tricycle for an entire day's sightseeing for P250.

AROUND BANAUE
Hapao & Hungduan
Between Banaue and Banaue View Point a seldom-used track turns off to Hapao (15 km) and Hungduan (25 km). It runs through magnificent countryside with scores of rice terraces all around. After only a few km, a sign informs you that you can see some mummies in a small village just off the track. And, lo and behold, you can. In an Ifugao house behind a big sheet of glass a mummified couple are on exhibit. Using his late grandparents as an example, the grandson willingly explains the intricacies of the traditional process of mummification to visitors.

It is said that General Yamashita, the commander in chief of the Japanese Imperial Army, held his last stand in Hungduan at the end of WWII, before finally surrendering in Kiangan, a few km south-east of Hungduan.

Getting There & Away There are probably only a few jeepneys that make the trip every day from Banaue to Hapao or Hungduan. A Special Ride to Hapao and back costs P600.

Batad & Cambulo
The wonderful village of Batad is about 16 km east of Banaue. It is surrounded by breathtakingly beautiful rice terraces which

are in the shape of an amphitheatre. It is an impressive sight to see them slowly emerge from the low-lying cloud early in the morning. Many Ifugao houses now have corrugated iron roofs, but luckily these have not yet been generally accepted. Batad must be one of the most impressive places in Central Cordillera and is a 'must see' spot. There is the beautiful Tapplya waterfall, with a natural swimming pool, only about an hour's walk from Batad, but it would be better to stay overnight in Batad rather than include it in a day trip from Banaue.

If you want to photograph villagers in Batad, you should ask them first as they either object or will demand payment.

About two hours on foot from Batad is Cambulo, a typical little Ifugao village, in the midst of rice terraces. From there a trail, which takes about four hours, leads to Kinakin on the main road, where a jeepney might pass by on its way to Banaue (P20). It is another eight km back to Banaue.

Places to Stay & Eat Accommodation is basic throughout the area, but the atmosphere is always very friendly. You can stay the night in Batad for about P50 at the *Batad Pension*, *Cristina's Guest House*, *Shirley's Inn*, *Foreigner's Inn*, *Rita's Mount View Inn*, *Summer Inn*, or *Simon's Inn* and *Hillside Inn*. The Hillside Inn has good meals, especially Middle-Eastern dishes. If you're dying for a huge pizza, then *Simon's Inn*, where the sandwiches are also excellent, is the place for you.

In Cambulo, the *Riverside Guest House* has overnight accommodation for P40. Lydia, the owner, also cooks for her guests (P40 per meal).

Getting There & Away For the first 12 km from Banaue to Batad you can go by vehicle, but the rest you have to walk. There may be a bus from Banaue to Mayoyao between 10 am and noon, which stops at the turn-off (referred to locally as the 'junction') to Batad. Returning, it passes between 9 and 11 am.

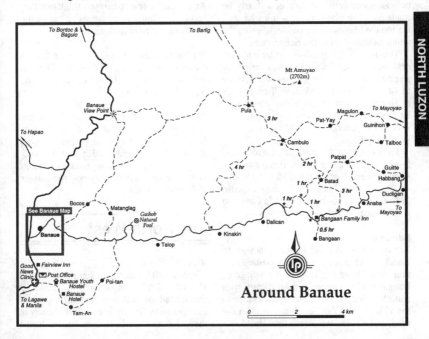

Around Banaue

The 'junction' is between Dalican and Bangaan. From there, it's a two-hour trek up the steep path over the saddle, youngsters do a roaring trade selling drinks.

Another path leads from Bangaan (coming from Banaue, 50m before the Bangaan Family Inn) up to the saddle. At first it takes you up a steep path through high grass, further on you can walk in the shade of lush vegetation if you're there in the forenoon. The view of Bangaan valley from the path is magnificent.

On the way back to Bangaan, there is a path that takes you the longer way, but it has the advantage of not having any steep bits to negotiate. The path leads along the mountain chain you climbed over on the way there. It later rejoins the road to Mayoyao about one km east of Bangaan. This path is shaded in the afternoon and is difficult to find in its early stages. Best ask one of the local boys from the first little village (you can see where it is from Batad) to act as guide for you. For a few pesos he'll accompany you for about half an hour, until the path can clearly be made out. The place where it joins up with the road to Mayoyao can be identified by the white painted wall in the rice terraces.

The Tourist Information Center and several guesthouses will organise trips by jeepney for P500. The jeepney will take up to 14 people and the driver will come back to pick up his passengers at the 'junction' at an agreed time in the late afternoon. One-way to the junction costs P350; by tricycle you'll pay P150.

Jeepneys with the destination Anaba and Ducligan make the run in the Batad direction daily between 1 and 5 pm (P35 per person).

An attractive alternative for the return trip to Banaue is to go from Batad via Cambulo and Kinakin, which takes six hours.

Bangaan

Not quite two km east of the 'junction' to Batad, a track takes you in the opposite direction down from the road to the village of Bangaan. The scenery is magnificent, with countless rice terraces forming a backdrop to the village. You can see Bangaan from the road, and it's easier to reach than Batad.

Places to Stay & Eat The *Bangaan Family Inn* is not in the village of Bangaan itself, but on the main road before it goes downhill. Expect a family atmosphere, where pleasant rooms cost P40/80. They also rent five original native Ifugao houses for P50 per person. The food is excellent, and views from the big patio restaurant are wonderful.

Getting There & Away Buses and jeepneys from Banaue to Mayoyao go via Bangaan (one hour). Special Rides by jeepney cost P350.

Mayoyao

Situated about 30 km east of Bangaan, Mayoyao is a rather unattractive place with a small recognisable centre and numerous houses spread higgledy-piggledy over the valley. You can see that a corrugated iron salesman must have made a killing here, as the metal of the Ifugao house roofs glints in the sunlight from a distance. The rice terraces in Mayoyao were built with masonry walls. An incredible feat, when you think that they had to drag millions of stones up the mountain from the river beds to do it.

Places to Stay & Eat Only private accommodation is available in Mayoyao. The nice lady who owns the *Travelers Canteen* will be glad to fix you up.

Getting There & Away A few buses and jeepneys travel every day from Banaue to Mayoyao (4½ hours). You get the best view if you sit on the right-hand side of the bus.

If you don't want to go back to Banaue, you can get a bus from Mayoyao to Santiago at 7 am (five hours).

The North-West

VIGAN

Vigan is 130 km north of San Fernando (La Union) and, after Intramuros in Manila, is the second greatest architectural legacy of the Spaniards. The difference is that many of the old houses still stand in Vigan. In the latter half of the 16th century, after the young conquistador Juan de Salcedo won a naval battle against the Chinese, Legaspi, his grandfather, gave him the commission to govern Ilocos Province. Vigan thus became a Spanish base.

In planning the layout of the town, Salcedo was no doubt influenced by the secure fortifications of Intramuros. Today Vigan is the best preserved Spanish town in the Philippines. You can almost sense history here. It is well known as the birthplace of several national heroes, including Diego Silang and his brave wife Gabriela, Padre Jose Burgos, Isabelo de los Reyes, Leona Florentina and Elipido Quirino.

Vigan is especially impressive in the early morning, when the diffused light transforms the old town with its colonial houses and calesas into a scene reminiscent of the 17th century. Mena Crisologo St is a particularly beautiful place. UNESCO has already approved money for the redevelopment of the old town centre, also known as 'Heritage Village'.

Telephone
The area code for Vigan is 077.

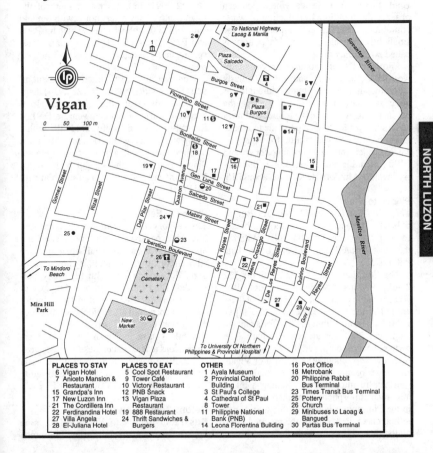

PLACES TO STAY
6 Vigan Hotel
7 Aniceto Mansion & Restaurant
15 Grandpa's Inn
17 New Luzon Inn
21 The Cordillera Inn
22 Ferdinandina Hotel
27 Villa Angela
28 El-Juliana Hotel

PLACES TO EAT
5 Cool Spot Restaurant
9 Tower Café
10 Victory Restaurant
12 PNB Snack
13 Vigan Plaza Restaurant
19 888 Restaurant
24 Thrift Sandwiches & Burgers

OTHER
1 Ayala Museum
2 Provincial Capitol Building
3 St Paul's College
4 Cathedral of St Paul
8 Tower
11 Philippine National Bank (PNB)
14 Leona Florentina Building

16 Post Office
18 Metrobank
20 Philippine Rabbit Bus Terminal
23 Times Transit Bus Terminal
25 Pottery
26 Church
29 Minibuses to Laoag & Bangued
30 Partas Bus Terminal

NORTH LUZON

Things to See & Do

The partially restored old town is the birthplace of Padre Jose Burgos, who was executed by the Spaniards in 1872. The house in which he was born has housed the **Ayala Museum** since 1975. It is open Tuesday to Sunday from 9 am to noon and 2 to 5 pm. Admission is P10. You can also get information there about the Tingguian, who live east of Vigan.

The **Cathedral of St Paul** near Plaza Burgos, built in 1641, is one of the oldest and biggest churches in the country.

Along Rizal St, as it crosses Liberation Blvd, there are **potteries** where you can observe the traditional production of water containers. The fat-bellied pots with the small lids are called *burnay* (a pottery is called *pagburnayan*).

Mindoro Beach, about four km southwest of Vigan, is grey and not particularly recommended for swimming, although it is quite suitable for lonely walks along the ocean. On the way, there is a **tobacco factory** and a small **pottery**. It's a good idea to make this short trip (in a way fitting for Vigan) by calesa, which should be possible for around P100 (including a one-hour stop at the sea). A tricycle to Mindoro Beach costs about P15.

Places to Stay

The *Vigan Hotel* (☎/fax 722 3001) on Burgos St has fairly good accommodation, although some of the rooms are a bit stuffy. With fan they cost P275/375 and with air-con and bath P500/675.

The Cordillera Inn (☎ 722 2526; fax 722 2840), 29 Mena Crisologo St, is a good place with passable rooms, although some of them are not in the best of condition. You'll pay P400 for a room with fan, P800 for a fan and bath, and P900 for air-con and bath. The owners have also opened the *Teppeng Cove Beach Resort*, about 40 km north of Vigan, which has rooms from P300 to P650.

If you're interested in catching a bit of historical atmosphere – and there's nowhere in the Philippines better for this than Vigan – then check in at one of the restored colonial-style hotels and soak in the atmosphere.

Expect Spanish colonial houses with original tile roofs, hardwood floors, and balustrades you could imagine Zorro jumping from.

The *RF Aniceto Mansion* (☎ 722 2382; fax 722 2384) in Mena Crisologo St has the most inexpensive rooms in this category. Doubles with fan are P250, rooms with fan and bath P250/350, and with air-con and bath P550/650. Situated on the Plaza Burgos diagonally across from the cathedral, this is an authentic Vigan building with really good rooms. They also have a swimming pool.

The friendly *El-Juliana Hotel* is at the corner of Liberation Blvd and Quirino Blvd (☎ 722 2994) in a quiet area south of the town centre. They offer rooms with fan and bath for P400, with air-con and bath for P500 and P750 (with TV). This place has atmosphere, and you can always cool off in their pool.

However, the most attractive of them all must be the *Villa Angela* (☎ 722 2914) diagonally across from the El-Juliana Hotel between Quirino Blvd and Ventura De Los Reyes St. This is a beautiful old villa with a really well preserved interior, furniture from colonial times and a magnificent garden. Singles/doubles with fan and bath go for P250/500 and doubles with air-con and bath for P800.

Places to Eat

The *Victory Restaurant* on Quezon Ave offers inexpensive Filipino food. The *Cool Spot Restaurant*, a lovely half-open-air place adjacent to the Vigan Hotel, is known for its good Ilocano cooking. But for really outstanding food and big portions, the place to go to is the *888 Restaurant* in Del Pilar St, which is open until after midnight. They also offer cheap pool at P2 per game.

While you're in Vigan you should try empanadas at least once; these are tasty vegetable-filled pasties of Spanish origin. You can get them from around 4 pm until quite late at night at the Plaza Burgos for P3 each.

Getting There & Away

Bus From Manila to Vigan (P180; nine hours), there are several Partas, Philippine

Rabbit, Times Transit, Fariñas Trans and Maria de Leon buses daily. Some buses continuing north to Laoag bypass the town, in which case you will have to take a tricycle from the highway (P5) or walk (10 minutes).

From Baguio to Vigan (P80; 4½ hours) there are a few Times Transit buses a day.

From San Fernando several Philippine Rabbit buses go to Vigan daily (2½ hours), leaving from the plaza. You can also board a bus from Manila to Vigan or Laoag there.

From Aparri to Vigan there are only a few buses a day (nine hours).

From Laoag to Vigan, there are many minibuses daily as well as Partas, Philippine Rabbit, Times Transit, Fariñas Trans and Maria de Leon buses bound for Manila or San Fernando (two hours). You may have to get off the bus on the highway outside the town and complete the last stretch to Vigan by tricycle (P5) or walk (10 minutes).

BANGUED

Bangued was founded in 1598 by Augustinian monks and is the capital of Abra, which has been a province since 1917. From little Victoria Park, on Casmata Hill, you can get a good view of the town and of the Abra River flowing through the wide valley.

Every year from 5 to 10 March, Bangued celebrates the Abry Abra Festival with parades, colourful cultural presentations and folklore displays, including some from the Ilocanos and the Tingguian.

Telephone
The area code for Bangued is 074.

Places to Stay
Though basic, the best hotel in town is the *Marysol Pension House* (☎ 752 8590) on Taft St, where rooms with fan go for P250, with fan and bath for P300 and with air-con and bath for P400/500. Their restaurant only serves meals if they are ordered in advance.

The unpretentious *Tingguian Lodge* (☎ 752 8384) is a bit outside of town in Calaba. They will give you a room with fan for P150 and with air-con and bath for P250. Make enquiries at the convent near the church if you are interested in staying at the *Diocesan Pastoral Center* (☎ 752 8092) on Rizal St. They charge P165/200 for rooms with fan and bath, and P385/440 with air-con and bath. The Center is not a hotel but church-run accommodation.

Places to Eat
Good restaurants are hard to come by in Bangued. Worth mentioning perhaps are *Jade's Restaurant* and the *Yan Yan Mami House*. They also serve food in the *Bene Disco*, which is open until after midnight.

Getting There & Away
From Manila to Bangued there are Partas, Philippine Rabbit and Times Transit buses daily (nine hours).

From Vigan to Bangued there are several minibuses daily from the terminal at the new market. Large Times Transit buses are also likely to be there.

Four Philippine Rabbit buses go from Baguio to Batad daily (five hours).

AROUND BANGUED
About 30 km south-east of Bangued, near the little town of **Manabo**, there are several villages of the Tingguian tribe that you can visit by walking through Boliney, Bucloc and Sallapadan. In Boliney are the **Bani Hot Springs** and the **Nani Waterfalls**. Bucloc has rice terraces, and, if you are lucky, you may see the Grand Tingguian Festival at Sallapadan. This is the most important cultural event in Abra Province and is usually held in March or April each year. The exact date is fixed only shortly beforehand.

Getting There & Away Several minibuses travel from Vigan to Bangued daily, leaving from the bus terminal at the new market. They take three hours. There is also an irregular connection between Bangued and Tubo via Manabo several times a week. A jeepney leaves Bangued at about 6 am. If you ask the driver the day before, you will be picked up at your hotel and you might get to sit at the front. The jeepney does not go beyond Tubo.

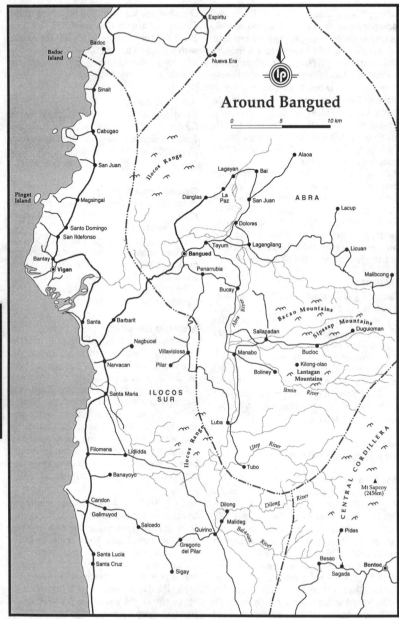

Around Bangued

0   5   10 km

CURRIMAO

Currimao, with its D'Coral Beach Resort, a particular favourite of the Filipinos, is about 75 km north of Vigan and 25 km south of Laoag. Slightly farther north, the long bay of Pias Sur curves along the coast with a beautiful deserted beach. The beach itself is unfortunately not framed by appropriately romantic palm trees, but by a shaggy mixture of vegetation.

Telephone
The area code for Currimao is 077.

Places to Stay
On the outskirts of Currimao, the *Villa na Pintas* (☎/fax 792 2917) has rooms with fan for P700 and with fan and bath for P1200. They have a swimming pool in the neatly trimmed green of their garden and offer sea diving. Run by Swiss management, the building is in tip-top condition, set on a low rise with a view down to the ocean. It costs P15 by tricycle to get there from the main road.

To get to the *D'Coral Beach Resort* (☎ 772 1133) get out at Port Currimao and walk about 500m. Their rooms with fan and bath go for P500, cottages with fan and bath from P1100, and cottages with air-con and bath from P1600. The cottages are OK, but a bit spartan.

Getting There & Away
Bus From Vigan to Currimao, there are lots of minibuses daily as well as several big Partas, Times Transit and Philippine Rabbit buses bound for Laoag (1½ hours).

From Laoag to Currimao, there are also plenty of minibuses daily as well as several big Partas, Philippine Rabbit, Times Transit, Fariñas Trans and Maria de Leon buses (30 minutes), all going on to Vigan and Manila.

LAOAG

In 1818, when Ilocos Province was divided in two, Laoag, on the Laoag River, became the capital of Ilocos Norte, one of Luzon's most beautiful provinces. Worth seeing is **St Williams Cathedral**, which was built between 1650 and 1700, and is one of the many old Spanish churches in this province. Also interesting is the mighty sinking belltower, which stands apart from the cathedral.

You get a good view over this city of 100,000 inhabitants from **Ermita Hill**. Day trips into the nearby countryside are recommended. (See the Around Laoag section later in this chapter.)

Telephone
The area code for Laoag is 077.

Places to Stay
The *City Lodging House* on General Antonio Luna St must be doing something right. They have small, loud and basic rooms with fan for P100/200, but the place is, amazingly, often fully booked.

A well-maintained hotel, and really good for this price category, is the *Texicano Hotel* (☎ 772 0606) on Jose Rizal St. Rooms in the old building with fan cost P110/140, and with fan and bath P145/165. If you want air-con and TV, then accommodation in the new building will cost you P500/540. The actual entrance is on General Hizon St.

The *Casa Llanes Pension* (☎ 772 1125) on Primo Lazaro Ave is a pleasant, tidy establishment. Spacious rooms with fan and bath go for P170 and with air-con and bath for P270. They can also be rented for three and 12 hours.

On Primo Lazaro Ave, the *Pichay Lodging House* (☎ 221267) has rooms with fan and bath for P200 and with air-con and bath for P280/330. They are adequate, although some are a bit run-down.

The *Fort Ilocandia Resort Hotel* (☎ 772 1166; fax 772 1411) is an exclusive hotel on Suba Beach, south of the airport. Singles with air-con and bath cost P4130 and doubles P4500. Suites are P5800. They have a disco, casino, three swimming pools and a tennis court. You can take a jeepney going from Laoag to Calayab there.

Places to Eat
You can get good and cheap Chinese and Filipino dishes at the no-frills *Noodle House* on FR Castro Ave and at the *City Lunch &*

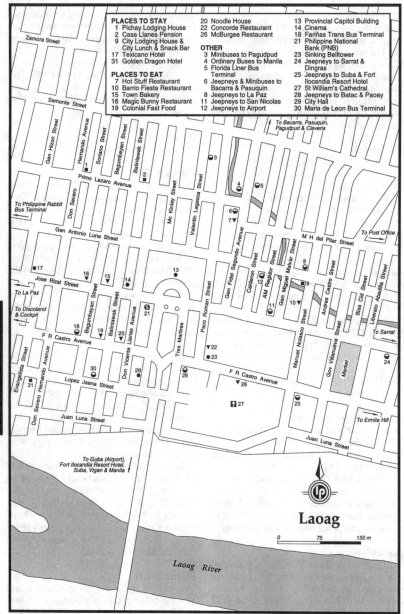

PLACES TO STAY
1 Pichay Lodging House
2 Casa Llanes Pension
9 City Lodging House &
   City Lunch & Snack Bar
17 Texicano Hotel
31 Golden Dragon Hotel

PLACES TO EAT
7 Hot Stuff Restaurant
10 Barrio Fiesta Restaurant
15 Town Bakery
16 Magic Bunny Restaurant
19 Colonial Fast Food

20 Noodle House
22 Concorde Restaurant
26 McBurgee Restaurant

OTHER
3 Minibuses to Pagudpud
4 Ordinary Buses to Manila
5 Florida Liner Bus
  Terminal
6 Jeepneys & Minibuses to
  Bacarra & Pasuquin
8 Jeepneys to La Paz
11 Jeepneys to San Nicolas
12 Jeepneys to Airport

13 Provincial Capitol Building
14 Cinema
18 Fariñas Trans Bus Terminal
21 Philippine National
   Bank (PNB)
23 Sinking Belltower
24 Jeepneys to Sarrat &
   Dingras
25 Jeepneys to Suba & Fort
   Ilocandia Resort Hotel
27 St William's Cathedral
28 Jeepneys to Batac & Paoay
29 City Hall
30 Maria de Leon Bus Terminal

NORTH LUZON

Laoag

Laoag River

0   75   150 m

Snack Bar, on the corner of General Antonio Luna and Manuel Nolasco Sts. It also serves very reasonably priced breakfasts.

On Jose Rizal St is the good and cheap *Dohan Food & Bake Shop*. *McBurgee* is a small inexpensive fast-food restaurant on FR Castro Ave. The *Concorde Restaurant* on Paco Roman St and the *Barrio Fiesta* on Manuel Nolasco St belong to the mid-price range.

The *Town Bakery* in Jose Rizal St between Balintawak St and Bagumbayan St, has good cakes, plus doughnuts for only a peso.

Entertainment

To the relief of Chinese tourists, the introduction of flights to and from Taiwan brought about the re-opening of the Casino in the Fort Ilocandia Resort Hotel.

Cockfighting takes place on the edge of town on Sunday and public holidays from 2 pm onwards. Next door, you will find Laoag's nightlife at *Discoland*, consisting of about 10 discos.

Getting There & Away

Air PAL flies on Monday and Friday from Manila to Laoag (P1350; one hour); and on Monday from Basco to Laoag (P811; one hour).

PAL has an office at Laoag international airport (☎ 772 0537) and on Jose Rizal St (☎ 220135).

Bus From Manila to Laoag, there are many Partas, Philippine Rabbit, Fariñas Trans, Maria de Leon and Times Transit buses daily (11 hours). The buses go via San Fernando and Vigan. Vigan is off the highway and not all buses make the detour into town. If you're in a hurry, get a tricycle for P5 to the highway and stop one of the buses there (two hours).

There are also many minibuses travelling from Vigan to Laoag daily (three hours).

From Aparri to Laoag, there are only a few buses, going via Pagudpud. Of the ones that do go, some are bound for Vigan. You will probably have to take a jeepney to the new Marcos Bridge on the highway and catch a bus coming from Tuguegarao to Laoag or Vigan.

From Tuguegarao to Laoag you can take a Florida Liner bus; they leave daily at 4 and 9 am and 6 pm (seven hours).

From Baguio to Laoag via San Fernando and Vigan, Philippine Rabbit buses go every hour, unfortunately seldom with air-conditioning. The trip takes six hours.

From Laoag to Aparri via Pagudpud, there are few daytime buses, leaving from the corner of Primo Lazaro and General Fidel Segundo Aves. There is also a night bus to Aparri at 10 pm (Florida bus) (five hours), but travel by day to see the spectacular landscape and beautiful views over the South China Sea. The views along Pagudpud to Claveria are especially worth seeing.

Getting Around

The Airport The Laoag international airport is at Gabu, about five km south-west of Laoag. Jeepneys to the airport (P4; 15 minutes) leave from the corner of AM Regidor and General Luna Sts.

AROUND LAOAG
North

North of Laoag, **Bacarra** has a massive belltower which stands next to the town's church. It dates back to 1783 and was partly destroyed in the severe earthquake of 1930. The top of the spire was crooked and, until 1984, was held in place solely, as they said then, by 'the hand of God'. Another earthquake then caused its complete collapse.

NORTH LUZON

Salt Shakers

From December to March you can see women strenuously at work harvesting salt in the late afternoon. At low tide, the top layer of salt, mixed with sand, is scraped together and put in a light hanging basket. Water is then poured in and runs out through the bottom of the basket into an earthenware pot, now with a high salt content. This water is taken to the village and boiled in a large pot until it has almost completely evaporated. The remaining slurry is then ladled out of the pot into a hanging basket, which the remaining water seeps through to form a long, hanging white cone of the finest salt. ■

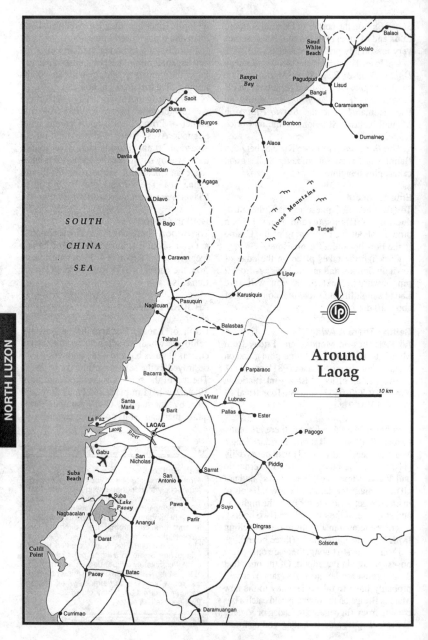

Ten km farther north is Pasuquin; from there you can go to **Seksi Beach**, which is four km outside the town and can be reached by tricycle.

West
The nearest good beach to Laoag is in **La Paz**, an unhurried, long drawn-out place at the mouth of the Laoag River. Hardly any vegetation exists on the wide beach, but there are very extensive sand dunes that eventually end up in a beautiful pebble beach at the north end.

South-East
A country road leads to Sarrat, the birthplace of former president Marcos. In the centre of town is the restored **Sarrat Church & Convent**, built in 1779 by Augustinian monks.

Only ruins remain of the church in Dingras, which was destroyed by fire in 1838.

South
There is a **church** in San Nicolas which was built in the latter part of the 17th century and restored in the 19th century. About 15 km further south, in Batac, another building attracts the attention of the Filipinos: **Marcos Mansion** is full of Marcos memorabilia, including the refrigerated remains of the former president.

A few km to the south-west is the fortress-like church of **Paoay Church**, which is worth a stop. Its side walls are supported by strong posts. Styled in 'earthquake baroque', this church is probably the most famous in Ilocos Norte. You can also see scenic Lake Paoay. Going from Paoay through bamboo forests, along the western shore of the lake to Suba, you could make a detour to **Suba Beach**. The road there is hilly and winding and there are high, extensive sand dunes, more imposing than those at La Paz, where many Philippine films have been shot. It is usually windy on this wide beach and there is good surf.

If you have come up from Paoay by tricycle and want to return to Laoag by jeepney, ask the driver to drop you off at the Fort Ilocandia Resort Hotel or at the Suba Golf

Course. The last regular jeepney leaves the hotel at about 4 pm and passes the golf course on the way back to Laoag. The exclusive hotel is about five km south of Gabu, where Laoag international airport is located. Marcos had it built especially for guests on the occasion of the wedding of his daughter Irene to Greggy Araneta in 1983. The tables and seats under cover on the beach belong to the hotel and there is a P100 charge for their use.

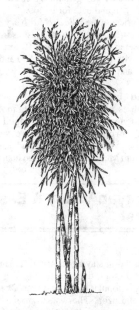

Many kinds of bamboo are useful in everyday life, eg for building, weaving or cooking. The shoots (*labong*) closest to the ground are chopped and boiled and used as a basic vegetable in many local dishes.

PAGUDPUD
Pagudpud lies on beautiful Bangui Bay, about 60 km north of Laoag, and could become a tourist destination in the near future. The beautiful **Saud White Beach** at Pagudpud is probably the best and most attractive in North Luzon and has been used

as the backdrop for many a Philippine film. Unfortunately, there is not a large enough selection of resorts at reasonable prices to really get the place going. If you go by tricycle to Saud Beach, have the driver wait until you've negotiated an acceptable room price before he leaves.

Places to Stay

About four km out of Pagudpud, the *Saud Beach Resort* has generously sized rooms with air-con and bath for P1400.

The prices at the *Villa del Mar Ivory Beach Resort* (☎/fax 928 8296) are just as inflated as those at the Saud Beach Resort, with rooms with fan and bath at P1500 and with air-con and bath at P1900.

Getting There & Away

Bus Buses from Vigan and Laoag to Aparri and Tuguegarao go via Pagudpud (two hours). From Laoag there are several minibuses which travel to Pagudpud daily and leave from McKinley St (P24; two hours).

Cagayan Valley & East Coast

APARRI

It's not worth staying in Aparri, unless you want to do some deep-sea fishing. Big-game fishing is popular in the **Babuyan Channel**, north of Luzon. The waters around **Point Escarpada**, near San Vicente, are well known as the best Philippine fishing grounds for marlin.

If you want to explore this north-eastern corner of Luzon, you should take the bus from Aparri to Santa Ana. You will have to continue by tricycle to San Vicente if there is no bus or jeepney. From there you can get somebody to take you across to Palaui Island by outrigger boat.

Telephone

There are two area codes for Aparri: 078 and 07822.

Places to Stay & Eat

Before Aparri, you come to the *Pipo Hotel* (☎ 22122) at 37 Macanaya St, on the right hand side. Simple rooms with fan go for P120/240 and with fan and bath for P270/380. Jeepney drivers will halt if requested.

The *Ryan Mall Hotel* (☎ 22369) on Rizal St has good rooms with fan and bath for P275 and with air-con and bath from P400 to P600. Apart from the *Magnolia Restaurant*, down near the river, the hotel restaurant is the only decent one in town.

Getting There & Away

Bus From Manila to Aparri, Baliwag Transit and Victory Liner buses leave daily from the Cubao terminal. They go via Ilagan, Tuguegarao and Gattaran (13 hours).

From Vigan and Laoag, there are few buses to Aparri. The trip takes seven and five hours respectively (see the Getting There & Away sections under Vigan and Laoag earlier in this chapter).

From Aparri to Manila (13 hours) via Gattaran (one hour) and Tuguegarao (two hours), there are Baliwag Transit and Victory Liner buses daily. The minibuses from Aparri to Tuguegarao stop frequently and leave from opposite the Victoria Hotel; the first leaves at 7 am.

Getting Around

Bus Only a few buses go to or from Aparri directly. Most of them stop 30 km further south at the big Marcos Bridge at Magapit. There is a jeepney route between Magapit and Aparri. If you want to go from Aparri to Laoag, for example, you have to go to Marcos Bridge first and then wait for a bus coming from Tuguegarao.

GATTARAN

You can break the journey from Manila or Tuguegarao to Aparri, get down in Gattaran and make a lengthy detour to the **Tanlagan Waterfalls**, which have a drop of over 100m. This is only for dedicated lovers of waterfalls, for this natural spectacle is almost 40 km to the east, beyond Cumao, which you can only reach by jeepney from Gattaran.

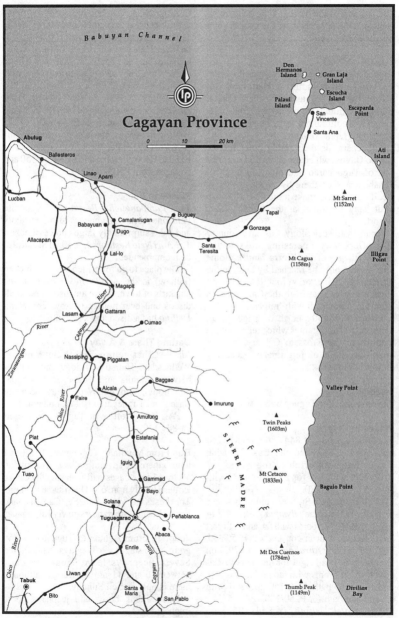

Cagayan Province

The last part of the trip can only be done by vehicle in the dry season, as there are several rivers to be crossed.

TUGUEGARAO

Tuguegarao is the capital of Cagayan Province. The **Cagayan Museum & Historical Research Center**, next to the Provincial Capitol Building, exhibits archaeological finds, historical and cultural artefacts, liturgical items and ethnographic objects.

Tuguegarao is the starting point for the **Callao Caves**, which are about 15 km northeast of Tuguegarao and nine km north of Peñablanca. Get there by jeepney or tricycle. If you want to make more than a day trip of it, stay the night at the Callao Caves Resort.

Apart from speleology, this cave country also offers very interesting treks to the distant villages of the **Sierra Madre**. Some villages can only be reached by boat on the Pinacanauan River or on foot. It takes about 30 minutes by boat from the Callao Caves Resort to a waterfall with 'mineral water'.

In **Iguig**, slightly north of Tuguegarao, there are 14 large statues which represent the Stations of the Cross to Calvary. It is an important place of pilgrimage, especially during Easter week.

Telephone

The area code for Tuguegarao is 078.

Places to Stay

The *Hotel Leonor* (☎ 844 1806) on Rizal St was previously called the Casa Lavadia. Basic, but comfortable, rooms go for P100/170, with fan for P120/200 and with air-con for P180/280.

On Washington St, you could do worse than stay at the basic *Olympia Hotel* (☎ 844 1805), where OK rooms with fan and bath cost P150/200 and with air-con and bath P250/350.

The *Pensione Abraham* (☎ 844 1793) on Bonifacio St is all right for the money. Relatively good rooms with fan go for P80/110, with fan and bath for P150/280 and with air-con and bath for P250/300.

The *Hotel Delfino* (☎ 844 1953) on Gonzaga St is clean and has a disco. Rooms with air-con and bath cost from P300 to P500.

The rooms at the *Hotel Lorita* (☎ 844 1390) on Rizal St are passable; those with air-con and bath cost between P500 and P880, and it has a coffee shop. They also offer an airport service.

On the corner of Luna and Bonifacio Sts, the friendly *Pensione Roma* (☎ 844 1057) has pleasant rooms with fan and bath for P250 and with air-con and bath from P550/600.

Near the caves, the *Callao Cave Resort* (☎ 844 1057) in Peñablanca has rooms from P150 to P300, with fan and bath for P350 and cottages from P500 to P700.

Places to Eat

The *Pampangueña Restaurant*, opposite Pensione Abraham, changes its menus daily and has a surprisingly large choice of cakes. The *Adri Nelo Restaurant* in Rizal St can also be recommended.

The place to go for grilled meat or chicken (inihaw) is the *Apollo Restaurant* on the outskirts of town. There are also some small discos and beer houses nearby. The *Hotel Delfino* has a disco and a restaurant.

Getting There & Away

Air PAL has return flights on Monday, Wednesday, Thursday, Friday and Sunday between Manila and Tuguegarao (P1208; one hour); and on Wednesday between Basco and Tuguegarao (P942; one hour).

PAL has an office at Tuguegarao airport (☎ 844 1201).

Bus From Manila to Tuguegarao (P170; 11 hours) there are several Baliwag Transit and Victory Liner buses daily, leaving the Cubao terminal hourly from 6 to 11 am and 6 to 11 pm. The buses go via Santa Fe, Cauayan and Ilagan. Manila-Aparri buses go via Tuguegarao.

Jeepney From Bontoc to Tuguegarao you go in three stages via Tinglayan and Tabuk. Several jeepneys leave Tinglayan daily between 6 and 11 am for Tabuk, although there is only one on Sunday.

From Tabuk buses and jeepneys go to Tuguegarao.

Getting Around

The Airport Tuguegarao's airport is about four km from the centre of town. A tricycle costs about P20.

ROXAS

Roxas is in Isabela Province. You can enjoy real Philippine country life here. The mayor will be happy to make his resthouse available.

There is a connection by bus from Roxas to Manila.

CAUAYAN

Cauayan is a busy little town on the National Highway with a large market which is worth seeing, and a surprising number of restaurants. Buses belonging to different companies leave there daily for Manila.

Telephone

The area code for Cauayan is 076.

Places to Stay

The *Amity Hotel* (☎ 634 5392) on the National Highway next to the market, has rooms with fan from P85/105, with fan and bath from P200/250 and with air-con and bath from P325 to P925. At night you can

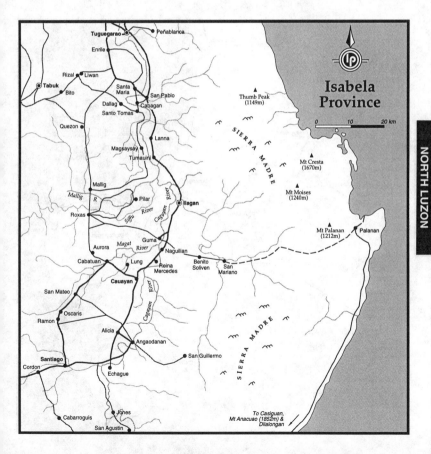

NORTH LUZON

listen to live folk music while you enjoy beer and a barbecue on the roof garden.

SALINAS

There are salt springs in Salinas whose deposits have created a white hilly landscape. To get here, you have to break the journey about halfway between Manila and Tuguegarao in Bambang, south of Bayombong. From there you can get a jeepney to Salinas.

SANTA FE

Santa Fe is in the mountains of Nueva Vizcaya Province and has a pleasant, dry climate. You can buy all sorts of handcrafts here, especially basketware.

Places to Stay & Eat

Tony's Hotel has rooms for P100/200. It is basic but has a restaurant. The *Golden Rose Hotel* has reasonable rooms for P150/230 and a good restaurant with plenty of choices.

BALER

Baler is the capital of Aurora Province. Some key scenes in Francis Ford Coppola's *Apocalypse Now* were shot there on the wild east coast of North Luzon. The town itself is not

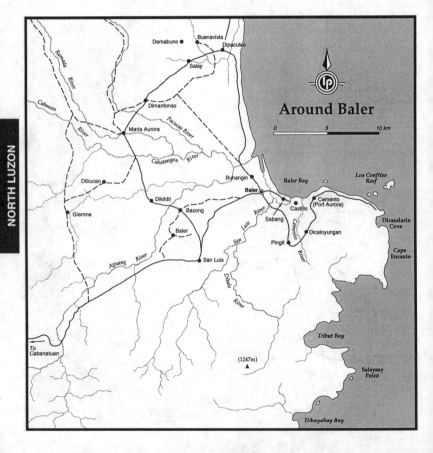

very interesting, but you can go on excursions to the surrounding mountains, visit the seafaring Negrito tribes (Dumagat), or spend a few days snorkelling or just lazing on the beach. In December the strong surf should attract surfers.

You may also be able to talk the Baler fishermen into taking you on fishing trips in the open Pacific in small, fully equipped fishing boats. On the way from Baler to the radar weather station on Cape Encanto there are several refreshing springs, such as the **Digisit Springs**. In **Dibut Bay**, a bit farther south, you can find beautiful coral. You can get there by boat, or on foot across the mountains. **Dipaculao**, north of Baler, is a starting point for mountain treks; some Ilongot tribes live in the mountains.

Places to Stay
If you want to get an early start, the roosters next door crow pretty early in the morning at the *Amihan Hotel* on Bitong St. Basic and clean rooms with fan cost P90/180 and with fan and bath P200.

There are various places offering accommodation along the beach in Sabang. The rooms at the *Baler Guest House* cost P120 with fan, and P200 with fan and bath. The *Ocean View Lodge* offers rooms with fan and bath for P180/250 and also has a restaurant. The *MIA Surf & Sports Resort* will give you a room with fan for P150/200 and with fan

and bath for P250/300. You can hire surfboards there and take surfing lessons.

If you want bigger surf than that at Sabang Beach, you can get a surf guide to take you to another beach.

Getting There & Away
Bus There are several Baliwag Transit and a few Five Star buses from Manila to Cabanatuan daily (2½ hours). You can either take a direct bus or one indicating San Jose, Tuguegarao or Aparri.

The last bus from Cabanatuan to Baler leaves at 3 pm and is a Sierra Madre Transit bus (4½ hours). The road across the Sierra Madre is bumpy but the views are beautiful. Going towards Baler, the best views are from the left-hand side of the bus. The trip will take you four hours or more.

There are several Baliwag Transit and E Jose Trans buses daily from Olongapo to Cabanatuan which also stop in San Fernando (Pampanga). From San Fernando to Cabanatuan, Arayat Express buses run several trips daily, leaving from the bus terminal next to the Philippine National Bank.

Baler to Cabanatuan
Roughly halfway, you will come to the entrance to the **Aurora Memorial Park**, where there are a few restaurants. The bus stops there for half an hour, long enough for a scrumptious eggcaldo soup in *Lorelyn's Restaurant*.

South Luzon

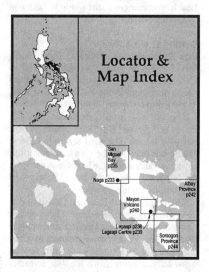

Locator & Map Index

San Miguel Bay p235

Naga p233

Albay Province p242

Mayon Volcano p240

Legaspi p236
Legaspi Centre p239

Sorsogon Province p244

This peninsula which twists its way south from Manila has an impressive, volcano-studded landscape including the giant Mayon Volcano. Mayon's symmetrical cone is said to be the most perfect in the world. It's one of the symbols of the Philippines and the most imposing feature of South Luzon. North of Mayon, the slopes of Mt Isarog, near Naga, and Mt Iriga, near Iriga, are home to several Negrito tribes. Between Sorsogon and Matnog, Mt Bulusan, with its long spurs, has helped earn the area the name the 'Switzerland of the Orient'.

Forget the little-known beach resorts from Atimonan to Gumaca on Lamon Bay east of Lucena; those at Daet and San Miguel Bay are better. Good beach weather is rarer here than in other parts of the islands, as the Pacific climate is usually rough. The best time to travel is in April and May.

South Luzon is also a convenient departure point for travel to the islands of the Visayas.

GETTING THERE & AWAY

Most transport from Luzon to other islands goes through Manila. See Getting There & Away in the Manila chapter earlier in this book.

Bus

A wide selection of BLTB, Cedec Transport, Inland Trailways, JB Bicol Express Line and Philtranco buses go south from Manila via Lucena, Daet, Naga, Iriga and Legaspi daily. To travel right through to Legaspi takes 12 to 13 hours. It's wise to make a reservation, especially for air-con buses.

An air-con Gold Line Tours bus leaves Manila daily at 7.30 pm from the company's office on the corner of MH del Pilar and Pedro Gil Sts, Ermita, heading for Legaspi (P295; 12 hours). It's advisable to book (☎ 524 0506).

The road to Legaspi, the main town in the south, is long and winding – particularly the stretch to Daet. If you want, you could take one of the large Cedec Transport, Philtranco and Inland Trailways buses and follow the Philippine Highway all the way to Matnog at the southern tip (17 hours). There you could take the ferry to Samar. Some of the buses even carry on to Tacloban and Ormoc on Leyte, Naval on Biliran and Davao on Mindanao.

Train

The journey by train from Manila to South Luzon is quite an experience. Leaving from the Tayuman railway station, Philippine National Railways (PNR) runs two trains every day bound for the region of Bicol. At the moment the last stop is Ragay (about 60 km before Naga). At 2 pm, it's the rickety economy-class train (P100), and at 7 pm the only slightly better air-con tourist-class train (P140). The departure from Paco railway station is an hour later in each case. It takes 3½ hours to San Pablo, 4½ hours to Lucena and 9½ hours to Ragay. Don't expect a smooth and comfortable journey – the coaches were imported from India, Japan and Romania over 20 years ago, and the tracks they travel on are museum pieces at over 100 years old! Absolute top speed is 50 km per hour, and even that is only on short stretches like San Pablo to Lucena. Otherwise, the fastest they go is around 35 to 45 km per hour. They have, however, been putting a lot of effort for some time into modernising the track, so it is possible that in a few years time the journey from Manila to Legaspi by train will once more offer a viable alternative to the bus.

ATIMONAN & GUMACA

If you travel by motorcycle or car along the Maharlika Highway, note that the only places to stay between Lucena and Daet are at Atimonan and Gumaca, where there are a couple of reasonable beach resorts.

Places to Stay

On the Maharlika Highway at Atimonan, the *Victoria Beach Resort* offers rooms for P150, with fan and bath for P270/380 and doubles with air-con and bath for P500.

In Gumaca, 25 km east of Atimonan, the well-maintained *Pinky's Lodge* on Maharlika

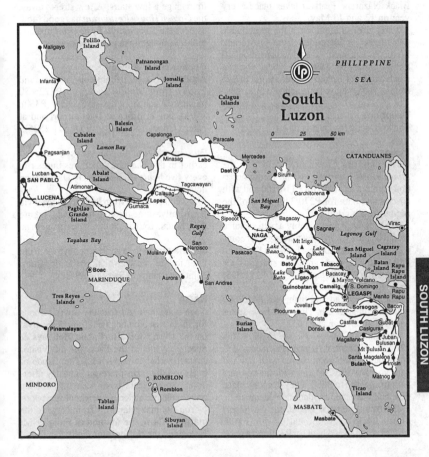

SOUTH LUZON

Highway, outside the centre of town, has comfortable rooms with fan for P70/140, with fan and bath for P180 and with air-con and bath for P350.

DAET & APUAO GRANDE ISLAND

Daet is a good overnight stop if you're heading to San Miguel Bay for a few days on the beach. **Bagasbas Beach** is the best in the vicinity of Daet. It is 4½ km away and is simpler and cheaper to get to than the beaches on San Miguel Bay. You can also visit the gold fields of **Paracale** and **Mambulao**. In **Caplonga**, farther west, the Black Nazarene Festival takes place every year on 12 and 13 May.

Early risers should catch the remarkable fish market in **Mercedes** from 6 to 8 am. Mercedes is a small coastal village about 10 km north-east of Daet from where you can reach beautiful Apuao Grande Island in San Miguel Bay, where the beach is white.

Telephone

The area code for Daet is 054.

Places to Stay

On the outskirts of town on Vinzons Ave, the *Mines Hotel* has basic, clean accommodation with fan and bath for P110/160 and with air-con and bath for P270/320; some of the rooms are a bit dingy.

On Vinzons Ave, probably a better choice would be the *Dolor Hotel* where good rooms with air-con and bath cost between P450 and P800, some of them are quite spacious. Or you could try the *Wiltan Hotel* (☎ 721 2525) near the Mines Hotel where rooms cost P200/300 with fan and bath, and P450/600 with air-con and bath. They also have suites with TV and fridge at P1100.

On Moreno St, the *Karilagan Hotel* (☎ /fax 721 2314) is central, which also means it is quite loud. Quite good rooms with fan and bath go for P150/200 and with air-con and bath from P400 to P800. They keep the place tidy, and the accommodation is adequate.

On Apuao Grande Island, the *TS Resort* offers dorm accommodation for P100, singles with fan and bath for P350 and a good

number of cottages with fan and bath for P500/700. The resort has a tennis court, golf course and swimming pool as well as a restaurant, and you can go water skiing, windsurfing, diving or sail Hobie Cats. Complete tours, including return travel, can be booked and reservations made in Manila with Swagman Travel (☎ 522 3650; fax 522 3663), 1133 L Guerrero St, Ermita.

Places to Eat

Near the Karigalan Hotel, a pleasant place with very good food is the *Sandok at Palayok*. It's on the second floor, so you have to manage a few stairs. A few streets away, the *Golden House Restaurant* has good food, as does the *Sampaguita Restaurant* upstairs in the Sampaguita department store.

Getting There & Away

Air PAL has return flights on Tuesday and Friday from Manila to Daet (P772; 50 minutes). Asian Spirit flies on Tuesday (P360).

PAL has an office at Daet airport and at Allega Optical, Vinzons Ave (☎ 511 2525).

Bus In addition to the buses mentioned earlier in this chapter, Superlines buses run every two hours from Manila to Daet (seven hours).

Several buses go from Legaspi to Daet via Naga daily, some through to Manila, taking three hours. You can get minibuses from Naga.

Jeepney It's only a short jeepney ride from Daet to Mercedes, which is the departure point for islands in San Miguel Bay.

NAGA

Naga is a clean and friendly town, famous for its late-September Peñafrancia Festival on the river. (See also Public Holidays & Special Events in the Facts for the Visitor chapter earlier in this book.) The parade of boats usually takes place on Saturday afternoon. Some years have seen the wooden bridge collapse under the weight of spectators.

You can make day trips from Naga to the **Inarihan Dam**, the **Malabsay Falls** at Mt Isarog and the **Nabontalan Falls**.

Telephone

There are two area codes for Naga: 054 and 05421.

Places to Stay

Naga draws loads of visitors during the Peñafrancia Festival and the hotels are booked solid in spite of the increased prices (twice to three times as much as usual). Rooms should be booked by the middle of August at the latest.

The friendly *Sampaguita Tourist Inn* (☎ 214810) on Panganiban Drive has clean, although small, singles with fan and bath for P185 (good value), singles with air-con and bath for P265 and doubles with air-con and bath for P395 and P500. It also has a disco.

At the well-kept *Crown Hotel* (☎ 212585) on Burgos St, a single room with fan costs P150 and with fan and bath P200. Rooms with air-con and bath cost P380 to P650 and suites are P800. The beds in the fan-cooled rooms are rather narrow.

The pleasant *Midtown Travellers Pension* (☎ 738255) at 31 General Luna St provides rooms with fan and bath for P350/500 and with air-con and bath for P400/550.

On Elias Angeles St, the *Aristocrat Hotel* (☎ 738832, 8111284) keeps reasonably comfortable rooms which cost P245 with fan, P340 with fan and bath, and P430 and P610 with air-con and bath. Suites for up to six people are P1170.

A little bit more expensive, but noticeably better, the *Moraville Hotel* (☎ 811 1807; fax 811 1685) on Dinaga St offers singles/doubles with fan and bath for P175/275 and with air-con and bath from P400 to P600, all good value. It is quiet, comfortably furnished and all rooms have TV. The more expensive doubles have a fridge. It also have a nightclub.

The *Grand Imperial Plaza* (☎ 736534; fax 739003) on Burgos St will let you have

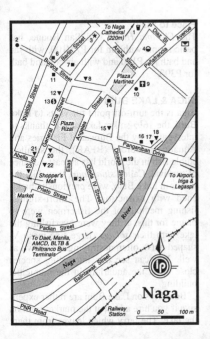

Naga

Railway Station   0   50   100 m

PLACES TO STAY
6   Rodson Garden Hotel
7   Midtown Travellers Pension
11 Grand Imperial Plaza Hotel & Karihan Restaurant
14 Crown Hotel
16 Sampaguita Tourist Inn & Ball Room Disco
19 Moraville Hotel
24 Aristocrat Hotel & Shakey's Pizza
25 Fiesta Hotel & Fiesta House Restaurant

PLACES TO EAT
8   Graceland Bakeshop
12 Graceland Fast Food
15 Ming Chun Foodhouse
17 Wok Food Garden Restaurant
18 Pawlene Foodstreet Restaurant
20 Carl's Diner
21 McDonald's
22 Café Candice
23 New China Restaurant

OTHER
1   Flower's Disco
2   University of Nueva Careres
3   Police Station
4   Jeepney Terminal
5   Post Office
9   San Francisco Church
10 Galleria de San Francisco & PAL
13 PCI Bank & Philippine National Bank (PNB)

a comfortable and cosily furnished room with air-con and bath for P720 and P880. Suites are P1350 and P1800. The suites are spacious and have a fridge and TV, otherwise TV costs P50 extra. It has a restaurant and coffee shop. Airport service is available.

Places to Eat
The clean *Ming Chun Foodhouse* on Peñafrancia Ave serves good Filipino and Chinese dishes, dim sum among them. You'll find a fresh menu every day at the *New China Restaurant* on General Luna St. The Chinese food in the pleasant *Wok Food Garden*, by the river next to the bridge, is outstanding. You can get Bikolano food in the *Karihan Restaurant* on the ground floor of the Grand Imperial Plaza.

Carl's Diner at Plaza Rizal is a 1950s-style fast-food restaurant and is clean, inexpensive and popular. It serves a wide choice of sandwiches, Korean spare ribs with kimchi, chili con carne, filet mignon and various dishes of the day. You can find hamburgers and ice-cream at *Graceland Fast Food*, also near Plaza Rizal. And if you feel like a pizza, *Shakey's Pizza* is on the ground floor of the Aristocrat Hotel on the south end of Elias Angeles St.

Things to Buy
Pili nuts are a popular favourite of the Bicol region. There is a shop in the market at Naga which sells all varieties of pili nuts.

Getting There & Away
Air PAL has return flights daily between Manila and Naga (P811; one hour).

PAL has an office at Pili airport and in the Galleria de San Francisco, Peñafrancia Ave (☎ 732277).

Bus From Manila, several different companies operate to Naga daily (8½ hours).

From Daet, several buses leave daily, either for Naga only or for Legaspi or Matnog via Naga (1½ hours). There are also minibuses.

Similarly, from Legaspi, buses go daily to Naga or through Naga on the way to Daet or Manila. It is a two-hour trip. Also from Legaspi to Naga, every hour from 6 am to 4 pm and at 7.30 pm, AMDG air-con buses leaves from the Shell petrol station in Peñaranda St, taking 2½ hours (many stops!).

Getting Around
The Airport Pili airport is about 12 km south-east of Naga, just off the road to Pili. The Aristocrat Hotel has an airport service for P200, for guests and non-guests. Otherwise, jeepneys (Naga-Pili) are an alternative, although they can only drop you as close as the airport turn-off on the main road.

Bus The bus terminals of the bigger companies are all on the bypass at the southern edge of town. A tricycle to the town centre costs P10.

PILI
Pili, to the east of Naga, is noted for its nuts and is an access point to Mt Isarog National Park.

Place to Stay
The *El-Alma Hotel*, Old San Roque, has basic rooms with fan for P75/100, with fan and bath for P150 and with air-con and bath for P300.

IRIGA & LAKE BUHI
Iriga is the turn-off point for visits to **Lake Buhi**, the 16½-sq km lake where, thanks to intervention by the Bureau of Fisheries and Aquatic Resources (BFAR), the smallest edible fish in the world has at least a chance of survival. Called *sinarapan*, they, like the *tabios* in Lake Bato, were previously threatened with extinction. The short-sighted fishing methods of the fishermen were to blame for this, as they were overfishing the lake with their *sakags* (large fine-mesh V-shaped nets), often destroying the spawn as well. You can see this interesting species close up at the aquarium in the municipal building.

Boat trips on Lake Buhi are rather expensive if you hire a boat at the market right on the lake. The ferry which leaves from there

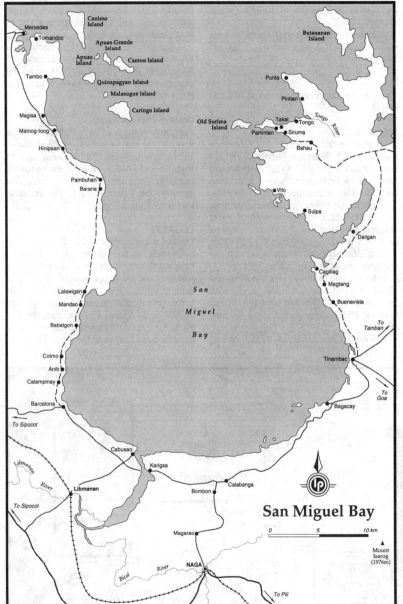

San Miguel Bay

0   5   10 km

Mount
Isarog
(1976m)

SOUTH LUZON

and runs to the other side of the lake is much cheaper.

A Negrito tribe, the Agta, lives on Mt Iriga – also called Mt Asog – between Iriga and Lake Buhi.

Telephone

There are two area codes for Iriga: 054 and 05431.

Places to Stay

A pleasant no-frills place to stay is *Lemar's Lodge* (☎ 92594) on San Nicolas St, where rooms with fan go for P100/120, with fan and bath for P150/190 and with air-con and bath for P250. The air-con rooms have wide beds.

Close to the railway station on Governor Felix Alfelor St, the *Bayanihan Hotel* offers singles with fan for P100 and singles/doubles with air-con and bath for P200/225. It's a reasonably comfortable place with air-con singles that are big enough for two.

In San Roque near the plaza, the *Parkview Hotel* (☎ 92405) provides OK rooms with fan and bath for P200 and with air-con and bath for P550. Some rooms are a bit run-down.

The small *Ibalon Hotel* (☎ 92352) on San Francisco St is the best hotel in town. Rooms with air-con and bath cost from P350 to P600, and suites are P800.

A real alternative in San Isidro, about three km north-west of Iriga in the direction of Naga, is the *Baao Recreation Center*, which offers rooms with air-con and bath for P250/450.

Getting There & Away

Jeepney Jeepneys to Lake Buhi leave from opposite the Petron station, which is diagonally across from the church. Going back to Iriga, they do not leave from the centre of town but from the entrance to Buhi, also opposite the Petron station. The last one leaves for Iriga at 7 pm.

LEGASPI

Legaspi is the capital of Albay Province. The town itself has no must-see sights, the only ones worth mentioning at all is the bustling port area and the headless statue in front of the post office, a monument to the unknown heroes who died at the hands of the Japanese in WWII. St Rafael Church, opposite the Plaza Rizal, has a 10-tonne chunk of volcanic rock from Mayon as the altar.

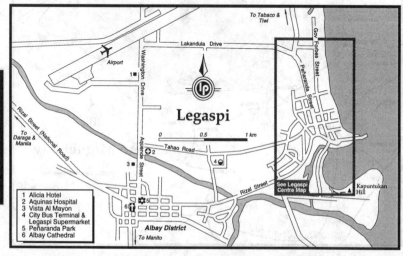

1 Alicia Hotel
2 Aquinas Hospital
3 Vista Al Mayon
4 City Bus Terminal & Legaspi Supermarket
5 Peñaranda Park
6 Albay Cathedral

However, there are many interesting attractions to see in the Legaspi area, including the ruins of **Cagsawa**, the **Hoyop-Hoyopan Cave** in Camalig, and of course the mighty **Mayon Volcano**. In the rainy season the volcano is often draped with clouds, but even then the views are clear at sunrise.

From the top of the **Kapuntukan Hill** you can get a fascinating panoramic view of the port area, with the impressive Mayon in all its glory in the background. Early morning hours and sunset are the best times for views and photographs.

A tricycle from the centre of town to the hill costs P10; negotiate the fare beforehand. On foot, the following route should be taken. Go down Quezon Ave in the direction of the wharf and cross over the little bridge opposite the beginning of Elizondo St; this takes you to the idyllic fishing village of Victory Village. At the south end of the village next to the barangay toilet turn left, then after about 50m at the *sari sari* store, turn left again and head on up the steps. A few metres before the concrete path leads down to the water, you will see a fairly overgrown path on the right, which will take you to the top of the hill.

Orientation
Legaspi is divided into two parts: the centre or downtown area around the port and, further inland, the Albay district. The two areas are linked by Rizal St.

Information
Tourist Office The tourist office (☎ 243215; fax 243286) is in the Meliton Dy building on Rizal St.

Telephone The area code for Legaspi is 05221.

Places to Stay – bottom end
There are plenty of cheap hotels around Legasi but none of them will win any prizes for high accommodation standards. There is quite a choice along Peñaranda St, parallel to the waterfront.

Catalina's Lodging House, on Peñaranda St,

is a friendly establishment offering goodsingles/doubles with fan for P80/120, with fan and bath for P140 and with air-con and bath for P300/400.

Also on Peñaranda St, the *Hotel Xandra* (☎ 22688) has basic and reasonably clean rooms with fan for P100/120, with fan and bath for P180/200 and with air-con and bath for P210/280.

The *Legaspi Tourist Inn* (☎ 23533) on Lapu-Lapu St, in the V & O Building (3rd floor) opposite the post office, has rooms with fan and bath for P210/250 and with air-con and bath for P350/400. Suites are P500. The rooms are really quite good for the money, and the hotel has a small restaurant.

The rooms at the friendly *Tanchuling Hotel* (☎ 22747) on Jasmin St, Imperial subdivision, are basic, clean and spacious, and there is a pleasant roof garden. Good-value rooms with fan cost P280 and with air-con and bath P550/650. It is in a quiet area, south of the town centre, but unfortunately not too easily accessible.

Places to Stay – top end
On Lapu-Lapu St, the *Legaspi Plaza Hotel* (☎ 243085) has passable rooms with fan and bath for P340/500 and with air-con and bath for P550/670, and it has a disco. Check-out time is always 24 hours after check in.

The *Hotel Casablanca* (☎ 23130) on Peñaranda St has adequate rooms with air-con and TV for P770, some with a big balcony. It also has a 24-hour coffee shop and a disco. It offers a free service to the airport.

At the *Victoria Hotel* (☎ 243476; fax 243246) on Rizal St the rooms are very comfortable and have TV. Singles/doubles with air-con and bath are P825/880. It offers a free airport service.

The *Hotel La Trinidad* (☎ 22951; fax 243148) is the best hotel in town, centrally located on Rizal St, with a swimming pool, coffee shop and even a cinema in the complex. Rooms with air-con and bath are P720/820 and suites are from P1000; there is a free airport service.

SOUTH LUZON

Places to Eat
Good Chinese and Filipino food is served in the *Shangrila Restaurant* on Peñaranda St, and in the *New Legaspi Restaurant* on Lapu-Lapu St, where the special meal for P60 is to be recommended. The food is basically Chinese with some Filipino dishes. Try the New Legaspi's pineapple pie for a special treat.

Mike's Oakroom Restaurant, next to the Xandra Hotel on Peñaranda St, offers economical menus. Unfortunately, at least in the hot summer months this place is not sufficiently ventilated. A few metres farther north the *Mamalola Bakery & Snack House* will surprise you not only with its plucky karaoke singers but also with its excellent cooking. The *Waway Restaurant* on the Peñaranda St Extension in the north of town serves good Filipino dishes. Among others, the spicy local specialities á la 'Bikol Express' and the vegetarian meals can be recommended.

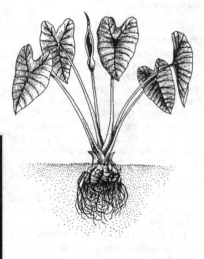

The protein-rich leaves of the yam (*cocoyam*) are combined with onions, garlic and coconut milk and served as a side vegetable (*pinangat na gabi*) with 'Bikol Express', a local speciality prepared with green and red chilli peppers.

In the evenings it's pleasant to sit in the *Garden Restaurant* on Rizal St, which specialises in chicken, steaks and seafood in the mid-price range. In the charming little *Café Old Albay* at the Victoria Hotel on Rizal St, they serve a passable American breakfast, among other things. The *Alibar Foodland* in Mabini St at the corner of Rafael St is a clean fast-food restaurant. The *Legaspi Ice Cream House*, a clean establishment on Magallanes St, makes wonderful ice cream.

Entertainment
Nightly from 8 pm, you can often hear refreshingly good live music in the *Aura Music Lounge* at the Legaspi Plaza Hotel, Lapu-Lapu St, and in the new *Momento Music Hall* next to the Hotel Casablanca in Peñaranda St. In Magallanes St, *Peppers* is a pleasant pub with modern fittings.

Getting There & Away
Air Air Philippines and PAL have return flights daily between Manila and Legaspi (P1134; 50 minutes). PAL has an office at Legaspi airport (☎ 44746).

Bus From Manila, buses of different companies run daily to Legaspi via Daet, Naga and Iriga. See Getting There & Away at the beginning of this chapter.

From Naga to Legaspi an AMDG air-con bus leaves every hour from 6 am to 4 pm and at 7.30 pm, taking 2½ hours (repeated stops!).

Minibuses and jeepneys run frequently from Tabaco to Legaspi every day, taking about an hour.

If you want to go from Legaspi to Matnog (and then perhaps on to Tacloban via the west coast of Samar), it may be better to do the trip in stages, changing somewhere like Sorsogon or Irosin. Few buses make this trip, possibly only two a day, and they come from Manila, pulling in to Legaspi for a short stop at about 3 am and 5 pm. However, it is possible that they will be fully booked. There are a few small restaurants at the bus terminal where you can wait; they are also open at night.

Several BLTB buses go from Legaspi to Manila daily, departing between 2.15 and

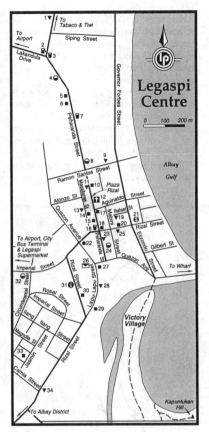

Legaspi Centre

0   100   200 m

PLACES TO STAY
5   Hotel Casablanca & Monumento Music Hall
6   Shirman Lodge & Lady Ann Nightclub
10   Catalina's Lodging House
14   King's Lodge & Pepper's
15   Hotel Xandra & Mike's Oakroom Restaurant
17   Rex Hotel
18   Mayon Hotel
20   Hotel La Trinidad
27   Legaspi Tourist Inn
29   Legaspi Plaza Hotel
30   Victoria Hotel & Café Old Albay
33   Tanchuling International House

PLACES TO EAT
1   Waway Restaurant
9   Cindy's Fastfood
11   Mamalola Bakery & Snack House
13   Legaspi Ice Cream House
19   Alibar Foodland
23   Shangrila Restaurant
25   Quick'n Hearty Restaurant
28   New Legaspi Restaurant
34   Garden Restaurant

OTHER
2   Caltex Petrol Station
3   Paayahayan Beer Garden
4   BLTB Bus Terminal
7   Small Bars
8   AMDG-Buses to Naga & Shell Petrol Station
12   St Rafael Church
16   VIP Pub House
21   Philippine National Bank (PNB)
22   LCC Department Store
24   JB Bicol Express Line Bus Terminal
26   Post Office & Headless Monument
31   Tourist Office
32   Philtranco Bus Terminal

7.40 pm; air-con buses leave at 5.20, 5.30, 6.20 and 6.30 pm.

Gold Line Tours air-con buses leave for Manila (P295;12 hours) from the La Trinidad Hotel in Legaspi at 8.30 pm.

Getting Around
The Airport Legaspi airport is about three km north-west of the town centre. A tricycle costs P20. You can also take a jeepney heading to Daraga from the centre, get out in the Albay District and take a tricycle from there to the airport for P5. A short journey within the town should cost P2 per person.

AROUND LEGASPI
Mayon Volcano
Mayon stands 2462m high and is famed for its perfectly symmetrical cone. The name Mayon is a derivation of the Bikolano word *magayon*, which means beautiful. Beauty can also become dangerous, as the clouds of smoke rising from the crater indicate.

The last serious eruption was at the beginning of February 1993 when, without any warning, the volcano spewed ash and steam five km into the atmosphere. Rivers of glowing hot mud, rocks and stones rushed down the south-east slope, totally destroying villages and farmland on the way. Seventy people died, a further 50,000 had to be evacuated. Only after a series of smaller eruptions lasting until late March did the volcano calm down again, but weeks later the glowing lava was still flowing, offering a fascinating spectacle at night. The most violent eruption to date took place on 1 February 1814 (see the following Daraga & Cagsawa section).

If you want to climb Mayon, the tourist office in the Albay District of town will supply detailed information and organise the climb. The usual cost for two people is P1800 for guide, porter and tent; each addi-

tional person costs P500. To that P300 must be added per person for food and a second porter, who the guide brings along. Anyone thinking of saving a few pesos by carrying everything themselves would definitely regret the decision.

You can try hiring a guide and porters in Buyuhan. The standard daily rate is about P500. To try the ascent without a guide is reckless and irresponsible–as it's easy to get lost at the foot of Mayon and many canyons turn out to be dead ends with sheer drops.

To reach Mayon, you get a jeepney in the market to Buyuhan (this is not included in

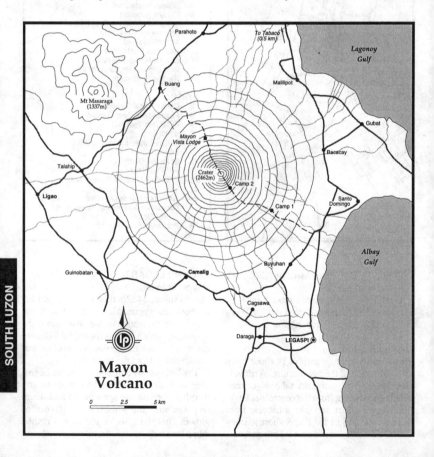

Mayon
Volcano

the price), from where it is a 2½ hour climb to Camp 1 (Camp Amporo) at about 800m. If you start late, you will have to spend the night at the simple hut there; a spring is nearby.

It's another four hours to Camp 2 (Camp Pepito) at about 1800m. Here you have to use a tent, as there is no hut and the nights can be fairly cold. In the morning you have another four-hour climb to the summit. The last 250m is a scramble through loose stones and over steep rocks, and it is advisable for climbers to be roped.

Going down it takes about three hours from the crater to Camp 2, almost two hours from Camp 2 to Camp 1 and over two hours from Camp 1 to the road.

Take warm clothing, a sleeping bag and provisions for two days. On some days you'll need sunscreen lotion as well.

Getting There & Away To get from Legaspi to the Mayon Vista Lodge on the northern slope, take a bus or jeepney to Tabaco, then a bus or jeepney to Ligao. Get off at the turn-off to halfway to Ligao. From there you've got about an eight-km walk up to the lodge. You can hire a jeepney in Tabaco but it's cheaper to persuade the regular Ligao jeepney drivers to make a small detour to the lodge and drop you there. The tourist office advises people not to climb the north slope of the volcano as it is apparently too dangerous.

Note: the Mayon Vista Lodge provides an excellent view point on the northern slope halfway to the top of the volcano, but it looks like it's going to be closed for the foreseeable future.

Daraga & Cagsawa

The magnificent baroque church in Daraga, built by Franciscan monks in 1773, offers an excellent view of Mayon from its vantage point on the top of a hill overlooking the town. On Sunday and public holidays Daraga is the scene of heated cockfights, which take place in the cockpit at the edge of town, near the petrol station. The atmosphere at Daraga's night market is very pleasant with its sounds and smells of frying and cooking. Along the road between Daraga and

Cagsawa you can find small workshops where they make whole furniture suites from used car tyres.

The catastrophic eruption of Mayon on 1 February 1814 totally destroyed the villages of Camalig, Cagsawa and Budiao on the southern side of Mayon. About 1200 people perished as ash fell as far away as the China coast. Many local residents took shelter in the church at Cagsawa, only to be smothered by falling ash. Today, only the church steeple stands as a reminder of 'The Beautiful One's' terrible powers. The rest of the village was buried under ash and lava. Today, plants, including orchids, are offered for sale near the church tower, and with the grandeur of Mayon in the background the scene is idyllic.

Getting There & Away From Legaspi, several jeepneys leave the old market or the city bus terminal daily for Daraga. The turn-off to the Cagsawa ruins is on the right, two km west of Daraga. A tricycle from Daraga to the ruins shouldn't cost more than P10. Buses and jeepneys for Camalig, Guinobatan, Ligao, Polangui and Naga also drive through Daraga, directly past the turn-off to the Cagsawa ruins where you can get out. (Don't forget to tell the driver in good time!) From there, it is about 10 minutes to the ruins on foot.

Camalig

The town of Camalig is famous for the **Hoyop-Hoyopan** limestone caves which are in Cotmon, about eight km to the south. There is an admission fee of P50. The name Hoyop-Hoyopan means 'blow-blow' from the sound of the wind rushing through. Bones have been found in the caves as have potsherds, which are over 2000 years old. They are now on display in a small museum in the Camalig Catholic church.

Ask for Alfredo Nieva, who will guide you to the Calabidogan Cave, about two or three km (a 45-minute walk) away from the Hoyop-Hoyopan caves. It is best to have a word with Alfredo the day before, to work out times and prices. It is possible that he himself will not be the guide as he may give the job to one of his sons.

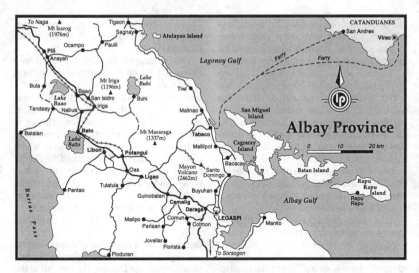

The **Pariaan Cave**, known as the 'Fountain of Youth', is near Pariaan. Eduardo (Eddie) Nalasco is an experienced guide – he lives opposite the town hall in Camalig but you can also catch him now and again in Mike's Oakroom Restaurant in Legaspi. To get there take a jeepney either from Legaspi or Camalig to Guinobatan, where you can get a jeepney for Pariaan. Ask the driver to drop you at the path for the cave and, after a 10-minute walk, you will come to a hut where the cave's 'owner' lives. For a few pesos he'll look after excess clothing – it's very hot and humid inside the cave. A strong torch or, even better, a kerosene lamp is necessary for exploring the cave. There's a natural pool in the cave with warm water, surrounded by beautiful stalactites. After some time in the cave, it's a pleasure to jump into the privately owned swimming pool on the left side of the road towards Jovellar; admission is P2. The property is in an idyllic setting, surrounded by palm-covered hills. There are actually three pools, all at different heights.

Getting There & Away Camalig is about 14 km north-west of Legaspi. Jeepneys and buses go there from the old market or the bus terminal, either directly or en route to Guinobatan, Ligao, Polangui or Naga. From Camalig, you have to take a tricycle to the cave. Occasionally it is possible to find a jeepney in the market going to Cotmon. After 6 pm the only way to return to Camalig is to arrange a Special Ride.

Santo Domingo

About two km outside of Santo Domingo town, 15 km north-east of Legaspi, is a **black-sand beach** which occasionally has quite high surf. The beach resorts on the so-called 'Mayon Riviera' vary considerably in size and price. The *Reyes Beach Resort* with its inexpensive restaurant is popular; the *Sirangen Beach Resort* is basic and nicely laid out. Local day trippers like to use the beach at Santo Domingo for long, drawn-out picnics, but the beach is not really suitable for bathing and is actually quite disappointing.

Getting There & Away To get to Santo Domingo, take a jeepney from the old market in Legaspi or ask if there's a direct bus to Santo Domingo, as some of the Tabaco buses take the route around the outskirts. Tricycles go from Santo Domingo to the beach resorts.

Malilipot

For lovers of waterfalls in more or less unspoiled nature, a day trip from Legaspi to Malilipot can be warmly recommended. From here, on the north-east foothills of Mayon, a path leads in the direction of the volcano to the **Busay Falls**, also known as the Malilipot Falls; admission P2. These falls descend in stages from a height of 250m, on the way flowing into seven pools that tempt you to swim. If you don't want to jump straight into the first pool, then turn off onto the path on the right just before it. After about a 15-minute walk this will take you to the second pool. The waterfalls are popular with day-trippers at the weekends.

Getting There & Away Go from Legaspi to Malilipot by a jeepney or bus travelling to Tabaco. Then it's about another hour on foot. It would be a good idea to have a guide show you the way for about P20.

TABACO

Tabaco is the departure point for the boat to San Andres and Virac, both on Catanduanes Island (see Getting There & Away in Manila chapter). Probably the only thing worth seeing in Tabaco is the two-storey market, where some interesting knives are sold.

Places to Stay & Eat

The *VSP Lodge* on Riosa St has simple, but fairly good rooms with fan and bath for P175 and with air-con and bath for P350. Opposite the town hall is the *Royal Crown Canteen* – a very clean restaurant.

Getting There & Away

Bus Several Philtranco buses go from Manila to Tabaco daily. Some go via Legaspi (12 hours).

From Tabaco to Manila, an air-con bus leaves at 4.50 pm; the last bus for Manila leaves Tabaco at about 7 pm.

Jeepney Jeepneys run frequently between Tiwi and Tabaco in about half an hour, and

plenty of buses and jeepneys from Legaspi to Tabaco leave from the city bus terminal (45 minutes).

TIWI

North of Legaspi, Tiwi is noted for its hot springs, which were for many years a small health resort or spa. Some of the springs were so hot that the locals stood their pots in them to cook their dinners. Nowadays six geothermal power stations have reduced the underground water pressure and most of the springs have dried up. It would be a waste of time to go there just to see the few remaining springs.

Two well-known but not particularly good beaches, with black sand, are **Sogod Beach** and **Putsan Beach**. If you walk to Putsan, take a look at the primitive potteries on the way.

Places to Stay

The *Baño Manantial de Tiwi Youth Hostel & Mendoza's Resort* has basic rooms with fan and bath for P350/400 and with air-con and bath for P500/600. There's a swimming pool that can get very busy at the weekends, and a pretty good restaurant.

Getting There & Away

Bus For Manila, a Philtranco bus leaves Tiwi market daily at 9 am and 3 pm (12 hours).

Jeepney To get from Legaspi to Tiwi, take a minibus or a jeepney from the city bus terminal, and from Tabaco continue on by jeepney. Jeepneys also go regularly and directly to Tiwi from Peñaranda St in Legaspi. From Tiwi to the resort – a distance of about three km – take a tricycle. The whole trip takes about 1½ hours.

Leaving Tiwi, if you want to go beyond Legaspi to Matnog the same day, you must depart early in the morning or you'll have connection problems in Irosin.

SORSOGON & GUBAT

Sorsogon is the capital of Sorsogon Province, an area at the eastern tip of South Luzon which is subject to frequent violent typhoons.

From there, you can make a little detour to Gubat and the long, broad **Rizal Beach** on the Pacific. A jeepney or tricycle will take you the five km south from Gubat to Rizal Beach for P3.

Telephone
The area code for Sorsogon is 056.

Places to Stay
The *Dalisay Lodge* at 182 VL Peralta St, Sorsogon, is a simple, but fairly clean place with a restaurant. It has rooms with fan for P75/130 and with fan and bath for P100/150.

The *Rizal Beach Resort Hotel*, Gubat, (☎ 211 1056) although beginning to show its age, has passable singles with fan for P365, rooms with fan and bath for P450/550 and with air-con and bath for P750. The restaurant here is open until 10 pm.

Also in Gubat, the *Veramaris Resort* is a good alternative to the Rizal Beach Resort Hotel. It has good, variously furnished rooms

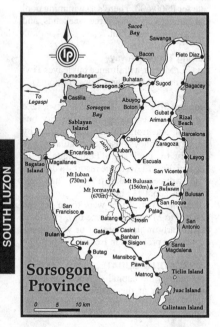

Sorsogon Province

with fan and bath from P400 to P900, the more expensive ones with a sea view.

Getting There & Away
Bus From Legaspi, JB Bicol Express Line buses run to Sorsogon roughly every half hour throughout the day. It's a 1½ hour trip. There are also BLTB, Ceres Transport, Inland Trailways and Philtranco buses, but they are not so frequent. They come from Manila, go via Matnog and Samar as far as Tacloban; they are usually full.

BULAN
Bulan, a little coastal village on the west coast, is simply a departure point for a daily boat to Masbate. (See under Boat in the Getting There & Away section in the Manila chapter earlier in this book.)

Places to Stay
Mari-El's Lodging House, on the pier site, is a basic place with rooms with fan for P60/120.

Getting There & Away
Bus Philtranco and JB Bicol Express Line buses leave from Legaspi for Bulan about every hour between 4.30 am and 3 pm. Take a bus by 8 am if you want to be on time for the boat to Masbate. It takes 3½ hours.

BULUSAN & IROSIN
You can't help but see Mt Bulusan, the 1560m-high volcano at the centre of the Juban-Bulusan-Irosin triangle. Nearby, surrounded by lush vegetation, is a small **crater lake** of the same name, at a height of 600m with a three-km-long path around it called Lovers' Lane. For the walk around the lake, which in parts is fairly difficult and tiring, you will need 1½ hours, including rests.

From Bulusan to Lake Bulusan is about eight km. Only a few jeepneys make the trip between Bulusan and Irosin; the first one leaves at 7 am, the last one at 4 pm. They will stop at the turn-off for the crater lake if requested to. The walk up to it is very pleasant.

The refreshingly cool **Masacrot Springs**, complete with big swimming pool, are in the foothills of the volcano, near San Roque. Unfortunately, the way there is not signposted.

Apart from Bulusan, there is another good base for a stay in the so-called 'Switzerland of the Orient': the Mateo Hot & Cold Springs Resort. This pleasant establishment is in a forest about four km north-east of Irosin (three km in the direction of Sorsogon and then one km north-east). There is a signpost at the point where the path leaves the road. The resort has two pools to jump into (luke-warm and hot) and there is a small restaurant and a variety of cottages. It's easy to get from the resort to Irosin. Unlike Bulusan, there are more than enough tricycles in Irosin, so it should be easy to negotiate the fare for a Special Ride from there to the volcano. It's a good idea to have the tricycle wait for you, then you don't have to worry about the return trip.

Places to Stay

In Bulusan you can stay at the *Bartilet's Lodging House* belonging to the friendly teacher Mrs Nerissa Bartilet. It's directly behind the town hall. Rooms with fan are comfortable and cost P100/200.

The pleasant *Villa Luisa Celeste Resort* in (☎ 211 1083) Dancalan, Bulusan, has clean and spacious rooms with fan and bath for P300/P500 and with air-con and bath for P500/700. A cottage with bath and kitchen costs P600, and there's a restaurant and pool.

At the *Mateo Hot & Cold Springs Resort*, San Benon, Monbon, Irosin, the rooms are basic but passable. With fan they cost P125/250 and with fan and bath P250. Cottages with fan, bath and kitchen are P250. The resort is a pleasant and peaceful place with a restaurant.

Getting There & Away

Bus JB Bicol Express Line buses run from

Legaspi daily to Irosin or to Bulan via Irosin (2½ hours). Philtranco buses also go from Manila through Irosin to Matnog and on to Tacloban or even to Mindanao, but these are usually full. Jeepneys go from Irosin to Bulusan in an hour, roughly at 15-minute intervals.

MATNOG

Matnog is the last stop on Luzon. This little coastal town, on the south-eastern side of Sorsogon, is the departure point for ferries to Allen and San Isidro on Samar, the next big island. During bad typhoons all shipping is stopped, so you could be held up in Matnog for a few days – not a cheerful prospect. It's better to wait somewhere like Bulusan or Legaspi until the seas settle down.

On sunny days, a trip to the little offshore island of **Ticlin**, with its palms and beautiful white sand beach, would be well worthwhile.

Places to Stay

The only place to stay is the basic *Mely's Snack House*, which charges around P50 per person. You could always do what many Filipinos do who have missed the last ferry: sleep on a bench in the big waiting room.

Getting There & Away

Bus In Legaspi you could try to board a bus arriving from Manila and going through Matnog en route to Tacloban or Mindanao. As the seats are usually occupied, it's better to do the trip in stages using other means of transport. It takes 3½ hours. For more details see Getting There & Away in the Legaspi section earlier in this chapter.

Jeepney Several jeepneys run daily from Irosin to Matnog (one hour).

Around Luzon

Locator &
Map Index

Batanes
Islands
p247

Puerto Galera p262
Puerto Galera Beaches p266
Sabang Beach p267
White Beach p269

Catanduanes
p248

Lubang
p252

Virac p250 ●

Marinduque
p253

Pandan Bay p275

Masbate
p258

San Jose p272

Mindoro
p260

Several islands around the main island of Luzon are also generally grouped with Luzon. They include the Batanes, which are scattered off the far northern coast of Luzon; Catanduanes, off the south-eastern coast near Legaspi; and the smaller islands of Lubang, Marinduque and Masbate and the larger island of Mindoro, all off the western coast.

Batanes

The Batanes Islands are the northernmost islands of the Philippines. Y'ami is only 100 km from Taiwan. The biggest and economically most important islands are Batan, Itbayat and Sabtang. Dinem Island is uninhabited. The climate of the Batanes Islands is fairly changeable. Compared with other parts of the Philippines, all 10 of these islands are hit by typhoons relatively frequently between June and September. From October to February or March it is often wet and stormy. The best months to visit are April and May.

Geographically isolated from the big important islands and archipelagos of the country, the Batanes Islands are surprisingly unspoilt and different. Many houses are built of solid rock and have roofs thickly thatched with cogon grass to resist the weather. They are low, with few windows, and are usually found in small groups in niches protected from the wind. If you know your Asterix, you sometimes feel here as if you had been transported back to a village populated by stubborn Gauls. You would probably not be in the least surprised if around the next corner you came across a venerable druid brewing his potions.

People here protect themselves from sun and rain with a *suot*, a head-covering made from *voyavoy* leaves which reaches right down the back. The leaves are first processed into a rough, straw-like fibre, which is then used to make the hats.

Goods which aren't produced on the islands are slightly more expensive here than in Luzon, as they have to be flown in or shipped on the occasional freighter. The main crops are garlic, onions, taro yams and camotes. The main occupations are cattle farming and fishing.

GETTING THERE & AWAY

You can get to the Batanes Islands from Laoag and Tuguegarao on Luzon (see the Getting There & Away section of the Manila chapter earlier in this book). Travel in and out depends first and foremost on the weather. On rainy days, if the partly concreted runway at Basco is wet, planes can neither land nor take off. Delays may also occur even in the summer months of March, April and May.

Air

Luzon PAL flies from Basco to Laoag on Monday, from Basco to Manila on Monday

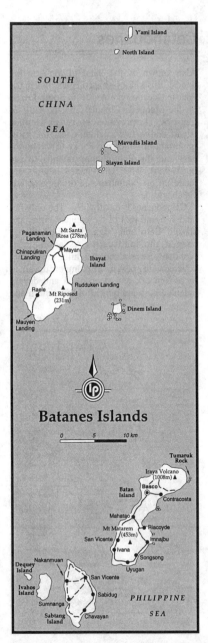

Batanes Islands

0   5   10 km

and Wednesday, and from Basco to Tuguegarao on Wednesday.

Boat
Luzon The Avega Exchange Services' MV *LSD* goes from Basco to Manila two or three times a year.

BATAN ISLAND
Don't expect very much in the way of sights; in fact, this is part of the island's charm. About the only activity is the Sunday cockfight. There are a couple of white beaches on the western coast; the southern and eastern coasts are rocky. To the north the landscape of this green and hilly island is dominated by the raw beauty of the 1008m high Iraya Volcano, which can be climbed in about five hours from Basco.

A seldom-travelled and only partly surfaced road runs from Basco to Riacoyde (via Mahatao, Ivana and Uyugan) and then straight across the island back to Mahatao. It's a good track for walking and you come across lovely little villages inhabited by friendly Ivatan, the natives of Batan Island.

Basco
Basco is the capital of the province of Batanes, which is the smallest in the Philippines, both in area and population. Next to the big church, with its beautiful façade, are numerous governmental buildings which dominate this neat town at the foot of Mt Iraya. Roughly 5000 people live here.

Information The Philippine National Bank here will cash travellers cheques.

The area code for Basco is 078.

Places to Stay *Mama Lily's Pension House* has rooms with fan for P400 per person. It is basic but clean and the price includes full board. Guests can use the living room and patio. You can also stay at the *Iraya Lodge* which has rooms with fan for P100/200.

Getting There and Away In Basco you can hire private jeepneys, motorcycles and bicycles. Enquire at Mama Lily's Pension House.

SABTANG ISLAND

In contrast to Batan Island, there are no cars on Sabtang. It is worth the effort to go around the island on foot and visit the four villages. The mayor will place at your disposal a guide who knows the paths and the shortcuts. With his help you will find it easier to get to know the villagers and to see how things such as suots are made. On the eastern coast of the neighbouring island of Ivahos there is an extensive coral reef. You can get there by boat from Nakanmuan or Sumnanga.

Places to Stay

There are no hotels on Sabtang, but it is possible to stay with the mayor or the director of the Fishery School (both in the main town of San Vicente). You can get something to eat here, but since no-one will charge you money or accept it, it's handy to 'happen' to have a small gift on hand.

Getting There & Away

Boat A boat goes once a week from Basco to San Vicente. If you don't want to wait, you will have to go to Ivana, but the jeepney to Ivana usually only goes when a plane lands. In good weather a boat goes daily from Ivana to San Vicente on Sabtang at about 8.30 am and takes about 30 minutes. It should return the next morning.

ITBAYAT ISLAND

Itbayat is the largest island of the group. It has few beaches and a rocky coast. A feature of the island is the *tatus*, the coconut crab, which is so fond of coconuts that it will climb trees to get them. You can stay with the mayor.

Getting There & Away

Air East of Raele is a landing strip for small aircraft.

Boat The boat service from Basco to Paganaman Landing or Mauyen Landing on Itbayat is irregular. Travel time is about four hours. The boats only go in good weather and are unpredictable – not so good if you are on a tight schedule.

Catanduanes

Also known as the 'land of the howling winds', this kidney-shaped island lies in the Pacific Ocean, separated from South Luzon by the Maqueda Channel and the Gulf of Lagonoy. The province consists of the main island and a few smaller ones, the most important of which are Panay to the northeast and the Palumbanes Islands to the north-west. The Palumbanes Islands are made up of Palumbanes, Porongpong and Calabagio.

Catanduanes is mostly hilly. The only flat land is found east of the capital, Virac, and around Bato and Viga. The climate has shaped the landscape. As a result of typhoons, several coastal hills are barely covered with grass, many palms are uprooted or broken off, and steep cliffs and deeply indented bays are typical of the eastern and

north-eastern coasts. The typhoons blast into this part of the Philippines straight off the Pacific. In Catanduanes you have to expect rain throughout the year, particularly from November to January, with not quite so much from April to June.

The main industries are fishing and farming. The most prolific fishing grounds are the Maqueda Channel, the Gulf of Lagonoy and Cabugao Bay. The main agricultural products are abaca (Manila hemp), rattan and coconuts, rice, sweet potatoes, cassava and fruits such as avocados, jackfruit, papaya and oranges. Mining has not been developed much, although there are deposits of coal, gold, silver, manganese and copper.

Many islanders have left Catanduanes in search of work, most settling in Manila. The greatest migrations take place after typhoons when houses and crops have been destroyed. People only come back then to visit on

The papaya, or pawpaw, tree is actually a giant herb. It's also one of the most common fruit trees in the Philippines.

important occasions like festivals or family gatherings.

The people are friendly and very religious. They are Bikolano, and speak Bikolano, the language of South Luzon. English is also spoken and understood. Visitors are nearly always invited into homes, and you'll have to depend on this hospitality because, with few exceptions, there is no commercially run accommodation on the islands.

GETTING THERE & AWAY
You can travel to Catanduanes Island from Manila, Legaspi and Tabaco (see Getting There & Away in the Manila chapter earlier).

Air
Luzon PAL flies Monday and Wednesday from Virac to Legaspi and daily from Virac to Manila. Asian Spirit flies daily from Virac to Manila (P1100).

Boat
Luzon The Bicolano Lines' MV *Eugenia* leaves Virac daily at 1 pm for Tabaco (P50; four hours). Another small boat leaves every second day at 9 am.

The Regina Shipping Lines' MV *Regina Calixta* leaves San Andres daily at 9 am for Tabaco (2½ hours).

VIRAC
The cosy and clean little town of Virac is the capital of Catanduanes Province. Popular destinations for day trips from there are the **Luyang Cave** at Lictin (15 km west), which is said to reach as far as the coast and even has lighting at the beginning, **Igang Beach**, eight km south-west, and the **Binanuahan Falls** in Cabugao, a little south of Bato; they are easily reached by tricycle and a short walk. A trip to the Balongbong Falls in Bato is, however, hardly worth the effort, especially because they are not easily accessible.

Information
Money The Philippine National Bank at the town plaza will change travellers cheques.

Telephone The area code for Virac is 052.

Places to Stay

Virac The *Cherry Don Resthouse* on San Pedro St has basic rooms with fan for P75/150. *Sandy's Blossoms Pension House* (☎ 811 1762) near the pier has rooms with fan for P100/200 and with air-con and bath for P380. It is basic and has a restaurant with a small terrace. The *Catanduanes Hotel* on San Jose St has rooms with fan and bath from P250 to P400. It is unpretentious but quite cosy and is the best hotel in town.

Around Virac The *Bosdok Beach Resort* at Magnesia has cottages with fan and bath for P600 and with air-con, refrigerator and bath for P1000. The resort is made up of a group of solidly built, roomy, clean cottages on the side of a hill. It covers an extensive area in an idyllic bay and boasts a beautiful little sandy beach with a gorgeous view of Mayon Volcano in the distance. There is also a big restaurant and a swimming pool. Bosdok Beach itself is a bit out of the way, 12 km south-west of Virac. A Special Ride by tricycle costs about P200. A service jeep belonging to the resort leaves daily from Virac market and it also meets the plane and the ferry boat.

Places to Eat

It is possible to eat good, inexpensive Filipino food at the *Catanduanes Hotel Restaurant* on the roof of the hotel. Also good value are the fine dishes served at the *Café de Paul* on the corner of A Surtida and San Jose Sts, worth trying are the sizzling blue marlin and the wanton soup. The *Trellis Garden Café* not only serves coffee, but also ice-cold beer and dishes like spaghetti and lasagne. *Sandy's Restaurant*, in the Sandy's Blossoms Pension House at the pier, serves snacks and non-alcoholic drinks.

Getting There & Away

Air The PAL office (☎ 811 1385) is at the airport, not in town, so you might as well confirm your return flight when you first arrive.

Jeepney Transport connections within Catanduanes are fairly limited. Three jeepneys run daily from Virac market to Pandan, in the north of the island, and back. One jeepney runs daily from Virac to Tambugnon via Viga, leaving there at 9 am and returning at midnight. Two jeepneys go from Virac to Gigmoto via Puraran, leaving between 9 and

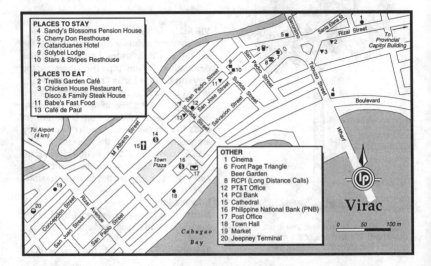

PLACES TO STAY
4 Sandy's Blossoms Pension House
5 Cherry Don Resthouse
7 Catanduanes Hotel
9 Solybel Lodge
10 Stars & Stripes Resthouse

PLACES TO EAT
2 Trellis Garden Café
3 Chicken House Restaurant, Disco & Family Steak House
11 Babe's Fast Food
13 Café de Paul

OTHER
1 Cinema
6 Front Page Triangle Beer Garden
8 RCPI (Long Distance Calls)
12 PT&T Office
14 PCI Bank
15 Cathedral
16 Philippine National Bank (PNB)
17 Post Office
18 Town Hall
19 Market
20 Jeepney Terminal

Virac

To Provincial Capitol Building

Boulevard

To Airport (4 km)

Town Plaza

Cabugao Bay

0   50   100 m

10 am and returning between 2 and 3 am. A regular service of jeepneys and buses runs between Virac and Baras. The bumpy but scenic road from Virac to Gigmoto follows the coast and winds around one bay after another. The dirt road from Bato to Viga, goes through forest and little villages in the centre of the island. This and the Virac to Gigmoto coast road are good for hiking.

Car Rodino Molina, owner of the small Halik-Alon Restaurant opposite the Provincial Capitol Building, hires out his jeep for around P1000 per day, including driver and petrol.

Getting Around
The Airport The airport is about four km south-west of Virac. The trip into town by tricycle should normally cost P2 per person. The least they will charge, however, is P10.

PURARAN
Puraran is a small place on the wild Pacific coast about 30 km north-east of Virac. It is a good stopover on a journey to the north of the island. However, many of the few foreigners who have visited Catanduanes up till now take one look at its long white beach and decide to finish the journey right there. Surfers especially like to stay in Puraran for the excellent breakers which usually start at the beginning of July. In September and October the surfing is good, while from November to January the particularly high breakers even provide a challenge for experts.

It is safe to swim at high tide in front of the reef, but be careful: there is a dangerously strong current near the beach, and especially over the reef itself – you have been warned! Even excellent swimmers have been known to get into serious trouble in this current. Only when the water is calm is it worth snorkelling. Typhoons can put an end to all thoughts of water sports. So, unless you're a surfer, the best time to stay would probably be from the middle of March until the middle to end of June.

Places to Stay
The *Puting Baybay Resort* has rooms for P100/150, or P350 including three meals daily. It's a basic place with rustic cottages directly on the beach.

The *Puraran Beach Resort* has nice cottages for P300/600. Three meals a day cost an extra P250. There is a restaurant with a beautiful view of the beach. This pleasant resort with a lawn at the south end of the bay is run by a Japanese-Philippine corporation.

Getting There & Away
Jeepney Two jeepneys leave Virac market for Puraran between 9 and 10 am daily, going on to Gigmoto. Another may leave after the arrival of the boat from Tabaco. You can also go to Baras by jeepney and then travel the following five km by tricycle (about P30). A tricycle for the whole trip from Virac costs at least P250. There is a pathway leading from the street in Puraran down to the beach which takes about five minutes on foot.

From Puraran to Virac, there is a regular jeepney service at about 3.30 am (it can even be as late as 4.30 am). This jeepney comes from Gigmoto.

Lubang

The Lubang Islands are part of the province of Mindoro Occidental. They hit the world headlines in 1974 when the Japanese soldier Hiroo Onoda, who had been hiding in the mountains of Lubang for 30 years, finally decided it was time to give himself up as a WWII prisoner of war. Fumio Nakahura, a captain in the Japanese Imperial Army, held out for another six years before being discovered in April 1980 on Mt Halcon on Mindoro. When the 74-year-old Hiroo Onoda paid a sentimental return visit to his island hideout in 1996 after many years, he was confronted over and over again by blunt hostility. Either some people still had a chip on their shoulder, or a few badly mannered yobbos grasped the opportunity to let off steam about the sons of Nippon.

The people of Lubang earn their income mainly from the sale of garlic. They would like to share in the profits from tourism but at present visitors may only be inspired to leave for Manila or Mindoro as soon as possible. I found people in Tilik and farther south-east to be less forthcoming than elsewhere. As you go from Tilik towards Lubang, attitudes become noticeably more relaxed.

Places to Stay
There is no commercial accommodation available in Lubang, so you will have to find a family who will rent you a room. Just ask at the church or one of the shops in Tilik.

GETTING THERE & AWAY
You can get here from Luzon (see the Getting There & Away section of the Manila chapter).

Air
Luzon Air Ads flies on Tuesday, Thursday, Saturday and Sunday from Lubang to Manila.

Boat
Luzon The Asuncion Shipping Lines' MV *Catalyn B* leaves Tilik for Manila on Tuesday, Friday and Sunday at 10 am (eight hours).

GETTING AROUND
Tilik is the port for this area. When a boat docks, a regular jeepney runs to Lubang and a truck takes freight and passengers to Looc. There is no other public transport. Once in a while there may be a *carretela* (a horse-drawn cab) from Tilik to Lubang. If you don't want to wait around, you could take a Special Ride, which costs about P70 and takes one hour. Transport costs on Lubang are at least twice those on other islands. This applies also to the short trip by *banca* from Balaquias across to Ambil Island, for which they now ask P250. It's not worth it, especially if you are expecting to look for and find the jade which the Philippine technical literature claims is there.

The airport is along the road from Lubang to Tagbac.

TILIK
You can't travel around much here because of the lack of transport, but the country around Tilik is good for walks, such as the one to Como Beach near Vigo. It's no tropical paradise, but there's some real surf and it's not crowded. There's a beautiful sandy beach at Tagbac, west of Lubang, but the sea

Lubang

0   5   10 km

LUZON

SEA

floor is muddy. If you go by paddle boat from Tilik to the other side of the bay, make sure there is at least a 15 cm clearance above the water line. The centre of the bay is exposed and even a light wind can blow water into the boat. It's easy to get thoroughly drenched.

Marinduque

Marinduque is the near-circular island between South Luzon and Mindoro. The Marinduquero are Tagalog people, and most of them come from Batangas and Quezon provinces.

Coconuts and rice are the main agricultural products. Two mining companies extract iron ore and copper; there are large copper deposits at Labo near Santa Cruz. The main tourist attraction is the Moriones Festival at Easter, which is great fun and everyone joins in with good humour (see the Public Holidays & Special Events section of the Facts for the Visitor chapter earlier in this book). This is when Marinduque gets most of its tourists. At other times there aren't many around, as the tourist industry here is just getting going.

Marinduque

GETTING THERE & AWAY
You can get to Marinduque from Luzon and Mindoro (see also Getting There & Away in the Manila chapter earlier in this book and Getting There & Away in the Mindoro section later in this chapter).

Air
Luzon PAL flies daily from Boac to Manila.

Boat
Luzon From Balanacan to Lucena (P65; 2½ hours), the Viva Shipping Lines' MV *San Agustin Reyes* leaves daily at 11 am and 5 pm.

From Buyabod, the harbour for Santa Cruz, two ferries leave daily for Lucena at 9 and 10 pm (4½ hours). Cars and motorcycles can be carried.

Mindoro A boat leaves Gasan for Pinamalayan on Mindoro daily at 8.30 am (3½ hours).

BOAC
Boac, on the Boac River, is the capital of Marinduque Province. It is a pretty little town towered over by a massive church with a richly decorated altar built on a hill. Of the passion plays performed all over the island at Easter, each claiming to be the best, the star production of the Moriones Festival is the one staged in Boac from Easter Thursday to Easter Sunday.

South of Boac there are a few beach resorts on pebbly beaches.

Telephone
The area code for Boac is 042.

Places to Stay
Boac *Cely's Lodging House* (☎ 332 1519) at 10 de Octobre St has basic, clean rooms with fan for P200.

The *Boac Hotel* (☎ 322 1121) on Nepomuceno St offers simple rooms with fan for P150/300, singles with fan and bath for P200 and doubles with air-con and bath for P375.

Right behind the market, the friendly people at the *Susanna Inn* (☎ 332 1997) provide quite comfortable rooms with fan for P250/300, with fan and bath for P300/400 and with air-con and bath for P500/700.

Around Boac A short way out of Boac, towards Mogpog, is the *Swing Beach Resort* (☎ 332 1252) on Deogracias St. Rooms (with four beds) cost P250 per person or P400 per person for full board.

The friendly *Marinduque Marine* (cellular ☎ 0912-311 1438) in Balaring about four km south of Boac, offers good accommodation. Cottages with fan and bath go for P380. The owner, Keith Gardner, is British. It has a good restaurant and an open-air garden bar. Diving facilities, dive courses and several-day diving tours are also offered.

The *Cassandra Beach Resort* in Caganhao, on the beach between Boac and Cawit, lets rooms with fan for P150 and cottages with fan and bath for P175. The guests are allowed to use the kitchen.

Also in Caganhao is the *Aussie-Pom Guest House* with pleasant, spacious rooms with fan for P200. Weekly and monthly rates can be arranged. The kitchen can be used by the guests. You can hire snorkelling equipment for P30 a day (there is a fairly good coral reef not far from the pebbly beach).

Also in Caganhao, the *Pyramid Beach Resort* (☎ 322 1493) is good value, with basic but adequate rooms for P150/200 and rooms with fan for P200/250. Meals should be ordered in advance.

In Cawit, the *Sunraft Beach Hotel* (☎ 332 1491) has basic rooms for P120/200 and with fan and bath for P200/300. The hotel is in the middle of a garden, right on a pebbly beach. The *Sea View Hotel* (☎ 332 2840) has adequate rooms with fan and bath for P400.

Getting Around
The Airport Boac airport is 12 km to the south of Boac, near Masiga.

BALANACAN
This small town in north-west Marinduque has a little harbour in a sheltered bay which provides shipping services to and from Lucena on Luzon.

Places to Stay

The *LTB Lodge* is a basic place near the wharf, where there are a few small restaurants. Rooms are P60/120 and with fan P100/150.

Getting There & Away

Jeepney There aren't many jeepneys between Boac and Balanacan daily. It's safer to rely on those that meet the boats.

Boat From Lucena, Balanacan is as close as you'll get to Boac by boat (see Getting There and Away in the Manila chapter).

SANTA CRUZ

Although Boac is the capital of Marinduque, Santa Cruz has the most inhabitants. Its great church, built in 1714, is very impressive with its old paintings and sculpture.

Equipment for diving trips from Santa Cruz can be hired from Franco Preclaro, though it's a good idea to have your own regulator. He can also advise on good areas for diving and arrange trips there.

Places to Stay

Across from the market, the *Model's Lodging House* has basic, clean accommodation with fan for P100/200 and with air-con for P175/350. The people are friendly, and it has a restaurant.

Places to Eat

Probably the best place to eat is the *Tita Amie Restaurant*, on the corner of Palomares and Pag-asa Sts. The choice is limited but special dishes can be ordered in advance.

Getting There & Away

Jeepney Several jeepneys run daily from Boac to Santa Cruz via Mogpog.

Boat There's a connection by ship from Santa Cruz and Lucena on Luzon. Buyabod is the pier for Santa Cruz and is a few km to the east.

IPIL

The **Bathala Caves**, about 10 km north-west of Santa Cruz in Barrio Ipil, are a complex of seven caves in all, only four of which are accessible. They're on the private property of the Mendoza family, so before a visit you should ask for permission (admission costs P50; guided tours P150). You may enjoy a swim in the natural pool behind the house – especially after visiting the bats in the caves!

Places to Stay

The Mendoza family rents a fairly big cottage for five to six people.

Getting There & Away

Jeepney Jeepneys travel from Santa Cruz to Ipil about every half hour (P5).

MANIUAYAN ISLAND

The three Santa Cruz islands north-east of the town of Santa Cruz have long beaches and good snorkelling, particularly Maniuayan Island.

Places to Stay

Lucita Perlada offers a room in a *cottage* on the beach for P200 per day, including meals.

Getting There & Away

Boat A boat leaves Bitik, on the north-eastern coast of Marinduque, daily at about 7 or 8 am and makes the crossing in 45 minutes.

TORRIJOS

White Beach at near Torrijos is probably the best beach on Marinduque. The outlying coral reef is good for snorkelling and the beach has a magnificent view of **Mt Malindig**.

Maranlig and **Sibuyao**, both north-west of Torrijos, make good day trips. Maranlig has cockfights on Sunday; Sibuyao is on a plateau with rice terraces. A jeepney runs daily to Maranlig. There is only one to Sibuyao Sunday, market day.

You can reach the white beach on **Salomague Island** by boat in an hour, but the Salomague Island Resort, opened a few years ago, is no longer regularly open to guests. It is suffering from a lack of customers and is usually closed.

Places to Stay

At White Beach, *L & R* and the *Rendezvous Cottages* both have basic cottages for P100.

Some of the locals offer private rooms about 50m from the beach for P100, with cooking facilities. Try Leonard Pilar or Jose Roldan. In Torrijos, the mayor, Ben Cordero Lim, also rents rooms for P100.

Getting There & Away

Jeepney A few jeepneys run daily from Buenavista to Torrijos via the hill town of Malibago, but be careful, as from late afternoon they don't go beyond Malibago.

There aren't many jeepneys from Santa Cruz to Torrijos. It is safest to rely on those which meet the boat. For White Beach near Poctoy, ask the jeepney driver to make a short detour there.

BUENAVISTA

This town, on the southern coast of Marinduque, is the departure point for **Mt Malindig** at Marlanga Point, a 1157m high dormant volcano on which a telegraph station has been built. About five km by road inland from Buenavista are the **Malbog Hot Springs** – sulphur springs which are claimed to heal certain skin complaints (admission P3).

The **Buenavista Market** is especially worth seeing at weekends, when mountain people from all around bring their wares. Pigs and goats are sold, slaughtered and cut up on the spot.

Places to Stay

The *Three Kings Cottages* on the rugged beach at Buenavista is run by Manuel Sarmiento and his family, and has rooms with fan for P150 and a cottage with two bedrooms, cooking facilities, fan and bath for P350. All the rooms are comfortable. Trips in outrigger boats can be arranged.

The *Susanna Hot Spring Resort* at Malbog has rooms with bath for P500. There is a restaurant and a nice garden with a small swimming pool where the water is at least 40°C.

Getting There & Away

Jeepney Several jeepneys run daily between Boac and Buenavista via Cawit and Gasan.

ELEFANTE ISLAND

High up on the little Elefante Island, to the south of Marinduque, Japanese investors have built a club with extensive facilities set in its own grounds. Jeeps belonging to the hotel run from the club to the beach, saving guests a walk. The place was designed originally to be only for club members, but ordinary guests are accepted when occupancy rates are low. It is definitely worth a day trip there, to get an impression of just what can be done for tourism with an island of that size and the right amount of money.

Places to Stay

The *Fantasy Elephant Club* provides very comfortably furnished rooms with TV, aircon and bath from P3000 to P12,500 and cottages for P6000 and P7700. This is a well looked after establishment with a beautiful view. There is a restaurant, swimming pool, whirlpool, Japanese garden, golf course and tennis court; diving and windsurfing are available.

Getting There & Away

Boat A boat from Lipata to Elefante Island and back costs around P300. For security reasons guards of the Fantasy Elephant Club check visitors on arrival.

TRES REYES ISLANDS

It's a 30-minute trip in an outrigger boat from Buenavista to the outlying Tres Reyes (Three Kings) Islands. Although Balthazar and Melchor Islands are rocky and uninhabited, the third, Gaspar, has a small village and a lovely coral beach that is good for snorkelling and diving. In 1980 the wreck of a Chinese junk that sank 200 years ago was discovered about 100m north of Gaspar Island in 38m of water. Although most of its rich cargo of porcelain has already been salvaged, from time to time local divers bring up a few more finds, so the treasure hunt goes on.

JOHN PENNOCK

JOHN PENNOCK

JENS PETERS

JENS PETERS

Top: The Chocolate Hills, Bohol Province.
Middle Left: Mayon Volcano looms large over ricefields, Albay Province.

Bottom Left: Beach paradise on North Pandan Island, off Mindoro's west coast.
Right: Batanes women with headdress.

JENS PETERS

JENS PETERS

JENS PETERS

RICHARD I'ANSON

AROUND LUZON

Top: The jeepney, a Filipino highlight.
Middle Left: A family of easyriders.

Bottom Left: *Calesas* still ply the
    quieter corners of the Philippines.
Right: A capacity crowd, near Banaue.

GASAN

Like Boac and Mogpog, Gasan is heavily involved in the Easter passion play. Handcrafted basket ware and ornaments are made here. In the UNI Store you can see how the carved wooden birds are painted.

Places to Stay

The *Sunset Garden Resort* (cellular ☎ /fax 0973-795745) in Pangi is a well-kept place about two km north of Gasan. Cottages with fan and bath are P420. There is a tennis court and boat tours and diving are offered. Reservations can be made in Manila (☎ 801 6369).

Places to Eat

The *Sunset Garden Restaurant* belonging to the resort has European and Filipino food. At the market in Gasan, women prepare tasty corn pudding and rice and banana cake.

Getting There & Away

Boat There is a boat route connecting Gasan and Pinamalayan on Mindoro.

Masbate

The province of Masbate includes Masbate Island and the smaller Ticao and Burias Islands. Although the island group is officially part of the Bicol region, the influence of the Visayas is unmistakable, so the Cebuano and Hiligaynon languages are also frequently spoken.

Before WWII, Masbate was a leading gold field. Today it is noted for its meat production, having some herds of cattle as large as 4000 head. The island is also known in the Philippines as 'Cattle Country'. Fishing is also important economically.

Tourism doesn't mean much here, as few foreigners come to these islands, which are off the main traffic routes, so visitors accustomed to rusticity will have a pleasant time. Even basic, commercial overnight accommodation is really only available in the towns of Masbate, Mobo, Aroroy and

Mandaon. Lovers of *tuba* (palm wine) should try the white variety, which is a speciality of Masbate.

GETTING THERE & AWAY

You can get to Masbate from Cebu, Luzon, Romblon and Samar (see the Getting There & Away section of the Manila chapter earlier in this book and the Getting There & Away sections of the chapters on the other islands).

Air

Luzon PAL has flights from Masbate to Legaspi on Monday and Wednesday, and daily flights from Masbate to Manila. Asian Spirit flies daily from Masbate to Manila (P1130).

Boat

Cebu From Masbate to Cebu City, the MV *Asia-Taiwan* of Trans-Asia Shipping Lines leaves on Tuesday and Thursday at 6 pm (14 hours). The Sulpicio Lines' MV *Cebu Princess* leaves on Saturday at 4 pm (36 hours, via Ormoc on Leyte). The boat comes from Manila.

Apparently, a boat goes from Cataingan to Hagnaya twice a week on Monday and Thursday, and from Cawayan to Hagnaya twice a week on Wednesday and Saturday.

Leyte From Masbate to Calubian, the Sulpicio Lines' MV *Palawan Princess* leaves on Thursday at 10 pm (eight hours). It goes on to Baybay and Maasin.

From Masbate to Ormoc, the Sulpicio Lines' MV *Cebu Princess* leaves on Saturday at 4 pm (P200; 16 hours).

From Masbate to Palompon, the MV *Sacred Heart* of WG & A leaves on Tuesday at 8 pm (P160; 10 hours). It goes on to Ormoc.

Luzon From Masbate to Bulan, the MV *Matea* leaves Masbate daily at 5 am (3½ hours). There may be a second boat some other time during the day.

From Masbate to Manila, the Sulpicio Lines' MV *Palawan Princess* leaves on Monday at 3 pm (19 hours). Their MV *Cebu Princess* leaves on Wednesday at 4 pm (19 hours). The MV *Sacred Heart* of WG & A leaves on Thursday at 9 pm (P280; 19 hours).

Romblon There is one ship a week from Mandaon to Sibuyan Island in Romblon Province, leaving on Wednesday or Thursday at 7 pm. After a short trip, it anchors in Maolingon Bay (about 15 to 30 minutes by boat from Mandaon), before finally departing about 1 am for Cajidiocan on Sibuyan, which takes another five hours. From Sibuyan another boat runs to Romblon Island. You can only find out the exact departure time in Mandaon. Information given in other places varies widely and is not reliable.

MASBATE

The town of Masbate is the capital of the province but doesn't have a great deal of note beyond the harbour, the market and numerous stalls which line the streets. It is the base for air and sea travel to places like South

Luzon. A few km south-east, in Mobo, is Bitu-on Beach, a popular place to visit, with a beach resort whose cottages are a good alternative to the hotels in the town.

Every year in the second week in April, the Rodeo Masbateño takes place in the Masbate Sports Complex. There are even cowboys from the USA participating.

Telephone

The area code for Masbate is 056.

Places to Stay

The only halfway decent hotel in town is the *St Anthony Hotel* on Quezon St, where simple rooms with fan cost P150/200, with fan and bath P250/300, and with air-con and bath P350/400.

Places to Eat

For a good, reasonably priced meal try the *Peking House* in the port area or the *Petit Restaurant* opposite the St Anthony Hotel

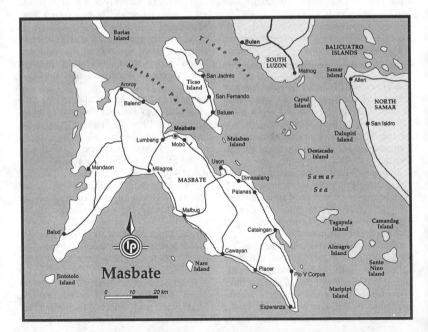

on Quezon St. The clean *Kapihan Restaurant* on Mabini St is known for good seafood.

CATAINGAN
Cataingan is a small harbour town at the head of a narrow bay which reaches quite a way inland, on the south-east of the island. Boats leave there for Cebu.

Getting There & Away
Jeepney A few jeepneys run daily from Masbate to Cataingan. The trip takes five hours on the bad road.

MANDAON
Boats go from Mandaon to Sibuyan Island in Romblon Province. Near the town is Kalanay Cave, the site of several archaeological finds.

Places to Stay
Mesa's Lodging right on the beach has basic accommodation, with rooms for P50/100.

Getting There & Away
Jeepney Several jeepneys and buses run daily from Masbate to Mandaon (two hours). Try to get a seat on the roof if you want a good view of some lovely countryside.

Mindoro

Mindoro is the next big island to the south of Manila. It is divided into the provinces of Mindoro Occidental, which is the western part, and Mindoro Oriental, the eastern part. Only the coastal strip is heavily populated. In the jungles and mountains inland there are various groups of the Mangyan tribes (see under Cultural Minorities in the People section of the Facts about the Country chapter earlier in this book).

Fishing and the cultivation of rice and coconuts are the main economic activities, with some cattle-raising around San Jose. While the name Mindoro is a contraction of the Spanish *Mina de Oro* ('gold mine'), no major gold discovery has been made. The difficult terrain has also limited Mindoro's

potential for copper and iron-ore mining, the main mining activity being the quarrying of marble. There has, however, been some promising oil prospecting in the south-west.

The tourist route is from Puerto Galera to Roxas and Mansalay, via Calapan. Around Puerto Galera there are popular beaches and coral reefs. Roxas is the starting point for boat trips to Tablas and Boracay Islands.

It's a fair bet that it will not be long before the northern stretch of coastline from Mamburao to Sablayan in Mindoro Occidental becomes an important centre of tourism. Unfortunately, there is still no regular shipping route from Sablayan or San Jose to Coron on Busuanga in the north of Palawan. Such a route would really add to the attractions of island hopping in the region.

GETTING THERE & AWAY
Buses leave the BLTB terminal in Manila daily for Batangas. An air-con bus leaves the Centrepoint Hotel in Ermita every day at 9 am. You can get combined bus and boat tickets to Mindoro from an office in the hotel.

There are boats daily from Batangas to Abra de Ilog (docking at Wawa), Calapan and Puerto Galera. For more information about getting to Mindoro from Luzon, see the Getting There & Away section of the Manila chapter earlier in this book.

You can also get to Mindoro from Marinduque, Panay and Romblon (see the Getting There & Away sections of the chapters on the other islands).

Air
Luzon PAL has flights on Wednesday and Saturday from Mamburao to Manila, on Monday, Wednesday, Thursday and Saturday from San Jose to Manila. Asian Spirit flies from San Jose to Manila (p880). Pacific Airways plans to have flights on Monday, Wednesday and Friday between Sablayan and Manila (P1100).

Bus
Luzon Combined bus and boat tickets for the journey from Puerto Galera to Manila via Batangas can be bought, and reservations

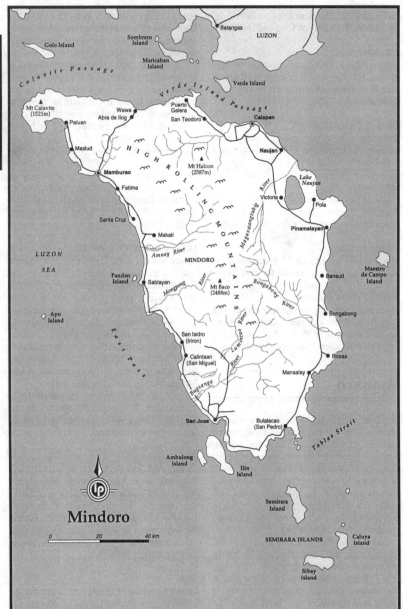

Mindoro

0   20   40 km

made, at the docks. If you want to buy your tickets separately, you can catch an ordinary public bus or air-con bus for Manila in Batangas (see the Batangas section of the Around Manila chapter earlier in this book).

Boat

Luzon From Puerto Galera to Batangas (P45; 1½ hours), Santo Domingo Shipping Lines' MV *Santa Peñafrancia VI* (car ferry) leaves daily at 5 and 10.30 am and 2.30 pm. Departure is from Balatero, 2½ km west of Puerto Galera. The MV *Si-Kat II* of Si-Kat Ferry leaves daily at 9.30 am (P150; 2½ hours). An air-con bus waits at the dock in Batangas and goes direct to the Centrepoint Hotel in Manila.

A big outrigger leaves Sabang, outside Puerto Galera, for Batangas daily at 6, 7 and 8 am (P60; 1½ hours). The 8 am *Sabang Princess* is the most comfortable. A Special Ride with an outrigger should be about P800.

From Calapan to Batangas, the MV *Supercat* of Universal Aboitiz leaves daily at 5.30 and 9.30 am and 1 and 4 pm (P150; 45 minutes). The fast ferries MV *Lourdes* and MV *Fatima* make the crossing eight times a day from 5.15 am until 4.30 pm. Between 6 am and 6 pm there are about 12 regular ferries (two hours).

From Abra de Ilog to Batangas, a car ferry of Montenegro Shipping Lines or Viva Shipping Lines leaves daily at 6.30 am, noon, 4.30 and 6 pm (P60; 2½ hours). A big outrigger also leaves at 11 am.

From Sablayan to Batangas, Viva Shipping Lines' MV *Viva Peñafrancia or* MV *St Christopher* sails on Monday, Wednesday and Saturday (P150; nine hours).

From San Jose to Batangas, Viva Shipping Lines' MV *Santo Niño* sails on Monday, Wednesday and Saturday at 6 am (13 hours). The MV *Marian Queen* leaves on Tuesday, Thursday and Sunday at 6 am (12 hours). RN Hi Speed Ferries' MV *Florida I* sails on Tuesday, Friday and Sunday at 9pm (6 hours).

Marinduque One boat goes daily from Pinamalayan to Gasan, leaving at 5 am or 2 pm (3½ hours).

Panay A big outrigger boat goes from Roxas to Boracay on Monday and Thursday at about 10.30 am (P260; five to six hours). From December to May it can even leave as often as every other day. If it goes via Looc on Tablas Island in Romblon Province it takes at least 10 hours and you may have to stay overnight in Looc. In bad weather the sea in the Tablas Strait is rough and crossing is not recommended. Small boats sometimes sail over, but they are completely unsuitable and often dangerously overloaded.

From San Jose to Buruanga there is another big outrigger boat which leaves on Thursday and Sunday at 9 am (P100; eight hours) This trip is also not recommended when the waves are high in Tablas Strait.

From San Jose to Lipata, the MV *Princess Melanie Joy* and the MV *Aida* sail once or twice a week (24 hours). They go via Semira and Caluya Islands, where they lie up to 10 hours at anchor. Lipata is five km north of Culasi on the west coast of Panay.

Romblon From Bongabong, an outrigger boat runs irregularly to San Agustin on Tablas Island, possibly on Sunday at 2 pm (six hours). It continues to Romblon on Romblon Island.

A big outrigger boat runs irregularly from Pinamalayan to Sibali Island (Maestro de Campo Island) and then continues to Banton Island.

From Roxas to Looc on Tablas Island, a big outrigger boat goes on Tuesday, Wednesday and Sunday at 10.30 am (four hours).

From Roxas to Odiongan on Tablas Island, a big outrigger boat goes on Monday, Wednesday and Saturday at 10.30 am (three hours).

PUERTO GALERA

The fine beaches and excellent diving at Puerto Galera have been attracting travellers for some time. For about 60 years, it has been regarded by zoologists, botanists and students of the University of the Philippines as an ideal place to study the ecostructure of animals, plants and micro-organisms in almost undisturbed natural conditions. In 1934, the UP Marine Biological Station was set up. Forty years later, the United Nations Man & Biosphere Program International declared Puerto Galera a nature centre. It was at this time that the media also discovered the attractions of Puerto Galera as a tourist resort, and the place took off.

The town's new wealth has attracted foreign interest and investment. It has also split the population into two opposing camps: the developers and the environmentalists. The developers see tourism as the business opportunity of a lifetime and advocate expansion at any price. The environmentalists are concerned about the detrimental effects development is having on the customs and morals of the inhabitants and on the natural features of their environment.

It's a popular destination which tourism could easily destroy. The adage that tourism is like fire – it can cook your food but it can also burn down your house – should be heeded in Puerto Galera. Considering the tourism potential of this little beauty spot, the disruption of the environment has so far been kept within bounds. However, the Department of Tourism has added Puerto Galera to

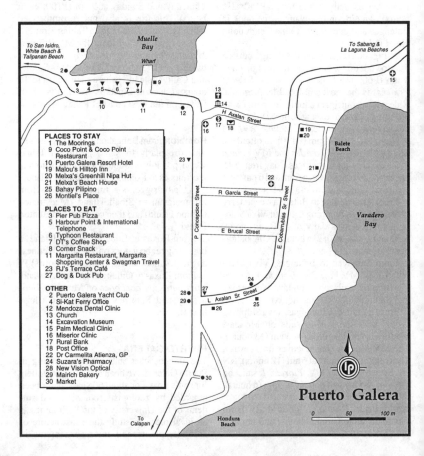

PLACES TO STAY
1 The Moorings
9 Coco Point & Coco Point Restaurant
10 Puerto Galera Resort Hotel
19 Malou's Hilltop Inn
20 Melxa's Greenhill Nipa Hut
21 Melxa's Beach House
25 Bahay Pilipino
26 Montiel's Place

PLACES TO EAT
3 Pier Pub Pizza
5 Harbour Point & International Telephone
6 Typhoon Restaurant
7 DT's Coffee Shop
8 Corner Snack
11 Margarita Restaurant, Margarita Shopping Center & Swagman Travel
23 RJ's Terrace Café
27 Dog & Duck Pub

OTHER
2 Puerto Galera Yacht Club
4 Si-Kat Ferry Office
12 Mendoza Dental Clinic
13 Church
14 Excavation Museum
15 Palm Medical Clinic
16 Miserior Clinic
17 Rural Bank
18 Post Office
22 Dr Carmelita Atienza, GP
24 Suzara's Pharmacy
28 New Vision Optical
29 Mairich Bakery
30 Market

Puerto Galera

0   50   100 m

the list of special development areas, so that means the go-ahead for more sophisticated tourist resorts. New developments include the comfortable Heaven on Earth Club on Talipanan Beach and The Moorings, an apartment complex with clubhouse, tennis courts and swimming pool, on a hill overlooking Muelle Bay. There's no doubt that increased tourism will see the face of Puerto Galera change out of all recognition in the next few years.

Puerto Galera has a most beautiful natural harbour, and the view from the deck of the ferry as you come through the Batangas Channel or the Manila Channel is a delight. Spanish galleons once sought shelter here from typhoons, and the name dates from that era, when this was the gateway for Spanish traders on their way to China, India, Sumatra and Java. In the small, so-called **Excavation Museum** by the church you can see pieces of pottery from various Chinese dynasties as well as a fine collection of shells.

In the hinterland are some interesting alternatives to beach living. There is a Mangyan village barely one km behind White Beach. Near Dulangan, about six km towards Calapan, villagers pan for gold in the river. The **Tamaraw Waterfalls** are about 15 km towards Calapan. You can visit a marble quarry or climb **Mt Malisimbo** and explore the nearby jungle.

The Ponderosa Golf & Country Club is run by members and has a nine-hole golf course. It is south-west of Puerto Galera at about 600m above sea level. There is a tremendous view, and guests are welcome. It's about five km from the village of Minolo up to the club. Transport can be requested at the Ponderosa waiting station in Minolo.

The journey from Manila to Puerto Galera by bus and boat is comfortable by Philippine standards and only lasts about five hours. Although it can be rainy and somewhat cool, most visitors come to Puerto Galera in December and January. Tourist numbers have usually declined by mid-March, but sunny and exceptionally calm weather can still be enjoyed between the months of June and October.

Information

Money The Rural Bank in Puerto Galera changes cash and may also change travellers cheques, albeit at a less favourable rate than the moneychangers and banks in Manila. It is sometimes possible to change both travellers cheques and US dollars cash at the Margarita Shopping Center.

Post & Communications The small post office is diagonally opposite the church on H Axalan St.

There is a telephone for international calls at the pier. Many of the resorts also have cellular telephone links.

Travel Agencies Swagman Travel has an office near the Puerto Galera pier which handles bookings and reconfirmation of national and international flights, and visa extensions. It also has an office with Asia Divers, Sabang Beach.

Medical Services The Palm Medical Clinic is a little out of town on the way to Sabang. It is open Monday to Friday from 8 am to 5 pm.

Dr Carmelita Atienza, a GP on R Garcia St, consults Monday to Saturday from 8 am until 5 pm.

Dr Jiolita Mendoza runs the Mendoza Dental clinic near the pier (☎ 788518). She is available Monday to Saturday from 8.30 am until noon, and 1 to 5 pm.

Diving

Among other diving activities available, five-day diving courses for around P7000 are on offer. One dive usually costs around P500, including equipment. The shops all have top facilities and equipment; and nearly every one can provide its own dive boat. Most diving excursions take place near Puerto Galera.

A number of dive shops also undertake diving trips from February until May to places such as Busuanga in the north of Palawan and the spectacular Apo Reef to the west of Mindoro.

Dive shops to be recommended are:

Action Divers (cellular ☎ 0912-751968) at Small La Laguna Beach: courses are available in English and German.

Asia Divers (cellular ☎ 0912-3050652) at Small La Laguna Beach: courses are available in English, German and Japanese.

Atlantis Dive Resort (cellular ☎ 0912-3080672) at Sabang Beach: courses are available in English, French and German.

Capt'n Gregg's (cellular ☎ 0912-3065267) at Sabang Beach: courses are available in English, German and Swedish.

Cocktail Divers (cellular ☎ 0912-3065828) at Sabang Beach and Big La Laguna Beach: courses are available in English, German and Swedish.

Encenada Dive Club at Encenada Beach: courses are available in English.

La Laguna Dive Centre (cellular ☎ 0912-3065622) at Big La Laguna Beach: courses are available in English, French, German, Spanish and Swedish.

Octopus Divers at Sabang Beach.

Pacific Divers (cellular ☎ 0912-304 3984) at White Beach: courses are available in English, French and Tagalog.

Philippine Divers (cellular ☎ 0912-304 7017) at Coco Beach.

Whitetip Divers at White Beach.

Reef Raiders Dive Center at Big La Laguna Beach: courses are available in English, German and Japanese.

Scuba World at Big La Laguna Beach.

South Sea Divers at Sabang Beach: courses are available in English, German and Tagalog.

Places to Stay

Puerto Galera The fan-cooled rooms at *Malou's Hilltop Inn* are basic, costing P150. *Melxa's Greenhill Nipa Hut* offers rooms with fan from P150 to P400. On Balete Beach, *Melxa's Beach House* provides spacious rooms with kitchen, fan and bath from P250 to P450. Monthly rates are available.

The *Coco Point* is right at the wharf and good value for the money. Their pleasant and tidy rooms with fan and bath go for P250/300.

The *Puerto Galera Resort Hotel* (cellular ☎ 090-309 0905)is a big place with a view of Muelle Bay. Comfortable rooms with aircon and bath cost between P1000 and P3000.

Around Puerto Galera There are several places in walking distance of Puerto Galera that you can choose from.

Rooms with bath at the *Sandbar Beach Resort* cost P300/450, and cottages with bath P400. This friendly place is about two km out of town on the narrow land bridge connecting the mainland and Boquete Island on the Muelle Bay side. It also offers windsurfing.

If you keep on walking, you'll come to the *Coral Aquaria* on the south-west coast of Boquete Island. Cottages with fan and bath cost P300 and P500 (with kitchen). It's quiet here, only a few minutes from the beach, and ideal for people with children. You can get information at the Pier Pub Pizza.

The *Fishermen's Cove Beach Resort* (cellular ☎ 0912-306 8494) is on a quiet bay (no beach) about one km out of town towards White Beach. The place is under Italian management and rooms with fan and bath go for P400/500. It has an Italian restaurant. Windsurfing is also offered.

The *Encenada Beach Resort* (cellular ☎ 0912-301 2289) is about 1½ km out of town towards Sabang. Their spacious rooms and cottages with fan and bath go for P2200 per person (full board); some have a fridge. Hobie Cats, windsurfing, water skiing and diving are available. It is a pleasant, beautifully laid out place with its own beach.

The *Tanawin Lodge* (cellular ☎/fax 0912-328 7692) is about one km out of town on the way to Sabang, near Encenada Beach (a short descent). It has small, fully-furnished two-storey houses with living rooms and bedrooms. They are all individually furnished and cost P800 to P1800 depending on facilities. The atmosphere is like staying with friends, and there is a restaurant and a swimming pool with bar. The grounds are the nicest in Puerto Galera, with a beautiful view of Varadero Bay. Bookings can be made in Manila at Afro-Asian Tours & Travel (☎ 525 4374; fax 521 8167), 1006 San Luiz Building, Maria Orosa St, Ermita.

Places to Eat

Around the docks at Puerto Galera various restaurants serve European and Filipino dishes. Among these are the *Typhoon Restaurant* and the *Harbour Point Restaurant*. The *Pier Pub Pizza* not only has pizzas, but also tasty seafood. Just across from the school, *RJ's Terrace Café* has good breakfast and small snacks. British traditions are kept alive at the *Dog & Duck Pub*, especially on Sundays when the special is roast beef and Yorkshire pudding.

Getting There & Away
Bus Several BLTB buses leave from Pasay City in Manila daily for Batangas (P60; three hours). An air-con bus leaves the Centrepoint Hotel in Ermita every day at 9 am. You can get combined bus and ferry tickets (P300) at the Si-Kat Ferry Office in the hotel (☎ 521 3344).

Combined bus and ferry tickets from Puerto Galera to Manila can be obtained in the Si-Kat Ferry Office at the pier. Bus seats should be reserved at least one day in advance.

For more information about getting to Mindoro from Luzon, see the Getting There & Away section of the Manila chapter earlier in this book.

Dangers & Annoyances
Despite what many maps say, the road between Abra de Ilog and Puerto Galera was never built.

Jeepney
Jeepneys run from Calapan to Puerto Galera (P30; two hours) every day between 7 am and 4 pm, leaving from the market.

The trip from San Jose to Puerto Galera has to be done in several stages. The jeepney from San Jose to Bulalacao leaves between 6 and 7 am from the Metrobank; it's a rough trip of four hours. Alternatively, you could make this part of the trip by outrigger boat, leaving at 11 am (3½ hours). From Bulalacao, you travel by jeepney or bus to Roxas, a one-hour journey along a road which is bad as far as Mansalay. A big bus then takes you from Roxas to Calapan in four hours. The final stage of the journey is done by jeepney and takes two hours. The last jeepney leaves Calapan for Puerto Galera at about 4 pm.

Boat
From Batangas to Puerto Galera the Ski-Cat ferry departs daily at noon (P150; two hours).

From Batangas to Balatero, 2½ km west of Puerto Galera, a car ferry departs daily at 8.30 am, 12.30 pm and 5 pm (P45; 1½ hours). A jeepney to town costs P5 per person. A Special Ride with an outrigger from Balatero to Sabang costs P150.

Big outriggers travel daily from Batangas to Sabang (P60; 1½ hours), leaving at 9.30 and 10.30 am, noon and 1.30 pm.

A Special Ride by outrigger boat from Batangas to Puerto Galera costs about P800.

There are lots of fast ferries daily from Batangas to Calapan (P150; 45 minutes). From Calapan to Puerto Galera you can take a jeepney (P30; two hours). The last one leaves about 4 pm. (See also the Getting There & Away section of the Manila chapter earlier in this book.)

From Mamburao to Abra de Ilog and on to the wharf at Wawa at least one jeepney runs daily at about 6 am (P35; two hours). From Wawa, boats leave at irregular intervals for Puerto Galera, as long as there are enough passengers (P75; 2½ hours). A Special Ride costs about P800.

There is another route to Puerto Galera from Abra de Ilog, via Batangas. Catch the morning ferry from Wawa to Batangas (P60; 2½ hours) and carry on at noon or in the afternoon, with the ferry to Puerto Galera.

PUERTO GALERA BEACHES
In almost every bay with a beach that's at all useable, you'll find cottages for local and foreign tourists. To the east, resorts have sprung up at Sabang Beach, Small La Laguna Beach and Big La Laguna Beach. To the south, they go as far as Tabinay Beach. To the west, Talipanan Beach development has almost reached its limit. While the main beaches have electricity, considering the number of power failures, it's a good idea to have a torch handy.

Beaches just outside Puerto Galera, such as Balete Beach and Hondura Beach, are rather undeveloped and may disappoint some pampered beachlovers. Most travellers prefer the ones a few km farther away.

Sabang is a more 'happening' place for the visitor, especially after dark, and it might not be everybody's scene. It can get very hectic and loud at night around the discos and bars. Some restaurants have been built on sites close to the water and the remaining beach is almost completely blocked by outrigger boats. A hill path takes you through a palm grove and over a grassy meadow to Escarceo Point, two km east of Sabang. There you can go to the top of the 14m high lighthouse where you can get a gorgeous view, especially at sunrise and sunset.

There is also some action to be found on **Small La Laguna Beach**, although it is maybe a bit more relaxed. The beach itself is not particularly impressive. The most popular activities during the day are snorkelling and diving. Many travellers prefer to stay overnight at Small La Laguna Beach, or just spend the days there, and go out at night at the nearby Sabang Beach.

At **Big La Laguna Beach** there's a lot of activity. Some of the cottages here are packed close together, but the coral reef is worth seeing and is good for snorkelling.

The reefs at **Balete Beach**, **Long Beach** and **Halige Beach** are also good for snorkelling, but careful: strong currents can make **Boquete Beach** dangerous for swimmers.

There's not much action on the beaches between San Isidro and Talipanan Point, a few km west of Puerto Galera. The busiest one of them all is **White Beach**. On the other hand, the adjoining beaches of **Aninuan** and **Talipanan** in the next bay are extremely quiet. All three of them are good bathing beaches, although – unlike the beaches mentioned above – snorkelling is not particularly interesting there. The water at White Beach gets very deep a few metres from shore – too deep for children and non-swimmers.

Places to Stay

The following list of resorts is only a small cross section of the accommodation available. If you want to stay more than a few days and are willing to pay in advance, you can negotiate quite reasonable rates. But to save embarrassing your landlord, keep quiet about the rates you get – especially to other landlords!

Prices can vary, depending on how successful the season is. Especially around Christmas time and during the Easter week price hikes of up to 100% are possible, while the off-season from June until November is occasionally good for big discounts.

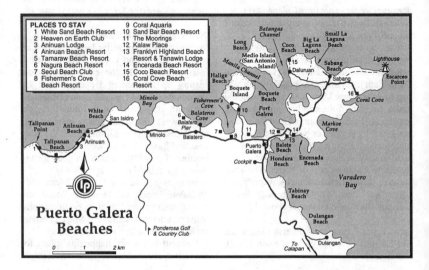

PLACES TO STAY
1 White Sand Beach Resort
2 Heaven on Earth Club
3 Aninuan Lodge
4 Aninuan Beach Resort
5 Tamaraw Beach Resort
6 Nagura Beach Resort
7 Seoul Beach Club
8 Fishermen's Cove Beach Resort
9 Coral Aquaria
10 Sand Bar Beach Resort
11 The Moorings
12 Kalaw Place
13 Franklyn Highland Beach Resort & Tanawin Lodge
14 Encenada Beach Resort
15 Coco Beach Resort
16 Coral Cove Beach Resort

Puerto Galera Beaches

0   1   2 km

Sabang Beach *Tina's Upstairs* has cottages from P100 to P180, and cottages with fan and bath from P150 to 400; the more expensive have kitchen and TV. The buildings are basic but good, and are on a hill with a beautiful view. *Capt'n Gregg's Divers Lodge* (cellular ☎ 0912-306 5367) has rooms with fan and bath for P350 and with air-con for P450. The atmosphere is pleasant and there is a restaurant. Divers prefer it.

Angelyn's Beach Resort (cellular ☎ 0912-306 5332) is a quiet place on the side of a hill, with a good view. Cottages with fan and bath go for P400, each with kitchen and fridge.

Situated a bit higher up than most places and with a good view, the *Seabreeze Vista Lodge* offers cottages with fan from P250 to P500; the more expensive ones have cooking facilities. The grounds are green and pleasant.

Cathy's Cottages (cellular ☎ 0912-305891) are cosy with fan and bath, costing from P250

to P500. There is also a restaurant. *At Can's Inn* has cottages with kitchen, fan and bath from P250 to P400. The cottages at the *Seashore Lodge* cost P350, 450 and P600 including fan and bath. At the above three resorts, the more expensive cottages have a kitchen, fridge and TV.

The *Big Apple Dive Resort* (cellular ☎/fax 0912-308 1120) is a bigger place where cottages with fan and bath go for P350 and with kitchen and TV for P500 and P900. There is a restaurant, billiards, mini golf and a swimming pool with poolside bar.

The *Terraces Garden Resort* (cellular ☎ 0912-308 0136) has clean, quiet and comfortable rooms with fan and bath for P350/450. The surroundings are pleasant – small houses among tropical plants on a slope above Sabang.

There is a beer garden at *Villa Sabang* (cellular ☎ 0912-313 4486), which has nice cottages with fan and bath from P400 to P650. All have a kitchen and refrigerator.

AROUND LUZON

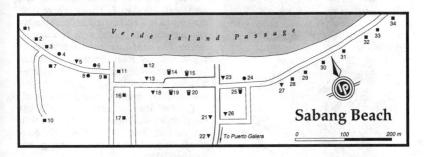

Sabang Beach

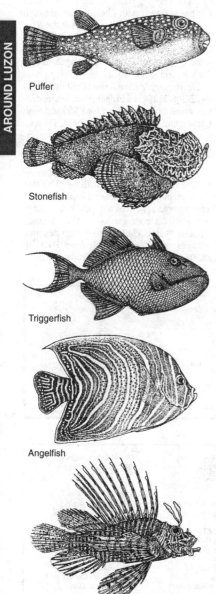

Puffer

Stonefish

Triggerfish

Angelfish

Lionfish

The *Atlantis Dive Resort* (cellular ☎ 0912-308 0672) has very good rooms in a white, Spanish-Mexican style building. With air-con and bath they cost P1250/1750. It have a pool with waterfall, and diving facilities. This is the best place in Sabang so far.

Coral Cove Beach The *Coral Cove Beach Resort* (cellular ☎ 0973-797836) has immaculate rooms with fan for P250 and with fan and spotless bath for P700. This is a big, tastefully designed building in a small, remote bay, about one km from Sabang. There is a restaurant and diving available, and staff can arrange day trips by boat. This is a great place if you want to get away from it all. Air-con rooms should be ready by 1997, and a swimming pool is planned for then as well.

Small La Laguna Beach *Nick & Sonia's Cottages* (cellular ☎ 0973-751 968) is a friendly place with cottages with fan and bath for P200 and P300. The more expensive cottages have a kitchen and fridge. Monthly rates are available. Boat trips can be arranged.

The *Havana Moon* is a comfortable, quiet resort, with big rooms in really good cottages. Rooms with fan cost P200, cottages with fan and bath P300, cottages with air-con and bath P600 (with kitchen and refrigerator).

The *Full Moon* (cellular ☎ 0973-75968) has plain but well-maintained cottages with fan and bath from P200 to P400. The *Sha-Che Inn* is good value. Cottages with fan and bath cost P150.

The *Sunsplash* has spacious cottages with fan and bath for P350 and P600, and it has a restaurant and billiards. *El Galleon Beach Resort* (cellular ☎ 0912-308 3190; fax 305 0652) has large rooms with fan and bath for P500 and with air-con, bath and TV P800. It is comfortable and will soon have a swimming pool. Diving is also available.

Carlo's Inn (cellular ☎ /fax 0912-301 0717) is on a rise right at the beach. It has comfortable rooms with fan and bath from P350 to P650, and with kitchen, fridge, fan and bath for P450 to P950. Well appointed rooms with TV, fridge, air-con and bath cost

P1500. It also has weekly and monthly rates, and has billiards and a restaurant with international cuisine.

Big La Laguna Beach The spacious rooms at the *Paradise Lodge* (cellular ☎/fax 097-375 6348) are in really good condition. With fan and bath they cost P350 and P550. Enjoy live music in the bar at the weekends. It also has windsurfing, diving and organise boat trips. The lodge is under Austrian management.

Set in a beautiful garden, the *El Oro Resort* (cellular ☎ 0912-306 6642) offers cottages with fan and bath for P400.

The *La Laguna Beach Club* (cellular ☎ /fax 0912-306 5622) provides rooms with fan and bath for P470/630, and with air-con and bath for P900. There is a pool, and diving and windsurfing are available. Reservations can be made in Manila at the Park Hotel (☎ 521 2371; fax 521 2393) on Belen St, Paco.

Finally, *Miller's Corner* (cellular ☎ 0912-305 7127) at the west end of the beach has rooms with fan and bath from P500 to P800. All rooms have a refrigerator and TV.

Coco Beach The *Coco Beach Resort* (cellular ☎ 0912-305 0476; fax 304 7017) has beautifully decorated rooms with fan and bath for P1300/2600 including breakfast. It is well maintained with a restaurant, big, attractive swimming pool, and a quiet private beach with drop-off. Windsurfing, sailing, diving and tennis are available. Reservations can be made in Manila at the Coco Beach Booking Office (☎ 521 5260; fax 526 6903), Legaspi Towers, Roxas Blvd, Malate.

White Beach The popular *White Beach Lodge* (cellular ☎ 0912-311 6127) provides several fairly roomy cottages with fan and bath for P250/350, while rooms with kitchen, fridge and TV are P500. There is also a good restaurant.

Estrella's Resort is adequate accommodation where rooms with fan and bath cost P250/300.

Delgado's Cottages has fairly roomy cottages with fan and bath for P300. It's a good place with a restaurant. *Cherry's Inn* has adequate cottages with kitchens, fan and bath for between P300 and P500.

The *Lodger's Nook* (cellular ☎ 0912-305 7011) offers several single and duplex cottages with fan and bath from P300 to P600, and also has a restaurant, billiard hall and windsurfing.

Simon's Place (cellular ☎ 0912-311 3555) has various cottages, each a different size, with fan and bath from P350 to P600. One larger one has a kitchen and fridge. This is a pleasant little establishment with a beach bar.

The *White Beach Nipa Hut* (cellular ☎ 0912-305 9343) is a fairly large establishment with lots of little cottages with fan and bath for P350/500 and with air-con and bath P600/800; some of them have cooking facilities.

At the western end of White Beach, the *Summer Connection* (cellular ☎ 0912-312 6837) is a pleasant, quiet little place, where cottages with fan and bath go for P400. The restaurant is pleasant.

Warren's Seaview (cellular ☎ 0912-318 4890) has spotless rooms with and without kitchen. They are all equipped with fan and bath, and cost P450 and P600.

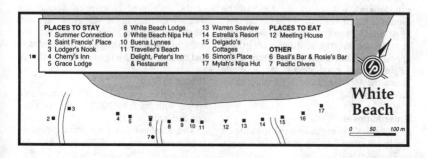

PLACES TO STAY
1 Summer Connection
2 Saint Francis' Place
3 Lodger's Nook
4 Cherry's Inn
5 Grace Lodge
8 White Beach Lodge
9 White Beach Nipa Hut
10 Buena Lynnes
11 Traveller's Beach
　 Delight, Peter's Inn
　 & Restaurant
13 Warren Seaview
14 Estrella's Resort
15 Delgado's
　 Cottages
16 Simon's Place
17 Mylah's Nipa Hut

PLACES TO EAT
12 Meeting House

OTHER
6 Basil's Bar & Rosie's Bar
7 Pacific Divers

White Beach

0   50   100 m

Aninuan Beach The *Aninuan Lodge* is a small, fairly quiet place directly on the beach, with a few cottages of different sizes. All have baths and cost between P250 and P350.

The *Tamaraw Beach Resort* (cellular ☎ 0912-306 6388) has cottages with bath for P350 and P600, and there is a good restaurant. This is a popular place shaded by trees and with several cottages of different sizes. Next to the Tamaraw Beach Resort, the *Aninuan Beach Resort* (cellular ☎ 0912-330 8683) has comfortable rooms with fan and bath from P350 to P750. The atmosphere is family-like and the grounds are well maintained. There is also a small gym.

Talipanan Beach The *White Sand Beach Resort* offers rooms with fan and bath for P250 and P350. It is a fairly large establishment with duplex cottages and rooms in terrace houses (townhouses), and it has a restaurant.

The *Bamboo House* (cellular ☎ 0912-330 1722) is a pleasant little place with a family atmosphere. Cottages cost P350 to P450.

Places to Eat

Practically every resort has its own restaurant. Various places at the beaches also offer international specialities.

In Sabang, *Le Bistro* can be recommended. It serves excellent pizzas and good French food. The tasty Philippine and European food at the *Tropicana* is inexpensive, as is the case at the *Sabang Fastfood*, said to be one of the best places to eat. Both are on the way into town. Lovers of Indian and Japanese cooking will enjoy the food in the *Sunshine Coast Restaurant* right at the sea.

At Small Laguna the *Full Moon Restaurant* serves mostly seafood and grilled specialities. The *Paradise Restaurant* at Big Laguna serves good steaks, and at White Beach the *Meeting House* is the place to try Korean cooking.

Entertainment

If you enjoy the nightlife more than life on the beach, then Sabang is the place to go.

Sabang has open-air bars like the *It's OK Bar* where things heat up to the sounds of karaoke. In spite of their names, the *Sunset Disco*, *Umbrella Disco* and *Sabang Disco* are not so much discos, but nightclubs with go-go dancers.

Getting There & Away

Jeepney Jeepneys run between Puerto Galera and Sabang (P10), or you can walk it in about 1½ hours. The unsealed road can be impassable after heavy rains. The last jeepney back to Puerto Galera leaves Sabang in the late afternoon. From Sabang, you can walk along the beach and over a few rocks and stairs to Small La Laguna Beach and Big La Laguna Beach (15 minutes).

Several jeepneys run daily between Puerto Galera and White Beach in San Isidro (P10). Some of them go on to Talipanan Point (P15). The last one back from San Isidro to Puerto Galera leaves at about 5 pm. The fare for a Special Ride is between P100 and P150. You can walk along the beach from White Beach to Talipanan Beach in about 45 minutes.

Boat From Puerto Galera, Special Rides by outrigger boat (with four passengers per boat) cost: to Sabang (P150; 30 minutes), Small Laguna (P120), Big La Laguna (P100), White Beach (P440) and Talipanan Beach (P500).

CALAPAN

Calapan is the capital of Mindoro Oriental Province. The Sanduguan Festival was first held in 1981, and was such a success that it is now a yearly event in the middle of May or the middle of November. *Sanduguan* means friendship in the Mangyan language. At the festival the locals re-enact the first meeting between seafaring Chinese traders and the indigenous Mangyan at Aroma Beach.

Places to Stay

The *Travellers Inn* on Leuterio St has simple rooms with fan for P100/120 and with air-con and bath for P350.

The *Riceland Inn I* on Rizal St offers fan-cooled rooms for P120, with bath for

P180/300 and with air-con and bath for P380/480. It's reasonable but none too clean. The restaurant is good value and some rooms have wide beds. The *Riceland Inn II* on MH del Pilar St has similar rates and is the best choice in Calapan. There is a restaurant and a disco.

Getting There & Away
Bus Big buses from Roxas to Calapan (P100; four hours) run hourly until 3 pm. You can also do it in stages by minibus and jeepney.

Jeepney From Puerto Galera to Calapan (P30; two hours), several jeepneys depart between 7 am and 5 pm from the market.

PINAMALAYAN
From Pinamalayan boats go to Sibali Island, the local name for Maestro de Campo Island, and to Banton Island, both in Romblon Province. You can also take a boat from here to Marinduque. You can ask about timetables at the coast-guard station, 200m beyond the market.

BONGABONG
Bongabong is a small, not very interesting place. Now and then, boats run from there to Tablas Island in Romblon Province (see Getting There & Away at the beginning of the Mindoro section).

Places to Stay
Mabuhay Lodging House near the market has basic rooms with fan for P75/150.

The *D & J Pension House* has friendly staff and good, clean rooms. Those with fan cost P100, with fan and bath P150/200. The building has a big patio.

ROXAS
From Roxas, big outrigger boats run to Tablas Island in Romblon Province and Boracay north-west off Panay (see Getting There & Away at the beginning of the Mindoro section). That's probably the only reason for coming to this basically uninviting place. Some of the waiting time can be spent at the nearby Melco Beach.

Places to Stay
The *Hotel Dannarosa* is a neighbour of the Santo Niño Hotel and has basic rooms with fan for P75/150.

The *Santo Niño Hotel* has basic rooms with fan for P80/160, with fan and bath for P150/200 and with air-con and bath for P350/500.

The *Catalina Beach Resort* at Bagumbayan, 1½ km from Roxas, has simple rooms with fan for P60/120 and rooms with fan and bath for P100/200.

Getting There & Away
Bus Big buses leave the wharf at Calapan every hour from early morning to 3 pm daily, bound for Roxas via Pinamalayan and Bongabong (P2 by tricycle from the centre). It takes two hours to reach Pinamalayan, three hours to Bongabong and four hours to Roxas (P100).

Minibuses in the market at Calapan go to Bongabong. From Bongabong to Roxas, the last jeepney or minibus goes at about 6 pm from the market. The only reliable information about departure times comes from the drivers; information that the waiting passengers give you will usually be useless.

MANSALAY
This is a good starting point for visits to the Mangyan tribes, but be warned that rubber-necks or camera-happy tourists are not appreciated. A visit without reason is intrusive and unnecessary. If, however, you are genuinely interested in the problems of these minority groups, the members of the mission are informative and co-operative. Father Antoon Postma, a Dutch missionary, took care of the Mangyan around Mansalay for many years and published a number of books and articles on this peaceful tribe.

Getting There & Away
Jeepney Several jeepneys run daily from Roxas to Mansalay. If you want to go on into the mountains to visit the Mangyan, go early or you'll be walking in the noon heat.

SAN JOSE

Among other things, San Jose is one of the starting points for diving excursions to Apo Reef. It is in the south-western part of Mindoro Occidental and those with time to spare can catch a boat trip to Palawan. (Boats only leave occasionally for Coron on Busuanga and for islands of the Quiniluban Group, which is the northernmost part of the Cuyo Islands.) However, San Jose lacks the kind of appeal that could tempt you to stay longer; the amount of comfortable hotels to choose from is limited, and good restaurants are a rarity.

In Mindoro Occidental there are many cultural minorities, the most remote tribes having little contact with civilisation. Occasionally some come into town and with luck you may meet Mangyans who will guide you to their village.

Queen's Ranch is a good place for a day trip. It is two hours away by jeepney and you can stay there overnight for about P100 per person. From there it takes about eight hours on foot to reach the Mt Iglit Tamaraw Reservation.

Boats can also be hired in San Jose for swimming and snorkelling on the nearby islands of Ilin and Ambulong (P700 to

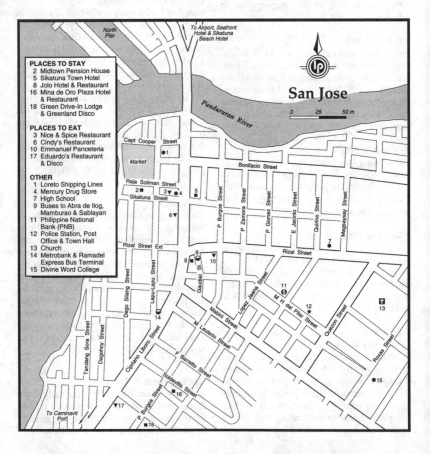

PLACES TO STAY
2 Midtown Pension House
5 Sikatuna Town Hotel
8 Jolo Hotel & Restaurant
16 Mina de Oro Plaza Hotel & Restaurant
18 Green Drive-In Lodge & Greenland Disco

PLACES TO EAT
3 Nice & Spice Restaurant
6 Cindy's Restaurant
10 Emmanuel Panceteria
17 Eduardo's Restaurant & Disco

OTHER
1 Loreto Shipping Lines
4 Mercury Drug Store
7 High School
9 Buses to Abra de Ilog, Mamburao & Sablayan
11 Philippine National Bank (PNB)
12 Police Station, Post Office & Town Hall
13 Church
14 Metrobank & Ramadel Express Bus Terminal
15 Divine Word College

San Jose

Ambulong). Both islands have white beaches. On Ilin Island is the Mina de Oro Beach Resort.

Information
Money The Metrobank in Cipriano Liboro St changes travellers cheques.

Telephone The area code for San Jose is 046.

Swimming
Across from the Green Drive-in Lodge there is a public swimming pool. Admission is P35 from 6 am to 6 pm and P45 from 6 to 10 pm.

Places to Stay
San Jose The *Sikatuna Town Hotel* on Sikatuna St has rooms with fan for P70/100, with fan and bath for P145 and with air-con and bath for P410. This place is basic, but fairly good at this price. A modest breakfast is included, however the restaurant doesn't open until 7 am, after the early buses have already left.

The *Mina de Oro Plaza Hotel* (☎ /fax 491 1595) in Soldevilla St has basic, fairly small plain rooms, some of which are a bit stuffy. Singles with fan are P240 and singles/doubles with air-con and bath are P570/890. The air-con rooms are expensive. The most impressive thing about this hotel is its name.

Around San Jose The *Sikatuna Beach Hotel* on Airport Rd outside of town at the beach near the airport, has basic, clean accommodation. The rooms are from P100 to P160, with fan and bath from P180 to P250 and with air-con and bath from P450 to P500. The air-con rooms are overpriced, however. This is a more pleasant place to stay than the hotels in the town.

The *Seafront Hotel* also on Airport Rd has modest rooms with fan and bath for P150/200 and with air-con and bath for P420, and there is a restaurant.

The *Mina de Oro Beach Resort* at Inasakan on Ilin Island has pleasantly furnished rooms in a big bamboo house. Singles/doubles with bath are P1300 to P1800. The restaurant is

rather expensive. Diving and windsurfing are available. This is a cosy resort in a small, palm-lined bay with a white sand beach.

Places to Eat
Cindy's Restaurant on Cipriano Liboro St offers a small selection of simple Filipino dishes, as does the spotless *Emmanuel Panciteria* on Rizal St – however, guests are rationed to two bottles of beer each! *Nice & Spice* on Sikatuna St serve pizzas, ice cream and cakes, starting in the late afternoon, but it doesn't have coffee.

Getting There & Away
Air PAL has an office at San Jose airport (☎ 491 1343).

Bus & Jeepney Few buses go from Roxas to Bulalacao, so it's better to go by jeepney to Mansalay and then get another jeepney to Bulalacao (P75; two hours). Leave early if you don't want to stay in Bulalacao overnight. From Bulalacao a boat goes to San Jose (see below). In the dry season, from December to May, it is also possible to travel by jeepney from Bulalacao to San Jose (P80; four hours), leaving at 4 am.

Three rickety Ramadel Express buses travel daily from Mamburao to San Jose via Sablayan (P80; six hours). From San Jose to Mamburao the buses leave at 5, 6.30, 8.30, 10.30 and 11.30 am from Gaudiel St near the Jolo Hotel.

Buses to Abra de Ilog via Mamburao depart at 1 and 3 am.

Boat A boat leaves Bulalacao for San Jose in the morning at around 8 am. The trip takes six hours, usually finishing at South Pier, Caminawit Port.

Departure from San Jose to Bulalacao is at 11 am every day.

Getting Around
Tricycle A tricycle to San Jose airport, north of the town, or to Caminavit Port, four km outside San Jose, costs P5 per person.

APO ISLAND & APO REEF

Right in the middle of the busy Mindoro Strait, which separates Mindoro from the Calamian Group in the north of Palawan, you will find the little flat island of Apo with the vast Apo Reef to the east of it. A 36m high lighthouse warns passing ships off the reef, where countless rocks and coral heads jut out of the water at low tide. What is for mariners a highly dangerous area, is for divers one of the most spectacular areas in the Philippines, in spite of the enormous number of coral reefs destroyed in recent years by dynamite fishing. In the summer months of March, April and May, several diving expeditions head for Apo Island and Apo Reef. However, this is a paradise not only for divers but also for snorkellers and latter-day Robinson Crusoes.

The only place to camp is at the southeastern end, but make sure your tent is closed up before sunset or you will be tortured by sandflies. Take your own food and about five litres of water per day.

Don't confuse this island with the other Apo Island loved by divers, just off the south-east coast of Negros.

Getting There & Away

Boat There is no regular connection to Apo Island so you will have to charter a boat. A return trip in a big outrigger boat from Sablayan, including a trip round the island, shouldn't cost more than P2500. Arrange a pick-up time beforehand.

SABLAYAN

This friendly, clean little town is at the mouth of the Bagong Sabang River in the south of Pandan Bay. There are several shops and a lively market with a few simple local restaurants along the riverside, where boats can take you to the islands of Pandan Bay. Larger boats dock at the Sablayan Pier, in a sheltered little bay near the lighthouse.

Places to Stay & Eat

The *Emely Hotel* on Rosario St has clean rooms with fan for P75/150 and with fan and bath for P200. Meals can be arranged. The restaurants at the market close about 7 pm. North of the market on the other side of the Bagong Sabang River, *Albert's Place* has pleasant rooms from P250 to P400. To get there, cross the river by boat (P2) and walk up, or ask the boatman to take you directly upstream.

Getting There & Away

Bus & Jeepney Buses and jeepneys pass through Sablayan to and from San Jose (bus: P40; three hours), Abra de Ilog (bus: P60) and Mamburao (bus: P40; three hours). Jeepneys are more expensive than buses. Note: the track along the west coast of Mindoro is very dusty.

NORTH PANDAN ISLAND

North Pandan would be near the top of my personal Top 10 Philippine islands. This gorgeous spot has a beautiful white sand beach with palms. The northern part of this island is covered by jungle which reaches to the beach, and the animal population is still intact.

Places to Stay

The *Pandan Island Resort* has rooms for P230/280, cottages with fan and bath for P400 and a house for four people for P800. The cottages are very spacious and supplied with solar energy. This quiet, rambling establishment is managed by French people. There is a restaurant with a communal buffet for P150, a beach bar and diving available.

Getting There & Away

Boat The resort service boat leaves for North Pandan Island around 10 am from the river landing place at the market in Sablayan. A Special Ride costs P100 (30 minutes).

Arrangements to be picked up by boat from Mamburao (P4000), and reservations, can be made in Manila at Asiaventure Services (☎ 522 2911, 598379; fax 583323), Holiday Inn Manila Pavilion, Room 501, United Nations Ave, Ermita.

MAMBURAO

The not very appealing community of Mamburao is the capital of Mindoro Occidental Province. The stone church in the

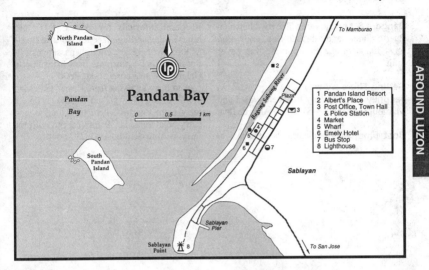

AROUND LUZON

Pandan Bay

0   0.5   1 km

1 Pandan Island Resort
2 Albert's Place
3 Post Office, Town Hall
  & Police Station
4 Market
5 Wharf
6 Emely Hotel
7 Bus Stop
8 Lighthouse

centre with its twin spires is not uninteresting, but there is really little else to see. Jeepneys and tricycles run along the road between the two markets looking for passengers.

The surrounding countryside offers plenty of opportunities for good walks. One hour's drive north, not far from Paluan and a Mangyan village, you can marvel at the freshwater pools at Calawagan in the foothills of the mountains.

Telephone
The area code for Mamburao is 043.

Places to Stay
Mamburao The *Traveller's Lodge* is a passable place with restaurant, where rooms with fan go for P100/170, with fan and bath for P180/280 and with air-con and bath for P500/800. The rooms are slightly more expensive, but better, at the Hotel Mindoreños. As of 1998, look out for the *Tamaraw Hotel*.

Around Mamburao The *Tayamaan Palm Beach Club* (☎ 711 1657), about four km north-west of Mamburao, has cottages with

fan and bath for P500; full board is available on request. The cottages are clean, well-built stone buildings under palm trees on a beautiful bay with a sandy beach suitable for bathing. There is also a restaurant. It costs P40 to get there by tricycle from the airport.

Getting There & Away
Air There are flights to and from Manila at least twice a week.

PAL has an office at Mamburao airport.

Bus From San Jose to Mamburao via Sablayan (P80; six hours) rickety Ramadel Express buses leave at 1, 3, 5, 6.30, 8.30, 10.30 and 11.30 am from Gaudiel St near the Jolo Hotel.

WAWA
The little port of Wawa, 30 km north-east of Mambuaro, is the wharf for Abra de Ilog. A car ferry runs between here and Batangas in Luzon (see Getting There & Away at the start of the Mindoro section). If you are stranded, the clean *Lodging House*, about 500m from the pier, has rooms for P120/150.

Dangers & Annoyances The road between Puerto Galera and Abra de Ilog, shown on most maps of the Philippines, was never built.

Getting There & Away
Jeepney Jeepneys ply between Wawa and Mamburao (P35; 2½ hours) via Abra de Ilog.

Boat From Puerto Galera, boats leave at irregular intervals for Wawa (P75; 2½ hours) – the landing place for Abra de Ilog – as long as there are enough passengers. A Special Ride by outrigger boat from Puerto Galera to Wawa costs about P800.

Another way to get from Puerto Galera to Abra de Ilog is to go via Batangas: take a ferry from Puerto Galera to Batangas and carry on at 9am, 11:30 am or 3 pm with the ferry to Abra de Ilog (P60; 2½ hours).

The Visayas

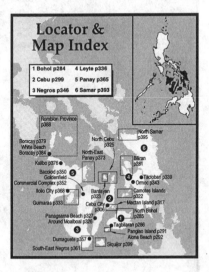

Locator &
Map Index

1 Bohol p284	4 Leyte p336
2 Cebu p299	5 Panay p365
3 Negros p346	6 Samar p393

Romblon Province p388

Boracay p379
White Beach
Boracay p384

Kalibo p376

Bacolod p350
Goldenfield
Commercial Complex p352

Iloilo City p368

Guimaras p333

Panagsama Beach p327
Around Moalboal p326

Dumaguete p357
South-East Negros p361

North Cebu p325

North-East
Panay p373

Bantayan p323

Cebu City p306

North Samar p395

Biliran p281

Tacloban p339
Ormoc p343

Camotes Islands p322

Mactan Island p317

North Bohol p285

Tagbilaran p286

Panglao Island p291
Alona Beach p292

Siquijor p399

THE VISAYAS

South of the island of Luzon, north of Mindanao and east of Palawan is the main island group of the Philippines, the Visayas. The major islands in this group are Bohol, Cebu, Guimaras, Leyte, Negros, Panay, Romblon, Samar and Siquijor, and there are countless little islands scattered between them. The Visayas offer by far the best possibilities for island hopping in the Philippines. Observant travellers will notice the way the islands differ from each other, whether it be in their topography, state of economic development, nature of the locals or even in the design of the tricycles.

ISLAND HOPPING

A possible circuit of the Visayas could take you to most of the places of interest with minimal backtracking. Starting from Manila, you could travel down to the Bicol Region and, from Matnog at the southern tip of Luzon, there are ferries every day across to Allen, at the northern end of Samar. The new

road down the west coast of Samar means it is now a quick and relatively easy trip through Calbayog and Catbalogan across the bridge to Tacloban on the island of Leyte. This was where MacArthur returned in 1944 to free the country from the Japanese occupying forces. From Tacloban or Ormoc there are regular ships to Cebu City. You can also take one of the larger outrigger boats from San Isidro to Maya in the north of Cebu, from where boats leave for the little island of Malapascua. If you first want to get from Leyte to Bohol, however, best take a boat from Maasin or Bato to Ubay.

Bohol's main attraction are the Chocolate Hills. Another popular destination is the little island of Panglao, which is just offshore from the capital, Tagbilaran. Ships travel daily from Tagbilaran to Cebu City, the third largest city in the Philippines and the centre of the Visayas.

Cebu was where Magellan arrived in the Philippines, and you can still find a number of reminders of the Spanish period. From Cebu City there are connections by air and sea to nearly all of the important places in the country, including Puerto Princesa on Palawan.

Several small ferries make the trip every day between Toledo on the west coast of Cebu and San Carlos on the east coast of Negros. Buses from San Carlos take the route along the coast north to Bacolod, where ferries leave for Iloilo City on Panay. The bus trip from Iloilo City via Kalibo to Caticlan only takes a few hours, and in just another half an hour you're on Boracay.

If you're looking for something a shade more adventurous, the following trip through the Visayas will fit the bill. Starting off in Manila, take a bus heading south to Batangas or Lucena, from where boats leave more or less regularly for Romblon on Romblon Island. Although this island is famed for its marble and does boast a few beautiful beaches, travellers are still fairly thin on the ground. Boats leave from

277

THE VISAYAS

Romblon daily for the adjacent island of Tablas and on from there to the popular little island of Boracay. If you're in a hurry and you're keen to avoid some of the more tedious aspects of terrestrial travel, you can always catch a plane direct from Manila to Tablas.

After a few lazy days on the beach you can carry on by bus right across Panay to Iloilo City and from there take the ferry to Bacolod on Negros, the sugar island of the Philippines. Take a bus or jeepney to Cadiz, a small harbour town on the north coast of Negros, and from there hop on a boat to Bantayan Island, which is already in Cebu Province. This friendly island in the centre of the Visayas can be best explored by bicycle. The ferry from Santa Fe to Hagnaya on Cebu is met on arrival by a bus or jeepney which will take you on to Maya, the most northerly settlement on Cebu Island. From there, outrigger boats will take you to the offshore island of Malapascua. If you find Boracay a bit too overrun with tourists, you'll feel right at home on this beautiful little island paradise.

Next stop is the island of Leyte. From San Isidro in the north-west you can carry on in two or three stages by bus via Ormoc and Baybay along the scenic coastal route south to Bato or Maasin, where a boat will take you to Bohol. After you've visited the bizarre Chocolate Hills, the smaller islands of Cabilao, Balicasag and Panglao west of Bohol are well worth a visit for a few days relaxation. From Cabilao Island you can have yourself taken over to Argao on the south-east coast of Cebu and take a bus from there to Bato, where several ferries leave daily for the big island of Negros.

The pleasant provincial capital of Dumaguete is a departure point for trips over to Siquijor Island where – according to many Filipinos – magic and witchcraft still flourishes. If you can drag yourself away from the attractions of this island, there is a ship to Cebu City three times a week. From there you can carry on your journey, for example, to the provinces of Mindanao or Palawan, or back to Manila.

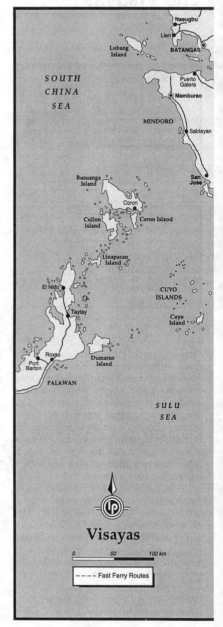

Visayas

0   50   100 km

- - - - Fast Ferry Routes

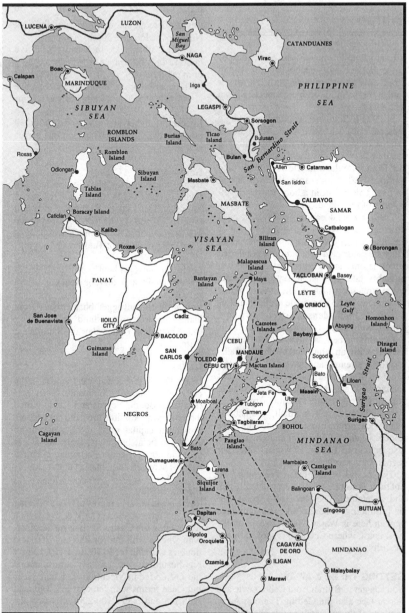

Biliran

Biliran Island lies just off the north coast of Leyte. Between both islands runs the Biliran Strait, only a few km wide. At its narrowest part in the south, a bridge connects Biliran with Leyte.

In 1992 Biliran succeeded in becoming a separate political entity from its neighbour and has been an autonomous province since that date. It was a wise decision, as economic aid from Manila now flows directly and without deductions into the provincial coffers. This has been a boon for the development of the island.

The provincial capital is Naval, a busy little harbour town on the west coast. All of the other larger towns are also on the coast. They are connected by a bumpy coastal road which is only surfaced in parts as yet; it'll probably take another few years until the entire stretch is finished. The interior of this 32 km long and 18 km wide island is mountainous, rough, densely overgrown and dotted with extinct volcanoes. Biliran is noticeably green, a pleasure for nature lovers, with an abundance of waterfalls, countless streams and several hot springs. Most of the rain falls in December, but January also gets its fair share. According to statistics, the sun shines most in April.

In addition to a few small, uninhabited islands just off the coast, the somewhat more remote islands of Maripipi and Higatangan also belong to Biliran Province. There are regular boat services to them.

The locals live mainly from catching fish, but there is some agriculture, principally rice and vegetables. They have also specialised in producing coconut oil. The language spoken here is Waray-Waray, except on the west coast, where Cebuano is spoken by the majority.

GETTING THERE & AWAY

You can get to Biliran from Cebu, Leyte and Samar (see also the Getting There & Away sections of those islands in this chapter).

Bus

Leyte There are about 10 buses daily from Naval to Tacloban (P50; three hours).

From Caibiran to Tacloban (P50; five hours) a daily bus leaves early in the morning or in the forenoon.

JD buses for Ormoc (P45; three hours) leave Naval daily at 5.30 and 8 am, noon and 3 pm.

Luzon From Naval to Manila (P560; 30 hours), a daily Liberty Transport bus leaves at 8 am.

Boat

Cebu From Naval to Cebu City, the San Juan Shipping Lines' MV *San Juan* leaves on Tuesday, Thursday and Sunday at 9 pm (P100; 7½ hours). The MV *Katarina* or the MV *Michael* of MY Shipping leaves daily at 8 pm, but possibly not Tuesday (12 hours).

Leyte An outrigger boat goes from Naval to Calubian daily at 9 am (one hour).

Samar A big outrigger boat crosses from Danao on Maripipi Island to Calbayog (three hours) on Wednesday and Saturday at 5 am.

NAVAL

Legend has it that Naval was founded in the early 18th century by Cebuanos. Later, settlers from Bohol, Negros and Panay joined them. This modest little town did not become provincial capital until 1992. Apart from various official buildings, there are a few shops, a hospital and a Philippine National Bank. There is a daily market at the jetty.

Places to Stay

There is a handful of places in Naval offering basic accommodation. The *V & C Lodge*, a few metres off Castin St, is a rustic place, with singles with fan for P50 and P60, and doubles with fan for P140 and P170. Expect real hospitality and a family atmosphere at the *LM Lodge* in Vicentillo St, where basic but clean rooms with fan cost P70/140, and with fan and bath P100/200, all worth the money.

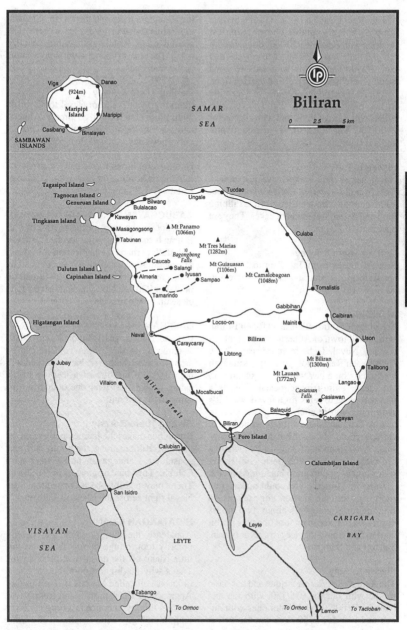

The *Bay View Lodge* in Castin St is a simple, but acceptable, hotel. Singles/doubles with fan cost P50/110, doubles with fan and bath cost P150 and with air-con and bath P250. The rooms with fan are good value. There is a small patio on the first floor.

The *Rosevic Lodging House* in Vicentillo St has basic, quiet and slightly expensive rooms with fan for P250 and with air-con for P400/500. There is a small inner courtyard, and a restaurant.

Places to Eat

Naval has several inexpensive restaurants. The friendly *Gemini Coffee Shop*, about 100m into town from the jetty, offers Filipino food and a small selection of cakes. They are open until 8.30 pm.

Getting There & Away

Bus All buses from Tacloban to Kawayan and further to Tucdao and Culaba (and return) go via Naval.

ALMERIA

The place most travellers head for on Biliran is the small town of Almeria, about eight km north of Naval. To be more precise, it's the Agta Beach Resort not quite three km north of Almeria on a bay with an unexceptional, but clean, palm-fringed beach. This is a pleasant place to relax for a few days. If it's swimming you're after, take a boat over to nearby Dalutan Island with its white beach. Or you could always head for Masagongsong, two km north of Agta Beach, where a big swimming pool with fresh, cool spring water invites you to jump in. Admission P2.

Based in Almeria, you could make a few short trips into the interior. For example, to Bagongbong Waterfall about two hours north-east of Caucab on foot (the way is a bit hard to find), or to the rice terraces at Iyusan, Salangi and Sampao.

Places to Stay

The *Agta Beach Resort* is quiet and has basic rooms with fan for P75/150, with fan and bath for P100/200 and better ones with air-con and bath for P350. You can eat well at the restaurant there and the owner, Clemencio Sabitsana, will gladly try to meet any special orders. Paddleboats for hire cost P20 a day. The resort is popular with day visitors at the weekends.

Getting There & Away

Jeepney Jeepneys from Naval to Kawayan in the north of the island, go through Almeria and pass the resort (20 minutes). There are only a few a day so you might have a long wait.

Bus Several buses travel daily from Naval to Almeria heading for Kawayan, Tucdao or Culaba (P5; 30 minutes).

CABUCGAYAN

This dot on the map on the south coast of Biliran is the starting point for the Casiawan waterfall, perhaps the highest on the island. In a picturesque location, it is surrounded by rich, green vegetation and forms a natural pool. For P20 you have yourself driven quite close up by motorcycle.

CAIBIRAN

Caibiran is the largest town on the east coast. A climb up to the Biliran volcano can be arranged from there. The barrio captain will help organise the hire of a jeep up to the camp. It takes just over one hour from the camp to the summit.

Getting There & Away

Bus A bus makes the journey daily from the town of Biliran along the south and east coasts via Cabucgayan and Caibigan to Caluba. This bus originates in Tacloban. There may possibly be a connection from Naval right across the island to Caibaran.

HIGATANGAN ISLAND

Apparently, the future president Marcos temporarily took refuge during WWII on this little island off the north-west tip of Leyte. That's why the highest point on the island (46m) is still called Marcos Hill to this day. Approaching Higatangan Island from Naval, the first thing you notice is a roughly 200m long, blindingly white sandbank, stretching out like a gigantic tongue from the little town of Mabini. Along the south coast you'll come across attractive little white stretches of sand tucked in between decorative, angular cliff faces.

Getting There & Away
Boat Several outrigger boats travel daily from Naval to Mabini (45 minutes).

MARIPIPI ISLAND
Once you have made it to Biliran Island, you should make a detour to Maripipi Island. Because of its relative isolation, about eight km north-west of Biliran, this exceptionally beautiful island has so far been little affected by civilisation. There is no telephone, and only a few villages have electricity for a few hours in the evening. The hospitable inhabitants seem to be happy with their simple and caring way of life.

This exotic island is dominated by an extinct volcano that is almost 1000m high and partly covered by dense jungle. A narrow road circles around the island, connecting picturesque little villages – ideal hiking or cycling territory. Maripipi is less suitable for lazing around on the beach, as the coast is almost entirely rocky and offers few bathing opportunities. In the villages of Casibang and Binalayan on the south coast, the women make clay utensils, which are renowned for their good quality, to sell to other islands.

Getting There & Away
Boat A big outrigger boat makes the trip from Naval to Viga, leaving daily at noon (P25; three hours). Departure time from Viga to Naval is 5 am. Because of the frequent stops, it may be 10 am before it arrives in Naval.

A big outrigger boat leaves at 10 am Monday to Friday from Naval heading for Danao (two hours). Departure time from Danao to Naval is 5 am.

SAMBAWAN ISLANDS
These two elongated, rocky islands lie close together to the west of Maripipi. The northern one turns into three even smaller islands

at high tide. You can see the dazzlingly white coral beach from quite a distance away. There are no palms and therefore no shade on the islands, so if you're going there for the day don't forget to take along means of protecting yourself from the sun.

Bohol

Between Leyte and Cebu, in the south of the Visayas, Bohol is the 10th largest island of the Philippines. Its historical significance goes back to the blood pact between the Spanish conqueror Legaspi and the Boholano chieftain Sikatuna. Today most visitors go to Bohol to see the Chocolate Hills. The Swiss author Erich von Däniken would have a field day with this strange hilly landscape. Tourism on this attractive, scenic island with its friendly people has only recently begun to be developed. Another 72 small islands belong to the province of the same name.

Agriculture is the main source of income of the Boholano. The main crop is coconut, but maize and rice are also grown. They even have small rice terraces near Lila, 25 km east of Tagbilaran. The Manila souvenir shops are well stocked with woven and plaited goods and basket ware from Bohol, but the prices are much lower in Tagbilaran and other places on Bohol itself.

A few km north-east of Tagbilaran, near Corella, live the rare, shy tarsier, the smallest primates in the world, with large, round eyes and long tails.

GETTING THERE & AWAY
You can get to Bohol from Cebu, Leyte, Luzon, and Mindanao (see the Getting There & Away section of the Manila chapter and the relevant Getting There & Away sections of this chapter and of the chapters on the other islands).

Air
Cebu PAL flies on Monday, Wednesday, Thursday, Saturday and Sunday from

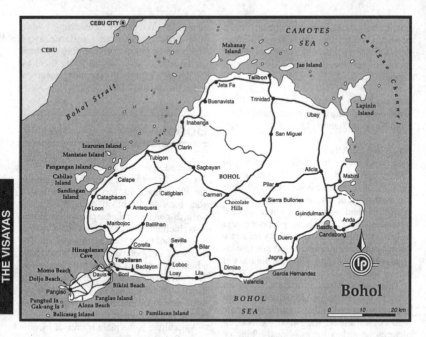

Bohol

Tagbilaran to Cebu City. You should reconfirm at least three days before flying.

Luzon PAL has daily flights from Tagbilaran to Manila.

Boat

Cebu From Tagbilaran to Cebu City there are several fast boats daily (P150; 1½ hours). The MV *Star Ruby 1* leaves at 6 am; Water Jet Shipping's MV *Water Jet 2* leaves at 6:30 am; the MV *Supercat* of Universal Aboitiz leaves at 7 am and 1 pm; Socor Shipping Lines' MV *Oceanjet 1* leaves at 11 am; and the MV *Bullet Xpress* of Bullet Xpress leaves at noon and 5 pm; and Water Jet Shipping's *Water Jet 1* leaves at 7pm.

The crossing with regular ships from Tagbilaran to Cebu City takes about four hours: Cokaliong Shipping Lines' MV *Filipinas Dumaguete* leaves daily at 7.30 am; Lite Shipping's MV *Santiago de Bohol*

leaves daily at 10.30 am; their MV *Lite Ferry I* leaves on Monday at 12.30 pm.

Trans-Asia Shipping Lines' MV *Asia-Japan* leaves Tagbilaran for Cebu City on Monday and Friday at midnight. The MV *Asia-Thailand* sails Tuesday, Thursday and Sunday at midnight. From Jeta Fe to Cebu City, the MV *Star Ruby 1* sails at 4 pm (P100; one hour).

From Tubigon to Cebu City, the MV *Charing* leaves daily at 9 am (P60; 3½ hours); the MV *Rayjumar* leaves daily at 11 am (P50; 2½ hours); the MV *Betchie* leaves daily at noon (2½ hours); the MV *Queen Leonora* or the MV *Queen Vicki* leaves daily at 4 pm (2½ hours); and the MV *Harvey* leaves daily at midnight (three hours).

From Talibon to Cebu City MV *Krishia* leaves daily at 8 am (3½ hours); the MV *Talibon Cruiser* leaves daily at 9 am; and the MV *Andy* leaves daily at 10 pm (both four hours).

From Loon through to Argao, Lite Shipping's MV *LCT Barge St Mark* (car ferry) sails every Monday, Wednesday and

Friday at 7 am and 1 pm; on Tuesday, Thursday and Saturday at 10 am; and on Sunday at 8.30 am. The crossing takes 2½ hours (P45 to P75).

Leyte From Ubay to Bato, a big outrigger boat leaves daily at 10 am, sometimes going via Lapinin Island (three or four hours). The MV *Star Ruby 1* leaves daily at 11 am (P100; 1¼ hour). From Ubay to Maasin, an outrigger boat leaves daily at 10 am (four hours).

Luzon From Tagbilaran to Manila, the MV *Superferry 7* of WG & A leaves on Monday at 8 am (P550; 26 hours). Their MV *Superferry 5* leaves on Thursday at 7 am (26 hours).

Mindanao From Jagna to Butuan, the MV *Lady of Fatima* of Cebu Ferries leaves on Sunday at midnight (six hours).

From Jagna to Cagayan de Oro, the MV *Lady of Lourdes* of Cebu Ferries leaves on Monday at midnight (P150; six hours). Their MV *Lady of Lipa* leaves on Sunday at 2 pm (four hours). The Sulpicio Lines' MV *Cagayan Princess* leaves on Saturday at 9 pm (five hours).

From Tagbilaran to Cagayan de Oro, Water Jet Shipping's MV *Water Jet* leaves daily at noon (P360; three hours). The MV *Superferry 7* of WG & A leaves on Sunday at 11 am (P150; seven hours). Their MV *Superferry 5* leaves on Wednesday at 11 am (seven hours).

The Trans-Asia Shipping Lines' MV *Asia-Thailand* leaves on Monday and Wednesday at 8 pm and Friday at 9 pm (eight hours).

From Tagbilaran to Dipolog, the Sulpicio Lines' MV *Dipolog Princess* leaves on Thursday at midnight (five hours).

Negros From Tagbilaran to Dumaguete, the Trans-Asia Shipping Lines' MV *Asia-Japan* leaves on Tuesday and Saturday at 6 pm (P55; three hours).

TAGBILARAN

There are no special sights in Tagbilaran, the capital of Bohol Province on the south-west coast of Bohol. A popular meeting place at sunset is the Kay-Cee Promenade, also called the K of C Pier (Knights of Columbus).

Orientation

The main street is Carlos P Garcia Ave, or CPG Ave for short. During the day there is a never-ending stream of noisy tricycles, and

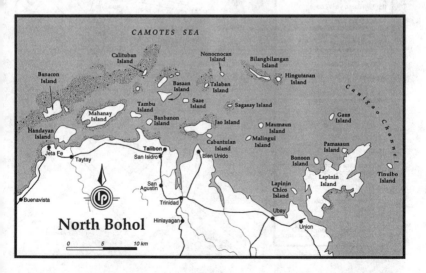

Tagbilaran

0   100   200 m

PLACES TO STAY
4 Sea Breeze Inn
5 Dagohoy Hotel & Seafood
   Restaurants
8 Gie Garden Hotel
10 LTS Lodge
14 Slim Pension House
20 Charisma Lodge
22 Nisa Travelers Inn
24 Executive Inn
25 Tagbilaran Vista Lodge

PLACES TO EAT
1 Coffee Garcia & Renés
   Swiss Gourmet Shop
15 Sayas Restaurant
27 BQ Garden Restaurant
30 Garden Café & Cruz Telephone
   Company (Cruztelco)

OTHER
2 University of Bohol
3 Trans-Asia Shipping Lines
6 Bohol Travel & Tours
7 Provincial Hospital
9 Mercury Drugstore
11 Metrobank & Tagbilaran
   Friendly Bazaar
12 Bombay Bazaar
13 Alturas Department Store
16 City Pharmacia
17 Ramiro Community Hospital
18 Post Office & Bohol Quality Store
19 Divine Word College
21 PCI Bank
23 Level Disco
26 Marbella Complex
28 Police Station & Town Hall
29 Post Office
31 Church
32 Philippine Long Distance
   Telephone Company (PLDT)
33 Philippine National Bank (PNB)

THE VISAYAS

the dust and exhaust fumes are choking. In this street you will find several hotels, restaurants and many shops, as well as the Agora Market and the Torralba Market where handcrafts and locally made products are sold.

Information
Money The Allied Bank on Carlos P Garcia Ave and the Philippine National Bank at the plaza will change travellers cheques.

The Indian gentleman in the Bombay Bazaar in Bernardino Inting St offers good exchange rates for cash and travellers cheques. Just round the corner on Carlos P Garcia Ave, on the ground floor of the Tagbilaran Friendly Bazaar at the back, there's a moneychanger who gives good rates.

Post & Communications The post office is on JS Torralba St, near the town hall. Another post office has been opened in the Bohol Quality Store on Carlos P Garcia Ave.

The PLDT office in Noli Me Tangere St offers inexpensive fax and long distance phone facilities. The Cruz Telephone Company (Cruztelco) in JS Torralba St does the same but is a bit more expensive. They also offer an incoming fax service for P22 per page. They stick up a list of incoming faxes every day.

There are two area codes for Tagbilaran: 038 and 03823.

Travel Agencies *Bohol Travel & Tours* on Carlos P Garcia Ave (☎ 411 3840; fax 411 2984) will arrange Bohol tours and take care of ticket and visa formalities.

Things to See
The best beach near the city is **Caingit Beach**, behind the Hotel La Roca, but it's nothing special. Some interesting trips include: Tagbilaran to Panglao Island, or along the west and east coasts of Bohol.

Places to Stay
Unpretentious, but OK for the money, the *Tagbilaran Vista Lodge* (☎ 411 3072) on Lesage St has singles/doubles with fan for P75/95, with fan and bath for P100/120 and with air-con and bath for P250/275. The rooms at the *Sea Breeze Inn* (☎ 411 3599) on Gallares St are simple but clean, with fan and bath for P160/200 and with air-con and bath for P300/400.

On Carlos P Garcia Ave the most inexpensive place to stay is the *Nisa Travelers Inn* (☎ 411 3731), which has singles/doubles with fan for P130/150, with fan and bath for P140/160 and with air-con and bath for P250/350. Also on Carlos P Garcia Ave, the *Charisma Lodge* (☎ 411 3094) has passable rooms with fan for P135/225, with fan and bath for P200 and with air-con and bath for P395.

One block east of Agora Market, the *Slim Pension House* on FR Ingles St has well maintained, fairly priced rooms with fan and bath for 350/450 and with TV, air-con and bath for P480/600. Free transport from airport and pier is available if you call.

Further along the road, the *LTS Lodge* (☎ 411 3310) has clean, comfortable rooms with fan for P100/160, with air-con for P200/300 and with air-con and bath for P300/400. The accommodation is pleasant; some of the rooms are quite roomy, although those overlooking the street are quite loud.

On MH del Pilar St just off the main street, the popular little *Gie Garden Hotel* (☎ 411 3182) has rooms with air-con and bath for P370/500. It's a pity some of the rooms are a bit dark and musty; the ones facing the inner courtyard are a lot quieter than those facing the street.

The next three hotels are all on Graham Ave, at the northern edge of town near the airport. The *Coralandia Resort* (☎ 411 3445) has reasonable cottages with two or three rooms situated in fairly big grounds at the ocean front. Those with fan and bath go for P250/475, while those with air-con and bath cost P375/635. Their Veranda Carolina Restaurant serves good pulutan, eg calamares.

Just south of the Coralandia, the *Hotel La Roca* (☎ 411 3179; fax 411 3009) has rooms with TV, air-con and bath from P530 to P880 and suites for P1210. This comfortable hotel also has a swimming pool on offer. The *Bohol Tropics Resort Club* (☎ 411 3510; fax

THE VISAYAS

411 3019), next to the La Roca, is a fairly large place with cottages directly along the waterfront. They charge from P980 to P1450 for pleasant, well-appointed rooms with TV, air-con and bath, and P2300 for suites with fridge. To top it off, it has a restaurant, swimming pool, fitness room and tennis court. This is the best hotel in Tagbilaran.

About three km east of Tagbilaran, you'll come to the *Island Leisure Inn* (☎ 411 2482) in the IIC Complex at Bohol. Their rooms with fan and bath go for P350/440 and with air-con and bath for P790/935. The rooms are quite good and have a balcony. This pleasant place has a bar and disco, and they also offer diving and whale spotting trips.

Places to Eat
An excellent breakfast can be had in the pleasant *Garden Café* next to the church, which is run by hearing-impaired people. Although the menu is not large, they are happy to do special orders such as mango and banana omelettes.

Good, inexpensive food can be found at the *Sayas Restaurant* in Dagohoy St, as well as at the restaurant in the *Gie Garden Hotel*, and in the seafood places at the K of C Pier, eg at *JJ's Seafood Village*. Well worth a recommendation is the friendly *BQ Garden Restaurant* in the south end of town in Gallares St. European specialities from Renés Swiss Gourmet Shop are available in the affiliated *Coffee Garcia* in Maria Clara St. In the evening, the appetising smell from the *barbecue stands* fills the air in front of the Agora Market.

Entertainment
Dedicated night owls will not be happy with what Tagbilaran has to offer after dark. If you want a change, you could try the pubs with billiards and bowling in the *Marbella Complex*, the *Zoom Disco* on A Clarin St or the *Level Disco* next to the Agora Market. In *JJ's Seafood Village* and *BQ Garden Restaurant* entertainment is provided in the evening with live music or karaoke.

Getting There & Away
Air PAL has an office at Tagbilaran airport (☎ 411 3102). Anyone wanting to leave Bohol by plane would be well advised to reconfirm the flight out immediately on arrival. PAL does not have an office in town.

If you want to leave the Visayas with Grand Air from Cebu, you can book your flight at Grand Air, Aquarius Press Building, 25 Maria Clara St (☎ 411 3615; fax 411 3840).

Bus Most of the transport on the island is taken care of by the Arples Line, St Jude Bus and Dory Lines. Their buses depart from Tagbiliran's new bus terminmal on E Butalid St.

Friday is market day in Tagbilaran and on that day there are bus and jeepney connections in practically every direction.

Car Nick Rent-a-Car is a reliable company for hiring a car with driver. You can find Nick and Riza Almedilla (Cruztelco ☎ 53394) at 51-5 Pamaong Extension. Best call ahead and make an appointment. Cruztelco, in case you're wondering, is an independent telephone company with its own lines.

Boat Trans-Asia Shipping Lines is on R Palma St, near the corner with Carlos P Garcia Ave. All the other shipping lines calling at Tagbilaran have their ticket offices at the jetty.

Getting Around
The Airport The airport is at the northern edge of the city. A tricycle from the airport to the city centre (Agora Market) costs P3 and to Alona Beach P100 to P150.

Private taxis will make the run to Alona Beach for between P200 and P250, even if they start off by asking for P500. You can order a van or minibus in advance by telephone from Cebu City or Manila. This will cost P250 for two to six people. Reservations can be made with Kapirig (☎ 411 2773).

Philippine Airlines has an office at the airport (☎ 411 3102).

Making a point at the colourful Ati-Atihan Festival in Kalibo, Panay Island.

JENS PETERS

RICHARD I'ANSON

JENS PETERS

VISAYAS
Top Left: Traditional home on Apo Island, Negros Oriental Province.
Top Right: Beach hawker, Boracay Island.
Bottom: White Beach, Boracay Island.

Tricycle From the wharf to the city centre is only one km and costs P2 by tricycle.

AROUND TAGBILARAN

There are some historical sights to the north and east of Tagbilaran. It is best to hire a car and do a round trip, possibly starting at Alona Beach on Panglao Island. There would also be time to include a detour to the Chocolate Hills. The following places can be reached by public transport from Tagbilaran.

Maribojoc

About 15 km north of Tagbilaran near Maribojoc stands the old **Punta Cruz Watchtower**, built in the time of the Spaniards in 1796 to look out for pirates. It gives a good view over other islands of the Visayas.

Loon

Loon, a few km north-west of Maribojoc, has a beautiful old church dating back to 1753. It has noteworthy ceiling frescoes. There is a daily connection by car ferry between Loon and Argao on Cebu (see Getting There & Away earlier in this section).

Antequera

Various kinds of basket ware are for sale on Sunday in the market at Antequera, about 10 km north-east of Maribojoc. Little more than a km out of town and situated in a forest you will find the beautiful **Mag-Aso Falls** with a deep natural pool to swim in. Admission is P2. The last bus from Antequera to Tagbilaran departs at 3 pm.

Corella

The woods around Corella are home to the rare, monkey-like tarsier, which is an endangered species. These tiny primates have extraordinary, immobile eyes and jump from branch to branch with an almost frog-like motion. They are nocturnal hunters and are seldom seen during the day.

In Barrio Cancatac, about four km east of Corella, a few tarsier are being held in a generously proportioned cage, for study purposes. Visitors are welcome at this project, run by the Department of Environment and Natural Resources (DENR), although the sleeping animals must not be disturbed during the day. Donations are also welcome.

Bool

The memorial at Bool, barely three km east of Tagbilaran, is a reminder of the blood compact between Legaspi and Sikatuna, who sealed their bond of friendship on 16 March 1565 by making a cut in their skin, letting the blood drip into a cup of wine and then emptying the cup together. At Bool there is also the Ilaw International Center, with its open-air restaurant, bar and disco. Big weddings are often held here on Saturday.

Baclayon

About four km to the east of Bool is Baclayon, the oldest town in Bohol. It is the location of one of the oldest churches in the Philippines, the **Parish Church of the Immaculate Conception**, built in 1595. The small museum adjoining it is open Monday to Saturday from 9 to 11 am and from 2 to 4 pm. Admission is P10.

There are a few cheap restaurants in the market, and boats go from Baclayon to nearby Pamilacan Island.

Loay & Loboc

At Loay, where the Loboc River flows into the Mindanao Sea, there is an old church with an adjoining convent school which are worth seeing. While you're here, you can take an exciting river trip in a chartered outrigger boat from the Loay bridge until just before the Tontonan Hydroelectric Power Station, about two km north of Loboc. In Loboc itself it's worth seeing the large old **San Pedro Church**, built in 1602, because of the remarkable naive painting on the ceiling.

Sevilla and Bilar

A few km north of Loboc, roughly between the turn off to Sevilla and the small town of Bilar, the road leads through a dark mahogany forest, which was planted a few years ago by students. Near Sevilla a primitive hanging bridge spans the Loboc River. From this bridge you can jump into the water from a height of several metres.

JAGNA

Jagna is a busy, clean little town about 60 km east of Tagbilaran. About three ships a week sail from here to various destinations in north Mindanao. Departure times are usually late at night; the atmosphere at the wharf is best then. Don't miss having a look at the old church, with its ceiling frescoes. **Ilihan Hill**, four km north from Jagna, can be reached by a winding road and is frequently a place of pilgrimage.

Places to Stay

The *DQ Lodge* (☎ 328 2350)in the port area near the landing stage has fairly basic rooms with fan for P60/120 and with air-con and bath for P275/375.

Getting There & Away

Bus There are no direct buses from the Chocolate Hills area to Jagna. From Carmen, you have to take the bus to Tagbilaran, get off in Loay and then wait for a bus or jeepney from Tagbilaran to Jagna.

Several buses leave the St Jude bus terminal in Tagbilaran daily for Jagna (P23; two hours).

From Tubigon, on the west coast, there are several buses a day going to Jagna via Talibon. They go along the coast instead of going through Carmen.

ANDA

Anda is a clean, somewhat sleepy little community on a peninsula in the south-east of Bohol. Right on the doorstep there is a long, wide beach with white sand that strangers seldom happen onto. Only two commercial accommodation possibilities exist, but that could change quickly considering the attractions of this coastline.

The picturesque scenery begins just outside Guindulman, where lonely bays with little white beaches and crystal-clear water tempt the visitor to stay. The ideal way to explore here is by boat, as the unsurfaced road which runs about 500m from the ocean has few paths offering access to the coast.

One of these idyllic bays is **Bugnao Beach** near Candabong, which has little stretches of white sand sectioned off by rocky cliffs eaten away at their bases by the sea.

Places to Stay

The friendly *Dapdap Beach Resort* in Candabong (☎ 419 8291) is about three km west of Anda and has a few cottages with fan and bath for P250/300. About five km west of Anda, the *Bituon Beach Resort* in Basdio, offers cottages with fan and bath for P1800 per person; including three meals. This family-style establishment has attractive bungalows just up some steps from a little beach. Under German-Philippine management, they have diving facilities here, as well as boat trips.

Getting There & Away

Bus Coming from Tagbilaran, instead of stopping at Jagna, you can carry on in the direction of Ubay, get out at Guindulman and take a tricycle from there.

Jeepney There are only a few jeepneys that go from Jagna to Anda, taking 1½ hours for the 40 km trip. The last trip back to Jagna is at about 5 pm. A Special Ride costs about P250 one way.

Tricycle A tricycle from Guindulman to Dapdap Beach Resort costs about P100.

PANGLAO ISLAND

Several beach resorts have recently opened on Panglao Island. There are two bridges you can use to cross over to the island from Bohol. The older bridge is near Tagbilaran Town Hall. The newer one is almost two km south-east of Tagbilaran and connects the district of Bool on Bohol with Dauis on Panglao.

Information

Money There is neither a bank nor a moneychanger on Panglao Island, so bring enough pesos.

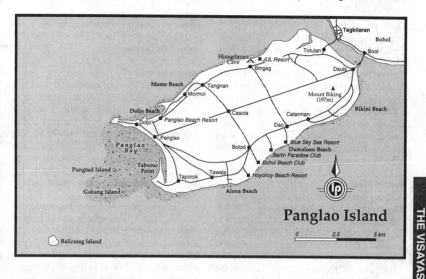

Panglao Island

0   2.5   5 km

Things to See

The lake in **Hinagdanan Cave** at Bingag on the north-east of the island has refreshingly cool water. However, as all kinds of disease-spreading bacteria thrive in still waters, it is best to do without that tempting swim. For a few coins the caretaker will switch on the light in the cave.

The white sand **Alona Beach** is the most beautiful, most popular and the most developed beach on the island. Spread along the beach for 1½ km there are small, individually designed resorts, cosy restaurants, rough-and-ready beach bars, and several dive shops. The bathing is unfortunately hampered a bit by knee deep sea grass. It is inhabited by sea urchins, so you can't go in for more than a few metres without being careful. Still, this beach is good for snorkelling (swim out to about 100m from the shore) and especially (with a bit of luck) for watching sea snakes. There are several places to stay at Alona Beach in different price categories.

On a beautiful part of **Dumaluan Beach**, 2½ km east of Alona Beach, the exclusive Bohol Beach Club is open for business.

Doljo Beach is also good, although the water there is pretty shallow; however, it's largely clear of sea grass. From there you can have someone take you over to **Pungtud Island** in Panglao Bay (30 minutes).

Momo Beach is another shallow beach, where the Gie Garden Hotel lets several large cottages, though only to groups.

Serpents of the Sea

It would be wise to assume that all of the sea snakes (*walo walo*) in the Philippines are venomous. Fortunately however, these creatures are seldom aggressive and only have tiny mouths. Richly patterned and with paddle-like tails, they congregate regularly around the Cervera Shoal, between Panglao and Pamilican Islands. ■

Sea snake

Diving

There are several dive shops on Alona Beach, including the Atlantis Dive Center, Genesis Divers, Sea Quest Scuba Diving Center, Sea Explorers Scuba Diving Center, Sharky's Diver and Sunshine Dive Center. A five-day diving course (PADI) at the Atlantis Dive Center costs US$275. Further prices include one dive at the drop-off for US$19; a dive from a boat for US$25; and two dives from a boat, eg off Balicasag Island, for US$40.

Whale Watching

Although whales and dolphins can be seen all year in the Mindanao Sea south of Bohol, the best time to watch them is from April to July. A few resorts and dive shops on Alona Beach, eg the Atlantis Dive Center, organise trips out to watch the whales for between P300 and P1000 per person. The Island Leisure Inn (☎ 411 2482) also offers tours lasting one day or more (ask for Juny Binamira).

Organised Tours

Several resorts organise, or will arrange for you, half-day trips round Panglao Island for P300 (tricycle) or whole-day trips by jeepney (including a boat trip on the Loay river and lunch at the Chocolate Hills) for about P800 per person.

Places to Stay

Alona Beach You can choose from several places at Alona Beach. The accommodation is basic but acceptable at the *Alonaville Beach Resort*. Rooms with fan cost P150/200, cottages with fan and bath P300/400, and with air-con and bath P400/600. The resort restaurant has a good view of the beach and the ocean. It also has motorcycles for hire, diving facilities, and offers diving courses.

A pleasant place to stay is *Peter's House* with its family atmosphere and spacious, clean rooms for P200/400. Mountain bikes are available for hire. At the *Pyramid Resort* the rooms are pleasantly decorated and cost P300 with fan. Unique two-storey cottages set in a beautiful garden cost P500 and P650 with fan and bath. You can enjoy sea views from the balcony of your cottage.

The *Bohol Divers Lodge* (☎/fax 411 4983) has cottage accommodation with fan and bath from P300, P600 and P800 (the expensive ones also have a fridge). You can go

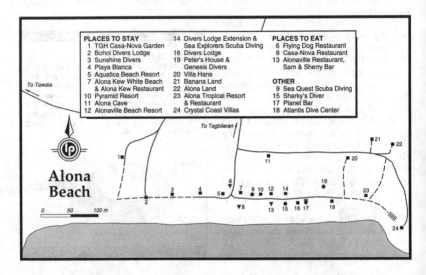

PLACES TO STAY
1 TGH Casa-Nova Garden
2 Bohol Divers Lodge
3 Sunshine Divers
4 Playa Blanca
5 Aquatica Beach Resort
7 Alona Kew White Beach & Alona Kew Restaurant
10 Pyramid Resort
11 Alona Cave
12 Alonaville Beach Resort
14 Divers Lodge Extension & Sea Explorers Scuba Diving
16 Divers Lodge
19 Peter's House & Genesis Divers
20 Villa Hans
21 Banana Land
22 Alona Land
23 Alona Tropical Resort & Restaurant
24 Crystal Coast Villas

PLACES TO EAT
6 Flying Dog Restaurant
8 Casa-Nova Restaurant
13 Alonaville Restaurant, Sam & Sherry Bar

OTHER
9 Sea Quest Scuba Diving
15 Sharky's Diver
17 Planet Bar
18 Atlantis Dive Center

To Tawala

To Tagbilaran

Alona Beach

0   50   100 m

Whale Meat Again, Don't Know Where, Don't Know When...

'Towards thee I roll, thou all-destroying but unconquering whale...from hell's heart I stab at thee.'
– Moby-Dick, *by Herman Melville*

This rather unfriendly attitude to the whale makes for a vivid reminder of how we humans once regarded these magnificent giants of the sea. Whales were nothing but monsters, profitable booty, only there to be slaughtered for pride and profit.

In Melville's classic novel, published in 1851, it is most likely a full-grown bull sperm whale (top right) that is portrayed as something akin to an ocean-going drug pusher and serial killer.

Modern-day whale-watching tours aside, all sorts of lucrative business has emanated from the whale: spermaceti, a wax-like substance from the head of the sperm whale, was sought after as a base for cosmetics and candles; whale oil was used to produce soap and margarine; lubricating grease was made from the lard; ambergris provided the foundation for expensive perfumes; baleen (whalebone) was used to bolster corsets and umbrellas; the offal was processed into manure; and the skin was used to make laces and bicycle saddles.

In 1946 the International Whaling Commission (IWC) was founded to bring about the non-depletive use of the remaining whale population. Initially, the commission only regulated the cull quota, but in 1979 the decision was finally reached to ban whaling completely. Whale numbers have since recovered somewhat, despite countries like Japan and Norway riding roughshod over international agreements.

In the mid-1960s, the whale's fortunes changed as ocean mammals were introduced to the public in various oceanariums. The playful nature and intelligence of whales and dolphins made people look at them in a whole new way, and awareness grew that these animals had to be protected. People also became more interested in seeing them in their natural surroundings.

Whales and dolphins are no strangers to the waters of the Philippines. Various species appear in the deep water south of Bohol all year round, particularly between the months of April and June. The little island of Pamilacan is home to several smart ex-whalers who know where and when the most magnificent specimens can be found. There is no question that the ex-hunters have learnt how to show care and consideration in approaching the animals. ■

Sperm whale

Humpback whale

Minke whale

Killer whale

Short-finned pilot whale

THE VISAYAS

diving with the French proprietor Jacques, who also speaks English and German. He will organise day trips by boat or jeep on request.

The *Playa Blanca* has cottages with fan and bath for P350/400. The staff will arrange day excursions by boat and jeep.

You will find the next few places a bit set back from the beach. The *Alona Cave* is a small set-up with three pleasant little cottages with fan, bath and fridge which go for P350. Under Belgian-Philippine management, it has its own restaurant and rents out motorcycles. The immaculate cottages of *Banana Land* all have fan, bath and refrigerator, and cost P400, P600 or P1100. The better cottages also have cooking facilities. Set in quiet, spacious grounds, the cottages have plenty of space between them. Right next to Banana Land, *Alona Land* is a pleasant little place offering cottages with fan and bath for P500.

About 300m inland from Alona Beach, the *TGH Casa-Nova Garden* has rooms with fan and bath for P400/475, with air-con and bath for P600/700 and a cottage with two bedrooms, living room and cooking facilities for P800. It is a well-kept place and besides having its own restaurant, the premises have a disco, tennis court and swimming pool. Motorcycle hire can be arranged.

Getting back to the beach front, we come to the *Alona Tropical*, a pleasant, quiet resort at the east end of the beach. They have cottages with fan and bath at P450 and have a very good, popular restaurant. The friendly *Aquatica Beach Resort* has rooms with fan and bath for P550/600. The cottages are pleasant, while the rooms are spacious and clean, if a little spartanly furnished. To make up for it, the well-run restaurant has a good selection of French wines!

Set in fairly large grounds with a trim garden, the *Alona Kew White Beach* (☎ 411 2615) has rooms with fan and bath for P650 and P900, plus a variety of different cottages with fan and bath for P650 and P700 and with air-con and bath for P1500. There is a fine, big restaurant here. You can also hire a car or motorcycle.

Clean and comfortable two-level rooms are available at the *Crystal Coast Villas*; including air-con and bath they cost P750/935, albeit in an unimaginatively designed building. There is a pool. The villas are situated on a flat clifftop at the east end of the beach and actually belong to the La Roca Hotel in Tagbilaran.

Other Beaches The *Palm Island Beach Resort* on Doljo Beach has seen better days. Their rooms with fan go for P200.

Three km further east, on Momo Beach, the *Momo Beach Resort* has cottage accommodation with fan and bath for P1400 per person, including meals and transfer. Only groups of at least six people staying for three days or longer are accepted. You can book at the Gie Garden Hotel, Tagbilaran.

In Bingag on the north coast of Panglao Island, the *JUL Resort* offers cottages with fan and bath for P600 and with air-con and bath for P1500 and P2500, all including breakfast. This tranquil resort is located a few metres up from a white beach. The cottages are all well maintained and tastefully decorated, the air-con ones being particularly generously appointed. On the ocean side there is a large terrace built on stilts over the beach, which offers a beautiful sea view. If you want to eat in the restaurant it's best to order well beforehand. A tricycle from the airport or Tagbilaran to the resort will cost you P75. The resort has an office in Tagbilaran (☎/fax 411 2697).

In Tawala, about 1½ km east of Alona Beach, the *Hoyohoy Beach Resort* has several roomy cottages which cost P300 with fan and bath. They stand together in a row on an isolated flat stretch of ground, with stairs leading down to the white beach below. The whole set-up is starting to show its age ever so slightly.

The *Bohol Beach Club* set on its own beach in Bolod, about 2½ km east of Alona Beach, has singles with fan and bath for P1500/2800 and doubles with fan and bath for P1700/3000. It has an expensive restaurant, swimming pool, tennis court and sauna. Diving and windsurfing are also available.

Getting There & Away
Bus Several JG Express buses go from Tagbilaran to Panglao Island daily, leaving from the new bus terminal on E Butalid St. Not all go to Alona Beach. Those marked 'Panglao' go right across the island to Panglao town near Doljo Beach. Those marked 'Panglao-Tauala' go along the southern coast and detour to Alona Beach. The first departure is at about 7 am, but it may be advisable to confirm. The trip as far as Alona Beach takes 45 minutes (P10), the last bus leaving about 5 pm. The first bus from Alona Beach to Tagbilaran leaves between 6 and 6.30 am, while the last leaves at about 4.30 pm. This is important if you are just making a day trip as normally there are no tricycles waiting for passengers at the beach.

Car Private cars will make the journey from the airport to Alona Beach for between P200 and P250.

Tricycle From Tagbilaran to Doljo Beach or Alona Beach by tricycle costs between P100 and P150, but you'll often be asked for twice as much. The trip takes one hour.

Car & Motorcycle A car with driver for a day trip to Bohol (Chocolate Hills etc) costs P1500. Motorcycle hire costs P600 per day (eight hours). Both can be arranged at the Alona Kew White Beach.

BALICASAG ISLAND
The small island of Balicasag lies about 10 km south-west of Panglao Island. It is surrounded by a coral reef which offers excellent diving and snorkelling. This underwater world is a marine sanctuary which the local fishermen know and respect. Strangers have so far been very scarce on this somewhat remote island. One of them didn't want to leave and shot himself at the top of the lighthouse. Since then, the lighthouse has been closed to visitors.

Places to Stay
The *Balicasag Island Dive Resort* has pleasantly designed duplex cottages with bath for P1400/1600, as well as a mediocre and expensive restaurant. Diving costs US$40 for two dives, plus P150 for the boat. A diving course costs US$300 and diving equipment can be hired. Reservations can be made in Manila (☎ 812 1984; fax 812 1164) and in Tagbilaran at the Philippine Tourism Authority (PTA) (☎ 411 2192) in the Governor's Mansion, Carlos P Garcia Ave. Transfer to the resort from the airport or hotel in Tagbilaran costs P500 payable at the time of registration. There is a transport boat which makes the journey twice weekly and costs only P50.

Getting There & Away
Boat A proposal has been made to run boats regularly from Tagbilaran to Balicasag Island, which would take two hours. Please make enquiries. Otherwise the Alona Beach resort proprietors offer Special Rides for about P600.

Traders often travel between Balicasag Island and Panglao Island and take passengers with them to their island.

PAMILACAN ISLAND
The peaceful little island of Pamilacan lies about 20 km south-east of Tagbilaran and is surrounded by an extensive coral reef, which unfortunately has been severely damaged by dynamite fishing. Strangers don't come here often. If you want to cross over for a few days, you should take provisions for the first day, as the locals are unlikely to be prepared for visitors. From the second day on, you should be able to arrange for supplies from the fishermen.

Pamilacan is also known as a whalers' island. If you want to observe dolphins and whales in the Mindanao Sea you'll find experienced boatsmen among the islanders who know where and when they can be spotted.

Places to Stay
In the northern part of the island, on a white beach near the old Spanish watchtower, you can stay at *Nita's Nipa Hut* for P250, including three meals. The accommodation is basic but the people are friendly.

Getting There & Away

Boat There are boats almost daily from Baclayon to Pamilacan Island (one hour). Your best chance of a cheap trip over is on Wednesday, which is market day, and Sunday when the fishermen and their families return home from church. That will cost you only a few pesos. Even on weekdays there are often people from Pamilacan in Baclayon. They always anchor their boats on the right-hand side of the landing stage looking towards Pamilacan and leave for home shortly before 3 pm. If you can wait for them, you won't have to pay the P350, which is about what a Special Ride (round trip) costs.

A Special Ride from Alona Beach on Panglao Island to Pamilacan Island and back costs around P800.

CABILAO ISLAND

Cabilao Island is 30 km as the crow flies, north-west of Tagbilaran in Cebu Strait between Bohol and Cebu. The nearby reef offers excellent snorkelling and diving. Several large beach resorts on Cebu prefer these diving grounds for their guests and send diving boats, usually full of Japanese tourist groups, practically every day.

Places to Stay

The pleasant *La Estrella Beach Resort* (cellular ☎ 0912-502 0286), located under the palm trees on a white sand beach, offers really good, quiet accommodation. Dorm beds are P100 and rooms with bath cost P250. The newer, bigger rooms for P350 and P450 are located on the neighbouring beach. There is a restaurant which serves Filipino and German cuisine, as Babie, the owner, spent several years in Germany. Their well-stocked Sea Explorers Dive Shop is run by Chris who's from Switzerland.

Getting There & Away

Boat From Catagbacan, on Bohol, to Cabilao Island, several regular boats run daily for P10 per person, going to the landing stage at Talisay or Cambaquis. From there it's about 30 minutes on foot to La Estrella Beach Resort adjoining the lighthouse in the north-west of the island. A Special Ride from Catagbacan directly to the resort costs about P200. Two boats leave Cabilao Island every morning at 8 am for Catagbacan. There are buses between Tagbilaran and Catagbacan.

If you go by car ferry from Taloot near Argao on Cebu to Bohol, you can walk to the landing stage in Loon after you arrive (which should take about 10 minutes) to get an outrigger boat from Catagbacan to Cabilao Island. Up to three outrigger boats leave Cabilao Island every Tuesday and Saturday between 8 and 10 am heading for Argao (Looc)/Cebu – the landing place of Argao is at Looc, just outside Argao. Departure from Argao (Looc)/Cebu for Cabilao Island is on Tuesday and Saturday between noon and 3 pm (P25 per person).

CHOCOLATE HILLS

Exactly 1268 in number (so they say!), the Chocolate Hills are between 30 and 50m high and covered in grass. At the end of the dry season the grass is quite dry and chocolate coloured, hence the name.

If you're not in a hurry, you should spend the night in the **Chocolate Hills Complex** and experience the bizarre effect of the sunrise in this mysterious landscape the following morning. Admission to the complex is P3 for non-residents.

Chock-a-block

Boring old geological explanations aside, there are two legends concerning the origin of the Chocolate Hills. The first legend tells of a fight between two giants who threw stones and sand at each other for days, until they were so exhausted and sore from fighting that they made friends and left the island. They didn't, however, tidy up the battlefield, leaving the Chocolate Hills. The second legend is a lot more romantic. Arogo, a young and unusually strong giant, fell in love with an ordinary mortal, Aloya. After Aloya's death, Arogo cried bitterly. The Chocolate Hills are proof of his grief, for his tears turned into hills. ■

According to some geologists, Bohol lay under water in prehistoric times. Volcanic eruptions caused unevenness on the bottom of the sea which was gradually smoothed and rounded by the movement of the water. Most serious geologists, however, regard such an explanation as nonsense. Even though the geological origin of the hills has not yet been explained beyond doubt, the consensus is that they are weathered formations of a kind of marine limestone lying on top of impermeable clay soils. Comparisons have been made with the Hundred Islands of North Luzon. On the top of the observation hill there are plaques containing what is probably the correct explanation of the hills' origin in relief lettering on them.

Places to Stay
The *Chocolate Hills Complex* has dorm beds for P100 and double rooms with bath and balcony (and a beautiful view) for P250. The rooms are unpretentious but OK. There is a restaurant and a swimming pool (which is unfortunately unusable most of the time).

Getting There & Away
Bus There are several St Jude Bus and Arples Line buses a day, practically hourly, from Tagbilaran to Carmen (P20; two hours). As you have to get out four km before Carmen, don't forget to tell the driver. It is about a one km walk from the main road to the Chocolate Hills Complex. The last bus leaves Carmen for Tagbilaran at about 4 pm.

From Tubigon to Carmen, there are several buses a day. They leave fairly reliably after the arrival of a ship from Cebu (P30; two hours). They may continue beyond Carmen and pass the turn-off to the Chocolate Hills Complex. Otherwise, take the next bus or jeepney going to Bilar, Loay or Tagbilaran to the turn-off. From there it is about a one km walk.

Tricycle The tricycle operators in Carmen ask for at least P40 for the four km to the Chocolate Hills Complex, P30 only to the turn-off. They like to claim that neither buses nor jeepneys make the journey to the turn-off, which is of course absolute rubbish.

Getting Around
Amiable motorcycle riders wait at the turn-off for the Chocolate Hills Complex to take people on half or whole day tours for between P300 and P500. After such a tour, you could have them take you to Tagbilaran or Panglao Island, including a few sightseeing stops along the way.

TUBIGON & INARURAN ISLAND
Tubigon is a small place with a wharf for ships to and from Cebu.

Just under 10 km west of Tubigon is the island of Inaruran, which has a white-sand beach fringed by palm trees, and a small resort.

Places to Stay
The *Cosare Lodging House* in Tubigon has simple, clean rooms with fan for P60/120. The spacious cottages at the *Inaruran Island Beach Resort* have a fan, bath and big veranda for P2600 per person, including three meals. The restaurant serves Filipino and French dishes; it's a bit expensive, even for drinks. The resort closes down from the beginning of October until 20 December.

Getting There & Away
Bus There are several buses from Carmen to Tubigon daily (two hours). The last bus leaves at about 2 pm.

UBAY
Ubay is a little place on the eastern coast of Bohol from where boats leave daily for Maasin and Bato on Leyte.

Places to Stay
Unpretentious, but comfortable accommodation is available at the *Royal Orchid Pension House*, where singles/doubles with fan go for P100/200. The *Casa Besas Pension House* has fairly good rooms with fan for P80/160, singles with fan and bath for P160, and doubles with air-con and bath for P300.

Getting There & Away

Bus From Carmen to Ubay via Sierra Bullones, there are several buses daily. They either come from Tagbilaran (you can board these at the turn-off on the main road) or from Carmen. An alternative route would be to go first to Loay and change to a bus heading along the coast to Ubay.

From Tagbilaran to Ubay (four hours), there are a few buses going via Jagna or via Carmen and Sierra Bullones daily.

A few buses travel daily from Ubay to Tagbilaran via Sierra Bullones and Carmen or via Jagna. The last bus via Carmen departs at 2 pm.

TALIBON

With its 55,000 inhabitants, Talibon is the largest town on the island. Located on the northern coast of Bohol, it has a wharf for ships to and from Cebu City. You can also cross to nearby Jao Island from here.

Places to Stay

There's a family feeling at the friendly *Lapyahan Lodge*. Basic rooms cost P50/100 and P100/180 with fan and bath.

Getting There & Away

Bus Several buses coming from Tagbilaran leave daily from the Chocolate Hills Complex turn-off to Talibon between 8 am and 4 pm (2½ hours).

From Tagbilaran to Talibon via Carmen, there are several St Jude Bus and Arples Line buses (possibly also JG Express buses) daily between 6 am and 2 pm (4½ hours).

JAO ISLAND

Jao (pronounced 'how') Island is one of the many small islands off the northern coast of Bohol. Unfortunately, a severe typhoon has destroyed the coral reef, so there is nothing for snorkellers to see. Even the swimming is not especially good. At the south-eastern corner of the island the German-Canadian Heinz Kunzemann and his Filipina wife operate a small resort on a lagoon near the beach. Yachts can moor here and you can hire outrigger boats. Heinz is a passionate sailor who decided to sell his ship after a long trip from Canada via the South Seas, so he dropped anchor at Jao. He is a radio ham and has contacts around the world.

Places to Stay

The *Laguna Escondido Resort & Yacht Haven* has dorm beds for P100 and cottages with bath for P300. There is a beer garden/disco and you can enjoy generous portions of European-Filipino food in the restaurant. Full board can be arranged.

Getting There & Away

Boat From Talibon, boats leave regularly for Jao Island (P5; 15 minutes). Special Rides are offered for P50. Every day at 9 am the 'service boat of Mr Heinz' usually comes to Talibon and returns to Jao Island after a short stop, so you can hitch a ride on it.

Cebu

This island, more than 200 km long and just 40 km across at its widest point, is at the centre of the Visayas, locked between Negros, Leyte and Bohol. It is the main island of Cebu Province and the location of the capital, Cebu City. Of the smaller islands which are also part of the province, the most important are Mactan, Bantayan and Camotes. Cebu is a hilly island and flat areas are only to be found on the coast and in the north.

When the Spaniards arrived in Cebu, it was called Sugbu and trade was already being carried on with China. Today, many different industries contribute to the province's economic importance. There are large copper mines near Toledo, and coal, iron ore, gold and silver are also mined. Cement has been produced in Cebu for some years, but oil is the hope of the future. At the moment, Cebu supplies the West with fashionable shell and coral jewellery and also with rattan furniture.

The cultivation of maize is the dominant agricultural activity. However, there are also

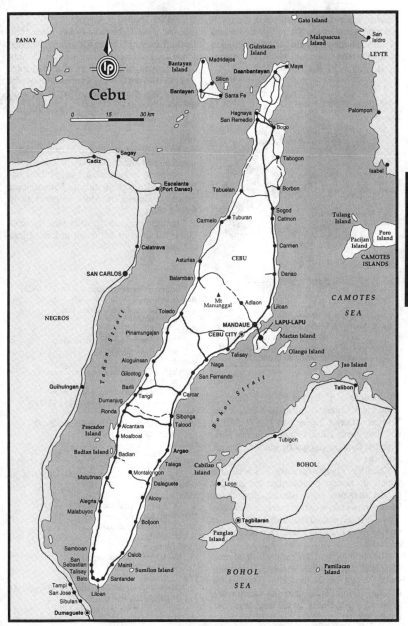

THE VISAYAS

Cebu

0   15   30 km

PANAY

LEYTE

Gato Island

San Isidro

Malapascua Island

Guintacan Island

Bantayan Island

Madridejos

Daanbantayan

Maya

Silion

Bantayan

Santa Fe

Hagnaya

San Remedio

Bogo

Palompon

Sagay

Cadiz

Escalante
(Port Danao)

Tabogon

Borbon

Isabel

Tabuelan

Sogod
Catmon

Carmelo

Tuburan

Calatrava

Carmen

Tulang Island

Asturias

CEBU

Danao

Pacijan Island

Poro Island

SAN CARLOS

Balamban

CAMOTES ISLANDS

NEGROS

Toledo

▲ Mt Manunggal

Adlaon

Liloan

CAMOTES SEA

Pinamungajan

MANDAUE

LAPU-LAPU

CEBU CITY

Mactan Island

Aloguinsan

Talisay

Olango Island

Jao Island

Giloogot

Naga

San Fernando

Tañon Strait

Barili

Tangil

Carcar

Bohol Strait

Talibon

Guihulngan

Dumanjug

Ronda

Sibonga

Talood

Pescador Island

Alcantara

Moalboal

Badian Island

Badian

Argao

Tubigon

BOHOL

Talaga

Cabilao Island

Matutinao

Montalongon

Loon

Dalaguete

Alegria

Alcoy

Malabuyoc

Boljoon

Tagbilaran

Samboan

Oslob

San Sebastian

Mainit

Sumilon Island

Panglao Island

BOHOL SEA

Talisay

Bato

Santander

Pamilacan Island

Tampi

San Jose

Sibulan

Liloan

Dumaguete

sizeable sugar cane plantations in the north and more are planned. The mangoes of Cebu are famous; they only cost a few pesos each during the harvest season, which is in March, April, May and June.

The majestic mango tree represents the most important crop on Cebu. A member of the cashew family, its luscious fruit provides a rich source of vitamins A, C and D.

The people of Cebu are all very friendly. They speak Cebuano, the main dialect of the Visayas. Many Chinese live in Cebu City, and they speak Chinese among themselves. Visitors, though, can get by quite well with English.

Cebu has many expensive beach resorts which are always promoted in the island's tourist literature. Those who can do without luxury, however, will feel more comfortable on the less developed beaches, such as those on Bantayan Island or Malapascua Island for example.

The coral gardens at Pescador Island near Moalboal and around Sumilon Island are worth seeing, as are the guitar factories on Mactan Island. Treks into the interior are growing in popularity, as are lazy days near the refreshing waterfalls.

GETTING THERE & AWAY

You can get to Cebu from Bohol, Camiguin, Leyte, Luzon, Masbate, Mindanao, Negros, Palawan, Panay and Samar (see the Getting There & Away section of the Manila chapter and the relevant Getting There & Away sections of this chapter and of the chapters on the other islands).

Air

As a result of the opening of Mactan international airport and of the boom in tourism and the economy in general, not only inland airlines but also foreign airlines have opened offices in Cebu City. More will inevitably follow soon.

The following are the addresses and telephone numbers of the major airline offices in Cebu City:

Air France
    Borromeo Arcade, F Ramos St (☎ 253 1623)
British Airways
    Ayala Center, Cebu Business Park
    (☎ 232 0006)
Cathay Pacific
    The Rivergate Mall, Maxilom Ave
    (☎ 254 0821, 254 0476)
Cebu Pacific
    Capitol Commercial Complex, Escario St
    (☎ 255 0201-04)
Continental Airlines
    QC Pavilion, Gorordo Ave (☎ 253 1753)
Grand Air
    Capitol Commercial Complex, Escario St
    (☎ 253 6499, 253 1670)
Gulf Air
    Cebu Plaza Hotel, Lahug (☎ 231 1205)
KLM Royal Dutch Airlines
    Capitol Commercial Complex, Escario St
    (☎ 52080, 231 2655)
Malaysian Airlines
    QC Pavilion, Gorordo Ave (☎ 253 4731)
Northwest Orient Airlines
    QC Pavilion, Gorordo Ave
    (☎ 73011-13)
Pacific Airways
    Mactan international airport
    (☎ 92854, 340 8204)
PAL
    Capitol Commercial Complex, Escario St
    (☎ 53927, 254 4036)
    Plaridel St (☎ 254 4136, 254 4879)
    Mactan international airport (☎ 340 0422)

Qantas
   Ayala Center, Cebu Business Park (☎ 232 0004)
Scandinavian Airlines System (SAS)
   QC Pavilion, Gorordo Ave (☎ 73015, 212573)
Singapore Airlines
   Silkair Office, Royal Wings Inc, 424 Gorordo
   Ave (☎ 253 1343)
Thai Airways International
   QC Pavilion, Gorordo Ave (☎ 73014, 231 1227)

Bohol PAL flies on Monday, Wednesday,
Thursday, Saturday and Sunday from Cebu
City to Tagbilaran.

Camiguin PAL flights from Cebu City to
Mambajao have been cancelled because of
lack of demand. An alternative is to fly from
Cebu City to Cagayan de Oro or Butuan, then
travel by bus to Balingoan and by ship to
Benoni, where jeepneys wait at the wharf for
passengers to Mambajao.

Leyte PAL has flights from Cebu City to
Tacloban on Monday, Wednesday and Saturday.

Luzon Cebu Pacific and Grand Air fly daily
from Cebu City to Manila.
   PAL flies daily from Cebu City to Manila
and on Monday, Wednesday, Thursday and
Sunday to Legaspi.

Mindanao From Cebu City, PAL flies daily
to Davao, General Santos, Pagadian and
Zamboanga. It also has flights on Monday,
Wednesday and Saturday to Cagayan de
Oro; Monday and Wednesday to Cotabato;
daily except Wednesday and Sunday to
Butuan; Tuesday, Thursday, Friday and Satur-
day to Dipolog and Surigao; Tuesday, Thursday,
Friday and Sunday to Ozamis; and on Monday,
Wednesday and Saturday to Tandag.

Negros PAL flies daily from Cebu City to
Bacolod and on Monday, Tuesday, Wednesday, Friday and Saturday to Dumaguete.

Palawan PAL flies on Thursday and Saturday from Cebu City via Iloilo City on Panay
to Puerto Princesa.

Panay PAL flies daily from Cebu City to
Iloilo City and on Monday, Wednesday,
Friday and Saturday to Kalibo. Air Philip-
pines flies daily from Cebu City to Kalibo
(P800).

Bus
Negros Five Ceres Liner buses leave Cebu
City daily for Bacolod between 5 and 7.30
am from the Southern bus terminal. They
meet the ferry going from Carmelo/Tuburan
to Escalante (Port Danao) and go on to
Bacolod. The trip takes eight hours (P80/110).

Boat
The shipping lines in Cebu City are pretty
relaxed about keeping to timetables. Ships
are cancelled and others put on without any
notice. Even the people on the ticket counters
seem to be quite clueless. The announcements in the daily *Sun Star* are more or less
reliable. Information from the shipping lines
is more accurate, but probably only if you
phone and say you are a foreign tourist.
   The following are addresses and telephone
numbers of the shipping lines in Cebu City:

Aznar Shipping Corporation
   T Padilla St (☎ 253 5523)
Bullet Express Company
   Pier 1 (☎ 91272)
Cebu Ferries
   Pier 4, Reclamation Area (☎ 232 0490)
Cokaliong Shipping Lines
   46 Jakosalem St (☎ 253 2262, 71220)
George & Peter Lines
   Jakosalem St (☎ 75914, 74098)
Lite Shipping Corporation
   L Lavillas St (☎ 253 7776, 253 6857)
K & T Shipping Lines
   MacArthur Blvd (☎ 62359, 90633)
Socor Shipping Lines
   MacArthur Blvd (☎ 253 6531)
Sulpicio Lines
   Reclamation Area (☎ 73839, 99723)
Trans-Asia Shipping Lines
   Cuenco Ave (☎ 254 6491-98)
Universal Aboitiz
   Pier 4, Reclamation Area (☎ 91542)
Water Jet Shipping Corporation
   Pier 4, Reclamation Area (☎ 232 1356)
WG & A
   Pier 4, Reclamation Area (☎ 232 0490)
Western Samar Shipping Lines
   V Sotto St (☎ 255 0930)

THE VISAYAS

Biliran From Cebu City to Naval, the San Juan Shipping Lines' MV *San Juan* leaves on Monday, Wednesday and Friday at 9 pm (7½ hours). The MV *Katarina* or the MV *Michael* of MY Shipping leaves daily at 8 pm, but possibly not on Tuesday (12 hours).

Bohol Several fast boats go daily from Cebu City to Tagbilaran (P150; 1½ hours). Water Jet Shipping's MV *Water Jet 2* leaves at 4.3) pm, their MV *Water Jet 1* leaves at 10.30 am. The MV *Supercat* of Universal Aboitiz leaves at 5 and 11 am; the Socor Shipping Lines' MV *Oceanjet 1* leaves at 9 am; and the MV *Bullet Xpress* of Bullet Express Corporation leaves at 10 am and 3 pm; the MV *Star Ruby 1* leaves at 5.30 pm.

The crossing with regular ships from Cebu City to Tagbilaran takes about four hours. The MV *Filipinas Dumaguete* of Cokaliong Shipping Lines leaves daily at 6.30 pm. The MV *Santiago de Bohol* of Lite Shipping Corporation leaves daily at 9.30 pm and their MV *Lite Ferry 1* leaves Sunday at 12.30 pm. Trans-Asia Shipping Lines' MV *Asia-Thailand* leaves Monday, Wednesday and Friday at noon.

From Cebu City to Talibon, the MV *Andy* leaves daily at noon (3½ hours); the MV *Krishia* leaves daily at 7 pm (3½ hours); and the MV *Talibon Cruiser* sails daily at 9 pm (four hours). You can sleep onboard until morning.

From Cebu City to Tubigon, the Anco Shipping Lines' MV *Tubigon* leaves daily at 9 am, noon and 4 and 10 pm (2½ hours); and the Charisse Shipping Lines' MV *Charisse* leaves daily at noon (two hours); the Roble Shipping Lines' MV *Betchie* leaves daily at 7 pm (two hours).

From Argao to Loon the Lite Shipping Corporation's MV *LCT Barge St Mark* (car ferry) leaves daily at 10 am, on Tuesday and Saturday also at 4 am (2½ hours).

A big outrigger boat goes from Argao to Cabilao Island on Tuesday and Saturday at 2 pm (P20; 1½ hours).

Camiguin From Cebu City to Mambajao, the MV *Doña Lili* of Cebu Ferries leaves Sunday at 10 pm (10 hours).

Leyte From Bukog on Camotes Islands to Ormoc, a big outrigger boat leaves daily at 7 am (three hours). From Carmen to Isabel, an outrigger boat leaves daily at 8 am (four hours).

From Cebu City to Baybay, the Cokaliong Shipping Lines' MV *Filipinas Siargao* leaves daily at noon (P60; six hours). The MV *Gregorai May* of Western Samar Shipping Lines leaves on Monday, Wednesday and Friday at 11 pm (five hours), and the K & T Shipping Lines' MV *Samar Queen* leaves on Tuesday, Thursday and Saturday at 10 pm (six hours).

From Cebu City to Liloan, the K & T Shipping Lines' MV *Guiuan* sails on Monday and Friday at 8 pm (six hours); Water Jet shipping's Water Jet 2 sails on Tuesday, Thursday, Saturday and Sunday at 4.45 pm.

From Cebu City to Maasin, the MV *Supercat* of Universal Aboitiz leaves daily at 9 am and 1.30 pm (P200; two hours). Water Jet Shipping's *Water Jet 2* leaves on Tuesday, Thursday, Saturday and Sunday at 8.30 am.

There are also several regular ships from Cebu City to Maasin (P86; six to seven hours). The Cokaliong Shipping Lines' MV *Filipinas Surigao* leaves on Monday, Tuesday and Thursday at 7 pm; their MV *Filipinas Dapitan* leaves on Sunday at noon: and the Trans-Asia Shipping Lines' MV *Asia-Singapore* leaves on Thursday at 9 pm.

From Cebu City to Ormoc, there are several fast boats daily (P200; two hours). The MV *Bullet Xpress* of Bullet Express leaves at 5 am; Water Jet Shipping's MV *Water Jet 1* leaves at 5:30 am. The MV *Supercat* of Universal Aboitiz leaves at 6, 8.30 and 11.15 am and 2, 4.15 and 6.30 pm; and the Socor Shipping Lines' MV *Oceanjet* leaves at 1 pm. Water Jet Shipping's *Water Jet 2* leaves on Tuesday, Thursday, Saturday and Sunday at 4.45 pm.

Regular ships make the trip from Cebu City to Ormoc (P76; six hours). The Sulpicio Lines' MV *Cebu Princess* leaves on Monday at 10 pm. The MV *Iligan City* of Cebu Ferries leaves on Wednesday and Saturday at 1 pm, their MV *Doña Lili* leaves on Thursday and Friday at 1 pm and the MV *Lady of Carmel* leaves on Sunday at 1 pm.

From Cebu City to Palompon, the MV *Lady of Rule* of Cebu Ferries leaves on Monday at noon (P67; five hours); their MV *Doña Lili* leaves on Saturday at noon.

From Cebu City to Tacloban, the MV *Don Calvino* of Cebu Ferries leaves on Monday, Wednesday and Friday at 6 pm (13 hours). Their MV *Doña Lili* leaves on Tuesday at 6 pm (13 hours). The K & T Shipping Lines' MV *Leyte Queen* leaves on Tuesday, Thursday and Saturday at 6 pm (12 hours).

From Danao to Isabel, Aznar Shipping's MV *Meltrevic 3* sails daily at 2 pm (three hours).

From Maya in northern Cebu to San Isidro, a big outrigger boat leaves daily at 10.30 am (two hours). After the arrival of the boat in San Isidro a bus leaves for Ormoc and Tacloban.

Luzon From Cebu City to Manila, there are several ships a week (P520; 20 to 22 hours). The MV *Superferry 10* of WG & A leaves on Monday at noon, Wednesday at 5 pm and Friday at 8 pm. Their MV *Superferry 8* leaves on Tuesday at noon, Thursday at 5 pm and Saturday at 8 pm; the MV *Superferry 6* leaves on Sunday at 8 pm. Sulpicio Lines' MV *Princess of Paradise* sails on Monday at 9 pm. Their MV *Princess of the Orient* leaves on Wednesday at 8 pm and Sunday at 10 am; the MV *Filipina Princess* sails Friday at 10 am.

Masbate From Cebu City to Masbate, the MV *Asia-Taiwan* of Trans-Asia Shipping Lines leaves Monday, Wednesday and Friday at 6 pm (14 hours). The Sulpicio Lines' MV *Cebu Princess* leaves on Monday at 10 pm (48 hours, via Ormoc on Leyte).

Mindanao From Cebu City to Butuan, the Sulpicio Lines' MV *Nasipit Princess* leaves on Monday, Wednesday and Saturday at 8 pm (12 hours); their MV *Princess of Paradise* leaves on Thursday at 10 am (seven hours). The MV *Lady of Fatima* of Cebu Ferries leaves on Tuesday, Thursday and Saturday at 6 pm (11 hours); their MV *Lady of Lourdes* leaves on Friday at 6 pm (11 hours).

From Cebu City to Cagayan de Oro, Water Jet Shipping's MV *Water Jet 1* sails daily at 10.30 am (P510; 5 hours). Trans-AsiaShipping Lines' MV *Asia-China* or MV *Trans-Asia* sails daily at 7 pm (10 hours). The MV *Lady of Lipa* of Cebu Ferries leaves on Monday at 10 am, Tuesday, Thursday and Saturday at 8 pm (eight hours). Their MV *Lady of Lourdes* leaves on Wednesday and Sunday at 8 pm (10 hours). The Sulpicio Lines' MV *Cagayan Princess* leaves on Monday, Wednesday and Friday at 7 pm (10 hours).

From Cebu City to Dapitan, the MV *Dumaguete Ferry*, the MV *Georich*, or the MV *Pulauan Ferry* of George & Peter Lines leaves daily at 10 pm (12 hours, via Dumaguete on Negros). The Cokaliong Shipping Lines' MV *Filipinas Dinagat* leaves on Monday, Wednesday and Friday at 7 pm (16 hours, via Dumaguete on Negros).

From Cebu City to Davao, the Sulpicio Lines' MV *Filipina Princess* leaves on Monday at noon (26 hours, via Surigao).

From Cebu City to Iligan, Water Jet Shipping's MV *Water Jet 2* sails on Monday, Wednesday and Friday at 8.30 am (P510; 4 hours). The MV *Lady of Carmel* of Cebu Ferries leaves on Monday, Wednesday and Friday at 7 pm (13 hours, via Ozamis). Their MV *Doña Cristina* leaves on Tuesday, Thursday and Saturday at 7 pm (11 hours). The Sulpicio Lines' MV *Dipolog Princess* leaves on Saturday at 9 pm (nine hours).

From Cebu City to Ozamis, the MV *Water Jet 2* of Water Jet Shipping Corporation leaves on Monday, Wednesday and Friday at 8.45 am (P525; 4¼ hours). The MV *Lady of Carmel* of Cebu Ferries leaves on Monday, Wednesday and Friday at 7 pm (10 hours); their MV *Lady of Rule* leaves on Thursday and Saturday at 7 pm (10 hours). The Sulpicio Lines' MV *Philippine Princess* leaves on Saturday at 10 pm (seven hours).

From Cebu City to Surigao, Water Jet Shipping's MV *Water Jet 2* sails on Tuesday, Thursday, Saturday and Sunday at 8.45 am (P425; 3½ hours). Sulpicio Lines' MV *Filipina Princess* leaves on Monday at noon (nine hours). Cokaliong Shipping Lines' MV *Filipinas Dapitan* sails on Monday, Wednesday and Friday at 7 pm (11 hours); their MV *Filipinas Surigao* leaves on Saturday at 7 pm (11 hours). Trans-Asia Shipping Lines' MV

Asia-Singapore leaves on Tuesday at 8 pm and Saturday at 10 pm (10 hours).

From Cebu City to Zamboanga, the George & Peter Lines' MV *Zamboanga Ferry* leaves on Monday at 10 pm and Friday at noon (24 hours, via Dumaguete on Negros and possibly via Dapitan). The Trans-Asia Shipping Lines' MV *Asia-Japan* leaves on Saturday at 6 pm (22 hours, via Dumaguete on Negros).

Negros Several ferries leave Bato for Tampi daily (P28; 45 minutes), the last one at about 4.30 pm. A boat may go from San Sebastian and Talisay to San Jose, where jeepneys for Dumaguete wait at the wharf (P7). ABC Liner air-con buses leaving daily at 6, 7, 8 and 11 am and 1.30, 2 and 3 pm from the ABC Liner bus terminal in Cebu City for Bato will meet the ferries for Tampi. The buses also stop at the Southern bus terminal (which is not so good, because the best seats will probably already be taken). The trip takes three hours.

From Cebu City to Dumaguete, the MV *Supercat* of Universal Aboitiz leaves daily at 5.45 am and 3 pm (P200; 2¼ hours).

You can also go by the George & Peter Lines' MV *Dumaguete Ferry*, MV *Georich* or MV *Pulauan Ferry*. The boats leave daily at 10 pm and possibly at 9 pm on Monday (eight hours). The Cokaliong Shipping Lines' MV *Filipinas Dinagat* leaves on Monday, Wednesday and Friday at 7 pm and on Sunday at noon (six hours). The MV *Asia-Japan* of Trans-Asia Shipping Lines leaves Tuesday and Saturday at 6 pm (six hours).

From Liloan to Sibulan, a big outrigger boat leaves daily about every 30 minutes. The last departure is at about 3 pm (20 minutes). A jeepney from Subulan to Dumaguete costs P5.

From Tangil to Guihulngan boats leave daily at 6 am (two hours).

From Toledo to San Carlos, a ferry leaves daily at 9 am and 2 pm from Monday to Saturday, and at 1.30 pm on Sunday. There may be different departure times on holidays. Only one boat goes on Maundy Thursday and none on Good Friday. The timetable on this route changes frequently. Buy your ticket from the kiosk at the entrance to the pier and not from the shady men offering tickets. The trip takes 1¾ hours.

The last bus from San Carlos to Bacolod waits for the last boat from Toledo. A combined bus and boat ticket is cheaper than two single tickets.

From Tuburan to Escalante, the MV *Melrivic 2* of Aznar Shipping Corporation leaves daily at 8 and 10 am (P35; 1¾ hours).

From Bantayan town on Bantayan Island, a big outrigger boat leaves daily between 10 am and noon for Cadiz on the northern coast of Negros (P65; 3½ hours).

Panay From Cebu City to Iloilo City, the Trans-Asia Shipping Lines' MV *Asia-Brunei* or MV *Asia-Indonesia* leaves daily at 6 pm (P230; 12½ hours). The MV *Iligan City* of Cebu Ferries leaves Monday and Saturday at 7 pm (12 hours); their MV *Tacloban City* leaves Tuesday and Thursday at 7 pm (12 hours).

From Cebu City to Roxas, the MV *Iligan City* of Cebu Ferries leaves Thursday 7 pm (12 hours); their MV *Tacloban City* leaves Saturday at 7 pm (12 hours). Both ships continue on to Dumaguit (near Kalibo).

Samar From Cebu City to Catarman, the Western Samar Shipping Lines' MV *Elizabeth Lilly* leaves on Saturday at 6 pm (14 hours). The same ship leaves Cebu City for Catbalogan on Tuesday at 6 pm (13 hours).

Siquijor From Cebu City to Larena, the MV *Doña Cristina* of Cebu Ferries leaves on Saturday at 7 pm (24 hours, via Iligan on Mindanao).

CEBU CITY

Cebu City is the capital and the main town on Cebu, with a population of about 675,000. Even though a fairly big city, the so-called 'Queen City of the South' is easy to get to know. The busy city centre, called Downtown, includes Colon St, the oldest street in the Philippines. It has unfortunately lost some of its charm in recent years. The houses and streets are only just being maintained, and the easy and natural friendliness of many of the locals has obviously suffered because of their economic difficulties. The many beggars and homeless who camp in the streets and in doorways bear witness to their privations.

In contrast to the depressed Downtown, Uptown – the area north of the Rodriguez St, Fuente Osmeña, Maxilom Ave axis – has obviously gained in prosperity. Smart restaurants, varied places of entertainment and a well cared-for townscape provide a marked contrast with the very busy Colon area, particularly in the late afternoon. The densely populated outer suburbs and adjoining barrios are gradually joining up with Cebu City. According to the projections of the city's progressive town planners, its appearance will change considerably in the near future. An imposing new city is being planned in the Reclamation Area in the harbour, with numerous skyscrapers, shopping centres, leisure and recreation centres and a new city hall.

Life in Cebu City is more leisurely than in Manila. There are, of course, many jeepneys and taxis and even a few *tartanillas* (horse-drawn carriages), but you can get almost anywhere in this city on foot. There are plenty of hotels, restaurants and cinemas, while beaches are great for leisure activities. Transport facilities to other islands are excellent.

Orientation
Recently several streets in Cebu City were renamed, but people also still use the following names in brackets: Osmeña Blvd (Jones Ave, Juan Luna St), Maxilom Ave (Mango Ave), V Gullas St (Manalili St), Bacalso Ave (Rizal Ave, South Expressway) and Fuente Osmeña (Osmeña Circle).

Maps Bookmark has published an illustrated *Cebu Landmarks* map which offers a bird's-eye view of the city's most important streets and noteworthy buildings.

Information
Tourist Office The tourist office (☎ 254 2811) is in the GMC Building on Plaza Independencia near Fort San Pedro. It has a service counter at Mactan international airport (☎ 340 8229), where room reservations and other travel arrangements can be made.

The monthly tourist bulletin *What's on in The Visayas and Mindanao* has interesting articles and useful advertisements, and is handed out free at the airport and in various hotels and restaurants. The advertising pages of the Cebu City daily *Sun Star* contain up-to-date information on entertainment and shipping connections.

Visas The Immigration Office (☎ 253 4339) is in the Customs Building near Fort San Pedro. You can get your visa extended here from 21 to 59 days. If you want a visa for more than 59 days, your application and passport could be sent to Manila for processing and will not be available for at least two weeks. You should bring a pen to fill out the forms. It also wouldn't hurt to be dressed respectably and look as if you had spent the night actually sleeping.

Foreign Consulates The Thailand Consulate is in the Eastern Shipping Lines Building, MJ Cuenco Ave (near the Plaza Independencia) (☎ 93013). A visa for Thailand can be processed within 24 hours.

The United States Consulate is located in the PCI Building, Gorordo Ave (☎ 231 1261).

The following countries all have consulates here: Austria, Belgium, Chile, Denmark, Netherlands, Norway, Spain, Sweden and Turkey.

Money The Philippine National Bank, the Standard Chartered Bank and the Bank of the Philippine Islands, all near Cebu City Hall, can change travellers cheques and foreign currency.

The place to change American Express travellers cheques is the Amex office (☎ 232 2970) at the Ayala Center (2nd floor), Cebu Business Park. You can also get an American

THE VISAYAS

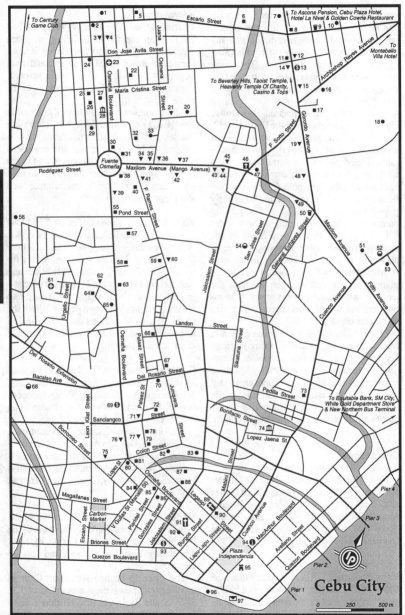

Cebu City

0   250   500 m

PLACES TO STAY
5 Mayflower Pension House
6 Cebu Grand Hotel, The Apartelle, Bouraq Airlines, Grand Air, KLM, PAL & Hertz Rent-a-Car
8 Kukuk's Nest Pension House & Restaurant, Tonros Apartelle & Duty Fee Shop
11 West Gorordo Hotel & Family Choice Restaurant
17 St Moritz Hotel & Disco-Nightclub & L'Oasis Garden Restaurant
22 Cebu Mintel
25 Jasmine Pension
26 Verbena Pension House
27 Casa Loreto Pension House
30 Elegant Circle Inn
31 Park Place Hotel
32 Fuente Pension House
38 Cebu Midtown Hotel, Metrobank Plaza & Robinson's Department Store
40 Kan-Irag Hotel, Bachelor's Too, Love City Disco & Thunderdome
55 Emsu Hotel & McDonald's
57 Jasmine Pension
58 Arbel's Pension House
59 Diplomat Hotel, Europa Delicatessen & Butcher Shop
63 YMCA
64 Jovel Pension House
66 Teo-Fel Pension House
67 Cebu Elicon House
72 Golden Valley Inn
73 Cebu Harbour View Hotel
78 Hotel de Mercedes & McSherry Pension House
79 Century Hotel
81 Cebu Hallmark Hotel
84 Pacific Tourist Inn
85 Centrepoint Hotel

87 Hotel Victoria de Cebu & Visayan Restaurant
88 Ruftan Pensione & Café
90 Patria de Cebu

PLACES TO EAT
3 Food Street
4 Boulevard Restaurant
12 Pistahan Seafood Restaurant
14 Europa Delicatessen & Butcher Shop, Continental Airlines, Malaysian Airlines, Northwest Airlines, SAS – Scandinavian Airlines, Thai Airways International & QC Pavilion
15 Royal Concourse Restaurant
19 Alavar's Seafoods House
21 Govinda's
34 Ginza Restaurant & McDonald's
35 Old Cebu Restaurant
36 Mikado Japanese Restaurant, Mango Plaza & National Book Store
37 Ding Qua Qua Dimsum House & Rustan's Department Store
39 Sammy's Restaurant & Silver Dollar Bar
41 Ric's Food Express
42 Mister Donut
43 La Dolce Vita Restaurant, Vienna Kaffee-Haus & Web Link Internet Café
44 Shakey's Pizza & Puerto Rico Bar
45 Swiss Restaurant, Ball's Disco & Robinson's Foodorama
48 Grand Majestic Restaurant
49 Lighthouse Restaurant
60 Café Adriatico
62 Cosina sa Cebu Restaurant
71 Our Place Restaurant
75 Snow Sheen Restaurant
76 Snow Sheen Restaurant

77 Pete's Kitchen & Pete's Mini Food Center

OTHER
1 Provincial Capitol Building
2 Bikes R Us
7 Singapore Airlines (Silkair)
9 Frankfurter Hof Folkhouse
10 Cebu Holiday & Fitness Center
13 PCI Bank & US-Consulate
16 Avis Rent-a-Car
18 Ayala Center, American Express & Qantas Airways
20 Habagat Outdoor Shop
23 Cebu Doctors Hospital
24 JC Bike Shop
28 Rizal Memorial Library & Museum
29 Fruit Stalls
33 Off-Road Bicycling
46 Iglesia Ni Kristo Church
47 Cathay Pacific Airways & The Rivergate Mall
50 Steve's Music Bar
51 Caretta Cemetery
52 Old Northern Bus Terminal
53 Chinese Cemetery
54 ABC-Liner Bus Terminal
56 Anzar Coliseum
61 Sacred Heart Hospital
65 Bookmark
68 Southern Bus Terminal
69 Central Bank
70 San Carlos University
74 Casa Gorordo Museum
80 Gaisano Metro Department Store
82 Gaw Department Store
83 Gaisano Main Department Store
86 PAL
89 Cebu Cathedral
91 Basilica Minore del Santo Niño
92 Magellan's Cross
93 Philippine National Bank (PNB) & City Hall
94 Tourist Office
95 Fort San Pedro
96 Immigration Office
97 GPO

Express cash advance there. It is open Monday to Friday from 8.30 am to 4 pm for cash advances and to 5.30 pm for travellers cheques, and Saturday from 9 am to noon.

Thomas Cook Travel has an office on the ground floor of the Metrobank Plaza on Osmeña Blvd, where you can change Thomas Cook travellers cheques.

The Equitable Bank (☎ 232 0320) on Port Center Ave at the corner of San Jose dela Montana Ave (next to SM City), Reclamation Area will give you a cash advance on your Visa or Eurocard/MasterCard. They offer the same service at their two downtown branches on Gonzales St at the corner of Magallanes St (☎ 254 8191), and on Borromeo St at the corner of Magallanes St (☎ 253 0430).

Department stores like Gaisano Metro and Rustan's will also change cash, even at the weekends, and sometimes even at a better rate than the banks. You can also change up to US$200 travellers cheques in SM City. You'll need to show your passport and the receipt of purchase.

Citibank on Osmeña Blvd near Fuente Osmeña (☎ 255 9333) has an ATM which takes Visa and MasterCard, as does the Equitable Bank in the Reclamation Area. Access to the ATM is only during bank opening hours.

Post & Communications The GPO is near Plaza Independencia. The poste restante service is apparently not very reliable here. There are branch offices in the Cebu City Hall, Briones St, at the University of the Visayas (UV), Colon St, and at the University of San Carlos, Del Rosario St.

To prove the Web really is world-wide, you can enjoy surfing the Net and taking care of your email at the Web Link Internet Café on Manros Plaza, Maxilom Ave. Coffee, tea and juices are available, as is one-on-one tuition if you need it.

The area code for Cebu City is 032.

Bookshops There is a good branch of the National Book Store on Maxilom Ave. Bookmark has a branch on Osmeña Blvd.

Dawn Subscriptions, downstairs in Robinson's Department Store, Fuente Osmeña, has a small but good selection of PC literature (software and hardware).

Medical Services If you are seriously in need of medical attention go to the Cebu Doctors Hospital (☎ 253 7511) on Osmeña Blvd, near the Provincial Capitol Building.

If it's dental care you're in need of, then you'll get relief from Dr Lorna Tipon-Sabandal, Sabandal Dental Clinic, Colon St at the corner of Pelaez St (☎ 255 0845). She consults Monday to Saturday from 8 am until 6 pm.

A professional shiatsu massage costs P300 at the Cebu Holiday Health & Fitness Center (☎ 231 0408), Molave St. It's open daily from 1 pm to midnight.

Also worth recommending is the inexpensive Guardo Shiatsu & Reflexology Center on Bacalso Ave (next to the Southern bus terminal) (☎ 254 1487), and in the Adela Building on Maxilom Ave (☎ 253 7963).

Emergency The Tourist Assistance Unit (TAU) can be reached at ☎ 96518, 61625.

Dangers & Annoyances A big city and traffic interchange such as Cebu City is obviously a lucrative field for pickpockets. They usually work in the late afternoon and evening in the vicinity of Colon St and Osmeña Blvd, and in the harbour area during the arrival and departure of big passenger ships.

Even in Cebu City it is best not to take apparently friendly invitations at face value!

Our friends the moneychangers, who offer a seductively high rate of exchange but more or less never stick to it, are active at the Plaza Independencia in front of the tourist office.

Fort San Pedro
Legaspi himself turned the first sod of earth on 8 May 1565 for this fort, which was built to keep out the marauding pirates who were giving the Spanish quite a bit of bother. He gave it the name of the ship in which he crossed the Pacific.

At the end of the Spanish era, in 1898, the fort was taken over by the freedom fighters of Cebu. Later, it served as a base and barracks for the Americans, and from 1937 to 1941 it was used for training purposes. In WWII the fort was used as a prison camp by the Japanese. The bitter liberation struggle towards the end of the war took its toll, and much of Fort San Pedro was destroyed.

Restoration work began in the late 1960s and a well-tended garden was laid out in the inner courtyard – a beautiful little place of refuge not too far from the hustle and bustle of the harbour. Admission is P10; it is closed on Mondays.

Magellan's Cross

The first Catholic Mass on Cebu was celebrated on 14 April 1521, when Rajah Humabon, his wife, sons and daughters and 800 islanders had themselves baptised by Father Pedro de Valderrama. Magellan marked this beginning of Christianity in the Philippines with the erection of a cross. The original cross is said to be inside the present, hollow cross, which stands in a pavilion near the Cebu City Hall.

Basilica Minore del Santo Niño

The present basilica – formerly San Agustin Church – was finished in 1740, three earlier wooden structures having been destroyed by fire. Undoubtedly, the focal point of the slightly weathered stone church is **Santo Niño**, a statue of the infant Jesus, but if you want to admire this valuable object on the left of the altar you either need a telescope or have to wait in a long queue. In 1565 this treasure, with its jewelled crown and gem-covered clothes, was found undamaged by Juan de Camus, one of Legaspi's soldiers, in a hut near the basilica. Since then Santo Niño has been the patron saint of the Cebuano.

Casa Gorordo Museum

The Parian district in today's Downtown area was the residential home of Cebu's wealthy at the turn of the century. Of the remaining four houses, the Gorordo residence has been restored and furnished in the style of the period. The Gorordo family produced the first Bishop of Cebu. Apart from furniture, you can see porcelain, liturgical items, clothes and old photographs of Cebu. New exhibits and written material on the same theme are being added all the time. The museum is open daily except Sunday from 9 am to noon and 2 to 6 pm. Admission P15; students P3. Photography is not allowed.

University of San Carlos Museum

The museum of the University of San Carlos (founded 1595) was opened in 1967. Its divisions cover ethnography, archaeology, natural sciences and the Spanish colonial period. Filipino objects from different epochs and exhibits from other Asian countries are also displayed. The museum is open Monday to Friday from 9 am to noon and 2 to 5 pm, and Saturday until noon. It is closed during vacations.

Carbon Market

The agricultural produce and the many and varied handcrafts of Cebu Province are on offer at this big and colourful market. There are also products from other Visayan islands, such as basket ware from Bohol.

Caretta Cemetery

A visit to this large cemetery on MJ Cuenco Ave near the old Northern bus terminal is probably only of significance on 1 November – All Saints Day – or perhaps the night before, when everyone is pretty wound up (see the Public Holidays & Special Events section in the Facts for the Visitor chapter earlier in this book). Opposite is the Chinese Cemetery. To get there, catch a jeepney from Colon St going towards Mabolo.

Taoist Temple

Some six km from the city centre lies Beverly Hills, the millionaires' quarter of Cebu City. The impressive, highly ornate temple of the Taoist religious community is also located here. Its size and architecture are evidence that a considerable part of the population of Cebu is Chinese. You can get a good view of the city from this magnificent temple.

The taxi fare to the temple from the Downtown area should be about P40, but agree on the fare first. It is cheaper by Lahug jeepney, which will get you fairly close. Catch it in Jakosalem St and get off at the Doña M Gaisano Bridge in Lahug (don't forget to tell the driver in good time), cross the small bridge, turn right and walk for another 1½ km or so. At the split in the road behind the guard-post with the sign 'Beverly Hills Estate', take the left fork.

Cebu Heavenly Temple of Charity

On the way to the Taoist Temple you will see on your left the Cebu Heavenly Temple of Charity. It is built on a hill which provides a stunning view. A natural spring flows underneath the building. The middle altar of this beautiful temple houses the statues of the Supreme God and of Milagrosa Rosa, the temple's patron saint.

To get there, take a jeepney from the Downtown area just as you would to the Taoist Temple. Just after the little bridge go right, then after 200m there's a path leading off to the left in the direction of the temple.

Tops

To enjoy probably the best panoramic view of Cebu City, with Mactan Island and Bohol in the background, you have to make the trip to Tops. This is a lavishly built viewpoint on Busay Hill, around four km north of the Cebu Plaza Hotel and 15 km from Downtown. The view is particularly impressive at sunset, when the lights of the city below come on. At this time of day, however, it can get cool, so take a pullover or a jacket with you. But beware: there is no public transport back to Cebu City in the evening! The place is owned by the Lito Osmeña family, whose domed, glittering silver residence is not far away. Admission to Tops is P25.

You can get there by taking a Lahug jeepney as far as the La Nival Hotel, changing across the road from there at the turn-off for the Cebu Plaza Hotel to a jeepney heading in the Tops direction (P5). Some of the jeepney drivers turn back 500m after the Cebu Plaza Hotel, so ask before you get in if it actually does go to Tops. After about five km get out at the top of the pass, and walk up the last stretch to the summit. If you don't take a break, the walk should take about 20 minutes on this rather steep, but well-maintained road.

The trip by taxi from the Downtown area to Tops is decidedly more comfortable and should cost around P80.

Special Events

The colourful and crowded Sinulog Festival takes place in Cebu City every January. (See also the section on Public Holidays & Special Events in the Facts for the Visitor chapter.)

Places to Stay – bottom end

Across from the Cebu Cathedral, the *Patria de Cebu* (☎ 72084) on P Burgos St has very basic, unpretentious rooms with fan for P150/200. It's an old place with its own restaurant and offers billiards and bowls.

Already in its dotage, the *YMCA* (☎ 214057, 215217) at 61 Osmeña Blvd has uninspiring rooms with fan for P120/200, with fan and bath for P150/300 and with air-con and bath for P240/480. OK for the money though. Couples may be accepted. It has a restaurant, swimming pool, billiards, table tennis and bowls.

Upstairs from the Elicon Café, the friendly staff in the *Cebu Elicon House* (☎ 253 0367; fax 73507) on General Junquera St will provide you with clean and comfortable rooms with fan for P130/200 and with air-con and bath for P360/430. The accommodation is all right at these prices.

The basic but popular *Ruftan Pensione* (☎ 79138; fax 254 9261) on Legaspi St is an amiable place to stay, with unassuming but clean singles with fan for P135, and doubles with fan from P165 to P440. They have their own restaurant. The rooms looking out on to the courtyard are the quietest.

About 50m from Osmeña Blvd down a little side street, *Arbel's Pension House* (☎ 62393) will let you have a modest, but clean, single with fan for P150 and a double with fan for P280.

At the East Capitol Site near the Provincial Capitol Building, the *Mayflower Pension House* (☎ 253 7233; fax 253 6647) has quiet, fairly small rooms with fan for P180/230 and singles with fan and bath for P250. Rooms with air-con and bath are P350/410 and P455/515, the more expensive air-con ones with TV.

The *McSherry Pension House* (☎ 52749) is a pleasant central place to stay, in a quiet lane off Pelaez St next to the Hotel de Mercedes. Rooms with fan and bath cost P250/300 and with air-con and bath P350/450. Monthly rates are available. It changes money and there are safe-deposit boxes.

The rooms at the *Verbena Pension House* (☎ 253 4440; fax 253 3430) at 584-A Don Gil Garcia St are clean and of varying sizes; all with air-con and bath, they cost from P370/430.

The jovial owner of the *Jovel Pension House* (☎ 253 5242) at 24-K Uytengsu Rd will let you have quiet and comfortable rooms with fan for P250/300 and with air-con and bath for P385/450. There is a coffee shop in the building.

The rooms would have to be cosy to call a place the *Kukuk's Nest Pension House* (☎/fax 231 5180). At 157 Gorordo Ave, this is a pleasant old bourgeois house with clean, cosily furnished rooms with fan for P225/395, with air-con for P450 and with air-con and bath for P620.

Quietly located in the north of Cebu City on Salinas Drive Extension, the *Ascona Pension* (☎ 231 5971; fax 231 2780) provides friendly accommodation. The Swiss management make sure the big rooms are kept well up to par. Rooms with fan and bath go for P380, with air-con and bath for P580. The restaurant has Philippine and Mediterranean style food.

Right on the corner of Don Gil Garcia and Filimon Sotto Sts, the *Jasmine Pension* (☎ 54559) has pleasant, variously sized rooms with fan and bath for P290/350 and with TV, air-con and bath for P350/410. Its namesake and affiliate, the *Jasmine Pension*

(☎ 213757) at 395 Osmeña Blvd, is more centrally located.

In Junquera St, the *Teo-Fel Pension House* (☎ 212482) has rooms with air-con and bath for P400/450 and for P500/550. The accommodation is in good condition, although the more costly rooms have more comfort and a TV. There is a small restaurant.

In a quiet little side street, the *Golden Valley Inn* at 155-A Pelaez St (☎ 253 8660; fax 253 8482) has well-maintained, tidy rooms with air-con and bath for P450/520, and doubles with air-con and bath for P640/980. There is a coffee shop.

Under Austrian management, the *Cebu Mintel* in Maria Cristina St (☎ 254 6200) will provide you with immaculate, friendly rooms with air-con and bath for P500 to P800; TV is P50 extra. They too have a coffee shop.

The friendly *Fuente Pension House* (☎ 253 4133; fax 253 4365) is a natty little place on Don Julio Lloreno St, in a quiet area near Maxilom Ave and Fuente Osmeña. The rooms are pleasant and clean, costing P560/680 with air-con and bath. It has a roof-top coffee shop and a restaurant.

Places to Stay – middle

Right in the heart of downtown, the *Century Hotel* (☎ 255 1341; fax 255 1600) on Pelaez St at the corner of Colon St, has quite good rooms, some of them getting a bit on the shabby side, with air-con and bath from P400/500. The single rooms on the 4th floor are good for two people, while those on the 5th floor next door to the disco night-club are noisy.

The *Pacific Tourist Inn* (☎ 253 2151; fax 254 5674) on the corner of V Gullas and Balintawak Sts has singles with air-con and bath from P380 to P480 and doubles with air-con and bath from P450 to P800. Suites are P1100. Of varying degrees of comfort, the more expensive accommodation has windows, fridge and TV. Hard to put a finger on it, but there's a kind of run-down feeling to the whole place.

In a handy location for getting to Maxilom Ave and Fuente Osmeña, the *Kan-Irag Hotel*

(☎ 253 1151; fax 253 6935) on F Ramos St has good enough rooms with air-con and bath for P720/770 and with TV and fridge for P890/980; the ones overlooking the street are, however, a bit on the noisy side. Their excellent restaurant is open round the clock.

The *Hotel de Mercedes* (☎ 253 1105; fax 253 3880) on Pelaez St has singles with air-con and bath for P500 and P600 and doubles with air-con and bath for P700 and P800. Suites are P900 and P1000.

As the name suggests, quite impressive rooms can be found at the *Elegant Circle Inn* on Fuente Osmeña (☎ 254 1601; fax 254 1606). Those with air-con, bath and TV cost P930 to P1200, and they have a few slightly less comfortable ones for P480/580.

Priding itself in immaculately tended rooms, the *Diplomat Hotel* (☎ 254 6341; fax 254 6346) on F Ramos St charges P1000 to P1500 per night for air-con, bath and TV.

You have to pay a bit more to get a window to look out of at the *Park Place Hotel* (☎ 253 1131; fax 253 0118) on Fuente Osmeña. Pleasant, quality rooms with TV, air-con and bath cost between P1150 to P2400. Suites are P3050. There is a coffee shop and a restaurant.

On the corner of Osmeña Blvd, the *Centrepoint Hotel* (☎ 211831-39; fax 210695) on Plaridel St, provides comfortable rooms with air-con and bath for P1200/1500. They all have a TV, but are still a bit pricey. There is a restaurant and a disco.

Places to Stay – top end
As you would expect in this price range, the *West Gorordo Hotel* (☎ 231 4347; fax 231 1158) on Gorordo Ave has very comfortable, immaculate rooms with TV, air-con and bath from P1030. Suites are P2500. There is a fitness room and a sauna.

Pleasant, tastefully furnished rooms with air-con and bath await you at the *St Moritz Hotel* (☎ 74371-74; fax 312485) on Gorordo Ave, for P1345 and P1590; suites are P2075. This quality hotel has a restaurant and a disco cum night-club.

An attractive, somewhat older establishment on the outskirts of town, the *Montebello Villa Hotel* (☎ 313681; fax 314455) is in Banilad near the Gaisano Country Mall. Their singles with air-con and bath go for P1100 and P1625 and doubles with air-con and bath for P1250 and P1800. Suites are P1800 to P5300. They have a coffee shop, and a swimming pool set in beautiful gardens.

Directly above the Robinson's Department Store, the *Cebu Midtown Hotel* (☎ 253 9711; fax 253 9765) on Fuente Osmeña has very comfortable rooms with air-con and bath from P2700 to P3600. Suites are P3800 to P12,000. It has a swimming pool, jacuzzi, sauna and a fitness room.

Situated on a rise a little out of town is the best hotel in Cebu City, the *Cebu Plaza Hotel* (☎ 231 2064; fax 231 2069) at Nivel Hills, Lahug. A night will cost you P3750/4700 for a room with air-con and bath. Suites are from P6800 to P30,000. It has a restaurant, coffee shop, disco, swimming pool and tennis court.

Apartments It is possible to get apartments for a longer stay in Cebu City – look at the ads in the local daily, the *Sun Star*. Usually what is being offered are furnished air-con apartments with kitchen or cooking facilities, a fridge and TV. Electricity has to be paid separately.

The following two places are good examples of what is available, both providing two-room apartments. The *Apartelle* (☎ 76271, 61944) on Escario St charges P900 a day, P9000 a fortnight and P14,000 a month. The *Tourists' Garden Lodge* (☎ 461676, 93770; fax 70518) at 27 Eagle St in Santo Niño Village, Banilad, costs P750 a day, P5300 a week and P18,200 a month.

Places to Eat
Filipino *Pete's Kitchen* on Pelaez St is a clean restaurant with amazingly inexpensive food – probably why it is crowded from the early morning hours on. The nearby *Pete's Mini Food Center*, also on Pelaez St, is a big, semi-enclosed restaurant where the guests can choose their food at a long buffet and have it warmed up if they want. *Ric's Food Express* on F Ramos St has good, cheap meals, with mainly barbecue dishes.

The *Ruftan Café* in the pension of the same name on Legaspi St is good for breakfasts and also serves Filipino meals.

Sammy's on Osmeña Blvd is open 24 hours a day. This unassuming restaurant next to the Silver Dollar Bar is very popular with the Cebuanos, especially in the evening. They are drawn by excellent pochero, a strong tasting soup made with leg of beef and bone marrow. There is seating both inside and out.

The *Boulevard Restaurant* on Osmeña Blvd is a popular café and garden restaurant, and at the same time a favourite meeting place for young people, especially in the evenings.

Always sure of a good crowd is *Food Street* on Osmeña Blvd, where several small, cheap restaurants across from the Boulevard Restaurant compete for custom. One of them is called *Arnold's* and makes what is probably the best kinilaw in town (P65 or P75, depending on the current price of fish).

The *Royal Concourse* on Gorordo Ave is a big, very clean self-service restaurant with inexpensive Filipino, Japanese and Chinese dishes. A lunch might cost you about P80. They are open from 10 am until 10 pm. For fresh seafood, try the *Pistahan Seafood Restaurant* on the same street. Their specialities, such as sizzling squid, are in the medium price range. It is open daily from 11 am to 2.30 pm and 6 to 10.30 pm.

Cosina sa Cebu on Ascension St is a clean restaurant serving inexpensive Cebuano meals. It is popular with students.

The *Fuente O* on Fuente Osmeña is a coffee shop on the 1st floor of the Park Place Hotel. Cebuano specialities are served, and among other things a first-class green mango shake. It is open 24 hours daily.

A long-time favourite of gourmets, the *Golden Cowrie* on Salinas Drive, Lahug, has inexpensive seafood dishes which can be heartily recommended. Popular orders are baked mussels and green mango shakes. This one-off, rustic bamboo restaurant has a great atmosphere and is always busy. It is open from 11 am to 2 pm and 6 to 10 pm.

The *Lighthouse Restaurant* on Maxilom Ave is a pleasant, well-looked after restaurant with laid-back live music. Apart from Filipino dishes – mostly seafood – which are usually eaten with the fingers here, standard Japanese dishes such as tempura and sushi are also served. It is open daily from 10.30 am to 2 pm and 5.30 to 10.30 pm.

Alavar's Sea Foods House on Gorordo Ave is an excellent restaurant specialising in food from Zamboanga on Mindanao, such as blue marlin. It's open daily from 11 am to 2.30 pm and 5 to 10.30 pm.

Chinese Deservedly so, the big *Snow Sheen Restaurant* on Osmeña Blvd has been popular for years for its good cooking. Another, somewhat smaller *Snow Sheen Restaurant* can be found round the corner on Colon St.

A place really worth checking out is the *Visayan Restaurant* on V Gullas St, which has earned a good reputation for providing excellent, inexpensive food, big portions and friendly service.

Downstairs in Robinson's Department Store on Fuente Osmeña, there is a dim sum restaurant which is worth trying and really good value.

A pleasant place to eat, especially if you're shopping anyway, is at the *Food Center* on the top floor of the Gaisano Metro Department Store at the corner of Colon and Lopez Sts. Here you have the opportunity to wander round and try something different. A variety of self-service restaurants serve excellent food like dim sum, but also cakes and ice cream etc.

Japanese The *Ginza Restaurant* in Belvic Complex, Maxilom Ave, is good with friendly service. They also prepare Korean food. It's open daily from 10 am to 2 pm and 6 to 11 pm.

The *Mikado Restaurant* in Mango Plaza, Maxilom Ave, serves authentic Japanese dishes; favourites are sushi and sashimi. It is open daily from 10 am to 2 pm and 4 to 10 pm.

Western *Shakey's Pizza* on Maxilom Ave is a favourite local rendezvous for pizzas and live music. On the same street, the golden arches of *McDonald's* invite you to try their well-known fast food. There is another McDonald's on the ground floor in the new Emsu Hotel.

The *Europa Delicatessen* in the QC Pavilion, Gorordo Ave, sells meat, gourmet cheese, caviar and smoked salmon, and also has a cosy restaurant on the premises. Wine and champagne is sold. There is another *Europa Delicatessen* on Ramos St which is open Monday to Saturday from 9 am to 10 pm.

The *Master Key Restaurant*, a charming old-fashioned restaurant in the Hotel de Mercedes, Pelaez St, is the place to go for international cuisine and good American breakfasts.

Slake your thirst with a cold beer at *Our Place* on Pelaez St, which also has relatively cheap Filipino, US and European meals for about P75. A narrow staircase leads up to this pub/restaurant above street level. It's open Monday to Saturday from 9 am to 10 pm.

Although anything but cheap, the *Café Adriatico* on F Ramos St is an attractive place to eat, with a pleasant atmosphere. They specialise in steaks, seafood and salads, and also keep a selection of wines to wash them down. It is open daily from noon to 2 am.

In a pleasant garden on the corner of Gorordo and Escario Sts, you can enjoy good European and Filipino cuisine at the *Kukuk's Nest*.

Any time of day or night, a chef at the *La France*, the excellent restaurant in the Park Place Hotel, Fuente Osmeña, will prepare you French cuisine and other European specialities.

In Salinas Drive Extension, the friendly *Ascona Restaurant* can be found in the Pension of the same name. They specialise in Mediterranean cooking, mainly French.

The *L'Oasis Garden Restaurant* on Gorordo Ave in the centre courtyard of the St Moritz Hotel is a good setting for excellent European and Filipino meals. They are open daily between 8 am and 10.30 pm.

On General Maxilom Ave, the *Swiss Restaurant* dishes up good Swiss and Filipino meals. The generous portions on the menu of the day cost P125. This is a well-run place with a civilised atmosphere, open daily from 9 am to 11 pm.

In Banilad, between Cebu City and Mandaue, in the Hotel Wayne's Inn, it's no surprise that the *Vienna Kaffeehaus* prides itself on its Austrian specialities. Breakfast, cakes and several sorts of coffee are available here. The prices are a bit on the high side, but actually worth the money. This is the original Vienna Kaffeehaus that used to be on Maxilom Ave (that location still has a Vienna Kaffee-Haus in it, but it's run by an Italo-Philippine corporation). They are open daily from 8.30 am until midnight.

Vegetarian About five minutes' walk from Maxilom Ave, on Don Ramon Aboitiz St near the corner of Juana Osmeña St, *Govinda's* is the place for well-cooked vegetarian dishes at reasonable prices (student meal P30).

Self-Catering The fruit stalls on Don Julio Llorente St, near Fuente Osmeña, have an excellent selection of tropical fruits. At the weekends in the Ayala Center, they have Farmers Day with fruit, vegetables and flowers on sale.

Entertainment
There are night-clubs and karaoke bars spread out all around the town, and more are being opened all the time. Nevertheless, a few pubs have managed to survive, eg *Our Place* on Pelaez St. The *Frankfurter Hof Folkhouse* in Escario St at the corner of Acacia St has live music from 5 pm until 2 am. The youth of Cebu City often meet at the *Boulevard* on Osmeña Blvd where the beer is cheap and new video clips are shown on a large screen. Also on Osmeña Blvd the *Silver Dollar Bar* attracts mainly foreign guests, as does the *St. Moritz Disco-Nightclub* in Gorordo Ave.

There is a wide selection of entertainment available on Maxilom Ave, including the *Puerto Rico Bar*, which is a show disco; *Ball's Music Lounge*, which features good, live music; and the big *Steve's Music Bar*.

There's excellent live music at *Pards* in the Cebu Plaza Hotel in Lahug, where three or four bands entertain the guests every evening. The *Bai Disco* in the same hotel is the most popular in Cebu City. It is open from 9 pm and admission costs P100 (minimum consumption). Staying in Lahug, you can get a fantastic view of Cebu by night from the *Club Circus Disco Bar* in Fulton St; they charge P50 admission, which includes one free drink. Downtown, you can experience a similar panoramic view, plus pounding rhythms, from the aptly named *Motions Disco* on the revolving top (15th) floor of the Centrepoint Hotel. It's a safe bet that gamblers would prefer the *Casino* opposite the Cebu Plaza Hotel in Lahug, where there is a full house every evening until the wee small hours.

On Sunday in the *Century Game Club* in M Velez St near the Provincial Capitol building in Banawa you may get a chance to watch 'high rollers' place their bets. The first cockfights take place in the forenoon.

Things to Buy

In Cebu you'll find lots of shell jewellery and guitars. The interesting Carbon Market south of Magellanes St sells produce and handcrafts. Making guitars is big business on Mactan Island near Cebu City. They vary widely in price and quality. Among the biggest and best department stores are the Ayala Center in the Cebu Business Park; SM City (with an ice-skating rink, several restaurants and eight cinemas with both English and Tagalog films for P20), and White Gold, both in the Reclamation Area; Gaisano Main and Gaisano Metro, both Downtown on Colon St; Robinson's on Fuente Osmeña; and Rustan's on Maxilom Ave.

A first-class place to go for all sorts of top quality equipment from knives to rucksacks is the *Habagat Outdoor Shop* (☎ 253 6292) on Don Ramon Aboitiz St. The friendly people there will contact all sorts of clubs for you, and also organise trekking tours. In the building behind the shop they offer a reliable maintenance and repair service for mountain bikes.

Getting There & Away

Bus There are three important bus terminals in Cebu City: the Northern bus terminal in Soriano St, Mabolo, for trips in a northerly direction (note: some buses still leave from the old Northern bus terminal in MJ Cuenco Ave, but probably not for much longer); the Southern bus terminal on Bacalso Ave for trips in a southerly direction; and the ABC Liner bus terminal on San Jose St for trips in a southerly direction to catch the ferry to Negros. Buses of the ABC Liner company also stop at the Southern bus terminal.

See also Getting There & Away at the beginning of this section.

Car The most reliable places for car hire would probably be Avis (☎ 310930, 231 7317) on Archbishop Reyes Ave, Lahug and Hertz (☎ 254 5004) in the Cebu Grand Hotel, Escario St

Getting Around

The Airport Mactan international airport is on Mactan Island, about 15 km from Cebu City. The PAL inland flights use this airport, as do the few international flights from places such as Singapore and Japan.

From Mactan international airport to Cebu City there are shuttle buses which cost P80 per person. They go to the Park Place Hotel at Fuente Osmeña.

From Cebu City to Mactan international airport the shuttle buses leave from the Park Place Hotel at Fuente Osmeña at 5.30 and 6.45 am, then approximately hourly from 8 am until 5 pm (one hour). If you have an early plane to catch, it could pay to spend the night near the airport instead of in town (see Lapu-Lapu in the following Mactan Island section).

An air-con taxi or air-con limousine from Mactan international airport to the city should cost P150, but make sure the price is agreed upon before departure. Hardly any taxis will switch on their meters, unless they have been fixed beforehand. From the town to the airport you might get away with paying P100. If there are no traffic jams a taxi should take around 20 minutes.

Tricycles are prohibited in the airport area, but you will find them waiting nearby. They cost about P10 as far as the Mandaue-Mactan Bridge or the jeepney terminal, where you can board a jeepney to Cebu City for P4.50.

The airport tax for inland flights is P40 and a whopping P400 for international flights!

Jeepney Of the many jeepney routes available, the following ones are probably the most important for tourists: Capitol (Uptown at the end of Osmeña Blvd), Lahug (Lahug district in the north of the city), Carbon (Carbon Market, Downtown) and Colon (Colon St, Downtown). The charge is P1.50.

Taxi Taxis cost P20 for the first 500m, thereafter P1 for every extra 200m. Mind you, not every taxi driver switches on the meter if it is not pointed out to him. It is worthwhile trying to negotiate a fare in advance for longer trips. If you're leaving by ship, remember that taxis have to pay a fee of P5 to get into the dock area.

Walking If you get caught jay-walking in Cebu City it can cost you P20. On the other hand, for that money an official ticket issued by the Republic of the Philippines is a neat souvenir.

Bicycle If you're looking for a bicycle for rent you could check the following bike shops for further information: Bikes R Us (☎ 214769), Escario St; Off-Road Bicycling (☎ 214561), Century Plaza Commercial Complex, Juana Osmeña St; and JC Bike Shop (☎ 213637), Don Jose Avila St, where you will be personally served by no other than Janice, the Philippine champion in mountain biking.

Boat The piers are not far away from the city centre, so a taxi to a hotel in Downtown should cost P30. If you want to stay in Uptown a taxi should cost about P40. It is not unusual to be charged P100; after the arrival of a bigger ship you will scarcely find a taxi driver who will switch on his meter..

MACTAN ISLAND

When people talk about the boom in tourism on Cebu, they are usually talking about Mactan Island, which is connected with Cebu by the 864m-long Mandaue-Mactan Bridge. On the south-east coast of the island there is a row of exclusive beach hotels like nowhere else on the Philippines. No expense was spared during the building of these resorts – they even constructed beaches with tons of imported sand. About 80% of the guests are Asian, especially Japanese, who fly in direct from Narita (Tokyo), avoiding Manila completely. In the meantime, convenient non-stop flights to Mactan International airport are available from Hong Kong, Malaysia and Singapore.

There is a memorial on the beach at Punta Encaño in the north-east of the island, dedicated to Chief Lapu-Lapu, who killed Ferdinand Magellan in the battle of Mactan Island on 27 April 1521.

Lapu-Lapu

Lapu-Lapu was founded in 1730 by Augustinian monks. About 150,000 people live today in the former administrative centre of Opon. The town is experiencing a boom, and there is even a Gaisano department store.

Places to Stay The *Mactan Bridgeside Hotel* (☎ 340 1704; fax 340 8569) at the Mandaue-Mactan Bridge is a basic place, but has good rooms with TV, fan and bath for P385 and with air-con for P700. There is a restaurant and beer garden and they have motorcycles for rent.

On the road between Lapu-Lapu and the airport, the *HR Tourist Hotel* (☎ 340 0048; fax 340 0158) at Pusok near the Mandaue-Mactan Bridge has singles/doubles with fan and bath for P400/500 and with air-con and bath for P600/P850. The rooms are quiet and are just OK for the money; the more expensive ones have fridges and TV. There is a garden restaurant, pool and free airport service.

The nearby *Cesar's Mansion* (☎ 340 0211; fax 340 0615) at Pusok has comfortable rooms with air-con and bath from P1500 to P2000. The ones looking down on the courtyard inside are quieter. The less expensive rooms in an annex diagonally across the street cost P600/730. It also has a restaurant, and cars for rent.

Places to Eat For a wide selection of Philippine and European dishes – ranging from pancit canton for P50 to cordon bleu for P140 – the place to head is the *Mactan Bridgeside Restaurant* at the Mandaue-Mactan bridge. The *Ristorante Italiano* serves (guess what?) Italian food and, just as predictably, the *Sunburst Fried Chicken* will sell you fried chicken. Also to be recommended is the *Café Cesario* in Cesar's

Mansion Hotel, Pusok, where good Filipino and international food is served. You can eat in comfort at the *Swiss Chalet Restaurant* which offers inexpensive four-course lunch and dinner menus with all the trimmings from P125. You could make it a long lunch, then participate in the 'longest happy hour in Mactan' from 3 until 7 pm. Near the markets there are two *Lechon* restaurants.

Entertainment There is a whole selection of more or less basic night-clubs, starting with the *1890* next to the town hall; then there's the *Miami*, *Brown Bear*, *Muffin Bar*, and the discos *More* and *Watergate*.

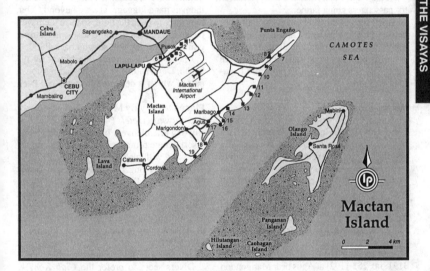

Mactan Island

PLACES TO STAY			
1	Hotel Clubhouse	11	Tambuli Beach Club & Villa
2	HR Tourist Hotel	12	Costabella Tropical Beach Hotel
3	Cesar's Mansion Hotel	13	Buyong Beach Resort & Maribago Bluewater Beach Resort
6	Mactan Bridgeside Hotel	14	Cebu Beach Club
7	Golden Views Beach Resort	15	Club KonTiki
9	Shangri-La's Mactan Island Resort	16	Hadsan Beach Resort
10	Mar Y Cielo Beach Resort		

17	Bahia Beach Club
18	Coral Reef Hotel & Golden Sunrise Beach Resort
19	Kalingaw Beach Resort

OTHER	
4	Lapu-Lapu City Hall
5	Gaisano Mactan
8	Lapu-Lapu Monument & Magellan Marker

Getting There & Away

A lot of jeepneys go from Cebu City to Lapu-Lapu daily – just listen for the 'opon-opon' call. They leave from the SM City department store. The seats next to the driver are best, as the ones behind get very crowded. The fare is P4. You can take a jeepney from Colon St to SM City for P1.50.

The last jeepney from Lapu-Lapu to Cebu City leaves at 11 pm, and the next does not go till about 4 am the following morning. The jeepney terminal is a bit outside of town, towards Cebu City.

A taxi from Cebu City to Lapu-Lapu costs about P70, but if you want to go to the beach you have to pay another P20.

At the Lapu-Lapu Market the tricycles wait for passengers going farther.

Small ferries travel about every half hour between Cebu City and Lapu-Lapu (P5; 30 minutes) and are a pleasant alternative to the overcrowded jeepneys. Last departure from Cebu City (Pier 3) is at 5.30 pm; from Lapu-Lapu at 5 pm.

Marigondon

The next public beach you come to after Cebu City is **Marigondon Beach**. It is a favourite with the locals and is especially popular at the weekends. There is ample roofed seating for P50 where day visitors can eat freshly grilled fish at low prices and drink beer and tuba. The beach itself is not too exciting but will do at a push. You could always hire a boat and go out to Olango Island for a bit of snorkelling. Fix the price beforehand.

Places to Stay The *Coral Reef Hotel* (☎ 253 3191; fax 253 1192) at Agus near Marigondon has rooms with air-con and bath from P4500 to P5600. Suites are P11,300 and P20,000. It is a luxurious but somewhat dreary establishment, with a restaurant, pool, tennis court, Hobie Cats, diving, water skiing, windsurfing and a private beach only for hotel guests.

Getting There & Away Lapu-Lapu to Marigondon Beach by tricycle usually costs no more than P3 per person, though sometimes you can't get the price down to that figure no matter how hard you bargain. A fair price for a tricycle is P25. It may be advisable to agree on a pick-up time for the return.

Maribago

At Maribago, between Marigondon and Punta Engaño, you can inspect some **guitar factories**. The biggest is probably Lilang's Guitar Factory, but the smaller factories also make quite good and well-priced guitars; it pays to compare them. If you want a guitar that will last, it is worth spending a few pesos more and buying an export guitar, as the ones that are made for the local market are dirt cheap but give up the ghost quickly once out of the tropics. You can get a good export guitar from P3000. Since PAL will not accept them as hand luggage, at least beyond Cebu, they have to go in the hold, so have them well packed. It is even better to invest in a strong guitar case which will set you back P800.

Maribago has several fine hotels by the beach. Day visitors have to pay admission, a part of which is deducted from the bill later.

Places to Stay By Mactan Island standards, the *Buyong Hotel* (☎/fax 253 7337) at Buyong is a relatively basic and inexpensive resort, where rooms with fan and bath go for P395 and with air-con and bath for P1220.

Also in Buyong, the *Hadsan Beach Resort* (☎ 72679, 70247) has singles with air-con and bath from P850 to P2400 and doubles with air-con and bath from P1000 to P2500. The more expensive, and newer, rooms are in the new wing or facing the sea. There is a swimming pool and a small beach, and diving and windsurfing are available here.

Divers seem to prefer the *Club KonTiki Resort* (☎ 340 0310; fax 340 0306) at Maribago. They charge from P750 to P1300 for singles with fan and bath, and P800 to P1500 for doubles with fan and bath. The grounds are respectable, but have almost no vegetation or beach.

In Agus, the *Bahia Beach Club* (☎ 206 0406) has rooms with air-con and bath and TV for P880. They have a sea-water pool for which costs P25 for non-residents of the hotel.

A popular place with Japanese tourists is the clubby *Costabella Tropical Beach Resort*

(☎ 253 0828; fax 231 4415) at Buyong. Singles with air-con and bath cost between P1600 and P2500, doubles with air-con and bath from P1900 to P2700 and suites from P3600 to P5000. The restaurant is a bit expensive. There is also a swimming pool and tennis court, and windsurfing and diving are offered, as well as table tennis, darts, billiards etc.

An altogether wonderful place to stay is the *Tambuli Beach Club & Villa* (☎ 253 1543; fax 253 1545), where singles with air-con and bath cost from P1750 to P2250 and doubles with air-con and bath from P1950 to P2400. Consisting of two distinct sections, there is a well groomed garden and four swimming pools. The more expensive rooms belong to the Tambuli Beach Villa. They are very spacious, tastefully decorated and noticeably better than the cheaper ones in the older Tambuli Beach Club. Admission for day visitors is P200, of which P150 are later deducted from the bill.

On a noticeably clean beach, the *Maribago Bluewater Beach Resort* (☎ 253 7617; fax 501 0633) in Maribago will put you up in comfortable rooms with air-con and bath for P3600/3900 and spacious cottages with a living room, bedroom, air-con and bath for P5800. You can have a dip in their beautiful swimming pool, and there is also a tennis court. Diving, water skiing and windsurfing are available for the active types. This is a pleasant, generously laid out establishment. Admission for day visitors is P250.

Getting There & Away A tricycle from Lapu-Lapu to Maribago costs P3 per person. A Special Ride costs P25, but you will have to do some hard bargaining as the drivers are used to guests at the beach resorts paying around P60.

Punta Engaño
Punta Engaño is the north-eastern corner of Mactan Island. On 27 April 1521, the conquering explorer Ferdinand Magellan lost his life in battle while attempting to make a landing here. In 1866 a memorial, the **Magellan Marker**, was erected to commemorate

the spot where he fell. A few metres away, a statue of a bold-looking Chief Lapu-Lapu, complete with sword and shield, keeps the memory of this popular hero alive.

The historic battle for Mactan (Kadaugan sa Mactan) is re-enacted each year on the beach at Magellan Bay by amateur actors, providing a sponsor can be found. The Tourist Office should be able to provide you with up-to-date information.

Places to Stay Standing on its own on a small private beach, the *Mar Y Cielo Beach Resort* (☎ 253 2232; fax 501 1268) will charge you between P2500 and P3400 for a room with air-con and bath. There is a swimming pool with a bar, and diving, water skiing and windsurfing are available. This is a large, well maintained establishment with tastefully designed, spacious cottages. The admission for day visitors is P250, which includes one meal; at the weekends it's P350.

Built on a simply gorgeous beach, *Shangri-La's Mactan Island Resort* (☎ 231 0288; fax 231 1688) is a big first-class hotel, with around 350 spacious rooms from P5500 to P8300; suites are from P9000 to P22,000. You have

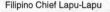
Filipino Chief Lapu-Lapu

THE VISAYAS

four restaurants to choose from, a swimming pool, and a tennis court, and diving, water skiing, windsurfing and parasailing are available. An airport service is also provided.

Getting There & Away A tricycle from Lapu-Lapu to Punta Engaño costs P3 per person. You should be able to get a Special Ride for P30 by bargaining skilfully.

OLANGO ISLAND

Olango Island is the long island visible from Maribago and Marigondon. It has small white beaches and beautiful stands of palms providing shade. The bungalow hotel Santa Rosa by the Sea, which is closed at present, is in the south-western corner. North of the village of Santa Rosa there is an extensive lagoon which has been declared a sanctuary for migratory birds, the first of its kind in the Philippines. Plovers, sandpipers and egrets are some of the birds which can be seen here, stopping over on their flight from the rigours of the Siberian winter on their way to Australia. Their return journey in the spring also brings them to this area as they rest their wings from the exhausting flight.

As humans have similar needs, there is a resthouse for them too, located on the lagoon with four double rooms costing P300. Reservations can be made through the Kukuk's Nest Pension House in Cebu City.

The island is surrounded by a reef stretching another 10 km in a south-westerly direction, where the islands of Panganan, Caohagan, Lassuan (Kalassuan) and Hilutangan mark the drop-off. Much of the coral has unfortunately been destroyed by dynamite fishing.

Getting There & Away
Boat The trip from Maribago to Olango Island costs P10 per person by outrigger boat. A Special Ride should cost about P150, but operators have been known to ask up to P500 without blushing.

TALISAY
This is a nice day trip from Cebu City but not much more. The Talisay beaches, such as Tangque Beach and Canezares Beach, are anything but impressive.

Places to Stay
The *Tourist Seaside Hotel* (☎ 97011) was obviously at its best a few years ago. You'll pay P250 and P350 for a room with fan and bath, and P480 and P600 with air-con and bath. There are two pools to cool off in.

Getting There & Away
Jeepney A lot of jeepneys make the trip from Cebu City to Talisay daily (30 minutes).

TOLEDO
Toledo is on the west coast of Cebu and has a population of about 120,000. Many of the people are economically dependent on the Atlas Consolidated Mining & Development Corporation. This mine, which is one of the biggest in the world, often employs several members of one family.

Little egrets from Japan migrate to the Philippines, where they spend the winter feeding on mudflats and waterways.

You can go by ship from Toledo to San Carlos on Negros (see Getting There & Away earlier in this section).

Places to Stay
You can enquire at the Vizcayno Restaurant near the wharf whether the basic *Lodging House* has rooms available.

Getting There & Away
Bus Several buses leave the Southern bus terminal in Cebu City for Toledo daily (two hours).

LILOAN
The road from Cebu City along the east coast heading north takes you through several inviting provincial towns. It's about 20 km to Liloan, not to be confused with the Liloan at the southern tip of Cebu (or the *other* Liloan at the northen tip of Panaon Island).

Places to Stay
A pleasant place to stay, *Franziska's Beach Resort* at Jubay, Liloan, will let you have a passable cottage with fan and bath for P700 and with air-con and bath for P950. There is a swimming pool on the grounds, and you can eat both Filipino and Swiss food in their restaurant.

Getting There & Away
Bus There are several buses from Cebu City to Liloan daily, leaving the Northern bus terminal (30 minutes).

DANAO
About 20 km north of Liloan you come to the town of Danao, the gun town of the Philippines. Under the shadow of the big, old colonial style church, in quiet back rooms, skilful hands busily work away at producing illegal weapons. The production consists mostly of revolvers, but exact copies of well-known makes of pistol are also made to order here.

Basically, Danao is a peaceful place, and the casual observer would never even notice the obscure activities going on behind the scenes. As it is, probably only one hundredth of the population of 75,000 is involved in the clandestine production of weapons, but that's enough to keep Danao's dubious reputation alive all over the country.

Boats leave daily for the Camotes Islands from the jetty near the hospital. There is also a daily connection to Isabel on Leyte.

Places to Stay
Located near the jetty, *Nancy's Pension House* is a basic little place that charges P200 for a room with fan and bath, and P300 with air-con and bath.

Places to Eat
The Philippine dishes are quite good at *Roxanne's Restaurant*, where you can also sit outside in the pleasant little garden. At the weekend rock bands sometimes performs.

CAMOTES ISLANDS
The Camotes Islands are located in the middle of the Camotes Sea, about halfway between Cebu and Leyte. The two main islands, Pacijan and Poro, are connected by a causeway. North-east of Poro lies Ponson Island, known locally as Pilar, after the largest town on the island. Tulang, the smallest of the four Camotes islands, is located just north of Pacijan Island and is blessed with idyllic beaches. A few years ago a group of Japanese investors were so impressed by these beaches they bought the island, although since then they have remained reticent to develop their business potential.

All along its west coast, Pacijan Island is also adorned with a row of very attractive white sand, palm-lined beaches interrupted every now and then by rocky promontories. In the interior of the island Lake Lanao is a fairly large, fresh-water lake that is up to four metres deep in places. The Camotes Islands are also riddled with scores of caves, eg at MacArthur on Poro Island and Consuelo on Pacijan Island. From San Francisco ('San Fran') a road leads over to Poro on Poro Island, curving past the Boho Rocks, a deeply fissured, craggy stretch of coastal rock with roofed picnic facilities every now and then.

THE VISAYAS

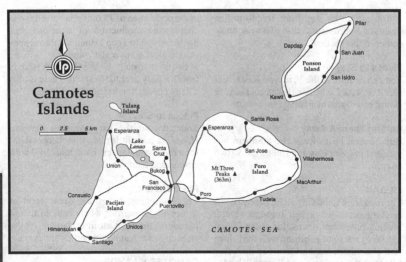

The lack of commercial accommodation (a tent would come in handy) and the inadequate infrastructure between the towns have left the Camotes Islands pretty well untouched by tourism up till now. However, you can include this attractive group of islands in your island hopping itinerary, as there are boats not only to Cebu, but to Ormoc on Leyte.

Information
Money There is neither a bank nor a money-changer on the islands, so make sure you have enough pesos with you.

Getting There & Away
Boat The MV *Oceanjet 1* of the Socor Shipping Lines leaves Cebu City for Poro daily at 6 am and 5 pm (one hour). The departure from Poro to Cebu City is daily at 7.30 am and 6.30 pm.

Getting Around
Motorcycle Although jeepneys travel between Poro, where the fast boat from Cebu City arrives, and San Francisco (P10), for transport you will usually have to depend on

relatively expensive motorcycles, eg from San Francisco to Esperanza for at least P30.

SOGOD
The Cebu Club Pacific Beach Hotel in Sogod was one of the few beach resort hotels on the north-east coast of Cebu for many years. It now has stiff competition from the exclusive Alegre Beach Resort.

Places to Stay
You can stay at the attractive, well maintained *Cebu Club Pacific Beach Resort* (☎ Cebu City 76598; fax 314621) in a cottage with air-con and bath for P1850. In addition to its own restaurant, there is a tennis court on the grounds. The resort also offers Hobie Cats, windsurfing, water skiing and diving. Day visitors pay P100 admission, which is deducted afterwards from their purchases.

The accommodation at the *Alegre Beach Resort* at Calumboyan is very comfortable. Fitted with TV, fridge, air-con and bath, rooms cost P5800. Suites are P11,000. There is a restaurant and tennis court, and Hobie Cats, diving, water skiing and windsurfing are available. Information is available in Cebu City (☎ 231 1231; fax 231 2961).

Getting There & Away

Bus There are several buses daily from Cebu City to Sogod, leaving the Northern bus terminal (two hours).

BANTAYAN ISLAND

Located in the north-west of Cebu Province a little off the usual tourist route, Bantayan Island basks in the sunshine with its beautiful beaches. Especially on the southern coast, between Santa Fe and Maricaban, Sugar Beach, Paradise Beach and the picturesque beach near Tingting-on all beckon the visitor. Near Paradise Beach you will find the small Ogtong Cave with its freshwater spring. Right next to it is a pool belonging to the Santa Fe Beach Club. Admission is P20.

So far, only a few tourists have come to this friendly island. There are only two beach resorts, both of which can be comfortably reached on foot from Santa Fe, where the ferries from Hagnaya on Cebu arrive. A small airport was built about two km east of Santa Fe. It's hoped this will encourage a tourism boom. Until this happens, local fishermen will continue to make a living supplying squid to the Cebu mainland, while the farmers use their land for raising poultry. They ship millions of eggs to other islands, so it's no wonder all the roads are free of bumps and carefully asphalted!

Bantayan

With its 60,000 inhabitants, Bantayan is the largest town on the island of the same name. It has a nice plaza, a clean and lively market (mercado) where the meat is good value, a picturesque port, a hospital, three lodges to stay at and some simple restaurants along the pier. There is a boat service daily between this small harbour town and Cadiz on Negros, so you can include Bantayan Island in a round trip through the Visayas.

Information The Rural Bank has a branch where you can cash travellers cheques, albeit at an unfavourable rate.

Places to Stay A simple but relatively good room with fan at the *Saint Josef Lodge* on President Osmeña Sr St will cost you P50/100. Also providing basic accommodation, the *Island Pension House* on Rizal Ave charges P75/150 for rooms with fan. A little bit further along Rizal Ave on the way into town the *Admiral Lodging House* is another cheapie with basic rooms for P90/180 and with fan for P125/220.

Santa Fe

Santa Fe is the third-largest community on Bantayan. Day trips can be made to the islands of Hilantaga-an, Jibitnil, Guintacan and other destinations. In and around Santa Fe there is a cottage industry producing lampshades and hanging decorations made from the shells of tiny sea snails. In the rustic *Ten Wee Wee Bros Restaurant* down by the pier (a good place to spend a few pleasant hours, by the way) members of the family and staff thread countless snail shells together and make little objets d'art from them.

Places to Stay Bantayan Island is popular for short visits, especially in the Easter week when prices can double! The *Santa Fe Beach Club* (☎ 254 4765) in Talisay, a beautiful little village just north of Santa Fe, has

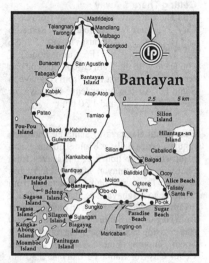

simple cottages with fan and bath for P400 and good, well-kept rooms with air-con and bath for P900 to P1700. The staff are very attentive. The beach here is nothing special, but the excellent restaurant, Majestic By the Sea, is probably the best on the island, and worth the money. Coming from the pier the cottages are on the right next to the big oil tanks.

The friendly *Budyong Beach Resort* next to the Kota Beach Resort has cottages with fan and bath for P300/500 and with air-con and bath for P600/1000. Compared to some places, good value for money; the owners, Norma and Dodong Zaspa really look after their guests' welfare. The food here is outstanding and also a good deal (from P40 on up). Advance meal orders are appreciated.

The well-appointed *Kota Beach Resort* is a pleasant resort on a beautiful beach on the south-eastern tip of Bantayan, about one km south of Santa Fe pier. You can get a room with fan here for P480 and P540, cottages with fan and bath for P720 and with air-con and bath for P1080. It has a restaurant where it is better to order beforehand if you can, and they have diving facilities. Information is available in Cebu City (☎ 254 2726).

Getting There & Away

Bus There are several buses a day from Cebu City's Northern bus terminal to San Remedio and Hagnaya. Air-con buses leave at 5 and 6 am, 1.30 and 2.30 pm (P65; three hours). If you leave with the 5 am air-con bus you can connect with the first ferry from Hagnaya to Santa Fe. Air-con buses leave Hagnaya for Cebu City at 7 am and 1.30 pm.

Boat From Hagnaya to Santa Fe, there are regular ferries daily at 8 and 9.30 am, 6 and 8 pm (P44; one hour). A bus leaves from Santa Fe to Bantayan after the ferry has arrived. There are daily departures from Santa Fe to Hagnaya at 5.30, 6.30, 9.30 and 10 am. A Special Ride with an outrigger boat from Hagnaya to Santa Fe costs around P600 (the crossing can be a bit on the rough side!). Socor Shipping Lines' *Oceanjet 2* leaves Cebui City for Santa Fe daily at 5.30 am

(P300; three hours). Departure time from Santa Fe to Cebu City is daily at 9 am.

The Lapu-Lapu Shipping Lines' MV *Honey* leaves Cebu City for Bantayan or Santa Fe every Monday and Thursday at 9 pm (nine hours). Departures from Bantayan or Santa Fe to Cebu City are every Wednesday and Saturday at 9 pm.

To Negros, there is a daily connection by boat between Bantayan and Cadiz.

Getting Around
A bus leaves from Santa Fe to Bantayan after the ferry arrives. There are also a few buses daily from Bantayan to Madridejos (P5) on the northern tip of the island.

A tricycle from Bantayan to Santa Fe costs P50, or P10 per person.

As the roads are good and the traffic is minimal, a bike offers a great way to explore the island. Many locals own bikes, and for a few pesos it's no problem to rent one.

There's no commercial rental, but some motorbike owners (eg the barrio captain of Santa Fe) are willing to hire out their machines for about P100 per hour or P400 daily.

MALAPASCUA ISLAND
Malapascua Island is about eight km northeast of Cebu and 25 km west of Leyte. It is sometimes referred to as Logon, after Barangay Logon, the main community in the south of the island. A walk around the island, which is 2½ km long and about one km wide, will take you to friendly little fishing villages and deserted idyllic bays. In 1994 a lighthouse was built on the island, and the panoramic view from the top is a sight worth seeing. There is a cloud on the horizon, however. It's a pity the fishermen in this area have still not grasped the simple fact that fishing with dynamite is a wanton act of destruction. Maybe the dollars brought in by tourism will bring them to their senses, so the coral reefs can have a chance to regenerate.

If you've been to Boracay, you'll recognise that not only the outline of little Malapascua, still practically unknown, is similar, the rest of the island can also stand comparison. Admittedly everything on Malapascua is a bit smaller and let's say rural

– the palms, the beach, the local huts – but the ingredients are all there in the right basic proportions. The fine sand of the blindingly white **Bounty Beach** on the south coast makes it a gorgeous bathing beach. You will find a few basic, but pleasant places to stay there. A deserted bay on the east coast is to be the site of an exclusive beach hotel to be opened in 1997, with a pool and diving station.

The three Japanese wrecks lying at 30 to 40m depth between two to five sea miles west and north-west of Malapascua will probably end up being favourite destinations for divers. What's more, the nearby tiny little island of Gato and its underwater caves with swarms of sea snakes will also be an unusual attraction for divers.

Places to Stay

Two basic little places in the village of Logon, both with singles for P100 and doubles for P150/200, are *BB's Lodging House* and *Nita's Lodging House*. Just behind the Cocobana Beach Resort and a little way from the beach, *Ging Ging's Flower Garden* charges P200 for doubles with bath. Two rooms share a bathroom. Directly on the beach, the *Monteluna Beach Resort* is a basic, but pleasant place to

stay. You'll pay P300 for a double with bath. The *Bluewater Beach Resort* is between the Monteluna and Cocobana resorts. It charges P350 for a roomy cottage with bath and large veranda. Two further places to choose from are *Monteruibo* and *Peter & Hilda*, which charge P350 and P500 respectively.

Once the only establishment of its kind on Malapascua, the *Cocobana Beach Resort* asks for P850 (two persons) for a roomy cottage with bath and large veranda; in the off season, from the beginning of May until the end of November, you'll pay P700. Prices include half board (two meals). Guests who require overnight accommodation only will be turned away. If you tire of lazing on the beach, there's a sunset bar.

Places to Eat

A friendly welcome awaits you at *Ging Ging's Flower Garden* where inexpensive fish dishes (which they would like you to order beforehand) cost around P50. Breakfast is accompanied by bread baked in their own ovens. A bit away from the beach, the *La Isla Bonita Restaurant* will feed you local fare as well as pizzas, pasta, wines and filter coffee.

THE VISAYAS

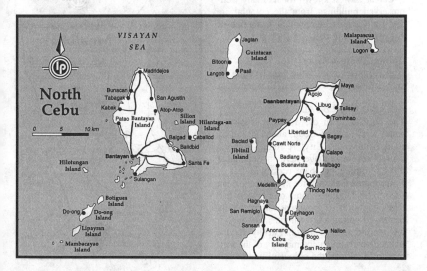

Getting There & Away
Bus D'Rough Riders air-con buses leave from Cebu City's Northern bus terminal for Maya at 5 and 6 am (P65; 3½ hours). If possible take a direct bus to Maya, because buses that make a detour to Hagnaya allow for 30 minutes extra. The last D'Rough Riders and Cebu Autobus ordinary buses leave at noon (4½ hours).

Boat Two outrigger boats leave Maya for Malapascua daily between 10 and 11.30 am. They go directly to Bounty Beach (regular boat P15, Bounty Beach-Express P30; 30 minutes). A Special Ride costs P300.

A big outrigger boat leaves Maya for San Isidro on Leyte daily at 11 am (P45; two hours). Departure from San Isidro to Maya is around 8 am.

A Special Ride from Malapascua to Santa Fe on Batayan Island costs P1300.

CARCAR
In Carcar, 33 km south of Cebu City, the road forks. One road leads along the east coast south to Bato, the other first goes over the mountains and then along the west coast to Bato.

Carcar is well known for its many well-preserved buildings from the colonial era and the Parish Church of St Catherine of Alexandria, built between 1860 and 1875.

Getting There & Away
Bus All buses from Cebu City heading for Bato or Moalboal go via Carcar (P15; one hour).

AROUND MOALBOAL
The popular town of Moalboal is on the south-west coast of Cebu, about 90 km by road from Cebu City. A fierce typhoon caused severe damage here in September 1984. Nothing but bare rock was left of **Panagsama Beach**, three km from the main road. The fabulous coral reef which had taken centuries to grow was almost totally destroyed within a few minutes, although it has started to regenerate. Luckily for the many divers who are the majority of the visitors to Moalboal, the colourful underwater world of nearby **Pescador Island** survived the fierce hurricanes and still offers good diving opportunities. All of the diving shops on Panagsama Beach offer tours there.

If it's a sandy beach you're looking for, it takes about 15 minutes by outrigger boat from Panagsama Beach to the nearby **White Beach** (P150 including pick-up service). You could also use the beach belonging to the Moalboal Reef Club for P20, although you are expected to order something to eat or drink if you do this.

As well as seeing itself as a base for diving outfits, Moalboal is trying to get established as a start-off place for mountain biking. There are already exciting tours on offer.

Information
Money Practically every resort will change cash, although not always at the best rates. It is better to take enough pesos with you. Only a few dive shops and the more expensive hotels and resorts accept credit cards.

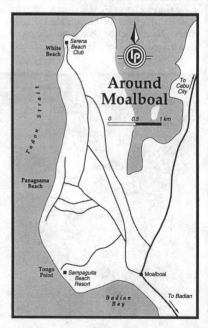

Post & Communications There is a post office in the town hall in Moalboal, but it's not unusual for them to be out of postage stamps.

You can make phone calls from the telephone exchange in the same building, although it's more convenient to go to the dive shops. They all have telephones, and you can either pay by credit card or make a collect call.

Cycling
Jochen Hanika of the Last Filling Station (cellular ☎ 0918-770 8686) rents out mountain bikes that are in top shape mechanically for P40 per hour or P250 a day. He also organises one-day or longer cycle tours through the interior of the island, eg:

- hill trip to Batat Batat (30 km, highest point 400m, 2½ hours cycling time)
- trip to the Busay Caves (26 km, highest point 350m, four hours cycling and walk through the caves)
- panorama tour of Moalboal via Ronda, Argao, Dalaguete and Badian and back to Moalboal (120 km, highest point 1800m, 14 hours cycling time)

Diving
Diving and diving instruction are very cheap in Moalboal. A one-day introduction costs P650 including equipment. You'll pay P450 for a diving trip, which includes the hire of a boat. A week's diving course will cost you about P6000.

A favourite destination is the Pescador Island Marine Park. Trips to Alegria Marine Park are also available, where Father Ray, a keen diver, will marry couples underwater if they wish. Diving equipment is available at the various diving centres, but, as usual, it is best to have your own.

You can hire a mask, snorkel and flippers for P100 per day. Enquire with Nelson of Ocean Safari Philippines at Nelson's Dive Shop, next to Eve's Kiosk; Bert Schaap of Seaquest Dive Center at the Sumisid Lodge; Karl-Heinz at the Savedra Divecenter (one of the best dive shops in the village); Jürgen of Visaya Divers; or Thomas of Neptune Diving Unlimited, or at the Moalboal Reef Club.

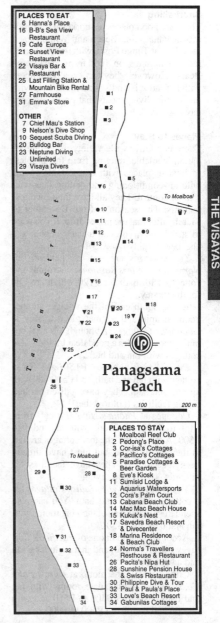

THE VISAYAS

THE VISAYAS

Snorkelling

There are good places to snorkel at the drop-offs at Panagsama Beach and White Beach as well as at Tongo Point, with its intact coral reef 20 minutes on foot from Panagsama Beach. However, they can't really compete with Pescador Island's coral reef. A trip with one of the diving boats that go there every day costs P50.

Places to Stay

There is a fairly wide variety of accommodation available, ranging from the simplest of huts to places with comfortable rooms with air-conditioning and ceiling fans with remote control. They all have their own restaurants. The season is from December to March; after that the prices drop. If you want to stay longer, you can usually negotiate a cheaper monthly rate.

The cottages are not the newest, but *Norma's Travellers Resthouse* has rooms and cottages with bath for P120 which are OK for the money.

At the south end of the village, another good cheapie and a quiet place to stay is *Gabunilas Cottages*. Although it's a bit out of the way, it offers a good deal for their nice cottages with fan and bath.

Eve's Kiosk charges P150/200 for a cottage with fan and bath, and P500/650 with air-con and bath. They have a disco bar and diving facilities (not together!).

Cottages at *Pacita's Nipa Hut* cost from P150 to P250, and rooms with fan and bath P500. A few of the cheaper cottages are not in the best of shape, but most have already been redecorated. They have facilities for billiards, sailing and diving.

You'll pay P200 at *Paradise Cottages* for a cottage with fan and bath. You can also spend the night in one of their big rooms with fan and bath for P350.

Accommodation in one of *Pacifico's Cottages* goes for P250, and that includes a fan and a bath.

Good value is the motto at *Cora's Palm Court*, where immaculate rooms with fan and bath cost from P300 to P550 and with air-con and bath from P500 to P900.

Next door to Cora's, the *Sumisid Lodge* (☎ 82761; fax 246 0592) has good accommodation with fan and bath for P350/450 and with air-con and bath for P650/750, including breakfast. Diving facilities are available.

The friendly *Sunshine Pension House* is in a quiet area away from the beach, and has pleasant attic rooms with fan for P150/200, with larger rooms with fan and bath for P350/400. There's also a swimming pool here.

Philippine Dive & Tour will put you up in a room with fan for P100/200 and in a passable cottage with fan and bath from P300 to P550. Tax may be added to those prices. You must pay in advance and no refunds are given.

In the southern part of Panagsama, *Love's Beach Resort* has adequate rooms with fan and bath for P350/450. The nearby *Paul & Paula's Place* has really pleasant rooms with fan and bath that cost P300, as does *Kukuk's Nest* halfway along the beach.

The *Marina Residence & Beach Club*, under Italian-Filipino management, will give you a cottage with fan and bath for P300 and a room with air-con and bath for P1000.

At the northern end of Panagsama Beach, the *Moalboal Reef Club* has very comfortable rooms with fan for P500 and with air-con and bath for P1000 and P1600. This is the only place here with a proper white beach.

Spacious accommodation at the *Savedra Beach Resort* (cellular ☎ 0912-501 9034) costs P1000 in a stone-built, comfortable cottage with air-con and bath.

The *Cabana Beach Club* (cellular (☎ 0918-770 7599) has attractively furnished rooms with air-con and bath from P1300 to P2100 (all with TV).

About two km south of Panagsama Beach, the *Sampaguita Beach Resort* at Tongo Point offers cottages with fan and bath for P1600 a night. The management is Italian.

Heading off in the opposite direction, about three km north of Panagsama Beach, the *Serena Beach Club* at White Beach offers very good accommodation. The quality is reflected in the price, at P2100 to P2700 for a room with air-con and bath.

Places to Eat

Most of the restaurants here offer similar fare and the prices don't vary much either. And remember, this is not the big city: service is not always snappy, and the food may take a while to arrive.

You can eat Philippine food cheaply and well at *Emma's Store*. Most of the resorts provide reasonably priced international food, eg *Norma's Restaurant* and the *Sunset View Restaurant*, where they have a barbecue party every Friday for P75. The garlic dishes at *Hannah's Place* are a bit more expensive, but excellent. The *Swiss Restaurant* and the *Café Europa* are both good addresses for German and Swiss cuisine.

If you're dying for a pizza, then the very popular *Visaya Bar* definitely will not disappoint you, it's marvellous. Equally good is the *Farmhouse* with tasty pizzas from the stone oven and delicious vegetarian dishes. The *Cabana Beach Club* will serve you outstanding Italian food at up-market prices. Last but not least, if you want to give your system a rest from bacon and eggs, the *Last Filling Station* will serve you a healthy breakfast with freshly roasted coffee, home-made muesli, pita bread and other goodies.

Entertainment

In the evening, you can watch video films in *Pacita's Nipa Hut*, while the *Bulldog Bar* offers pool (billiards) and darts. If you're itching to dance, then *Chief Mau's Station* is the place to head for.

Getting There & Away

Bus Buses for Moalboal leave the Southern bus terminal in Cebu City roughly hourly every day (P26; 2½ hours). If in a good mood, your driver may even take you straight to the beach. Otherwise you will have to take a tricycle from the main street to Panagsama Beach, at a cost of P5 per person or about P20 for the tricycle. The ABC Liner air-con buses leave daily at 7 am and 2 pm from the ABC Liner bus terminal in Cebu City for Bato, going via Barili and Moalboal (P32; two hours). The buses also stop at the Southern bus terminal.

The connection between Toledo and Moalboal along the west coast is a bit frustrating. You have to allow for three changes of bus, and waiting around. It's better to go from Toledo to Naga and get the next bus from Cebu City to Moalboal.

To go from Argao to Moalboal, first take a bus in the direction of Cebu City to Carcar, then get a bus from Cebu City to Moalboal. The trip takes two hours.

BADIAN & BADIAN ISLAND

About 10 km south of Moalboal you will find the small community of Badian. Just offshore in a lagoon-like bay is Badian Island, a peaceful island with a white sand beach and the Badian Island Beach Hotel. This hotel can be found in more and more tour catalogues these days.

In Lambug, about two km south of Badian and a further two km from the main road, there is a peaceful, palm-lined white sand beach, which has few resorts on it. It can be reached by tricycle from the main road.

Places to Stay

You can get a room with fan and bath for P300/400 at the *Stockli Beachhouses* in Lambug, as well as a two-bedroom house with kitchen and bath for P9000 all inclusive. Run by a Swiss-Philippine couple, this is a friendly, welcoming place with a neat tropical garden. It's absolutely idyllic here, just the place for peace and relaxation. The restaurant is good, but it's only for hotel guests. The coral reef just off the white beach is perfect for snorkelling.

The nearby *Lambug Beach Resort* charges P400 for their cottages, and they have a fairly expensive restaurant. This is a small, Philippine-American establishment where you can snorkel, go diving or try water skiing.

Practically next door, at the *Green Island Golf & Beach Resort* the spacious and comfortable rooms with air-con and bath go for P2500. Suites are P5000. There is a restaurant and swimming pool, and water skiing and diving are offered. The grounds are quite extensive and include an 18-hole golf course. The place is run by the Cebu Green

Island Club (☎ 73980, 95935; fax 311269), Suarez Building, Gorordo Ave at the corner of Escario St, Lahug, Cebu City.

At the *Badian Island Beach Hotel* on Badian Island you'll pay P2800 per person for a tastefully furnished room with fan and bath. This is an attractive place under Philippine-German management. The restaurant here is expensive (dinner will set you back P600 to P800). They have a swimming pool, and they also offer windsurfing and diving. Reservations can be made in Cebu City at the Badian Island Office, Capitol Commercial Complex A, Escario St (☎ 216364; fax 213385).

MATUTINAO

In the midst of lush tropical vegetation in the mountains near Matutinao you can find the refreshingly cool, crystal-clear **Kawasan Falls**. They are probably the best waterfalls on Cebu, and the natural pools are great for swimming. This idyllic place is a good starting point for mountain treks. There is a P10 entrance fee, and they charge P50 for the use of the tables, even if you order a drink with the owner.

Places to Stay & Eat

There are about 20 cottages near the waterfalls costing P100 to P250. There is also a small restaurant which serves cold drinks as well as simple meals. As these cottages may be booked out, it is probably a good idea to organise a day trip first to check them out. Heraldo, a German who has created his own little paradise next to a waterfall, dedicating himself to the art of just living, could possibly help.

Getting There & Away

Jeepney There are no problems getting from Moalboal to Matutinao by jeepney or bus during the day, but you could have trouble getting transport in the late afternoon. The trip takes 45 minutes. Get off at the church in Matutinao and follow the trail upriver on foot. This will take you about 15 minutes.

Motorcycle Motorcycles can be parked at the church for P5.

SAMBOAN

Samboan got its first claim to fame from the 'Escala de Jacob' (Jacob's Ladder), built there in 1878. This flight of stone stairs leads up to an old watchtower on a plateau about 65m above the town. From that vantage point there is a magnificent view over the Tañon Strait, the narrows between Cebu and the neighbouring island of Negros. Whales and dolphins can often be seen passing by through the straits. A roughly four hour spotting trip by boat with a fisherman from Samboan will cost about P500 (for six to eight participants).

Just off Samboan there's a majestic coral reef. Arguably Cebu's best, it stretches from Ginatilan to Bato and is ideal for snorkelling. The coast itself is fairly rocky, with occasional small bays and a few pebbly beaches.

Where to Stay

The *Samboan Coral Garden Resort* in Dalahikan provides neat rooms with fan and bath for P250, each with a big veranda overlooking the ocean. A friendly place, they are active supporters of nature conservancy and eco-tourism. Snorkelling equipment is available for P50 per day, and they are going to start renting out mountain bikes in 1997. They also plan to offer diving in the future.

Getting There & Away

Bus ABC Liner buses travel from Cebu City to Samboan with a destination of Bato via Barili (three hours). You can also take a bus to Bato via Oslob and carry on to Samboan by jeepney.

SAN SEBASTIAN & BATO

Several ships go from San Sebastian and Bato to San Jose or Tampi on Negros daily (see Getting There & Away earlier in this section).

Getting There & Away

Bus ABC Liner air-con buses leave daily at 6, 8, 10.30 am, noon, and at 2 and 5 pm from the ABC Liner bus terminal in Cebu City for

Bato. The buses also stop at the Southern bus terminal. The trip takes you along the east coast via Argao, Dalaguete, Mainit and Lilian to Bato, and there is a direct transfer to a boat heading to Tampi on Negros. Additional buses leaving at 7 am, 1 pm and 3.30 pm go along the west coast via Barili, Moalboal, Samboan and San Sebastian to Bato.

As departure times change frequently, it's a good idea to phone and check the times with the ABC Liner Company (☎ 254 0245).

LILOAN

Liloan is situated at the beautiful southernmost point of Cebu. The roads are lined with lush bougainvillaea bushes, and their vibrant colours make the area a joy for flower lovers.

There are several outrigger boats from Liloan to Sibulan on Negros daily for P15 per person and at least P200 for a Special Ride. If you don't want to go right through, you can spend the night at the Manureva Beach Resort. A 10 minute walk from Liloan pier, it is right on the white beach and is managed by Jean-Pierre Franck, who is French. Apart from jeepney trips into the surrounding country, he offers diving trips to Apo Island, Sumilon Island and Dako Island. A day trip to Sumilon Island costs P600 by boat.

Places to Stay

The *Manureva Beach Resort* has tastefully decorated rooms with fan and bath for P300/380 and with air-con and bath from P500 to P1000. They all have balconies with a view onto the ocean. If you want full board, it'll cost P1300 per person. The resort is a well-designed, large building with a restaurant which serves tasty local and French dishes. Diving and windsurfing are offered.

SUMILON ISLAND

Sumilon Island, off Cebu's south-eastern coast, is a favourite with divers and snorkellers. On the western side of this little island south of the sandbank the water is only two to five metres deep and 200m wide, which makes it ideal for snorkelling, while drop-off plunges into the darkness are only about 100m off the south-west coast.

The Marine Research Center no longer exists, and the former Sumilon Marine Park is being fished day and night. That could mean the end of the coral reef: fishing with dynamite is so easy. Perhaps tourism will help stop to this senseless destruction.

Places to Stay

The large cottages at the *Sumilon Island Resort* cost a hefty P2500 with bath and are a bit overpriced. Reservations can be made at the Sumilon Island Office in Oslob.

Getting There & Away

Boat For about P300 you can get from Mainit to Sumilon Island by small outrigger boat and be picked up again. You pay almost twice that for a round trip from Liloan or Santander, although the boats are sturdier.

MONTALONGON

Montalongon is a few km inland from Dalaguete, south of Argao at an altitude of about 700m. It is also called the 'Little Baguio of Cebu'. The **market** held here every Thursday has a remarkable range of vegetables. The extensive chrysanthemum fields a little outside Montalongon are beautiful.

Getting There & Away

Jeepney Several jeepneys go from Dalaguete Market to Montalongon daily, taking an hour or more. The last jeepney for Montalongon leaves Dalaguete at 3 pm, though there is a very wobbly bus at about 4 pm.

It's a pleasant 14 km walk from Montalongan down to Dalaguete, with good views and almost no sound of traffic.

ARGAO

Argao is a small provincial town on the southern coast of Cebu, which became known to tourists when the exclusive Argao Beach Club opened in the early 1980s, though it is now closed. Just along the coast is the **Dalaguete Public Beach**, which is free. Showers are available and the daily rent for sun shelters is P15, or P25 on Sundays and holidays. You can also eat cheaply here.

There is a daily car ferry between Argao

(leaving from five km north of town) and Loon on Bohol (see Getting There & Away at the beginning of this section).

Places to Stay

The friendly *Luisa's Place* will let you have a cottage with fan and bath for P300. Accommodation is pleasant, and the restaurant is good.

The rooms at the *Bamboo Paradise* are good value at P300/350 with fan and bath. There's a family atmosphere, and the restaurant is excellent. The owners, Carola, who is German, and Rey Rubia will organise trips round the island and boat trips on request.

A night at the *Sunshine Beach Club* will cost you P300/350 for a room with fan and bath; singles with air-con and bath cost from P700 up, and doubles with air-con and bath from P900. It's a functional kind of building, built into the sea and meant to represent a ship.

Places to Eat

You can eat well and cheaply at *Luisa's Place*. At *Carmen's Kitchen* the food is good and inexpensive. They'll be glad to cook any fish you've bought at the market. The *Bamboo Paradise* has outstanding German and Filipino cuisine.

Getting There & Away

Bus There are several ABC Liner buses daily from Cebu City going to Argao. They leave from the ABC Liner bus terminal bound for Bato. The buses also stop at the Southern bus terminal. The trip takes 1½ hours. The air-con buses are a bit faster, leaving at 6, 8 and 10.30 am, noon, 2 pm and 3.30 pm.

Guimaras

Until 1992 Guimaras was a sub-province of Iloilo Province but then became an independent province, with Jordan as the capital. Several smaller islands off the south and south-east coast of Guimaras also belong to the province, such as the islands Inampulugan

and Nagarao, which have both already been developed for tourism.

Situated as it is between Panay and Negros, the island makes a good day trip from Iloilo City. Loads of boats make the crossing over to Jordan every day. Only about five percent of the island's roads are surfaced, the rest are tracks, so this is ideal country for hikers and mountain bikers. The Iloilo Mountain Bike Association (IMBA) realised this too, and started the annual Guimaras International Mountain Bike Festival in February 1995.

Among the attractions is **Daliran Cave**, just outside Buenavista. The walk to get there is better than the cave itself. You can only go by tricycle between Jordan (pronounced Hordan) and Buenavista; this should cost about P50.

On **Bondulan Point**, about 40 minutes on foot from Jordan, there is a giant cross which attracts many pilgrims during Easter week. You will get a good view from here of Iloilo City and the Iloilo Strait. The re-enactment of the crucifixion of Christ, Ang Pagtaltal sa Guimaras, which takes place on Good Friday, is now a growing tourist attraction in Jordan.

At the Barrio San Miguel, between Jordan and Nueva Valencia, is a small **Trappist monastery**. The monks have been busy cultivating kalamansi, which has become an important source of income for Guimaras. The best beaches on the island are west of Nueva Valencia, where several resorts have already established themselves.

Tourists rarely visit the small village of Cabalagnan, in the south of the island. A couple of idyllic islands lie offshore.

GETTING THERE & AWAY

You can get to Guimaras from Negros and Panay (see the relevant Getting There & Away sections of this chapter).

Boat

Negros A small boat leaves Cabalagnan for Valladolid in the early morning around 3 to 4 am, stopping at several different islands en route. This boat will also pick up passengers on Nagarao Island. As there is no jetty in Valladolid the boat anchors a bit out to sea, and the passengers have to wade ashore.

Panay Several small ferries run daily from Jordan (P5; 30 minutes) and Buenavista (one hour) to Iloilo City almost every hour between 5 am and 5.30 pm.

Several small boats travel daily from Jordan to the Ortiz wharf, near the Iloilo City central market (15 minutes).

Most of the resorts on Guimaras offer a transfer service from Iloilo City, but it can cost as much as P1000.

GETTING AROUND

Jeepneys run between Jordan and Nueva Valencia, a few going as far as Cabalagnan. They return to Jordan only in the morning. You can go to Valladolid on Negros by boat daily. It leaves Cabalagnan at 3 or 4 am and stops at several islands. You can also board the boat on Nagarao Island.

Once a day at about noon, a jeepney runs from Jordan to San Isidro, where you will be able cross to Nagarao Island. The ride costs P10, but the asking price for a Special Ride is at least P250. There's a small signal post in San Isidro which you have to

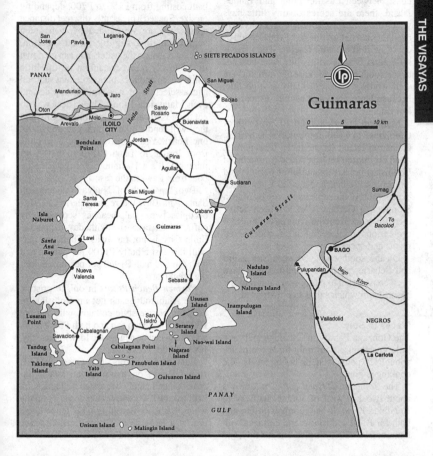

wave to get the boat to come across. The crossing costs P40.

Boat Trip around Guimaras

The best way to do this trip is by outrigger boat, which can take two to three days, depending on the number of stops. It is essential to take along drinking water and food, and make sure your boat is equipped with a roof for sun protection.

The trip could start in Iloilo City and continue around the island in an anti-clockwise direction. All along the south-west coast, between Lusaran Point and Tandug Island, there are scores of tiny little bays which are perfect for snorkelling. Plans have been mooted to turn this coral-rich section of coastline into a nature reserve. The various little coral islands with white sand beaches to the south and south-east of Guimaras are well worth a visit, especially at high tide, because large areas are usually exposed at low tide.

Malingin Island, a good 10 km south of Guimaras, is ideal for outdoor activities. Guiuanon Island (pronounced Giwanon) is good for hiking. Ususan Island (pronounced Usu-usan) houses a handful of hermits and has a passable beach. Nagarao Island has a beach resort of the same name, run by Martin Stummer, a German who has been active there for years in encouraging environmental protection and looking after endangered plants and species.

On the south coast, between San Isidro and Sebaste, primitive wind turbines have been constructed to pump sea water into flat basins from which salt is later extracted.

Places to Stay

The Gonzaga Family in Cabalagnan have a little guesthouse with only three rooms for about P150 per person, including meals. The cooking is good.

The *Colmenaras Hotel & Beach Resort* is about two km west of Jordan, halfway to Bondulan Point. It has rooms with fan and bath for P120 and rooms and cottages with bath for P100/200. It's pleasant and tidy, and

has a restaurant and disco in a building on stilts. There are three swimming pools which are, however, usually empty or blocked with algae. Windsurfing is available, although the beach is not suitable for bathing.

The *Isla Naburot Resort* on Isla Naburot has cottages for P2000 per person, including meals. This is a small, rustic establishment, without electricity. For further information, see the PAL office in Iloilo City.

Nestled into a little bay on the west coast of Guimaras, the *Baras Beach Resort* (cellular ☎ 0912-520 0820) comprises six comfortable, beautifully built cottages with bath costing from P450 to P700, depending on size. Spaced a pleasantly discreet distance apart, they are surrounded by lush green vegetation in a slightly raised location, looking down on the water. You can go down to the lovely resort restaurant on the little white beach and tuck in to excellent seafood and a selection of western, Philippine and even Malaysian dishes. The easiest way to get there is to call them from Iloilo City and they will send a boat to pick you up (P600; one hour). You could also hire a jeepney from Jordan to Lawi (P150 to P200; 45 minutes). It's a 10 minute Special Ride by boat from Lawi to the resort.

Two km north of Nueva Valencia, on Santa Ana Bay, the resort *Puerto del Mar* occupies two small beaches separated by cliffs. It's a favourite with day trippers – Iloilo City is not far away. Their cottages with fan cost a hefty P1100 per person and with fan and bath P1900 per person, including breakfast.

Raymen Beach Resort in on the pristine white Alubihod Beach not far from Puerto del Mar. Native-style cottages with fan are P300/500 and with fan and bath P500/1000, a discount can be negotiated for a longer stay. It's quiet on weekdays.

East of Guimaras, the *Costa Aguada Island Resort* on Inampulugan Island has spacious and nicely decorated cottages with bath from P1300/1400. This property on the white Bamboo Beach is well tended and covers a large area. There is an attractive restaurant, a pool and tennis courts. There are outrigger sailboats for rent, and horseback riding is also available.

The *Nagarao Island Resort* (☎ 0912-5200343) on Nagarao Island has pleasant, spacious cottages with bath for P1250/2500, including meals. The resort has a restaurant and a swimming pool, and offers windsurfing and boat trips. For further information, ask at the Nagarao Island Office (☎ 320 6290; fax 329 2139) at 113 Seminario St, Jaro, in Iloilo City.

Leyte

Leyte is in the eastern part of the Visayas and lies between Bohol, Cebu, north-east Mindanao and Samar. The San Juanico Bridge, over two km long, joins the islands of Leyte and Samar across the San Juanico Strait, is one of the most beautiful bridges in southeast Asia. Central and southern Leyte are mountainous, with plains in the northern and western parts of the island. Administratively, it's divided into the province of Leyte, where the capital is Tacloban, and Southern Leyte, with its capital Maasin.

Copra is Leyte's most important export. More than 30% of cultivable land is planted with coconut palms. Other important exports are rice, maize and sugar cane. These are mostly shipped from Tacloban, making it unnecessary to send exports via Manila.

Leyte is particularly remembered as the place where General MacArthur fulfilled his 'I shall return' pledge. On 20 October 1944, US troops landed at Red Beach in Palo, a little south of Tacloban, and started pushing the Japanese out of the Philippines. A little further south, Tolosa is a town also sure of a future place in history, as the birthplace of the former First Lady, Imelda Marcos. Another place of historical significance here is the little island of Limasawa in the deep south of Leyte. The famous explorer Ferdinand Magellan landed there after a long voyage of discovery and celebrated his first holy mass on Philippine soil on Easter Sunday, 1521.

The main dialect in and around Tacloban is Waray-Waray, whereas in the north-west and the south it is Cebuano. You can get by quite well with English.

GETTING THERE & AWAY

To reach Leyte you can go from Biliran, Bohol, Cebu, Luzon, Mindanao and Samar (see the Getting There & Away section of the Manila chapter and the relevant Getting There & Away sections of this and the Mindanao & Sulu chapter).

Air

Cebu PAL flies from Tacloban to Cebu City on Monday, Wednesday and Saturday.

Luzon Cebu Pacific, Grand Air and PAL fly daily from Tacloban to Manila.

The Filipino coconut palm (*niyog*) yields much of the world's copra, a raw material used in the making of magarine and vegetable shortening.

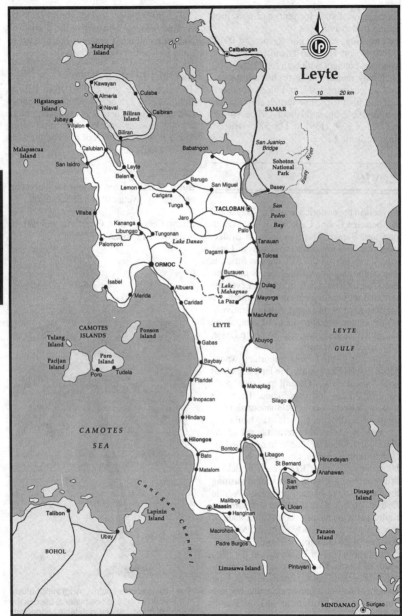

Leyte

Bus

Biliran There are about 10 buses a day leaving Tacloban for Naval (P50; three hours). Last departure is 3 pm. Some of the buses may carry on as far as Almeria, Kawayan, Tucdao or Culaba. You can also take a bus heading for Ormoc and change in Lemon to a bus for Naval.

A bus leaves Tacloban to Caibiran (P50; five hours) every day between 9 and 11 am from the bus terminal.

Buses leave from the bus terminal at the wharf in Ormoc daily at 3 and 4 am for Caibiran (three hours). You may have to change in Lemon.

JD Company buses go from Ormoc to Naval every day, leaving at 4.30 and 5.30 am, and possibly noon (P45; three hours).

Luzon Philtranco Company air-con buses leave from the Philtranco bus terminal in Tacloban daily for Manila at 5.30 am and 4 pm. Travel time is 28 hours (P490), including the ferry from San Isidro to Matnog. It is advisable to reserve a seat. Cedec Transport and Liberty Transport buses also make the trip daily from the bus terminal.

Samar Air-con Philtranco buses leave Tacloban for Manila daily at 5.30 am and 4 pm, going through Catbalogan and Calbayog. Travel time to Catbalogan is three hours and four hours to Calbayog. It's best to book. There are also Cedec Transport and Liberty Transport buses from the bus terminal.

Boat

Bohol From Bato to Ubay, a big outrigger boat leaves daily at 10 am (P50; three hours). The MV *Star Ruby 1* leaves daily at 1 pm (P100; 1¼ hour). From Maasin to Ubay, a big outrigger boat leaves daily between 8 and 10 am (P50; four hours).

Cebu There are numerous ships to Cebu City, leaving from various towns in Leyte.

From Baybay, Cokaliong Shipping Lines' MV *Filipinas Siargao* sails at midnight (six hours). The MV *Gregoria May* of Western

Samar Shipping crosses on Tuesday, Thursday and Saturday (five hours).

From Liloan, the MV *Guiuan* of K & T Shipping Lines leaves on Thursday and Sunday at 6 pm (six hours).

From Maasin, the MV *Supercat* of Universal Aboitiz leaves daily at 11.30 am and 4 pm (P200; two hours); Water Jet Shipping's *Water Jet 2* sails on Tuesday, Thursday, Saturday and Sunday at 2.15 pm; Cokaliong Shipping Lines' MV *Filipinas Surigao* leaves on Tuesday at 10 am, Thursday at 2 am and Saturday at 1 am (six hours); their MV *Filipinas Dapitan* leaves Wednesday at 2 am and Sunday at 10 pm (5½ hours). Trans-Asia Shipping Lines' MV *Asia-Singapore* leaves on Friday at midnight (five hours); and the MV *Asia-Taiwan* leaves on Sunday at midnight (six hours).

From Ormoc, there are several fast boats daily (P200; two hours). The MV *Supercat* of Universal Aboitiz leaves at 6, 8.30 and 11 am and 1.45, 4.30 and 6.45 pm; the MV *Bullet Xpress* of Bullet Express Corporation leaves at 7.30 am; Socor Shipping Lines' MV *Oceanjet* leaves at 3.30 pm; Water Jet Shipping's Water Jet 1 sails at 8 am and their Water Jet 2 sails Tuesday, Thursday, Saturday and Sunday at 7.15 pm.

The trip with regular ships from Ormoc to Cebu City takes six hours: The MV *Lady of Rule* of Cebu Ferries leaves on Monday at midnight; their MV *Iligan City* leaves on Wednesday and Saturday at midnight; the MV *Doña Lili* sails Thursday and Friday at midnight; and the MV *Lady of Carmel* leaves on Sunday at midnight. Sulpicio Lines' MV *Cebu Princess* leaves Sunday at 11 pm.

From Palompon, the MV *Lady of Rule* of Cebu Ferries leaves on Monday at 7 am (10 hours, via Ormoc); their MV *Doña Lili* leaves on Saturday at midnight (five hours); and the MV *Don Calvino* leaves on Sunday 11 pm (six hours).

From Tacloban, Cebu Ferries' MV *Don Calvino* sails Tuesday and Thursday at 4 pm (13 hours). The MV *Doña Lili* goes Wednesday at 4 pm (13 hours). K & T Shipping Lines' MV *Leyte Queen* sails Wednesday, Friday and Sunday at 5 pm.

If you're not heading for Cebu City, the MV *Meltrivic 3* of Aznar Shipping Corporation leaves Isabel daily at 10 am for Danao (three hours). There is also a big outrigger boat that leaves Isabel daily at 4 pm for Carmen (four hours). Another big outrigger boat leaves Ormoc daily at 1 pm for Bukog on Camotes Islands (three hours). And finally, a big outrigger boat leaves San Isidro for Maya in northern Cebu daily at 8 am (two hours). For an additional payment of P200 the boat will make a stop at Bounty Beach on Malapascua Island. After the arrival of the boat in Maya a bus leaves for Cebu City.

Luzon From Calubian to Manila, the Sulpicio Lines' MV *Palawan Princess* leaves on Sunday at midnight (34 hours, via Masbate). It leaves Maasin on Sunday at 6 am and Baybay at noon.

From Ormoc to Manila, WG & A's MV *Sacred Heart* sails Wednesday at 5.30 pm (P470; 47 hours, via Palompon and Masbate).

From Palompon to Manila, the MV *Sacred Heart* of WG & A leaves on Thursday at 7.30 am (P435; 33 hours, via Masbate).

From Tacloban to Manila, the Sulpicio Lines' MV *Tacloban Princess* leaves on Monday at 4 pm (24 hours) and on Friday at 5 am (35 hours, via Catbalogan on Samar). The MV *Masbate Uno* of WG & A leaves on Wednesday at noon (29 hours, via Catbalogan on Samar) and on Saturday at 4 pm (P470; 24 hours).

Masbate From Calubian to Masbate, the Sulpicio Lines' MV *Palawan Princess* leaves on Sunday at midnight (six hours). It leaves Maasin on Sunday at 6 am and Baybay at noon.

From Ormoc to Masbate, the Sulpicio Lines' MV *Cebu Princess* leaves on Tuesday at 10 am (24 hours). The MV *Sacred Heart* of WG & A leaves on Wednesday at 5.30 pm (P200; 23 hours, via Palompon).

From Palompon to Masbate, the MV *Sacred Heart* of WG & A leaves on Thursday at 7.30 am (P160; 13 hours).

Mindanao From Liloan to Lipata, 10 km

north-west of Surigao, the MV *Maharlika II* (car ferry) of Bernard Services leaves daily at 8 am (three hours).

From Maasin to Surigao, Water Jet Shipping's *Water Jet 2* sails Tuesday, Thursday, Saturday and Sunday at 10.45 (P210; 1-2 hours); Cokaliong Shipping Lines' MV *Filipinas Surigao* leaves on Wednesday at 6 am and Friday at 3 am (four hours). Trans-Asia Shipping Lines' MV *Asia Singapore* leaves on Friday at 5 am (four hours); their MV *Asia-Taiwan* leaves on Saturday at 3 am (four hours). Sulpicio Lines' MV *Palawan Princess* sails Friday at 9 pm (four hours). It leaves Calubian at 7 am and Baybay at 4 pm.

Samar From Tacloban to Catbalogan, the MV *Masbate Uno* of WG & A leaves on Wednesday at noon (P80; four hours). The Sulpicio Lines' MV *Tacloban Princess* leaves on Friday at 5 am (four hours).

From Tacloban to Guiuan in southern Samar, the MV *Stacey* of K & T Shipping Lines leaves every other day at 11 pm (six hours).

TACLOBAN

The capital of Leyte is a port town with about 140,000 inhabitants. It has an excellent harbour with facilities for handling large ships and overseas trade. The colourful market at the western end of the wharf is full of life.

A large relief on the wall of the Provincial Capitol Building depicts MacArthur's return to the Philippines. This historic event is celebrated each year on 19 and 20 October with cockfights and parades.

The museum in Tacloban's Divine Word University has rare and priceless artefacts from Leyte and Samar, which date from the early trade with China, and from the Sohoton Cave diggings. The museum opens at 1.30 pm. Another good museum is the colonial-style , that also gives an impression of the state of luxury the Marcos clan lived in. A guided tour for up to five persons costs P200. If you are on your own, there are usually other people to join in with. Tours start every hour from 8 to 11 am and 1 to 4 pm. Next door is

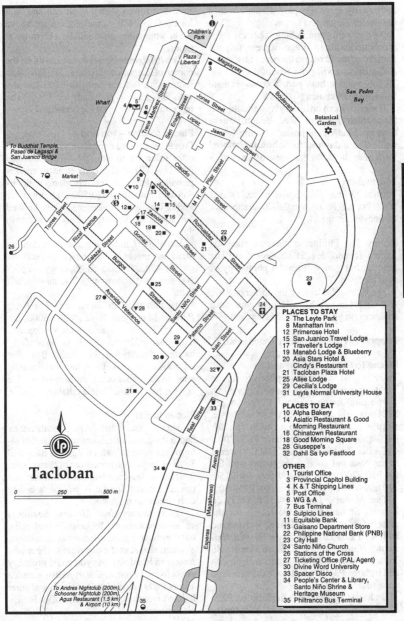

THE VISAYAS

Tacloban

0 ___ 250 ___ 500 m

PLACES TO STAY
2 The Leyte Park
8 Manhattan Inn
12 Primerose Hotel
15 San Juanico Travel Lodge
17 Traveller's Lodge
19 Manabó Lodge & Blueberry
20 Asia Stars Hotel &
     Cindy's Restaurant
21 Tacloban Plaza Hotel
25 Allee Lodge
29 Cecilia's Lodge
31 Leyte Normal University House

PLACES TO EAT
10 Alpha Bakery
14 Asiatic Restaurant & Good
     Morning Restaurant
16 Chinatown Restaurant
18 Good Morning Square
28 Giuseppe's
32 Dahil Sa Iyo Fastfood

OTHER
1 Tourist Office
3 Provincial Capitol Building
4 K & T Shipping Lines
5 Post Office
6 WG & A
7 Bus Terminal
9 Sulpicio Lines
11 Equitable Bank
13 Gaisano Department Store
22 Philippine National Bank (PNB)
23 City Hall
24 Santo Niño Church
26 Stations of the Cross
27 Ticketing Office (PAL Agent)
30 Divine Word University
33 Spacer Disco
34 People's Center & Library,
     Santo Niño Shrine &
     Heritage Museum
35 Philtranco Bus Terminal

the equally large People's Center, with a library for Samar and Leyte.

As a reward for climbing the many steps (decorated with 14 statues representing the Stations of the Cross) to the base of the statue of Christ, you will get a beautiful view over Tacloban and its busy port. You can get there from the market along Torres St.

If you are keen on history, you should visit **MacArthur Park** on Red Beach, where General MacArthur landed. Nature lovers will enjoy a day trip to **Sohoton National Park** near Basey on the island of Samar.

Information
Tourist Office The tourist office (☎ 321 2048; fax 325 5807) is in the Children's Park on Senator Enage St.

Money The Philippine National Bank on Justice Romualdez St changes travellers cheques but you will need a photocopy of your passport.

The Equitable Bank on the corner of Rizal Ave and Gomez St will give you cash advances on your Visa and MasterCard.

Telephone The area code for Tacloban is 053.

Places to Stay – bottom end
There is a wide variety of places to stay in Tacloban, particularly of the budget variety.

The *San Juanico Travel Lodge* (☎ 321 3221) at 104 Justice Romualdez St is a simple place with rooms with fan for P100/150, with fan and bath for P150/200.

Cecilia's Lodge (☎ 321 2815) at 178 Paterno St has basic but good value rooms with fan for P100/200, with fan and bath for P150/230 and with air-con and bath for P250/300.

The *Manabó Lodge* (☎ 321 3727) on Zamora St has reasonable rooms for the price: with fan for P150/230 and with fan and bath for P220/320. The *Leyte Normal University House* (☎ 321 3175) on Paterno St, has spacious, good value rooms with air-con and bath for P310/465. It has a cafeteria and a tea-room.

On Justice Romualdez St, the *Tacloban Plaza Hotel* (☎ 321 2444) has clean, pleasantly furnished rooms with TV, air-con and bath for P300 to P470. Some of them are above the bowling alley and could be a bit noisy at times.

The *Primerose Hotel* (☎ 321 2248), on the corner of Zamora and Salazar Sts, has clean rooms with fan and bath for P200/250 and with TV, air-con and bath for P500. The restaurant is only open for breakfast.

Places to Stay – top end
Proving that more expensive places can still offer value for money, the *Manhattan Inn* (☎ 321 4170) on Rizal Ave near the market provides clean, comfortable rooms with air-con and bath for P420/500 and suites for P600. This well-run hotel is often booked out, so it is advisable to make reservations in advance.

Just above Cindy's Restaurant in Zamora St, a fairly recent arrival, the *Asia Stars Hotel* (☎ 321 4942; fax 325 5889), charges P600/900 for good rooms with TV, air-con and bath.

The best hotel in Tacloban is *The Leyte Park* on Magsaysay Blvd (☎ 325 6000; fax 325 5587) where rooms with air-con and bath cost P2200/2600. It is beautifully located, directly on San Pedro Bay. For relaxation and exercise it has a swimming pool and a tennis court. An airport service and car hire facilities are available.

Places to Eat
Adequate Chinese and Filipino meals can be had at the *Asiatic Restaurant* and the *China-town Restaurant*, both on Zamora St. *Dahil Sa Iyo Fastfood* on the corner of Burgos and Real Sts is clean and popular, but closes at 8 pm. The house special is pakdol, a hearty dish similar to meat stew.

The restaurant *Good Morning Square* is an air-conditioned McDonald's look-alike but they have a good selection of breakfasts. You can also start the day right at the *Alpha Bakery* in Rizal Ave. As you could probably guess from the name, *Giuseppe's* in Avenida Veteranos is a cosy place for pizzas and other Italian favourites, but they also offer Philippine cuisine.

The best place to go for seafood is undoubtedly the *Agus Restaurant*, a bit outside of town on the south side, and directly on San Pedro Bay. They are open 24 hours and well worth the visit, especially if you are in a small group. Look forward to enjoying excellent, inexpensive food here with a view onto the ocean.

If you suddenly get the urge for a scrumptious bowl of ice-cream, then head for *Blueberry* in Zamora St.

Entertainment
The nightlife is fairly limited here. Two of the best places to dance are the *Volare Disco* at The Leyte Park hotel and the *Spacer Disco* on Real St. Late shows are on offer at the night-clubs *Schooner*, *Andres* and *Corkeez*, all nearly two km further south on Real St.

Getting There and Away
Air PAL has an office at Romualdez airport (☎ 321 2212) on Romualdez St.

Bus Philtranco air-con buses are often booked out when heading for Manila, so try to book a seat at least one day before leaving. Philtranco has its own terminal in the south of the city. All other buses leave from the bus terminal at the market.

The ride to a hotel in the city with a tricycle should cost P5.

Getting Around
The Airport It is 11 km from Romualdez airport to the centre of town. The trip should not cost more than P20 per person by jeepney; going back, the trip should cost a little less.

AROUND TACLOBAN
Sohoton National Park & Basey
Although Sohoton National Park (also known as Sohoton Natural Bridge National Park) is on the island of Samar, the simplest way to get there is from Tacloban via Basey. It has waterfalls, underground waterways and a labyrinth of **caves**, which are also called 'wonder caves' because of their glittering stone formations. The biggest and

most beautiful are Panhulugan I, Bugasan III and Sohoton. A park ranger lives at the entrance to the park and will, on request, guide you through the caves with a kerosene lamp. You can stay overnight with the ranger, but you have to take your own provisions. The best time to see the caves is from March to July, as you can only visit them when the water level is low, and not after prolonged rainfall.

Basey is well known for its colourful mats and other woven goods, which are sold in the markets in Tacloban.

Staff at the tourist office in Tacloban should be able to help you arrange trips to Sohoton National Park.

Getting There & Away The first jeepney leaves Tacloban for Basey at about 7 am, the second not till 9.30 am, each taking over an hour. A day trip from Basey to the Sohoton National Park is only worthwhile if you arrive early in Basey, as the last jeepney leaves for Tacloban at about 3 pm and then only if there are enough passengers. Failing that, a Special Ride with a tricycle from Basey to Tacloban costs about P60, even in the late afternoon.

Boats leave the market in Tacloban for Basey in the morning (P5; 30 minutes).

You can obtain the necessary permit from Francisco Corales or Arnulito Viojan in Basey, who will also arrange a boat. The permit, which has to be shown at the entrance to the national park, costs P2.50, the rental charge for a kerosene lamp P50, and a guide and boat P500. The guide also expects a small tip.

The beautiful trip upriver to the park takes about 1½ hours.

Palo
A monument (Leyte Landing Memorial) and a plaque on Red Beach at Palo commemorate the return of General MacArthur to the Philippines on 20 October 1944 after a major naval battle. He liberated the country from Japanese occupation roughly 2½ years after fleeing from the island fortress of Corregidor in Manila Bay.

Palo Cathedral, built in 1596 with an altar covered in gold leaf, was temporarily converted to a hospital by the Americans during the early days of the liberation of the Philippines.

On the outskirts of Palo, Guinhangdan Hill looks down on the town. Also known as **Hill 522** (because it is 522 feet above sea level), this was the scene of bitter fighting in 1944 when many American and Japanese soldiers lost their lives. A huge wooden cross now graces the top of the hill, with a path leading up to it. From up there you can get a good view of the historic area and of Palo Cathedral.

Places to Stay The *City Lodge Pension* has rooms with air-con and bath for P350. It's fairly comfortable, relatively clean, and you can rent rooms by the hour.

The *MacArthur Park Beach Resort* (☎ 323 3015), about 300m south of the Leyte Landing Memorial, has rooms with air-con and bath for P1400/1600 and suites for P2600. The rooms are comfortable and tastefully furnished. They have a swimming pool.

Getting There & Away Several jeepneys leave the bus terminal for Palo daily, but not all make the detour to MacArthur Park about 1½ km from the main road.

SAN ISIDRO
San Isidro is a small community in the northwest of Leyte, with boat connections to northern Cebu. You can also go to the small island of Malapascua from San Isidro (see Cebu under Getting There & Away at the beginning of this section).

There are only two small, basic places to stay at in San Isidro.

Getting There & Away
Bus Buses go from Tacloban to San Isidro via Calubian four times a day, leaving at 6, 7 and 10 am, noon and 3 pm (3½ hours including a short stopover in Calubian). A Special Ride by motorcycle from Calubian to San Isidro costs P100.

One bus and some jeepneys leave Ormoc

in the early morning for San Isidro, taking 4½ hours.

PALOMPON
Palompon is a coastal town north-west of Ormoc and three hours away by jeepney. Ships go from Palompon to Cebu and Panay. If you follow the road from Palompon northwards along the coast, you will reach Jubay (pronounced 'hu-bye'), where you can get a boat to small Higatangan Island, which is off the usual routes and belongs to Biliran Province.

Places to Stay
The *Russell Lodging House* on Rizal St, not far from the pier, has rooms with fan for P85/110 and with air-con and bath for P250/350. This place is simple and fairly tidy.

Getting There & Away
Jeepney There are several jeepneys from Ormoc to Palompon daily, taking 2½ hours.

ORMOC
This port town is connected to Cebu by ship. The wharf area is always lively, especially in the late afternoons and evenings, when a lot of people meet for a yarn on the wall of the wharf.

On 5 November 1991 Ormoc experienced the blackest day in its history, when the typhoon Uring stormed over Leyte, leaving in its wake massive quantities of water raging down into the town from the mountains, taking everything with it that couldn't get out of its way. Over 5000 people died from injuries or drowned, while almost 50,000 were made homeless. There is no doubt these floods were made possible by the activities of illegal logging operators who for many years got away scot-free with denuding the slopes, leaving them stony and barren as a result. There is a memorial to the tragedy in the cemetery at Ormoc.

South-west of Ormoc are the Camotes Islands, which belong to Cebu Province and can be reached by outrigger boat in about three hours.

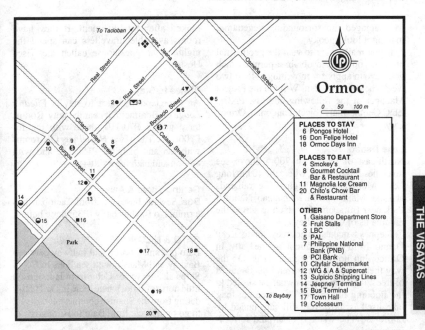

Ormoc

0   50   100 m

PLACES TO STAY
6 Pongos Hotel
16 Don Felipe Hotel
18 Ormoc Days Inn

PLACES TO EAT
4 Smokey's
8 Gourmet Cocktail
   Bar & Restaurant
11 Magnolia Ice Cream
20 Chito's Chow Bar
   & Restaurant

OTHER
1 Gaisano Department Store
2 Fruit Stalls
3 LBC
5 PAL
7 Philippine National
   Bank (PNB)
9 PCI Bank
10 Cityfair Supermarket
12 WG & A & Supercat
13 Sulpicio Shipping Lines
14 Jeepney Terminal
15 Bus Terminal
17 Town Hall
19 Colosseum

THE VISAYAS

Telephone
The area code for Ormoc is 05351.

Places to Stay
The *Pongos Hotel* (☎ 2482, 2211) on Bonifacio St charges P200/310 for basic but adequate rooms with fan and bath, and P385/550 for rooms with air-con and bath. They also run *Pongos Lodging House*, which has basic, clean rooms with fan at P100.

Until now, the best hotel in Ormoc has been the *Don Felipe Hotel* (☎ 64661; fax 64306) on Bonifacio St, near the jetty. It has clean, good value rooms with fan and bath for P190/290 and with air-con and bath for P800/910.

But from mid-1997, the *Days Inn Hotel* on Ciriaco Ariles St should have won the title. Rooms are P2000; suites with jacuzzi P2700.

Places to Eat
Chito's Chow Bar & Restaurant on the harbour promenade offers fine dishes. The *Bahia Coffee Shop* in the Hotel Don Felipe and the *Filipino*

Fastfood Restaurant in the Gaisano department store on Lopez Jaena St are both recommended. The *Gourmet Cocktail Bar & Restaurant* on Ciriaco Ariles St does good seafood.

Getting There & Away
Bus Buses for Ormoc (P40; 2½ hours) leave Tacloban bus terminal daily from 4 am until the early afternoon, roughly every hour.

After the arrival of the boat from Maya on Cebu, a bus leaves San Isidro around noon for Ormoc (4½ hours). The first bus leaves Ormoc for Tacloban from the jetty at 5.30 am.

AROUND ORMOC
Tongonan
In Tongonan, a little north of Ormoc, a hot spring has been developed to provide geothermal energy and is well on the way to making Leyte much less dependent on energy imports. The steam from the spring

has damaged the surrounding vegetation, making it look spooky.

If you really want to visit the geothermal project, you need to obtain a permit which you have to apply for in writing at least two weeks before your visit. Write to the Project Manager at the following address: PNOC EDC Geothermal Project, Tongonan, Ormoc City.

Lake Danao

North-east of Ormoc at 700m above sea level, lies Lake Danao, where the 40 km long Leyte Mountain Trail begins. The trail ends at Lake Mahagnao in Mahagnao National Park near Burauen, after snaking across the mountains of Central Leyte.

Jeepneys make the journey up to Lake Danao from the terminal at the jetty in Ormoc, but not on a regular basis. On the way there through the barren hills denuded of trees, it becomes plain what causes led to the flooding of Ormoc. The three km long lake itself is, however, still surrounded by rainforest. The water is clean and refreshingly cool.

If you want to want to hike the Leyte Mountain Trail from the east coast of Leyte to Lake Danao, first take the bus from Tacloban south to Burauen via Tanauan and Dagami. You can then have yourself driven by motorcycle (P100) from Burauen to the entrance to Mahagnao Volcano Mountain Park, where the hike finally begins. It's about 1½ km to Lake Mahagnao.

The last bus from Burauen to Tacloban leaves about 3 pm.

BAYBAY

Baybay is a little harbour town on the central west coast of Leyte, where ships leave for Cebu and other islands. With mountains in the background and an old Spanish church dominating the town, it makes a most attractive picture seen at dawn from a ship just arriving in port.

About seven km north of Baybay is the modern Visayan State College of Agriculture (VISCA) which was financed by the World Bank. This is a surprisingly spruce, well-looked after establishment. If they have rooms available, travellers can spend the night in the guesthouse called the Visca Hostel.

Places to Stay

An unpretentious place to stay is *Ellean's Lodge* on Bonifacio St near the jetty. Rooms there go for P70/110, those with fan for P100/150. The *Visca Hostel* has OK rooms with fan and bath for P150/250 and with air-con and bath for P400/450.

Getting There & Away

Bus Several buses go from Tacloban bus terminal to Baybay daily (P35; three hours).

BATO & HILONGOS

Bato is a small port about halfway between Baybay and Maasin with sea links to Cebu. Ships also leave for Cebu from Hilongos, a little north of Bato, where there is a tall belfry dating from the Spanish conquest. It costs P2 to go by tricycle from Bato to Hilongos.

Places to Stay

The *Green House Lodging* on Rizal St in Bato is a simple place with rooms with fan for P50/100.

Getting There & Away

Bus Several buses go from Tacloban bus terminal to Bato daily (P48; four hours).

From Ormoc to Bato (three hours), the first bus leaves at 6 am. There are several buses daily.

MAASIN

Maasin is on the south-west coast of Leyte and is the capital of Southern Leyte Province. If you're feeling active, hikes can be taken from here into the mountainous hinterland.

The more religious traveller can also take part in the Friday morning pilgrimage by the faithful up to the Shrine of St Francis Javiar in Hanginan.

There are connections by ship from Maasin to Bohol, Cebu and Mindanao.

Places to Stay

There's a family atmosphere at the *Verano Pension House* on Kangleon St in Matahan (☎ 381 2253) about 10 minutes by tricycle from Maasin. Their tidy, pleasantly furnished rooms with fan cost P60/120, with air-con and bath P250. They will prepare breakfast on request.

Not far from the Provincial Capitol in Mambajao, the *Maasin Country Lodge* will give you an adequate room with fan and bath for P200, with air-con and bath for P350.

Places to Eat

The *Valtenian Restaurant* and the *Avenue Restaurant* both have good Filipino food, the former with live music in the evenings.

Getting There & Away

Bus Several buses leave Tacloban for Maasin daily (P55; five hours). The last bus leaves Maasin for Tacloban around 1 pm.

LILOAN

Liloan is at the northern tip of Panaon Island in the south of Leyte. The waters there are good for diving and snorkelling. A ferry service operates between Liloan and Lipata, 10 km north-west of Surigao in north-east Mindanao.

Places to Stay

The *Liloan Hillside Lodge* behind the ferry terminal has rooms with fan for P75/150. Don't expect luxury here, and it can get loud.

Places to Eat

The *Annie & Boys Carenderia* on Quezon St offers tasty, cheap food.

Getting There & Away

Bus There are several buses daily from Tacloban to Liloan (P50; five hours). The buses may terminate in Sogod, however, or carry on from there to Maasin. In that case, you can carry on by jeepney from Sogod to Liloan. Several buses travel from Maasin to Liloan between 4 and 7.30 am ($3\frac{1}{2}$ hours).

LIMASAWA ISLAND

About 20 km west of Panaon Island you will find the fairly remote island of Limasawa. Ferdinand Magellan landed here at the end of March 1521 after setting foot for the first time on the Philippines two weeks earlier on the island of Homonhon, to the east of Leyte. A huge cross dominates Limasawa in memory of this event. Every year on 31 March the islanders also commemorate the event by getting dressed up and celebrating mass on the beach at Triana in a riot of colour.

The inhabitants of Butuan on the north coast of Mindanao are not at all pleased at the goings on north of them. The way they see it, the conquering hero did not land at Limasawa, but right round the corner at Masao, on the Agusan river estuary. They simply reject the claim made by later historians that Pigafetta (Magellan's chronicler) was referring to a place on Limasawa when he mentioned the landing at 'Mazauna'.

Places to Stay

In honour of the 475th anniversary of Magellan's landing, a small guesthouse was erected on Limasawa. Visitors may stay there if they don't want to use private accommodation.

Getting There & Away

Boat An outrigger boat leaves Padre Burgos every day at noon for Limasawa (P10; one hour).

Departure from Limasawa to Padre Burgos is at 6.30 am.

Negros

Sandwiched between Cebu and Panay in the south-west of the Visayas, Negros consists of the provinces of Negros Occidental and Negros Oriental, which are separated by mountain chains in the centre of the island. The south takes its character from the Tablas Plateau. There are wide plains west of an imaginary line from Ilog to Cadiz.

Negros is the sugar island of the Philippines, producing about 60% of the country's

THE VISAYAS

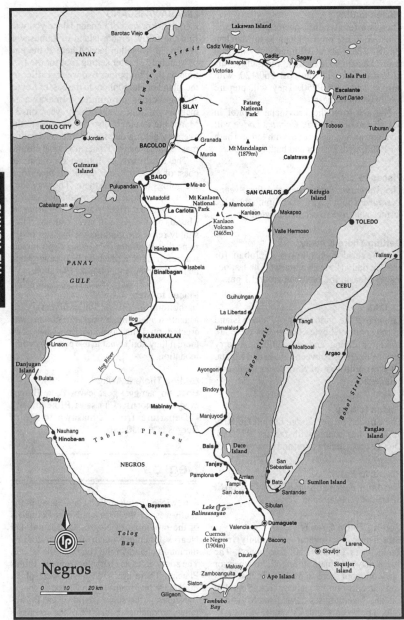

Negros

0   10   20 km

total sugar production. Around 450,000 hectares, or more than half of the total land area, is used for the production of sugar. There are big sugarcane plantations and refineries in Victorias and Binalbagan.

Sugar exportation began in the middle of the 19th century, when the production from the first plantations was shipped to Japan, China, Australia, the UK, Canada and the USA. From then on it brought great wealth and political power to the few sugar barons living on their haciendas. At least during the years of the sugar boom the seasonally employed field workers were able to earn just enough to support their families. This irresponsible system of exploitation and social indifference existed until 1985, when the world market price of sugar fell so drastically that it wasn't even worth cutting the cane.

Sugarcane (*tubo*), thought to have originated in what is now Papua New Guinea, has produced a bittersweet harvest for the field workers of the Philippines.

Negros, with its single product economy, was economically at rock bottom. About a quarter of a million Sacada (the name of the plantation workers) were out of work. Because of the absence of any government relief programme and the unwillingness of most *hacienderos* to make some land available for grain planting by their needy workers, many desperate Negrenses took to the mountains to join the antigovernment NPA in its underground fighting.

If government figures are to be believed, conditions on Negros have improved with rising sugar prices in the last few years. Widespread prawn cultivation (Black Tiger Prawn, *Penaeus monodon)* and the manufacture of rattan furniture, both strongly export oriented, have also aided economic improvement.

'Sugarland', of course, also aims to develop tourism, but leisure facilities like those of the Mambucal Summer Resort in the central part of the island are still too rarely visited to talk about a boom yet. Kanlaon Volcano may, it is hoped, become an attraction similar to the famous Mayon Volcano in South Luzon. The east and south-east coasts offer Spanish-style charm – perhaps a reason why foreign tourists often spend a few days in the pleasant little town of Dumaguete. Pretty good beaches can be found around Hinoba-an in the south-west of the island; this is also where you will come across inveterate adventurers seeking their pot of gold by panning for it in the mountains.

Among the main attractions of Negros are the old steam locomotives, some of which were still being used until recently to bring home the sugar cane, side by side with modern diesel locomotives. During the milling season between October and April, you may still be able to hitch a ride for a few km on one of these working museum pieces. There are only a few steam locomotives left today, but you can see them near the sugar mills. The best of these old-timers belong to the Hawaiian-Philippine Sugar Co in Silay, Vicmico in Victorias, Central Azucarera de la Carlota in La Carlota, and the Ma-ao Sugar Central in Bago. Also worth seeing are those belonging to Biscom in Binalbagan, Sagay

Sugar Central and Lopez Sugar Central in Toboso, and San Carlos Milling Co in San Carlos. Colin Carraf describes them all in his book *Iron Dinosaurs*.

The aborigines of Negros are called the Negrito, hence the name of the island. Some tribes of this cultural minority still live in the mountain regions. The main dialect in Negros Occidental is Ilongo, whereas Cebuano is spoken in Negros Oriental.

GETTING THERE & AWAY

You can get to Negros from Cebu, Guimaras, Luzon, Mindanao, Panay and Siquijor (see Getting There & Away in the Manila chapter and the relevant Getting There & Away sections of this and the Mindanao & Sulu and Palawan chapters).

Air

Cebu PAL flies daily from Bacolod to Cebu City and on Monday, Tuesday, Wednesday, Friday and Saturday from Dumaguete to Cebu City.

Luzon Cebu Pacific flies daily from Bacolod to Manila. PAL flies daily to Manila from Bacolod and Dumaguete.

Siquijor Pacific Airways flies fairly regularly to Siquijor from Dumaguete on Monday and Thursday (P250; 15 minutes).

Bus

Cebu Ceres Liner buses leave Bacolod daily at 6.30, 7.30 (air-con), 7.45 (air-con), 8, 9, 9.30 (air-con) and 10 am for the ferry from Escalante (Port Danao) to Carmelo/Tuburan and on to Cebu City. The trip, including the ferry, takes eight hours (P80/110).

Boat

Cebu From Cadiz on the north coast of Negros to Bantayan town on Bantayan Island in northern Cebu, a big outrigger boat leaves daily between 10 am and noon (P65; 3½ hours). The river port in Cadiz is several km long, so it's best to take a tricycle from the bus terminal to the wharf.

From Dumaguete to Cebu City, the MV *Supercat* of Universal Aboitiz leaves daily at 8.30 am and 5.45 pm (P200; 2¼ hours). The Cokaliong Shipping Lines' MV *Filipinas Dinagat* leaves on Tuesday, Thursday, Saturday and Sunday at midnight (P100; six hours).

The MV *Dumaguete Ferry*, the MV *Georich* or the MV *Palauan Ferry* of George & Peter Lines leaves Dumaguete for Cebu City daily at 10 pm (eight hours).

From Tampi to Bato, a ferry runs several times a day. The last departure is at about 3.30 pm (45 minutes). The boat from San Jose may also go to Talisay. Jeepneys and minibuses run from Real St, on the corner of Locsin St, in Dumaguete, to the wharf. ABC Liner air-con buses meet boats in Bato and leave immediately for Cebu City (three hours). They go along the east coast via Oslob and Argao at 5, 6.30, 8 and 10 am, noon and 2.30 pm, they take the west-coast route via Moalboal and Barili at 6.30 and 9 am and 2.30 pm.

From Sibulan to Liloan, a big outrigger boat leaves daily around every 30 minutes. The last departure is at 3 pm (20 minutes).

From Guihulngan for Tangil, a boat leaves daily at 11 am (three hours). The connection from Tangil to Moalboal is better than the one from Toledo to Moalboal.

From San Carlos to Toledo, a ferry leaves daily at 5.30 am and 1.30 pm, and on Sunday usually at 10.30 am (1¾ hours). The departure times may be different on holidays. On Maundy Thursday there may only be one boat and on Good Friday there are none. The times of departure are liable to change. For reliable information ask at the wharf rather than the trishaw drivers in town.

From Escalante to Tuburan, the MV *Melrevic 2* of Anzar Shipping Corporation leaves daily at 10.30 am and 12.30 pm (P35; 1¾ hours)

Guimaras As an alternative to the popular connection by boat from Bacolod via Iloilo City on Panay, you can go to Guimaras Island by boat from Valladolid, about 30 km south of Bacolod. Coming by bus or jeepney from Bacolod, you have to get off at the first bridge. A boat goes daily from Valladolid to

Cabalagnan, on Guimaras, at about 11 am, stopping at several small islands on the way, including Nagarao Island. From Cabalagnan a jeepney leaves in the morning for Jordan.

Twice a week a boat sails from Pulupandan, a little north of Valladolid, to Suclaran on Guimaras.

Luzon From Bacolod to Manila, the MV *San Paolo* of Negros Navigation leaves on Tuesday at 2 pm and Saturday at 10 am (P480; 19 hours). Their MV *Princess of Negros* leaves on Wednesday and Sunday at 4 pm (23 hours).

From Dumaguete to Manila, the Sulpicio Lines' MV *Philippine Princess* leaves on Monday at noon (26 hours). The MV *Medjugorje* of WG & A leaves on Wednesday at 8 am (P545; 27 hours). Their MV *Maynilad* leaves on Friday at 8 am (32 hours).

Mindanao From Bacolod to Cagayan de Oro the MV *San Paolo* of Negros Navigation leaves on Thursday at 4 pm (14 hours).

From Dumaguete to Dapitan, the Cocaliong Shipping Lines' MV *Filipinas Dinagat* leaves on Tuesday, Thursday and Saturday at 7 am (P62; four hours). The MV *Dumaguete Ferry*, the MV *Georich*, or the MV *Palauan Ferry* of George & Peter Lines leaves Dumaguete for Dapitan daily at 8 am (P62; four hours). On Tuesday and Saturday the boat goes on to Zamboanga.

From Dumaguete to Dipolog, the MV *Maynilad* of WG & A leaves Tuesday at 5 am (P65; four hours). The Trans-Asia Shipping Lines' MV *Asia-Japan* leaves on Wednesday at 8 am (3½ hours).

From Dumaguete to Iligan, the MV *Superferry 7* of WG & A leaves Wednesday at 9 pm (P140; six hours).

From Dumaguete to Ozamis, the Sulpicio Lines' MV *Philippine Princess* leaves Thursday at 10 pm (seven hours).

From Dumaguete to Zamboanga, the Trans-Asia Shipping Lines' MV *Asia-Japan* leaves on Sunday at 2 am (14 hours).

Panay From Bacolod to Iloilo City, the MV *St Rafael*, the MV *St Michael* or the MV

SM/DV of Negros Navigation leave daily at 6, 7, 7.30, 9.45 and 10.30 am, noon and 2, 3, 4 and 5 pm (P55 to P160; one to two hours, depending on the ferry). Note that these times change frequently. Tickets are on sale at the wharf; the queue can take up to 30 minutes.

The MV *Bacolod Express* leaves daily at 8.45 am (Sunday at 9 am) and 3.45 pm (Friday and Sunday at 4.30 pm) (P100; one hour). Tickets for this fully air-conditioned catamaran are on sale at the wharf.

From Da-an Banwa, the port of Victorias, the MV *Queen Rose* or the MV *Princess Jo* leaves daily between 9 and 11 am for Culasi, and the MV *Seven Seas* or the MV *San Vicente* leaves daily between 9 and 11 am for Malayu-an, both near Ajuy on the east coast of Panay (two hours).

Siquijor From Dumaguete to Tambisan, a big outrigger boat leaves daily at 10 and 11 am (2½ hours). For safety reasons, this trip is not recommended in bad weather. A tricycle from Tambisan to Siquijor costs P5 per person.

From Dumaguete to Larena, fast Delta Lines' ferries leave daily at 6 and 8.30 am and 1 and 3.15 pm (P62; 45 minutes). The MV *Doña Cristina* of Cebu Ferries leaves on Sunday at 11 pm (1½ hours).

From Dumaguete to Siquijor, a big outrigger boat leaves daily at 7 am (two hours). the MV *Catherine* of Marjunnix Shipping Lines leaves daily at 2 pm (three hours). A tricycle from Siquijor to Larena costs about P5 per person.

BACOLOD

The capital of Negros Occidental Province, Bacolod has about 300,000 inhabitants and is the sugar capital of the Philippines. The name Bacolod is derived from the word *buklod*, or hill, which refers to a rise on which the town's first church stood.

Information
Tourist Offices The helpful tourist office (☎ 29021) is in the city plaza.

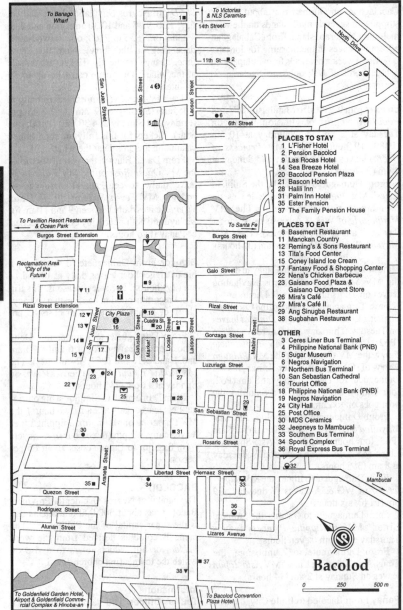

THE VISAYAS

PLACES TO STAY
1 L'Fisher Hotel
2 Pension Bacolod
9 Las Rocas Hotel
14 Sea Breeze Hotel
20 Bacolod Pension Plaza
21 Bascon Hotel
28 Halili Inn
31 Palm Inn Hotel
35 Ester Pension
37 The Family Pension House

PLACES TO EAT
8 Basement Restaurant
11 Manokan Country
12 Reming's & Sons Restaurant
13 Tita's Food Center
15 Coney Island Ice Cream
17 Fantasy Food & Shopping Center
22 Nena's Chicken Barbecue
23 Gaisano Food Plaza &
   Gaisano Department Store
26 Mira's Café
27 Mira's Café II
29 Ang Sinugba Restaurant
38 Sugbahan Restaurant

OTHER
3 Ceres Liner Bus Terminal
4 Philippine National Bank (PNB)
5 Sugar Museum
6 Negros Navigation
7 Northern Bus Terminal
10 San Sebastian Cathedral
16 Tourist Office
18 Philippine National Bank (PNB)
19 Negros Navigation
24 City Hall
25 Post Office
30 MDS Ceramics
32 Jeepneys to Mambucal
33 Southern Bus Terminal
34 Sports Complex
36 Royal Express Bus Terminal

Bacolod

0   250   500 m

Money The main office of the Philippine National Bank on Lacson St changes travellers cheques.

Telephone The area code for Bacolod is 034.

Things to See

The former Provincial Capitol Building in Lacson St, known as the *capitolio* and built in the 1930s, has housed the informative **Sugar Museum** since 1996. The main exhibits are objects and machinery closely connected with the development of the sugar industry in Negros Occidental, including models of a steam locomotive and hacienda furniture. Worth seeing are the large paintings with scenes taken from village life on Negros before the arrival of the Spaniards.

Next to the old **San Sebastian Cathedral** is the **Bacolod City Plaza**, with benches under shady trees, where cultural events are often held on Sunday afternoons and special occasions.

Bacolod is a leading producer of ceramics in the Philippines. Most of the workshops, like **NLS Ceramics** and **Bilbao Ceramics**, are on the edge of town. Only **MDS Ceramics** at 26 Rosario St has a central location.

You can take quite a few interesting day trips from Bacolod, eg to Silay and Victorias. Lovers of old locomotives especially will not be disappointed.

Special Events

Every year in October or November Bacolod boisterously celebrates the MassKara Festival. (See also the section on Public Holidays & Special Events in the Facts for the Visitor chapter earlier in this book.)

Places to Stay – bottom end

There are lots of different places to stay in Bacolod. South of the town centre, the *Halili Inn* (☎ 81548) on Locsin St has singles with fan for P60, with fan and bath for P100, doubles with air-con for P180, and with aircon and bath for P400. The beds in the cheaper rooms are narrow, and the place could do with renovating. If you want to stay in this part of town, you'd be better off at the

Palm Inn Hotel, also in Locsin St (☎ 435 0543), although it's a bit more expensive. Singles/doubles with fan and bath cost P220/330, with air-con and bath P415/525 and P605. The accommodation is spotless and the more expensive rooms have TV. Enjoy a drink in the roof-deck lounge bar with live music in the evenings.

Rooms on peaceful 11th St north of the town centre, the *Pension Bacolod* (☎ 23883; fax 27734) is further down market and offers good value for money. Immaculate rooms with fan cost P95/145, with fan and bath P155/200 and with air-con and bath P260/335. No wonder it's often fully booked.

The small, well-managed *Ester Pension* (☎ 23526) on Araneta St charges P150/200 for its tiny rooms with fan and bath, and from P300 for rooms with air-con and bath. It's OK for the money.

Places to Stay – middle

Centrally located, the *Bacolod Pension Plaza* (☎ 27076; fax 433 2203) on Cuadra St is a quiet place with clean rooms with air-con and bath from P575 to P790. The more expensive rooms have TV and refrigerator.

You can enjoy the friendly service at the *Bascon Hotel* (☎ 23141-43; fax 433 1393) on Gonzaga St. Pleasant, clean rooms with air-con and bath cost from P450/540.

Although you might not think so from the lobby and restaurant, the *Sea Breeze Hotel* (☎ 24571; fax 81231) on San Juan St is a clean and pleasant place to stay. They have singles with air-con and bath for P665 and doubles with air-con and bath from P740 to P880 (with TV).

Places to Stay – top end

The well looked after *Goldenfield Garden Hotel* (☎ 433 1111; fax 433 1234), in the Goldenfield Commercial Complex near the airport, has very comfortable rooms with air-con and bath for P1500 and suites for P2500 and P2900, including refrigerator and TV. There is a disco and a swimming pool.

The elegant and tastefully decorated *L'Fisher Hotel* (☎ 433 3731; fax 433 0951) is on Lacson St, on the corner of 14th St in the northern part of town. Their pleasant rooms with TV, air-con and bath go for P1920/2400 and suites from P4000 to P6400. You can also enjoy their pool.

No doubt the best hotel in town, the *Bacolod Convention Plaza Hotel* (☎ 83551; fax 83392) on Magsaysay Ave on the corner of Lacson St, has attractive rooms with TV, fridge, air-con and bath from P2000 to P2500. Suites are P3600. There is a swimming pool and a tennis court; they also offer a free airport service.

Places to Eat

The popular *Reming's & Sons Restaurant* in the city plaza prepares the best Filipino fast food. Reming himself even runs a weekly cooking course. Another favourite for fast food is the *Gaisano Food Plaza* on Luzuriaga St. This fully air-conditioned centre has several different kinds of small restaurant and also features videos and live music.

Mira's Café on Locsin St will brew you a cup of native coffee. If you want cakes with your coffee, you can get them at the bakery on the corner. Nearby, *Mira's Café II* has the same selection and excellent service.

The clean and well-kept *Ang Sinugba*

Restaurant on San Sebastian St is well known for its superb seafood.

A pleasant ambience, wide variety of good steaks and expertly prepared Filipino dishes cooked á la Negros distinguish the *Basement* on Gatuslao St at the corner of Burgos St. You can breakfast in style at the *Café Marinero* on the ground floor of the L'Fisher Hotel on Lacson St, on the corner of 14th St.

Within the Goldenfield Commercial Complex are the *Old West Steakhouse*, with its cosy atmosphere, *Shakey's Pizza* and *Carlo Pizza Garden*, the open-air *Foodland* and the more expensive *Seafood Market Restaurant*.

You can get barbecues and beer at the many all-night restaurants at the *Manokan Country* in the Reclamation Area. Also in the Reclamation Area, at the western end of Burgos St Extension, you can spend a breezy evening in the *Pavillion Resort Restaurant*. Make sure to arrange for a taxi to pick you up afterwards as there is almost no transport back to the city at night.

Entertainment

The pleasant *Ang Sinugba Restaurant* on San Sebastian St entertains its guests with folk

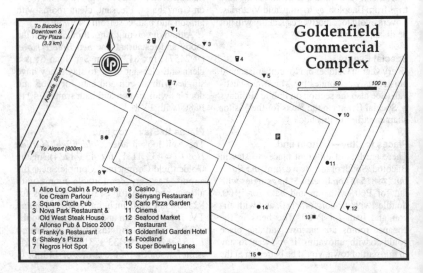

Goldenfield Commercial Complex

To Bacolod Downtown & City Plaza (3.3 km)

Araneta Street

To Airport (800m)

0   50   100 m

P

1	Alice Log Cabin & Popeye's Ice Cream Parlour	8	Casino
2	Square Circle Pub	9	Senyang Restaurant
3	Nova Park Restaurant & Old West Steak House	10	Carlo Pizza Garden
4	Alfonso Pub & Disco 2000	11	Cinema
5	Franky's Restaurant	12	Seafood Market Restaurant
6	Shakey's Pizza	13	Goldenfield Garden Hotel
7	Negros Hot Spot	14	Foodland
		15	Super Bowling Lanes

music every evening until 9 pm. The *Spectrum Disco* downstairs in the Sea Breeze Hotel seems to have missed the boat on every trend going and is not very inviting.

Among the most popular places in the Goldenfield Commercial Complex are *Disco 2000* and the big *Negros Hot Spot* with live music nightly and a cheery atmosphere. Within the complex, there are also entertainment venues like the *Casino* (admission P150), the 40-lane *Super Bowling Lanes*, the biggest in the Visayas, and the *Quorum Disco* in the Goldenfield Garden Hotel, which opens at 9 pm (admission P70).

Getting There & Away
Air PAL has an office at Bacolod airport (☎ 83529, 83579).

Bus Ceres Liner express buses leave Dumaguete for Bacolod daily at 6.45, 8.30 and 10.30 am, noon and 2 pm (nine hours). You can book seats.

A few Ceres Liner buses travel from Hinoba-an to Bacolod daily. The last departure is generally in the early afternoon. The bus terminal is in Nauhang, a little north of Hinoba-an (seven hours).

Royal Express Line buses travel from Dumaguete via Mabinay and then along the west coast to Bacolod (5½ hours).

Several Ceres Liner buses go from San Carlos to Bacolod daily. The last one leaves after the last ship arrives from Toledo on Cebu (four hours).

There are jeepneys to Mambucal, Ma-ao, Silay and Victorias (see the Getting There & Away sections for these towns).

Car You can hire a car at Parmon Transportation & Tours (☎ 29593; fax 23222) at the USB Building on 6th St. They have branches at the Bacolod Convention Plaza Hotel, Goldenfield Garden Hotel and L'Fisher Hotel.

Getting Around
The Airport Bacolod's airport is about five km south of the city. On leaving the terminal, turn left to go towards the city. You can stop a jeepney, as they all go to the city plaza.

A PU-Cab from the airport to the city centre should cost no more than P30, but it is best to agree on a price with the driver beforehand.

Bus Buses from Dumaguete and San Carlos arrive at the Northern bus terminal or in the Ceres Liner bus terminal about 200m farther on. Jeepneys marked 'Libertad' leave both bus terminals for the city centre and cost P2. In the other direction the destination is marked 'Shopping'. A PU-Cab from the bus terminal to the city centre should cost no more than P15.

Buses from South Negros and Dumaguete via Mabinay (the west coast route) arrive at the Southern bus terminal or at the Royal Express bus terminal a little further south-east.

Boat Banago Wharf is about seven km north of the city. A jeepney will cost you P7 plus P3 for baggage, and a PU-Cab about P40, but determine the price first. After the arrival of a ferry from Iloilo City the following Negros Navigation air-con buses go into town: 'Plaza' to the city centre, 'Libertad' to the Southern bus terminal, and 'Shopping' to the Northern bus terminal and Ceres Liner bus terminal (all P20).

MAMBUCAL
With its hot sulphur springs, Mambucal is the best known resort on Negros, yet it's not overcrowded. The so-called **Summer Resort** has swimming pools, waterfalls and accommodation. However, the places are all a bit run-down, so you wouldn't be missing much if you didn't come here. You can't go from Mambucal across the island to the east coast as, in the central area of Negros, all roads end at the Kanlaon massif.

If you want to climb the 2465m high Kanlaon, you need to allow three to four days for the round trip. Edwin Gatia of the tourist office (☎ 29021) in Bacolod can organise guides from the Negros Mountaineering Club (NMC). An excellent guide himself, he advises those who intend to climb the volcano or visit the national park for bird-watching or whatever to inform the club or the tourist office beforehand for co-ordination and safety purposes. There is good reason behind this, as the volcano can by no means be described as benign. In August 1996 it suddenly erupted without any warning, catching a group of mountaineers totally by surprise. Quite a few of the party were injured, some fatally. A tour for two people organised by NMC will cost P3500 (via Mambucal) or P2500 (via La Carlota).

You can also find knowledgeable guides on your own in Mambucal who will also provide a tent and cooker.

Places to Stay
The *Mambucal Health Resort* is fairly basic and has rooms with bath for P100/150, suites for P250, and also has a swimming pool.

Getting There & Away
Jeepney Several jeepneys go from Bacolod to Mambucal daily, leaving from Libertad St. The trip takes one hour (P10), but the morning trip from Mambucal to Bacolod can take up to two hours because of the many stops. The last jeepney back leaves at about 5 pm.

MA-AO
The sugarcane fields of Ma-ao stretch to the foot of the Kanlaon Volcano, criss-crossed by about 280 km of railway tracks. Just as exciting as the bridges that cross the rivers and ravines are the old steam locomotives, which were used until recently for harvesting.

These old-timers were recently pensioned off and pushed on to the 'old-timer tracks' of the **Ma-ao Sugar Central (MSC)**, where they may possibly still be available for inspection (check at the tourist office in Bacolod). There are two American Locomotive Company (Alco) 2-6-0s: one is the TS 1-3, dated 1921, and the other is the BM 5, dated 1924.

Getting There & Away
Jeepney Several jeepneys go from Libertad St in Bacolod to Ma-ao daily (one hour). The last trip back is at 4 or 5 pm.

SILAY
An excellent way to get a picture of life on Negros in its heyday at the turn of the century is to visit the **Balay Negrense Museum** in 5-Novembre St. Providing a glimpse particularly of the lifestyle and culture of the upper classes in days past, the museum is open every day except Monday from 10 am until 6 pm.

A little outside Silay is the **Hawaiian-Philippine Sugar Company**, one of the largest plantations on Negros, which has a rail network that is about 180 km long.

Nicknamed 'Red Dragons', the steam engines used here are in excellent condition. The name goes back to the time when they were bright red, but today they are blue-black in colour. In WWII, most of them were hidden from the Japanese by being run on special rails into the wooded mountains. They include a 1920 Henschel 0-6-0 and six Baldwin 0-6-0s built in 1919, 1920 and 1928. Check at the tourist office in Bacolod to see if it is still possible to inspect the locomotives, and if so, at what times.

Getting There & Away
Jeepney Several jeepneys leave from Lacson St, on the corner of Libertad St, in Bacolod for Silay daily, taking 30 minutes. Buses and jeepneys from the Northern bus terminal also go through Silay.

Jeepneys go from the market in Silay to the Hawaiian-Philippine Sugar Company.

VICTORIAS
The Victorias Milling Company, **Vicmico**, is open for inspection from Tuesday to Friday. It's part of a large complex where sugar is processed in several stages for the consumer. To get permission for a guided tour (2pm; P5 per person), you have to go to the Public Relations Office next to the Urban Bank on the factory grounds. Men wearing shorts and women wearing shorts or miniskirts will be refused admission. Sandals and thongs (flip-flops) are not permitted for safety reasons.

Vicmico's 349 km railway track is the longest on Negros and possibly the longest two foot gauge track in the world. As with the Hawaiian-Philippine Sugar Company on Silay, the diesel and steam locomotives are directed by radio remote control from a central point, but the dark-green old-timers are now used only during the peak season from January to February. The rolling stock includes eight Henschel 0-8-0Ts, dating back to 1926 to 1928, and two Bagnall 0-4-4Ts, which were built for the Kowloon (Hong Kong) to Canton Line in China.

Apart from the sugar mill, the **St Joseph the Worker Chapel** is worth seeing. The unusual coloured mural showing an angry Filipino Jesus. The 'Angry Christ' received international attention after an article about it appeared in *Life* magazine.

Getting There & Away
Bus Buses run daily at irregular intervals from the Bacolod Northern bus terminal to Victorias (P13; 45 minutes).

Jeepney Several jeepneys run from Bacolod to Victorias daily (P8; 45 minutes). Several jeepneys marked 'VMC' also go daily from Victorias market to the Vicmico sugar mill (P1.5; 15 minutes).

LAKAWON ISLAND
Just over two nautical miles from the north coast of Negros lies the delightful little island of Lakawon. The actual name is Ilacaon, but it is pronounced Lakawon, and the locals only know it under this name. The island is in the shape of a banana and is just under one km long and 100m wide. It is only two metres high and forms the tip of an extensive reef which for a short time at full moon and new moon is almost completely exposed to the elements.

Nature has provided Lakawon with a gorgeous white beach consisting of coarse coral sand, and the island is covered with palm trees and in places dense bushes. There is a picturesque village on the west side of the island which is home to some friendly fishermen. Lakawon Island is popular at the weekends with day trippers.

Places to Stay
The *Lakawon Island Resort* has cottages with bath for P400. The huts are basic, but acceptable. Tents can be hired for P200. The restaurant's menu varies according to the local fishermen's catch for the day. The Sales & Booking Office, Casa de Amigo II (☎ 453 0808) on Libertad St, Bacolod, is the place to go to find out the availability of beds and their cost.

Getting There & Away
Bus, Tricycle & Boat Take a bus from the Northern bus terminal in Bacolod in the direction of Cadiz or San Carlos. Get off at the Caltex petrol station in Cadua-an, a few km after Manapla (you definitely have to ask the bus driver to drop you there, because the place is hardly recognisable from the road). The trip takes one hour. Carry on from there by tricycle to the little coastal town of Cadiz Viejo. It takes about 15 minutes to get there, and the fare is P40, or P7 per person. The 15 minute trip over to the island by boat shouldn't cost more than P200.

CADIZ
The little port of Cadiz lies at the estuary of the river of the same name on the north coast of Negros. There is a daily boat connection from there to Bantayan Island in the north of Cebu.

Places to Stay
Right next to the Ceres bus terminal you can be confident the *RL Apartelle* will provide clean, no-frill rooms with fan for P75/100.

Getting There & Away
Bus Several Ceres Liner company express buses make the trip daily from Bacolod to Cadiz from the Northern bus terminal (P24; 1½ hours).

ESCALANTE
Every year on 20 September, Escalante remembers the 1985 massacre of sugar cane workers, with speeches, street theatre and memorial services. The striking workers were marching through the streets in protest

when soldiers opened fire, killing 20 of them at random.

There is a daily boat service between Escalante and Tuburan on the north-west coast of Cebu. The harbour (Port Danao) is a little bit out of town.

Places to Stay
Across from the bus terminal, *Laida's Lodge* provides basic rooms for P50/100, fan P20 extra.

Getting There & Away
Bus Several Ceres Liner Company buses go from Bacolod to Escalante daily from the Northern bus terminal. Those leaving between 6.30 and 10 am take people to the ferry then carry on to Cebu City (2½ hours).

SAN CARLOS
There is a shipping service between San Carlos and Toledo, Cebu. The offshore **Sipaway Island** (or Refugio Island) is supposed to have a few beautiful beaches and walking tracks. There are sari sari stores, but their stock is limited, so it's advisable to bring your own provisions from San Carlos.

Telephone
The area code for San Carlos is 03440.

Places to Stay
The *Coco Grove Hotel* (☎ 2560) on Ylagan St, about 150m from the Ceres Liner bus terminal has rooms with fan for P150/280, with fan and bath for P250/380, and with air-con and bath for P650/750. The hotel has a restaurant and is quiet and fairly clean, although a bit on the shabby side.

Getting There & Away
Bus Several Ceres Liner express buses leave the Northern bus terminal at Bacolod for San Carlos daily, some going on to Dumaguete (P53; 3½ hours).

From Dumaguete there are Ceres Liner express buses going to Bacolod via San Carlos, leaving daily at 6.45, 8.30 and 10.30 am and at noon (four hours).

DUMAGUETE
Dumaguete is a very pleasant town with neat little park areas and what must be the cleanest market in the Philippines. It's the capital of Negros Oriental Province and also a university town. **Silliman University**, whose extensive campus is on the northern edge of town, is the only Protestant university in the Philippines and was named after its founder, Dr Horace B Silliman. It has an interesting and informative **anthropological museum** (admission P5) and a post office.

Silliman Beach near the airport is no great shakes as a bathing beach, but it's actually not bad and quite popular with students.

Information
Money The Equitable bank on the corner of Perdices and San Juan Sts gives cash advances on Visa and MasterCard.

The Philippine National Bank on Silliman Ave will change travellers cheques, although it can take up to an hour.

Telephone The area code for Dumaguete is 035.

Laundry The Brightwash Laundry on Silliman Ave charges P20 per kg (minimum 5 kg) for washing, drying and ironing. It takes one to two days.

Medical Services The medical care at the Holy Child Hospital, Legaspi St, and at the Silliman University Medical Center (SUMC) is better than at the Provincial Hospital.

Diving
Members of the marine laboratory near Silliman Beach run diving courses there twice a year. They also use a boat that you can charter for diving excursions. Favourite destinations are Sumilon Island in southern Cebu, and Apo Island, south of Dumaguete.

About 150m from the Panorama House & Beach Resort (see Places to Stay in this section) you will find the well-equipped dive shop, Dive Sibulan, which offers diving courses and dive trips.

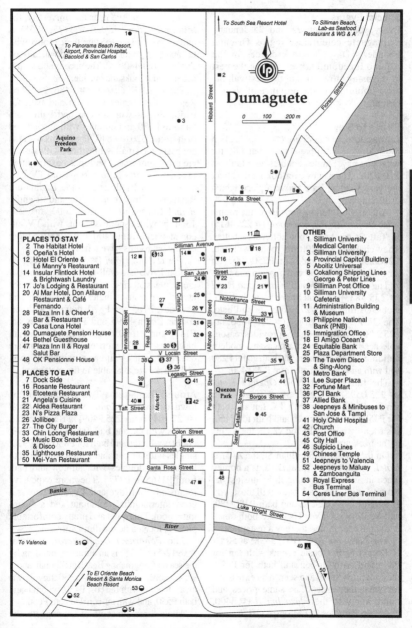

THE VISAYAS

PLACES TO STAY
2 The Habitat Hotel
6 Opeña's Hotel
12 Hotel El Oriente &
   Lé Manny's Restaurant
14 Insular Flintlock Hotel
   & Brightwash Laundry
17 Jo's Lodging & Restaurant
20 Al Mar Hotel, Don Atilano
   Restaurant & Café
   Fernando
28 Plaza Inn I & Cheer's
   Bar & Restaurant
39 Casa Lona Hotel
40 Dumaguete Pension House
44 Bethel Guesthouse
47 Plaza Inn II & Royal
   Salut Bar
48 OK Pensionne House

PLACES TO EAT
7 Dock Side
16 Rosante Restaurant
19 Etcetera Restaurant
21 Angela's Cuisine
22 Aldea Restaurant
23 N's Pizza Plaza
26 Jollibee
27 The City Burger
33 Chin Loong Restaurant
34 Music Box Snack Bar
   & Disco
35 Lighthouse Restaurant
50 Mei-Yan Restaurant

OTHER
1 Silliman University
  Medical Center
3 Silliman University
4 Provincial Capitol Building
5 Aboitiz Universal
8 Cokaliong Shipping Lines
  George & Peter Lines
9 Silliman Post Office
10 Silliman University
   Cafeteria
11 Administration Building
   & Museum
13 Philippine National
   Bank (PNB)
15 Immigration Office
18 El Amigo Ocean's
24 Equitable Bank
25 Plaza Department Store
29 The Tavern Disco
   & Sing-Along
30 Metro Bank
31 Lee Super Plaza
32 Fortune Mart
36 PCI Bank
37 Allied Bank
38 Jeepneys & Minibuses to
   San Jose & Tampi
41 Holy Child Hospital
42 Church
43 Post Office
45 City Hall
46 Sulpicio Lines
49 Chinese Temple
51 Jeepneys to Valencia
52 Jeepneys to Maluay
   & Zamboanguita
53 Royal Express
   Bus Terminal
54 Ceres Liner Bus Terminal

Special Events

Every year between 21 and 25 January, Dumaguete celebrates Negros Oriental Founder's Day. The folk dances in the Aquino Freedom Park are among the best of the many attractions of this festival, the most important in the province of Negros Oriental.

Places to Stay

Dumaguete *Jo's Lodging* (☎ 225 4412) on Silliman Ave is unpretentious but OK for what you pay. Singles/doubles with fan cost P100/200. The rooms overlooking the street are very loud and are above a place which grills chickens.

Although a bit more expensive, the rooms at the *Dumaguete Pension House* (☎ 225 4615) in Taft St are basic, but noticeably better. They charge P150/200 for rooms with fan, P200/250 with fan and bath, P250/300 with air-con, and P300/400 with air-con and bath.

The rooms at the nearby *Casa Lona Hotel* (☎ 225 4833) on Real St are basic, but spacious, costing P175/275 with fan and bath. The *OK Pensionne House* (☎ 225 4636; fax 225 2480) on Santa Rosa St provides reasonable accommodation in a pleasant, modern building. Rooms with fan and bath go for P280 and with air-con and bath from P390/440.

The fairly comfortable *Opeña's Hotel* (☎ 225 0595) on Katada St has singles with fan for P150, rooms with TV, fan and bath for P350 and with air-con and bath for P450. It's friendly here and good value; the rooms at the back are quiet.

On the corner of San Juan St, the *Al Mar Hotel* (☎ 52567) on Rizal Blvd, is a homey place in an older building in Spanish style. Rooms with fan and bath will cost you P190/280, with air-con and bath P380/480, and P530 (with TV). There are both small and large rooms, and there is a restaurant.

The *Plaza Inn I* (☎ 3103, 3538) at 50 Dr V Locsin St has basic rooms with fan for P375 and with air-con and bath for P490; they are fairly small and seem a bit expensive for what they offer. The same prices and rating apply to the *Plaza Inn II* (☎ 3400, 4441) on Percides St (Alfonso XIII St).

On Silliman Ave near the university, the *Insular Flintlock Hotel* (☎ 3495, 4255) is quite a good place to stay; their rooms with fan and bath go for P400/450 and with air-con and bath for P480/570. The accommodation is better than it looks the outside.

The *Hotel El Oriente* (☎ 3486, 2539) on Real St has singles with fan and bath for P250, singles with air-con and bath from P450 to P680 and doubles with air-con and bath from P520 to P840. The rooms with fan are basic and small, while those with air-con are tidy, comfortable and spacious; the more expensive rooms have a fridge and TV.

On Rizal Blvd, next to the Lighthouse Restaurant, the comfortable and friendly *Bethel Guesthouse* (☎ 225 2000; fax 255 1374) provides spotless rooms with TV, air-con and bath from P400 to P1200 (the more expensive rooms have a fridge).

The *Habitat Hotel* (☎ /fax 225 2483) on Hibbard Ave is a well-kept hotel with spacious, pleasant air-con rooms. In a quiet area at the university, singles with air-con and bath cost P765 and P870, doubles with air-con and bath P995 and P1100. Suites are P1400 and P1680. Some rooms have small balconies, and the more expensive rooms are equipped with TV. It has a swimming pool, and snacks are available in the restaurant.

Around Dumaguete Two km north of the town centre, the *South Sea Resort Hotel* (☎ 225 0491; fax 225 2409) in Bantayan has singles with fan and bath for P725 and P790, doubles with fan and bath for P830 and P920, singles with air-con and bath from P1030 to P2400 and doubles with air-con and bath from P1165 to P2775. The more expensive rooms have a fridge and TV, and there is a good international restaurant and a swimming pool. This quiet and pretty comfortable place is located near Silliman Beach.

The *Panorama Beach Resort* (cellular ☎ 0912-515 0275) is an attractive building by the sea on Cangmating Beach at Sibulan, about six km north of Dumaguete – a P30 tricycle ride away. Rooms with fan cost P450, with fan and bath P550, and with air-con and bath P650.

About three km south of Dumaguete, the

El Oriente Beach Resort (☎ 225 0668; fax 225 4914) in Mangnao offers fairly good rooms with fan and bath for P400 and with air-con and bath from P650. There is a pool.

In Banilad, about four km south of Dumaguete, the *Santa Monica Beach Resort* (☎ 225 0704; fax 225 7801) provides good rooms with fan and bath for P705/780 and with air-con and bath from P910/1100. The resort is popular, although the grounds are no longer the newest; it is located on a grey part of the beach which is not particularly well looked after, but is at least quiet.

Places to Eat

There's excellent Chinese food in the *Chin Loong Restaurant* on Rizal Blvd; the special menu is especially good value at around P60. Another good and inexpensive Chinese restaurant is the *Mei-Yan Restaurant* in the southern outskirts of Dumaguete, south of the Banica River, directly on the sea next to a little Chinese temple. They also serve Philippine food.

Jo's Restaurant on Silliman Ave has what is probably the best chicken dish in town: the delicious Chicken Inato. Just round the corner on Percides St, the *Rosante Restaurant* prepares good Filipino dishes. A good selection of food is available in the department store *Lee Super Plaza*, where several local restaurants have fast-food stalls on the first floor. Inexpensive Filipino food is available in several small, clean restaurants in the covered market near the church.

If you get the munchies late at night, then the *Dock Side* near the jetty is the place to go. It's functionally furnished, but very good value, and you don't have to wait long. They are closed during the day.

The roof-garden restaurant *Aldea* on the corner of Percides and San Juan Sts is extremely pleasant and offers good, inexpensive Filipino and Chinese food; there is live music in the evenings. *N's Pizza Plaza* on Percides St is popular and always busy. They don't just make pizzas, but also several international dishes, a selection of cakes, and excellent fruit juices.

You can eat the best steaks in town in the air-conditioned comfort of the *Don Atilano Restaurant* on Rizal Blvd, where the ambience is Spanish and the service superb. The *Music Box Snack Bar* in the disco of the same name on Rizal Blvd serves Philippine and European snacks. This is a popular meeting place, especially for expat Europeans.

For those who like seafood, the *Lab-as Seafood Restaurant* can be recommended; on Friday evening they have an inexpensive buffet. It is on the corner of Flores and EJ Blanco Rds, two km north of Silliman Ave along the water. Another good restaurant for seafood, which also serves Filipino and western cuisine, is the rustically romantic *Baybay Restaurant* in the South Sea Resort Hotel near Silliman Beach.

Entertainment

There are few places open in the late evening, the big *Music Box* disco on Rizal Ave being one. It's under Swiss management and can get really busy, although not until after 10 pm, when most people start arriving. The *Ocean's* restaurant in Silliman Ave is mostly frequented by Filipinos, who like to watch basketball or boxing on TV. In *El Amigo* right next door, the clientele is mostly students who obviously like the loud music.

Getting There & Away

Air PAL has an office at Dumaguete airport (☎ 225 1352).

Bus Several Ceres Liner express buses go daily to Dumaguete via San Carlos from the Northern bus terminal in Bacolod. The trip takes 7½ hours from Bacolod (P150) and four hours from San Carlos.

It's quicker to go from Bacolod to Dumaguete via Mabinay using the Royal Express Lines buses which leave at 6 am and 1.30 pm (5½ hours).

A few buses go daily to Dumaguete via Hinoba-an, leaving from the Southern bus terminal in Bacolod. The last departure is at 8 am and the trip takes 12 hours.

A few buses go daily to Dumaguete from the Nauhang bus terminal near Hinoba-an. The last bus is supposed to leave at 2.45 pm, possibly earlier. The trip takes six hours with a one hour stop in Bayawan. If you're in a hurry, buy a ticket only as far as Bayawan where you will usually find buses ready to leave for Dumaguete.

Getting Around
The Airport A tricycle from the airport into town should cost no more than P5 per person, but considerably more is often demanded (P20 will do).

Bus Buses heading north (San Carlos, Bacolod) and south (Bawayan, Hinoba-an) leave from the Ceres Liner bus terminal on the southern outskirts of town, where the Royal Express bus terminal is also located. A tricycle from the town centre costs P2 per person.

AROUND DUMAGUETE
Twin Lakes
About 25 km west of Dumaguete there are two crater lakes surrounded by dense rainforest: Lake Balinsasayao and the smaller, adjoining Lake Danao, at a height of about 800m. Environmentalists are demanding that these lakes (also known as Twin Lakes), located in what is for Negros rare forestland, be declared a national park. This would prevent the possible construction of a hydroelectric power station in this area. There is a basic nipa hut for overnight stays, but you have to bring your own provisions.

Getting There & Away You can get to Twin Lakes from Dumaguete by bus or jeepney going north. Get off about two km before San Jose, or travel back from San Jose by tricycle to the small track leading from the road up to Twin Lakes. You have to walk the remaining 15 km or so as it is impossible for jeepneys or tricycles. Motorcyclists without cross-country experience would have difficulty because of the steep slope and rough track.

San Jose & Tampi
Ships for Bato on Cebu leave from San Jose and Tampi, north of San Sebastian (see also Getting There & Away earlier in this section).

Getting There & Away Jeepneys and minibuses for San Jose and Tampi leave Dumaguete from the corner of Real and Locsin Sts (P7).

Valencia
Valencia's town park is pleasantly laid-out, as is the suburb of Dumaguete where people live in up-market housing comfort, under the shade of the many trees. From there, you can take a tricycle for about P100 (return journey) up to Camp Look-out at the extinct volcano Cuernos de Negros. Unfortunately, what was a beautiful view of Dumaguete, Cebu and Siquijor Island has become more and more hampered as the viewing area has become almost completely overgrown.

In Terejo, about two km out of Valencia, you'll find the Banica Valley Resort, which has a small creek, a swimming pool and a few resthouses. It's popular with the locals, especially at weekends. If you want to go there on foot, ask for the swimming pool, which is near a shrine.

Further upstream from the swimming pool you can have a wonderful dip in the natural pool at the Casiroro waterfall, surrounded by huge rocks and unspoilt vegetation. The turn-off from the road is hard to find so it would be best to have someone point it out to you. A narrow path leads up to the pool, and it gets quite steep in places, but the climb is worth it. Don't forget to wear sturdy shoes.

Getting There & Away Several jeepneys run daily to Valencia from Dumaguete from the Valencia turn-off south of the Banica River.

SOUTH-EAST COAST
Along the coast from Dumaguete to the southern tip of Negros there are several places that will tempt you to stay a bit longer.

Getting There & Away
Bus/Jeepney Several jeepneys leave from Dumaguete every day from the first road junction south of the Banica River and head along the south coast via Dauin (30 minutes), Maluay and Zamboanguita (45 minutes) as far as Siaton (P15; one hour).

Bacong

In the small coastal village of Bacong, about seven km south of Dumaguete, they have a beautiful church with an old altar and organ, and the beach is clean here. If you're feeling adventurous, you could spend the night in a comfortable tree-house (complete with bath!). Information can be obtained from the office in the village hall next to the church.

Dauin

The township of Dauin, about 15 km south of Dumaguete, was founded back in the 18th century and is one of the oldest communities in the province. The charming church was built back then, as were a few watchtowers where they used to keep a look-out for plundering pirate ships. The quality of the beach here is OK.

Places to Stay The attractive *El Dorado Beach Resort* (☎ 225 7725; fax 225 4488) has comfortable rooms with fan and bath for P520, with air-con and bath for P650 (with TV), cottages and tree-houses with cooking facilities and refrigerator for P650. Discounted weekly and monthly rates are available. The excellent restaurant offers outstanding Philippine and European cuisine round the clock. It has a swimming pool and diving is offered from the Sea Explorers Dive Shop; diving instruction can be arranged. The management is Swiss. A shuttle bus goes between the resort and the Music Box in Dumaguete several times daily (20 minutes).

Maluay

Maluay (Malatapay) has a large **market** on Wednesday which is worth seeing. Farmers come from the mountains, and fishermen from the coast and nearby islands tie their boats up there. The market trades in agricultural produce, livestock and seafood. Chickens and fish are grilled, and whole pigs roasted on the beach, amid much chattering, gossiping, laughing, eating and drinking.

Although the sand is black on the beaches near Maluay (Malatapay) and Zamboanguita, the water is clean and clear. You can get to the offshore island of Apo from either place.

Places to Stay Right on the beach, *Hans & Nenita's Malatapay Cottages* (cellular ☎ 0918-740 0038) is a friendly set-up under German-Philippine management. Their roomy cottages with fan and bath go for P300. There is a restaurant, and bicycle and motorcycle hire can be arranged. They also have their own boat service over to Apo Island (P500) at the appropriate jetty for boats to and from the island. Get out at Malatapay Crossing, head towards the sea for 200m, then 100m to the right.

Zamboanguita

Just on the outskirts of Zamboanguita, a centre for the 'World Peace & Life's Survival' organisation was built in the mid-80s, called Spaceship 2000. Its members' main concern is encouraging reforestation and trying to restore the ecological balance. They are very open and are obviously glad to show visitors around 'Zoo Paradise World', as they call it. They also show people the grave of the peripatetic founder of the establishment, Father Tropa, who passed away in 1993.

Places to Stay Two km past Zamboanguita coming from Dumaguete, the *Salawaki*

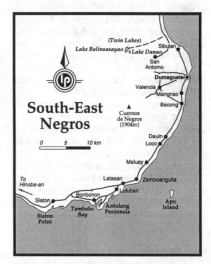

Beach Resort has cottages right on the beach with fan and bath for P400 and P600. The well-furnished accommodation is spacious, and you can enjoy good cheap meals and home-grown native coffee in their restaurant. The resort is about 200m from the large sign on the road. A boat for a day trip to Apo Island costs from P500 to P600.

Tambubo Bay

Also known as Tambubo Yacht Harbour and Port Bonbonon, this bay in the deep south of Negros is only 300m wide at its broadest point, but is 2½ km long. The mouth of the Paliohan river is at the head, that of the Talocoy nearer the entrance to the bay.

The eastern end of the bay is marked by the elongated Antulang Peninsula, which helped by the shape of its narrow sound provides a protected anchorage all year round. The first beach resorts have already been opened on the shores of this picturesque bay.

Places to Stay The *Tambubo Beach Club* is idyllically located on the beach near the village of Tambubo at the entrance to the bay. The club is run by Lars from Sweden and his Philippine wife May. A cottage will cost you between P150 and P360, depending on its size and fittings. The restaurant has good, inexpensive Philippine and European food. They hire out snorkelling equipment and paddle boats. Take a jeepney as far as Siaton (P15), carry on from there by tricycle over the occasionally bumpy road to Tambubo (P10 per person, or P50 for the tricycle).

The pleasant little *Kookoo's Nest Beach Resort*, run by the Australian Mark and his Philippine wife Felly, is on a peaceful stretch of sand at the tip of the Antulang Peninsula, not far from the entrance to the bay. Basic, but adequate cottages go for P290, with bath P490. The restaurant is good, and three big meals a day cost P270. If you stay here, don't miss the resort's main 'attraction': probably the smallest swimming pool in the Philippines. They also have four paddleboats for guests, and a nearby still-intact reef is excellent for snorkelling. To get there, follow the

instructions for the Tambubo Beach Resort, then make the crossing from Tambubo by boat. You could also take a taxi from Dumaguete airport (P500; one hour) and go the last 100m on foot.

APO ISLAND

Little Apo island, about eight km south-east of Zamboanguita, has about 1000 inhabitants. The island is slightly hilly, and in the north can get as high as 120m. Here they erected a lighthouse which provides a beautiful panoramic view. In the flatter, southern part of the island near the village there's a little lagoon which is separated from the sea by a sandy beach. To protect some unusual coral formations and rare fish, the waters up to 300m around Apo Island have been declared a sanctuary and placed under the protection of Silliman University in Dumaguete.

A part of the Apo Island Marine Reserve is the strictly regulated 'Fish Sanctuary' off the lagoon at the south coast of the island, where even anchoring is not allowed. The conditions here are excellent for diving and snorkelling, although the strength of the currents and undertow should not be underestimated.

Places to Stay

Nomen non est omen: The *Divers Paradise* near the lagoon consists of two extremely drab cottages which go for P100 each.

Attractively located, under palm trees on a slope, the *Kan-Upi Cove Beach Resort* has dorm beds for P200, and comfortable cottages with bath for P500/600. The restaurant here is good, and they offer diving for P700 per dive including boat rental. The little white sand beach is framed by decorative rock formations. Reservations can be made in Dumaguete at the Paradise Travel Center on Silliman Ave (☎ 225 3299; fax 225 5490).

Getting There & Away

Boat A boat leaves Maluay daily at 4 pm to Apo Island. The fare is P20. Departure from Apo Island for Maluay is at 7.30 am.

You can hire boats in Zamboanguita and

Maluay from about P400 to P600 to go to Apo Island. It's better to leave before 8 am and return after 4 pm because of the swell.

BINALBAGAN
Binalbagan is on the west coast of Negros, about 65 km south of Bacolod. This is where you will find one of the biggest sugar refineries and plantations in the world. It is called **Biscom**, which is short for Binalbagan Sugarmill Company. The two Baldwin locomotives 2-6-2T No 6, dated 1924, and Davenport 0-4-0T No 28, dated 1929, are no longer used, but you may inspect them.

KABANKALAN
Kabankalan is about 30 km south of Binalbagan. This small town celebrates the Sinulog Festival on the third weekend (Friday, Saturday and Sunday) in January with parades, cultural events and horse fights. The Kabankalanons maintain that their Sinulog Festival more authentic than the better known one in Cebu City.

HINOBA-AN
As an interesting alternative to the usual route from Bacolod to Cebu via San Carlos and Toledo, you can travel along the west and south coasts via Hinoba-an and Dumaguete. However, the roads are rather difficult, so you will need two days if you take this route. The last section from Bayawan to Zamboanguita is particularly attractive, but the road is in poor condition.

Early in 1982 Hinoba-an experienced a gold rush. Both the national and international press published daily reports about new finds which brought numerous adventurers and optimists. Gold fever broke out in earnest when it was reported that a Filipino had found gold to the value of P23,000 in a single day. Soon afterwards an estimated 20,000 people were trying their luck along a 17 km stretch of the Bacuyongan River and many did find gold. The average daily yield at the peak of the rush is said to have been one gram per person; this sold at P80.

Unfortunately, there were disastrous events, too. One digger died in a landslide and another three in fighting over claims. Altogether, 17 victims were counted in two months. The most lucrative yields were those won by the buyers, merchants and traders, who soon made the sleepy village of Nauhang into a lively trading centre with a wild-west character. From the Crossing Golden Southbend (a junction near Nauhang), jeepneys run about seven km inland to Spar III at Sitio Sangke, where the well-trodden path to the promising river begins.

Places to Stay
The *Gloria Mata Lodging House* in Hinoba-an is reasonably good with rooms for P50. The *Mesajon Lodging House* on Gatuslao St, Hinoba-an, has simple but comfortable and clean rooms with fan for P75/150. Mrs Mesajon is very skilled in preparing an excellent chicken binakol. This chicken dish is a speciality of south-west Negros.

About 25 km north of Hinoba-an in San Jose/Sipalay, the unassuming and pleasant *Dadula's Lodging House* charges P75/150 for rooms with fan.

Getting There & Away
Bus Several Ceres Liner buses go from Bacolod to Hinoba-an daily from the Southern bus terminal. They are either direct or continue on to Dumaguete. The road is good until Kabankalan, after which it deteriorates, but the views are much better. The trip takes six hours. Some buses only go to Nauhang, and a tricycle from there to Hinoba-an costs P2 per person. The last bus from Bacolod to Dumaguete via Hinoba-an leaves at 8 am, taking 12 hours.

A few Ceres Liner buses run daily from Dumaguete to Hinoba-an (P50; five hours). The bus may stop for an hour in Bayawan. The last bus leaves Dumaguete for Hinoba-an at about 12.30 pm.

BAYAWAN
Anyone who happens to get stuck in the little village of Bayawan because of transportation problems can spend the night in the basic, but clean *Sacred Heart Pharmacy & Lodging House* at the market, for about P50.

Panay

Panay is the large triangular island in the west of the Visayas. It is subdivided into the provinces of Iloilo, Capiz, Aklan and Antique. The western half of the island is mountainous; the highest mountains being Mt Madja-as (2090m) and Mt Nangtud (2049m), both in the province of Antique. Iloilo City, with about 350,000 inhabitants is the biggest city on the island. The economy is predominantly agricultural, although there is also a textile industry in Iloilo City. Fabric made from piña, the fibres of the pineapple leaf, is used to make barong tagalog shirts.

Among the main tourist attractions in Panay are the Ati-Atihan Festival in Kalibo and the Dinagyang Festival in Iloilo City. Along the south coast there are also several massive old churches dating from colonial times.

The little dream island of Boracay is extremely popular, not only with the 'international travel set' but also with quite 'normal' holidaymakers. In the meantime, travel agents can make bookings with several different resorts with above-average facilities.

Before and after the Ati-Atihan Festival in Kalibo, Boracay can be full up.

GETTING THERE & AWAY

You can get to Panay from Cebu, Guimaras, Luzon, Mindanao, Mindoro, Negros, Palawan and Romblon (see the Getting There & Away section of the Manila chapter and the relevant Getting There & Away sections of this chapter and of the chapters on the other islands).

Air

Cebu PAL flies daily from Iloilo City to Cebu City and on Monday, Wednesday, Friday and Saturday from Kalibo to Cebu City.

Air Philippines flies daily from Kalibo to Cebu City.

Luzon Asian Spirit and Pacific Airways fly daily from Caticlan to Manila; Air Ads flies Monday, Friday and Saturday.

PAL flies daily to Manila, from Kalibo, Iloilo City and Roxas.

Air Philippines Flies daily from Kalibo and Iloilo City to Manila.

Cebu Pacific flies daily from Iloilo City to Manila; Grand Air flies daily except Sunday.

Mindanao PAL has a flight on Sunday from Iloilo City to General Santos.

Palawan PAL flies on Thursday and Saturday from Iloilo City to Puerto Princesa.

Boat

Cebu From Dumaguit (near Kalibo) to Cebu City, the MV *Iligan City* of Cebu Ferries leaves on Friday at 6 pm (11 hours). Their MV *Tacloban City* leaves on Sunday at 5 pm (14 hours, via Roxas).

From Iloilo City to Cebu City, the Trans-Asia Shipping Lines' MV *Asia-Brunei* or MV *Trans-Asia* leaves daily at 6 pm (12 hours). The MV *Iligan City* of Cebu Ferries leaves on Tuesday and Sunday at 7 pm (12 hours). Their MV *Tacloban City* leaves on Wednesday and Friday at 7 pm (12 hours).

From Roxas to Cebu City, the MV *Tacloban City* of Cebu Ferries leaves on Sunday at 7 pm (12 hours).

Guimaras Several small ferries run daily from Iloilo City to Guimaras almost every hour between 5 am and 5.30 pm. They leave for Jordan (P5; 30 minutes) from the wharf near the post office and for Buenavista (one hour) from Rotary Park. Several outrigger boats travel daily from the Ortiz wharf, near the central market, to Jordan (15 minutes).

Luzon From Iloilo City to Manila there are several ships a week (P510; 18 to 23 hours). The MV *Santa Ana* of Negros Navigation leaves on Monday at noon and Thursday at 10 am (20 hours). Their MV *Saint Francis of Assisi* leaves on Wednesday at 10 am and Friday and Sunday at noon (18 hours). The MV *Superferry 1* of WG & A leaves on

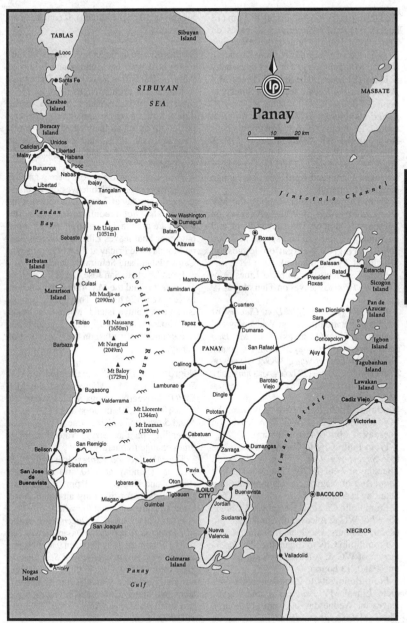

THE VISAYAS

Wednesday at 11 am and Friday at 3 pm (18 hours). Their MV *Superferry 2* leaves on Thursday at 8 am (23 hours); the MV *Superferry 6* leaves on Saturday at 8 am (23 hours); and the MV *Superferry 5* leaves on Sunday at 11 pm (21 hours). The Sulpicio Lines' MV *Princess of the Pacific* leaves on Sunday at noon (19 hours).

Various ships go to Manila from different towns in Panay. From Caticlan (near Boracay), the MV *Romblon Bay* of MBRS Lines leaves Wednesday at 1 pm (22 hours). The MV *Superferry 1* of WG & A goes once a week in March and April if there is enough demand (11 hours).

From Dumaguit (near Kalibo), the MV *Our Lady of Naju* of WG & A leaves on Tuesday at 3 pm, on Thursday at 5 pm, and on Sunday at 3 pm (15 hours). The MV *Don Julio* of Negros Navigation leaves on Monday at 3 pm (16 hours).

From Estancia, the Sulpicio Lines' MV *Cotabato Princess* leaves on Thursday at 10 pm (17 hours).

From Roxas, the MV *Don Claudio* of Negros Navigation leaves on Wednesday and Saturday at 5 pm (17 hours). Their MV *Don Julio* leaves on Thursday at 3 pm (16 hours). The MV *Our Lady of Naju* of WG & A leaves on Thursday at 12.30 pm (20 hours, via Dumaguit).

Mindanao From Iloilo City to Butuan, the MV *Superferry 2* of WG & A leaves on Tuesday at 3 pm (P410; 17 hours).

From Iloilo City to Cagayan de Oro, the MV *Superferry 9* of WG & A leaves on Thursday at 7 pm (P370; 15 hours). The MV *Santa Ana* of Negros Navigation leaves on Saturday at 5 pm (14 hours).

From Iloilo City to Davao, the MV *Superferry 1* of WG & A leaves on Sunday at 2 pm (P650; 32 hours, via General Santos).

From Iloilo City to Iligan, the MV *Superferry 5* of WG & A leaves on Saturday at 2 pm (P350; 13 hours).

From Iloilo City to Zamboanga, the Sulpicio Lines' MV *Princess of the Pacific* leaves on Wednesday at 3 pm (14 hours). Their MV *Cotabato Princess* leaves on

Sunday at 10 pm (14 hours). It continues on to Cotabato.

Mindoro From Caticlan to Roxas, a big outrigger boat goes on Monday and Friday at 9.30 am (P280; five hours). From December to May it can even leave as often as every other day. In bad weather the sea in the Tablas Strait is very rough and the crossing is not to be recommended. Small vessels sometimes sail across, but they tend to be completely unsuitable and often dangerously overloaded.

From Buruanga to San Jose there is another big outrigger boat which leaves on Wednesday and Saturday at 7 am (eight hours). This trip is also not recommended when the waves are high in Tablas Strait. Another big outrigger boat leaves Libertad for San Jose on Monday and Friday at 3 am (11 hours, via Caluya Island and Semirara Island).

From Lipata to San Jose, the MV *Princess Melanie Joy* and the MV *Aida* leave once or twice a week (24 hours). They go via Semira Island and Caluya Island, where they lie up to 10 hours at anchor. Lipata is a small place five km north of Culasi on the west coast of Panay.

Negros From Iloilo City to Bacolod, the MV *St Rafael*, the MV *Michael* and the MV *SM/DV* of Negros Navigation leave daily at 6, 7, 8, 9 and 11.30 am, noon and 12.30, 3.30, 4 and 5 pm (P55 to P160; one to two hours, depending on the ferry). Note that these times change frequently.

The MV *Bacolod Express* leaves daily at 7.15 am (Sunday at 7.30 am) and 2 pm (Friday and Sunday at 3 pm) (P100; one hour). Tickets for this fully air-conditioned catamaran are on sale at the wharf.

From Culasi, the MV *Queen Rose* or the MV *Princess Jo* leaves for Da-an Banwa, the port of Victorias, daily between 9 and 11 am, and the MV *Seven Seas* or MV *San Vicente* leaves from Malayu-an for the same destination daily between 9 and 11 am. Either trip takes two hours. Culasi and Malayu-an are two small places near Ajuy on the east coast of Panay.

Palawan From Iloilo City to Cuyo and Puerta Princesa, the Milagrosa Shipping Lines' MV *Milagrosa-J-Tres* leaves on the 2nd, 12th and 22nd of each month at 6 pm. It takes 12 hours to reach Cuyo (P170), and 38 hours (including an eight hour stopover in Cuyo) to reach Puerto Princesa (P360). Their MV *Milagrosa-J-Dos* sails on the 6th, 16th and 26th of the month at 6 pm.

Romblon From Boracay to Looc on Tablas, a big outrigger boat leaves about twice a week (two hours), and for Santa Fe on Tablas daily at 6.30 am (1½ hours). At Santa Fe, you can get a jeepney to Tugdan, Tablas Island's airport.

From Caticlan to Looc on Tablas, a big outrigger boat leaves on Tuesday and Saturday at 8.30 am, and Friday at 3.30 pm (two hours).

ILOILO CITY

Apparently the name Iloilo stems from the expression 'Ilong-Ilong', which means 'like a nose'. This refers to the outline of the city centre, which lies between the mouths of the Iloilo and Batiano rivers.

Iloilo City is not very different from other Philippine port towns of a similar size, but its image has recently been improved. Of interest, apart from some lovely old houses in the side streets, are the modern jeepneys and those loosely styled after the American street cruisers of the 1950s.

Information

Tourist Office The tourist office (☎ 337 5411) is on Bonifacio Drive.

Money The Chartered Bank gives a good rate of exchange, but charges a P33 handling fee per cheque. You might get yourself a better deal at the Philippine National Bank, on the corner of General Luna and Valeria Sts.

Telephone The area code for Iloilo City is 033.

Things to See

The small 'Window on the Past' **Museo Iloilo** on Bonifacio Drive is worth a visit. On request, visitors are shown videos of the attractions of Panay and various Philippine festivals. It's open daily from 9 am to noon and 1 to 5 pm. Admission is P10.

Six km west of the city is the suburb of **Arevalo**. Until a few years ago, it was well known as a centre for the production of woven fabrics from *jusi* and piña. Today only one loom still exists at the Sinamay Dealer on Osmeña St. You can buy clothes and fabrics here. It is in a beautiful old house partly furnished with valuable carved furniture – something that only wealthy Filipinos can afford. On the way to Arevalo, you pass through **Molo**, which has a 19th-century church constructed from blocks of coral.

Special Events

Every year on the weekend after the Ati-Atihan Festival in Kalibo, the people of Iloilo City celebrate the city's greatest festival, the Dinagyang. The paraw regatta, a race between outrigger sail boats in the Iloilo Strait, between Iloilo City and Guimaras Island, is held on the second Saturday or Sunday in February.

In Pavia, a little north of Iloilo City, water buffalo races take place each year on 3 May from 8 am. To get there, take a jeepney from the SM Shoemart on Valeria St.

Places to Stay – bottom end

Located on the corner of Aldeguer and JM Basa Sts, the *Iloilo Lodging House* (☎ 72384) has rooms with fan for P130/ 180, with fan and bath for P160/230 and with air-con and bath for P230/310. The fittings are basic, plus it's cramped and anything but comfortable; bathrooms are shared between two rooms. The accommodation at the *Eros Travellers Pensionne* (☎ 71359) on General Luna St, is basic and nothing special; rooms with fan and bath cost P160/200 and with air-con and bath P220/290. They have their own restaurant.

There's a friendly atmosphere at the popular *Family Pension House* (☎ 270070) also on General Luna St. They will let you have a clean, adequate room with fan and bath for P200/225 and with air-con and bath for between P350 and P700.

Places to Stay – middle

A pleasant hotel is the *Villa Rosa by the Sea* (☎ 76953) in Calaparan, Villa, about six km west of Iloilo City. Rooms with air-con and bath cost P400 to P800. This is a well-run beach resort hotel with basic, but pleasant rooms. The beach is not particularly inviting. They also have a restaurant and a pool. A taxi here from the airport should cost about P80.

Centrally located in a lane between JM Basa and Iznart Sts, the *Centercon Hotel* (☎ 73431) provides noisy rooms with fan for P300 and comfortable ones with air-con and bath for P390/495. The standard at the *Madia-as Hotel* (☎ 72756) is decidedly better than the modest entrance stuck in a hallway off Aldeguer St would lead you to expect. Worth the money charged, the rooms are clean and comfortable, costing P300/325 with fan and bath, and P395/485 with air-con and bath.

The rooms at the *Original River Queen Hotel* (☎ 270176; fax 200854) on Bonifacio

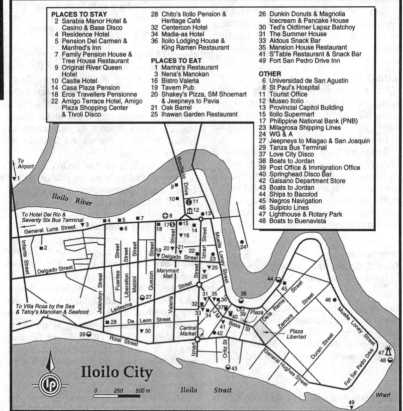

PLACES TO STAY
2 Sarabia Manor Hotel & Casino & Base Disco
4 Residence Hotel
5 Pension Del Carmen & Manfred's Inn
7 Family Pension House & Tree House Restaurant
9 Original River Queen Hotel
10 Castle Hotel
14 Casa Plaza Pension
18 Eros Travellers Pensionne
22 Amigo Terrace Hotel, Amigo Plaza Shopping Center & Tivoli Disco

28 Chito's Iloilo Pension & Heritage Café
32 Centercon Hotel
34 Madia-as Hotel
36 Iloilo Lodging House & King Ramen Restaurant

PLACES TO EAT
1 Marina's Restaurant
3 Nena's Manokan
16 Bistro Valeria
19 Tavern Pub
20 Shakey's Pizza, SM Shoemart & Jeepneys to Pavia
21 Oak Barrel
25 Ihawan Garden Restaurant

26 Dunkin Donuts & Magnolia Icecream & Pancake House
30 Ted's Oldtimer Lapaz Batchoy
31 The Summer House
33 Aldous Snack Bar
35 Mansion House Restaurant
41 S'Table Restaurant & Snack Bar
49 Fort San Pedro Drive Inn

OTHER
6 Universidad de San Agustin
8 St Paul's Hospital
11 Tourist Office
12 Museo Iloilo
13 Provincial Capitol Building
15 Iloilo Supermart
17 Philippine National Bank (PNB)
23 Milagrosa Shipping Lines
24 WG & A
27 Jeepneys to Miagao & San Joaquin
29 Tanza Bus Terminal
37 Love City Disco
38 Boats to Jordan
39 Post Office & Immigration Office
40 Springhead Disco Bar
42 Gaisano Department Store
43 Boats to Jordan
44 Ships to Bacolod
45 Negros Navigation
46 Sulpicio Lines
47 Lighthouse & Rotary Park
48 Boats to Buenavista

THE VISAYAS

Iloilo City

Drive are all right, if a little worn. With fan and bath they cost P215/300 and with air-con and bath P420/520. Also on Bonifacio Drive, close to the Original River Queen Hotel, *The Castle Hotel* (☎ 81021) is an older, refurbished building with an imposing façade. Small, clean singles with fan and bath cost P325, with air-con and bath P435 and doubles with air-con and bath cost P525 to P935.

A good deal, and worth recommending, *Chito's Iloilo Pension* at 180 Jalandoni St at the corner of De Leon St near the Tanza bus terminal (☎ 76415; fax 81186) offers rooms with air-con and bath for P530/650. All equipped with TV, the more expensive ones have a refrigerator. You can eat in the restaurant on the premises and enjoy a swim in the small, well-designed swimming pool. Service to the airport is available for P40.

The tastefully decorated *Pension del Carmen* (☎ 81626) on General Luna St, on the Iloilo River across from the Universidad de San Agustin, offers a pleasant family style atmosphere. Rooms with TV, air-con and bath cost P650/720. Right next door, *Manfred's Inn* (☎ 73788; fax 70736) has decent rooms with air-con and bath from P600 to P1050, and there is a restaurant. Also on General Luna St about 250m further east, *The Residence Hotel* (☎ 81091; fax 72454) has nice singles/doubles overlooking the river, with TV, air-con and bath from P550/600 to P1230/1400. It has a restaurant and a coffee shop.

Places to Stay – top end

Situated a little outside the centre of town on the Iloilo River, the *Hotel del Rio* (☎ 271171; fax 70736) on MH del Pilar St is a lovely, older place with a restaurant and swimming pool. The service is friendly. The rooms are all right, although of differing standards; those with air-con and bath cost P700/750, while suites cost P1400 and P1680.

The best hotel in the centre of town is the *Amigo Terrace Hotel* (☎ 74811; fax 270610) on Iznart St. An air-con room with bath goes for P900, and suites with TV from P1600 to P3000. The accommodation is comfortable, although some parts of the hotel are a bit

noisy. There is a restaurant and a swimming pool.

On General Luna St, the *Sarabia Manor Hotel* (☎ 271021; fax 79127) is a well-run establishment with pleasantly furnished rooms with TV, air-con and bath from P700 to P900 and suites from P2500 to P3800. To while away the time, you can visit the casino, disco and swimming pool.

Places to Eat

The most popular, and probably the best, native restaurant is called *Tatoy's Manokan & Seafood*, at Villa Beach on the western edge of town, about eight km from the city centre. The short drive there by jeepney or taxi will be well worth the effort. Hundreds of Filipinos make the trek there everyday, many of them only because of the tasty chicken, which gave Tatoy's its reputation in the first place. But the other items on the menu are also excellent. First you go to the buffet and pick out your food, then you wash your hands and wait only a few minutes until the waitress serves the tasty morsels. Here the food is eaten with the fingers, a struggle the locals particularly enjoy watching from the neighbouring tables.

However, there are also some cosy little rustic restaurants serving Filipino food nearer the city centre. These include *Nena's Manokan* restaurant on General Luna St, where the food is also eaten with the fingers; the airy *Tree House Restaurant* (good steaks) belonging to the Family Pension House with its very pleasant atmosphere; and the popular *Marina's Restaurant*, a beautifully situated garden restaurant on the north bank of the river.

You can get good Chinese and Filipino meals on JM Basa St, upstairs in the *Mansion House Restaurant* and in *The Summer House*, which also serves a 'mean' western breakfast. Iloilo City has several Batchoy restaurants – two of the best are *Ted's Oldtimer Lapaz Batchoy* on Mabini St and the *Oak Barrel* on Valeria St. (Batchoy is a speciality of the western Visayas and consists of beef, pork and liver in noodle soup.)

The air-conditioned *Tavern Pub*, on the corner of Quezon and Delgado Sts is well kept and cosy. The prices are a bit steep, but the fish dishes are fairly inexpensive and the choice of cocktails impressive. The *Golden Salakot*, one of three good restaurants in the Hotel Del Rio, serves fairly cheap buffet lunches and dinners daily.

The *Aldous Snack Bar* keeps long hours, and is a popular night-time rendezvous. In good weather, the open-air restaurant *Fort San Pedro Drive Inn* is popular for beer and barbecues.

If you have a sweet tooth, don't miss the *S'Table Restaurant & Snack Bar* on JM Basa St, which probably has the best selection of cakes in Iloilo City.

For snacks and ice cream, try the *Magnolia Icecream & Pancake House* on Iznart St. Right next to it, the *Dunkin Donut* is open 24 hours.

Entertainment
The best and most popular discos in Iloilo City are *Tivoli* in the Amigo Terrace Hotel and the *Base Disco* in the Sarabia Manor Hotel.

Among the simplest discos are the rustic *Fountain Head*, *Kuweba* and *Love City Disco*. The *Ihawan Garden Restaurant* on Delgado St features live music and is packed every evening.

Getting There & Away
Air PAL has an office at Iloilo airport (☎ 320 3131, 70925) and on General Luna St (☎ 75925, 78471).

Bus Ceres Liner buses from Iloilo City to Estancia, Roxas, Kalibo and Caticlan leave from the Tanza bus terminal on Rizal St near the corner of Ledesma St. There is a daily bus at 3 and 9 am direct to Caticlan.

As a rule, the 11 am bus to Kalibo should arrive in time for the last connection from Kalibo to Caticlan and Boracay, but it could be dark when the boat from Caticlan reaches Boracay. The trip takes about four hours to Kalibo (P60), and six hours to Caticlan (P80).

Getting Around
The Airport It's about seven km from the airport to the centre of town. If you take a PU-Cab, it should cost about P100. Private cars cost about half.

SOUTH COAST
Although there are several beach resorts with cottages along the south coast, between Arevalo and San Joaquin, the beaches are not up to much. A good base for short trips to other coastal places or the Nadsadan Falls near Igbaras is the *Coco Grove Beach Resort* at Tigbauan. It has cottages with fan and bath for about P500.

Getting There & Away
Buses from the Seventy Six Company run daily from Iloilo City to San Jose de Buenavista (two hours), leaving about every hour from 5 am to 5.30 pm from MH del Pilar St, in the Molo district.

Although buses travel along the south coast, most don't go via Anini-y and Dao (see Anini-y & Nogas Island later in this section). Numbered tickets are on sale at a kiosk before departure.

Guimbal
'Home of the sweetest mangoes in Iloilo Province', Guimbal is also famous for its sandstone church, which dates back to the time of the Spaniards. It also has three watchtowers built in the 16th century, from which smoke signals used to be sent to warn against pirates.

Miagao
Miagao, 40 km west of Iloilo City, has a mighty church resembling a fortress that dates back to 1787. It has unusual reliefs on the façade mixing European elements (St Christopher) and Philippine plants (coconut palms and papaya trees).

San Joaquin
The most 'military' church in the Philippines is in San Joaquin. The façade, built of blocks of coral, shows the battle of the Spanish against the Moors in Tetuan, Morocco, in

1859. Every second Saturday in January, water buffalo fights take place in San Joaquin.

Places to Stay The *Talisayan Beach Resort* has cottages with fan and bath for P800 and with air-con and bath for P1000. Although basic, this is a pleasant resort; the staff can arrange meals for you.

Anini-y & Nogas Island

Anini-y has a massive old church of white coral built by Augustinian monks during the Spanish colonial period. Private overnight accommodation is available with Mrs Magdalena Cazenas.

From Anini-y you can go to Nogas Island, which has white beaches and excellent diving areas. Although there is no regular service, you can get a paddle banca to take you across for about P50.

Getting There & Away There is a daily bus through Anini-y that goes as far as Dao, leaving from the corner of Fuentes and De Leon Sts in Iloilo City at 7 am. There may also be others leaving at 11 am and noon (three hours). The return bus leaves Anini-y at 12.30 pm; there are sometimes others at 4.30 and 6.30 am.

A daily jeepney goes from San Joaquin to Anini-y at 10 am, taking one hour and possibly going on to Dao. The return jeepney from Anini-y leaves at 1 pm.

WEST COAST
San Jose de Buenavista

San Jose de Buenavista is the capital of Antique Province, so Filipinos know the town not by its official name but as San Jose Antique.

Places to Stay The *Susana Guest House*, across from the Seventy Six bus terminal, has basic rooms with fan and bath for P100/200. The *Annavic Plaza Hotel* (☎ 558) is relatively good in its price range, offering rooms with fan and bath for P200/250 and with air-con and bath for P450/550.

Places to Eat The handful of restaurants closes very early in the evening. After 7 pm the only place open is *Nina's Pizza & Restaurant* near the Seventy Six bus terminal. It is possible that the good *Diamond Garden Restaurant* will still be open; it's 500m outside of town in a northerly direction.

Getting There & Away There are few jeepneys and buses from San Jose de Buenavista to Culasi (three hours) and Pandan (five hours). Some jeepneys only go as far as Culasi. From Pandan you can get connections to Malay and Kalibo.

Culasi

You may like to break the trip along the west coast of Panay at Culasi and spend a few days on Mararison Island. Although there is no regular boat service there, one or two crossings a day are possible. A Special Ride costs around P100 and takes approximately 30 minutes.

A boat makes the trip from Lipata, about five km north of Culasi, once or twice a week to San Jose, Mindoro, via the Semirara Islands. A tricycle to Lipata takes 10 minutes and costs P5.

Places to Stay The *Balestramon Lodging House* in Culasi is a simple place and has rooms for P75/150.

There is only private accommodation on Mararison Island, at about P200 per night, including three meals.

Getting There & Away From Culasi to San Jose the last bus departs daily at 1.30 pm.

THE NORTH-EAST
Concepcion, San Dionisio & Pan de Azucar Island

Concepcion and San Dionisio are small places on the east coast of Panay with quite big markets. There is a string of beautiful islands lying offshore which you can reach quickly by outrigger boat.

The most conspicuous island is Pan de Azucar – its 573m high 'sugar loaf' can be seen from a long way off. For the time being, it will continue only to attract visitors who are prepared to put up with its basic amenities. Little **Agho Island**, too, a little farther south-east, is among the more attractive of the islands. However, this island is the private property of the mayor of Concepcion, who issues permits to visitors before they can go there.

Places to Stay In Concepcion, the *SBS Iyang Beach Resort* has passable cottages with fan and bath for P250/350. It also has a restaurant, and the owners, Sandy and Betty Salcedo, will organise trips to offshore islands on request (P2500 a day!). You can only stay in private houses in San Dionisio, for example, with the Magsongsong family on JM Basa St; it's about P100 per person.

On Pan de Azucar Island you also have to depend on private hospitality, but as the locals are friendly, this should not be too difficult. You could ask for Anidlina de Julian who is glad to put up travellers (about P50 per person). She doesn't mind preparing the fish you bought from the fishermen at the beach for your meal. If you turn up unannounced, take provisions with you, including drinking water. There's only room for two people, unless you are willing to sleep in the open.

Getting There & Away From Iloilo City to Concepcion, there are a few Ceres Liner buses, taking 2½ hours. The last departure could be as early as 3 pm. There is no direct bus from Iloilo City to San Dionisio. The best way to get there is by Ceres Liner bus from the Tanza bus terminal on Rizal St to Estancia. They leave every hour from 4 am to 4 pm. To go to San Dionisio, get off at Sara and take a jeepney, or you can also catch one coming through at the turn-off in Deveria.

Outrigger boats leave from Dionisio to Pan de Azucar Island between 9 and 11 am (P10; 45 minutes). Apparently the boats leave Concepcion on Thursday, market day. A Special Ride should cost around P200.

Estancia

This unassuming little town serves mainly as a jumping-off point for the offshore islands.

Boats cross from here to the Sicogon, Gigante Islands and other destinations.

Places to Stay The *Terry & Em Lodge* (☎ 388) on Cement St, has simple rooms for P80/140 and with fan for P100/150. The *Fuentes Lodging House* on Inventor St offers basic accommodation with rooms with fan and bath for P120/200. The *Vila Lily Beach Resort* (☎ 429) is a fairly large establishment on a hill near Estancia. It has rooms with fan and bath for P250/350 and cottages with air-con and bath for P560.

The *Pa-on Beach Resort* (☎ 444), just a bit out of town, has dorm beds for P75 and clean rooms with fan and bath for P230/325 and with air-con and bath for P445/535.

Places to Eat Estancia's few restaurants close very early. Only *Melbert Restaurant* in Reyes Ave stays open after 8 pm. The *Together Restaurant* across from the Ceres Liner bus terminal is good and fairly inexpensive.

Getting There & Away Ceres Liner buses leave daily from Iloilo City to Estancia (five hours) every hour between 4 am and 4 pm from the Tanza bus terminal on Rizal St.

From Roxas to Estancia, there are several jeepneys or minibuses every morning. You may have to change at President Roxas. Apparently two Ceres Liner buses leave between 7.30 and 9 am (three hours).

Sicogon Island

On the idyllic island of Sicogon, on the magnificent white sand Bantill Beach, stands the Sicogon Island Club, one of the first beach resort hotels in the Philippines to achieve international recognition. It's hard to believe it, but this luxurious establishment with its 120 cottages, swimming pool, tennis court etc, has been closed for quite some time. Among many factors contributing to its demise, perhaps its peculiar policy of trying to minimise all contact between locals and tourists had a lot to do with it. (Sicogon's 3000 inhabitants were strictly forbidden to let rooms to tourists. They also were not

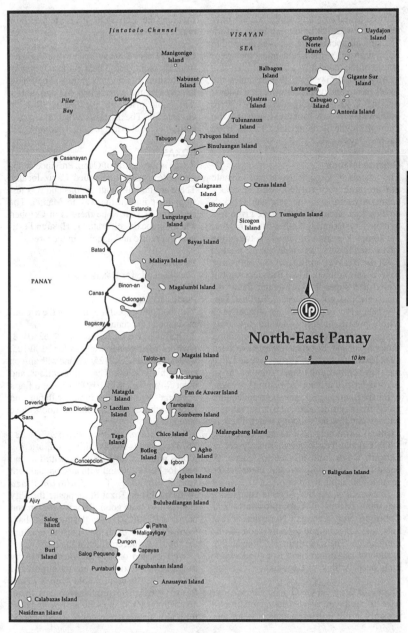

allowed to sell anything, so the island's only restaurant was that belonging to the resort. To cap it all, locals were not even allowed to bring strangers to the island unless they were guests of the resort.)

Any touristic venture that excludes the locals has to end up creating social tensions, not the kind of background considerate holidaymakers are looking for. But, who knows? Maybe Sicogon Island will soon see happier days again.

Gigante Islands

The islands of Gigante Norte and Gigante Sur are both very rugged. Massive rocks, commonly known as the 'enchanted rocks', contain lots of caves which have given rise to many mysterious tales. It is rumoured that the complex system of tunnels between the caves used to serve as a hide-out for pirates.

Of the 10 caves on Gigante Sur, only three have been explored. Most islanders are too scared and superstitious to enter them and many are just not interested. **Turtle Cave**, also called Pawikan, has a huge antechamber where white monkeys swing on roots hanging down from the top of the opening. Tiniphagan and Elephant caves have been even less explored than Turtle Cave and they may have connecting tunnels to other caves. A good departure point for visiting the caves is Barrio Lantangan. It's recommended that you hire a guide and take stout shoes, torches, candles and drinking water. There is a natural swimming pool near the caves.

On Gigante Norte you can easily get to **Langub Cave** from the Barrio Piagao. A beautiful beach with crystal clear water stretches all along the barrio.

Just south of the two Gigante Islands are the small islands of **Cabugao Norte** and **Cabugao Sur**. Cabugao Norte has a few huts, a small cave and a pretty good swimming beach. The settlement on Cabugao Sur is slightly larger and there is a good swimming beach with very fine sand.

Places to Stay On the Gigante Islands you have to find your own accommodation – possibly at the Barrio Lantangan – but this shouldn't be a problem. It's up to you how much you pay.

Getting There & Away To go to the Gigantes from Estancia, you'd best get in touch with Mr Rustum Tan and his family. They have relatives on the islands and can negotiate a reasonable price for the Special Ride to Gigante Sur. The trip takes 2½ hours. Apparently, there is also a regular daily connection.

ROXAS

Roxas is the capital of Capiz Province and is therefore usually just called Capiz locally. There are no tourist attractions and it is just stopping point on the way to Manila. The best time of year to be there is in October, when the locals celebrate the Halaran Festival with music and dancing in the streets.

Telephone

The area code for Roxas is 036.

Places to Stay

You shouldn't expect too much of the accommodation in the centre of town.

On Roxas Ave, the *Beehive Inn* (☎ 6210418) provides basic rooms with fan for P100/125, with fan and bath for P125/200 and with air-con and bath for P300. The unpretentious and quiet *River Inn* (☎ 6210809) on Lapu Lapu St charges P120/140 for rooms with fan, and P260 for those with air-con. The doors close here at 9 pm.

The *Halaran Avenue Pension* (☎ 621 0675) on Roxas Ave is fairly good, offering rooms with fan for P150/200, with fan and bath for P200/250 and with air-con and bath for P300/350. The *Halaran Plaza* (☎ 6210649) on Rizal St, opposite the City Hall, is also quite good. Rooms with fan and bath cost P230/290 and with air-con and bath from P340/390. Although not outstanding, the rooms are acceptable for the money.

Well located on Baybay Beach (P15 by tricycle from Roxas) between the airport and Culasi port, the comfortable *Marc's Beach Resort* (☎ 6210103) provides rooms with fan and bath for P400 and with air-con and bath for P500. It has a tennis court. Another good place in Baybay is *Villa Patria Cottages* (☎ 6210180), where singles/doubles with air-con and bath cost P680/780.

Places to Eat
Of the few restaurants in Roxas only two are worth mentioning. *John's Fast Foods* on Roxas Ave, opposite Halaran Avenue Pension, is remarkably cheap and has a large selection of Filipino and Chinese dishes. *Halaran Restaurant* in the Halaran Avenue Pension serves well-priced comida (the daily special) but no beer. There are a few beer gardens and eateries with live music near the church: from Roxas Ave, go over the river, then turn off to the right when you come to the church.

Getting There & Away
Air PAL has an office at Roxas airport (☎ 210618).

Bus From Iloilo City to Roxas, Ceres Liner buses leave every 30 minutes from 4 am to 5.30 pm from the Tanza bus terminal on Rizal St (four hours).

The last bus for Iloilo City usually leaves Roxas at about 11 am.

Several buses go from Roxas to Kalibo daily, departing between 5 am and noon (3½ hours).

Getting Around
Roxas airport is about four km west of Roxas.

Culasi Port is about six km west of Roxas. The ride by tricycle from there to the city takes 10 minutes and costs P15.

KALIBO
The oldest town in Aklan, Kalibo is also the capital of the province. Well known for the piña textiles and intricately woven abaca shoes and handbags it manufactures, Kalibo is even more renowned for the annual Ati-Atihan Festival held in January. This is the Mardi Gras of the Philippines. Long before the show begins, the people of Aklan can think of nothing but the vibrant tom-toms, the sound of which dominates the festival's

activities from beginning to end. Other villages and towns in the Philippines hold similar festivals but the one in Kalibo is the most popular.

About 20 km north-west of Kalibo are the **Jawili Falls**, which cascade down the valley, forming several basins where you can have a refreshing swim. To get there, take a bus or jeepney from Kalibo going to Nabas or Caticlan, get off at Tangalan and go on by tricycle.

Just under 20 km south-west of Kalibo, there is a long, grey beach with fine sand called Aroma Beach. Overnight accommodation is available. You can get there from Kalibo by taking a jeepney or tricycle to Dumaguit (30 minutes), then by boat over the bay to Batan (10 minutes), then another tricycle from Batan on to Aroma Beach (10 minutes).

In **Banga**, a few km south of Kalibo, you can visit the Aklan Agricultural College with its well-equipped experimental station. If you want to stay, there is a guesthouse.

Telephone
The area code for Kalibo is 036.

Places to Stay
During the Ati-Atihan Festival, prices in Kalibo may triple, and it can be almost impossible to find a hotel room.

Basic, clean rooms at *Gervy's Lodge* on G Pastrana St cost P80/160. *RB Lodge* on the same street, has basic, fairly good rooms with fan for P100/200, and with air-con and bath for P350.

The *Apartel Marietta* on Roxas Ave offers basic and noisy accommodation. Rooms with fan go for P200/400, with fan and bath for P300/500 and with air-con and bath for P800.

A warm welcome awaits you at the spruce *Garcia Legaspi Mansion* on Roxas Ave (☎ 662 3251), where rooms with fan go for P300/350, with fan and bath for P350/450, with air-con and bath for P600/700; suites cost P850. This is immaculate accommodation on the third floor with good rooms. They are planning to open a coffee shop and pool.

There are a couple of passable hotels on S Martelino St. The *Glowmoon Hotel* (☎ 662 3073) offers adequate rooms with fan for P250/350, and with air-con and bath from P500 to P700. The food in the restaurant here is excellent, if not that cheap. About 50m further south, the *Casa Alba Hotel* has rooms with fan for P300/400 and with air-con and bath for P700/800. This is a fairly basic hotel with slightly overpriced rooms.

In a residential area in a side street off the main road, the *Beachcomber Inn* on Roldan St (☎ 868 4765) is a pleasant, quiet place to stay. They charge P750 for well maintained rooms with fan, and P850/950 for those with air-con and bath.

About 10 minutes away from Kalibo (P20 by tricycle), the *Hibiscus Garden Club* (☎ 868 4488) in Andagao, is probably the best accommodation in and around Kalibo. Inviting rooms with loads of plants all around cost P800 with fan and bath, and P950 with air-con and bath. They have a very good restaurant and a pool where you feel like you are swimming in a forest glade. A free airport service is offered.

Just outside Kalibo in Napti, the *Aroma Beach Resort* has roomy cottages with fan

and bath for P500. The resort only has three two-room cottages that are big enough for four people. Their restaurant serves German and Philippine cooking.

Places to Eat
Enjoy outstanding Chinese food at the *Peking House Restaurant* on Martyrs St. The set menu for P65 can be recommended. The *Hibiscus Garden* in Andagao (see Places to Stay) is like a sanctuary. This inviting restaurant by the pool also has a friendly bar. It serves excellent Filipino and international dishes, European specialities and desserts like vanilla ice cream with mango flambé.

Getting There & Away
Air PAL has an office at Kalibo airport (☎ 662 3260). The flights from Kalibo to Manila are often hopelessly overbooked. This could also happen on flights to Cebu City, so you would be well advised to confirm your return flight or connecting flight at the PAL counter as soon as you arrive. There is also a PAL office on Boracay which will deal with flight confirmations and changes of itinerary.

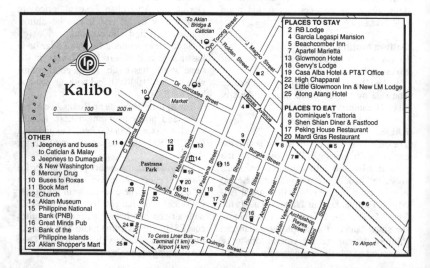

PLACES TO STAY
2 RB Lodge
4 Garcia Legaspi Mansion
5 Beachcomber Inn
7 Apartel Marietta
13 Glowmoon Hotel
18 Gervy's Lodge
19 Casa Alba Hotel & PT&T Office
22 High Chapparal
24 Little Glowmoon Inn & New LM Lodge
25 Atong Atang Hotel

PLACES TO EAT
8 Dominique's Trattoria
9 Shen Shian Diner & Fastfood
17 Peking House Restaurant
20 Mardi Gras Restaurant

OTHER
1 Jeepneys and buses to Caticlan & Malay
3 Jeepneys to Dumaguit & New Washington
6 Mercury Drug
10 Buses to Roxas
11 Book Mart
12 Church
14 Aklan Museum
15 Philippine National Bank (PNB)
16 Great Minds Pub
21 Bank of the Philippine Islands
23 Aklan Shopper's Mart

Kalibo

0   100   200 m

Sooc River

To Aklan Bridge & Caticlan

Oyo Torong Street
Roldan Street
J Magno Street
Dr Gonzales Street
Market
Legaspi Street
Pastrana Park
Maristela Street
Pastrana Street
Roxas Avenue
Burgos Street
Martyrs Street
Luis Barrios Street
G Ramos Street
Acevedo Street
Aklan Veterans Avenue
Archbishop Reyes Street
Mabini Street
Rizal Street
Jose Street
F Quimpo Street

To Cares Liner Bus Terminal (1 km) & Airport (4 km)

To Airport

Bus From Iloilo City to Kalibo, Ceres Liner buses leave every hour from 3 am to 3 pm (five hours). An express bus leaves at 7 am (P60; four hours). After heavy rain the journey can easily take up to twice as long, as the road becomes a mud track in places.

From Kalibo, several Ceres Liner buses go to Iloilo City daily. The last trip may be at about 2 pm. Express buses leave at 7 and 10.30 am and noon and perhaps 1 pm, but not all are air-conditioned buses, which have more comfortable seats.

Buses run from Kalibo to Roxas (3½ hours) at 8 and 11 am and 2 pm from C Laserna St. Minibuses run in between.

After flight arrivals, jeepneys and comfortable air-con buses leave the airport for Caticlan (P150; two hours), where boats for Boracay leave. Tickets for the air-con buses are on sale outside the airport, and include the boat transfer which costs P15.

Jeepney Several jeepneys make the trip from Kalibo to Caticlan (P30; two hours) daily from Roxas Ave.

Boat Boats leave from Dumaguit port to Manila and Cebu (see Getting There & Away at the start of this section). Jeepneys ply between Dumaguit port and Kalibo (P5; 30 minutes).

Getting Around
The Airport It's only a few km from the airport to town. Normally, a tricycle costs P4 per person, and a Special Ride for two people P10 (however, you could be asked for P50 or more).

Bus The Ceres Liner bus terminal is at the southern edge of town. A tricycle from there to the departure point of the jeepneys for Caticlan/Boracay costs P2 per person.

IBAJAY
Ibajay (pronounced Eebahi) is a small town halfway between Kalibo and Caticlan. Each year on the weekend after the Kalibo festival, the 'really original' Ati-Atihan Festival (according to the locals) is held here. It is more authentic and traditional than the commercialised Kalibo festival. Sunday is the main day. The festival is very colourful and offers great opportunities for photos.

CATICLAN
This small town in the north-west corner of Panay is the starting point for outrigger boats to offshore Boracay Island. Before boarding, you have to register at the ticket counter. As it has no pier, you will have to wade through the water to get to the boats. Apart from the wharf, Caticlan also has an airstrip for small planes, which are being used increasingly to go to and from Manila.

The best day for day trips from Boracay to Caticlan is Sunday, when the market and the cockfights take place.

About 25 km south-west of Caticlan the **Ignito Cave** (Elephant Cave), a dripstone cave, was discovered as late as 1966. It is open to the public and can be crossed in half an hour (admission P150). Tours are on offer on Boracay. If, however, you want to make a day trip under your own steam, eg by mountain bike, then take the coast road from Caticlan to about five km past Buruanga. At that point, a track breaks off from the road to the left and takes you up the three km to the cave. Wooden steps take you the last few metres up to the cave entrance.

Getting There & Away
Bus There is a direct daily Ceres Liner bus to Iloilo City via Kalibo departing from Caticlan at around 6.30 am and noon. It takes two hours to reach Kalibo and six hours to reach Iloilo City. The last bus from Kalibo to Iloilo City leaves at about 2 pm. There are also several jeepneys from Caticlan to Kalibo daily.

Several air-con buses go daily from Caticlan to Kalibo airport. Tickets are on sale on Boracay.

Boat Several large outrigger boats make the trip from Caticlan to Boracay (P15; 30 minutes) daily until late in the afternoon. They tie up at three places, the so-called boat stations on White Beach, provided for them by the tourist office.

Getting Around

The Airport A tricycle between the small Malay airport and the Caticlan wharf 500m away costs P30.

BORACAY

Boracay Island is a great place for just lazing around. Seven km long, it is only one km wide at its narrowest point. Boracay's largest villages or *barangays* are Yapac, Balabag and Manoc-Manoc. They, and several smaller hamlets called *sitios*, are connected by a confusing network of paths and tracks, so the map of Boracay can only serve as a general guide. Slightly more than half the 5200 population live in Manoc-Manoc.

There is a beautiful beach on the west coast with very fine white sand, particularly near Balabag. The water is quite shallow, however. For snorkelling the east coast is better but beware of rips. There are scores of little sandy bays scattered around the island; they make an attractive alternative to the ever popular White Beach.

The atmosphere on Diniwid Beach is also pleasant and peaceful, just to the north of White Beach. There are a few places offering inexpensive accommodation there that would cost twice as much at White Beach. Also well worth the visit is the immaculate Punta Beach.

Boracay is also well known for its now very rare gleaming white puka shells, said to be the best in the world. For years puka shells were dug out of the beach at Yapak and then sold. It's already a *fait accompli* that large masses of land are soon going to be moved in the north of the island. The most important Philippine property developers, Ayala Land, Fil-Estate and Primetown Property Group have bought up 205 hectares of land. There they intend to build resorts and housing for the better-off; construction on the obligatory golf course is already well under way.

It cannot be denied that the island has lost its innocence. But, in spite of the odd incident and various sins against the environment, it still has that certain something about it. Among its good points, the friendly locals being one of them, are the carefully tended gardens, the individually designed resorts, and the tastefully decorated cottages.

Every day seems to be a holiday on Boracay – all you need to do is relax and enjoy yourself. Just get up, make some coffee and decide whether to go sailing, windsurfing or perhaps snorkelling and looking at corals. If you're curious you may get as far as the 'Caves of the Flying Dogs of Yapak' or **Bat Caves** (admission P20) on the other side of the island, where there are still fishermen who have nothing to do with tourism, except that they too have to pay higher prices in the stores.

For many people, Boracay is the typical Pacific island paradise. Whether this will change in the foreseeable future depends on how much building development goes on, which will inevitably change the face of the island out of all recognition. The new slogan seems to be 'concrete instead of bamboo'. Fortunately, so far most architects have succeeded in designing buildings which do not dominate their environment and fit in with the island around them.

Information

Tourist Office The Department of Tourism runs a small office in Manggayad, at about the middle of White Beach.

Money Travellers cheques and cash can be changed at the Boracay Tourist Center, the foreign exchange counter at the Allied Bank next to the Queen's Beach Resort in Angol, and the Boracay branch of the Allied Bank (☎ 288 3026). At the latter, you can open a peso or dollar account (minimum opening balance of P1000 or US$200). The Boracay Tourist Center will give cash advances on all popular credit cards (for a 7.5% fee). The Allied Bank will only accept American Express.

Post & Communications There is a small post office in Balabag on the basketball court. It would be a good idea to have some

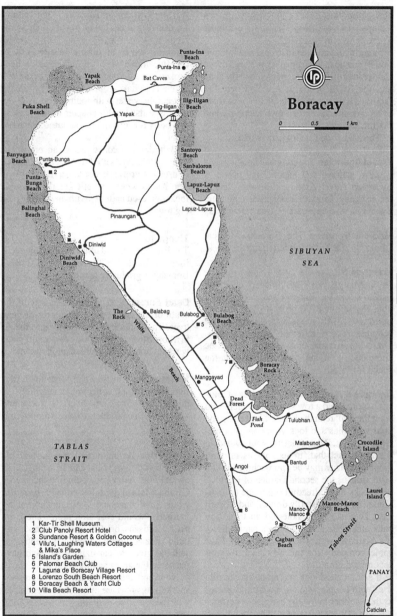

Boracay

0   0.5   1 km

THE VISAYAS

Punta-Ina Beach
Punta-Ina
Yapak Beach
Bat Caves
Ilig-Iligan
Ilig-Iligan Beach
1
Puka Shell Beach
Yapak
Santoyo Beach
Banyugan Beach
Punta-Bunga
2
Sanbaloron Beach
Punta-Bunga Beach
Lapuz-Lapuz Beach
Balinghai Beach
Pinaungan
Lapuz-Lapuz
3
4 Diniwid
Diniwid Beach
SIBUYAN SEA
The Rock
Balabag
Bulabog
5
Bulabog Beach
White
6
7
Boracay Rock
Beach
Manggayad
Dead Forest
TABLAS STRAIT
Fish Pond
Tulubhan
Malabunot
Crocodile Island
Angol
Bantud
Laurel Island
8
Manoc-Manoc
Manoc-Manoc Beach
9 10
Cagban Beach
Tabon Strait
PANAY
Caticlan

1 Kar-Tir Shell Museum
2 Club Panoly Resort Hotel
3 Sundance Resort & Golden Coconut
4 Vilu's, Laughing Waters Cottages
   & Mika's Place
5 Island's Garden
6 Palomar Beach Club
7 Laguna de Boracay Village Resort
8 Lorenzo South Beach Resort
9 Boracay Beach & Yacht Club
10 Villa Beach Resort

change on you. Better still, bring your own stamps with you, from Manila for example. There is no parcel service.

Long-distance calls (national and international) can be made from the Boracay Tourist Center in Manggayad, at Pantelco in Balabag and the RCPI office in Angol, where fax facilities are also available. In the meantime, several resorts have their own telephone and fax links.

The area code for Boracay is 036.

Travel Agencies You can make bookings and confirm national and international tickets at Swagman Travel, Angol and Balabag, and at the Boracay Tourist Center in Manggayad. Swagman also take care of visa extensions.

Medical Services The Boracay Medical Clinic (☎ 288 3147) is open round the clock.

Massage Next to the Titay Theater Restaurant in Manggayad Vibes Shiatsu Center and Fausto's Shiatsu Massage will take care of you. For about P200 an hour well-trained, licensed blind masseurs will provide acupressure and reflexion zone massages. These professional massages should not be compared with the ones available at the beach for P150.

Dangers & Annoyances The influx of tourists has attracted a few shady characters who want their share in the boom. Keep an eye on your valuables and lock your cottage, especially at night. If possible, use your own lock. It's a sad fact that, in security as in other things, Boracay may be approaching the end of its time as the second Garden of Eden.

Attacks have already been made on individuals at night (usually drunk), and women have been sexually molested on their way back alone late at night from a bar or disco. It's better to wait a few minutes and have some company for the way back to your accommodation.

It's not a good idea to arrange snorkelling trips with people who are not from Boracay, as they neither know the dangerous currents nor where the good coral can be found.

The tap water on Boracay is not suitable for drinking at all. I even avoid brushing my teeth with it. Nearly every store carries drinking water in plastic bottles, but be careful, make sure the seal hasn't been broken before you buy any! The best alternative is to have your own water bottle and to treat the water with iodine. This is 100% safe. See the Health chapter at the back of this book for information about iodine treatment.

Batteries are consumed at an enormous rate on Boracay, with the result that disposal of used batteries is becoming a real problem. The island would benefit greatly if people took their used batteries with them to the next big town.

Things to See & Do
The list of sports and other leisure time facilities available on the holiday island of Boracay is gradually getting longer.

Dead Forest Next to the fishponds in the south of the island there are scores of dead trees. Their silhouettes jut eerily into the air in a horribly fascinating way (especially at the witching hour on the night of a full moon).

Museum The Kar-Tir Shell Museum in Ilig-Iligan has a small collection of sea shells on display as well as arts & crafts works and various woven products to see. Admission is P20.

Boat Trips An unhurried trip around the island by outrigger boat can be arranged for about P500. A day trip, including the nearby Carabao Island with its equally beautiful white sand beaches – still unspoiled by tourism – would cost a bit more. There are skilful artisans on Carabao who not only build snazzy *paraw* (a small, fast outrigger sailboat given to capsizing), but also have mastered the art of sailing them well.

Now and then, boat trips to interesting snorkelling areas are available, for example, with the MB *Blue Dolphin*, which costs P150 per person for four hours. The Boracay

Tourist Center in Manggayad rents out safe deposit boxes.

Diving A diving trip, including one dive, the boat and equipment, will cost you P600; four-day courses cost P7500. The equipment at the different dive shops is of varying quality; it's worthwhile making a comparison, and paying particular attention that the equipment is new. For further information, check with Aqualife Diving Center, Aquarius Diving, Asia Divers, Beach Life Diving Center, Boracay Scuba Diving School, Calypso Diving, Far East Scuba Diving Institute, Lapu-Lapu Diving, Nautilus Diving, Ocean Deep Diver Training Center, Sea World Dive Center and Victory Divers.

Horseback Riding A one hour ride, with a guide if necessary, costs about P350 at the Boracay Horse Riding Stables (☎ 288 3311), Balabag, near Friday's. Riding lessons are available.

Sailing On White Beach you can hire a paraw. It costs P100 an hour, or P500 per day.

Snorkelling There are good snorkelling areas at Ilig-Iligan Beach in the north-east and at little Crocodile Island just off the south-east coast. But beware of the strong currents that can often be encountered on the east coast of Boracay. Especially off Crocodile Island and Laurel Island the undertow has been known to put the wind up even strong swimmers. Laurel Island offers a unique attraction for snorkellers. Through an opening in the rocky floor, an iron ladder leads into a partly flooded cave. The cave is open to the sea, and fish and coral can be observed.

Tennis Tennis is available at the Tirol & Tirol Resort, Manggayad (next to the tourist office) for P140 an hour, including rackets and balls.

Windsurfing It costs between P220 and P250 an hour to rent a board. One-week courses cost around P2000. Rental and

courses are available at the restaurant Zur kleinen Kneipe and elsewhere. There are other companies on Bulabog Beach on the east of the island, which is also the venue every January for The Boracay Funboard Cup, one of the leading windsurf competitions in Asia.

Places to Stay

Most of the accommodation is on White Beach, between Balabag and Angol. There are so many of them and they are so alike, it's probably easiest to simply be dropped off in the middle of the beach and wander around until you find a suitable place. Usually the cottages are all equipped with either two single beds or a double bed, and nearly always have their own veranda and bathroom. If you are staying on your own, you may get the price lowered in the off season. But to save embarrassing your landlord, keep quiet about the prices you get – especially to other landlords!

Prices can vary, depending on how successful the season is. Especially around Christmas time when price hikes of up to 200% are possible, while the off season from June until November is good for, at times, big discounts. It's not unusual at this time to get cottages for P150, while during the on season on the other hand, you'll be hard pushed to find any accommodation for under P400.

Out of about 200 beach resorts, a selection has been made of some 50 clean and comfortable places to stay. Each of the villages along White Beach is represented in the different price brackets. The prices shown are for cottages or rooms with fan and bathroom for two people. It would be worthwhile comparing the resorts, because sometimes there is a big difference in what is being offered for the same money (size, furnishing and setting of a cottage, for instance).

Places to Stay – bottom end

There are several good, relatively cheap places in Angol. *Tin-Tin's Cottages*, a small place conveniently just off the beach, has cottages with fan and bath from P150 to

P300. *Sea Side Cottages* is a basic place about 100m behind the Sulu Bar. Cottages with fan and bath cost P250 to P300. Next door, *Charlie's Place* also has cottages with fan and bath from between P250 and P300. The *Highland Spring* is a pleasant, quiet place between Boat Station 3 and the main road. They offer cottages with fan and bath for P300. *Moreno's Place* is good value, with cottages with fan and bath for P300. The *Austrian Pension House* has rooms with fan and bath for P350. It's a friendly place at the south end of Angol.

Moving up the beach to Manggayad, there's the *St. Vincent Cottages* in an alleyway behind the larger Lorenzo Resort. Their cottages go for P300 and P400, with fan and bath. This is an OK place in the interior of the island.

In Balabag, *GP's Resort* next to Lapu-Lapu Diving is good value at P350 for a cottage with fan and bath.

The next four places are all in Diniwid on the little bay just north of White Beach. *Vilu's* is a small set-up, where cottages with fan and bath cost P300. *Laughing Water Cottages* also go for P300, with fan and bath. *Mika's Place* is a friendly place, where they charge P350 for cottages with fan and bath. They also have basic rooms without bath for P250. The *Golden Coconut* has cottages with fan and bath for P350 and P500. It's located on a slope just below the Sundance Resort, with a beautiful view onto the beach.

Places to Stay – middle

There are several places in this category, up to P800 or a bit more.

Melinda's Garden in Angol has cottages with fan and bath for between P450 and P750. It's a pleasant place, set back a little from the beach.

Manggayad has many places in this price range. The *Sunset Beach Resort* has cottages with fan and bath from P400 to P600. The *Bahay Kaibigan* behind the Dalisay Village Resort also offers cottages with fan and bath for P400/600. *Roque's Place* (☎ 288 3356) is a well-run place, and their cottages with fan and bath at P500 are OK for the money.

The *Dalisay Village Resort* has roomy cottages and the service is very helpful. Their cottages with fan and bath go for P700, while those with air-con and bath cost P1750. The *B & B Beach Resort* (☎ 288 3235) has roomy stone-built cottages with fan and bath for P750 and with air-con and bath for P1200.

Balabag also has its fair share of places in this price range, starting with *Bans Beach House*, which has a long row of basic, but adequate cottages with fan and bath for P500. *Fiesta Cottages* will rent you immaculate cottages with fan and bath for P400 and P500, which is relatively good value. *Sunshine Cottages* are good value at P400 and P500 for cottages with fan and bath. *Serina's Place* is a small set-up with passable cottages with fan and bath for P500. All four of them are near the beach. Set back from the beach a little, the family-style *Mistral Beach Resort* will charge you P700 for a pleasantly furnished cottage with fan and bath.

Near Bulabog Beach (east side) in Bulabog, *Island's Garden* provides pleasant accommodation in cottages with fan and bath for P650, and with air-con and bath for P1600. Some of them have two storeys.

Back in Angol, the cottages belonging to the *A-Rock Resort* (☎ 288 3201; fax 288 3002) are all in the second alleyway back from the beach. Of varying standards, those with fan and bath cost P600 to P800, with air-con and bath P1400 (including TV and refrigerator).

Getting closer to the P1000 mark, an excellent choice in Angol is the *Villa Camilla Apartel*, an attractive building with tastefully furnished rooms with fan and bath from between P800 and P1100. They also have a small swimming pool with a bar. Also in Angol, the *South Sea Beach Resort* (☎ 288 3131) has cottages with fan and bath for P800, with air-con and bath for P1800.

Manggayad has several places in the P1000 range. The *Morimar Boracay Resort* has cottages with fan and bath from P800 to P1000. The rooms are spacious and the cottages are set in peaceful grounds about 150m from the beach. *La Isla Bonita Cottage* has cottages with fan and bath for P800, with air-con and bath for P1800. This is an OK place, although a few of the cottages are bit tired looking. A bit more expensive, the *Nigi Nigi Nu Noos* (☎ 288 3101) covers a fairly wide range of prices, with cottages with fan and bath between P800 and P1200. You could always ask for a discount. The cottages are pleasant and of various sizes in a green setting. Finally, the *Tirol & Tirol Resort* has roomy cottages with fan and bath for P800. Depending on occupancy, they can be flexible with their pricing.

In Balabag, the long established *Galaxy Beach Resort* offers cottages with fan and bath for P700 and P1000. There is a mixture of new and old cottages. In the same area but a bit up-market, the well-kept *Cocomangas Hotel Beach Resort* (☎ 288 3409) has cottages with fan and bath for P1000, with air-con and bath for P1800. It's a popular and comfortable place to stay.

At Bulabog Beach, on the east side of Boracay, the *Palomar Beach Club* offers rooms with fan and bath for P900, and with air-con and bath for P1700, in a trim and tidy setting. The wind conditions here are excellent, and you can windsurf practically up to your door.

Places to Stay – top end

Heading for the P2000 mark, we start with Angol, which has the *Angol Point* where cottages with fan and bath will cost you P1500. There are only six of these tastefully furnished cottages, all with big verandas, set in generously laid-out grounds.

Manggayad has quite a few places in this category too. The *Nirvana Beach Resort* (☎ 288 3140) is in the interior of the island, about five minutes from the beach. They offer rooms with fan and bath for P1350 in well furnished cottages. The *Mona Liza White Sand* (☎ 288 3205) has good cottages with fan and bath for P1500 in well-tended grounds at the beach, but it's a bit expensive for what you get. Set in pleasant grounds with lots of plants, the big cottages at the *Lorenzo Main Resort* cost P1500 with fan and bath. The Inso Disco is in the basement of the resort.

The last few places in this price range are all in Balabag. The *Red Coconut* is a neat place, just behind the restaurant of the same name. Their cottages with fan and bath go for between P800 and 1500, with air-con and bath for P1700 and P2000. *Joni's Place* has pleasant grounds with lots of plants. They charge P1200 here for cottages with fan and bath, and P1800 for those with air-con and bath. The *VIP Lingau* (☎ 288 3150),has the best location on the beach, and this is reflected in the prices. Rooms with fan and bath cost P1250 to P1750, with air-con and bath P2300.

Over the P2000 mark, Manggayad has *Boracay Paradise Garden Resort Hotel* (☎ 288 3411), an exclusive, well-maintained resort with pool. Their rooms with fan and bath cost P3000, with air-con and bath P4000.

Balabag has more than its share in this category. Accommodation at *Mila's Boracay Beach Resort* (☎ 288 3536) starts at P2000/ 2250 for spotless rooms with air-con and bath. The whole place has a kind of Spanish atmosphere. The tastefully furnished rooms at the *Crystal Sands Beach Resort* go for P2200, including breakfast. *Sand Castles* (☎ 288 3207) is a comfortable place to stay, with cottages with air-con and bath for P2600. *Friday's* (☎ 288 3427) is an older place (in fact, it was the first in this category on Boracay) with cottages with fan and bath for between P2750 and P4800.

Diniwid has the exclusive *Sundance Resort*, on a hill, with a beautiful view right down onto Diniwid Beach. Obviously expecting loads of Japanese guests, they charge P3200 for rooms with fan and bath.

We end up in Punta-Bunga, where the *Club Panoly Resort Hotel* will set you back P4000/6000 for a room with air-con and bath. This is a first-class establishment with a swimming pool. Popular with package tours, it is by itself in the north of the island.

Places to Eat

There are so many restaurants that some have to tempt customers with surprisingly inexpensive, yet quite sumptuous buffets, ranging from P75 to P120. Others have concentrated

THE VISAYAS

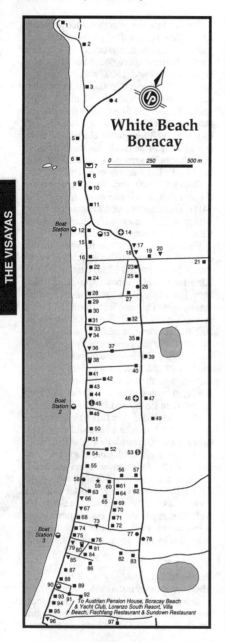

PLACES TO STAY
1 Golden Coconut, Laughing Water Cottages, Mika's Place, Sundance Resort & Vilu's
2 Boracay Terraces
3 Costa Blanca Resort, Friday's, Moonshiner's, Naro's Place & Raintree Resort
5 Pearl of the Pacific & Seawind
6 Boracay Plaza Beach Resort, VIP Lingau & Willy's Place
8 Boracay Dive Lodge, Cocomangas Hotel Beach Resort, Asia Divers, Moondog's Shooter Bar & Swagman Travel
11 Jony's Place & Restaurant
12 Sun Coast Resort
15 Mila's Boracay Beach Resort & El Toro Restaurant
16 Bans Beach House & Zorbas
19 Nena's Paradise Inn
21 Island's Garden
22 Fiesta Cottages, Jomar's Place & Scuba Diving World
23 Villa Felicitas
24 Serina's Place & Sunshine Cottages
25 Pink Patio Beach House
27 Mistral Resort
28 Sand Castles
29 Galaxy Beach Resort & Aquarius Diving
30 Crystal Sand Beach Resort
31 La Reserve Resort & Restaurant
32 Lion's Den
33 Red Coconut
35 Romaga's
37 Nora's Resort & Villa Lourdes
39 Blue Moon Cottages, Datu's Bowling Lanes
40 Casa Filipina, Nirvana Beach Resort & Viking Inn Restaurant
41 GP's Resort, Golden Sun Restaurant, Mango Ray, True Food & Lapu-Lapu Diving
42 Bahay Kaibigan & Dalisay Village Resort
43 Family Cottages, Chez Deparis Restaurant, Summer Place Bar & Restaurant & Sea World Dive Center
44 La Playa Blanca Beach Resort
47 Green Hill Cottages & Froggy Bar
48 Boracay Peninsula & Seoul Korean Restaurant
49 Green Paradise Inn
50 Tirol & Tirol Resort
51 Nigi Nigi Nu Noos, Palm Beach Lanai, Sunset Beach Resort, Victory Bar & Restaurant, Baracuda Bar & Victory Divers
52 Ati-Atihan Resort & Restaurant & Benross Cottages
54 Sanders White, Greenyard Restaurant & Calypso Diving
55 Alice in Wonderland & Country Inn
56 Green Valley Homes & Shangrila Oasis Cottages

57	Rainbow Villa Resort	89	Melinda's Garden &	79	Sulu Tha Thai
60	Morimar Boracay		Roy's Rendezvouz		Restaurant, Swiss
	Resort	91	Moreno's Place		Inn Restaurant,
61	Roque's Place & St	92	Mountain View Inn		Aqualife Diving &
	Vincent Cottages		& The Orchids		Sulu Bar
62	B & B Beach Resort		Resort	85	Lea's Restaurant
63	Bamboo Beach	93	Angol Point		& Star Fire
	Resort &	94	Villa Camilla, Dada's		Restaurant
	Restaurant		Restaurant,	96	Dutch Pub &
64	Alice in Wonderland		English Bakery,		Ristorante Italiano
	Beach Resort		Jolly Sailor, White		
65	Lorenzo Main Resort		Beach Divers &	**OTHER**	
68	Casa Pilar		Swagman Travel	4	Boracay Horse Riding
69	Boracay Imperial	95	Boracay Surfside		Stables
	Beach Resort		Resort, Tin-Tin's	7	Post Office & William
70	Tonglen Beach Resort		Cottages & Flying		Shiatsu Massage
71	Lea's Homes &		Dog		Center
	Paradise Garden	97	The Music Garden	9	Beachcomber Bar &
	Resort		Resort & Music		Jonah's Snack Bar
72	Holiday Homes		Garden	10	Far East Scuba
74	La Isla Bonita, Mona				Diving Institute
	Lisa White Sand,	**PLACES TO EAT**		13	710 Boracay
	Beach Life Bar &	17	Island Delight		Shuttle Office
	Restaurant, Pizza	18	Kain Na Restaurant	14	Boracay Medical
	da Baffo & Beach	20	English Bakery &		Clinic
	Life Diving Center		Tea Room	26	Pa-ama Minimart,
75	Oro Beach Resort,	34	Zur kleinen Kneipe		Pantelco & PAL
	Queen's Beach	36	Sea Lovers		Booking Office
	Resort, Allied Bank		Restaurant &	38	Ofukurosan
	Money Changer &		Creek Bar		Japanese
	Ocean Deep Diver	66	Dalisay Bar &		Restaurant,
	Training Center		Restaurant &		Bazura Bar &
76	Tropical Cottages		Guitar Bar		Nautilus Diving
81	Charlie's Place,	67	English Bakery &	45	Tourist Office
	Jhovir Place, M &		Titay Theater	46	Hospital & Aloja the
	E Guest House &		Restaurant,		Shop
	Sea Side Cottages		Boracay Scuba		(Delikatessen)
82	Highland Spring		Diving School,	53	Allied Bank
83	Percy's English Place		Fausto's Shiatsu	58	Boracay Tourist
84	A-Rock Resort		Massage & Vibes		Center
86	Nikko's Place		Shiatsu Center	59	Police Station
87	Pearl of the Pacific,	73	Alvarez Restaurant,	77	Abrams Supermart
	La Capannina		Honey Bee	78	WG & A
	Italian Restaurant		Restaurant, Lolit's	80	Jungle Bar
	& Coco Loco Bar		Restaurant, Nene	90	PAL & RCPI
88	South Sea		Bell Food's House,		
	Beach Resort &		Vinjo Indian		
	Dive Right Dive		Restaurant &		
	Shop		Talipapa Market		

on one particular kind of food to attract customers.

In Angol the *Starfire* can be recommended for its inexpensive menu of the day. *Melinda's Garden Restaurant* is a pleasant place with excellent Filipino cooking and typical European dishes. The fruit salads and fruit juices are particularly good in the *Jolly Sailor*. Next door, in *Dada's Restaurant*, the fish can be recommended. The *Sundown Restaurant* has

good German, Austrian and Swiss food, especially its popular dinner buffet (seafood) every Wednesday and Sunday, costing about P200. The *Swiss Inn*, not surprisingly, offers almost exclusively Swiss food. The Thai food in the *Sulu Tha Thai Restaurant* is excellent. For about P25 you can eat marvellous Philippine food in the *Honey Bee Restaurant* and *Nene Bell Food's House*, both in Talipapa Market St.

Manggayad seems to have more European restaurants than anything else. You can eat good German food in pleasant surroundings at the *Victory Bar & Restaurant*. They also have seafood from the grill and a daily set menu for about P100. *Chez Deparis* is a place for French food, and the *Bamboo Restaurant* for Swiss. The *Green Yard* features Mongolian barbecue every evening, where you can eat as much as you want for P135, while *Nigi Nigi Nu Noos* has an excellent four-course meal every evening for P100. The daily set menu at *Alice in Wonderland* for P95 can also be recommended, as can their fish dishes. If you can find it, the *Atihan Restaurant* is good value.

In Balabag, the modest *Sea Lovers Restaurant* next to the little bridge serves an excellent bulalo, a strong tasting vegetable soup with beef shank, as well as other outstanding Filipino dishes. On the other side of the bridge, the restaurant *Zur kleinen Kneipe* is popular for good, filling German food, and the daily set menu in the *Golden Sun Restaurant* is excellent value at P75. *Zorbas* has Greek and Filipino food, *La Reserve* serves real French cuisine (wines and cognac too), while the *El Toro Restaurant* offers Spanish food like paella, plus sangria by the carafe for about P100. The ambience is part of what makes *True Food* popular; they are near the Bazura Bar and offer Indian and vegetarian food. The *Red Coconut* serves Chinese and European dishes, *Jony's Place* has Mexican food (and excellent Margaritas, happy hour is between 5 and 7 pm), while *Jonah's* is popular for its fruit juices. A superb breakfast can be had at the *English Bakery & Tea Room*, which also has establishments in Angol and Manggayad.

Imported delicacies and red or white wines are available at the *Island Delight* and *Aloja the Shop*.

Entertainment

There are lots of opportunities for entertainment and diversion on Boracay. Those of us too lazy to walk can indulge in the pleasure of 'bar-hopping' by tricycle, for example from the Sulu Bar to the Beachcomber.

After dinner many guests like to listen to music or go dancing at their favourite place. *Moondog's Shooter Bar* in the Cocomangas Beach Resort in Balabag is very popular at happy hour. Many people head from there later on to the *Beachcomber*, where the dancing can become very animated when things warm up. Others prefer the big *Bazura* disco one km farther south, which is particularly busy at weekends. The atmosphere in the *Baracuda Bar* next to the Nigi Nigi Nu Noos is pleasant. Also popular in Angol is the *Sulu Bar*, with billiards and videos. A few metres away the *Jungle Bar* occasionally breaks out in a spontaneous party. For a change of pace, the *Titay Theater Restaurant* in Manggayad offers free cultural shows every evening together with a dinner buffet, and the *Beachlife* shows videos after dark.

Getting There & Away

Air The quickest (and most expensive) connection between Manila and Boracay via Caticlan is by Air Ads, Asian Spirit and Pacific Airways; the one-way fare is about P1700.

Asian Spirit and Air Ads bookings can be made at the Red Coconut, Balabag.

Pacific Airways bookings can be made at the Dublin Resthouse in Angol, the Red Coconut in Balabag and at the Boracay Tourist Center.

The little PAL office is next to the South Sea Resort in Angol. Apart from taking care of changes in itinerary and flight confirmations PAL also sells tickets for P150 for the air-con bus from Caticlan to Kalibo, which includes the boat trip from Boracay to Caticlan. The office is open from 8.30 am to noon and 2 to 4 pm. PAL flights can also be booked at the Boracay Tourist Center and at Pantelco, above the Pa-am Minimart near the Mistral Resort.

PAL flies from Manila to Kalibo on Panay and Tugdan on Tablas Island, in Romblon Province. The connection from Kalibo to Boracay via Caticlan is better than the one from Tugdan to Boracay via Santa Fe. After the aircraft arrives there are air-con buses from Kalibo to Caticlan. PAL also flies from Cebu City to Kalibo.

The trip with a bus belonging to the companies Southwest Tours or 7107 Boracay Shuttle cost P150. Southwest Tours sells tickets at the domestic airport in Manila. The price includes the boat transfer from Caticlan to Boracay.

Boat & Bus Many boats cruise along White Beach heading for Caticlan; just wait at one of the boat stations if you want to go there. The first boat comes along at about 6 am. There are three so-called boat stations on White Beach for boats to and from Caticlan (P15; 30 minutes): Boat Station 1 at the Mila's Boracay Beach Resort, Boat Station 2 at the tourist office and Boat Station 3 at the Sulu Bar. From June to November, during the south-west monsoons, the sea on the west side of Boracay can grow too rough for outrigger boats. They then have to leave from Tabon (to the east of Caticlan) instead of from Caticlan itself, and drop anchor on the east coast in the bay near the Dead Forest, or near Bulabog.

As almost all passengers have to wade through the water to get to the boats or back to shore, patent-leather boots and well-pressed long trousers are definitely not the things to wear.

On arrival in Caticlan, you can get a jeepney or bus to Kalibo (two hours).

A bus leaves Caticlan for Iloilo City via Kalibo at around 6.30 am (six hours). Anyone wanting to take this bus will have to take either the first boat at 6 am or a Special Ride for about P175 from Boracay.

Air-con buses make special trips from Caticlan to Kalibo airport, timed to catch the departures of PAL flights. Tickets for the Southwest Tours bus can be obtained at the PAL office on Boracay; the 7107 Boracay Shuttle Office is located near Boat Station 1.

There are shipping services between Manila, New Washington and Dumaguit, both are near Kalibo on Panay. (See the section on getting to Panay in the Getting There & Away section of the Manila chapter.)

Getting Around
Tricycle Several tricycles ride along the narrow road which runs through the middle part of the island from Manoc-Manoc in the south to Yapak Beach in the north. They charge from P5 to P20 per person, depending on the distance and number of passengers. There is a stop for tricycles at the turn-off to Boat Station 3, the first stop for boats from Caticlan.

Bicycle Various resorts along White Beach rent out bikes. A mountain bike costs P50 an hour, or P300 per day. You could also check out Van's Bicycle Works (there's a contradiction there somewhere!) in Manoc-Manoc, where they sell and repair bicycles.

Romblon

Almost in the centre of the Philippine archipelago, Romblon Province comprises around 20 islands and islets, the largest of which are Tablas, Sibuyan and Romblon. All three are hilly, and Sibuyan is thickly forested.

Because of its large marble deposits, Romblon is also called 'Marble Country'. Experts consider that Romblon marble is at least equal in quality to Italian marble. It is usually sold as large blocks, but several families make a few pesos by selling handmade ashtrays, chess pieces, vases and statues. When passenger ships visit, people set up stalls on the wharf of Romblon town to sell marble souvenirs.

GETTING THERE & AWAY
You can get to Romblon from Luzon, Masbate, Mindoro and Panay (see Getting There & Away in this chapter and the Manila chapter).

Air
Luzon PAL flies on Tuesday, Thursday and Saturday from Tugdan on Tablas Island to Manila; Asian Spirit flies Tuesday, Thursday and Sunday (P860).

Boat

Luzon There's a boat four times a week from Magdiwang on Sibuyan Island to Lucena (12 hours).

The MV *Viva Peñafrancia VIII* of Viva Shipping Lines leaves Tuesday, Friday and Sunday at 11 am from Magdiwang to Batangas (21 hours, via San Agustin on Tablas Island and Romblon on Romblon Island). It leaves San Agustin at 3 pm (17 hours) and Romblon at 9 pm (11 hours).

From Romblon town to Manila, MBRS Lines' MV *Salve Juliana* sails Wednesday at 8 pm and Sunday at 3 pm (15 hours).

From Romblon town to Lucena, the Kalaayan Shipping Lines' MV *Del Rosario* leaves on Wednesday and Friday, while the Transmar Shipping Lines' MV *Transmar* leaves on Monday (12 hours).

From Odiongan on Tablas Island to Batangas, RN Hi Speed Ferries' MV Florida 1 sails Monday and Saturday at 9 pm (5 hours). Viva Shipping Lines' MV *Viva Peñafrancia VIII* leaves Tuesday, Friday and Sunday at 8 pm (seven hours); their MV *St Kristopher* leaves on Monday, Thursday and Saturday at 6 pm (eight hours).

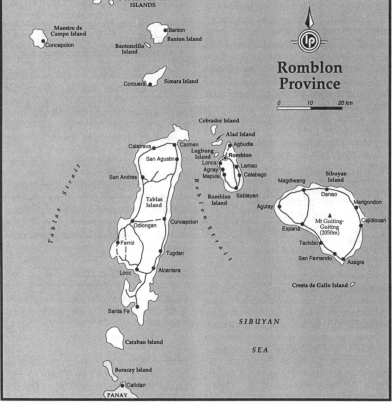

From San Agustin to Lucena, the Kalaayan Shipping Lines' MV *Kalayaan* leaves on Tuesday, Wednesday and Thursday (10 hours).

Masbate A big outrigger boat goes from Cajidiocan (on Sibuyan Island) to Mandaon three times a week (five hours).

Mindoro From Looc on Tablas Island to Roxas, a big outrigger boat goes on Saturday at 10.30 am (3½ hours). Additional trips may be run on Monday and Thursday and even daily if required. Sometimes it may run from Odiongan, also on Tablas Island, instead of Looc.

In bad weather the sea in the Tablas Strait is very rough and the crossing is not to be recommended. Small boats sometimes sail over, but they are completely unsuitable and often dangerously overloaded.

Panay From Looc on Tablas Island to Boracay, a big outrigger boat goes daily (P100; two hours).

A big outrigger boat goes from Santa Fe on Tablas Island to Boracay on Tuesday, Thursday and Saturday, soon after the Manila plane's arrival in Tugdan. The boat then waits for the jeepney from the airport and goes on to Caticlan (P80; 1½ hours).

ROMBLON ISLAND
Romblon

The small port town of Romblon is the capital of Romblon Province. In the typhoon season, ships often take cover in its sheltered bay. The two forts of San Andres and Santiago Hill were built by the Spaniards in 1640 and are said to have underground passages leading to the coast. Today, San Andres is used as a weather station. From the forts there are good views of San Joseph's Cathedral and the town with its Spanish-style houses. Dating back to 1726, the cathedral houses a collection of antiques that you can see on request.

A trip to one of the two lighthouses, **Sabang** and **Apunan**, makes a good outing. If you don't mind heights and trust in the stability of the lighthouses, you can climb to the top and enjoy the view over palm forests, rocky cliffs and marble quarries.

The bay of Romblon is sheltered by small **Lugbung Island**, which you can quickly reach by outrigger boat from the harbour. The island has a beautiful white beach and a few cottages, but you should bring your own provisions. **Alad Island** is located north of Lugbung, with **Cobrador Island** further out.

Diving The dive shop, Romblon Sea Divers, in Roxas St next to the RCPI office, has a speedboat and offers diving courses for P6500. A regular diving trip costs P700. The Sub-Aqua diving Center in the D'Marble Cottages resort in San Pedro only charges P500 for a diving trip.

Places to Stay Near the church, the *Feast-Inn* has basic but clean rooms with fan and bath for P100/200. A better choice, and excellent value, the *Marble Hotel* has outstanding rooms with fan and marble bathrooms for P120/150.

Places to Eat Both at the harbour, the *Tica Inn* is better than the well-known *Kawilihan Food House*. The *Marble Dust Restaurant* is also good.

Getting There & Away A boat does the trips between Romblon and Magdiwang on Sibuyan Island every day, departing at 11 am (two hours).

Outrigger boats leave daily from San Agustin on Tablas Island for Romblon at 8 am and 1 pm (45 minutes).

Getting Around A round trip of the island by tricycle, including a tour of marble quarries and works, can be arranged for P300 in Romblon.

Lonos

The village of Lonos, about four km southwest of Romblon, has an attractive white sand beach.

Places to Stay The *Palm Beach Resort* has rooms for P100/200 and cottages with fan and bath for P150 per person. The cottages are basic but OK and have a big veranda. The food here is Philippine and European. They offer motorcycle hire and have diving facilities.

Agnay

About eight km south-west of Romblon before Mapula, Agnay has a few tree-houses directly above the water on a beautiful beach.

Places to Stay The *Selangga Tree Houses* cost P250 with shower and cooking facilities, but bring your own provisions from Romblon. Full board can be arranged. For information, ask Divina Festin Mortel in the Feast-Inn in Romblon. The private *Villa del Mar*, outside Agnay, has rooms with fan and bath for P350 and with air-con and bath for P550.

San Pedro

By far the most comfortable and pleasant set-up in Romblon at the moment must be the resort at Marble Beach, perched on an idyllic bay in San Pedro, two km south of Agnay.

Places to Stay *D'Marble Cottages* in San Pedro has cottages with bath for P200 and P250. Every cottage has a terrace, a small garden and its own access to the sea. This is a very quiet, well-looked after place. Staff will cook for guests on request, but self-catering is possible. Make enquiries to Robinson & Violeta Montojo, Governor Rios St, Romblon.

Getting There & Away A tricycle from Romblon to San Pedro costs P10 per person – they'll ask for P100 for a Special Ride (P75 if there's only one person).

Cobrador Island

Cobrador is a beautiful little island north-west of Romblon. It has a wonderful, palm-lined white beach and a 250m high mountain inland. The water is crystal clear and is great for snorkelling.

Places to Stay The *Cobrador Beach Resort* has cottages with bath for P150 per person.

The cottages are inviting, and some of them are built on the side of a hill. This is a neat place to spend time.

Getting There & Away The regular outrigger boat from Romblon to Cobrador costs P50 per person, a Special Ride P300 (30 minutes).

SIBUYAN ISLAND

Sibuyan is wilder, more mountainous, forested and less explored than Tablas or Romblon, the other two main islands in the Romblon archipelago. It has several waterfalls, such as the Cataga and Lambigan falls near Magdiwang, and the Kawa-Kawa Falls in Lumbang Este near Cajidiocan, the most densely populated town on the island. Nearby Mt Guiting-Guiting (2050m) is hard to climb because of its thick covering of moss. It was first climbed in 1982.

Offshore, the coral reefs around Cresta de Gallo Island, with its white sands, are well known for good diving.

Getting There & Away

Boat A boat runs every day between Magdiwang on Sibuyan Island and Romblon on Romblon Island, leaving at 9 am (two hours).

Mosses on the Mount

There are many myths surrounding Sibuyan Island's Mt Guiting-Guiting and its waterfalls. One story goes that the souls of rich landowners and corrupt politicians are gathered on the mountain, where they wait fruitlessly for the day when the proverb about the camel passing through the eye of a needle comes true (the Scriptures say that it is easier for a camel to go through the eye of a needle than for a rich man to enter the kingdom of heaven). The long wait is causing them great pain and their tears flow down to the living in majestic waterfalls. These souls cannot leave the mountain as their evil deeds have encouraged the growth of impenetrable moss and mud.

Another myth says that a giant magnet inside the mountain attracts climbers who then get caught in the moss and die of hunger. It also supposedly makes aircraft instruments go haywire, causing them to crash on the mountain. ■

Magdiwang

Magdiwang is a clean little town on the north coast of Sibuyan Island. The natural pool with crystal-clear water at nearby **Lambigan Falls** is ideal for a dip.

Places to Stay You can only stay in private houses in Magdiwang, such as the Muros family's house on Rizal St, which is basic but has a beautiful terrace right above the Dulangan River. They charge about P50 per person. Other places are the Ransay residence, also P50, and Mrs Geneva Rivas' place.

Taclobo

Taclobo, on the south-west coast of Sibuyan Island, is a good starting point for trips into the hilly jungles of the interior, such as the wild **Cantingas River Valley**. About 15 minutes outside of Taclobo (head from the main road and follow the sign 'Christ in the Mountain') there are the **Lagting Falls** with a natural pool, where you can have a refreshing dip. A simple guest house at the waterfall offers accommodation for P50 per person.

San Fernando

San Fernando, like Taclobo, is a good base for exploring the interior. You can also make trips from there to the little island of **Cresta de Gallo**, although you could also arrange such trips in Azagra at the southerly point of Sibuyan Island, for example, in the shop belonging to the friendly Mangarin family.

Places to Stay In the village, *Jenmar Lodge* has rooms for P75/140. *Bernie's Inn* on the edge of the village also has rooms for P75/140. This is a comfortable and pleasant inn built of bamboo, with four bedrooms, a living room and a kitchen. It is also known as *Bernie's Nipa Huts*.

TABLAS ISLAND

Tablas is the largest island in the Romblon archipelago. A tree-covered chain of mountains stretches across the north and the east of the island, reaching up to 600m on occasion. In contrast, the south is flat, as is the west coast with its many bays where most of the villages and small towns can be found.

Getting There & Away

Outrigger boats go daily from Romblon town to San Agustin on Tablas Island at 8 am and 1 pm (45 minutes).

San Agustin

San Agustin is a pleasant little town and has a wharf for boats to and from Romblon town. You can also do day trips to the **Bitu Falls** near Dabdaban and the **Cajbo-aya Ruins**.

Places to Stay The only really acceptable place to stay here is the *Kamella Lodge* which also has its own restaurant. They have rooms with fan for P100/200, with fan and bath for P350, and with air-con and bath for P450/650.

Getting There & Away Several jeepneys run from Looc to San Agustin daily (three hours). The 6 am jeepney from Looc connects with the boat to Romblon.

Calatrava & San Andres

Near Calatrava, in Kabibitan, you will find Tinagong Dagat, the 'hidden lake', where the water is salty, apparently due to being connected to the ocean somehow. Not far away there is another, slightly smaller lake with same properties.

A track runs from San Andres (Despujols) to the high Mablaran Falls.

Odiongan

Tricycles run a shuttle service to the small harbour which lies just outside the town of Odiongan. There are shipping services to Batangas (Luzon) and Roxas (Mindoro). Only large outrigger boats run to Mindoro.

Information Odiongan has a small post office which is, however, a bit hard to find – just ask your way there.

Places to Stay The *Shellborne Hotel* has simple rooms with fan and bath for P125/250 and with air-con and bath for P380/550.

Getting There & Away Several jeepneys run from the San Agustin wharf to Odiongan daily, via Calatrava and San Andres, taking 2½ hours.

Looc

The small port of Looc is located in the south-west of Tablas on the northern shore of Looc Bay. There are boat routes from there to many places, including Roxas on Mindoro and Boracay. The town has opened a tourist assistance centre at the market next to the Plaza, where travellers receive friendly and helpful advice.

Places to Stay Offering good accommodation, the *Morales Lodging Inn* near the wharf has rooms with fan for P95/170. Just across from the market, the *Tablas Pension House* has rooms with fan for P100/200. It is basic, but all right for the money.

Getting There & Away Several jeepneys run from Odiongan to Looc daily (one hour).

Santa Fe

An outrigger boat makes the trip three times weekly from Santa Fe to Caticlan on Panay, via Carabao and Boracay islands (two hours). The fare to Boracay is P80 per person.

Places to Stay Accommodation is simple throughout. You can stay for P75 to P100 per person at *Dolly's Place*, the *Tourist Inn*, the *White House* or the *Asis Inn*, which has a restaurant.

Getting There & Away There are several jeepneys daily from Looc to Santa Fe. They leave from the plaza and take 45 minutes.

Tugdan

You can get flights to and from Manila at Tugdan's airport. The planes to Manila are almost always booked out and it takes several days in Tugdan to get to the top of the waiting list.

Places to Stay The modest *Airport Pension* has big rooms with fan for P125/150 and

with fan and bath for P150/300. The accommodation is simple but clean, and you can arrange board with them.

Getting There & Away The plane in Tugdan is met by jeepneys going to San Agustin (1½ hours), to Santa Fe (one hour), and to Looc (45 minutes).

Samar

The second biggest island in the Visayas, Samar lies between South Luzon and Leyte and is connected with Leyte by the two km long San Juanico Bridge, which spans the San Juanico Strait. The island is divided into the three provinces of Eastern, Northern and Western Samar and is surrounded by about 180 small islands. One of these is Homonhon, where Ferdinand Magellan is reputed to have set foot for the first time on Philippine soil on 16 March 1521. Samar's landscape is hilly and steep and the greater part of the island is thickly wooded. Plains exist only along the coast and in the north, around Catarman.

Samar's climate is different from that of other islands in the Philippines, with dry periods only occurring occasionally in May and June. Apart from that, rainfall is possible throughout the year, although never for long periods. Most rain falls from the beginning of November until February. In early October to December there can be fierce typhoons. The best and sunniest time to visit Samar is from May to September, although surfers would probably prefer the time of the north-east monsoon, from November to February on the Pacific coast, when the surf is at its best.

The main crops are rice, maize and sweet potatoes, although Samar does not produce near enough of these to be self-sufficient. On the other hand, there are plentiful harvests of abaca and coconuts, and Borongan, in Eastern Samar, is the leading copra producer.

Sohoton National Park, near Basey in Southern Samar, is Samar's outstanding natural attraction. The best way to reach it is from Tacloban on Leyte (see the Sohoton National Park in the Leyte section earlier in this chapter for further information). Rather less exciting are the Blanca Aurora Falls near Gandara, between Calbayog and Catbalogan. The potential tourist attractions of Northern Samar should not be underestimated, although the infrastructure will have to be improved before people start taking notice of them.

Some parts of Central and Eastern Samar are still regarded as problem areas as fighting breaks out every now and then there between government troops and the NPA. Find out what the situation is before you venture there, although Northern Samar and the west coast are OK.

The inhabitants of Samar are Visayans who call themselves Waray and speak the Waray-Waray dialect.

GETTING THERE & AWAY

You can get to Samar from Biliran, Cebu, Leyte, Luzon and Masbate (see the Getting There & Away section of the Manila chapter and the relevant Getting There & Away sections of this and the Around Luzon chapter earlier in this book).

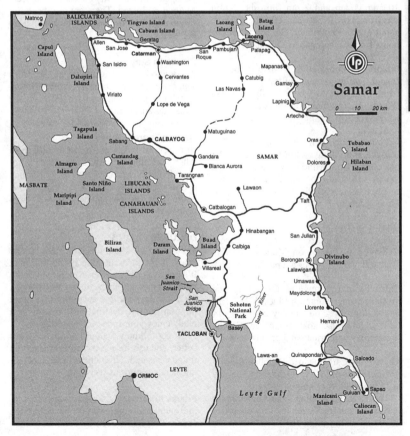

THE VISAYAS

Air

Luzon PAL flies daily except Wednesday and Sunday from Calbayog to Manila and on Tuesday, Thursday, Friday, Saturday and Sunday from Catarman to Manila. Asian Spirit flies on Tuesday, Friday and Saturday from Catarman to Manila.

Bus

Leyte Several Eagle Star, Philtranco and Philippine Eagle buses run daily from Catarman, Calbayog and Catbalogan to Tacloban along the west coast of Samar, either to Tacloban only or on the way to Ormoc or Mindanao. The buses leave Catbalogan at 4, 10 and 11 am and 2 pm from the Petron service station. In between, other buses leave about every 30 minutes. The trip takes 2½ hours from Catbalogan to Tacloban (P40).

Luzon Air-con Cedec Transport buses, Inland Trailways and Philtranco buses go from Catarman to Manila daily at 8 am (P390; 23 hours, including the Allen-Matnog ferry). The trip finishes at Pasay City (Edsa) in Manila.

Philtranco air-con buses run from Catbalogan and Calbayog to Manila daily. The bus comes from Mindanao or Leyte and is mostly full. The trip takes 25 and 26 hours respectively, including the San Isidro-Matnog ferry.

Boat

Biliran A big outrigger boat goes from Calbayog to Danao on Maripipi Island Wednesday and Saturday at 1 pm (three hours).

Cebu From Catarman to Cebu City, the Western Samar Shipping Lines' MV *Elizabeth Lilly* leaves on Sunday at 5 pm (14 hours), and from Catbalogan to Cebu City on Wednesday and Friday at 5 pm (14 hours).

Leyte From Catbalogan to Tacloban, the MV *Masbate Uno* of WG & A leaves on Tuesday at 11 am (P80; four hours).

The K & T Shipping Lines' MV *Stacey* leaves Guiuan for Tacloban every other day at 10 pm, taking six hours.

Luzon From Allen to Matnog, the ferries MV *Michelangelo* and MV *Northern Samar* leave daily at 6 am and 1 pm (1½ hours). The ferry MV *Marhalika I* of St Bernard Services leaves San Isidro for Matnog daily at 9 am and 4.30 pm (two hours). The Matnog and San Isidro terminal fee is P12 per passenger.

From Catbalogan to Manila, the MV *Masbate Uno* of WG & A leaves on Wednesday at 5 pm (P435; 23 hours). The Sulpicio Lines' MV *Tacloban Princess* leaves on Friday at 6 pm (22 hours).

ALLEN

Allen has a wharf for ferries to and from Matnog on Luzon. There are also boats for Capul and Dalupiri Islands, which both lie to the west.

Places to Stay

Accommodation is available at the *Mary Ann Lodge* and the *Laureens Lodging House*, both fairly basic with rooms for P75/100; the latter has a restaurant.

Getting There & Away

Bus Several buses go from Catbalogan to Allen via Calbayog daily, such as the Philippine Eagle buses at 9 and 10 am, which continue on to Catarman. The trip takes 3½ hours from Catbalogan and 1½ hours from Calbayog.

DALUPIRI ISLAND

South-west of Allen, not far off the Samar coast, is the pleasant little Dalupiri Island. It's known locally as San Antonio, after the village of the same name. If you want to relax for a few days and get away from the more popular tourist destinations, then you'll really enjoy your time on Dalupiri.

To get to know Dalupiri and its beaches better, you can have a motorcycle take you round the island. This will cost P150, including as many stops as you want.

Places to Stay

Surrounded by countless coconut palms, the *Flying Dog Resort*, run by Toni, an Italian, is a pleasant place to stay. A very comfortable cottage with bath will cost you P500.

Getting There & Away
Boat Outrigger boats make the short trip over to Dalupiri Island from San Isidro in the morning (P10). A Special Ride is possible for P50, if you can haggle them down.

GERATAG & SAN JOSE
Three km west of Geratag on the north coast of Samar, San Jose is a starting point for several boats which cross to the Balicuatro Islands offshore.

Places to Stay
Also known as the House of Mr Hans, the *House Schiefelbein (Mendoza)* near the beach at Geratag offers family-style accommodation. The rooms are quite comfortable and cost P150/200 with fan and bath. Food can be supplied on demand, and guests can do their own cooking if they want.

Getting There & Away
Bus & Jeepney Several buses and jeepneys depart from Allen daily and go through San Jose and Geratag on the way to Catarman and Rawis (for Laoang). The trip takes one hour.

BALICUARTRO ISLANDS
Biri and Bani islands are reckoned to be two of the most attractive diving areas in the eastern Philippines. In a move to promote tourism, the Northern Samar Tourism Council has applied to the Philippine Congress to have the Balicuatro Islands declared a protected area. In addition, the northern section of the Biri Island coast, with its small offshore limestone islands jutting out of the water by up to 37m, is to be declared a national marine park. During WWII, Biri Island had a Japanese garrison whose job was to observe the maritime traffic in the San Bernardino Straits.

Every two or three days, an outrigger boat goes from Biri on Biri Island to Gubat in South Luzon.

Places to Stay
There is no commercial accommodation as yet on the Balicuartro Islands, so visitors have to look for private alternatives. If you want to spend a few days in the picturesque village of San Antonio on Tingyao (Tinau)

THE VISAYAS

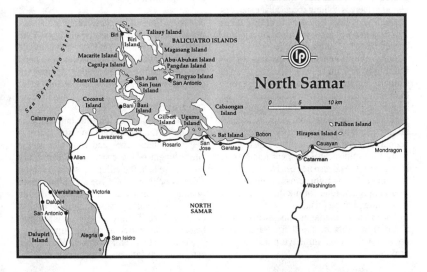

Island, you can organise an overnight stay at House Schiefelbein (Mendoza) in Geratag. See Places to Stay in the previous Geratag & San Jose section for further information.

Getting There & Away
Boat Outriggers travel daily from San Jose to Biri on Biri Island, San Antonio on Tingyao Island and San Pedro on Pangdan Island, leaving at 11 am and noon (45 minutes to 1½ hours). Departure from the islands is around 7 am.

An outrigger travels daily from Lavezares to Biri on Biri Island (one hour).

CATARMAN
Catarman, the capital of Northern Samar Province, is the starting point for travel in the north-east, for example, to Laoang or Batag islands. It should soon be possible to carry on from Catarman along the east coast to Guiuan in south Samar, as the coastal road from Laoang to Arteche via Palapag, Mapanas, Gamay and Lapinig is already partly finished. Up till now, the communities of Mapanas, Gamay and Lapinig could only be reached by boat.

An easy river cruise is to go along the Catarman River from Catarman as far as Washington, although there is nothing spectacular to be seen on the way. A boat leaves at 1 pm and takes less than two hours for the nine km trip. You can go back to Catarman by jeepney.

A lot more interesting is the trip up the Catubig river from Laoang to Las Navas via Catubig. It starts in the estuary, where several kilometres of mangrove thicket have to be negotiated, then continues upstream where the river is framed on both sides by breathtaking mountainous territory and mixed vegetation. The trip is meant to finish at the beautiful Pinipisacan Falls near Las Navas. However, it would also be possible to carry on from there, hiking right across the mountains to Matuguinao. Plan for another three days if you intend to do this.

The airport manager has information about the sights of Northern Samar and photos of the most attractive places in this province.

Money
The Philippine National Bank in Garcia St at the corner of Jacinto St changes travellers cheques.

Places to Stay
The rooms at *Joni's Hotel* on Jacinto St at the market (☎ 554 0224) are adequate for the money, costing P75/150 with fan, and P120/240 with fan and bath.

The *Diocesan Catholic Center (DCC)*, next to the Catholic church, lets pleasant rooms with fan for P80/160, and there is a restaurant.

By far the best accommodation in Catarman is available at the *Riverview Hotel* on Jose Rizal St. They charge P300 for good rooms with fan, and P500 and P600 with air-con and bath. It is at the bridge over the Catarman river which takes you to the University of Eastern Philippines (UEP), three km away at White Beach.

Places to Eat
Several restaurants in town offer Philippine food. The *Casa de Coco* is one of the best.

Getting There & Away
Air PAL has an office at Catarman airport and on Bonifacio St.

Jeepney Several jeepneys run from Catarman to Rawis (for Laoang) daily from 4 am until about 5 pm (1½ hours). Jeepneys to and from Laoang stop and depart from here. The destination marked on the jeepneys for Laoang is usually Rawis (not Laoang).

CALBAYOG
Calbayog, with its picturesque harbour, tops off one of the most scenic coastal roads in the Philippines. The road runs almost the entire length of the coast and is especially impressive near the village of **Viriato** (about halfway between Calbayog and Allen), with mountains, cliffs, distant islands and little bays with colourful boats. Sadly, the beaches don't look so inviting here as they seem to be occasionally used as garbage tips.

There is a large **waterfall** near Viriato that can be seen as far back as the bridge near the river mouth. The area around Viriato is good for a day trip and could include a hike along the coast. Getting back to Calbayog or Catarman shouldn't be a problem. The next jeepney will be coming round the corner any minute.

Approximately 50 km south-east of Calbayog are the **Blanca Aurora Falls**, the best known on Samar. To get there take the bus going to Catbalogan from Calbayog. Get out at the little community of San Jorge (pronounced San Horhay) about five km beyond Gandara. From there, you can carry on by tricycle to the waterfalls.

Telephone
The area code for Calbayog is 05541.

Places to Stay
On the corner of Nijaga and Orquin Sts at the market, the *San Joaquin Inn* (☎ 91125), charges P70/140 for basic rooms with fan, P280/350 with fan and bath, and P450/600 with air-con and bath. Despite its appearance, their restaurant serves very good food, and it's cheap too.

At the eastern edge of town, the *Seaside Drive Inn* is a relatively good hotel in Rawis, with rooms going for P80/160, with fan and bath for P200 and with air-con and bath for P350. You can relax on their small terrace overlooking the sea or boogie in the disco next door.

The best hotel in Calbayog is the *Central Inn* on Navarro St. The rooms are immaculate and cost P500 with air-con and bath. The restaurant is upstairs.

Getting There & Away
Air PAL has an office (☎ 255) on Navarro St.

Bus Philippine Eagle and Eagle Star buses run almost every hour between 5 and 9 am from Catarman to Calbayog via Allen daily. The trip takes 2½ hours to Catarman and 1½ hours to Allen. The buses go on to Tacloban on Leyte.

Several buses go from Catbalogan to Calbayog daily. You can get a Philippine Eagle bus at 9 or 10 am going to Allen and Catarman (two hours).

Jeepney There are also several jeepneys travelling between Catbalogan and Calbayog daily, taking an hour or more.

There are also several jeepneys daily, taking 3½ hours to Catarman and two hours to Allen.

Getting Around
The Airport Calbayog airport is about seven km north of the town, on the road to Allen. Jeepneys and buses are always driving by.

CATBALOGAN
The port of Catbalogan, the capital of Western Samar Province, is located on the west coast of Samar. It is the most important business centre on the island. You can get buses from here that go across the island to the east coast.

Calbiga is located almost 50 km south of Catbalogan. In 1987 a group of Italians discovered a five km long cave here, the **Langun-Gobongob Cave** which is home to the extremely rare gobinee fish *caecogobius cryptophtalmus*. Also worth seeing are the Literon Rapids and the Lulugayan Falls.

Places to Stay
After the inaptly named Fortune Hotel was closed down and Tony's Hotel burnt down, there is no longer a big choice in Catbalogan. If it's still open, *Kikay's Hotel* on Curry Ave will have basic singles/doubles with fan for P100/170 and one double room with air-con and bath for P280.

At the southern end of the town right on the ocean front, you can find the quite new *Maqueda Bay Hotel* where you can spend the night in clean, spacious air-con rooms with bath for P500 and P600 with TV. There's a gorgeous view of the sea from the restaurant.

Getting There & Away
Bus & Jeepney Several buses and jeepneys run daily from Catarman to Catbalogan via Allen and Calbayog, such as the Eagle Star and Philippine Eagle buses, which leave almost every hour between 5 and 9 am. Going to Catbalogan, the trip takes five hours from Catarman (P60), four hours from Allen and two hours from Calbayog.

BORONGAN

Borongan, the capital of Eastern Samar, is an important trading post for copra, rattan and bamboo. Situated as it is, near the mouth of the Lomo river and surrounded by numerous coconut palms at the edge of the jungle, Borongan could have just been taken out of one of the adventure stories from bygone days.

Outside on the bay, with the Pacific stretching out to the horizon in the background, the little island of Divinubo can be reached in 30 minutes. It could end up being a favourite with the surfers, as could several places south of Borongan, like Lalawigan (seven km), Umawas (17 km) and Llorente (26 km).

Places to Stay

The best place to stay in town is the *Domsowir Hotel* on Real St, where singles with fan go for P125 and doubles with fan and bath cost P250. There are a few others, but they're pretty basic.

Getting There & Away

Bus A daily SBL Lines bus runs from Catbalogan to Borongan at 9 am from Pier 1 (five hours). You can also catch Eastern Star Transport and Borongan Express buses travelling between Manila and Guiuan.

GUIUAN

A friendly little town on a peninsula in southeast Samar, Guiuan is fairly easy to reach by boat from Tacloban on Leyte. The Americans started their aerial attacks on the Japanese from here and the giant airport at the eastern edge was once one of the biggest US bases in the Pacific. Today the unused runways are overgrown with grass.

One of the most beautiful churches of the eastern Visayas can be seen in the centre of Guiuan. Its wonderfully carved doors, one of its most precious treasures, once caught the eye of a certain Imelda Marcos who was not averse to increasing her list of possessions. Thank God, even an offer of two million pesos didn't persuade the men of the cloth to give them up.

Near Guiuan are a couple of beautiful beaches which are hardly ever visited, as well as numerous small islands west of Guiuan in Leyte Gulf.

Places to Stay

Basic rooms at the *Arcenos Boarding House* on Managantan St cost P50/100 and P60/120 with fan.

You'll also pay P50/100 for rooms at the *Bluestar Lodging House* on Concepcion St, and P60/120 for those with fan. It's a reasonable place with a sing-along disco. Also on Concepcion St, the *Villa Rosario Lodging House* has dorm beds with fan for P50, rooms for P50/100 and with fan for P80/160. It is basic, and OK for the money.

Places to Eat

You can get very cheap meals at the clean *Sherly Tan Restaurant* on Concepcion St. The *Bluestar Eatery* in the lodging house of the same name serves meals if you order them in advance.

Getting There & Away

Bus Several buses travel daily from Catbalogan to Guiuan via Borongan (those coming from Manila), taking six hours.

Siquijor

The island of Siquijor is about 25 km east of southern Negros and is one of the smallest provinces in the Philippines. Until 1971 it was a sub-province of Negros Oriental. The 80,000 population of this likeable little island celebrate their Independence Day (Araw ng Siquijor) every year on 17 September. The Siquijodnons are remarkably friendly, but at the same time not in any way pushy.

The largest towns in the province are Siquijor, Larena, Enrique Villanueva, Maria, Lazi and San Juan. Siquijor is the capital, and Larena and Lazi have ports with connections to other islands. A surfaced road encircles this hilly island, connecting its well-kept villages and small towns. The main industries are agriculture and fishing. Manganese mining north-west of Maria reached its peak before WWII, and deposits of copper and silver have not yet been mined. The economic prosperity of the island is due to a large extent to the money sent back home by Siquijidnons working overseas.

Tourism is still not a major industry on Siquijor, although the potential is obviously there. Palm beaches, waterfalls and caves are just as worth seeing as the historical churches and old houses.

When the Spaniards discovered the island, they called it Isla del Fuego, which means island of fire. This suggests that they saw a large fire as they sailed past. It is believed that what they saw were countless glow-worms.

There is a legend that millions of years ago Siquijor lay completely under water. It emerged from the sea amid crashing thunder and flashing lightning. Fossils of mussels, snails and other underwater creatures can still be found in the mountainous interior and are quoted as evidence for this belief.

You can sense that there is something mysterious about Siquijor when you tell Filipinos that you intend to travel there. They will warn you of witches and magicians and healers with wondrous powers. Many strange events are said to take place on this singular island and are enhanced by the practice of voodoo and black magic. Filipinos will warn you that it is better to avoid it for your own safety's sake...

GETTING THERE & AWAY

You can get to Siquijor from Cebu, Mindanao and Negros (see the relevant Getting There & Away sections of this and the Mindanao & Palawan chapter).

Air

Negros Pacific Airways flies fairly regularly on Monday and Thursday from Siquijor to Dumaguete (P250; 15 minutes).

THE VISAYAS

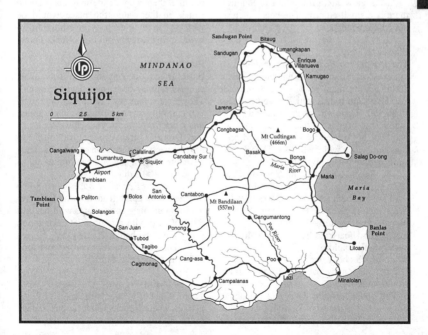

Mindanao Pacific Airways flies Wednesday from Siquijor to Dipolog, but not necessarily on a regular basis (P550; 30 minutes).

Boat
Negros Fast Delta Lines' ferries leave Larena for Dumaguete daily at 7.30 and 9.45 am and 2.15 and 4.30 pm (P62; 45 minutes).

The MV *Catherine* of Marjunnix Shipping Lines sails daily at 7 am from Siquijor to Dumaguete (three hours). A big outrigger boat goes daily at 6 am (two hours).

From Tambisan to Dumaguete, a big outrigger boat goes daily at 1 and 3 pm (2½ hours). For safety reasons, this service is not recommended in bad weather.

SIQUIJOR
The small town of Siquijor is the capital of the island. It has a Provincial Capitol Building, a church, a hospital, a post office and the St Francis de Assisi Church with its old belltower, which you can climb.

At Cangalwang, a little west of Siquijor, there is a small airstrip. The beach there is not recommended.

Places to Stay
The *Dondeezco Beach Resort* is about two km west of Siquijor in Dumanhug, about 200m off the main road. It has rooms for P200/280 and rooms with fan and bath for P280/350. There are small, stone-built cottages and bigger duplex ones made of bamboo. It's a friendly place, located on a long bay with a wide, white sand beach. The staff prepare meals on request.

The *Beach Garden Mini Hotel* in Catalinan has acceptable, if slightly small, rooms with fan and bath for P300, P350 and P400. A discount is given for longer stays. It offers bicycle and motorcycle rental as well as jeepney and boat trips. The owner of this big, comfortable building is Dutch. It is on a white beach about one km west of Siquijor (P2 per person by tricycle; P7 per person from Larena).

The *Tikarol Beach Resort* in Candanay Sur about 2½ km east of Siquijor is an idyllic little resort with pleasantly decorated, roomy

cottages with bath for P300. A narrow footpath leads from the ringroad to the beach (about 300m from the signpost). The place is run by two women, one from Switzerland, the other from the Philippines. If all you want is just to relax and feel good, this is the place for you.

Getting There & Away
Tricycle Short journeys from Siquijor with a tricycle cost P2 per person, P5 to Larena and San Juan. A Special Ride to Sandugan costs between P100 and P120.

LARENA
Larena is a quiet little place with a few beautiful buildings. The place only comes to life when a boat docks or departs.

If you walk to Congbagsa and go on along the road that branches off to the right about 100m west of the large, white National Food Authority building, you end up taking some steps down to a peaceful bay with a white beach. If there weren't so many sharp-edged stones in the water, the place would be perfect. There is even a refreshing freshwater spring flowing out of the rocks here.

Places to Stay
Basic, friendly accommodation is available at *Luisa & Son's Lodge* near the noisy wharf. They have rooms with fan for P100/150; if you can only sleep if it's absolutely quiet, this is not the place for you. However, Luisa and Douglas are very helpful and can provide useful information on the area. They have a restaurant and you can hire a motorcycle for P300 a day.

The *Larena Pension House* is just a few minutes' walk uphill from the wharf. Unpretentious but fairly good rooms with fan cost P75/150 and with air-con P250. Sanitation levels could be better. As they only have a limited choice, it's better to order your food beforehand in the restaurant.

Places to Eat
There is a fairly large restaurant near the market, where jeepneys wait for passengers. *Luisa & Son's Restaurant* near the wharf

serves good and relatively inexpensive Philippine food. It also has seating outside. The food at the Garden Orchid Bar opposite the bank near the market is also good and inexpensive, eg chicken curry with rice P45.

Getting There & Away
Jeepney Jeepneys leave the market in Larena to go to various spots around the island. Ask about the last trip back or you may have to walk, hire a tricycle or stay the night.

SANDUGAN
Sandugan Point is a fairly deserted beach, six km outside of Larena, with a coral reef just offshore. 'Fairly deserted' because a few resorts have already established a modest infrastructure. If you want peace and quiet but don't want to be completely alone, the northernmost tip of Siquijor will fit the bill.

Places to Stay
The accommodation is pleasant at the *Islanders Paradise Beach*, some 400m off the ring road. Cottages with bath are P300, with fan P25 extra. They offer discounts for longer stays, have a fairly good restaurant, and paddleboats can be hired for P25 a day.

A small, cosy place next to the Islanders Paradise Beach, the *Kiwi Dive Resort* (cellular ☎ 0912-5022597)has cottages with fan and bath for P300, and with refrigerator and cooking facilities and even a radio for P500. Run by Bruce from New Zealand and his Philippine wife Maritess, the atmosphere here is warm and inviting. They offer diving facilities (with their own dive shop and boat), and motorcycle and bicycle hire.

Right on the beach, the *Casa del Playa Beach Resort* (cellular ☎ 0918-740 0079) offers really peaceful accommodation. Sturdily built, beautifully decorated cottages with fan and bath go for P300, P350 including cooking facilities. The resort is built on a little rise that provides an unobstructed view of the sea below. The management is Philippine-German, which probably explains why the resort is also known as Emily and Terry's Beachhouses. Food is available on request. They have motorcycle and

bicycle hire here, and plan to offer yoga courses and painting workshops.

Eight km north-east of Larena, just before Enrique Villanueva about 300m off the ring road, the *Hidden Paradise* at Bitaug has cottages with bath for P200 and P250. A discount is given for longer stays. This is a friendly little place on an out-of-the-way bay with an attractive beach for swimming, although there are not many palms. The food in the family-style restaurant to be delicious.

Getting There & Away
Tricycle A tricycle from Larena to Sandugan costs P3 per person; a Special Ride down to the beach costs P20.

SALAG DO-ONG
Salag Do-Ong is on the northernmost point of Maria Bay. With its small swimming beach it is probably the most popular holiday resort of the Siquijodnons. There is no regular jeepney service and you have to walk the two km from the road to the beach. The last trip back to Larena is at about 4 pm.

LAZI
Lazi is a quiet little port on the south coast. Across from the massive St Isodore Parish Church built in 1884, behind a gnarled stand of acacias, the **St Isodore Labradore Convent** can be seen. Built in 1891, it's said to be the biggest and oldest in the country.

The coral beaches a little to the east are unsuitable for either swimming or snorkelling. **Lapac Beach**, north-east of Lazi on Maria Bay, opposite Salag Do-Ong, is said to be better. A few km inland from Lazi, set amidst beautiful scenery, there is a little waterfall with a natural pool.

SAN JUAN
One of the best beaches on the island is the palm-lined **Paliton Beach**, about two km north-west of the little town of San Juan, on the west coast of Siquijor.

Places to Stay
On Paliton Beach, the peaceful *Sunset Beach Resort* actually belongs to Luisa & Son's

Lodge in Larena. Rooms here go for P120/150, and cottages with bath for P250. The resort comprises a striking three-storey building with its own restaurant, and a few pleasant cottages standing under palm trees. You can hire a motorcycle for P300 a day.

On the beach at Tubod, two km south-east of San Juan about 100m from the road, the *Coco-Grove Beach Resort* has rooms with fan and bath for P500, and cottages with air-con and bath from P620 to P1000. The grounds are generous, with relatively few cottages all standing well apart from one another. It has a pleasant, inexpensive restaurant, and a jeepney and outrigger boat can be hired. Reservations can be made at the Paradise Travel Center on Silliman Ave, Dumaguete (☎ 255 3299; fax 255 5490).

Getting There & Away
Tricycle A tricycle from Siquijor to Paliton Beach costs P5 per person; a Special Ride from Larena should be available for P100.

SAN ANTONIO
San Antonio is in the mountainous interior of the island and is known as a centre for nature healers, also known locally as *mananambals*. But don't expect to find any witches' cauldrons. The work of these healers has nothing to do with magic, but is a novel attempt to effect cures through the use of coconut oil, herbs and other natural ingredients. By rubbing in the oils and lotions they try to relieve the most common complaints of the sufferers who consult them, mostly people with headaches and stomach pains. One of the best known medicine men in San Antonio is Jose Ponce, who lives in the woods in a simple hut.

A visit to the region during Holy Week should be interesting. That's when various quacks and 'druids' of the southern Philippines gather to exchange information and create dubious herbal potions accompanied by obscure rites. The necessary ingredients are collected during Holy Week, then on Good Friday a brew is brought to the boil in a large cauldron, sorry – vessel, known as a *kawa*, under a specially selected balete tree. Only after a long night of repeated communal praying and much discussion is the deed considered to be done and the healers share out the precious liquid among each other, filling up bottle after bottle with it. This is their precious ration for yet another year to come.

CANTABON
About three km east of San Antonio, the small township of Cantabon is known for its impressive dripstone cave. Coming from Siquijor, the road to Cantabon turns off left after San Antonio market; straight on would take you to Cang-asa and Campalanas. The cave entrance is about 200m north of the market in Cantabon, off the road. Ask at one of the sari sari stores across from the market if they know a guide.

The way down into the cave is a narrow, steep hole that leads about five to six metres deep into the mountain. After that you can work your way more or less upright, through the dripstones, to the end of the cave several hundred metres away. A crystal clear stream runs through the cave and you have to wade through it in places. Obviously, sturdy shoes and a torch (flashlight) are a 'must' here. Another good idea would be to take along a dry towel, which the guide could keep for you, because spelunking's a dirty business!

In Cantabon you're quite close to the highest point on the island, Mt Bandilaan, at 557m. It's good for a mountain hike.

Mindanao & Sulu

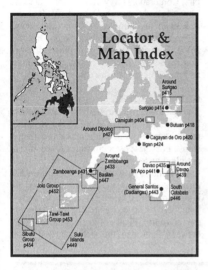

Locator & Map Index

Around Surigao p415
Surigao p414
Camiguin p404
Butuan p418
Around Dipolog p427
Cagayan de Oro p420
Iligan p424
Around Zamboanga p433
Zamboanga p431
Davao p435
Mt Apo p441
Around Davao p437
Basilan p447
General Santos (Dadiangas) p443
South Cotabato p446
Jolo Group p452
Tawi-Tawi Group p453
Sibutu Group p454
Sulu Islands p449

If you take a look at a map of the Philippines, the large landmass south of the Visayas known as the island of Mindanao seems to represent weight and stability, just as the island of Luzon does in the north. After all, the rest of the Philippine Archipelago appears like a jumbled mass of confusion in comparison.

Second only to Luzon in terms of square kilometres, the 'Promised Land', as Mindanao is often called, is anything but a pillar of strength and calming influence. For years the island has been the scene of constant upheaval as different ethnic groups, religions, economic interests and political ambitions have played havoc with the region's day to day existence.

Not quite part of this so-called land of promise, but still snuggled under the protective wing of Mindanao's northern coastline with its many bays, the little volcanic island of Camiguin meanwhile goes about its own unhurried, provincial business.

Camiguin

Camiguin lies off the north coast of Mindanao. Though relatively small, it has no less than seven volcanoes, as well as springs and waterfalls. The best known volcano is Hibok-Hibok, which last erupted in 1951. The volcanoes seem to attract clouds like magnets, and from December to mid-March short rain showers can be expected. The sunniest months are April, May and June. Camiguin is well known for its sweet *lanzones* fruit (called 'buahan' on Camiguin), which grows on the slopes of Hibok-Hibok and is the best in the Philippines.

The Camigueños are famous for their impressive hospitality. It is certainly one reason why so many of the visitors who have discovered it tend to come back again. (Camiguin is pronounced almost like 'come again'...) Unlike on other islands, strangers here are greeted not with 'Hi Joe', but with 'Hi friends'. Tourism is only just beginning to struggle to its feet on Camiguin. There are no plans as yet for incentives from the state, as other islands are obviously considered a priority. This is not necessarily a bad thing. If you're a friend of nature and can do without glittering hotels, your stay on Camiguin will definitely be a pleasure.

GETTING THERE & AWAY

You can get to Camiguin from Cebu and Mindanao (see the Mindanao Getting There & Away section in this chapter and the Cebu Getting There & Away section in the Visayas chapter).

Air

Cebu The Philippine Airlines (PAL) service has been cancelled because of lack of demand. The nearest airports for flights to Cebu City are in Butuan and Cagayan de Oro on Mindanao. Bookings can be made in

Mambajao at the PAL agents in the General Merchandise Caves Hardware & Auto Supply. Staff will also arrange the charter of a small aircraft for three or four passengers; the price from Mambajao to Cebu City should be around P3500.

Luzon PAL has flights from Butuan and Cagayan de Oro, both on Mindanao, to Manila.

Boat
Cebu From Mambajao to Cebu City, the MV *Doña Lili* of Cebu Ferries leaves on Monday at 8 pm (10 hours).

Don't leave it to the last minute to board. Depending on the load, and the captain's mood, departure may be early.

Mindanao From Benoni to Balingoan, the Tamula Shipping Lines' MV *Charles Brown* and *Ruperto Jr*, and the Corrales Shipping Lines' MV *Hijos* leave hourly from 6 am to 2 pm (P15 to P25; 1½ hours).

From Guinsiliban to Balingoan, Tamula Shipping Lines' MV *Anita* leaves daily at 6 and 11 am (one hour). The Philippine Shipping Corporation's MV *Yuhum* sails Tuesday, Thursday and Saturday at 2 pm, Wednesday at 5.30 am and Sunday at 10 am (one hour).

From Guinsiliban to Cagayan de Oro, the MV *Yuhum* of Philippine Shipping Corporation leaves Wednesday, Friday and Sunday at 3 pm (P50 to P95; three hours).

GETTING AROUND
You can travel right around the island, which has a circumference of about 65 km, in about three hours if you don't make too many stops. For the best connections, go in an anticlockwise direction, as there are not many vehicles between Yumbing and Catarman – the road between Benoni and Mambajao is most travelled by jeepneys and buses, and is your best prospect for getting transport on the return trip. Plenty of jeepneys also travel between Catarman, the second largest town

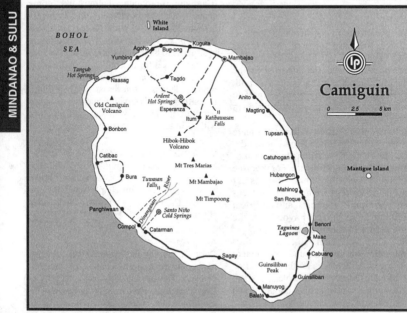

on the island, and Benoni. Along the west coast, however, be prepared to walk a few km, as only a few jeepneys run from Mambajao to Catarman and back.

For short distances you may be able to use tricycles, but the service is only good in and around Mambajao. A trip around the island by rented motorcycle is a great idea.

MAMBAJAO
The little town of Mambajao is the capital of Camiguin, which has been a province since 1966. The colourful Lanzones Festival, a sort of thanksgiving festival, takes place here every October.

Information
Tourist Office There is a tourist information centre in the Provincial Capitol building.

Money You can change travellers cheques at the Philippine National Bank (PNB), although the rate is not as good as in Cagayan de Oro or Cebu City, for instance.

Telephone The area code for Mambajao and Camiguin is 088.

Places to Stay & Eat
The friendly *RJ Pension* (☎ 870089) on J Neri St has good value accommodation. Rooms with fan go for P80/140; although a bit small, they are clean. It has a good restaurant, and offers motorcycle hire for P350 a day.

In a nice large building near the town hall, *Tia's Pension House* (☎ 871045) will give you quite a good room with fan for P75/150. You can order meals, or use the kitchen to prepare your own food for a small charge.

In Tapon, a few minutes from the town centre, *Shoreline Cottages* (☎ 871091) charge P85 per person for a cottage with fan. This is a pleasant place to stay, with basic but acceptable cottages. Nearby, *Tia's Beach Cottages* is a friendly, quiet place to stay; it charges P300 and up for a cottage with fan and bath.

About one km north-west of Mambajao, the *Tree House* (☎ 871044) at Bolok-Bolok, right on the seafront, offers rooms with bath

for P150/200 and a tree house big enough for two people for P350. The place definitely seems past its peak.

The best place in the area is the *Casa Grande* (☎/fax 870077) on Provincial Plaza, where rooms with air-con and bath go for P1000. It's planning to build a pool.

Getting There & Away
Jeepney Every day, several jeepneys travel from Benoni to Mambajao, the last one leaving at about 5 pm (P10; 30 minutes). A Special Ride should cost P80, although they'll ask for P150.

Tricycle A tricycle from Agoho to Mambajao costs P3 or P25 per tricycle.

AROUND MAMBAJAO
Hibok-Hibok Volcano
Hibok-Hibok (1320m) is the most active of Camiguin's seven volcanoes. On 5 December 1951 it erupted without warning, killing over 2000 people. A small collection of photos and newspaper clippings can be seen at the Comvol Station which monitors volcanic activity. This is about 400m up the mountain and takes a good hour to reach on foot. The staff at the station will be happy to show you around and explain the use of the seismographic instruments. They appreciate small gifts like bread, sweets and cigarettes. Comvol employees are not allowed to conduct tours from the station up to the volcano.

For trips to the volcano, the tourism office in the Provincial Capitol building in Mambajao or any resort can arrange an experienced guide for about P350. The climb is via Ardent Hot Springs and Esperanza, and takes about four hours. It begins with a gentle slope and takes you first through high cogon grass and fern groves, leading to a steeper section which takes you over scree, lava and rock faces to the summit. If you start your climb as early as possible – say 5 am but by 9 am at the latest – you should be able to make it back down again before sunset and save an overnight stay on the mountain (allow four hours for the descent). Some of the guides try to make it up and down again in record time, and don't like being held up for any reason. The tour loses a lot of its appeal when they do this, so you should not only agree on the price with the guide but also on the time available. Note: as there are no streams or wells on the way to the summit, take enough water with you.

Once at the top, you can climb down to a moss-encircled crater lake. This takes about 45 minutes. If you decide to go down to the lake, it would be wise to spend the nights before and after the trek at the Comvol Station to save time. In the dry season you can take a tent and camp beside the lake.

Katibawasan Falls
Surrounded by tropical vegetation, the falls thunder down from a height of 50m. The water is refreshingly cool. The best time to go there is from 10 am to 2 pm, when you can also sunbathe. There is a resthouse, although it's a bit tatty. You have to take your own provisions.

Getting There & Away To get to the falls, go first from Mambajao to the village of Pandan by tricycle. You then have to do the remaining three km from the fork in the road at the edge of town to the falls on foot. When it's dry, the track to the resthouse can be reached by motorcycle.

Ardent Hot Springs
The temperature of the crystal clear water in the beautifully designed swimming pool is around 40°C. The surrounding area is well tended and there are sheltered picnic places. It's a favourite for weekend outings; the pool is cleaned out on Monday and Friday from 8 am till noon. Admission costs P25; Filipinos pay only P10.

Places to Stay The *Ardent Hot Spring Resort* has dorm beds for P130 and P200, and cottages with bath for P560. There is a restaurant, and the food is good.

Getting There & Away The trip from Mambajao by tricycle and back costs around P150, including a few hours' waiting time.

There are numerous paths from the ring road to the hot springs, all of which take about an hour on foot.

White Island
White Island is a small island about three km north of Agoho. It consists of nothing but coral and sand, and there's no shade. A parasol or a tent would really come in handy. It's a good place for swimming and snorkelling, although the coral has been decimated in recent years by thoughtlessly destructive fishing methods.

Getting There & Away To get to White Island, go by tricycle or jeepney from Mambajao to Yumbing, Naasag or Agoho, then charter a boat. At the White Island terminal in Agoho and in the resorts there, you can organise a round trip for P200 per boat. Agree on a time for them to return for you.

AROUND THE ISLAND
Kuguita
The sandy beach at **Mahayahay** and **Turtles Nest Beach**, which has a few corals, are in Kuguita, three km west of Mambajao.

Places to Stay & Eat The *Turtles Nest Beach Cottages* (☎ 871000) provides rooms with fan for P170/300, and fairly large duplex cottages with fan and bath for P350 – but the place has seen better days. It offers a discount for stays of more than seven days. There is a garden and a restaurant. Mountain bikes (P150 a day) and motorcycles (P400 a day) are available for hire.

Agoho, Bug-ong & Yumbing
These small coastal towns, five to seven km west of Kuguita, are on most travellers' itineraries and all have their own beach resorts. At Agoho you can get a boat to the offshore White Island for P200.

Places to Stay & Eat Starting in Agoho, the peaceful *Camiguin Seaside Lodge* has dorm beds for P100 and P150, and cottages with bath for P275 and P300. The cottages are roomy but are beginning to show their age.

The restaurant closes at 8 pm, but most of the guests go elsewhere to eat anyway. Motorcycles are available for hire at P350 a day.

The *Morning Glory Cottages* (☎ 879017) in Agoho have rooms for P150/250 and cottages with bath for P350. It is fairly comfortable and has a restaurant, as well as good cooking facilities. The immaculate rooms at the *Paradise Palm Pension House* cost P250 with fan and bath. The pleasant looking building is directly on the sea, and has a big patio, kitchen and an exercise room.

The accommodation is adequate at the *Caves Resort* (☎ 879077), with rooms for P200/300 and cottages with bath for P350 and P500, although some of the rooms are no longer in the best condition. It has a restaurant, tennis court, and windsurfing equipment and a dive shop, Bubbles Diving (☎ 879040; fax 871009), under Italian-Austrian management. Mountain bikes can be hired.

The *Payag Cottages* have cottages with fan and bath for P250. There are not many of them, but they're looking good. A small rebate is offered for longer stays.

Jasmine by the Sea Beach Resort (☎ 879 015) in Bug-ong is a pleasant, shipshape place, which has cottages with bath for P300 and P400 (more spacious), and it has diving facilities.

Set in attractive grounds with a garden, the *Paras Beach Resort* (☎ 879008) in Yumbing offers tastefully furnished, bright rooms with air-con and bath from P1100 to P1950, and cottages with fan and bath for P2200 and P2750. The latter have two bedrooms with room for up to eight people. There is a big restaurant and a swimming pool, and diving facilities are available. All in all, the best accommodation on Camiguin.

Places to Eat There are a few no-frill eateries with inexpensive Philippine food on the 'Highway', as the main road from Agoho is called. The little family-run restaurant *Sagittarius Serve Food* is worth a mention, with its good food and big portions. The *Paradiso Bar & Restaurant* is in an old building, and specialises in Italian cooking, steaks and fish dishes; at the weekend it features live music. *Jasmine by the Sea* will prepare really good European food for you. The *Hexagon* has billiards, and is a favourite hang-out of Filipinos and foreign guests.

Getting There & Away The trip from Mambajao to Agoho by tricycle costs P3 per person; P25 for a Special Ride. A Special Ride by jeepney from Benoni to Agoho is P150.

Bonbon

Bonbon is mainly famous for its **Sunken Cemetery**, which disappeared under the waters after a volcano erupted in 1871. Some years ago, grave stones could be seen poking out of the water at low tide, so they say. Now, a large cross in the sea indicates where the Sunken Cemetery is, and that's about all you can see from the coast. If you want to get down to details, then diving would be an interesting way of seeing it. Every year on 21 May, the anniversary of the tragedy, Camigueños go to the spot in boats and strew flowers in the water.

A bit north of Bonbon you'll come across the old ruins of the **Guiob Church**, overgrown with moss. Further north again, starting at the ring road in a bay, the stations of the cross lead up to the **Old Camiguin Volcano** (Mt Daan), a favourite with pilgrims during Holy Week. There is a good view from each of the stations.

Catarman

Just under two km north-west of Catarman is a turn-off leading to the **Tuwasan Falls**, about four km from the ring road. When you get to the Dinangasan River, you have to head upstream a bit to find them. The local people compare the two main falls with two different women: one, Katibawasan, who wears lots of make-up; the other, Tuwasan, who has a natural, unspoilt beauty.

The nearby **Santo Niño Cold Springs** are refreshingly cool and you can swim in a nice large pool that is one to two metres deep; the pool is cleaned out on Wednesday. There are toilets and a picnic shelter. The place is also known as the Kiyab Pool and is over two km off the main road.

Places to Stay In Catarman you can stay in rooms at the high school for P50 per person if you're on a tight budget. Definitely more expensive, but a good alternative, would be the *Fisherman's Friend Resort* (☎/fax 877021), two km south of Catarman on the beach in Alga. You can have a native-style room with fan and bath for between P450 and P525. Other facilities include a restaurant, patio bar and a car available for rent.

Getting There & Away
Jeepneys leave Mambajao for Catarman at 6, 9 am, noon and 2 pm (P15; 1½ hours). The last one leaves Catarman for Mambajao at 4 pm.

Guinsiliban
There is a ferry route between Guinsiliban in the south of the island and Balingoan and Cagayan de Oro, both on Mindanao. The roughly 300-year-old **Moro watchtower** stands behind the elementary school.

Benoni
Benoni has a wharf for ferries going to and from Balingoan on Mindanao. From here boats also go to Mantigue (Magsaysay) Island, which lies offshore and is a favourite diving place (P350). About one km south of Benoni is a beautiful artificial lake, **Taguines Lagoon**, which is separated from the sea by a causeway.

Places to Stay A peaceful, cosy place right on the lagoon, the *J & A Fishpen* (☎ 874008) has simple but appealing cottages with large verandas, standing on stilts in the water. You'll pay P300 for rooms with fan and bath, P500/600 with air-con and bath. A tricycle ride there costs P15.

Places to Eat Highly recommended, the *LAB AS2 Restaurant* across the lagoon from the J & A Fishpen serves excellent food (mainly seafood) at agreeably low prices. The beautiful view is on the house.

Mahinog & Mantigue Island
Mahinog lies on the east coast of Camiguin, almost opposite Mantigue (Magsaysay) Island. The beach there is pebbly, but Mantigue Island has a white sandy beach and usually offers good snorkelling. Unfortunately, the rubbish lying around on the island has detracted from its original beauty. If you want to stay for a few days, bring your own provisions and drinking water. The round trip from Mahinog costs about P350.

Place to Stay The *Mychellin Beach Resort* (☎ 874005) in Mahinog has rooms with fan and bath for P250, and there are cooking facilities. It appears this place has seen better days.

Tupsan
Near Tupsan, about one km from the ring road, you can take a refreshing dip in the cold water of the **Macao Cold Spring**. The turn-off is signposted.

Mindanao

Mindanao is the second largest island of the Philippines. Its landscape is dominated by mountain chains running north-south. Close to Davao is Mt Apo (2954m), the highest mountain in the Philippines. Mindanao is one of the Philippines' richest islands, even though little of its mineral wealth has yet been tapped. There is an occasional gold rush sparked off by rumours of a sizeable find, but at present most of the island's income comes from agriculture, with large pineapple plantations in the north near Cagayan de Oro and banana groves in the south near Davao.

It is not quite true that all of the Mindanao population is Muslim but certainly most of the Muslim Filipinos live there and on the neighbouring Sulu Islands. The area around Lake Lanao in central Mindanao is predominantly Muslim.

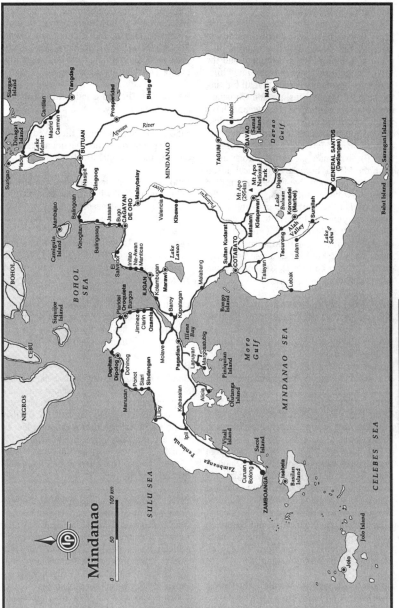

Dangers & Annoyances

The struggle of the Moro National Liberation Front (MNLF) for an autonomous Muslim state on the island lasted a quarter of a century. Although the government and the MNLF concluded a peace treaty in 1996, it is still not absolutely certain that all fighting has stopped. Many Muslims and Christians are totally against the treaty, and have announced their active opposition. Particularly serious are attacks by supporters of the radical Moro Islamic Liberation Front (MILF), a splinter group that broke away from the MNLF because of political differences and is responsible for causing its own brand of trouble. Although, as usual, the situation is often portrayed as being worse than it is, you should nevertheless enquire about possible disturbances before making overland trips in western Mindanao. Avoid buses carrying soldiers as these are especially likely to be shot at. Soldiers seldom take the air-con buses.

GETTING THERE & AWAY

You can get to Mindanao from Basilan, Bohol, Camiguin, Cebu, Leyte, Luzon, Negros, Panay and Siquijor (see the Luzon Getting There & Away section in the Manila chapter and the relevant Getting There & Away sections of this and the Visayas chapter).

Air

Cebu PAL has daily flights to Cebu City from Davao, General Santos, Pagadian, and Zamboanga.

PAL also has flights to Cebu City from Butuan daily, except Wednesday and Sunday; from Cagayan de Oro on Monday, Wednesday and Saturday; from Cotabato on Thursday and Sunday; from Dipolog on Monday, Tuesday, Wednesday and Friday; from Ozamis daily, except Monday, Wednesday and Saturday; from Surigao daily, except Monday, Wednesday and Sunday; and from Tandag on Monday, Wednesday and Saturday.

Luzon All planes go to Manila. Cebu Pacific and Grand Air fly daily from Cagayan de Oro and Davao. Air Philippines flies daily from Cagayan de Oro, Cotabato and Zamboanga. PAL has daily flights from Cagayan de Oro, Cotabato, Davao and Zamboanga. From Butuan, PAL flies on Monday, Wednesday Friday and Sunday; and from Dipolog daily, except Thursday and Saturday.

Panay PAL flies on Sunday from General Santos to Iloilo City.

Siquijor Pacific Airways flies Wednesday from Dipolog to Siquijor, but not necessarily on a regular basis (P550; 30 minutes).

Sulu Islands PAL flies daily from Zamboanga to Jolo and Tawi-Tawi. Tawi-Tawi airport is on Sanga Sanga Island, near Bongao.

Bus

Leyte From Davao, there are Philtranco aircon buses twice daily heading to Manila via Surigao, passing through Liloan and Tacloban on Leyte.

Luzon From Davao, Philtranco air-con buses leave twice daily for Manila. The 40 hours' travelling time includes ferries from Surigao to Liloan and from San Isidro to Matnog.

Boat

Basilan From Zamboanga to Isabela, Basilan Shipping Lines' MV *Doña Leonora* sails daily at 10 am and 4 pm, taking over one hour.

From Zamboanga to Lamitan, the Basilan Shipping Lines' MV *Doña Ramona* leaves daily at 3 pm, taking over one hour; the MV Don Julio leaves daily at 7 am and 1 pm, taking 2 hours. The wharf at Lamitan is on the outskirts of town.

Bohol From Butuan to Jagna, the MV *Lady of Fatima* leaves on Sunday at noon (six hours).

From Cagayan de Oro to Jagna, the MV *Our Lady of Lourdes* of Cebu Ferries leaves on Monday at noon (six hours). Its MV *Our Lady of Lipa* leaves on Sunday at 9 am (four hours). The Sulpicio Lines' MV *Cagayan Princess* leaves on Saturday at noon (five hours).

From Cagayan de Oro to Tagbilaran, Water Jet Shipping's MV *Water Jet 1* sails daily at 3.45 pm (P340; three hours). The MV *Superferry 5* of WG & A leaves on Wednesday at 11 pm (P150; seven hours). Its MV *Superferry 7* leaves Sunday at midnight (seven hours). Trans-Asia Shipping Lines' MV *Asia-Thailand* leaves Tuesday and Thursday at noon, and Saturday at 8 pm (eight hours).

From Dipolog to Tagbilaran, Sulpicio Lines' MV *Dipolog Princess* sails Monday at 9 am (five hours).

Camiguin From Balingoan to Benoni, the Tamula Shipping Lines' MV *Charles Brown* and *Ruperto Jr* and the Corrales Shipping Lines' MV *Hijos* leave hourly from 6 am to 4 pm (P15 to P25; 1½ hours).

From Balingoan to Guinsiliban, Tamula Shipping Lines' MV *Anita* leaves daily at 9 am and 2 pm (one hour). The MV *Yuhum* of Philippine Shipping Corporation sails Tuesday, Thursday and Saturday at 4 pm, Wednesday at 8 am and Sunday at noon (one hour).

From Cagayan de Oro to Guinsiliban, the MV *Yuhum* of Philippine Shipping Corporation leaves Tuesday, Thursday and Saturday at 8 am (P50 to P95; three hours).

Cebu Several ships go to Cebu City from various towns on Mindanao.

From Butuan, the MV *Lady of Fatima* of Cebu Ferries leaves on Monday, Wednesday and Friday at 6 pm (11 hours); the MV *Lady of Lourdes* leaves on Saturday at 6 pm (11 hours). The Sulpicio Lines' MV *Nasipit Princess* leaves on Tuesday, Thursday and Sunday at 8 pm (nine hours).

From Cagayan de Oro, Water Jet Shipping's MV *Water Jet 1* sails daily at 3.45 pm (P510; five hours, via Tagbiliran on Bohol). Trans-Asia Shipping Lines' MV *Asia-China* or the *Trans-Asia* leaves daily at 7 pm (10 hours). Sulpicio Lines' MV *Princess of Paradise* leaves Monday at noon (eight hours). Its MV *Cagayan Princess* leaves Tuesday, Thursday and Sunday at 7 pm (10 hours). The MV *Lady of Lipa* of Cebu Ferries leaves Monday, Wednesday, Friday and Sunday at 8 pm (eight hours). The MV *Lady of Lourdes* sails Tuesday and Thursday at 8 pm (10 hours).

From Dapitan, the Cokaliong Shipping Lines' MV *Filipinas Dinagat* leaves on Tuesday, Thursday and Saturday at 4 pm (14 hours, via Dumaguete on Negros).

From Davao, Sulpicio Lines' MV *Filipina Princess* leaves Wednesday at 7 pm (27 hours).

From Iligan, the MV *Doña Cristina* of Cebu Ferries leaves on Monday, Wednesday and Friday at 7 pm (11 hours). Its MV *Lady of Carmel* leaves on Tuesday, Thursday and Saturday at 4 pm (13 hours, via Ozamis). The Sulpicio Lines' MV *Dipolog Princess* leaves on Friday at 9 pm (nine hours).

From Ozamis, Water Jet Shipping's MV *Water Jet 2* sails Monday, Wednesday and Friday at 2.15 pm (P510; 4½ hours). The MV *Lady of Carmel* of Cebu Ferries leaves on Tuesday, Thursday and Saturday at 7 pm (10 hours). Its MV *Lady of Rule* leaves on Friday and Sunday at 7 pm (10 hours). Lite Shipping's MV *Lite Ferry I* sails on Tuesday, Thursday and Saturday at 8 pm (nine hours). The Sulpicio Lines' MV *Philippine Princess* leaves on Friday at 10 pm (seven hours).

From Surigao, Water Jet Shipping's MV *Water Jet 2* sails Tuesday, Thursday, Saturday and Sunday at 12.30 pm (P430; 4 hours, via Maasin on Leyte). The Cokaliong Shipping Lines' MV *Filipinas Dapitan* leaves on Tuesday (via Maasin on Leyte), Thursday and Saturday at 7 pm (10 hours). Its MV *Filipinas Surigao* leaves on Wednesday and Friday (via Maasin on Leyte) and Sunday at 7 pm (10 hours). Trans-Asia Shipping Lines' MV *Asia-Singapore* leaves on Wednesday at 11 pm and Sunday at 10 pm (10 hours). The Sulpicio Lines' MV *Filipina Princess* leaves on Thursday at 3 pm (seven hours).

Leyte From Surigao to Liloan, the MV *Maharlika II* of Bernard Services leaves at 5 pm from Lipata, 10 km north-west of Surigao (three hours).

From Surigao to Maasin, Water Jet Shipping's *Water Jet 2* sails Tuesday, Thursday, Saturday and Sunday at 12.30 pm (P210; 2 hours). Cokaliong Shipping's MV *Filipinas Dapitan* sails Tuesday at 7 pm (4½ hours); its MV *Filipinas Surigao* leaves Wednesday and Friday at 7 pm (4½ hours). Trans-Asia

Shipping Lines' MV *Asia-Singapore* leaves on Friday at 5 pm (four hours). The Sulpicio Lines' MV *Palawan Princess* leaves on Saturday at 8 pm (four hours). It goes on to Baybay and Calubian.

Luzon There are several ships that go to Manila from Mindanao.

From Butuan, the MV *Superferry 2* of WG & A leaves on Wednesday at 1 pm (P720; 42 hours, via Iloilo City on Panay). Its MV *Medjugorje* leaves on Saturday at noon (35 hours, via Surigao).

From Cagayan de Oro, the MV *Superferry 9* of WG & A leaves on Monday at midnight (P700; 31 hours) and Friday at 3 pm (39 hours, via Iloilo City on Panay). Its MV *Superferry 5* leaves on Wednesday at 11 pm (38 hours, via Tagbilaran on Bohol); the MV *Superferry 2* leaves on Saturday at midnight (31 hours); and the MV *Superferry 7* leaves on Sunday at midnight (32 hours, via Tagbilaran on Bohol). The Sulpicio Lines' MV *Princess of Paradise* leaves on Friday at noon (25 hours).

From Cotabato, the MV *Maynilad* of WG & A leaves on Wednesday at 10 pm (P815; 66 hours, via Dipolog and Dumaguete on Negros). Its MV *Superferry 3* leaves on Sunday at 9 pm (45 hours, via Zamboanga).

From Davao, the MV *Superferry 1* of WG & A leaves on Monday at midnight (P990; 53 hours, via General Santos). Its MV *Superferry 6* leaves on Thursday at noon (43 hours).

From Dipolog, the MV *Maynilad* of WG & A leaves on Friday at 1 am (P545; 39 hours, via Dumaguete on Negros).

From General Santos, the MV *Superferry 1* of WG & A leaves on Tuesday at 10 am (P910; 43 hours). Its MV *Doña Virginia* leaves on Thursday at 6 pm (42 hours, via Zamboanga).

From Iligan, the MV *Superferry 7* of WG & A leaves on Thursday at 9 am (P620; 40 hours, via Ozamis). Its MV *Superferry 5* leaves on Sunday at 9 am (35 hours, via Iloilo City on Panay).

From Ozamis, the MV *Medjugorje* of WG & A leaves on Tuesday at midnight (P615; 35 hours, via Dumaguete on Negros). Its MV

Superferry 7 leaves on Thursday at 1 pm (29 hours).

From Surigao, the MV *Medjugorje* of WG & A leaves on Saturday at 7 pm (P635; 28 hours).

From Zamboanga, the MV *Superferry 3* of WG & A leaves on Monday at 9 am (P645; 32 hours). Its MV *Doña Virginia* leaves on Friday at 8 am (28 hours).

Negros From Cagayan de Oro to Bacolod, the MV *San Paolo* of Negros Navigation leaves on Friday at 4 pm (16 hours).

From Cotabato to Dumaguete, the MV *Maynilad* of WG & A leaves on Wednesday at 10 pm (P480; 29 hours, via Dipolog).

From Dapitan to Dumaguete, the Cokaliong Shipping Lines' MV *Filipinas Dinagat* leaves on Tuesday, Thursday and Saturday at 4 pm (four hours). The MV *Dumaguete Ferry*, MV *Georich* or MV *Zamboanga Ferry* of George & Peter Lines leaves daily (five hours). The harbour for Dapitan and Dipolog lies between both cities and is called Dapitan Port. A tricycle from Dipolog or Dapitan costs about P30.

From Dipolog to Dumaguete, the MV *Maynilad* of WG & A leaves on Friday at 1 am (P65; four hours). The Trans-Asia Shipping Lines' MV *Asia-Japan* leaves on Friday at 8 am (four hours).

From Ozamis to Dumaguete, the MV *Medjugorje* of WG & A leaves on Tuesday at midnight (P125; six hours). The Sulpicio Lines' MV *Philippine Princess* leaves on Sunday at 4 pm (seven hours).

From Zamboanga to Dumaguete, the Trans-Asia Shipping Lines' MV *Asia-Japan* leaves on Sunday at midnight (eight hours).

Panay Several ships go to Iloilo City from various towns on Mindanao.

From Butuan, the MV *Superferry 2* of WG & A leaves on Wednesday at 1 pm (P419; 17 hours).

From Cagayan de Oro, the MV *Superferry 9* of WG & A leaves on Friday at 3 pm (P370; 15 hours). The MV *Santa Ana* of Negros Navigation leaves on Sunday at 4 pm (14 hours).

From Cotabato, the Sulpicio Lines' MV *Cotabato Princess* leaves on Tuesday at 10 pm (36 hours, via Zamboanga).

From Davao, the MV *Superferry 1* of WG & A leaves on Monday at midnight (P650; 33 hours, via General Santos).

From General Santos, the MV *Superferry 1* of WG & A leaves on Tuesday at 11 am (P600; 22 hours). The Sulpicio Lines' MV *Princess of the Pacific* leaves on Friday at 6 pm (36 hours, via Zamboanga).

From Iligan, the MV *Superferry 5* of WG & A leaves on Sunday at 9 am (P350; 12 hours).

From Zamboanga, the Sulpicio Lines' MV *Cotabato Princess* leaves on Wednesday at 8 pm (14 hours). Its MV *Princess of the Pacific* leaves on Saturday at 4 pm (14 hours).

Sulu Islands SKT Shipping Lines has three ships going from Zamboanga to Sitangkai. The MV *Lady Ruth* leaves on Tuesday at 8 pm (45 hours), going via Jolo (10 hours), Siasi (22 hours) and Bongao (36 hours).

The MV *Lady Helen* leaves on Wednesday at 6 pm (44 hours), going via Jolo, Siasi and Bongao.

The MV *Doña Isabel II* leaves on Saturday at 6 pm (45 hours), going via Jolo, Siasi and Bongao.

The Sampaguita Shipping Corporation also has three ships going from Zamboanga to Sitangkai. The MV *Sampaguita Grandeur* leaves on Monday at 8 pm (42 hours) going via Jolo (nine hours), Siasi (18 hours) and Bongao (33 hours).

The MV *Sampaguita Laei* leaves on Thursday at 8 pm (42 hours), going via Jolo, Siasai and Bongao.

The MV *Sampaguita Blossom* leaves on Sunday at 7 pm and (45 hours), going via Jolo, Siasi and Bongao.

The Zamboanga-based Magnolia Shipping Lines also has numerous ships on this route or parts of this route.

SURIGAO

Surigao, the capital of Surigao del Norte Province, is the starting point for trips to offshore islands like Dinagat and Siargao. What must be the best beach in the Surigao area, **Mabua Beach**, 12 km outside the city, is a favourite weekend resort. The water is clear and the swimming is great, although the beach has black pebbles instead of sand.

It's always a bit rainy in north-east Mindanao, and in December and January be prepared for heavy downpours. If you can put up with a few drops, however, you will be well rewarded by the magnificent landscape of the east coast. The best time to visit Surigao and its surroundings is from April to June.

Information

The telephone area code for Surigao is 08681.

Places to Stay

You can get simple but relatively good rooms with fan for P75/130 at the *Flourish Lodge* on Borromeo St, Port Area.

The rooms at the friendly *Dexter Pension House* at 309 San Nicolas St are basic and good value, costing P75 to P180 with fan, and P280/350 with air-con and bath.

The *Garcia Hotel* at 311 San Nicolas St has relatively clean rooms with fan for P75/150, and with air-con and bath for P250/300. You can have breakfast at the bakery across the road.

Although not really anything special, the best place in town is the *Tavern Hotel* (☎ 87300) on Borromeo St. You get OK rooms with fan for P80/160, with fan and bath for P150/200 and P180/230, and with air-con and bath from P400 to P600. You can arrange for the hotel boat to take you to the offshore islands.

Places to Eat

The restaurant at the *Tavern Hotel* on Borromeo St, where you can sit outside right on the water, is fairly pleasant. The *Cherry Blossom Restaurant*, on the corner of San Nicolas and Vasques Sts, has good food and live music. There are also small, reasonably priced restaurants on the waterside of the market near town hall.

A little outside the city, in the direction of the airport on Rizal St, dance enthusiasts gather every evening in the modern *Limelight*

Disco; you can eat cheaply in the restaurant downstairs.

Getting There & Away

Air The PAL office (☎ 96436) is at the airport; confirm your return flight when you first arrive.

Bus Several Bachelor Bus Liner and Surigao buses run daily from Cagayan de Oro to Surigao (P125; six hours) via Butuan (P48; 2½ hours).

From Davao to Surigao, Bachelor Bus Liner and Ceres buses run daily (P155; eight

hours). The last bus leaves around 1.30 pm. You may have to change in Butuan. Air-con Philtranco buses run from Davao to Surigao, going on to Tacloban and Manila.

Jeepney There are a number of jeepneys and minibuses from Butuan to Surigao (2½ hours).

Boat From Davao, the Sulpicio Lines' MV *Filipina Princess* leaves for Surigao on Monday at 9 pm (17 hours). From Dapa, on Siargao Island, the MV *Dua* or MV *Philippe* leaves for Surigao daily (possibly not on Sunday) between 9 am and noon (4½ hours),

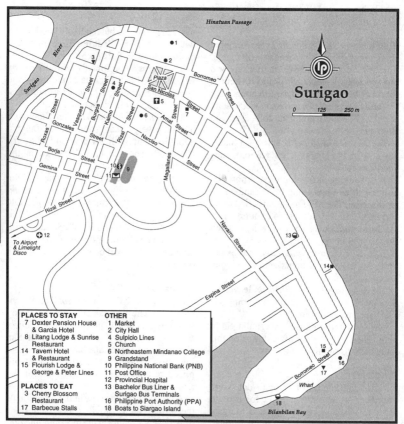

Surigao

0   125   250 m

PLACES TO STAY
7   Dexter Pension House
    & Garcia Hotel
8   Litang Lodge & Sunrise
    Restaurant
14 Tavern Hotel
    & Restaurant
15 Flourish Lodge &
    George & Peter Lines

PLACES TO EAT
3   Cherry Blossom
    Restaurant
17 Barbecue Stalls

OTHER
1   Market
2   City Hall
4   Sulpicio Lines
5   Church
6   Northeastern Mindanao College
9   Grandstand
10 Philippine National Bank (PNB)
11 Post Office
12 Provincial Hospital
13 Bachelor Bus Liner &
    Surigao Bus Terminals
16 Philippine Port Authority (PPA)
18 Boats to Siargao Island

depending on loading times. If you want a camp bed, get your ticket early at the Officina (Ticket Office) in Dapa. The jeepney driver will stop there on request.

From Del Carmen, an outrigger boat is said to go to Surigao daily at about 8.30 am.

From Sapao, a boat leaves for Surigao every other day at about 6 am.

Getting Around
The Airport Tricycles run from Surigao airport to town for P10.

Boat Most boats use the wharf south of town. The ferries to and from Liloan on Leyte use the wharf at Lipata, about 10 km north-west of Surigao.

Tricycle & Bus The regular price for a tricycle from Lipata to the centre of town is P5 per person; a Special Ride may be as high as P50. There are also some buses, such as those run by the Bachelor Bus Liner company.

SIARGAO ISLAND
Siargao is the biggest island in the group east of Surigao. Lots of travellers chiefly visit the island because of its excellent surf, especially from July to November on the east coast, facing the Pacific. At least a dozen breaks have become popular, including Horseshoes, Tuason Point, Cloud Nine, Tuesday Rock, Ventura and Pilar Point, all north of General Luna and reachable on foot or by boat. Just south of Union there's Pancit Reef, and further south out on the islands of Lajanosa and Antokon huge breakers are just waiting for surfers to experience them.

Dapa
Dapa is on the south coast of Siargao Island and is the most important town on the island. There are boat connections from there to Surigao and to Socorro on Bucas Grande Island.

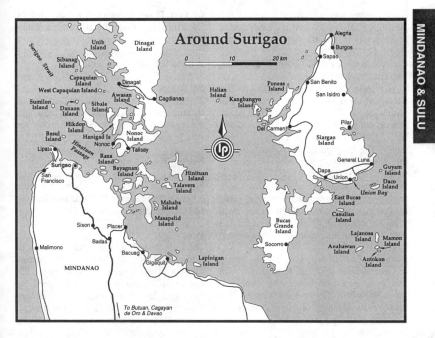

Information In Dapa there is a bank but you can't change travellers cheques or cash there, so bring enough pesos with you.

Places to Stay *Lucing's Carenderia* on Juan Luna St is about 300m from the wharf in the direction of the town centre. It has basic rooms for P50/80; rooms with fan cost P60/100.

Getting There & Away From Surigao, the MV *Dua* or MV *Philippe* leaves for Dapa daily (possibly not on Sunday) between 8 and 11 am (P40; 4½ hours), depending on loading times.

General Luna

General Luna, a laid-back small town on the south-east tip of the island, is the most popular destination on Siargao Island, especially for surfers.

Places to Stay Presently the best and most comfortable accommodation in General Luna is available at the *Siargao Pension House*, where rooms with fan cost P180 per person or P550 for full board. It has boats for island hopping, kayaks, windsurfers and a Hobie Cat. Apparently, it is also going to open the *Siargao Pacific Beach Resort* soon, five km out of town.

The *Pisangan Beach Resort* is about 300m outside of town and has basic, but adequate rooms for P150/300, including three meals. The fan-cooled rooms at *Maite's Beach Resort* cost P150/300 with bath, including three meals. The easy-going *BRC Beach Resort* offers wooden cottages set in grassy grounds with bath for P50 per head or P250 full board.

The *Jade Lodge & Beach Resort* is a friendly place about 350m outside of town on the way to Union, but not on the main road. Rooms cost P50/100, and with fan and bath P100/150. Full board is available.

Places to Eat The resorts and lodging houses in General Luna prefer to have guests with full, or at least half, board. One meal costs about P50 to P75. Try the marvellous fish dish poot-poot, a speciality of the area, which the local housewives pride themselves on.

Getting There & Away Jeepneys run from Dapa to General Luna in the morning at about 9 am from near the wharf (P5). Two more leave straight after the arrival of the boat from Surigao.

From General Luna to Dapa, jeepneys leave at 6 and 7 am, but only after a seemingly endless pick-up around the town.

Union

Between Dapa and General Luna, Union is a village with lovely beaches, a small bay and outlying islands. It is at the western end of the bay and is connected to Dapa by an eight km road. There is a jeepney service between the two places.

Places to Stay The *Latitude 9 Beach Resort* is in a beautiful location with a view of the offshore islands. It charges P50 per person for a cottage with fan and bath. Susan, the owner's wife, takes care of the cooking; P50 per meal.

Getting There & Away A jeepney leaves Dapa for Union every day at 7 am and sometimes at noon. Corresponding departure from Union for Dapa is between 10 and 11 am, and between 1 and 2 pm.

Del Carmen

There are said to be crocodiles at Del Carmen (Numancia), 25 km from General Luna, but the reports only seem to come from people who haven't been there!

Getting There & Away At least two jeepneys a day go from Dapa to Del Carmen between 7 and 9 am. There is a daily boat service between Surigao and Del Carmen leaving Del Carmen around 8.30 am.

Pilar

The little township of Pilar is on the north side of Port Pilar Bay on the east coast of Siargao Island. Similar to Del Carmen, the countryside around Pilar is covered by extensive mangrove swamps which are criss-crossed by a network of 'water streets'. You can take an interesting day trip there by

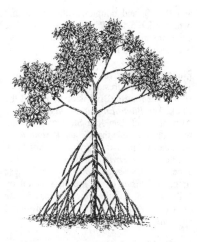

A tree that breathes through its knees? The above-ground roots, or knees, of the mangrove supply air to submerged nether regions.

boat from General Luna and cruise the water street.

Alegria

This is the northernmost community on Siargao Island, with a beautiful sandy beach. The first resorts have already established themselves there.

Places to Stay No-frills, but friendly accommodation is available at *Platil's Beach Resort*, where rooms cost P50/100. Meals can be arranged, and it even lets guests loose in the kitchen to cook for themselves.

Getting There & Away A jeepney makes the trip every day from Dapa to Sapao and, if there are enough passengers, another five km on to Alegria. An alternative would be to have a motorcycle take you for P20 (they'll ask for P50) from Sapao to Alegria.

Nearby Islands

You can reach the lovely little outlying islands of Guyam, Daco, Lajanosa, Anahawan, Mamon and Antokon, with their magnificent white sand beaches, by outrigger boat from Dapa, Union and General Luna.

Lajanosa is inhabited. Apart from the village of the same name in the north-east of the island, there is the fishing village of Suyangan where private accommodation is available. In the south of the island there's a beautiful beach with a magnificent coral reef which stretches to the next island, Mamon. In the meantime, it is possible that a little resort has opened up on the south-west side of Mamon, as an Australian had plans to do this.

BUTUAN

Butuan, on the Agusan River, is a port with many connections to the Visayan islands. Several Filipino historians assert that Butuan could be the site of the oldest human settlement in the country. This theory seemed to be confirmed in 1976 by the discovery near Butuan of a *balangay* (a large sea-going outrigger boat) thought to be over 1000 years old. You can see the balangay in a specially made glass showcase in the place it was found outside the town, half-way between Butuan and the airport, roughly 1.2 km from the main road.

In 1984, not far from the Agusan River, human bones, including skulls, were found together with death masks, porcelain, pottery and jewellery, which indicated an even earlier occupation of Butuan. The 1984 finds are displayed in a museum next to the town hall.

A *balangay*, or sea-going outrigger.

Information

There are two telephone area codes for Butuan: 08521 and 08522.

Places to Stay – bottom end

At the *Hensonly Plaza Inn* (☎/fax 225 1340) on San Francisco St, the rooms are OK, if a bit basic; they cost P85 with fan only, P150/200 with fan and bath, and P250/350 with air-con and bath. It has a disco.

The *Imperial Hotel* (☎ 2199) on San Francisco St is fairly good accommodation, with singles with fan for P85, singles with fan and bath for P125, and rooms with air-con and bath from P175 to P320.

The *Embassy Hotel* (☎ 3737) on Montilla Blvd is in a quiet area and has clean air-con rooms with bath for P300/400. The staff are friendly. The *Emerald Villa Hotel* on Villanueva St is a well-run place with immaculate fan-cooled rooms for P300/400 with bath, P400/500 with air-con and bath, including TV.

Places to Stay – top end

Centrally located on the little Rizal Park, the *Almont Hotel* (☎/fax 415010) on San Jose St has singles with air-con and bath for P650

and P1400, and doubles with air-con and bath for P775 and P1550. The rooms are adequate and have TV, the more expensive ones also have a fridge.

Places to Eat

The inexpensive restaurant in the *Embassy Hotel* on Montilla Blvd is open around the clock. The *Punta Engano Restaurant* in the Almont Hotel, San Jose St, serves international dishes, while the *Nicolite Restaurant & Bar* nearby will also give you a decent meal.

The *Golden Dragon Restaurant* on Concepcion St has a good reputation for Chinese food. *Jet's Sinugba* in the Jet's Hotel on Villanueva St and the *New Mansion House* on Concepcion St (both air-conditioned) specialise in seafood.

Getting There & Away

Air PAL has an office at Butuan airport (☎ 415144).

Bus There are several Philtranco and Bachelor Bus Liner buses running from Surigao to Butuan daily (two hours); they also go to Davao, Cagayan de Oro or Iligan via Butuan. The last bus usually leaves at about 6 pm.

Butuan

PLACES TO STAY	
3	Imperial Hotel
4	Jet's Hotel & Jet's Sinugba Restaurant
5	Emerald Villa Hotel
6	Hensonly Plaza Hotel
8	A & Z Lowcost Lodging House
10	Almont Hotel
19	Embassy Hotel & Philippine National Bank (PNB)

PLACES TO EAT	
7	New Mansion House Restaurant
9	Golden Dragon Restaurant

OTHER	
1	Shipping Agencies
2	Post Office
11	Market
12	St Joseph Cathedral
13	Urios College
14	Crown & Empress Cinema
15	Crown Thrift Market
16	Otis Department Store
17	MJ Santos Hospital
18	Police Station

MINDANAO & SULU

From Davao, Bachelor Bus Liner and Ceres Liner buses run daily to Butuan (P107; six hours), the last leaving at about 1.30 pm. Air-con Philtranco buses also run from Davao to Butuan and go on to Tacloban and Manila via Surigao.

From Cagayan de Oro, several Bachelor Bus Liner buses run daily to Butuan (P75; 3½ hours).

Getting Around
The Airport The Butuan-Cagayan de Oro road is about 200m from the airport. To the left it goes to Butuan and to the right it goes to Balingoan (for Camiguin) and Cagayan de Oro. Buses pass along here. A taxi from the airport to Butuan costs about P60; a jeepney costs P2.

Boat Not all boats from other islands come to the river port of Butuan. Trans-Asia Shipping Lines' vessels to and from Bohol use the seaport of Nasipit/Lumbacan. Jeepneys run between Nasipit/Lumbacan and Butuan, taking 30 minutes. They leave Butuan from the shipping agencies on RD Calo St.

BALINGOAN
A small coastal town on the road from Butuan to Cagayan de Oro, Balingoan is the departure point for ships going to nearby Camiguin Island. (See also the Mindanao Getting There & Away section earlier in this chapter.)

Places to Stay
Ligaya's Restaurant & Cold Spot has simple rooms with fan for P50/100, as do the *Balingoan Pension House* and the *Balingoan Hotel*.

CAGAYAN DE ORO
Cagayan de Oro has a population of around 500,000, and is a clean and friendly university city with numerous schools. An old legend tells how the name Cagayan is derived from the word *'kagayha-an'*, which means shame. The legend tells of an attack on a Manobo tribe by another tribe. The defeated villagers planned to retaliate, but,

before they could, their chieftain fell in love with the daughter of the enemy chieftain and married her. His disgusted subjects referred to their village as a place of shame, or kagayha-an. The Spaniards pronounced it Cagayan and, after they discovered gold in the river, it became Cagayan de Oro.

The Xavier University Folk Museum (Museo de Oro) on Corrales Ave near Golden Friendship Park, or Divisoria, is worth seeing; it is closed Monday.

Information
The tourist office (☎ 726394) is in the Pelaez Sports Complex on Velez St. The Philippine National Bank, on the corner of Corrales Ave and Tirso Neri St, will change travellers cheques. The area code for Cagayan de Oro is 08822.

Swimming
The Pelaez Sports Complex on Velez St is well equipped; its facilities include a large public swimming pool. The swimming pool in the Philtown Hotel is also open to the public.

Places to Stay – bottom end
On Borja St, the *New Golden Star Inn* (☎ 724079) provides simple, not exactly inviting rooms with fan for P150/190, with fan and bath for P180/240, and with air-con and bath for P250/350. The *Sampaguita Inn* (☎ 722640) also on Borja St has basic, acceptable rooms with fan and bath for P240/300, and with air-con and bath for P400. The rooms don't live up to the standard of the lobby.

East of town on Don Sergio Osmeña St, the *Bonair Inn* (☎ 725431) will let you have a passable single with fan and bath for P175, and room with air-con and bath for P280/380. Suites are P480 and P550.

Set in a quiet area next to the Golden Friendship Park, the *Parkview Lodge* (☎ 723223; fax 726656) on Tirso Neri St offers quite adequate accommodation with fan for P210/270, with air-con for P360, and with air-con and bath for P480. Some of the rooms could be bigger, but this is a popular place.

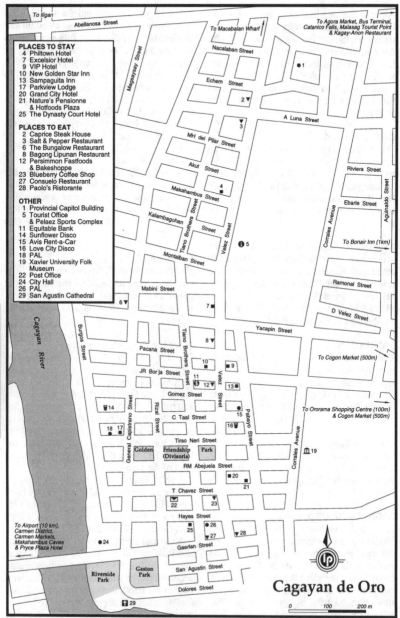

PLACES TO STAY
4 Philtown Hotel
7 Excelsior Hotel
9 VIP Hotel
10 New Golden Star Inn
13 Sampaguita Inn
17 Parkview Lodge
20 Grand City Hotel
21 Nature's Pensione
   & Hotfoods Plaza
25 The Dynasty Court Hotel

PLACES TO EAT
2 Caprice Steak House
3 Salt & Pepper Restaurant
6 The Bungalow Restaurant
8 Bagong Lipunan Restaurant
12 Persimmon Fastfoods
   & Bakeshoppe
23 Blueberry Coffee Shop
27 Consuelo Restaurant
28 Paolo's Ristorante

OTHER
1 Provincial Capitol Building
5 Tourist Office
   & Pelaez Sports Complex
11 Equitable Bank
14 Sunflower Disco
15 Avis Rent-a-Car
16 Love City Disco
18 PAL
19 Xavier University Folk
   Museum
22 Post Office
24 City Hall
26 PAL
29 San Agustin Cathedral

MINDANAO & SULU

Cagayan de Oro

You'll find big beds and clean rooms at *Nature's Pensionne* (☎ 723718; fax 726033) on T Chavez St. They cost P500 to P800 with air-con and bath.

Places to Stay – middle

On the corner of Makahambus and Velez Sts, the *Philtown Hotel* (☎ 726295; fax 723104) offers good accommodation, with comfortable rooms with TV, air-con and bath from P770 to P1100. There is a music lounge and a disco.

Near the corner of Velez and JR Borja Sts, the *VIP Hotel* (☎ 726080; fax 726441), has singles with air-con and bath for between P800 and P1420, doubles with air-con and bath from P1050 to P1170, and suites from P1420 to P2800. Most of the rooms are in good condition, the more expensive ones have a fridge and TV.

A pleasant hotel in the centre of town is the *Grand City Hotel Cagayan* (☎ 723551; fax 723658) on Velez St. Rooms with air-con and bath cost P775 to P1120 with TV; some of them have no windows.

You could describe the *Lauremar Beach Hotel* in Opol (☎ 735563), about seven km outside of Cagayan de Oro, as a fairly classy place. It has rooms with air-con and bath for P1050 (with TV), which look out onto the swimming pool and are kept in good shape. Its restaurant is pleasantly decorated with a sundeck open to the sea, and is open 24 hours. A taxi there costs P80 to P100 and a jeepney P5.

Places to Stay – top end

A very good, comfortable hotel in the centre of town is *The Dynasty Court Hotel* (☎ 724516; fax 727825) on the corner of Tiano Brothers and Hayes Sts. Rooms with air-con and bath cost P1050 to P1500, suites P1800 to P2250. All have TV, and the expensive rooms and the suites have refrigerators. The hotel has a coffee shop and restaurant.

The 1st class *Pryce Plaza* (☎ 722791; fax 726687), on Carmen Hill about four km west of the town centre, has singles with air-con and bath for P2100, doubles with air-con and bath for P2500, and suites for P3750. For

some reason this excellent hotel with its own swimming pool is not as busy as you would expect. From the vantage point of the hill you can get a magnificent view of Cagayan de Oro and the Mindanao Sea beyond.

Places to Eat

In Cagayan de Oro, probably the best restaurant for Filipino food is the surprisingly inexpensive *Kagay-Anon* at Lapasan, roughly north-east from the town centre. You get big meals which are very good value at the *Bagong Lipunan Restaurant* on Velez St, between the VIP and the Excelsior hotels.

About 100m south is the *Persimmon Fastfoods & Bakeshoppe*, an inexpensive self-service restaurant with sandwiches and good, standard Filipino dishes, like caldereta, kare-kare and sinigang.

If you like Chinese food, there is a choice of two good restaurants: *Sea King Garden* in the Grand City Hotel; and the *Dynasty Court Restaurant* in the hotel of the same name. At the north end of Velez St is the air-con *Caprice Steak House* and the small *Salt & Pepper Restaurant*, which has a limited menu but cheap beer.

Romantic candlelight and the gentle sounds of a piano lend *Paolo's Ristorante*, on the corner of Velez and Gaerlan Sts, a special ambience. Not surprisingly, it is a popular restaurant, with not only a good variety of pizzas and pastas, but also Spanish and Japanese food, seafood, steaks and sandwiches.

The *Consuelo Restaurant*, on the corner of Tiano Brothers and Gaerlan Sts, has a style of its own and is highly recommended. It specialises in steaks and sizzling spaghetti.

If you have a sweet tooth, the *Blueberry Coffee Shop* on the corner of Velez and Chavez Sts is well worth the visit. It specialises in coffee and cakes, and the menu runs from blueberry pie to cappuccino.

Getting There & Away

Air PAL flies from Cotabato to Cagayan de Oro on Monday and Wednesday (P814; 45 minutes); and from Davao to Cagayan de

Oro on Thursday, Friday and Sunday (P915; 35 minutes).

PAL has an office at Lumbia airport (☎ 725592) and at 21 Tirso Neri St (☎ 726216). It has also opened another office across from the Dynasty Court Hotel.

Bus Bachelor Bus Liner buses leave Butuan almost hourly from 4.30 to 11.30 am for Cagayan de Oro (3½ hours); after that the intervals are longer. The buses go via Balingoan (1½ hours), which is the berth for boats to and from Camiguin.

From Davao several Ceres Liner and Bachelor Bus Liner air-con buses run daily to Cagayan de Oro, leaving between 4 and 9 am and at 8 and 10 pm (P185; 10 hours).

Several Bachelor Bus Liner and Fortune Liner buses go daily between Iligan and Cagayan de Oro (1½ hours). Jeepneys and minibuses also cover this route.

From Pagadian, Bachelor Bus Liner and Fortune Liner buses leave daily for Cagayan de Oro, hourly between 4.30 am and 1 pm (4½ hours).

From Zamboanga, two Fortune Liner and Almirante buses leave daily at about midnight for Cagayan de Oro (15 hours). Each one leaves as soon as it's full, so you should get to the bus terminal early.

Car Avis Rent-a-Car has an office on the corner of Pabayo and C Taal Sts.

Getting Around
The Airport Lumbia airport is on a plateau, 185m above sea level, barely 10 km west of town. PU-Cabs may ask up to P100, but you can do the trip for P60 to P80.

Bus The bus terminal is on the outskirts in the north-east of the city, next to the Agora Market. Jeepneys going to the town centre, three km away, display the sign 'Cogon – Carmen'. Jeepneys going from the town centre to the bus terminal will display the sign 'Agora'. A taxi costs about P40.

Boat The Macabalan Wharf is five km north of the town centre. There is a jeepney service,

which usually goes direct to the bus terminal. The trip by taxi shouldn't cost more than P10.

AROUND CAGAYAN DE ORO
The **Makahambus Cave** is about 14 km south of Cagayan de Oro and can be reached by jeepneys going to Talacag. Make sure you take a powerful torch (flashlight) with you.

Even visitors who are not remotely interested in agriculture will enjoy a trip to the huge **pineapple plantations** at Camp Phillips, 34 km out of Cagayan de Oro. Jeepneys with the sign 'Phillips' go there (P5; one hour). If you're lucky, you may get on a tour of the plantation. On Wednesday and Saturday, jeepneys run the extra five km from Camp Phillips to the Del Monte Club House, where you can get a meal in the Golf Club which is not particularly cheap. The Del Monte Canning Factory is at Bugo, 15 km east of Cagayan de Oro, where the finished products are shipped away.

For a day at the beach, try **Raagas Beach** near Bonbon and **San Pedro Beach** in Opol, seven km west of Cagayan de Oro. They're nothing special but are OK for a quick dip.

About half-way between Cagayan and Iligan, **Timoga Springs** is a refreshing spot at the sea with several swimming pools.

Pineapple leaves are used to make piña cloth, the fabric of the *barong tagalog* shirt.

MALAYBALAY

The capital of Bukidnon, which is the largest province in the northern Mindanao region, Malaybalay is surrounded by mountain ranges in the valley of a tributary of the Pulangi River. Once a year, usually on the first Friday in September, the members of the various cultural minorities living in and around Malaybalay get together to celebrate the Kaamulan Festival. They meet in Pines View Park, dressed in traditional costumes, and play music, dance and put on craft demonstrations.

Telephone

The telephone area code for Malaybalay is 088.

Places to Stay

The staff offer real hospitality at the *Haus Malibu* (☎ 5714) on the corner of Bonifacio Drive and Comisio St. The rooms are comfortable and go for P160/220, with fan and bath for P275/350. It has a coffee shop.

Getting There & Away

Bachelor Bus Liner and Ceres Liner buses run daily between Cagayan de Oro and Malaybalay (two hours), leaving hourly.

There are also regular buses between Davao and Malaybalay (via Kibawe and Valencia.)

ILIGAN

Iligan is an industrial town surrounded by factories. The nearby **Maria Cristina Falls** will be the main source of power for the surrounding districts as far as Zamboanga, once the hydro-electric plant there is operating at full capacity. The power station so dominates the landscape that it's more likely to appeal to the technically minded than to nature lovers.

To get to the falls, take a jeepney from the pier to Agus Bridge, about seven km away, turn left after the bridge and walk for about half an hour. You can't swim in the pool and, as the river is a raging torrent, it's too dangerous; the attraction is to look down on the falls from above by going about 200m back towards Iligan from the Agus Bridge, where

a path and concrete steps lead straight to the waterfall.

On the other hand, the nearby **Tinago Falls** – also known as the Hidden Falls – have been left in their beautiful natural state and are not marred by construction. They must be among the most beautiful waterfalls on Mindanao. It is a real pleasure to go for a dip in the big, natural pool there, and admission is free. The easiest way to get to the Tinago Falls is with a PU-Cab (you have to walk the last 50m down to the pool), or with the jeepney as mentioned above. If you do take the jeepney, then go past the Agus Bridge for another two km to the turn-off (which is signposted) and cover the next couple of km on foot. You can even stay the night now near the waterfalls.

About 30 km north of Iligan on the Cagayan de Oro road is **Initao**, where there's a cave which you can explore, near the hospital. You'll need a good, powerful torch. There are cottages available for around P100 about 300m away on a white beach, which will appeal to guests wanting peace and quiet.

Telephone

The telephone area code for Iligan is 063.

Places to Stay

The *Iligan Star Inn* (☎ 881 5272; fax 881 5269) on Quezon Ave has basic, but OK rooms with fan and bath for P175/250, and with air-con and bath for P325/375; those facing Quezon Ave are noisy.

The *MC Tourist Inn* (☎ 5194) on Tibanga Highway is a reasonable place north of the town centre on Baslayan Creek. Its singles with fan go for P150, doubles with fan and bath for P250, and doubles with air-con and bath for P350.

Near the intersection of General Aguinaldo and Mabini Sts, the pleasant and attractive *Maria Cristina Hotel* (☎ 20645, 21082) is the best hotel in the town centre. It charges P500/650 for a room with air-con and bath, and P1200 for a suite. It also has a restaurant.

On the other hand, the best hotel near Iligan is the *Iligan Village Hotel* (☎ 21752),

MINDANAO & SULU

east of town in Pala-o, where very comfortable rooms with air-con and bath go for P650/850, and suites for P1400. It has a restaurant, fish ponds and an orchid garden.

Also in Pala-o, the well-kept *Iligan Day Inn Plaza* (☎ 881 3855; fax 881 3491), on the corner of Quezon Ave and BS Ong St, can be recommended. Singles with air-con, bath and TV are P790 and P985, doubles are P1310 and suites P1970, including breakfast.

Outside of Iligan at Tinago Falls, the *Tinago Residence* offers a whole range of accommodation from a simple tree house for P200 to a most comfortable Sultan Suite for P2800.

Places to Eat

Iligan has quite a few bakeries and restaurants, though most of them close at about 9 pm. You have a choice of reasonably priced Chinese meals at the *Big Dipper Restaurant* and the *Canton Restaurant*, both on Quezon Ave. *Enrico's Restaurant*, next to the PAL office on Quezon Ave, is clean. It has excellent food and the service is friendly. The *Bar-B-Q Inn* on the plaza is great for an evening meal.

In the mid-range category are the *Iceberg Café & Restaurant* and the *Bahayan Restaurant*, both serving Filipino food. The only problem with the well-run *Patio Alejandra*, on the corner of San Miguel and Luna Sts, is making your mind up from the wide choice of food and cuisines available; the seafood festival is highly recommended.

The partly open-air *Terrace Garden Restaurant* by the fish pond at the Iligan Village Hotel is a pleasant place.

Getting There & Away

Air PAL has an office at Iligan airport and on Quezon Ave (☎ 21095).

Bus From Cagayan de Oro, several Bachelor Bus Liner and Fortune Liner buses run daily to Iligan (1½ hours). There are also jeepneys and minibuses.

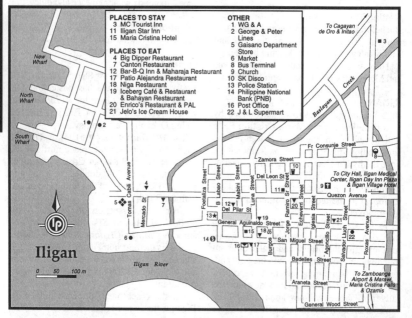

PLACES TO STAY
3 MC Tourist Inn
11 Iligan Star Inn
15 Maria Cristina Hotel

PLACES TO EAT
4 Big Dipper Restaurant
7 Canton Restaurant
12 Bar-B-Q Inn & Maharaja Restaurant
17 Patio Alejandra Restaurant
18 Niga Restaurant
19 Iceberg Café & Restaurant & Bahayan Restaurant
20 Enrico's Restaurant & PAL
21 Jelo's Ice Cream House

OTHER
1 WG & A
2 George & Peter Lines
5 Gaisano Department Store
6 Market
8 Bus Terminal
9 Church
10 SK Disco
13 Police Station
14 Philippine National Bank (PNB)
16 Post Office
22 J & L Supermart

Iligan

0   50   100 m

From Pagadian, several Bachelor Bus Liner and Fortune Liner buses run daily to Iligan (three hours). The last bus usually leaves in the early afternoon.

From Zamboanga, two Fortune Liner and Almirante buses leave daily around midnight to Cagayan de Oro via Iligan. (See also the Getting There & Away section under Cagayan de Oro earlier in this chapter.)

Getting Around
Iligan airport is 17 km south of Iligan, about 600m off the road to Marawi. The taxi to Iligan will cost you about P100.

MARAWI & LAKE LANAO
Marawi on Lake Lanao is the spiritual and cultural centre for the Filipino Muslims. Lake Lanao is the second biggest inland lake in the Philippines. During normal conditions the lake would be 112m deep, but it has often been considerably lower than this in recent years. More than 500,000 Maranao who live in one of the 30 towns around or near the lake, and whose lives depend on it, feel their way of life is being threatened. The culprit is apparently a power station in Marawi, run by the National Power Corporation (Napocor), which draws water from the lake (700m above sea level) to generate power. Napocor runs another five power stations along the Agus River, which drains naturally from Lake Lanao. They make use of the river current to generate power.

The Mindanao State University, usually referred to as 'Misyu' because of its initials, MSU, is here, as is the RP-Libya Hospital, the biggest and most modern hospital on Mindanao. On the MSU campus there is a small but interesting **Aga Khan Museum**, featuring the Muslim culture of Mindanao. It is open Monday to Thursday from 9 to 11.30 am and 1.30 to 5 pm, and on Friday until 10.30 am and 1.30 to 5 pm.

Don't expect a mysterious oriental bazaar in Marawi – there is a big **market** over towards the lake where you can buy brass ware, tapestries and Indonesian textiles. Good hand-woven tapestries at fixed prices are for sale at the Dansalan College Art Shop at MSU.

Information
Tourist Office Take a jeepney from Marawi to MSU, where there is a tourist office in Ford Guest House No 2.

Telephone The area code for Marawi is 063.

Dangers & Annoyances You may give offence if you photograph a Muslim woman without first asking permission.

Marawi and the region around Lake Lanao is a crisis area, so think at least twice before visiting the town of Tugaya, famous for its brass ware, or making boat trips to the small islands of Nusa-Nusa and Silangan. You can get an up-to-date situation report in Iligan.

Places to Stay & Eat
The *Marawi Resort Hotel* (☎ 520981) on the MSU campus is quite clean, comfortable and pleasantly furnished, although the sanitary facilities could do with some investment. Rooms and cottages with fan and bath go for P750/850. It has a restaurant, pool and tennis courts. The hotel is in extensive, park-like grounds, on a hill outside of Marawi from where you can get a beautiful view of Lake Lanao.

Getting There & Away
Several buses go from Iligan to Marawi daily, leaving from the bus terminal.

OZAMIS
There's not much for the traveller in Ozamis, a sea port in the south-east of Misamis Occidental Province. It is simply the port for ships to Cebu. (See also the Mindanao Getting There & Away section earlier in this chapter.)

Telephone
The telephone area code for Ozamis is 088.

Places to Stay
Quiet accommodation at reasonable prices can be found at the *Soriano Pension House* (☎ 21114) on Mabini St Extension. Its rooms with fan and bath go for P100/150, and with air-con and bath for P225/300.

Opposite the post office at 55 Abanil St, near the corner with Ledesma St, the *Grand*

Hotel is basic but fairly good. Fan-cooled rooms cost P125/150, with bath P180/240.

Near the Lilian Liner bus terminal on the Ledesma St Extension, the *Country Lodge* is quiet and good value. It offers rooms with fan and bath for P200/250, and with air-con and bath for P300/360.

The rooms are comfortable at the *Holiday Tourist Inn* (☎ 20073) on Blumentritt St. They cost P200/250 with fan and bath, and P350/400 with air-con and bath.

Getting There & Away
Bus From Dipolog, Lilian Liner buses go daily to Ozamis via Oroquieta, leaving almost hourly. The trip takes 2½ hours from Dipolog and one hour from Oroquieta.

From Pagadian, several Lilian Liner buses run daily to Ozamis (2½ hours). The last bus leaves in the early afternoon.

From Iligan, several Bachelor Bus Liner and Fortune Liner buses run daily to Kolambugan, some finishing there and some going on to Pagadian (one hour).

Boat There is a ferry service between Kolambugan and Ozamis almost every hour, between 7 am and 5 pm.

Water Jet Shipping's *Water Jet 2* sails for Ozamis on Monday, Wednesday and Friday at 1 pm, taking 45 minutes. WG & A's MV *Superferry 7* sails for Ozamis on Thursday at 9 am (two hours).

OROQUIETA
Oroquieta, on Iligan Bay, in the north-east of the Zamboangan Peninsula, is the provincial capital of Misamis Occidental, but most of the region's trade and industry is centred further south in Ozamis.

Telephone
The area code for Oroquieta is 088.

Places to Stay
Right on the river next to the hospital, *Sheena's Hotel* (☎ 31158) on the corner of Barrientos and G del Pilar Sts has trim and tidy rooms with fan for P170, with fan and bath for P200/300, and with air-con and bath

from P600/700. There is a restaurant and a garden.

The *Beach Resort Elvira* on Orbita St, on the beach at Plaridel, about 20 km north of Oroquieta, has dorm beds for P120 and rooms with fan for P300. It's fairly comfortable and guests can use the kitchen.

Getting There & Away
Several Lilian Liner buses run daily from Dipolog to Oroquieta, either finishing there or going on to Ozamis or Plaridel (1½ hours).

From Ozamis, several Lilian Liner buses run daily to Oroquieta, some going on to Dipolog (one hour).

DIPOLOG
Dipolog, the capital of Zamboanga del Norte Province, seems very clean and neat. The offshore **Aliguay Island** has white beaches and extensive undamaged coral reefs good for snorkelling and diving; you can reach it in about 45 minutes by outrigger boat. There's a chance of getting a lift out there with the boats that come in daily to Dipolog and Dapitan to get fresh water.

Information
Metro Shoppers on Rizal St will change money at a good exchange rate. The telephone area code for Dipolog is 065.

Places to Stay & Eat
There are several places you can choose from in Dipolog. Basic accommodation in adequate rooms is available at *Ranillo Pension House* (☎ 415 3536; fax 415 4712) on Bonifacio St. They go for P90/100 with fan, P200/250 with fan and bath, and P300/350 with air-con and bath.

Roughly in the same category, the *Ramos Hotel* (☎ 3299) on Magsaysay St has singles/doubles with fan for P120/240, with fan and bath for P250/300, and with air-con and bath for P360/500.

The best hotel in the centre of town is the *CL Inn* (☎ 3491, 4293) on Rizal Ave. Very comfortable, spacious and clean rooms with air-con and bath cost P400/650, and suites with TV and fridge cost P780.

The *Hotel Arocha* (☎ 415 2656) on Quezon Ave has fairly good rooms with fan and bath from P445 to P585, and with air-con and bath from P560 to P750; most of them are a bit on the loud side and many don't have windows.

The *Village Hotel* (☎ 415 2338) at Sicayab has passable, clean rooms of various sizes with fan and bath for P300, and with air-con and bath for P400. It also has a cottage with two doubles on the beach. The hotel is in a quiet area, about three km outside Dipolog towards Dapitan, shortly after the airport. A tricycle into town costs P3. It's only a few minutes on foot from the hotel to the long, fairly clean beach.

Getting There & Away
Air PAL flies from Zamboanga to Dipolog on Monday, Tuesday, Wednesday and Friday (P824; 50 minutes).

PAL has an office at Dipolog airport (☎ 415 2360).

Bus From Pagadian, several Lilian Liner buses run daily to Dipolog via Ozamis and Oroquieta. It takes five hours from Pagadian, 1½ hours from Ozamis and one hour from Oroquieta.

From Zamboanga, a few Fortune Liner or Almirante buses run daily to Dipolog via Ipil or Pagadian (13 hours). At Pagadian you may have to change to a Lilian Liner bus.

Boat The Trans-Asia Shipping Lines' MV *Asia-Japan* leaves Zamboanga for Dipolog on Thursday at 6 pm (15 hours).

Getting Around
The Airport The airport is about three km north of Dipolog, in Sicayab. A tricycle to the centre of town will cost you P20; for a ride in the town they charge P3 per person.

DAPITAN
Dapitan, 15 km north-east of Dipolog, is a quiet, clean town. The national hero, Jose Rizal, lived in exile here from 1892 to 1896. He made the big relief map of Mindanao in the town plaza, near St James Church. From the bridge over the river on the way to Rizal Park, you can catch a boat every 20 minutes going to **Dakak Bay**, which has a white beach and the luxurious, well-designed Dakak Park Beach Resort. There is a road from Dapitan to the bay. You can take a motorcycle taxi along this road to the beach

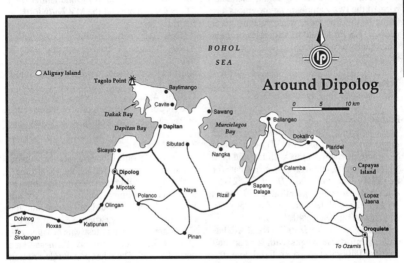

Around Dipolog

resort for P100. A minibus service for hotel guests has also been introduced.

Places to Stay & Eat

The newly opened *Dapitan Resort Hotel* on Sunset Blvd has comfortable rooms with air-con and bath for P100. *Dakak Park Beach Resort* is a decent place on Dakak Bay, where air-con rooms with bath cost P6000 and P8750. Tastefully furnished cottages stand in well-organised grounds, and there's an open-air bar, swimming pool, whirlpool, sauna and tennis court. Diving and horse-riding facilities are available. It charges day visitors P200 for admission.

Getting There & Away

Several jeepneys and minibuses travel every day between Dipolog and Dapitan (30 minutes).

PAGADIAN

The image of the province of Zamboanga del Sur is described by the Department of Tourism of Pagadian as a 'land of lakes, caves and waterfalls'. Sounds good, but is perhaps gilding the lily a bit. What may interest the traveller is that the small town of Lapuyan, 40 km from Pagadian, and other parts of the two Zamboangan provinces, are home to the Subanon, which means 'river people'. US Protestant missionaries brought Christianity and the English language to this isolated mountain world.

Telephone

The area code for Pagadian is 066.

Places to Stay

There's a real family atmosphere at the *Zamboanga Hotel* (☎ 214437) on Jamisola St, where passable rooms with fan and bath go for P160/200, and with air-con and bath for P275/350. The *Peninsula Hotel* (☎ 52115), also on Jamisola St, is good value with rooms at P175/225, with fan and bath for P250/300, and air-con and bath P400/ 500.

The *Pagadian City Hotel* on Rizal Ave has quite comfortable rooms with air-con and bath for P400/500. Also on Rizal Ave, the *Guillermo Hotel* has clean and comfortable singles/doubles with air-con for P550/650, and rooms with TV, fridge, air-con and bath for P850/950.

However, the best hotel in Pagadian is the *Hotel Camila* (☎ 214 2934) on Bonifacio Drive. Decent rooms with TV, air-con and bath cost P650 to P1250.

Getting There & Away

Air PAL has return flights daily between Zamboanga and Pagadian (P699; 40 minutes).

PAL has an office at Pagadian airport and in the Peninsula Hotel (☎ 52114) on Jamisola St.

Bus From Ozamis, several Lilian Liner buses run daily to Pagadian (2½ hours).

From Zamboanga, Almirante and Fortune Liner buses leave hourly from 5 to 10 am for Pagadian (eight hours).

From Iligan, several Bachelor Bus Liner and Fortune Liner buses run daily to Pagadian (three hours), the last one possibly leaving at about 2 pm.

Boat Three SKT Shipping Lines' ships sail from Zamboanga to Pagadian taking 12 hours. The MV *Lady Helen* leaves on Monday at 6 pm, the MV *Doña Isabel II* on Thursday at 6 pm and the MV *Lady Ruth* on Saturday at 7 pm.

The road from Cotabato to Pagadian passes through a crisis area and can be marred by broken bridges. Best take the daily ship that leaves Cotabato at 6 pm (eight hours).

Getting Around

The Airport Pagadian airport is on the east edge of Pagadian, two km from the town centre.

ZAMBOANGA

Some people find it hard to see why Zamboanga has been praised as 'the exotic pearl of the south Philippines'. A few Muslims in an otherwise Filipino-populated city are not what most people would call exotic, and the colourful – and very expensive – sails of the Vintas are only seen at festivals or when one of these boats is chartered. Plain sails are normally used. The other popular description of 'City of Flowers' comes from the Malay word 'jambangan', meaning 'land of flowers', and may have been used when the first Malays settled here. It is more likely that the name comes from 'samboangan', a word made up of 'samboang', meaning 'boat pole', and 'an', meaning 'place'.

As well as speaking English, Filipino, Cebuano, Tausug and Samal, the locals in Zamboanga also speak Chabacano, a mixture of Spanish and Philippine languages ironically known as Bamboo Spanish.

Information

The tourist office (☎ 991 0218) is at the Lantaka Hotel on Valderozza St. The telephone area code for Zamboanga is 062.

Fort Pilar & Rio Hondo

On the outskirts of town, to the east of Zamboanga, are Fort Pilar and the Muslim water village of Rio Hondo. The fort was built in 1635 by Jesuit priests as protection against Muslim, Dutch, Portuguese and English attacks. It was then called Real Fuerza de San Jose, but was renamed Fort Pilar after its overthrow by the USA at the end of last century.

For many years the only part of the ruins worth seeing was the altar on the outside, but in 1986 restoration began to make the building useable.

A visit to the extremely instructive **Marine Life Museum** is well worth the effort. The musuem has set up botanical, archaeological, anthropological and historical departments. The museum is open daily, except for Saturday, from 9 am to noon and 2 to 5 pm.

About 200m east of Fort Pilar, past a shining silver mosque, is a bridge leading to a village built on piles in the mouth of the river. This is known as Rio Hondo. The houses are linked by footbridges, some looking none too secure. The locals here are very friendly; however, for your own safety, it's probably not a good idea to visit Rio Hondo after nightfall.

Places to Stay – bottom end

The simple but fairly clean *Imperial Hotel* (☎ 991 1648) on Campaner St has rooms with fan for P90/120, with fan and bath for P160/190, and with air-con and bath for P230/300.

Set in spacious grounds on a side street off Mayor Jaldon St, *Atilano's Pension House* (☎ 991 0784) is good value with big, fan-cooled rooms for P130/160, with bath P160/170, and with air-con and bath for P270/300; some are a bit run-down.

The accommodation is immaculate and very good value at *L'Mirage Pension House* (☎ 991 3962) on Mayor Jaldon St. Rooms with fan go for P175/225, with fan and bath P225/275, and with air-con and bath for P350/385.

The *Mag-V Royal Hotel* (☎ 991 3054) on the corner of San Jose Rd and Don Basilio Navarro St, just out of town, has singles with fan for P100, rooms with fan and bath for P150/180, and with air-con and bath for P250/350. The rooms are spacious, but not all of them have windows. The arrival of morning is announced at 6 am by very loud jeepneys!

The *New Pasonanca Hotel* (☎ 991 5929), on the corner of Almonte and Tomas Claudio Sts, has small but comfortable single rooms with fan and bath for P190, and rooms with air-con and bath for P250/400. It also has a disco.

The service is friendly at the central *Hotel Paradise* (☎ 991 2026) on R Reyes St. Trim rooms with air-con and bath are good value at P360/450.

Places to Stay – middle

The *Paradise Pension House* (☎ 991 1054; fax 991 3465) is centrally located on the corner of Barcelona and Tomas Claudio Sts. Good rooms with air-con and bath cost P500.

The *Zamboanga Hermosa Hotel* (☎ 991 2040) on Mayor Jaldon St is getting on in years, but the rooms are OK, costing P200/250 with fan and bath, and P370/450 with air-con and bath.

Near the airport, the *Hotel Marcian Garden* (☎ 991 2519; fax 991 1874) on Governor

Camins Rd has good-value rooms with air-con and bath from P560 to P800.

The *Platinum 21 Pension House* (☎ 991 2514; fax 991 2709) on Barcelona St has fairly comfortable, though maybe not the cleanest, rooms with air-con and bath for P620 and P690. They all have TV; the more expensive ones also have a fridge. Its restaurant is open 24 hours.

The *Hotel Preciosa* (☎ 991 2020; fax 993 0055) on Mayor Jaldon St has really comfortable rooms with TV, air-con and bath for P560. Suites with a fridge and TV cost P900.

Places to Stay – top end

The *New Astoria Hotel* (☎ 991 2510; fax 991 2533) on Mayor Jaldon St has good accommodation, with comfortable rooms with air-con and bath for P850. Suites are P1600 and P4000.

Set in neat grounds with a garden, the popular *Lantaka Hotel* (☎ 991 2033; fax 991 1626) on Valderroza St at the waterfront is the No 1 place to stay in Zamboanga. Accommodation with air-con and bath goes for P800/1050, and suites from P1540 to P1970. The rooms are big and have a balcony, where you get a beautiful view of the sea and the harbour.

On Governor Camins Rd near the airport, the *Hotel Garden Orchid* (☎ 991 0031; fax 991 0035) has pleasant and comfortable rooms with air-con and bath for P1220/1490. There is also a disco, swimming pool and exercise room.

Places to Eat

You can eat cheaply and well at the *Flavorite Restaurant*, opposite the George & Peter Lines' office. Young Zamboangans meet in the popular *Food Paradise* on Mayor Jaldon St, where there are milk shakes and fast food on the ground floor and Chinese meals upstairs. In the Plaza Mall building not far from there, *Dunkin Donut* is the place if you have a sweet tooth, and it's open round the clock. Right next door is *Shakey's Pizza*. *Sunburst Fried Chicken* on Corcuera St, near the intersection with Pilar St, specialises in chicken meals.

Alavar's House of Seafood on Justice Lim Blvd is known for good Filipino and Chinese dishes, especially seafood, but is rather expensive. Equally good and in the mid-price range is the *Abalone Restaurant*, beside the New Astoria Hotel on Mayor Jaldon St. *Café Blanca* in the Platinum 21 Pension House is open day and night, and offers good Filipino and international food at reasonable prices.

A little further out of town is the *Boulevard Restaurant by the Sea*, where you sit right on the water – a good spot for sunset freaks. There are also numerous *food stalls* that open in the late afternoon along the Justice Lim Blvd. You can also sit near the water, by torch light in the evenings, at the *Lantaka Hotel Restaurant*, which often serves a reasonably priced buffet dinner; breakfast there is also pleasant.

The *Aldea Pasonanca Restaurant* at Pasonanca Park had the original idea of converting railways cars into a restaurant. It has excellent Filipino food.

Entertainment

Like most Philippine cities, Zamboanga has the best nightclubs on the outskirts of town. In Zamboanga there are some near the airport. Most clubs have a cover charge of P30 or P40 to get in, often including a drink.

At the airport, there is a generally cheery atmosphere in the *Lutong Pinoy* open-air restaurant, which has a bar and live music. The *Lutong Pinoy Airlanes Disco* is right next door. Nearby is the *Village Zamboanga*, a beer garden with fast food, just right for night owls.

In the city itself, there's a noisy band at the *King's Palace Disco*, on the corner of La Purisma and Tomas Claudio Sts. And if it all gets too exhausting, you can always recover in the soothing atmosphere of the open-air *Talisay Bar* at the waterside of the Lantaka Hotel, which is also a perfect place for a sundowner.

Things to Buy

You can shop cheaply at the market in the Alta Mall building, Governor Alvarez Ave

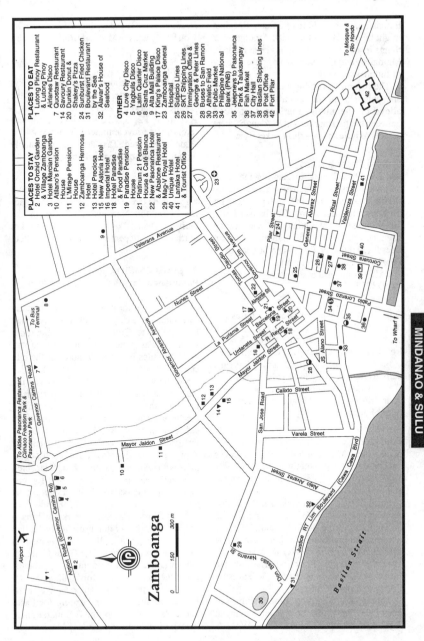

PLACES TO STAY

2 Hotel Orchid Garden
   & Village Zamboanga
3 Hotel Marcian Garden
10 Atilano's Pension
   House
11 L'Mirage Pension
   House
12 Zamboanga Hermosa
   Hotel
13 Hotel Preciosa
15 New Astoria Hotel
16 Imperial Hotel
18 Hotel Paradise
   & Food Paradise
19 Paradise Pension
   House
21 Platinum 21 Pension
   House & Café Blanca
22 New Pasonanca Hotel
   & Avalon Restaurant
29 Mag-V Royal Hotel
40 Unique Hotel
41 Lantaka Hotel
   & Tourist Office

PLACES TO EAT

1 Lutong Pinoy Restaurant
   & Lutong Pinoy
   Airlanes Disco
7 Quostaw Restaurant
14 Savoury Restaurant
20 Dunkin Donut &
   Shakey's Pizza
24 Sunburst Fried Chicken
31 Boulevard Restaurant
   by the Sea
32 Alavar's House of
   Seafood

OTHER

4 Love City Disco
5 Yagbulls Disco
6 Latin Quarter Disco
8 Santa Cruz Market
9 NBI Building
17 King's Palace Disco
23 Zamboanga General
   Hospital
25 Sulpicio Lines
26 SKT Shipping Lines
27 Immigration Office &
   George & Peter Lines
28 Buses to San Ramon
30 Athletic Field
33 Public Market
34 Philippine National
   Bank (PNB)
35 Jeepneys to Pasonanca
   Park & Taluksangay
36 Fish Market
37 City Hall
38 Basilan Shipping Lines
39 Post Office
42 Fort Pilar

Zamboanga

Extension, in the suburb of Tetuan. Receipts might be checked at the exits. Among other things it sells batik, which has been made in Mindanao and is not really up to the quality of Indonesian work.

The fish market at the docks is very lively and colourful in the late afternoon. In the alleys of the public markets next door, between the fish market and JS Alano St, there are lots of little shops – flea market style.

Getting There & Away
Air PAL has flights to Zamboanga from various towns in Mindanao. There are daily flights from Pagadian (P699; 40 minutes); on Tuesday and Friday from Cotabato (P1076; 40 minutes); on Monday and Wednesday from Davao (P1310; 50 minutes); and on Tuesday, Thursday, Friday and Sunday from Dipolog (P824; 50 minutes).

PAL has an office at Zamboanga airport (☎ 993257).

Bus From Cagayan de Oro, two buses run daily to Zamboanga via Iligan, leaving between 4.30 and 7 am, and taking 15 hours from Cagayan de Oro and 13 hours from Iligan.

From Dipolog, an early morning bus runs daily to Zamboanga via Ipil (15 hours).

From Pagadian, buses run about every hour from 4.30 to 10 am to Zamboanga (eight hours).

Boat From Cotabato to Zamboanga, the Sulpicio Lines' MV *Cotabato Princess* leaves on Tuesday at 8 pm (eight hours). The MV *Superferry 3* of WG & A leaves on Sunday at 9 pm (nine hours).

From Dipolog to Zamboanga, the Trans-Asia Shipping Lines' MV *Asia-Japan* leaves on Wednesday at 6 pm (13 hours).

From General Santos to Zamboanga, the MV *Doña Virginia* of WG & A leaves on Thursday at 6 pm (12 hours). The Sulpicio Lines' MV *Princess of the Pacific* leaves on Friday at 6 pm (12 hours).

Three SKT Shipping Lines' ships sail from Pagadian to Zamboanga, all leaving at 7 pm and taking 12 hours. The MV *Lady Helen* goes on Tuesday, the MV *Doña Isabel II* on Friday and the MV *Lady Ruth* on Sunday.

Getting Around
The Airport Zamboanga airport is two km from the city centre. The regular fare for the jeepney marked 'ZCPM' or 'Canelar – Airport' is P2, or P10 by tricycle, but you rarely get a tricycle under P20; up to P40 is sometimes asked. Taxi drivers, presumably without a licence, demand up to P60.

Bus The bus terminal for trips to and from Cagayan de Oro, Dipolog, Iligan and Pagadian is on the National Highway in the Guiwan District of town, about four km north of the city centre. A tricycle costs P20.

AROUND ZAMBOANGA
Pasonanca Park & Climaco Freedom Park
If the houses of the early settlers were really surrounded by a carpet of flowers, then today the nickname City of Flowers can only belong to Pasonanca Park, about seven km, or 15 minutes by jeepney, north of the city centre.

On the way there you pass prize-winning gardens, and in the 58 hectare park itself there are three swimming pools, an amphi-theatre and a tree house, where honeymooners can spend one night free. Since the demand is not great, tourists can also stay there by applying to the City Mayor's office. It's complete with two beds, a stereo, fridge, fan, bath and telephone, but remember, it's for one night only and open to all visitors during the day.

Not far from Pasonanca Park is Climaco Freedom Park, which used to be called Abong-Abong Park. It is now named in memory of a popular mayor Cesar Climaco, who was murdered by political opponents. From the big cross on Holy Hill, you get a wonderful view over Zamboanga and the Basilan Strait. Jeepneys heading for Pasonanca Park leave from the fish market near the wharf and cost P2.

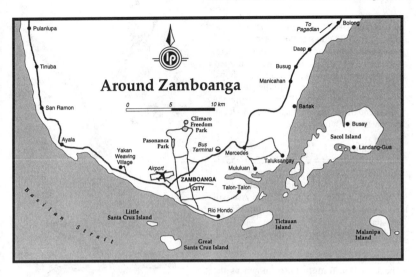

Around Zamboanga

0   5   10 km

Santa Cruz Islands

Great Santa Cruz Island has a lightly coloured sandy beach, peppered with fine, red pieces of coral; although it sounds perhaps a bit better than it is. Drinks are available at a small kiosk. Not far from the main beach are a small Samal cemetery tucked away in the bush and a Muslim village built on piles in a mangrove lagoon. Nearby Little Santa Cruz Island is off limits to visitors. A few soldiers are stationed there and there is an army guesthouse.

Sea gypsies try to sell shells and coral to tourists from their outrigger canoes beside the Lantaka Hotel. From here you can also hire boats to go over to Great Santa Cruz Island. It takes 15 minutes and the return fare is about P200 per boat. They also charge a landing fee of P5 per person.

San Ramon & Yakan Weaving Village

About 20 km west of Zamboanga is San Ramon Prison & Penal Farm – a good place to buy handcrafts made by the prisoners. You can get there by bus.

On the San Ramon road, seven km from Zamboanga on the right-hand side, is a **weaving village** of seven Yakan families who make and sell traditional fabrics, which you can see on the looms. You can get a bus there from Governor Lim Ave, near the corner of Mayor Jaldon St.

At **Pulanlupa**, eight km north-west of San Ramon, there is said to be a magnificent coral reef, but it is only suitable for diving from March to June. At other times heavy seas cause poor visibility.

Taluksangay

This Muslim town, 19 km north-east of Zamboanga, is partly built over the water. The Badjao live in houses on piles, while the Samal have settled on land centred around a minareted mosque. Their modest income comes mainly from fishing and collecting firewood. The children there can get quite aggressive if their begging doesn't produce results. Jeepneys leave Zamboanga for Taluksangay from the public market and the last one back is likely to leave before dark.

DAVAO

The fastest growing city in the Philippines after Manila is Davao, with a population of 900,000. There is plenty of room for newcomers, as this city covering 2440 sq km is one of the most sprawling cities in the world.

You can't miss the Chinese influence here, especially west of the wharf, where numerous businesspeople have set up little shops. Muslims have also set up the so-called Muslim Fishing Village, not far from the wharf and the nearby Magsaysay Park. It can be reached by a footbridge.

Information
The tourist office (☎ 221 6796, 221 6955) is within the Magsaysay Park Complex.

The two Equitable Bank branches on T Monteverde St and Claro M Recto Ave will give you a cash advance on your Visa or MasterCard.

The telephone area code for Davao is 082.

Things to See & Do
The **Lon Wa Temple** (also known as the Long Hua Temple) on Cabaguio Ave, three km in the direction of the airport, with its statues of Buddha and its woodcarvings, is the biggest Buddhist temple in Mindanao and a sight to be seen. Monks and nuns live on the temple grounds, and the Philippine Academy of Shakya (a Buddhist religious movement) is also here.

About 300m south of the temple, a **Taoist temple** with a beautiful pagoda stands on a side street off Cabaguio Ave. Jeepneys with the sign 'Sasa' will take you there.

A visit to the temple would be well rounded off with a tour of the **Puentaspina Orchid Gardens**, about one km south of the Lon Wa Temple on Cabaguio Ave (there's a sign pointing the way on the side street, Bolcan St).

From the **Shrine of the Holy Infant Jesus of Prague**, there's a good view over the town and the Davao Gulf. This small shrine is in the suburb called Matina, about six km west of Davao. It stands on a hill behind the Davao Memorial Park and can be reached by a road which branches off the MacArthur Highway. Take a jeepney from the NCCC department store, Magsaysay Ave, to the Bankerohan Market and change to a jeepney heading for Matina. The turn-off to the shrine is easy to

Bulbophyllum lobbii

Amasiella philippinensis

Vanda sanderiana (*waling waling*)

More than 1,000 species of orchid grow in the Philippines, and nearly all are endemic. The exquisite vanda sanderiana (above) is native to Mindanao. The word orchid, by the way, comes from the Greek word for testicle.

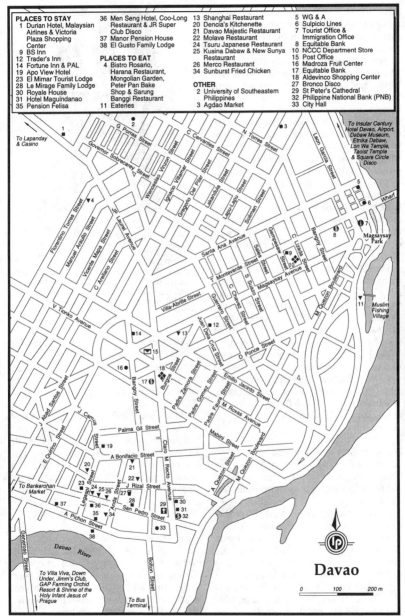

PLACES TO STAY
1 Durian Hotel, Malaysian Airlines & Victoria Plaza Shopping Center
9 BS Inn
12 Trader's Inn
14 Fortune Inn & PAL
19 Apo View Hotel
23 El Mimar Tourist Lodge
28 Le Mirage Family Lodge
30 Royale House
31 Hotel Maguindanao
35 Pension Felisa
36 Men Seng Hotel, Coo-Long Restaurant & JR Super Club Disco
37 Manor Pension House
38 El Gusto Family Lodge

PLACES TO EAT
4 Bistro Rosario, Harana Restaurant, Mongolian Garden, Peter Pan Bake Shop & Sarung Banggi Restaurant
11 Eateries
13 Shanghai Restaurant
20 Dencia's Kitchenette
21 Davao Majestic Restaurant
22 Molave Restaurant
24 Tsuru Japanese Restaurant
25 Kusina Dabaw & New Sunya Restaurant
26 Merco Restaurant
34 Sunburst Fried Chicken

OTHER
2 University of Southeastern Philippines
3 Agdao Market
5 WG & A
6 Sulpicio Lines
7 Tourist Office & Immigration Office
8 Equitable Bank
10 NCCC Department Store
15 Post Office
16 Madroza Fruit Center
17 Equitable Bank
18 Aldevinco Shopping Center
27 Bronco Disco
29 St Peter's Cathedral
32 Philippine National Bank (PNB)
33 City Hall

Davao

0   100   200 m

MINDANAO & SULU

miss, so the best thing to do is use the Matina cockpit (cockfighting arena) on the left-hand side as an orientation point. The ride by tricycle to the shrine costs P2.

Next to the Insular Century Hotel Davao near the airport is the **Dabaw Museum**, featuring the cultural minorities of south Mindanao, such as the Mansaka and the Bagobo; the latter are known as a proud and warlike people. The museum is open Tuesday to Sunday from 9 am to 5 pm. Behind the Insular Century Hotel Davao is **Etnika Dabaw**, where Mandaya people demonstrate their traditional skills in dyeing abaca fibres, weaving and decorating textiles.

Outside of the city, there are numerous **banana plantations** and **orchid farms** open to the public, such as the Lapanday Banana Plantation near Buhangin, 14 km north-west of Davao, and the Derling Orchids Farm near Toril, 12 km south-west of Davao.

The **GAP Farming Orchid Resort** can be found in Ma-a. Set in a park with a swimming pool, this is a popular place for day trips. It charges P7.50 for admission, and the swimming pool costs P25. Jeepneys go from Matina Crossing to Ma-a; carry on from there by tricycle or on foot (10 minutes).

The Tamolo Beach and Times Beach, south-west of Davao, are not worth a visit, but the white **Paradise Island Beach** on Samal Island makes a good day trip from Davao, as do **Talikud Island** and **Eagle Camp**. See the following Around Davao section for details.

Places to Stay – bottom end

Le Mirage Family Lodge (☎ 84334) on San Pedro St is good value. Its rooms with fan and bath cost P200, and with air-con and bath P330/400.

El Gusto Family Lodge (☎ 73662) at 51 A Pichon St has rooms with fan for P100/200, with fan and bath for P140/250, and with air-con and bath for P250/350. They are basic but acceptable, although some are a bit stuffy. Still, it's OK for the money.

On Juan Dela Cruz St, the *Trader's Inn* (☎ 221 4071; fax 64976) has acceptable singles with fan and bath for P240, and

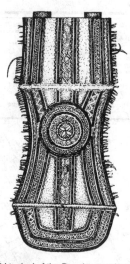

A shield typical of the Bagobo people, who live in the highlands north-west of Davao. Traditional warriors, this proud tribe believes a person's reputation should grow in proportion to the number of enemies they have killed.

singles/doubles with air-con and bath for P310/420.

The *Royale House* (☎ 73630; fax 221 8106) at 34 Claro M Recto Ave has fan-cooled rooms for P160/250, with bath P200/350, and with air-con and bath for P490/680 and P580/790. Though all fairly good, those with air-con are a bit too expensive.

A few km south of town, near the turn-off for the Shrine of the Holy Infant Jesus of Prague, the *Villa Viva* (☎ /fax 297 1411) is a friendly place on Willow St, Matina Heights. The owners are German-Philippine and charge P350/400 for rooms with fan, P550/650 with air-con, all including breakfast.

Places to Stay – middle

At the *BS Inn* (☎ 221 3980; fax 221 0740), on the corner of Monteverde and Gempesaw Sts, rooms of varying sizes are neat and good value. They all have air-con and bath, and cost P550/750. There is a well laid-out coffee shop and an open patio restaurant.

The *Manor Pension House* (☎ 221 2511; fax 221 2514) provides clean and good accommodation on a quiet little side street which leads off A Pichon St. Pleasantly furnished rooms with air-con and bath go for P650/780. The service is friendly and there is a restaurant.

Opposite the cathedral, the pleasant *Hotel Maguindanao* (☎ 78401; fax 221 2894) at 86 Claro M Recto Ave offers rooms with TV, air-con and bath from P850 to P1190. Suites cost P1430.

Places to Stay – top end

The *Apo View Hotel* (☎ 221 6430; fax 221 2281) on J Camus St is a long-established place, with very good rooms with air-con and bath for P1450/1700 and P2000/2250. There is a disco and swimming pool.

At the *Durian Hotel* (☎ 72721-25; fax 221 1835) on JP Laurel Ave, singles with air-con and bath cost between P1500 and P1700, doubles with air-con and bath from P1800 to P2000, and suites from P2600 to P4800. The rooms all have TV and fridge. It is very comfortable, tastefully decorated and there's a restaurant. Although the hotel is not directly in the town centre, transport is no problem as there are lots of jeepneys.

The *Insular Century Hotel Davao* (☎ 234 3050; fax 62959) at Lanang is on the northeast edge of the city towards the airport. Pleasant, comfortable rooms with air-con and bath go for P2900/3400, and suites from P6400 to P16,000. The hotel complex comprises several two storey houses in a beautiful garden setting and its own beach. It has boats to Samal and Talikud islands, a swimming pool, basketball, golf, and tennis and squash courts.

Places to Eat

Good cheap Chinese meals are available at *Dencia's Kitchenette* on Legaspi St, *Shanghai Restaurant* on Magsaysay Ave, which closes at 8 pm, and at the *Coo-Long Restaurant* on San Pedro St.

Other good restaurants on San Pedro St are the *Kusina Dabaw*, which serves Chinese and Filipino dishes, the ever crowded *New Sunya Restaurant* and the *Merco Restaurant*, which also has good ice-cream.

The Chinese food at the *Davao Majestic Restaurant* on A Bonifacio St is very popular. If it's fried chicken you're after, then *Sunburst Fried Chicken* on Anda St is the place to go to. You could also try the pleasant little *Molave Restaurant*, on Bangoy St close to the intersection with J Rizal St, where it specialises in 'greaseless chicken'.

There is a whole row of different restaurants on the corner of Florentino Torres St and JP Laurel Ave. Worth mentioning are the *Harana*, which has good barbecues and Filipino food, the *Sarung Banggi*, which is renowned for its steaks, prawns and salads, the *Mongolian Garden*, which specialises in Mongolian barbecue and spare ribs, the *Bistro Rosario*, with its excellent steaks, and the *Peter Pan Bake Shop*, which has wonderful cakes.

The *Eateries* at the Muslim Fishing Village near Magsaysay Park are strong on grills of almost anything that swims, mainly tuna and squid. A good spot for those who enjoy the romance of rustic life.

For lovers of Japanese food, the *Tsuru Restaurant* with sushi bar on Legaspi St serves excellent and surprisingly inexpensive meals.

If it has to be fast food, *McDonald's* and other members of this fraternity can be found in the Victoria Plaza shopping centre next to the Durian Hotel on JP Laurel Ave.

Entertainment

For a reasonable nightclub with live music and a floor show that is not too expensive, try *Jimm's Club*, a bit outside the city centre on the MacArthur Highway. Also out of town in the direction of the airport, on a side street to the right, 300m before the Taoist temple, is the *Square Circle Disco*. The *Casino* on Laurel St on the north-west outskirts of the city is open every night.

Bronco on J Rizal St has live and disco music, and there's a good lively atmosphere at the *Spam's Disco* downstairs in the Apo View Hotel (the entrance is at the back). By contrast, the *JR Super Club Disco* on San

Pedro St is quite simple, as is the *Hang Out* just next door. Expats tend to hang out in *Down Under*, about 150m south of Generoso Bridge.

Things to Buy
Davao boasts quite a few attractive markets and shopping centres with a wide variety of goods on offer. The Aldevinco Shopping Center on Claro M Recto Ave offers art work, antiques, products from cultural minorities, batik and lots more.

Fruit, vegetables, meat and fish are all sold at the Bankerohan Market, near Generoso Bridge, and at the Agdao Market on Lapu-Lapu St. The stalls of the Madrazo Fruit Center on Bangoy St offer a wide selection of tropical fruit, including, naturally, the infamous durian – a speciality of Davao. There is even a monument to it in Magsaysay Park. This prickly fruit that 'stinks like hell and tastes like heaven', has such a strong smell that it is banned from most hotel rooms and PAL won't allow it on its planes.

The NCCC is Davao's leading department store, and is better and less expensive than Gaisano.

Getting There & Away
Air PAL flies from Cagayan de Oro to Davao on Monday, Wednesday and Friday (P915; 35 minutes); and from Zamboanga to Davao on Thursday and Sunday (P1310; 50 minutes).

PAL has an office at Davao airport (☎ 234 0073, 234 6434) and in the Villa-Abrille building (☎ 221 5501, 221 5313) on Banyoy St.

Bouraq Airlines can be found at Davao Agritech Inc, Damosa Complex, Lanang.

Malaysian Airlines (☎ 224 1843) has an office at the Durian Hotel on JP Laurel Ave.

You have to pay a departure tax of P220 on international flights.

Bus Several Bachelor Bus Liner and Ceres Liner buses leave Butuan for Davao daily (6½ hours). The last bus might leave around noon.

From Cagayan de Oro, several Bachelor Bus Liner and Ceres Liner buses run to Davao daily (10 hours). The last departure may be quite early in the morning.

From Cotabato, numerous Mintranco and Weena Express buses run daily to Davao (six hours).

From General Santos, numerous Yellow Bus Line Bus Company buses run daily to Davao (P67; four hours). The last bus leaves at about 3 pm.

There are four Bachelor Bus Liner buses from Surigao to Davao daily between 4 and 9 am (8½ hours).

Car & Motorcycle Avis Rent-a-Car (☎ 234 2337) has an office in the Insular Century Hotel Davao.

Motorcycles can be hired for P450 a day (for a minimum of three days) at the Travel Service Center in Villa Viva (☎/fax 297 1411) on Willow St, Matina Heights.

Boat From General Santos to Davao, the MV *Superferry 1* of WG & A sails on Monday at 10 am (P90; 9 hours).

From Surigao to Davao, Sulpicio Lines' MV *Filipina Princess* leaves on Monday at 9 pm (P160; 17 hours) and WG & A's *Superferry 6* leaves on Wednesday at noon (18 hours).

Getting Around
The Airport Bangoy airport is 12 km northeast of Davao, between the districts of Lanang and Panacan. A taxi shouldn't cost more than P50 to P70. It's cheaper to take a tricycle (P2), 1.5 km along Airport Rd to the main road, then a jeepney marked 'San Pedro' or 'Bajuda' to Davao (P3.50); you may have to wait a few minutes. The jeepney travelling from the town centre to the airport has the sign 'Sasa'.

Bus The bus terminal for trips to and from Butuan, Cagayan de Oro, Cotabato, General Santos, Manila and Surigao is in the Ecoland District, about two km south of the town centre. Taxis charge P50 and jeepneys cost about P5.

Boat There are two piers you can use: Santa Ana Wharf next to Magsaysay Park; and

Sasa Pier a few km out of town. A jeepney from Sasa to the town centre costs P4.

AROUND DAVAO
Samal Island

A romantic pearl diving atmosphere is missing on Samal, as the prosperous times of the Aguinaldo Pearl Farm are over. Nowadays, a 1st class hotel complex – the Pearl Farm Beach Resort – sticks out into the picturesque bay, where only a few years ago thousands of oysters produced cultured pearls. However, make no mistake about it, it's exclusive; uninvited day guests don't even get their feet over the threshold.

The white **Paradise Island Beach** on the north-west coast is the best beach on Samal; north of it are the cottages of the Coral Reef Beach Resort, and south of it, a little out of the way, the Costa Marina Beach Resort.

Big and Little Cruz islands, north-east of Samal, are good for diving. They used to be called the Ligid Islands. There is another good diving area near the Pearl Farm Beach Resort at Malipano Island, where the wrecks of two WWII ships lie 30m below water.

Places to Stay The *Paradise Island Beach Resort*, which has extremely friendly staff and good service, provides attractive cottages with fan for P550, and with fan and bath for P700. The restaurant is good and inexpensive. It's quiet around here during the week, although popular on the weekend for day trips. Admission for day visitors is P30.

The *Pearl Farm Beach Resort* has cosily furnished rooms with fridge, air-con and bath for P2400, so-called Samal houses (standing on piles in the sea) for P3600 and spacious suites for P6300. The restaurant is expensive, and facilities on this extensive property include a swimming pool, tennis courts, water skiing, windsurfing and diving. Free transport is provided to the airport for guests. Reservations (☎ 832 0893; fax 832

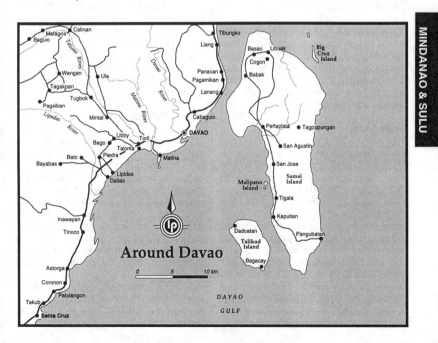

Around Davao

0044) can be made in Manila at the Anflocor building, 411 Quirini Ave, Parañaque.

Getting There & Away To get from Davao to Paradise Island Beach Resort, take a jeepney towards the airport with the sign 'Sasa' for P4. Ask the driver to stop at the Sasa Pier next to the Caltex oil tanks. From there it's a few steps to the boat that will take you over to Paradise Island Beach; it costs P5 per person, or P50 for the boat. Boats leave between 5.30 am and 5 pm.

From Santa Ana Wharf boats leave for Peñaplata on Samal Island (P20; 45 minutes). From the jetty in Peñaplata you can have a motorcycle take you to Paradise Island Beach Resort for about P80.

Talikud Island
This little island south-west of Samal has a cave with reputedly well-fed pythons and a couple of nice beaches with very hungry sharks. At least that's the story told by the friendly islanders.

Getting There & Away You can expect problems if you want to go to Talikud, but if you do decide to go there, get the boat in Davao from the left-hand side of Santa Ana Wharf. It leaves daily at about 10 am, but sometimes not until 2 pm, and the return trip may not be possible until the next day.

Eagle Camp
This camp (also known as the Philippine Eagle Nature Center) has been set up at Malagos, near Calinan in the Baguio District, about 36 km north-west of Davao by road. A trip to this establishment run by the Philippine Eagle Foundation Inc (PEFI) is really worth the effort (not only for ornithologists). The grounds are very well maintained and laid out like a botanical garden. It also has some typical Philippine animals in a small zoo, which includes the whole range of Philippine eagles (admission P12). In the whole country there are only 77 confirmed examples of the Philippine eagle, 16 of which live in Eagle Camp. Two of them hatched in the incubator and were successfully raised in the

camp. So there is a small spark of a chance that 'the air's noblest flier', as Charles Lindburgh called the Philippine national bird during a campaign to save the species back in the 1960s, will escape extinction.

The people at the camp, who observe the nesting habits of the Philippine eagle, are very friendly and have loads of information on these birds. For a fee, it may be possible to stay overnight and go trekking in the area, ie Mt Apo National Park. You should bring a sleeping bag, provisions and warm clothing, as it gets much colder up there than in Davao.

Two km south of Eagle Camp, you'll find the **Malagos Garden Resort**, with its pleasant restaurant, orchid garden and swimming pool. The resort is open from 9 am to 5 pm.

Getting There & Away Several jeepneys leave for Calinan daily from Agdao Market in Davao (you can also board them in San Pedro St or at the Bankerohan Market; P10). Take a tricycle for the remaining five km or so from Calinan to Malagos and the camp entrance (P40). The last jeepney from Calinan to Davao (with the sign 'Agdao') leaves at about 6 pm.

A taxi from Davao to Eagle Camp and back will cost you P600 (you can always negotiate), including waiting time (total time about five hours).

Mt Apo National Park
The tourist office in Davao has detailed information about Mt Apo National Park, the various routes up the mountain and recommended equipment. The personnel is competent to advise whether the climb is responsible and feasible. In April 1989, when around 300 local and foreign climbers took part in the annual organised climb, members of the New People's Army (NPA) made it blatantly clear who was boss on the mountain by seizing the whole group in a surprise raid, only to free them again shortly after.

In Digos, south of Mt Apo, you can obtain further information about climbing and security from the Mt Apo Climber Association at the office of the *Digos Times*. Guides and porters can be hired in Kidapawan for at least P250 a day. A water canteen and boots are essential. A warm sleeping bag is also necessary as the nights are cool – temperatures around freezing are not uncommon. Take your own provisions, not forgetting salt to prevent dehydration.

The climb is not easy. Even though sprinters have completed it in one day, five or six days is a more realistic schedule.

Kapatagan Route

Also known as the Davao del Sur Route, this can be managed in three days, although four would be more comfortable, including travel from and back to Davao.

Day 1 – Take a Yellow Bus Line, Mintranco or Weena bus from Davao to Digos from the bus terminal in Ecoland. You can take a direct bus or one heading for Cotabato or General Santos (one hour). From Digos bus terminal at the market take a tricycle to the jeepney station on the corner of Quezon St and Rizal Ave, then take a jeepney the 30 km up to Kapatagan (1½ hours). A motorcycle will take you for P120 (45 minutes).

Get in touch with a guide in Kapatagan, for example, through Guillermo Franco, Sampaguita Chapter. A written request in advance wouldn't harm: 8002 Kapatagan, Davao del Sur.

Buying your provisions is definitely cheaper in Kapatagan than in Digos or Davao, but there's not a big selection of tinned food available.

Around noon, set off for the village of Sabaug (four hours). Stay overnight in the hut. Drop off your sleeping bag and provisions.

Day 2 – Start off with your day pack at dawn. The first part of the route leads through tropical mountain rainforest and the slopes are steep by anybody's definition. The second section takes you through a rocky ravine and later through lava stone formations to the summit (five hours).

After a proper midday break on the summit, descend to Subuag (3 hours). Spend overnight in the hut.

Day 3 – It'll take about three hours to get back to Kapatagan in the morning. Go back to Davao via Digos. The last bus from Digos to Davao leaves at around 7 pm. Overnight accommodation is available in Digos at the *Digos Travel Lodge*, Rizal Ave, where a room with fan and bath will cost you between P250 and P400. You could also stay at the better quality *Hotel Yncierto*, 4440 Juan Luna St, where a room with air-con and bath will cost between P500 and P800.

Kidapawan Route
This recommended four day schedule includes travel to and from Davao:

Day 1 – Go from Davao to Kidapawan by Mintranco bus headed either for Kidapawan or Cotabato.

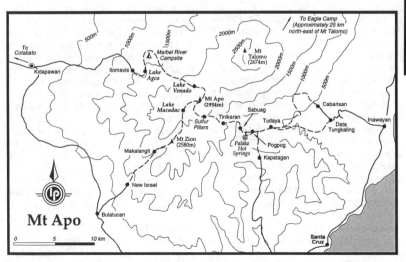

Mt Apo

0   5   10 km

This takes over two hours. Leave early as the last jeepney from Kidapawan to Lake Agco, via Ilomavis, usually leaves at about 3 pm. From Lake Agco, it's a good three hours uphill on foot to the Marbel River Campsite, where you can stay overnight in the shelter.

Day 2 – This section is six to eight hours' hard climbing; it's about five hours to Lake Venado. You will have to sleep outside, so take a plastic sheet or better still a small tent, as it's uncomfortable if it rains.

Day 3 – Allow for two hours to reach the summit, then return to Lake Venado or the Marbel River Campsite.

Day 4 – Return to Kidapawan or Davao.

GENERAL SANTOS (DADIANGAS)

Maguindanao Muslims and B'laans were the sole inhabitants of this city up to the beginning of the 20th century. The first influx of immigrants arrived between 1914 and 1915, and more followed in the 1930s. In 1939 pioneers from Luzon and the Visayas led by General Paulino Santos established a settlement on the Silway River in Sarangani Bay. In 1965 Dadiangas was renamed General Santos in his honour. The old name is also used today.

The city's economy depends mainly on pineapple, bananas (Dole Pineapple Plantation and Stanfilco Banana Plantation) and cattle (Sarangani Cattle Co).

The two islands of **Balut** and **Sarangani**, which still belong to the Philippines, lie off the coast of Mindanao, south of General Santos. Indonesia's territorial waters begin only a few miles away. Although there is a shipping route between Balut Island and Manado in the north of Sulawesi/Indonesia, they will only accept Filipinos and Indonesians as passengers. Other nationalities are not allowed on board, even with a valid Indonesian visa. The Indonesian border officials who check everybody before they leave Balut Island stick to the rules exactly. The outrigger boat from General Santos to Balut Island only goes at night, and the trip can be damp and cold. It takes seven hours.

Telephone
The telephone area code for General Santos is 083.

Places to Stay – bottom end
The unpretentious *Concrete Lodge* (☎ 552 4876) on Pioneer Ave has acceptable rooms with fan and bath for P135/210, and with air-con and bath for P300. At the *South Sea Lodge I* (☎ 552 2086), also on Pioneer Ave, relatively good rooms with fan go for P140/190, with fan and bath for P190/230, and with air-con and bath for P300/360. The *South Sea Lodge II* is on the corner of Salazar St and Magsaysay Ave.

There is a relaxed, family-style atmosphere at the friendly *La Azotea Inn* (☎ 552 3729) in a pleasant building on Salazar St. Good rooms with fan cost P200, with air-con P300/350. Its coffee shop is only open for breakfast.

The *Matutum Hotel* (☎ 552 2711; fax 552 4901) is centrally located on P Acharon Blvd. Quiet, adequate singles with fan and bath go for P200, singles with air-con and bath for P355 and P430, and doubles with air-con and bath for P520 and P700. It has its own disco.

Places to Stay – top end
At *Pietro's Hotel* (☎ 552 4831) on National Highway on the edge of town, really good rooms with fan and bath cost P230/340, with air-con and bath P350/460, and suites P700. It also offers hourly rates and has a disco.

The *Hotel Sansu* (☎ 552 7219; fax 552 7221) on Pioneer Ave is good value, with rooms with air-con and bath going for P460/580 and up to P800. The more expensive ones have a refrigerator and TV.

The rooms at the *Phela Grande Hotel* (☎ 552 4925; fax 552 2990) on Magsaysay Ave are really pleasant, costing P550/750 with air-con and bath, and P1500 for suites. It has a coffee shop. The pleasant and attractive *T'Boli Hotel* (☎ 552 3042,) on the National Highway on the edge of town, has comfortable rooms with air-con and bath for P600/800 and suites from P1000 to P1800. There is a restaurant and music lounge.

Places to Eat
The *Wok 'n' Chow* in the Hotel Sansu prepares a good selection of Chinese dishes.

You can find good Philippine food in the *Matutum Hotel Restaurant*. On the corner of Atis and Lucban Sts, *Flor's Restaurant* might not look much, but it's inexpensive and you combine your own choice of food from more than 20 pots filled with fish, meat and vegetables.

Getting There & Away
Air PAL has an office at Buayan airport (☎ (065) 415 2360) and in the Angkalian building on the National Highway (☎ 552 5905).

Bus From Davao numerous Yellow Bus Line buses run daily to General Santos (four hours). The last bus is likely to leave at about 3 pm.

From Koronadel (Marbel) numerous Yellow Bus Line buses run daily to General Santos, some going on to Davao (one hour). Last departure is around 7 pm. There are also minibuses.

Several Yellow Bus Line buses go from Surallah to General Santos every day. You may have to change in Koronadel (two hours).

Boat From Davao to General Santos, the WG & A *Superferry 1* leaves on Monday at midnight (nine hours).

From Zamboanga to General Santos, the WG & A MV *Doña Virginia* departs on Wednesday at 7 pm (P290; 12 hours) and Sulpicio Lines' MV *Princess of the Pacific* leaves on Thursday at 5 pm (12 hours).

Getting Around
The Airport The Buayan airport is about six km east of General Santos. A tricycle to the centre of town costs P30 to P50.

Boat Makar Wharf is four km south-west of the town centre. A taxi costs between P50 and P100.

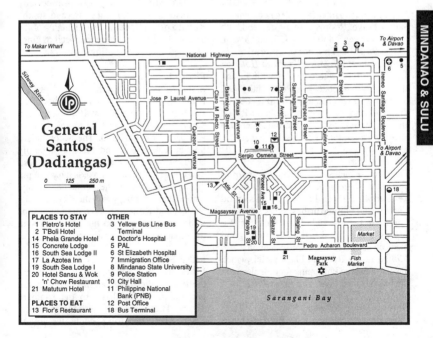

MINDANAO & SULU

General Santos (Dadiangas)

To Makar Wharf

0   125   250 m

PLACES TO STAY
1 Pietro's Hotel
2 T'Boli Hotel
14 Phela Grande Hotel
15 Concrete Lodge
16 South Sea Lodge II
17 La Azotea Inn
19 South Sea Lodge I
20 Hotel Sansu & Wok 'n' Chow Restaurant
21 Matutum Hotel

PLACES TO EAT
13 Flor's Restaurant

OTHER
3 Yellow Bus Line Bus Terminal
4 Doctor's Hospital
5 PAL
6 St Elizabeth Hospital
7 Immigration Office
8 Mindanao State University
9 Police Station
10 City Hall
11 Philippine National Bank (PNB)
12 Post Office
18 Bus Terminal

To Airport & Davao

National Highway

Jose P Laurel Avenue

Sergio Osmena Street

Magsaysay Avenue

Pedro Acharon Boulevard

Market

Magsaysay Park

Fish Market

Sarangani Bay

KORONADEL (MARBEL)

Koronadel, also known as Marbel, is the capital of South Cotabato Province. Mainly Maguindanao and B'laan, members of the original native ethnological groups, live here, but there are also immigrants from other parts of the Philippines. The Maguindanao call the town Koronadel, while the B'laan call it Marbel. It is a good starting point for a trip to Lake Sebu.

Telephone

The telephone area code for Koronadel is 08346.

Places to Stay

Alabado's Home, on the corner of Alunan and Rizal Sts, is a reasonable place and fair value for money. It has rooms with fan and bath for P120/220, and with air-con and bath for P280/330. It's possible the selection of rooms will be limited, as some of them are being used as offices.

A pleasant place to stay is the friendly *Ramona Plaza Hotel* (☎ 83284) on General Santos Drive. Rooms with air-con and bath go for between P450 and P750, and a suite costs P1200. The accommodation is immaculate at the *Marvella Plaza Hotel* on the same street, where singles with air-con and bath go for between P620 and P990, doubles with air-con and bath from P800 up to P1250, and suites are available for P1500 and P1750; all have TV, and the suites also have a refrigerator. The hotel has a disco.

Places to Eat

The Chinese meals at the *Capitol Restaurant* on Roxas St are good value. The *D'Breeze Restaurant* a little further on has good Chinese and Filipino dishes, as does the *Café Loretta* in the Marvella Plaza Hotel; it also serves good breakfasts. Worth a good mention is the self-service restaurant *Casa Illonga* in the Ramona Plaza Hotel, which has inexpensive Philippine food. It also runs the baker's next door, *The Fresh Baker*.

Getting There & Away

From Davao, several Yellow Bus Line buses run daily to Koronadel via General Santos, some going on to Tacurong. It takes four hours from Davao and one hour from General Santos. From General Santos, there are also minibuses to Koronadel.

To go from Lake Sebu to Koronadel via Surallah, you go first by jeepney to Surallah, then to Koronadel in a Yellow Bus Line bus bound for General Santos (2½ hours).

SURALLAH

Surallah is in the south of the Alah Valley. It provides access to Lake Sebu, perhaps the loveliest inland sea in the Philippines.

About 15 km south of Surallah are the impressive **Seven Falls**, which are surrounded by tropical rainforest. These thundering falls can be reached on foot in less than an hour along a well-cleared path, which begins at the road from Surallah to Lake Sebu and leads through dense jungle.

Day trips from Surallah can be recommended to **Buluan**, and from there to **Lake Buluan**, with its swamp areas – especially interesting for ornithologists, and to the **Kimato gold mines** in the mountains of the Tiruray Highlands, where the metal of kings is mined under hair-raising conditions.

Places to Stay & Eat

Bonns Haus in Surallah has basic rooms for P50/100, although redecorating should be finished soon and prices will probably rise. At *Vip Trading* on Camia St rooms with fan and bath cost P200/250. The accommodation is really good and there is a family atmosphere. Meals are provided on request. The owner, Ruth Lagamayo, is happy to put guests in touch with the Fernandez family, who will provide trips with their jeep to Lake Buluan and Kimato. It even organises trips lasting several days on horseback through the mountains and the rainforest.

LAKE SEBU

Lake Sebu, which is teeming with fish, and the two smaller neighbouring lakes Sultan and Lahit, are nestled into the southern Tiruray Highlands at an altitude of almost 300m. The T'boli tribespeople live around

Lake Sebu. They are in almost total seclusion, and produce rice, maize and sugar cane. They are well known for the quality of their brass ware and weaving. (For more details, see the section on Cultural Minorities in the Facts about the Country chapter.)

Try to arrange your schedule so as to include the colourful Saturday **market**, or, even better, the annual Lem-Lunay T'boli Festival on the second Friday in November, which lasts several days and concludes with wild horse fights.

You will only enjoy visiting the Lake Sebu area if you are interested in the traditional life and culture of the T'boli. Those looking for more modern attractions will soon be bored and will not be welcomed by the locals.

Warning

The area around Lake Sebu was extremely dangerous in 1996. Within a period of a few weeks, over twenty foreigners were kidnapped by Muslim extremists and held to ransom. After the military had sent in reinforcements in the shape of battle-hardened soldiers, the situation returned to normal. Nevertheless, it's advisable to check on the latest state of affairs around Lake Sebu, ie General Santos or Koronadel, before going there.

Places to Stay & Eat

The *Lakeview Tourist Lodge* near the market is run by Carlos and Irene Legaste. Basic cottages go for P40 and rooms for P50/100. It also owns a souvenir shop, where they sell T'Boli arts and crafts. The accommodation at the *Hillside View Park & Lodge* is basic but good; big rooms cost P40/80.

The *Bao Ba-ay Village Inn* by the lake has rooms for P125/150 and cottages for P350. Bao Ba-ay, the owner, is a pure T'boli (in fact, he's a justice of the peace) and can tell you a great deal about the T'boli culture. His wife, Alma, is an Ilokana and is a good cook. It also has its own fish farm, and can arrange boats and horses for outings (P25 per hour).

On a low rise with a good view down to the lake, the cosy *Punta Isla Resort* is a pleasure to stay at. Dorm beds cost P50, and friendly

rooms with fan and bath P250. Its cook's speciality is tilapia fish, prepared any way you want.

Getting There & Away

Several jeepneys go from the market at Surallah to Lake Sebu daily (1½ hours).

The last jeepney from Surallah to Koronadel (Marbel) usually leaves at about 3 pm.

COTABATO

Cotabato is on the Rio Grande de Mindanao, one of the country's longest rivers. The town appears to be predominantly Muslim, but statistics show that the population is 60% Christian and only 40% Muslim. The people here are known as Maguindanao. Islam came to Cotabato in 1371, when the Arab Sharif Muhammad Kabungsuwan, who is said to be the founder of Cotabato, arrived. The Jesuits didn't arrive until 1872 and settled in Tamontaka, seven km south-west, to build a church and establish Christianity in the area.

Information

The tourist office (☎ 211110, 217868) is in the Elizabeth Tan building.

The telephone area code for Cotabato is 064.

Places to Stay

The *Padama Pension House* (☎ 212625) on Quezon Ave, near the bus terminal, offers simple rooms with fan for P150/200 and with fan and bath for P180/250, but the rooms facing the street are noisy.

The *Hotel Filipino* (☎ 212307) in the city plaza on Sinsuat Ave has reasonable rooms for P200/230, with fan and bath P250/320, and with air-con and bath P390/520. Some rooms have a good view over the city.

Comfortable rooms at the *El Corazon Inn* (☎ 213035) on Makakua St go for P300/350 with fan and bath, and P400/450 with air-con and bath. Suites cost P650.

The *New Imperial Hotel* (☎ 212075) at 51 Don Rufino Alonzo St is the best hotel in town, with air-con rooms costing P750/850 with bath. It is a comfortable place to stay, and has a disco.

Places to Eat
The *Jay Pee's Dan Restaurant & Snack House* on Don Rufino Alonzo St has a reputation for good, reasonably priced food.

Entertainment
The disco upstairs in the *New Imperial Hotel* is relatively expensive but has a rather austere décor. The disco on the 1st floor of the *Sampaguita Hall* is better, and you can listen to folk music on the 2nd floor.

Getting There & Away
Air PAL flies from Cagayan de Oro to

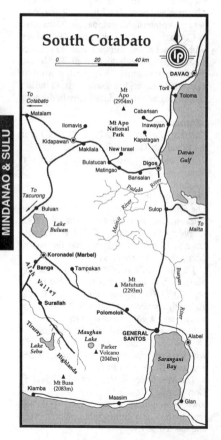

Cotabato on Tuesday and Sunday (P814; 45 minutes); and from Zamboanga to Cotabato on Tuesday and Friday (P1076; 40 minutes)

PAL has an office at Cotabato airport (☎ 211212) and on Don Roman Vilo St (☎ 212086).

Bus There are numerous Mintranco and Weena Express buses from Davao to Cotabato daily (5½ hours).

From Koronadel, many Maguindanao Express and JD Express buses run daily to Cotabato (three hours). Yellow Bus Line Company buses go at least as far as Tacurong, from where jeepneys run to Cotabato.

The bus trip from Pagadian to Cotabato is not advisable even if one is available. (See the Getting There & Away section under Pagadian earlier in this chapter.)

Boat A boat leaves Pagadian for Cotabato daily at 5 pm (eight hours).

From Zamboanga to Cotabato, Sulpicio Lines' MV *Cotabato Princess* leaves on Monday at 8 pm (eight hours). The WG & A MV *Superferry 3* leaves on Sunday at 7 am (9 hours).

Basilan

The southern end of Basilan meets the northern end of the Sulu Islands, and its northern end is just across the Basilan Strait from Mindanao. Since 1973 Basilan has been a province, comprising a main island and numerous smaller ones. About 230,000 people live here, roughly one-third of whom are Yakan, an ethnic minority found only on Basilan, except for some families living near Zamboanga on Mindanao. They are peace-loving Muslim farmers and cattle raisers, who are well known for their hospitality towards visitors and for their colourful and elaborate ceremonies, weddings and festivals. As well as the Yakan, Basilan is inhabited by the Chavacano, Visayan, Samal, Tausug and a few Badjao tribespeople.

Basilan is hilly and rugged, and its centre is virtually unexplored. In the north of the island, the climate is fairly stable and there is no obviously dry or wet season, but rain may fall at any time of the year. The southern part, by contrast, has a fairly dry season from November to April.

The area's main industry is the processing of caoutchouc for rubber. Basilan rubber is considered among the best in the world, and large international companies have invested in the plantations. Other crops are coffee, cocoa, pepper, African oil (a plant oil extracted from the dates of the African palm tree) and abaca; copper is also mined. Because the waters around Basilan abound with fish, mussels and seaweed, the province is one of the most important suppliers of seafood in the southern Philippines.

Warning

From 1993 until 1995 Basilan frequently hit the headlines in the Philippine press owing to kidnappings and other acts of violence. Many people lost their lives in shoot-outs between the military and members of the MNLF, who had set up camp in the Basilan mountains. That was the end of the bad news

reports, but that doesn't mean peace has suddenly broken out in the area. Even after the conclusion of a peace treaty, it is not unreasonable to expect the extremist splinter group, the MILF, to carry out violent attacks again in the future. For your own safety, think twice about visiting Basilan. Check with the tourist office in Zamboanga for the latest news on the situation there.

GETTING THERE & AWAY
Boat
Mindanao From Isabela to Zamboanga, the Basilan Shipping Lines' MV *Doña Leonora* leaves daily at 7 am and 1 pm (1½ hours).

From Lamitan to Zamboanga, the Basilan Shipping Lines' MV *Doña Ramona* departs daily at 7.30 am from the wharf outside town; the MV *Don Julio* leaves daily at 10 am and 4 pm. Both journeys take around 1¼ hours.

Sulu Islands Services to the Sulu Islands are irregular. It is probably better to go to Zamboanga and then on from there.

ISABELA
The capital of Basilan Province, Isabela is a small town with not much to see. You can go across the harbour in a few minutes in an outrigger boat to **Malamaui Island**, where a few Badjao live in pile houses. The beautiful **White Beach** is the best known beach on the island, but, in spite of this, is practically deserted. It's about an hour on foot from the landing place. You can get there by tricycle but there is no regular return service, so you either have to ask the driver to wait and order the tricycle for a fixed time, or walk. The last boat back to Isabela leaves around 4 pm.

A few km from Isabela are coffee, pepper and date plantations belonging to the Menzi family. On the way there you pass the **Menzi manufacturing plant**, where you can see exactly how rubber is produced from caoutchouc. Coffee beans are roasted there in the open air. It is closed on weekends. Before you reach the factory, you pass a mansion belonging to the wealthy Allano family, who

own the electricity plant and a shipping company, among other enterprises.

Places to Stay
The *New Basilan Hotel* on JS Alano St has rooms with fan for P100/200, and with fan and bath for P150/300. It is not far from the wharf and is better than the nearby *Selecta Hotel*.

Places to Eat
You can eat really well at the *New International Restaurant*. The food at *Awin's Icecream House* on Valderossa St is not exactly cheap, but the price of the beer makes up for it.

LAMITAN
Lamitan is a small town that is slightly inland but connected to the sea by an estuary. Every Thursday and Saturday from 6 to 11 am there is a large **market** that's really worth seeing. Ragged Badjao come with their boats to sell seafood, while Yakan bring farm produce and animals down from the hillside villages. Chinese merchants vie with local Chavacano and Visayan merchants in selling household goods and textiles.

In March 1983 the first Lami-Lamihan Festival took place. It was a pure Yakan folk festival and Yakan from the surrounding hills came in droves, dressed in their colourful costumes. The festival now takes place every year at the end of March or beginning of April.

Just off the main road, 12 km from Lamitan, you will find the **Buligan Falls**, which have a big, deep, natural pool – ideal for swimming.

Places to Stay
The *Traveller's Inn* has basic accommodation, with rooms for P100/200.

Getting There & Away
Several buses leave the market in Isabela for Lamitan from 5 am (45 minutes). There is also a white non-stop bus which does the 27 km stretch in 20 minutes.

JOHN PENNOCK

CHRIS MILES

JOHN PENNOCK

MINDANAO & SULU
Top: Yakan weaver, Basilan Province.
Bottom Left: Festive Muslim dress, Bongao Island.
Bottom Right: Rio Hondo, Zamboanga City, Zamboanga del Sur Province.

JENS PETERS

JENS PETERS

JENS PETERS

CHRIS MILES

MINDANAO & SULU

Top: Badjao (sea gypsies), Sulu Islands.
Middle Left: Gigantes at the Zamboanga
    Hermosa Festival.

Bottom Left: Fish, the staple diet of
    the Philippines.
Right: Beach boys, Tawi-Tawi Islands.

Sulu Islands

The Sulu Islands are at the southernmost tip of the Philippines. They stretch about 300 km from Basilan to Borneo, dividing the Sulu and Celebes seas. A well-known pirate haunt, these waters are avoided by wary sailors whenever possible. Even commercial trading ships have been boarded and plundered. Frequent bloody battles also occur between pirates and smugglers.

The Sulus consist of a group of 500 islands, which are subdivided into smaller groups: Jolo (pronounced Holo); Samales; Pangutaran; Tapul; Tawi-Tawi; Sibutu; and Cagayan de Tawi-Tawi (Cagayan Sulu). There are two provinces: Sulu, the capital of which is Jolo; and Tawi-Tawi, the capital of which is Bongao.

Attempts by the Spaniards to gain a foothold on these islands failed and the Americans were no more successful.

Among the most significant cultural minority groups are the Samal and the Badjao. Both seem very gentle and peaceful. The main islands inhabited by the Samal are Siasi, Tawi-Tawi and Sibutu islands. These people are Muslim, and make their living predominantly from fishing, agriculture and small- scale trading. Their houses are always close to the water, often standing in the water on piles.

The Badjao live on boats throughout the entire archipelago, but are concentrated around Tawi-Tawi and Sibutu. They are sea gypsies and their religion is generally thought to be animism. A lot of them, especially those who have ceased to be nomads and live in houses on piles like the Samal, have accepted the new way of life and converted to Islam. Of all the inhabitants of the Sulu Islands, the Badjao are on the lowest rung of the social ladder. Like the Samal, they feel oppressed by the Tausug, the largest and most politically and economically advanced tribe.

The Tausug are Muslim and are considered powerful, aggressive and independent. Quite a few generations have lived by piracy, smuggling and slave-trading. The original inhabitants of the Sulu Islands, the Buranun, are said to have been the forefathers of the Tausug. They too were converted to Islam and their descendants have remained so, except for small communities of Catholics and Buddhists.

From 1974 until the end of 1981, the Sulu Islands were totally out of bounds to tourists. You could sail there from Zamboanga but were not permitted to disembark without a permit. Now, however, foreigners are allowed into the area without permits or restrictions on where they go or how long they stay. This sounds good, but in fact many islands or parts of the islands are still inaccessible because of constant tension, such as between Tawi-Tawi and Jolo. There are other islands like Laa, near Simunul, or Sipangkot, near Tumindao, but no boat operators will visit because they fear or dislike the inhabitants.

It is essential to take warnings seriously. When I wanted to cross from Bongao to Bilatan, the boatman only gave a discouraging

'Maybe tomorrow'. That evening there was a real shoot out on Bilatan. A few days earlier I had been refused a ride from Bongao to Laa through fear of an ambush. That night you could clearly hear a long fusillade of shots from across the water. There was probably a good reason, too, for the naval escort given to our boat from Sitangkai to Bongao.

Added to this are accommodation and water shortages. Commercial accommodation is available only in Jolo and Bongao. Elsewhere you have to find private lodgings and you should pay a reasonable price for them. On the southern islands, there is a severe water shortage. You get a guilty conscience even brushing your teeth! Any washing is done in sea water polluted with sewage and refuse. You can almost feel the hepatitis threatening your liver.

Nevertheless, a trip to the Sulu Islands is a unique experience. The impressions gained are many and varied and well worth the effort.

GETTING THERE & AWAY

You can get to the Sulu Islands from Mindanao and probably also from Basilan. (See the Mindanao Getting There & Away section earlier in this chapter.)

Air

Mindanao PAL flies daily to Zamboanga from Tawi-Tawi (the airport is on Sanga Sanga Island, near Bongao) and Jolo.

Boat

Basilan Connections to Basilan from the Sulu Islands are irregular. However, merchant ships, which will also take passengers, are said to leave Jolo quite often for Isabela.

Mindanao See the timetable for SKT ships and the Sampaguita Shipping Corporation in the following Getting Around section in this chapter.

Palawan If you have time, you could try the route from Jolo to Pangutaran Island, then on to Cagayan de Tawi-Tawi, where you can occasionally get a freighter to Rio Tuba or Brooke's Point in southern Palawan.

GETTING AROUND

Ships ranging from vile little tubs to quite passable freighters that take passengers ply more or less regular routes between almost all of the larger islands. The better ships on the route from Zamboanga via Jolo, Siasi, and Bongao to Sitangkai and back are those of the SKT Shipping Lines and the Sampaguita Shipping Corporation.

SKT Shipping Lines Timetable:

MV *Lady Ruth*

Destination	Arrives	Departs
Zamboanga	Sat 5 pm	Tue 6 pm
Jolo	Wed 4 am	Wed 12 pm
Siasi	Wed 4 am	Wed 10 pm
Bongao	Thu 6 am	Thu 11 am
Sitangkai	Thu 3 pm	Thu 12 am
Bongao	Fri 4 am	Fri 6 pm
Jolo	Sat 6 am	Sat 9 am

MV *Lady Helen*

Destination	Arrives	Departs
Zamboanga	Mon 5 am	Wed 6 pm
Jolo	Thu 4 am	Thu 12 pm
Siasi	Thu 5 pm	Thu 8 pm
Bongao	Fri 5 am	Fri 10 am
Sitangkai	Fri 2 pm	Fri 12 am
Bongao	Sat 4 am	Sat 6 pm
Siasi	Sun 2 am	Sun 1 pm
Jolo	Sun 5 pm	Sun 9 pm

MV *Doña Isabel II*

Destination	Arrives	Departs
Zamboanga	Thu 4 am	Sat 6 pm
Jolo	Sun 2 am	Sun 12 pm
Siasi	Sun 4 pm	Sun 6 pm
Bongao	Mon 4 am	Mon 11 am
Sitangkai	Mon 3 pm	Tue 1 am
Bongao	Tue 5 am	Tue 6 pm
Siasi	Wed 2 am	Wed 2 pm
Jolo	Wed 6 pm	Wed 8 pm

Sampaguita Shipping Corporation Timetable:

MV *Sampaguita Grandeur*

Destination	Arrives	Departs
Zamboanga	Fri 6 pm	Mon 8 pm
Jolo	Tue 5 am	Tue 10 am
Siasi	Tue 2 pm	Tue 6 pm
Bongao	Wed 3 am	Wed 10 am
Sitangkai	Wed 2 pm	Wed 8 pm
Bongao	Wed 12 am	Thu 7 pm
Jolo	Fri 6 am	Fri 9 am

MV *Sampaguita Lei*

Destination	Arrives	Departs
Zamboanga	Mon 6 pm	Thu 8 pm
Jolo	Fri 5 am	Fri 10 am
Siasi	Fri 2 pm	Fri 6 pm
Bongao	Sat 3 am	Sat 10 am
Sitangkai	Sat 2 pm	Sat 8 pm
Bongao	Sun 12 am	Sun 7 pm
Jolo	Mon 6 am	Mon 9 am

MV *Sampaguita Blossom*

Destination	Arrives	Departs
Zamboanga	Thu 10 pm	Sun 7 pm
Jolo	Mon 7 am	Mon 11 am
Siasi	Mon 4 pm	Mon 6 pm
Bongao	Tue 6 am	Tue 11 am
Sitangkai	Tue 4 pm	Tue 8 pm
Bongao	Wed 3 am	Wed 7 pm
Jolo	Thu 7 am	Thu 10 am

JOLO

Jolo is the capital of the island of the same name and also of Sulu Province. It is the only place in the entire archipelago where the Spaniards, after a relatively short period of 20 years, finally gained a foothold and built a fortress. This was at the end of the 19th century, about 300 years after they first reached the Philippines.

In February 1974 Jolo was partly destroyed in fighting between Muslims and government troops. Even today the military is still present in the city. Although no permit is required for the city itself, foreigners need a military permit to travel around this volcanic island.

It is remarkable to see the many trishaws standing around the great mosque. Don't miss the colourful **fish market** and the **Barter Trade Market** in the halls next to the harbour, where goods that come mainly from Borneo are sold.

The lovely, sandy **Quezon Beach** is about three km north-east of Jolo. If it's not off limits for security reasons, you can get there by jeepney, getting out before Patikul. A little further east in **Taglibi** is another wide, sandy beach with crystal clear water.

It is possible there will be a curfew on Jolo from 7 pm every evening, which must be respected.

Places to Stay

Helen's Lodge (☎ 2278) on Buyon St has rooms with fan for P100/160, with fan and bath for P150/250, and with air-con and bath for P450. It is simple and relatively clean, and has a restaurant. Travellers passing through can use the sanitary facilities for a small charge.

Places to Eat

If you have just arrived from Zamboanga, you will have your first experience of the island's coffee shops in Jolo. Whether you order coffee or a Sprite (the popular soft drink in Sulu), you will be offered a large tray of all sorts of cakes.

Good restaurants are the *Bee Gees* on Sanchez St, the *Plaza Panciteria* on Sevantes St, which serves a mean milkshake among other things, and the *Plaza Restaurant*, which has quite passable toilet facilities.

SIASI

This island is a crisis area according to locals. I must admit, the little harbour town of the same name didn't make a particularly good impression on me either. It has many damaged or totally burnt-out houses, a boarded-up Sultan Hotel and lots of military personnel around. People are rather unforthcoming and language difficulties could be a problem.

TAWI-TAWI ISLAND GROUP
Bongao

Bongao, on Bongao Island, is the most important town in the Tawi-Tawi Island group. It's bigger than Siasi but smaller than Jolo, and has two harbours, a market, two cinemas and a main street with several side streets. The Provincial Capitol building stands out like a mosque on the hillside. The Badjao village of Tungkalang, on the southwest tip of Sanga Sanga, which has been described in some old travel books, no longer exists.

Sea gypsies have settled near Bongao, in the bay by the hospital, and Notre Dame College. As far as these friendly people are concerned, an 'Americano' isn't a 'Joe' (a holdover from 'GI Joe', popular after US troops

MINDANAO & SULU

helped liberate the islands from Japanese invaders in 1944 to 1945) but 'Milikan'.

Orientation

The military camp, Philippine National Bank and PAL are all on the outskirts of town. Beyond them, you come to quite a nice place to swim, where the road meets the shore. At low tide you can walk across to a sandbank that is good for snorkelling.

Mt Bongao

The little village of Pasiagan is five km from Bongao. This is the start of the trail leading up Mt Bongao, a 314m mountain worshipped by both Christians and Muslims. Anjaotals, a member of an old royal family, is buried on the summit. Prayers said in the four sq metre enclosure, with its wall draped in white cloth, are said to be more powerful than any medicine. (If you visit the enclosure, you must take off your shoes.) Paths right and left of the grave lead to good lookout points that are clear of trees. The climb takes about an hour, and is hot and tiring.

As this is a holy mountain, you should not defile it in any way and offensive behaviour

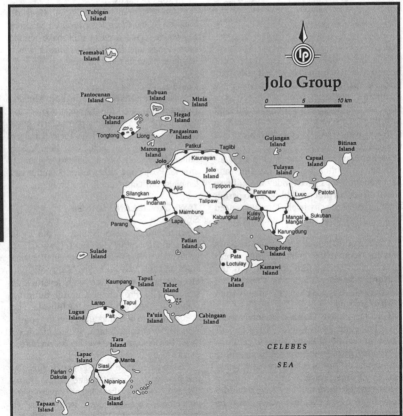

like swearing should be avoided. It is believed that people who touch a monkey here will soon die or lose their wits. It's a good idea to take some bananas for these inquisitive animals. There are numerous snakes, though they're not easy to see, so don't grab blindly at trees or vines. In early October, Bongao has a fiesta and the hill is alive with people.

Places to Stay

Staff are friendly at *Peping Cuarema's Residence* on Muslimin St, where basic, clean rooms go for P85/170.

The *Southern Inn* on Datu Halun St, opposite the mosque, has basic rooms for P250, and with fan and bath for P350. It has a restaurant and two pleasant balconies.

About two km out of town, the *Hill Stone Hotel* and the *Kasulutan Hotel* have rooms from P150.

Getting There & Away

From Bongao you can catch small boats to the islands of Bilatan, Simunul and Manuk Mankaw. Bunabunaan Island is the burial place of the Badjao people and it can only be reached by a Special Ride. When in Bongao,

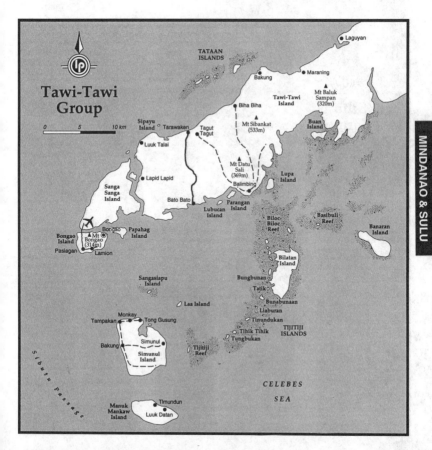

MINDANAO & SULU

I was constantly advised not to visit Tawi-Tawi.

Getting Around

The Tawi-Tawi airport is on Sanga Sanga Island, north of Bongao. The jeepney trip to the town costs P20, or P50 by tricycle.

SITANGKAI

It is said that more than 6000 people live in this 'Venice of the Far East', in houses built on piles on the giant reef. The water is so shallow that big ships have to anchor three km away in the Tumindao Channel and ferry their freight and passengers across in small boats (P25 per person).

There are more Badjao villages built on piles scattered over a large area west of Sitangkai. The largest, and furthest away, is called Tong Tong, and is made up of 50 houses. It's not far from the Meridian Channel, which is 50 to 100m deep. Here, as elsewhere, the Badjao have laid out underwater seaweed fields; sea cucumbers are another main source of income. A day trip there by boat can be arranged for P300 to P500.

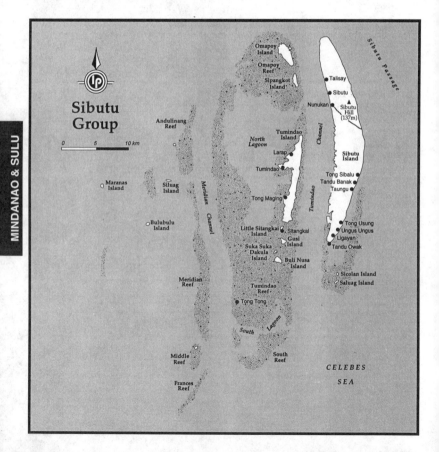

Warning

Because of the many people who travel illegally on smugglers' boats from Sitangkai to Sempora on Borneo (in the East Malaysian state of Sabah), for years tourists were only allowed to disembark at Sitangkai after showing a passport, a valid visa, and a permit from the Tawi-Tawi Task Force. This permit was issued in Bongao, where showing a return ticket (eg, from Zamboanga to Manila) saved a lot of interrogation time. Apparently these checks have now been scrapped, but it might be worth asking in Bongao whether it's possible to visit Sitangkai without all the red tape.

Places to Stay

You will have to look for private accommodation if you want to stay in Sitangkai. If you have the chance to stay with the Badjao for a few days, be generous with food and supplies, as these friendly people don't have much. Hadji Musa Malabong, the teacher at Sitangkai, and his brother, Hadji Yusof Abdulganih, can arrange private accommodation.

Getting There & Away

From Sitangkai, small boats run to the two bigger islands of Tumindao and Sibutu.

Palawan

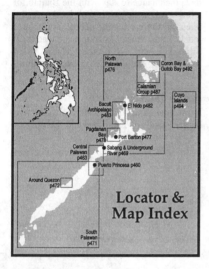

**Locator &
Map Index**

Palawan, in the south-west of the Philippines, is 400 km long but only 40 km wide, and separates the Sulu Sea from the South China Sea. Beautiful empty beaches, untouched natural scenery and friendly inhabitants make this a very attractive island. A further 1768 islands make up Palawan Province, the most important being Busuanga, Culion, Coron, Cuyo, Dumaran, Bugsuk and Balabac. Most of Palawan consists of mountainous jungle. At 2086m, Mt Mantalingajan is the highest mountain.

The El Nido cliffs and the limestone caves of Coron and Pabellones islands, off Taytay, are home to countless swallows' nests. Hotels and Chinese restaurants all over the country get their supplies from these places to make that oriental delicacy, birds' nest soup. If you like fish, you will think this is paradise, as the fruits of the sea are really plentiful here. You could try a different ocean meal every day, choosing from mussels, sea urchins, lobsters and many others. The jungles harbour plants and animals which are found nowhere else in the Philippines. These include the iron tree, mouse deer (chevrotain), king cobra, and many rare parrots and butterflies.

With the exception of the Underground River and the Tabon Caves, Palawan has no sights worth talking about. On the other hand, what makes the island so attractive and pleasant to visit are the friendly inhabitants, unspoilt nature and the outstanding, deserted beaches. Palawan also offers a wide variety of activities for the more adventurous visitor: you can try jungle expeditions; searching for gold; cave exploring; diving; hiking; searching for shipwrecks; or living like Robinson Crusoe, among other activities.

ECONOMY

Only a few coastal regions can be used for agriculture. Palawan's main crops are rice, coconuts, bananas, groundnuts and cashew nuts. For the economy, however, fishing is by far the most important activity. The richest fishing grounds in the Philippines are off Palawan's northern coast. About 60% of Manila's staple food is caught between Coron, Cuyo and Dumaran islands, and especially in Taytay Bay.

Since the discovery of oil off Palawan's north-west coast, the development of that industry looks promising.

Another important industry is forestry. Until 1989, when the Aquino government imposed a logging ban, Palawan had lost

The spiny lobster (*ulang*).

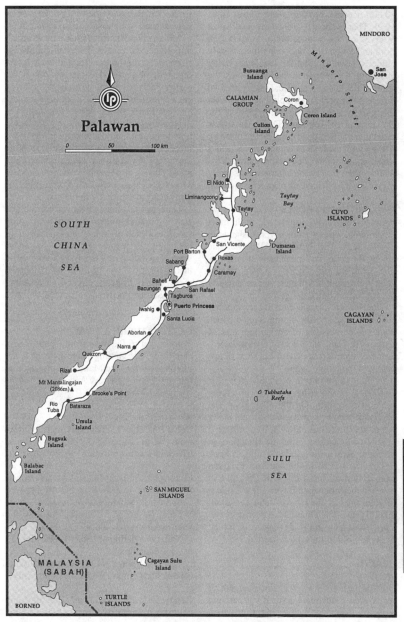

20,000 hectares of forests every year since 1979. That is about 2½% of the total forest reserves of this island, home to such rich flora and fauna. It is becoming increasingly obvious, however, that the law is not being observed. As so often in the Philippines, the letter of the law and practical reality are two different things. This stripping of Palawan is likely to frustrate the promising plans of the Department of Tourism (DOT). In a few years there will be dead coral reefs caused by fishing with explosives, and barren hillsides because of uncontrolled deforestation. This will alter the face of the island so drastically nature lovers will have no reason for visiting.

POPULATION & PEOPLE

Palawan is thinly populated, with most inhabitants coming from several islands in the Visayas. The Batak and Pala'wan are among the aboriginal inhabitants of Palawan. The Batak are very shy. If you want to find them and visit their villages, you need plenty of time and a competent guide.

The Negrito, nomads who live by hunting, are found in the north. Attempts to convince them of the benefits of agriculture and of settling the land have nearly always failed. Some of them go to school but then disappear into the jungle again.

In the extreme north of Palawan are the Tagbanua, a seafaring people who rarely settle in one place. On the other hand, the Tagbanua who live near the coast and along the rivers of central Palawan live in settled village communities. Like the Hanunoo on Mindoro, they use a syllabic writing system.

The Tau't Batu in the south of Palawan were only discovered in 1978. They live in caves in the Singnapan Basin, a few km east of Ransang, as they have done for about 20,000 years. Their habitat has been declared a protected area and is absolutely off limits. This prohibition must be respected.

HEALTH

Warning

Outside the capital, Puerta Princesa, medical services are inadequate. Even if you can find a doctor, there won't be a pharmacy which stocks the necessary medication. In case of illness, head straight for Puerto Princesa.

Malaria is widespread on Palawan, so it's important to take antimalarial tablets, always sleep under mosquito netting and use insect repellent. (See the Health section in the earlier Facts for the Visitor chapter.) If you get a fever, remember that it could be malaria and head straight for Puerto Princesa. The doctors there know more about malaria and how to treat it than doctors in Manila. On a more positive note, you won't see a mosquito during the dry season in large parts of Palawan. This is also when most people visit. Mosquitoes are usually only a problem in the rainy season, especially in the south.

Unfortunately, many Palawan beaches are also a popular home for 'nik-niks', tiny sandflies which often take pleasure in stinging lightly clad sun worshippers. An effective way of warding off these annoying little insects is to rub on coconut oil combined with a dash of insect repellent, such as Autan or Off. See also the Health chapter at the back of this book.

GETTING THERE & AWAY

You can get to Palawan from Cebu, Luzon and Panay. See Getting There & Away in the Luzon section of the Manila chapter and the relevant Getting There & Away section of the Visayas chapter.

Air

Cebu PAL flies on Thursday and Saturday from Puerto Princesa to Cebu City via Iloilo City on Panay.

Luzon Air Philippines and PAL have daily flights from Puerto Princesa to Manila; Grand Air flies daily except Sunday.

From Busuanga to Manila, Air Ads and Pacific Airways fly daily.

Soriano Aviation has daily flights from El Nido to Manila.

Pacific Airways has flights from Cuyo to Manila on Monday, Wednesday and Friday.

Panay PAL has flights on Thursday and Saturday from Puerto Princesa to Iloilo City.

Boat

Luzon From Puerto Princesa to Manila, Sulpicio Lines' MV *Iloilo Princess* leaves Tuesday and Friday at 8 pm (24 hours). WG & A's MV *Superferry 3* leaves Thursday at 2 pm (P455; 23 hours).

The Viva Shipping Lines has three ships going from Coron to Batangas (18 hours). The MV *Viva Peñafrancia IX* leaves on Monday at noon. The MV *Maria Socorro* leaves on Wednesday at noon, and the MV *Viva Santa Ana* leaves on Friday at noon. These ships all originate in Culion, leaving on their respective days at 6 am.

The Asuncion Shipping Lines has three ships going from Coron to Manila (22 to 26 hours). The MV *Asuncion XI* leaves on Wednesday at 4 pm. The MV *Catalyn A* leaves Culion on Saturday at 4 pm, and the MV *Asuncion X* leaves on Sunday at 4 pm.

The Asuncion Shipping Lines' MV *Asuncion IV* leaves El Nido on Thursday at 3 pm for Manila (28 hours), but not necessarily on a regular basis.

Panay The Milagrosa Shipping Lines' MV *Milagrosa-J-Dos* leaves Puerto Princesa for Iloilo City, via Cuyo, on the 1st, 11th and 21st of the month at noon. It takes 38 hours, including an eight hour stopover in Cuyo. Departure from Cuyo is on the 2nd, 12th and 22nd of the month at 6 am. The MV *Milagrosa-J-Tres* sails on the 7th, 17th and 27th of the month, leaving Puerto Princesa at 4 pm.

GETTING AROUND

Touring is a little bit difficult in Palawan. The roads between the villages are only good in parts but road works are progressing. There is only one 'highway', which is partly surfaced, leading from Brooke's Point via Puerto Princesa, Roxas and Taytay to El Nido. If you want to travel on side roads, you either need lots of time or lots of money. Jeepney drivers and boat operators always try to make you pay for a Special Ride. If you agree because you can't wait, you will certainly be paying for all the other passengers, so everybody will get in and enjoy the free ride.

It's difficult, and sometimes impossible, to travel by road in the rainy season as some of the routes become impassable after a few days' rain. If, as a result, you can only reach your destination by boat, you will probably have to pay through the nose to get anywhere.

Travel to North Palawan has been made considerably easier with the introduction of a boat service between Coron and Taytay a few years ago. With the addition of regular flights between Manila-Busuanga and Manila-El Nido, round trips are now possible without hassle, in an area where up until recently almost every trip ended up in a dead end.

Boat Tours

More and more visitors are discovering the pleasures of extended boat trips to Palawan's more interesting places and islands. So it is not surprising to find out that more and more large boats are being built.

A 10 day tour could look something like this: Puerto Princesa – Coco-Loco Island – Flowers Island – Elephant Island – El Nido – Port Barton – Underground River. This would cost around P1200 per day per person, with full board.

Mark Bratschi from Switzerland offers such trips from December until June with his MB *Moonshadow*. The boat is 20m long and has five cabins for eight to 10 passengers. He can be contacted at the Trattoria Inn and the Sonne Gasthaus in Puerto Princesa.

The Cruise & Hotel Center (☎ 815 4525), Shangri-La Hotel, Ayala Ave, Makati, offers four and seven day trips on the catamaran MV *Lagoon Explorer*. This extremely well-equipped ship (10 air-con cabins for 36 passengers in all) sails from Coron to El Nido and back, with frequent stops at anchor. Flights can be booked at the same time for Manila-El Nido and Manila-Busuanga (and vice versa). A four day trip in a double cabin, including return flight and full board, costs US$640 per person.

PALAWAN

Central Palawan

PUERTO PRINCESA

Puerto Princesa is a relatively new city with about 120,000 inhabitants. Although more houses are being built, you can still find beautiful buildings in the traditional style. The main buildings are the cathedral and the Provincial Capitol. At the waterfront there are fishers' huts built right over the water.

It is the second biggest city in the Philippines after Davao, in terms of area. Even Sabang and the St Paul Subterranean National Park, 50 km north of the city centre, belong administratively to the city.

The city is remarkable for its cleanliness, something the mayor Edwin Hagedorn is deservedly praised for. He managed to enthuse the locals with the idea of keeping their city clean. Refuse disposal and street cleaning both function immaculately, and many tricycles even have an ashtray in them (throwing away cigarette butts on the streets incurs a fine of 200 P!). The latest distinctions garnered by Puerto Princesa are the 1993 Earth Day Award and the 1994 Macliing Dulag Environment Award.

Information

Tourist Offices There is a City tourist office (☎ 433 2983) at the airport which specialises mainly in information on Puerto Princesa and transport connections from there.

The Provincial Tourist Office in the Provincial Capitol building, on the corner of Rizal Ave and Fernandez St, has information on the whole province of Palawan.

Underground River Office The St Paul Subterranean River National Park Office on Manalo St issues permits for the Underground River for P150.

Money The Philippine National Bank changes travellers cheques, although only up to US$300 per day.

AS Money Changer on Rizal Ave, diagonally across from the Café Puerto, changes cash and American Express (Amex) travellers cheques. Philippine Airlines may also change travellers cheques.

Outside Puerto Princesa there are practically no money-changing facilities on Palawan. This is especially true in El Nido, where many travellers have had to leave early because of lack of available funds.

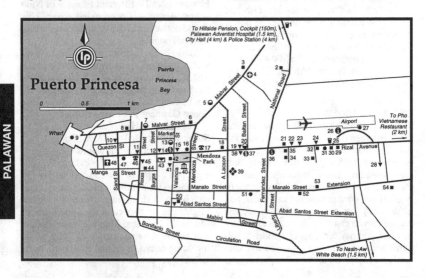

Telephone International telephone calls can be made at Piltel, Roxas Street, and RCPI, Rizal Ave.

The area code for Puerto Princesa is 048.

Travel Agencies The travel agencies Go Palawan (☎ 433 4570; fax 433 4580), Finest Travel and Princesa Tours, all on Rizal Ave, offer various day trips, such as island hopping in Honday Bay (P650) and trips to the Underground River (P1100). Go Palawan will also take care of flight confirmations and visa extensions.

Bookshops The Backpackers Café & Bookshop, Valencia Street, has a variety of books in eight languages, mainly English and German.

Bookshops may have the monthly bulletin *Bandillo ng Palawan*, written and published by local environmentalists, with interesting articles about ecotourism and conservation on Palawan. It costs P5 and is also available at the Ka Lui Restaurant and the Culture Shack, both on Rizal Ave.

Library The Palawan Museum at Mendoza Park houses a library which has books on Philippine and Palawan history, anthropology, ethnology, flora and fauna.

Medical Services The treatment, nursing care and medication are apparently much better at the Palawan Adventist Hospital than at the Provincial Hospital.

Palawan Museum
The Palawan Museum at Mendoza Park provides a good overview of the history, art and culture of Palawan. It is open Monday, Tuesday, Thursday and Friday from 9 am until noon and 2 to 5 pm.

PLACES TO STAY		
2	Asiaworld Resort Hotel Palawan	
3	Emerald Hotel	
6	Princesa Inn	
8	Puerto Pension	
18	Garcellano Tourist Inn, Zum Kleinen Anker & PCI Bank	
21	Trattoria Inn, Swiss Bistro & Go Palawan	
29	Airport View Inn	
30	Airport Hotel	
32	Palawan Hotel	
33	Ves Mansion	
34	Casa Linda	
35	Badjao Inn, Kubo Restaurant & Gold Mine Spirits	
42	Circon Lodge & Bang-Bang Disco	
44	Abelardo's Pension	
50	Duchess Pension House	
52	Paykyo Pension	
53	Swissippini International Guest House	
54	Sonne Gasthaus	

PLACES TO EAT		
10	Ignacio Restaurant	
11	Pink Lace Restaurant	
12	Roadside Pizza Inn & Folkhouse	
15	Edwin's Food Palace, Disco & Metrobank	
19	Café Puerto	
22	King's Court Restaurant & WG & A	
23	Ka Lui Restaurant & Island Divers	
24	Crystal Forest Grill Park, Disco & Coco-Loco Office	
28	Café Kamarikutan	
38	Kamayan Folkhouse & Restaurant	
41	Ph Vietnames Restaurant & Swissfood & Wines	
45	Lola Itang Restaurant	
49	Backpackers Café & Bookshop	

OTHER		
1	Nightclubs	
4	Provincial Hospital	
5	Jeepney Terminal	
7	Charing Bus Lines & Puerto Royale Bus Lines	
9	Milagrosa Shipping Lines	
13	Jeepneys to Iwahig	
14	Philippine National Bank (PNB)	
16	PTT Office	
17	RPCI (Long Distance Calls)	
20	Princess Transport Bus Stop	
25	Waltzing Matilda	
26	City Tourist Office, Caparii Dive Camp Office, Pacific Airways & Palawan Treasures & Gift Shop	
27	PAL	
31	Air Philippines & Princesa Tours	
36	Tourist Office & Provincial Capitol Building	
37	AS Money Changer & Culture Shack	
39	NCCC	
40	Museum	
43	Post Office	
46	Piltel (Long Distance Calls)	
47	Sulpicio Lines	
48	Cathedral	
51	St Paul Subterranean River National Park Office	

PALAWAN

Puerta Princesa Bay

The scene on the wharf at sunset is good fun. Puerto Princesa Bay also has some interesting places for diving. For about P300 you can hire an outrigger boat for a few hours and sail, swim, dive and fish in the bay. For trips on the MY *Lorca* see Places to Eat later in this section.

Nasin-Aw White Beach

On the eastern edge of town, Nasin-Aw White beach (admission P5) has surprisingly good snorkelling. Watch out for sea urchins when you're swimming. It's best to wear shoes for protection. You can get to the beach by tricycle.

Diving

Palawan is becoming more and more popular with underwater enthusiasts.

The Queen Ann Divers diving shop has a 23m-long outrigger diving boat with 10 complete sets of diving equipment. It offers diving instruction as well as one day or more diving trips with two dives daily for US$50 per day per person, including equipment. Also available are five day diving trips to the Tubbataha Reef in April, May and June for US$560. For bookings, contact Martin Gugi and Urs Rechsteiner, c/o Trattoria Inn, 353 Rizal Ave, 5300 Puerto Princesa.

The Palawan Diving Corporation offers one way or more diving trips on its 20m-long diving boat ML *Vicky*. It can handle one day trips or more, and up to three weeks on demand. The boat has three four bed cabins, shower and toilet. There is diving equipment for 15 people on board. The price of US$60 per day per person includes two dives daily (night diving is possible), equipment and full board. From July until October, the price is reduced to US$35. Contact Bernd Henke, c/o Zum Kleinen Anker, Rizal Ave, 5300 Puerto Princesa. The MB *Moonshadow* also has diving equipment on board (see Boat Tours in the Getting Around section earlier in this chapter).

For information about good diving places, you could also ask Norman Songco of Island Divers at 371 Rizal Ave. This diving shop

runs organised trips. Hiring a complete outfit costs P750 a day, and you can get goggles and a snorkel for P125 a day. Diving tours for two or more divers cost P1500 per person per day, including transport, two tanks, belt, backpack, two dives a day and a meal. You can do a one week diving course for P7500.

Special Events

Every year there is a week long festival which starts on 7 December. It includes concerts in Mendoza Park, Caracol boat processions, a beauty contest, quizzes, competitions and so on.

Places to Stay – bottom end

The unpretentious *Duchess Pension House* (☎ 433 2873) on Valencia St has good singles/doubles with fan for P100/150, and doubles with fan and bath for P250. The owners, Joe and Cecille, are friendly and the atmosphere is pleasant. They have a garden restaurant where they serve breakfast and snacks.

The *Princesa Inn* (☎ 433 2618), 169 Malvar Street, is near the market, with fan-cooled singles/doubles for P135/P150, with fan and bath for P250/P400, and with air-con and bath for P600 (with TV). It has good rooms with fan in the back building, while the air-con rooms at the front are a bit small.

The owners of *Abelardo's Pensionne* (☎ 433 2049) at 63 Manga St are very helpful and can give lots of tips on Palawan. Fairly good rooms with fan cost P150/200, doubles with fan and bath P300, and air-con and bath P450. The rooms are down to earth but more than acceptable.

As the name suggests, the *Airport View Inn* is across the road from the airport on Rizal Ave. Rooms with fan and bath go for P150/P200, with air-con and bath for P300. Though small, they have a veranda and are in a bamboo building in a quiet garden behind the main building.

The friendly, family atmosphere is what makes the *Swissippini International Guest House* (☎ 433 2540) at 263 Manalo St Extension. It charges P150 for singles/doubles with fan, and P180 for doubles with fan and bath (there is one bath for two rooms).

On the same street at No 366, the *Sonne Gasthaus* (☎ 433 4638) is a quiet place to stay. It is good value, charging P170/200 for basic, clean rooms with fan, and P300 for cottages with fan and bath.

At 35 Malvar St, you can't miss the *Puerto Pension* (☎ 433 2969). Its rooms with fan go for P175/225 (there is one bath for every two rooms). Doubles with fan and bath cost P275, and with air-con and bath P490. The building was thoughtfully designed using natural materials and has a roof deck drinking lounge with a view over Puerto Princesa Bay.

The friendly *Trattoria Inn* (☎ 433 2719; fax 433 4580) at 353 Rizal Ave is a place where people like to get together. Decent rooms with fan go for P190/290, and with TV, air-con and bath for P550/650. It has a garden.

Places to Stay – middle
Set back about 100m from Rizal Ave behind the Palawan Hotel, the *Ves Mansion* (☎ 433 2461) offers rooms with fan for P250/300, with air-con and bath for P450/500. You could check at the Gold Mine Shop next to the Badjao Inn to see if there are any vacant rooms.

The only peaceful rooms at the *Badjao Inn* (☎ 433 2380; fax 433 2180), 350 Rizal Ave, are those facing the back yard. Try to avoid the rooms on Rizal Ave, as they are too loud. Singles/doubles with fan and bath cost P180/260, singles with air-con and bath for P450 and P595, and doubles with air-con and bath for P510 and P660. The air-con rooms are neat and comfortable; the more expensive ones are tastefully furnished and have a fridge and TV. There is a nice big garden with a restaurant.

Highly recommended, the service at *Casa Linda* (☎ 433 2606) on Trinidad Rd is attentive and friendly. Expect clean, spacious rooms with fan and bath for P300/350, and with air-con and bath for P450/500. This is a pleasant place with a beautiful garden. All in all, a well-run establishment in a quiet area about 80m off Rizal Ave.

Near the airport on Rizal Ave, the *Palawan Hotel* (☎ 433 2326; fax 433 4961) is a comfortable place with a pleasant atmosphere. It has adequate rooms with air-con and bath for P460/540.

Places to Stay – top end
The *Airport Hotel* (☎ 433 2177) at 442 Rizal Ave will give you a cosy room with air-con and bath for P650/750, and comfortable suites with fridge and TV for P1400 and P1600. There is a coffee shop and a small swimming pool. It is, of course, handy to the airport.

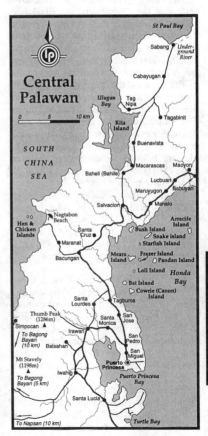

PALAWAN

Admittedly a bit expensive, the *Asiaworld Resort Hotel Palawan* (☎ 433 2111) on National Rd is the biggest and best hotel in town. Well-kept rooms with air-con and bath cost from P2750/2900. Suites are from P6500 to P19,500. It has a swimming pool, sauna and disco.

Places to Eat

There are lots of restaurants on the side streets, but Rizal Ave alone offers a bewildering assortment of places to eat, reflecting the cosmopolitan range of tourists in Puerto Princesa and Palawan.

You can enjoy a good meal in an attractive setting at the *Café Puerto* on Rizal Ave, where the English chef Andrew prepares excellent French dishes. It is open from 11.30 am to 2 pm and 5.30 pm to midnight. Italian food is available at the *Roadside Pizza Inn & Folkhouse*, also on Rizal Ave.

The cuisine at the friendly *Pink Lace Restaurant* includes Filipino, Chinese, Indian, Mexican and Vietnamese dishes and cakes. The Filipino dishes at the *Kamayan Folkhouse & Restaurant* are good, and you can eat on the terrace or in the tree house. The pleasant Filipino restaurant *Lola Itang* on Roxas St prides itself in preparing food the traditional way.

The unassuming *Ignacio Restaurant* on Quezon St also serves good-value Filipino dishes. The *NCCC Fastfood Restaurant* on the ground floor in the shopping mall of the same name on A Lacson St is always busy. It offers a wide choice of Filipino dishes and is self-service.

At the rustic cellar bar *Zum Kleinen Anker*, Achim and Honey serve Filipino and German meals and cold beer from 8 am to 10 pm. The friendly little *Backpackers Café & Bookshop* next to the Duchess Pension House on Valencia St offers a constantly changing daily menu for P75, as well as inexpensive vegetarian, Thai and western dishes.

Well worth a mention is the food at the popular *Swiss Bistro* in the garden of the Trattoria Inn, Rizal Ave. It serves steaks, pasta dishes, pizzas and grill specialities.

Just across the street, the *Kubo Restaurant* in the green backyard of the Badjao Inn, Rizal Ave, offers excellent sashimi for P40.

About 100m further in the direction of the airport, right next door to Island Divers, you will find the charmingly rustic *Ka Lui Restaurant*. In addition to having a refreshingly original look about it, there is an area in the restaurant where guests can simply read and relax. It is open daily, except Sunday, from 11 am to 2 pm and 5.30 to 11 pm. Instead of a menu, it has a meal of the day, always seafood served with vegetables and rice. The type of seafood depends on the catch.

Café Kamarikutan's architecture has that special something. Made entirely of bamboo, this big, decorative building has an airy feel to it and radiates a relaxed, almost meditative atmosphere. It is set back from the street, in a garden with lots of plants, and is a little out of town behind the airport on Rizal Ave Extension. On the menu you'll find a few vegetarian dishes, five different breakfasts and ten types of freshly brewed coffee, as well as expresso and cappuccino.

Two km further out of town, near the entrance to the former Vietnamese Refugee Camp, the popular *Pho Vietnamese Restaurant* is the place for good, albeit not cheap, Vietnamese food. There is a sister restaurant of this popular establishment, which can be found in Valencia St.

If you want a change from eating out in restaurants, try the buffet on the MY *Lorca* on its cruise around Puerto Princesa Bay. It has a Sunrise Breakfast Cruise from 6 until 9 am for P350, and a Sunset Dinner Cruise from 5 until 9 pm for P500. It charges extra for drinks and special orders. Reservations can be made at the Go Palawan travel agency at the Trattoria Inn on Rizal Ave.

Entertainment

Edwin's Food Palace & Disco shows films all day on a large screen. At around 9 pm this spacious Chinese restaurant is transformed into a disco where the guests can enjoy a mixture of music until midnight, ranging from sweet music to techno. The popular

Bang-Bang Disco across the street is open three hours longer and has live music.

One of the most popular dance clubs is the *Obsession Disco* in the Asiaworld Resort Hotel Palawan, while the *Kamayan Folkhouse & Restaurant* has male and female folk singers. In the evening, the *Swiss Bistro* has what must be the best recorded music in town.

There are several rustic nightclubs on the northern edge of town.

Things to Buy
Typical Palawan artwork is available from the Culture Shack on Rizal Ave. Also on sale is the tape *Palawan: At Peace with Nature*, which makes an excellent souvenir. It is 'A Musical Journey to the Last Frontier' by Sinika, a group using mostly native instruments. You can also buy souvenirs at the Palawan Treasures & Gift Shop next to the City tourist office at the airport.

Getting There & Away
Air PAL has an office at Puerto Princesa airport (☎ 433 4565). If you are flying back to Manila, Iloilo City and Cebu City, you should reconfirm your flight in advance as soon as possible, as flights are often hopelessly booked out.

At the airport compound, Pacific Airways (☎ 433 4872) has a six seater Cessna for charter at P7000 an hour; however, the organisation is not exactly reliable. A prebooked aircraft may be chartered to someone else at short notice, or a reserved seat given to another passenger. Air fares per passenger for (irregular) flights from Puerto Princesa to El Nido are P1500; Coron/Busuanga P2050; and Cuyo P2050.

Boat The following Shipping Companies have booking offices in Puerto Princesa:

Milagrosa Shipping Lines, at the entrance to the Port Area (☎ 433 4860)
Sulpicio Lines, Rizal Ave, near the cathedral (☎ 433 2641)
WG & A, Rizal Ave, next to the Trattoria Inn (☎ 433 4875)

Getting Around
The Airport The airport is on the eastern edge of town, about three km from the town centre. A tricycle trip into town costs P5 per person, or P15 to P20 if it's not shared.

Tricycle A trip in town by tricycle costs P2 per person. Chartering a tricycle should not cost more than P80 an hour.

The normal price by tricycle from the wharf to a hotel in the town centre should be P4 but P10 is often charged.

Motorcycle The travel agency Go Palawan on Rizal Ave, next to the Trattoria Inn, can arrange the hire of motorcycles for off-road riding from P600 to P800 per day. Don't forget you have to wear a helmet in Puerto Princesa.

Bicycle Backpackers Café & Bookshop, on Valencia Street, rents out mountain bikes for P50 an hour or P100 per day, depending on the condition.

AROUND PUERTO PRINCESA
Irawan
Irawan, halfway between Puerto Princesa and Iwahig, is the location of the **Irawan Crocodile Farming Institute**, which was founded in 1987. The goal of this project, financed by Japanese money, is to protect threatened species of the Philippines crocodile from extinction. On paper, this is of course a commendable idea. We can only hope that the project does not eventually fall victim to its original objective of making money for its backers. However, up till now

The local name of the Philippines crocodile is *buwaya*, which also means greedy.

it's still true to say that a visit to the 10 hectare farm will give you a good idea of what crocodiles are all about. Some of the reptiles here are up to five metres long. It also has examples of young animals belonging to different species of crocodile, as well as some impressive skeletons. Numerous notice boards provide information on the biology and habits of the various crocodiles in the collection. Apart from the crocodile pens and open compounds, the farm also has a small zoo which includes animals that can only be found on Palawan. It is open Monday to Friday and public holidays from 1 to 4 pm, Saturday from 8 am to 5 pm. Guided tours are available hourly. The farm is closed on Sunday. Admission is free.

Getting There & Away Buses and jeepneys to South Palawan go via Irawan (P5). A tricycle from Puerto Princesa to Irawan costs around P50.

Balsahan
There is a resort by the river in Balsahan which local Filipinos like to visit on short holidays to relax and celebrate family occasions.

Getting There & Away There is no direct connection between Puerto Princesa and Balsahan. At about 9.30 am a jeepney leaves Valencia St, near the market, for Iwahig. For a couple of extra pesos the driver may make the detour from the highway to Balsahan and pick you up again at about 1.30 pm.

Iwahig
The **Iwahig Penal Colony** is 23 km south of Puerto Princesa. Prisoners live here as in a normal village; there are no walls. They fish, cultivate rice and so on. The warders and administrators have a good time here and are never short of workers. Tourists are welcome as the souvenir shop sells handcrafts made by the prisoners. The prison colony also works as an advertisement for the government's modern and liberal penal policy. At the moment about 1700 prisoners, called colonists, live there. Many of them have their families with them. This penal colony is

self-supporting and needs no financial assistance from the state. The rate of recidivism of former prisoners is said to be markedly lower than in traditional prisons.

Getting There & Away A jeepney leaves Puerto Princesa for the Iwahig Penal Colony at 9.30 am from Valencia St, near the market, and returns at 1.30 pm. If you want to return later, you can walk to the highway and wait for a bus or jeepney coming from the south.

You can get a tricycle for the half-day trip to the Iwahig Penal Colony, the Balsahan Resort and the crocodile farm. You should pay no more than about P250 to P300 for the round trip.

Santa Lucia
Santa Lucia is a subcolony of Iwahig. There is a **hot spring**, but you'll have to walk the seven km there and back. It's a favourite for weekend outings, although, to be honest, it is by no means a 'must see'. The pool is cleaned out on Monday.

Several boats leave Puerto Princesa harbour daily for Santa Lucia (depending on demand).

Turtle Bay
Seven km directly south of Puerto Princesa, roughly on a line with Santa Lucia, Albin the German and his Filipina wife Mercedes run a small resort. It is near the shallow end of the isolated Turtle Bay, which is fairly hard to get to by land.

Places to Stay & Eat The *Turtle Bay Beach Resort* in Barangay Mangingisda has singles/doubles from P190 to P300, with bath for P310/370, and cottages with bath for P490. The resort, with its agreeably rustic setting, is a good place for people who want to get away from it all for a few days. You can get more information from staff at the Trattoria Inn in Puerto Princesa.

Getting There & Away Several jeepneys make the journey between Puerto Princesa and Mangingisda daily, leaving from the corner of Burgos and Malvar Sts (P15; one hour). The last one leaves at 6 pm.

Napsan

Around 70 km south-west of Puerto Princesa at **Labtay**, near Napsan on the South China Sea, there is a beautiful long beach (unfortunately spoiled in places by the sandflies) where you can find small, family-style accommodation. The somewhat adventure-packed journey there involves travelling right across Palawan, including climbing mountains covered in thick jungle on the second half of the journey.

Places to Stay & Eat The *Kiao Sea Lodge* has cottages with bath for P300. It is clean and comfortable, with a restaurant and a paddle boat. The place is run by the Frenchman Patrick and his Filipina wife Mary. It is only open in the dry season from November to May.

Getting There & Away Two or three jeepneys leave Puerto Princesa for Labtay/Napsan between 7 and 9 am from the jeepney terminal (P35; 3½ hours). From Labtay to Puerto Princesa the jeepneys leave between 10 am and 1 pm.

HONDA BAY

The islands in Honda Bay make a good day trip from Puerto Princesa. You can also stay there overnight. **Pandan Island**, populated by large numbers of fishermen, is one of the best-known islands in Honda Bay but hardly anyone ever visits it. There is a Coast Guard base on the island. An almost intact **coral reef** exists between Pandan and Cowrie (Canon) islands. Because of the strict control of fishing, snorkelling and diving are better in Honda Bay than in many of the areas around Palawan. **Snake Island** is sandy and has a shallow coral reef on the landward side which is ideal for snorkelling. Anyone wanting to camp for a few days on this island, where there is no shade, has to take drinking water and food.

A bit south-west of Snake Island is the small **Starfish Island**, the location of the Starfish Sandbar Resort; admission is P20. It's definitely no Fantasy Island, but a flat, treeless sandbar with a few simple huts. It also sports a modest, rustic restaurant (where the fish is excellent) and loungers for guests. You can hire a boat, snorkel and goggles if you want. There is a small coral reef at the end of the island where you can go snorkelling. In the late afternoon swarms of bats fly from Bat Island (where else?) to the mainland.

Places to Stay & Eat

The *Starfish Sandbar Resort* on Starfish Island has cottages with bath for between P500 and P800. These are simple huts with room for four people. This is by no means an idyllic resort.

Meara Marina Island Resort (☎ 433 2575) on Meara Island is under Austrian management, and has doubles for P500 and cottages with bath for P730. You can go water skiing, windsurfing and diving (courses for beginners and diving equipment are available), and it has ultralight flights at P800 for 15 minutes. For bookings write to Franz and Jane Urbanek, PO Box 04, 5300 Puerto Princesa.

Getting There & Away

You can go from Puerto Princesa to Santa Lourdes Pier (on the highway, north of Tagburos) by any jeepney (P10) or bus going north. They leave from the jeepney terminal or from the market. Get off at the big Caltex tank and walk towards the waterfront, where you can hire a boat. Prices range from P300 to P600, depending on the number and distance of the islands you want to visit. Jollibee Boat Hire has spotless outrigger boats with plenty of protection from the sun and cold drinks on board.

A tricycle from Puerto Princesa market to Santa Lourdes Pier costs about P50.

NAGTABON BEACH

White Nagtabon Beach lies on a beautiful calm bay on Palawan's west coast looking out on **Hen & Chicken Islands**. Unfortunately, there is a fly in the ointment, literally: sandflies just love it there.

PALAWAN

Places to Stay & Eat

The amiable *Pablico's Beach Resort* has a pleasant atmosphere. It charges P200 to P250 for cottages with bath. You can enjoy marvellous food for P80 per meal in its excellent restaurant. Reservations and pickup can be arranged in Puerto Princesa with Mrs Pablico (☎ 433 2267), 48-A Burgos St.

Georg and Lucy Bauer, a German-Filipino couple, run *Georg's Place*, which has singles for P150 and cottages with fan and bath for P400. The accommodation is adequate for the money. They also have a good restaurant. Their postal address is PO Box 67, 5300 Puerto Princesa. Reservations and pick-up can be arranged in Puerto Princesa (☎ 433 5773).

Getting There & Away

Two or three jeepneys are supposed to go from Puerto Princesa to Nagtabon Beach but this route is not always reliable. They leave between noon and 2 pm (one hour). Between 6 and 7 am, two or three jeepneys are supposed to make the journey between Nagtabon Beach and Puerto Princesa; however, it is possible that only one will actually turn up, and it may leave at 5 am! A Special Ride from Puerto Princesa to Nagtabon Beach costs around P800.

SABANG

The introduction of a regular jeepney service from Puerto Princesa brought an end to the role of the tiny community of Sabang as a kind of Sleeping Beauty. Sabang is near the **St Paul Subterranean National Park**, supported by the World Wild Fund for Nature (WWF). This beautiful piece of nature, with its thick covering of jungle, lies at the feet of the 1028m Mt St Paul. There is an amazing number of different varieties of tree; about 100 are marked around the Central Ranger Station and along the so-called 'Monkey Trail'. If you keep your eyes and ears open you will be aware of a rich and vocal community of birds, monkeys by the dozen and a few majestic 1.5 metre long monitor lizards. The imposing vertical grooves caused by erosion in the limestone cliffs are also well worth seeing. However, the main attraction of this well-run national park is, as the name would suggest, a subterranean one: the Underground River. The **Ren-Pat Cave** is another relatively unknown cave with impressive dripstone deposits. It was only discovered recently. This can be reached from Sabang by outrigger boat, provided the sea is calm.

If you head out from Sabang by foot along the beach in a westerly direction, after an hour you will come to a gorgeous waterfall, arching into the sea from a height of about 10m. You would be well advised to wear sturdy shoes as the beach is quite stony around this side.

Another fascinating trip from Sabang is by boat up the Puyoy-Puyoy River.

Places to Stay

If you arrive at the beach by jeepney, the modest little *Robert's Beach Cottages* is the first place to stay you'll see. It has cottages for P175, and cottages with bath for P200 and P250. The older cottages are a bit more basic than the newer, and better, ones. The restaurant is relatively expensive and the portions small.

A few metres further you'll come to the *Coco Slab*. Its cottages are of various sizes (some of them A-frame), all with bath, and cost P250 and P300.

Right next door, the *Villa Sabang* is basic, but OK for the money. Dorm beds go for P90, and cottages with bath for P160 and P190. The set-up belongs to an Italian, but is actually run by a group of friendly Filipinos.

On a small bay at the eastern end of Sabang Beach, just at the entrance to the National Park, *Mary's Beach Resort* has some small cottages with bath for P150 and a bigger one with bath for P250. This is easily the best place in Sabang, with immaculate cottages of various sizes. The most expensive ones form a row facing the beach. The beach itself is graced by a big, impressive tree which has hammocks slung in the shade of its extensive network of gnarled branches.

The *Bambua Jungle Cottages* has tastefully furnished cottages with bath for between P250 and P400. It has a generous amount of space

PALAWAN

separating them, and the view from its excellent restaurant is beautiful. The place is about 20 minutes on foot uphill from Sabang, in a dream setting at the foot of a mountain with jungle all around.

You can spend the night next to the *Central Ranger Station* in your own tent for P40 or hire one for P50. A dorm bed in a simple but clean room will cost you P75. You will have to take food and supplies with you.

About 1½ km north-east of the mouth of the Underground River is the pleasant little *Panaguman Resort*. Rooms cost P200 while cottages with bath cost P300. To get there catch a resort boat which leaves daily at 1 pm from Sabang Pier, or walk to the Central Ranger Station and have them order a boat to pick you up.

Places to Eat

The *Gonzales Seafoods Restaurant* is the place for good food at the right price. The Philippine food in the *Coco Grove Canteen* is also well worth the money. The *Villa Sabang Restaurant* offers a good choice of pasta and pizzas at reasonable prices.

A few metres west of Sabang Pier, *Silayan Restaurant* offers excellent food and views.

Getting There & Away

Jeepney Jeepneys from Puerto Princesa to Sabang via Baheli, Macarascas and Cabayugan leave at 8, 8.30, 9 am and 3 pm (P65; 3½ to as much as six hours). Tourists are expected to pay a few pesos more as a 'luggage fee'. It's a dusty ride! Departure from Sabang to Puerto Princesa is between 6.30 and 8.30 am, at 12.30 and possibly 2 pm. This route may not be available during the rainy season.

Boat Special Rides are the way to get from Sabang to Port Barton (P1200 to P1500; four hours) and El Nido (P4000 to P4500; seven hours). Be prepared to get wet, and definitely insist on your luggage being well-covered up.

Walking You can get to Sabang from San Rafael in a two to three day walk right across Palawan. Guides are available at Duchess Beachside Cottages in San Rafael.

UNDERGROUND RIVER

The Underground River, or its proper name, St Paul Cave, is Palawan's most fascinating network of caves. Carved by an underground

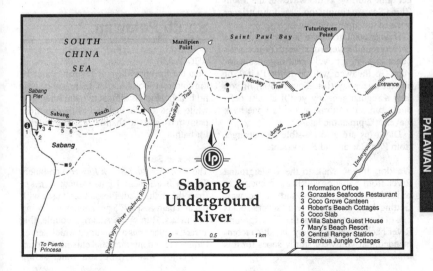

Sabang & Underground River

1	Information Office
2	Gonzales Seafoods Restaurant
3	Coco Grove Canteen
4	Robert's Beach Cottages
5	Coco Slab
6	Villa Sabang Guest House
7	Mary's Beach Resort
8	Central Ranger Station
9	Bambua Jungle Cottages

PALAWAN

river, the cave meanders for over eight km. Nature has provided it with a bewildering variety of enormous stalactites, fragile-looking columns, smooth-walled pipes, jagged caverns and big, impressive chambers. The entrance to the Underground River is set in a picturesque lagoon on the west coast of Central Palawan. You could almost overlook this deeply fissured, yawning opening in the grey limestone face. You can enter the dark maw of the cave in a *banca* (small boat). The light of the lamps reveals countless bats in the cave. You would need a pretty powerful flash to take photographs here.

Getting There & Away

Boat The easiest and best way to make a short trip to the Underground River is from Sabang. This takes about 20 minutes and costs P300 there and back (for the boat, irrespective of how many passengers).

From Baheli, on the other hand, the journey to the cave entrance takes about three hours and costs approximately P1200. It is worth noting that the trip from there is not possible during the south-west monsoon season from June to November, which can get quite stormy, as the waves of the South China Sea are simply too large for outrigger boats at this time.

If you want to make a day trip to the Underground River from Puerto Princesa it's better to have a travel agent organise it for you; Go Palawan will do it for P1100, or charter a jeepney (for about P2500). If you take a regular jeepney you'll almost definitely run out of time, as the last one back leaves at 2 pm at the latest.

Day trips are also possible by outrigger from Port Barton and San Vicente.

Walking If you walk to the Underground River from Sabang, you'll get a chance to walk through the jungle part of the way. Getting back is no problem: several boats make the journey from the Underground River back to Sabang every day. It's recommended that you wear sturdy shoes for this trip.

Leaving Sabang by foot, head along the long, palm-lined white sand beach to the right in an easterly direction. After about two km, or one hour through the jungle and over a little mountain, you will come to the park's Central Ranger Station. It's about another two km, or just over an hour on foot from the ranger station to the cave entrance. You can either take the so-called 'Monkey Trail', which has been laid out as naturally as possible and has steep, wooden steps in places, or the Jungle Trail, which is a bit longer and has some fairly overgrown stretches.

The permit for the journey into the Underground River should be obtained at the St Paul Subterranean River National Park office; however, in exceptional circumstances it is most likely possible to get one at the information office in Sabang before leaving, or even at the entrance to the Underground River. Admission costs P150, including the river trip with a paddle boat. This takes 45 minutes and ends up in the 60m-high 'Cathedral'. The trips are usually between 8 am and noon and 1 to 4 pm. The boatmen sometimes pack up for the day in the early afternoon, so it's safer to get there before 1 pm.

South Palawan

ABORLAN

Near the fishing village of Tigman, about 10 km south-west of Aborlan, there is a beautiful beach which is almost two km long. The white sand beach is lined with countless palm trees, and the shallow water is suitable for bathing.

Places to Stay

The *Villa Christina Beach Resort* is on lonely Tigman Beach near Tigman, about five km from the main road. Pleasant cottages with fan and bath cost P775 per person, including two meals. Run by an Austrian couple, this attractive place has a restaurant which serves Philippine and international cuisine. You can also enjoy windsurfing and water skiing here. If you want to go to the village of Tigman itself it's 1.5 km away, along the beach and over a footbridge.

Near the beach, about 300m from the village of Tigman, the *Camille Del Sol* (☎ 422 2562) is run by an American-Philippine couple. They'll let you a nice cottage with fan and bath for P350, P500 or P500, depending on size. The restaurant here is excellent.

Getting There & Away
Take a jeepney or a bus from Puerto Princesa in the direction of Narra, get off at the

Tigman turn-off in Plaridel, a little south of Aborlan (P25; 1½ hours). It'll cost you P50 to take a tricycle to the beach from there.

NARRA
Narra makes a good stop on the way to South Palawan. The **Estrella Waterfalls** are six km north at the foot of Victoria Peak; admission P5. You can get there by taking a tricycle from Narra market to Estrella village.

Places to Stay
The rooms at the basic *Tiosin Lodging House* on Panacan Rd are fan-cooled and cost

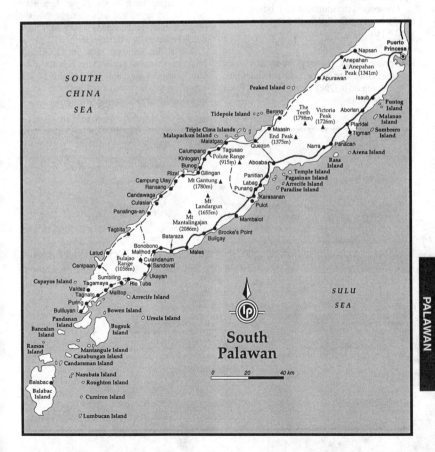

South
Palawan

0   20   40 km

PALAWAN

P60/120. Its restaurant serves good, well-priced meals.

Also on Panacan Rd, the *Gardeña Boarding House* offers fairly clean rooms with fan for P80/160. The *Victoria Peak Inn* on National Highway will give you a room with fan which is good value at P75/150.

Getting There & Away

Bus Princess Transport air-con buses leave at 7.30 am and 1 pm from the corner of Rizal Ave and Baltan St (two hours). Buses at 8 am and 1.30 pm heading for Brooke's Point also go via Narra.

Princess Transport air-con buses leave Narra heading for Puerto Princesa at 8.30 am and 4 pm.

Jeepney Many jeepneys run daily from Puerto Princesa to Narra, as do several buses, some going on to Quezon and Brooke's Point (P35; two hours).

QUEZON

Quezon is a small fishing village on Malanut Bay. It is the departure point for the **Tabon Caves**, whose main entrance is on the northwest side of Lipuun Point. By boat the trip to the caves takes only 30 minutes and should not cost more than P250.

This huge complex contains 200 caves. Only 29 have been explored and only seven are open to the public. Tabon Cave is the biggest and Diwata Cave, 30m above sea level, is the highest and most beautiful. Because of their prehistoric sites, the Tabon Caves are a kind of natural museum. Human bones dating back to the Stone Age have been found here, and it is thought that the original inhabitants, the Pala'wan, may have used the caves as a burial site.

Ask at the National Museum in Quezon for an experienced guide to the Tabon Caves. Don't expect too much from the caves, however, as all you can see are some large holes in the mountainside.

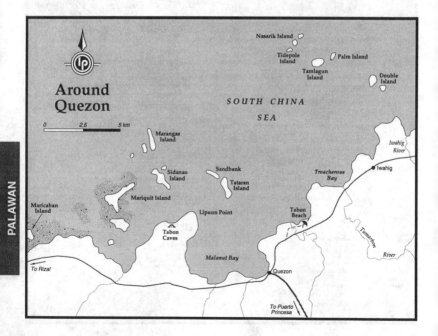

After you've gone cave exploring, you might be tempted to visit the nearby islands with their white beaches, for example, the islands of **Sidanao** or **Tataran**. Far offshore on **Tamlagun Island**, a German called Frederick lived a real-life Robinson Crusoe existence surrounded by all kinds of animals until his death in May 1994. A Philippine family now lives in his tropical Garden of Eden. It is doubtful whether the little huts Frederick built for guests will survive the next monsoon rains. A round trip from Quezon to Tamlagun Island costs P500.

A Belgian named Theo runs the Tabon Village Resort on Tabon Beach, four km north-east of Quezon. From here it's about an hour's walk to the **Tumarbon Waterfall**, or for P300 you can go by boat up the **Tumarbon River** through dense jungle. It takes 45 minutes to reach the mouth of the river and another 30 minutes to reach the waterfall.

The same Theo has also set up a four room cottage on the island of Malapackun, 20 km east of Quezon (see Places to Stay for details).

Places to Stay
The friendly *New Bayside Lodging House*, near the bus terminal and the wharf, has small rooms with fan for P100, and with fan and bath for P120. It is simple but clean, and on request staff will cook for guests. You can also obtain information about boats to the Tabon Caves, the offshore islands and other trips along the south-west coast of Palawan.

The *Villa Esperanza* is about 300m from the bus terminal towards Tabon Beach. It charges P80/160 for basic rooms with fan, and P350 for modest cottages with fan and bath, which seem to be a little bit overpriced, although the place is basically in good shape. It has a restaurant, though no alcoholic drinks are served.

The *Tabon Village Resort* on Tabon Beach, about four km north-east of Quezon, has simple rooms for P100/120 and cottages with bath for P250/350. This is a pleasant resort on a beautiful bay, but, unfortunately, the water at the beach is muddy and full of rocks which makes swimming impossible. A

tricycle from town to the resort costs P15 or P5 per person.

There is a four room cottage on Malapackun Island set up by Theo, who runs the Tabon Village Resort. He charges P150/200 per room. If you want to retreat there, take water and food with you. Fish is available from local fishermen, and the cottage has cooking facilities. The boat trip from Quezon takes 1½ hours and costs P400. You can get information at the Tabon Village Resort.

Places to Eat
The tastefully designed and furnished *Mutya ng Dagak* (Pearl of the Sea) is a bit expensive but has very good food. It is part of the Tabon Village Resort and is on an artificial island that is connected to the beach by a bridge.

Getting There & Away
Bus Buses belonging to the Charing Bus Lines depart daily, roughly hourly from 7 am until 3 pm, from Malvar St to Quezon (P60; four hours).

From Quezon to Puerto Princesa, the buses leave between 5 am and 3 pm.

Jeepney Several jeepneys leave early in the morning from both Quezon and Puerto Princesa.

BROOKE'S POINT
Halfway through the 19th century, British adventurer James Brooke had the imposing watchtower built here in the south of Palawan as a warning to the pirates of the Sulu Sea. A few years earlier pure wanderlust had driven the former officer of the East India Company to leave England for Borneo. At the head of a small private army, Brooke helped the Sultan of Brunei put down a local revolt. As a sign of his gratitude, the sultan made him Rajah of Sarawak. With the weight of his considerable authority behind him, the 'white rajah' – as Brooke became known – tried among other things to make the Sulu Sea safe for merchant vessels.

On nautical charts and in mariners' handbooks the light at Sir James Brooke Point is

PALAWAN

listed as a navigational aid. The township of Brooke's Point on the cape at the northern end of Ipolote Bay is, however, more important in terms of growing trade.

Several km inland there is a range of forested mountains with peaks around 1500m. Mt Mantalingajan, Palawan's highest mountain at 2086m, is roughly 25 km west of Brooke's Point.

About 10 km north-west of Brooke's Point, near Mainit, you could visit a small **waterfall** and hot **sulphur springs**, but missing them would be no great loss. You can get there by tricycle (P50 one way or P120 per day).

Places to Stay

The *Sunset Greenland Garden Lodge* offers rooms for P75/150, with fan and bath for P200 and P300, and with air-con and bath for P400 and P550. Although basic, it passes muster. There is a restaurant, disco and rather extensive grounds.

The unpretentious *Silayan Lodge* charges P50/100 for good rooms with fan, and P180/360 with air-con and bath. The owners are friendly.

A pleasant, generously appointed place, the *Cristina Beach Resort* is on a grey beach about seven km north-east of Brooke's Point, 1.5 km off the main road on Tagusao Shore. Rooms go for P100/200, and cottages with fan and bath for P250/300.

Places to Eat

Most of the few restaurants in town close early at night, but the *Islander* on the main road serves very good Filipino food until 10 pm.

Getting There & Away

Bus A few Puerto Royale buses run from the market at Puerto Princesa to Brooke's Point in the morning; last departure is at 1 pm. There is also a Mic Mac Trail air-con bus which leaves in the morning. Princess Transport air-con buses leave at 8 am and 1.30 pm from the corner of Rizal Ave and Baltan St (P75; 4½ hours).

Princess Transport air-con buses leave

Brooke's Point for Puerto Princesa at 6.30 am and 1.30 pm.

Jeepney Jeepneys travel between Puerto Princesa and Brooke's Point (five hours).

RIO TUBA

Apparently, freighters occasionally sail from Brooke's Point or Rio Tuba to Cagayan de Tawi-Tawi Island (Cagayan de Sulu Island), where there are sometimes opportunities for onward travel to Jolo or Zamboanga via Pangutaran Island.

Places to Stay

You can stay overnight at Rio Tuba in basic hostels at the wharf. The price is a matter for negotiation.

Getting There & Away

Bus Puerto Royale buses and jeepneys run from Puerto Princesa to Brooke's Point, possibly going on to Rio Tuba.

Jeepney Between 6 am and 1 pm, four jeepneys run from Brooke's Point to Rio Tuba via Bataraza (two hours).

Boat Outrigger boats travel between Rio Tuba and Balabac on Balabac Island.

URSULA ISLAND

Thousands of birds used to nest on beautiful Ursula Island, where they would return in swarms in the evening after foraging on other islands. However, the depredations caused by hunters with their shotguns have caused most birds to shift their nests, mainly to the faraway Tubbataha Reef. Ursula Island is uninhabited and there is no drinking water.

Getting There & Away

A Special Ride on an outrigger boat from Brooke's Point, Bataraza or Rio Tuba to Ursula Island costs P2000 at most.

North Palawan

SAN RAFAEL

San Rafael has only a few huts, which are strung out along the highway, a school and two small shops, where you can't buy much anyway. From San Rafael you can visit the Batak with a guide. Whether to visit the Batak or not is something you will have to decide for yourself. The few remaining tribes of these nomadic people certainly don't find contact with travellers important.

The Duchess Beachside Cottages and the adjacent Coral Island can be recommended for those seeking peace and quiet. It's also a good starting point for longer hikes, for example, right across Palawan to Sabang with its St Paul Subterranean National Park and the Underground River. This takes two to three days, and a guide costs P300 a day plus food.

Places to Stay

The *Duchess Beachside Cottages*, about 500m from the road, are simple but clean and cost P200. The cottages are built in a row on the beach. This well-looked after place also has a good restaurant.

Getting There & Away

Bus Between 5 and 7 am, three Puerto Royale buses run daily from the market in Puerto Princesa to San Rafael, going on to Roxas or Taytay (two hours).

Jeepney There are also several jeepneys in the morning, leaving from the market or the jeepney terminal.

ROXAS & COCO-LOCO ISLAND

Roxas is a quiet little place right by the sea. Fish and fruit are on sale in the relatively large market at reasonable prices. If you want to stay on a desert island in the north of Palawan, Roxas is the last opportunity to buy equipment. You can get things like canisters and buckets in out-of-the-way places such as El Nido, but not less common items like cookers. It's about 200m from the bus and jeepney terminal to the market and jetty.

The extensive bay beyond Roxas has several small islands, including beautiful Coco-Loco Island (Reef Island) surrounded by a coral reef, that are worth seeing.

Information

You can telephone and fax from the small Business Center (an agent of Globe Telecom) on the corner of Roxas and Sandoval Sts. It is open from 8 am until 9 pm.

Places to Stay

Gemalain's Inn is a basic place in Roxas, by the market, with rooms for P100/150.

A better choice would be the *Rover Pension House*, a few feet away from the bus and jeepney terminal. Although an unassuming place, its rooms are up to par and cost P200 with bath.

About three km north of Roxas, the *Retac Beach Resort* has comfortable rooms with fan and bath for P400, and cottages with fan and bath from P500 to P700, and there is a restaurant. A tricycle from Roxas costs P10.

The only place on the island, the *Coco-Loco Island Resort* has a wide selection of basic but good cottages at P200, and P400 with bath. It offers billiards, squash and table tennis, and there are also diving facilities (Tarawis Dive Shop offers a dive for P625) and water-skiing. Windsurfing, outrigger boats and paddle bancas complete the picture. Its pleasant restaurant has a well-thought out menu. You can enjoy breakfast for P100, and dinner for between P130 and P270 per person. Information can be obtained in Puerto Princesa at the Coco-Loco Office (☎ 433 3877) on Rizal Ave, opposite the Palawan Hotel.

Places to Eat

There are a few modest restaurants at the bus and jeepney terminal where you will be offered a limited choice of simple meals. The *Tia-Ver Restaurant* next to the Rover Pension House is a little bit better but you'll find them find them closing as early as 9 pm.

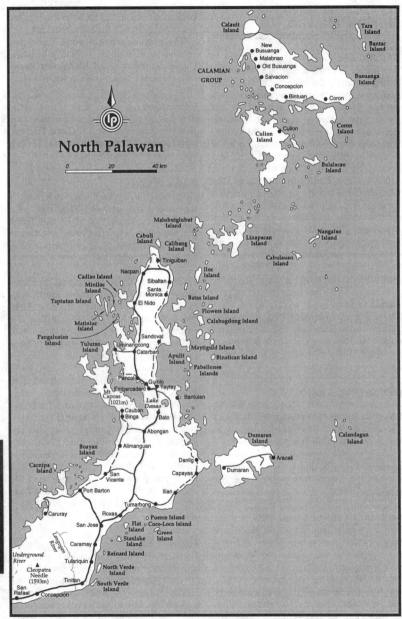

Getting There & Away

Bus Puerto Royale buses leave from Malvar St in Puerto Princesa for Roxas daily between 6 and 9 am and at 1 pm (P65; 4½ hours).

Jeepney In the morning between 6 am and noon several jeepneys also make the run from Puerto Princesa to Roxas (P70; five to six hours). Take something to cover your mouth and nose as it's a dusty trip.

Boat Every day around 9 am and 4.30 pm, the Coco-Loco Island Resort's outrigger boat returns to the island after buying supplies in Roxas (P80; 45 minutes). From December until June there may be another one leaving at noon. A Special Ride shouldn't cost more than P600.

The first boat from Coco-Loco Island to Roxas leaves at 7 am.

PORT BARTON

Port Barton is a small community on the picturesque Pagdanan Bay with a long, drawn-out beach. It has developed into a popular little meeting place in the north of Palawan.

Things to See & Do

There are several **waterfalls** in the beautiful countryside around Port Barton. Worth a special mention are those at Pamoayan, which you can reach in about 1½ hours on foot north of Port Barton. About halfway to Pamoayan a path breaks off to the right leading to a river which is shallow enough to wade through. Stick close to the river until you come to the first waterfall; just a bit further upstream there is a second waterfall.

You can hire outrigger boats in Port Barton for P500 a day and visit the nearby islands, some of which have strikingly beautiful white beaches. You can enjoy good snorkelling off **Inadawan Island** (formerly Tomas Tan Island) and in the so-called Aquarium. The colourful coral reefs off Exotica and Albaguin islands have, unfortunately, been largely destroyed by dynamite fishing.

Places to Stay

Port Barton A bit set apart, nestled into the north-east corner of the bay, the *Shangri-La of Scandinavian Beach Resort* has cottages with bath for P150 and P200. They are small and showing their age a bit. You can get there over a narrow wooden bridge.

Summer Homes has rooms for P100 and cottages with bath for P150. It's not a very big place, though it has a family atmosphere. It has three cottages directly on the beach and a house in the garden behind with two rooms.

At *Elsa's Beach Cottages* the pleasant little cottages cost P250, all with bath. It's a nice place to stay, and it has a restaurant.

Next to Elsa's, the *El Busero Inn* has basic accommodation, with rooms for P100/150 and cottages with bath for P300. It has a restaurant and diving facilities (El Busero Diving).

The *Swissippini Lodge & Resort* has cottages with bath costing between P350 and P600, depending on furnishings and size.

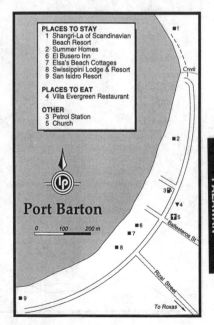

PLACES TO STAY
1 Shangri-La of Scandinavian
  Beach Resort
2 Summer Homes
6 El Busero Inn
7 Elsa's Beach Cottages
8 Swissippini Lodge & Resort
9 San Isidro Resort

PLACES TO EAT
4 Villa Evergreen Restaurant

OTHER
3 Petrol Station
5 Church

Creek

Port Barton

0   100   200 m

Ballesteros St

Rizal Street

To Roxas

PALAWAN

The neatly kept grounds have lots of plants. There is a pleasant restaurant, and billiards and diving facilities.

Finally we come to the *San Isidro Resort*, a small place in the south-west of the bay, which has rooms for P200 and P350, and cottages with bath for P500.

Around Port Barton On a white, palm-lined beach in the south-east of the island, the *Coconut Garden Island Resort* on Cacnipa Island has rooms for P175/225, cottages for P285, with bath P350 and P450. There is a long building with several rooms, as well as a bunch of different sized cottages with individual furnishings. It has tents available for P145. The pleasant grounds are quite extensive, and there is room for more cottages. Every Tuesday and Friday at 2 pm a boat goes from Port Barton to Cacnipa Island (P95 per person); a Special Ride shouldn't cost more than P500. A Special Ride to/from Sabang (Underground River) should be possible for around P1000.

The *Manta Ray Island Resort* on Capsalay Island has cottages for P1700 per person, including meals. There is a seasonal surcharge of around P300 from mid-December

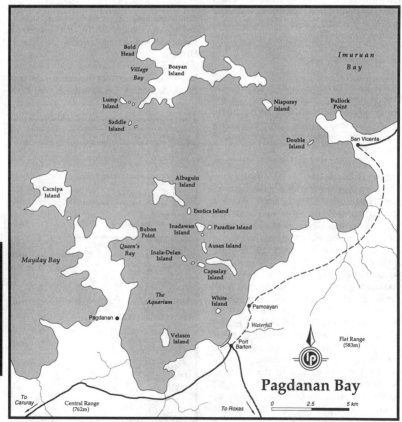

Pagdanan Bay

to mid-January. It has three tastefully designed cottages on attractive grounds with a neat garden which one enthusiastic traveller described as 'manicured'. The resort is run by an Italian woman by the name of Paola.

Places to Eat

The places to stay mentioned above serve good, generous meals, but the owners appreciate prior notice. The village itself has a small, inexpensive restaurant, the *Villa Evergreen Restaurant*, on Rizal St opposite the Petron station. It's open from 7 am until 9 pm.

Getting There & Away

Jeepney Several jeepneys run daily between 7 and 9 am to Port Barton from the jeepney terminal in Puerto Princesa (P80; six hours). There are occasionally faster jeepneys with relatively few passengers and ample space for luggage, but they charge double the normal fare. You can also go to Roxas first by bus or jeepney and then catch a jeepney going to Port Barton.

Only a few jeepneys leave Roxas market for Port Barton daily (P40; two hours). The first one leaves at 9 am.

A jeepney runs daily to Puerto Princesa from Port Barton at 5 am; a Special Ride costs P2500. A jeepney leaves Port Barton for Roxas daily at 6 am.

Boat At the time of writing the following prices were being charged: San Vicente, Boayan and Albaguin P700; Baheli P2000; El Nido P2500; and Underground River P1500. The charge for waiting time for the boat is P600 per day.

The boat trip from Port Barton to the Underground River takes at least four hours. It is important to leave early or you won't have much time to see the river.

SAN VICENTE

San Vicente lies on a peninsula about 18 km north-east of Port Barton. On the other side of the peninsula, Imuruan Bay, with its long beach, starts its sweep down to Alimanguan. The beach is actually 15 km long and is only interrupted once at Bokbok Point. If you

appreciate solitude and want to get away from inquisitive people, this is the place for you. A good idea for a day's outing is a hike to the **Little Baguio Waterfall**, about six km inland from San Vicente.

Places to Stay

The *Caparii Dive Camp* has comfortable duplex cottages with singles/doubles with fan and bath for P520, and with air-con and bath P800/920. The camp has its own restaurant and offers boat trips (including to the Underground River), bicycle hire, windsurfing (P125 an hour) and diving (including diving courses). This is a well-run resort on a small bay, two km north-west of San Vicente. There is a booking office at the airport in Puerto Princesa.

Getting There & Away

Jeepney A jeepney goes from Roxas to San Vicente two or three times daily (P30; 2½ hours). If requested, the driver will take passengers to Caparii Dive Camp.

Boat Now that the road from Port Barton to San Vicente has been closed for an indefinite period the only way to travel between them is by outrigger boat (P150 per person, P500 for the boat; one hour).

TAYTAY & EMBARCADERO

Taytay is the old capital of Palawan. You can still visit the ruins of the **fort** which was built by the Spaniards in 1667. The church is about 300 years old. There is a hospital and numerous shops which have a surprisingly wide range of goods.

Only a few km south of Taytay is **Lake Danao**, which is 62 hectares in size. It has small islands and is surrounded by unspoiled forest.

From Taytay you can go to the **Pabellones Islands** by outrigger boat, which takes about one hour. These are three small islands with sheer limestone cliffs. The many caves and cracks yield birds' nests for birds' nest soup. **Elefante Island** has a lagoon which is good for snorkelling. A round-trip costs about P500.

The new Sandoval domestic airport is

PALAWAN

being built at the northern end of Taytay Bay. When it's ready an enormous tourist boom is expected for the whole group of islands north-west of Palawan. Guests of the Club Noah Isabelle on Apulit Island are already being flown in here from Manila.

Embarcadero is about six km west of Taytay. Outrigger boats go almost daily, but at least twice a week, down the mangrove river to Malampaya Sound and on to Liminangcong.

Tricycles will take you between Embarcadero and Taytay for P15 per person or P60 for the tricycle; jeepneys occasionally also travel the route.

Places to Stay
Publico's International Guest House near the Taytay market is basic, but clean and comfortable, with rooms for P60/120, with bath for P150. It has a restaurant (order beforehand). The owner is helpful, and the courtyard is green and inviting.

Pem's Pension House on Taytay Bay near the fort has quite good rooms with fan for P75/120, and cottages with fan and bath for P250 and P500. The more expensive ones are roomier and better furnished. Its restaurant is good.

Places to Eat
There are several small restaurants and food stalls at the Taytay market, where you can eat inexpensive Philippine food.

Getting There & Away
Bus Buses belonging to the Puerto Royale company leave daily between 6 and 9 am and at 1 pm from Malvar St in Puerto Princesa for Taytay (P95; nine hours).

Two Puerto Royale buses leave Roxas twice daily for Taytay (P50; four hours).

Buses for Puerto Princesa leave Taytay at 3.30 am, noon and 7 pm. In addition, a jeepney might make the trip in the morning or evening.

Jeepney Several jeepneys make the trip between El Nido and Taytay during the day (P100; three hours). A jeepney occasionally leaves from Roxas at noon.

During the day jeepneys travel from El Nido to Embarcadero in three hours and cost P100.

Boat The trip from El Nido to Embarcadero by outrigger boat costs P150 per person or P1500 for a Special Ride (4½ hours).

The MB *Dioniemer*, a big outrigger boat, leaves from Coron on Busuanga for Taytay every Monday and Friday at 8 am (P350; eight hours). During heavy seas the boat anchors overnight in San Miguel on Linapacan Island and continues the next morning. The boat leaves Taytay on Wednesday and Saturday at 8 am.

APULIT ISLAND
In the middle of Taytay Bay, not quite 12 nautical miles north-east of Taytay itself, lies the idyllic Apulit Island. This island is enchanting – it's like something out of the backdrop of an overly romantic South Pacific film. Only 1.5 km long, Apulit is very narrow and not very high at the southern end, while a jagged 175m-high ridge runs along the middle of the wider, northern end of the 'dragon island'. Drawn by its exclusive resort, white beaches, local reef and the Royalist reef only half a nautical mile east, the island is a favourite with holidaymakers and divers.

Places to Stay
Club Noah Isabelle has comfortably decked out cottages, standing on pilons in the sea. Fully equipped with air-con and bath, these cottages cost US$170 per person. For your money you are entitled to full board, plus boat transfer, windsurfing, water-skiing and two dives per day. Reservations can be made in Manila at Noah's Century (☎ 810 7241; fax 818 2640), Basic Petroleum building, Carlos Palanka Jr St, Legaspi Village, Makati. The club has released strict environmental guidelines for the surrounding waters.

FLOWERS ISLAND
Flowers Island is a dream of a small island, around 50 km north-east of Taytay, with a white sandy beach and a still-intact reef. A Frenchman and his Filipina wife run a pleasant beach resort here with only a few

PALAWAN
Top: Coron Island, North Palawan.
Middle: Peaceful early morning at Taytay Bay, Palawan.
Bottom: Detail of Taytay Fort, Palawan.

JENS PETERS

JENS PETERS

JENS PETERS

PALAWAN
Top: Lake Cayangan, Coron Island, North Palawan.
Bottom Left: Nagtabon Beach, Palawan.
Bottom Right: Island of the Bacuit Archipelago off El Nido, Palawan.

cottages. For information on accommodation, check with Pem's Pension House in Taytay.

Places to Stay
The *Flowers Island Beach Resort* has roomy, pleasantly decorated cottages for P600 per person, with bath for P750, and full board. Paddleboats are available.

Getting There & Away
A Special Ride in an outrigger boat from Taytay to Flowers Island costs P800 to P1000, or P200 per person (three hours).

LIMINANGCONG
Liminangcong becomes a fishing centre during the north-east monsoons. The place itself is surprisingly peaceful as there are practically no cars. Even after the 22 km long access road has been opened there is little chance of there being much traffic, apart from a few jeepneys. Many of the well-tended houses have little gardens at the front, with the edge of the property marked by quaint red toadstools made with coconut shells.

From Liminangcong you can go to the small offshore **Saddle and Camago islands**. You can also get boats to islands further north. In addition, there are shipping connections to Manila at irregular intervals. Local shopkeepers often know more about departure times than the coastguard.

Places to Stay
Kaver's Inn has acceptable rooms in a well-constructed building for P200. The communal bath with its dark blue tub makes for an unusual feature.

Places to Eat
The big, two storey *Puerto Paraiso Restaurant* opposite the Lady Bug disco has good Philippine food on the menu. Built right on the water, there is a gorgeous view of the offshore islands.

Getting There & Away
Jeepney Apparently, there is going to be a jeepney connection between Taytay and Liminangcong soon.

Boat From Embarcadero several outrigger boats leave for Liminangcong weekly. The fare is P100 per person. A Special Ride costs P800.

To travel from Liminangcong to El Nido costs P80 per person, but you usually have to charter a boat. A Special Ride to El Nido should cost about P600.

EL NIDO & BACUIT ARCHIPELAGO
Picturesque El Nido is on a beautiful part of the coast, surrounded by rugged, steep limestone cliffs. The houses and streets are clean and well-looked after. There are scarcely any vehicles. More and more travellers have been attracted to this beautiful little town in the north of the 'Last Frontier' (as Palawan is often called) since the roads and transport were improved. Inevitably, some of these people will have been disappointed, because the transport and accommodation require not only flexibility, but also a willingness not to expect too much.

Information
Tourist Office The tourist office in El Nido (next to the post office) has albums on display with photographs of the various resorts.

Money There is neither a bank nor a money-changer in El Nido. At best you can change cash US dollars, albeit at an unfavourable rate. So, remember to bring enough pesos!

Post The small post office next to the tourist office is only open sporadically.

Things to See & Do
In El Nido you can take a trip to the fascinating islands of the Bacuit archipelago just offshore. Almost all of these grey islands jut steeply out of the crystal-clear water and have small, sandy bays. It costs around P800 per day to hire a boat, including petrol. A small paddleboat costs P10 an hour.

Anyone who finds it too expensive to hire a boat for a day or more, or join an excursion group, but wants to go snorkelling or to the beaches outside of El Nido, would be best advised to go to Corong-Corong Bay, about two km further south. The sunsets there are spectacular. From there it is possible to get a fisherman to drop you off for a few pesos on one of the sandy beaches on the south-west coast of the peninsula, for example, Lapus-Lapus Beach or Seven Commandos Beach.

You can also have a boat take you from El Nido to a beach or nearby island of your choice (don't forget to arrange when they are to pick you up again!). A few suggestions might be: Bocal Island (P150); Paradise Beach (P150); Pasandigan Cove (P250; good for snorkelling); Dilumacad (Helicopter) Island (P350); Ipil Beach (P150); Seven Commandos Beach (P250; excellent for snorkelling); and Lapus-Lapus Beach (P250). You can find out more about this service from Judith, a Swiss, in the El Nido Boutique.

El Nido's most important attraction for tourists is its living coral reefs and the multicoloured fish of the Bacuit archipelago. Consequently, if no-one manages to put an end to irresponsible fishermen dynamiting

vast areas of the underwater world into oblivion, tourism in El Nido has no chance of a future. By the way, the boats that do the damage with dynamite are not from El Nido, but come from further afield to wreak havoc in other people's local waters.

Diving

Snorkelling and diving equipment can be hired from Bacuit Divers. Goggles and snorkel cost P75, flippers are another P75. A five day diving course costs P7000; one diving trip with two dives costs P1600.

Islands of the Bacuit Archipelago

Cadlao Island Cadlao is the biggest and, at almost 600m, also the highest island in the Bacuit archipelago. Its massive cliff face, in places covered with thick green vegetation, is riddled with caves and fissures.

Miniloc Island Miniloc, south-west of El Nido, is the island where the well-known El

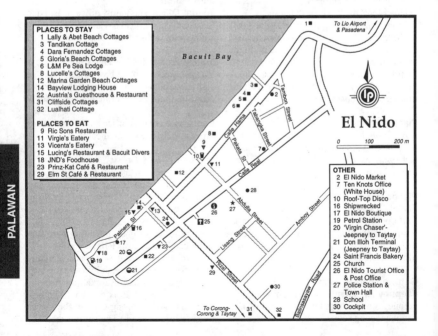

PLACES TO STAY
1 Lally & Abet Beach Cottages
3 Tandikan Cottage
4 Dara Fernandez Cottages
5 Gloria's Beach Cottages
6 L&M Pe Sea Lodge
8 Lucelle's Cottages
12 Marina Garden Beach Cottages
14 Bayview Lodging House
22 Austria's Guesthouse & Restaurant
31 Cliffside Cottages
32 Lualhati Cottage

PLACES TO EAT
9 Ric Sons Restaurant
11 Virgie's Eatery
13 Vicenta's Eatery
15 Lucing's Restaurant & Bacuit Divers
18 JND's Foodhouse
23 Prinz-Kat Café & Restaurant
29 Elm St Café & Restaurant

OTHER
2 El Nido Market
7 Ten Knots Office (White House)
10 Roof-Top Disco
16 Shipwrecked
17 El Nido Boutique
19 Petrol Station
20 'Virgin Chaser'- Jeepney to Taytay
21 Don Illoh Terminal (Jeepney to Taytay)
24 Saint Francis Bakery
25 Church
26 El Nido Tourist Office & Post Office
27 Police Station & Town Hall
28 School
30 Cockpit

El Nido

Bacuit Bay

To Lio Airport & Pasadena

To Corong-Corong & Taytay

PALAWAN

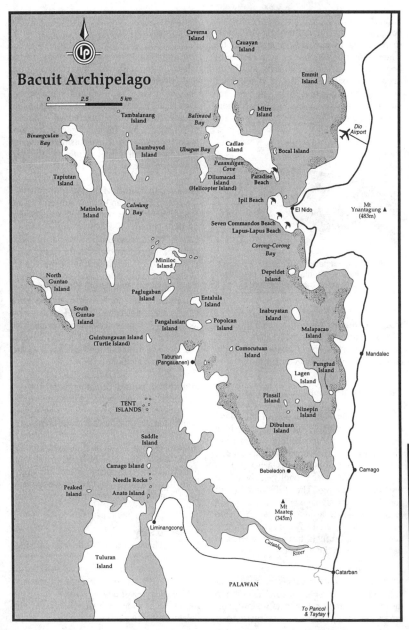

Bacuit Archipelago

0   2.5   5 km

Caverna Island
Cauayan Island
Emmit Island
Tambalanang Island
Balinaod Bay
Mitre Island
Binangculan Bay
Inambuyod Island
Ubugun Bay
Cadlao Island
Bocal Island
Dio Airport
Tapiutan Island
Pasandigan Cove
Diumacad Island (Helicopter Island)
Paradise Beach
Matinloc Island
Calmiug Bay
Ipil Beach
El Nido
Mt Ynantagung ▲ (483m)
Seven Commandos Beach
Lapus-Lapus Beach
Corong-Corong Bay
Miniloc Island
Depeldet Island
North Guntao Island
Paglugaban Island
Entalula Island
Inabuyatan Island
South Guntao Island
Pangalusian Island
Popolcan Island
Malapacao Island
Guintungauan Island (Turtle Island)
Comocutuan Island
Mandalec
Tabunan (Pangauanen)
Pungtud Island
Lagen Island
TENT ISLANDS
Pinsail Island
Ninepin Island
Dibuluan Island
Saddle Island
Camago Island
Needle Rocks
Bebeledon
Camago
Peaked Island
Anato Island
Liminangcong
Mt Maateg (345m)
Cataba River
Tuluran Island
Catarban
PALAWAN
To Pancol & Taytay

Nido Resort is located. The deeply indented coast, a little to the north of this establishment, leads to a beautiful lagoon in the island's interior which is only accessible by boat. There are said to be barracudas in the deep centre part of the lagoon which could possibly be dangerous to snorkellers and swimmers. Turtles have also been occasionally sighted there.

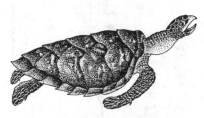

Paying dearly for having a large and colourful shell, the hawksbill turtle (*pawikan*) has been hunted to the brink of oblivion.

Matinloc Island Matinloc has numerous little bays along its coast, with sandy beaches and corals worth seeing. Calmung Bay on the east side of the island is worth a look.

Tapiutan Island Tapiutan runs for half of its length almost parallel and fairly closely to Matinloc Island. On this part of the island there is an attractively situated beach with a reef well suited for snorkelling. The extremely picturesque Binangculan Bay in the north-west of the island has a beach with some vegetation. Occasionally, sailboats use this for anchoring. The cliffs jutting out south of the bay signal one of the best diving areas in the waters around El Nido. There are several tunnels, archways and fissures that can be swum through; turtles, groupers and barracudas are quite common.

North Guntao Island This is the most westerly island of the archipelago. The climb to the top is rewarded with a breath-taking panorama. The little beaches on the west coast and at the south tip of the island are suitable for snorkelling breaks.

Pangalusian Island Unlike most of the islands in the archipelago, Pangalusian is flat and covered with thick vegetation in parts, and has a long, palm-fringed white beach. This island boasts the exclusive Pangalusian Resort. And this is meant literally. 'Exclusive' means non-resident guests are not welcome. As soon as an outside boat even looks like attempting a landing, guards warn it off immediately.

Malapacao Island Malapacao lies just off the coast of Palawan in the south-east of the Bacuit archipelago and surely counts as one of the Gardens of Eden of this group of islands. Malapacao can be recognised by its two striking giant rock faces standing sentry at both ends of a flat section of the island, overgrown with palms and other tropical plants on a beautiful beach. Lovers of relaxation need look no further than the little resort called Malapacao Island Retreat, with its friendly, family-style atmosphere. The superb resort of Marina del Nido on the east coast of the island offers sailors a secure place to drop anchor.

Inabuyatan Island The palm trees all over, and the white sandy beach at its southern tip, help make Inabuyatan another one of the South Seas dream islands in the archipelago.

Pinsail Island From a distance, Pinsail Island looks like a modest lump of rock until you come to an opening in the cliffs which leads to a cathedral-like cave, impressively illuminated from above by shafts of sunlight.

Places to Stay
El Nido There are several places in El Nido. *Austria's Guesthouse* is two streets away from the sea and has rooms for P40/50, with fan P50/70. It also has a beautiful garden.

The *Bayview Lodging House* has fine rooms with wide beds for P80/100. The balcony offers a good sea view.

Right on the ocean, the beautifully kept *Marina Garden Beach Cottages* has a family-style atmosphere. It charges P100/150 for rooms, and P250, P300 and P450 for cottages with bath.

Gloria's Beach Cottages offers a variety of rooms for P120, P150 and P200, while cottages with bath go for P450 and P500. Rooms facing the sea have big verandas.

Close by, *Tandikan Cottages* is a pleasant little place with tidy rooms for P100, with bath P200. A choice of different sized cottages with bath is available for between P300 and P400.

At the more peaceful, east end of the bay, *Lally & Abet Beach Cottages* is a bigger establishment with rooms for P300, and cottages with bath for P400 and P500.

At the southern edge of town, with a huge cliff towering over it, *Cliffside Cottages* will provide you with an excellent cottage with bath for P200.

Also at the southern edge of town on the way to Corong-Corong, *Lualhati Cottage* has rooms in a friendly atmosphere which are good value at P100/P150. There is a garden, and Mandy the owner will give you his half-hour massage for P100.

Around El Nido South of El Nido in Corong-Corong, at the northern end of Corong-Corong Bay, *Magos Cottage* has good accommodation. The rooms are well worth the cost of P100/200, and the atmosphere is cosy. Staff will cook for you if you ask them. You can hire a paddle boat for P10 an hour.

About five km south of El Nido, the *Dolarog Beach Resort* offers a roomy, tastefully decorated cottage with bath and big veranda for between P500 and P700. The resort is owned by Edo, an Italian, and Elena, his Filipina wife, and is about 1½ hours' walk along the Corong-Corong Bay beach from El Nido. You can also get there in half an hour by boat (P300).

The *Malapacao Island Retreat* on Malapacao Island has dorm beds for P600, singles/doubles for P700/1200 and P900/1450 with balcony. Cottages with bath will cost you P1150/1600. All prices include three

meals. The cottages are creatively built, with basic but adequate rooms which provide a beautiful view of the white beach. Lee Ann, an Australian, and Edgar, a Filipino, run this thoughtfully designed resort in the spirit of 'gentle tourism' and welcome guests (preferably non-smokers) who are, like themselves, friends of nature. Lovers of loud music and strong drink are absolutely persona non grata in this resort! Thanks to solar energy, the God-given peace is not even disturbed by sputtering generators. Snorkelling equipment is available (mask and snorkel P140; flippers P60 per day), and a paddle boat will cost you P100 a day. They also organise boat trips. Information about the accommodation can be obtained in El Nido at JND's Foodhouse near the jetty.

Also on Malapacao Island, cottages at the *Marina del Nido* cost US$125 with fan and bath. The stylish, round buildings are generously proportioned and stand in rambling, neatly maintained grounds with plants everywhere. The restaurant will serve you three meals a day for P1000. Yachts are available for charter. The resort management believe in acting in an environmentally responsible way and ask, among other things, that guests take their used lighters, batteries and such with them when they leave. In addition, each guest has to pay P400 into the resort's Environmental Guarantee Fund. Reservations can be made in Manila at Marina del Nido (☎ 831 1487, fax 831 9816), 2688 Park Ave, Pasay City.

The *Pangalusian Resort* on Pangalusian Island offers cottages with air-con and bath for US$110 and US$135. It offers diving, and only residents are allowed on the premises.

The *Club Noah El Nido* on Miniloc Island has cottages for US$190/300, including meals, diving gear, diving trips, water-skiing and windsurfing. It has a small beach which has been a bit overbuilt. Admission is only for residents.

Places to Eat

Surprisingly, El Nido has a few excellent restaurants, even if they don't always look too impressive from the outside. That's certainly the case with *Vicenta's Eatery* which offers excellent food and generous portions for around P60. It is recommended to order the evening meal at lunchtime.

Also on the recommended list is the modest-looking *JND's Foodhouse* near the jetty, where the restaurant doubles as the family living room. Your host, Nelda, cooks wonderfully, European-style cuisine if you want. It's also a good idea to order your food in good time here.

In the rustic little *Virgie's Eatery*, a few big pots of tasty Philippine food are prepared every day. A meal costs P30.

Definitely worth a mention is *Austria's Restaurant*, with its tasty dishes ranging from banana pancake to lobster. It's run by self-styled Mr Austria, the garrulous paladin and veteran of long-forgotten world wars, who has a vast store of incredible yarns up his sleeve. Also good are *Elm St Café & Restaurant*, a pleasant garden restaurant, that includes a daily changing set meal on its menu, and *Ric Sons Restaurant*, with its beautiful view over the bay.

After dinner many guests like to visit the tastefully decorated *Shipwrecked* bar for its astounding variety of cocktails and fine music.

Getting There & Away
Air At the Ten Knots Office (White House) in El Nido you can book Soriano Aviation flights to Manila.

Bus A direct bus belonging to the Puerto Royale company is said to leave Puerto Princesa at midnight for El Nido (P180; 10 hours).

It is possible to take the Puerto Royale bus at 5 am for Taytay and then take a jeepney from there to El Nido.

Jeepney At least one jeepney leaves Puerto Princesa daily in the early morning for El Nido (P200; 10 to 14 hours). During the rainy season the overland connection may terminate in Taytay.

Several jeepneys travel between Taytay

and El Nido daily – at least in the dry season (P100; three hours).

Boat From Embarcadero near Taytay you can also get to El Nido by boat (P150; 4½ hours). A Special Ride costs P1500.

Outrigger boats run from Port Barton to El Nido (P2500; five hours).

Getting Around
The Airport The small Dio airport is about four km north of El Nido right on the coast. Jeepneys go into town after the arrival of a scheduled flight (P50, although locals only pay about P20; 15 minutes). Boats sometimes also make the journey. A Special Ride by boat from El Nido to the airport costs P200.

Anyone arriving on a chartered flight can have a jeepney ordered by radio from El Nido. This is a Special Ride and shouldn't cost more than P200, although they ask up to P350 for it.

It is only possible to go along the beach from the airport to El Nido at low tide, and it should not be attempted with heavy baggage.

Calamian Group

The northernmost part of Palawan consists of the Calamian Group, whose main islands are Busuanga, Culion and Coron. The improvements made to the travel links with other islands and towns, together with the expansion in overnight accommodation, have brought about a modest upsurge in tourism in this beautiful island world. But so far, people still live mostly from fishing and selling *kasoy* (cashew nuts), which are mainly harvested on Busuanga and Culion.

The identical names of some of the towns and islands can certainly give the newcomer a headache. For example, there's the island of Busuanga with the towns Old Busuanga, New Busuanga and Coron. South of the town of Coron you can see the island of Coron in the east part of Coron Bay. To the west of the island of Coron the island of Culion is home to the town of Culion. Clear as mud, isn't it?

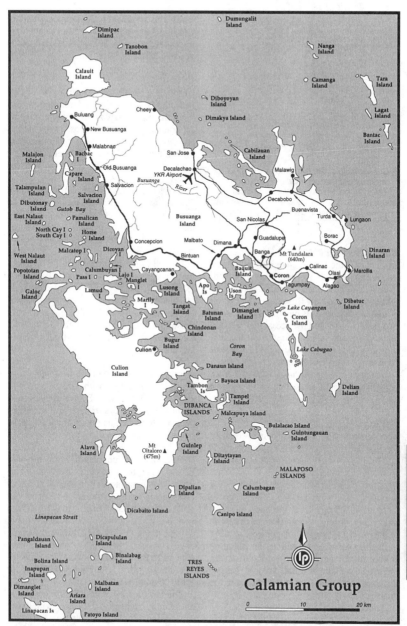

Calamian Group

A close relatve of the pistachio and mango, the cashew nut (*kasoy*) grows at the end of a fleshy 'drupe' which is very juicy and can be eaten as a fruit. Mildly toxic when raw, the nuts are lightly roasted before being eaten.

BUSUANGA ISLAND

Busuanga is the largest island in the Calamian Group. A partly surfaced road runs from Coron through Concepcion, Salvacion and Old Busuanga to New Busuanga. The amount of traffic on the roads is minimal. Before noon two rickety buses and the occasional jeepney leave Coron for Salvacion, returning the next morning. That makes Busuanga an ideal spot for nature lovers and hikers.

In the centre of the island are the Yulo King Ranch (said to be one of the largest cattle stations in Asia) and the YKR Airport.

Getting Around

The Airport Tiny YKR Airport is south of Decalachao in the north of the island. Air Ads and Pacific Airways aircraft land and take off from there. Several resorts, such as Club Paradise, pick up their guests with their own vehicles, otherwise all the jeepneys go to Coron (P75; 45 minutes to 1½ hours, depending on time of year). A roof seat guarantees an uninterrupted view of the magnificent scenery.

Pacific Airways is said to be planning flights in the near future to and from an airstrip behind the hospital in Coron. It's not quite one km from there to the market in the centre of town, and a tricycle costs P5.

Another airstrip is available near Old Busuanga in the north-west of the island.

Boat The wharf is in Tagumpay, a part of Coron. It takes about 20 minutes to get there on foot from the market, or for P3 per person you can take a tricycle.

Coron

Coron is a small town with about 35,000 inhabitants. The fishing and trading centre of the Calamian Group, it has a market, fishing school, hospital, two discos, two cinemas and several shops. Many of the houses here are built on piles in the sea. There are a few more shops and simple restaurants at the wharf in Tagumpay.

To get to the **Makinit Hot Spring**, go from Coron past the wharf to the ice plant, then go towards the water, not along the creek. The path soon leads away from the water through a cashew-nut plantation to a narrow beach. Turn left here.

Behind Coron hospital is a hill which provides a beautiful view of Coron Bay. It's a bit more difficult to climb the 640 metre high **Mt Tundulara**. You have to be fit to make it up there, and a guide would be a good idea (costing about P200). A path behind the Kokosnuss Garden Resort will take you to the summit.

Information You would be best advised to take as many pesos with you as you will need. In an emergency, PYY Hardware will exchange US dollars in cash and travellers cheques, however, its rate is about one peso below the official one.

Diving For many people, diving is the only reason to go to Busuanga; the waters between Busuanga and Culion islands are an El Dorado for wreck explorers. In Coron you will be charged P550 per dive; day trips (with two dives) and diving courses are available at Lapu-Lapu Divers and Discovery Divers.

Places to Stay & Eat The *Sea Coral Lodge* is a simple place with rooms with fan for P50/100 and P100/200.

The *Sea Breeze Lodging House* is a pleasant, family-style place to stay with basic fan-cooled singles/doubles for P60/120, with fan and bath for P250/300; the best have their own small veranda. Entirely built of wood, it stands on piles over the water.

The attractive *L&M Pe Lodge*, also built on piles over the water, has simple, very small rooms for P100/200, with fan and bath for P250, and a cosy veranda. It is right next to the market. Food must be ordered beforehand.

At the market, the *Bayside Divers Lodge* provides basic, adequate rooms with fan for P3500, with fan and bath for P400, including breakfast. It has a good restaurant, and a big terrace with a sea view. Reservations can be made in Manila with Swagman Travel (☎ 522 3650; fax 522 3663), 1133 L Guerrero St, Ermita.

Finally, the best accommodation in Coron is the *Kokosnuss Garden Resort*, with dorm beds with fan for P120, cottages with fan for between P180 and P350, and cottages with fan and bath for P600. The comfortable, charmingly furnished cottages are set in quiet grounds with a big garden. Full board is possible. Next to the hospital, it's only about 15 minutes on foot from Coron in the direction of the airport. The management is German. Rudolf and his Filipina wife, Fe, organise boat trips and jeepney tours.

Getting There & Away Three Viva Shipping Lines ships travel between Coron and Culion, leaving Coron every Monday, Wednesday and Saturday at 6 am, and Culion every Tuesday, Thursday and Sunday at 6 am. The trip takes two hours.

The MB *Dioniemer*, a big outrigger boat, leaves from Taytay for Coron every Wednesday and Saturday at 8 am (P350; eight hours). During heavy seas the boat anchors for the night in San Miguel on Linapacan Island and continues the next morning. Departure from Coron is on Monday and Friday at 8 am.

Concepcion

This pleasant little community, with only a few houses on a mangrove-lined bay, is a good starting point for boat trips to the offshore islands of Gutob Bay. On the way out of town heading towards Salvacion, just off the road, is a small waterfall with a natural pool where you can have a relaxing swim.

Places to Stay & Eat The *Sea Side Highway Lodging House* has simple, but clean rooms for P60/120. Food has to be ordered beforehand; the cooking is good. A day of island hopping costs about P600 per boat.

Pier House is an attractive place with rooms for P150/300. This pleasant, quiet accommodation is right at the pier, and is run by a Swede named Michael.

Also at the pier, but on the other side, *Concepcion Divers & Pier Cottages* charges P400 for cottages with fan and bath. The place is run by an Englishman Andy. The *Happy Edith Restaurant* here is cosy. Diving is available for P600 per dive, and boat trips for between P400 and P800.

Getting There & Away Two buses leave the cinema in Coron for Concepcion at around 10 am (two hours). From Concepcion to Coron the buses leave between 4 and 5 am, sometimes even earlier.

During the day the occasional jeepney will make the trip from Coron to Concepcion, but there is no precise timetable. From Concepcion to Coron the jeepney leaves between 4 and 5 am, sometimes earlier.

By motorcycle the trip costs around P300 from Coron to Concepcion.

Old Busuanga

The small town of Old Busuanga is at the mouth of the Busuanga River in the northwest of Busuanga Island. A long beach stretches south of the river mouth, where you will find the Las Hamacas Resort. A trip up the river in an outrigger boat is a wonderful way to experience nature and is highly recommended if you are staying in the area. Old Busuanga is also handy as a base for a short trip to Calauit Island.

Places to Stay & Eat

The *Las Hamacas Resort* has comfortable duplex cottages with rooms with fan and bath for P1850/3150, including three meals.

It is a pleasant place run by the Frenchman Daniel and his Filipina wife, Belen. They will be glad to organise boat trips.

Getting There & Away To get from Coron to Old Busuanga, first take a bus or a jeepney to Salvacion, where it is only a few minutes by outrigger boat to the Las Hamacas Resort. The bus leaves Coron around 10 am.

The bus leaves Salvacion for Coron between 3.30 and 4.30 am.

CALAUIT ISLAND
Large African animals are being raised on this small island, north of Busuanga Island, as an experiment which started in 1977 with eight African species and was carried on for 10 years in strict seclusion. The project has been successful: almost 500 African wild animals, including giraffes, zebras and gazelles, live together with rare Philippine animals, such as the mouse deer, bear cat and Philippine crocodile, in the 3700 hectare large **Calauit Island Wildlife Sanctuary**. Visitors are welcome. The manager is happy to drive guests around the national park in his jeep for a nominal fee (at the most P100 per head). Admission costs P300.

DIMAKYA ISLAND
There is a group of beautiful little rocky islands north of Busuanga Island, partially covered with various kinds of vegetation. If palms grew there, they would be veritable treasure islands. One of them is Dimakya Island. It is surrounded by a magnificent coral reef and boasts a beach with blindingly white sand which makes a seductive contrast to the turquoise, crystal clear water. This island is home to the exclusive Club Paradise which, among others, offers trips to Calauit Island and diving trips.

Places to Stay & Eat
The beautiful *Club Paradise* has rooms with fan and bath for US$100/180, and with air-con and bath for US$150/240. It has cosy, comfortable cottages and offers full board. The price also includes Busuanga YKR airport service, Hobie Cat sailing, windsurfing,

diving instruction (one hour) and a trip around the island in a speedboat. Its management is German-Filipino and reservations can be made at the Club Paradise (☎ 816 6871; fax 818 2894).

CORON BAY
The best way to explore the islands of Coron Bay is from Coron and Culion islands. Tiny Cagbatan Island, better known as CYC Island, is ideal for picnics, as is the slightly larger Dimanglet Island; both of them are near Coron. I especially liked the small Malcapuya Island among those east of Culion Island. It now belongs to a lawyer from Manila, who has built a weekend house on it.

In 1944 a convoy of 12 Japanese naval and merchant ships was sunk in the north-west of Coron Bay, most of them in the waters between Lusong and Tangat islands, where there are seven wrecks altogether in around 30m depth of water.

Coron Island
Wedge-shaped Coron Island is practically uninhabited and can be reached by boat from Coron on Busuanga Island in about 30 minutes.

The island consists of steep limestone cliffs with caves and numerous lonely sandy bays, where you may meet Tagbanua semi-nomads with Negrito blood. In the centre are hidden mountain lakes such as the turquoise Lake Cayangan (Barracuda Lake) and the large Lake Cabugao which has two islands. If you want to spend more than a few hours on Coron don't forget to take enough drinking water with you.

When exploring the island resist the temptation to have a quick look at Lake Cabugao. It's in an area reserved for the Tagbanua and is strictly *off-limits*. As it is, the Tagbanua are not wild about receiving uninvited guests in their little communities on the east coast, and it's best to simply leave them alone.

Tangat Island
Tangat Island (known locally as Sangat Island) is about four km south of Busuanga

and juts fairly steeply out of the sea. In the southern part it gets as high as 460m. In the little bays dotted around the island you will occasionally come across a shimmering white sand beach. A narrow mangrove glade stretches along roughly the middle of the west coast, and there is a coral reef offshore at this point. The island is home to a teeming, richly varied animal population, including monkeys and monitor lizards.

Places to Stay At the *Sangat Reserve* you'll find four cottages with bath for P500. Cooking and diving facilities are available. This little resort at the southern tip of Tangat Island belongs to the same Englishman Andy, who runs the Pier Cottages in Concepcion.

Tending Island
This ver small island is snuggled between Marily and Chindonan islands. It is also called Isla Migrosa. The coarse sandy beach is only of moderate quality but is all right for snorkelling.

Places to Stay At *Isla Migrosa Cottages* a cottage with bath costs P300 to P500, including full board. There are only three simple cottages, built well apart from each other on the side of the hill, with a beautiful view. Just the place for those who like to be alone.

GUTOB BAY
There are lots of lovely, deserted islands in Gutob Bay, between Culion and Busuanga islands. **Dibutonay**, **Maltatayoc** and **Horse islands** are only three among the many idyllic spots available.

The larger **Talampulan Island** is a complete contrast, with a town of 2000 people straggling along the east coast. There are two cinemas, and big ships often drop anchor off the town. Talampulan is a fishing centre, where the catches are brought and shipped to Manila two or three times a week. Note the chance of a ride!

One note of caution: after days and weeks at sea some of the fishermen get carried away with their alcohol consumption. Late afternoons

and evenings in the village can get a bit hair-raising.

Calumbuyan Island
Calumbuyan Island can be reached from Concepcion on Busuanga Island by boat in about 30 minutes (P150). As there is a pearl farm near this island, the reef is protected, which rules out dynamite fishing.

CULION ISLAND
Culion Island is the second largest island of the Calamian Group and is known in the Philippines as Leprosy Island. The colony is in Culion; about 600 lepers live here along with their relatives. Most of the many bays on the island, many of them quite deep, are lined with mangroves and are not very attractive when you take a good look at them.

Culion
Culion is a well-looked after picturesque community on the side of a hill, with a small harbour. Boats leave from there for Manila via Coron.

Places to Stay & Eat The *New Luncheonette Lodge* has a few simple rooms for P100, as well as a restaurant and two airy terraces overlooking the water. At the weekends there is live music (disco-type) on the larger of the two terraces. It's the second building on the right, coming from the jetty.

CUYO ISLANDS
In the north Sulu Sea, set apart from the large Palawan main islands but still part of Palawan Province, the Cuyo Islands consist of 40 islands, forming the Cuyo Group in the south and the Quiniluban Group in the north. This island world, which has been scarcely touched by tourism, offers an excellent environment for diving and snorkelling, particularly in the reefs around Manamoc, Pamalican and Tinituan Islands. The diving areas around the islands of Alcisiras and Quiniluban, as well as Agutaya and Oco, are also impressive.

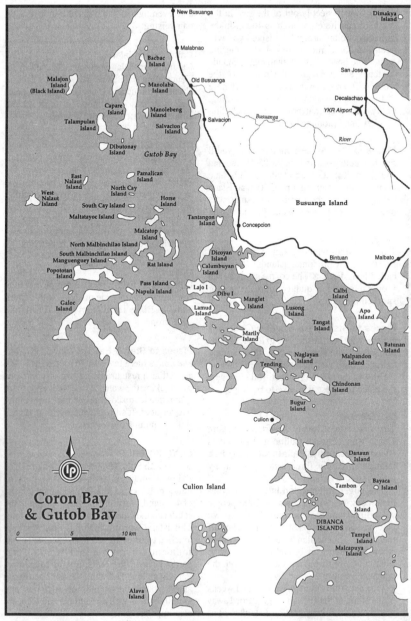

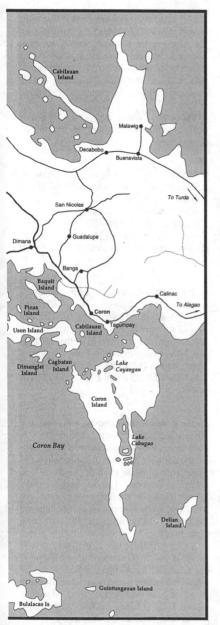

Manamoc Island

There is a broad, shallow lagoon in the south-west of this friendly island which welcomes guests who have a feeling for nature. Mt English, at 220m, is the highest point on the island; a bit of a challenge for hill-climbers, as there is no trail for the final stage of the climb. The coral reef surrounding the island is good for snorkelling. It runs quite some distance from the beach, so a small boat is required to get there.

Pamalican Island

This enchanting little island six km north-east of Manamoc Island belongs to the Soriano Group (the San Miguel Corporation), who have recently been getting involved in the tourism business. The extensive marine environment around the island has been declared a protected area, which means fishing and dropping anchor in this marine sanctuary are strictly forbidden.

Places to Stay The 1st rate *Amanpulo Resort* has cottages with air-con and bath for US$400 and $530. These superbly furnished buildings have living room, terrace, satellite TV, CD player and other goodies. Luxury is considered a necessity here. Savour the food in the restaurant after enjoying the swimming pool, tennis courts, diving, Hobie Cats and windsurfing. This must be the most exclusive resort in the Philippines, and it even has its own little airfield. Reservations can be made in Manila at the Amanpulo Resort (☎ 831 5876; fax 832 7964). A flight

Weeding Matter

Many of the Tinituan Island locals make their living by farming seaweed. The weed flourishes in underwater fields cultivated in the extensive neighbouring coral reefs. To protect these profitable plants, fishing with dynamite and poison is not tolerated in the waters around Tinituan Island. As a result, the underwater world can be viewed in all its pristine glory; snorkellers especially can usually make the most of perfect conditions here. ■

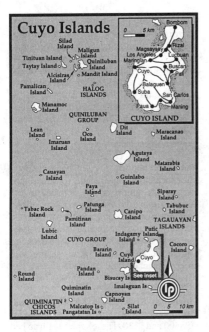

For economic reasons many Cuyonos have moved to Palawan where they make up the largest group of immigrants. Their economic, cultural, social and political influence on the entire province is considerable, and it is the main reason for Cuyo's solid reputation as a centre of traditional culture.

Tabunan Beach, between Cuyo and Suba, is probably one of the best beaches on Cuyo Island.

Places to Stay *Ireen's Lodge* is an unpretentious place, with basic rooms for P75/150. Its pub has a noisy jukebox.

The *Suba Resort*, a peaceful place on Tabunan Beach, charges P150 for a cottage. For more details contact Mr Milo Agustin at the Elda Store in Cuyo. A tricycle costs P10 per person.

Getting There & Away The Milagrosa Shipping Lines' MV *Milagrosa-J-Dos* sails from Puerto Princesa to Cuyo on the 1st, 11th and 21st of the month at noon (18 hours). The MV *Milagrosa-J-Tres* leaves on the 7th, 17th and 27th of each month at 4 pm. Departure from Cuyo to Puerto Princesa is on the 3rd, 7th, 13th, 17th, 23rd and 27th of each month at 2 pm.

Getting Around Transport between the islands is practically non-existent, and it is hard to avoid having to charter a boat. Generally, the only half-way reliable routes are those from the main town of Cuyo on Cuyo Island to Bisucay, Cocoro and Agutaya Islands. However, the direct route from Cuyo to the Quiniluban Group, especially between the months of December and March, can be quite rough.

It's a good idea to take along your own life jacket if you're thinking of island hopping, for example, from Agutaya Island via Dit Island to Tinituan Island (Concepcion). There is an irregular boat service from Manamoc Island, Tinituan Island and Quiniluban Island to San Jose, Mindoro Occidental.

can be arranged at Soriano Aviation (☎ 804 0760).

Tinituan Island

This island is one of the northernmost in the Cuyo archipelago. It is better known under the name Concepcion, after Barangay Concepcion, the largest town on the island on the south-east coast.

Anyone wishing to spend a few days on the little island of Tatay, with its blindingly white sand beach, just west of Tinituan, should ask the owner, Tony de los Angeles, for permission first.

Cuyo Island

The pleasant little town of Cuyo on Cuyo Island, with its population of about 30,000, has clean streets, lovely old houses and a fortress-church built in 1677 by the Spaniards as protection against the Moro pirates. The main sources of income are dried fish, copra and cashew nuts.

Health

State-owned hospitals and provincial private practices are often badly equipped. In case of an emergency, you should try to reach the nearest town and check into a private hospital. Dental treatment is adequate, at least in the towns and cities. In country areas on the other hand, dental problems are often simply solved by pulling the tooth.

You probably won't get any of the illnesses described here. However, you might be unlucky or need to help others, in which case the information in this section will be a useful starting point.

Travel health depends on your predeparture preparations, your day-to-day health care while travelling and how you handle any medical problem or emergency that does develop. While the list of potential dangers can seem quite frightening, with a little luck, some basic precautions and adequate information you will experience little more than an upset stomach.

Travel Health Guides

There are a number of books on travel health:

Staying Healthy in Asia, Africa & Latin America, Moon Publications. Probably the best all-round guide to carry, as it's compact but very detailed and well organised.

Travellers' Health, Dr Richard Dawood, OUP. Comprehensive, easy to read, authoritative and also highly recommended, although it's rather large to lug around.

Where There is No Doctor, David Werner, Hesperian Foundation. A very detailed guide intended for someone like a Peace Corps worker, going to work in an undeveloped country, rather than for the average traveller.

Travel with Children, Maureen Wheeler, Lonely Planet Publications. Includes basic advice on travel health for younger children.

Predeparture Preparations

Health Insurance A travel insurance policy to cover theft, loss and medical problems is a wise idea. There is a wide variety of policies and your travel agent will have recommendations.

The international student travel policies handled by STA or other student travel organisations are usually good value. Some policies offer lower and higher medical expense options, but the higher one is chiefly for countries like the USA which have extremely high medical costs. Check the small print:

1 Some policies specifically exclude 'dangerous activities' such as scuba diving, motorcycling, or even trekking. If such activities are on your agenda you don't want that sort of policy.

2 You may prefer a policy which pays doctors or hospitals direct rather than you having to pay on the spot and claim later. If you have to claim later, make sure you keep all documentation. Some policies ask you to call back (reverse charges) to a centre in your home country where an immediate assessment of your problem is made.

3 Check if the policy covers ambulances or an emergency flight home. If you have to stretch out you will need two seats and somebody has to pay for them!

Medical Kit A good medical kit is essential, particularly if you are going off the beaten track. Because you can't always get to your main luggage when travelling, for example on a flight, it's recommended that you keep a small medical kit in your hand luggage with medications such as pain-relieving tablets, diarrhoea tablets, eye drops and perhaps Alka Seltzer. Consult your doctor about individual medicines.

A possible kit list would include:

1 Aspirin or paracetamol (acetaminophen in the US) - for pain or fever.

2 Antihistamine (such as Benadryl) - useful as a decongestant for colds, allergies, to ease the itch from insect bites or stings or to help prevent motion sickness.

3 Antibiotics - useful if you're travelling off the beaten track. Choose a good broad-spectrum antibiotic.

4 Loperamide (eg Imodium) or Lomotil for diarrhoea

5 Rehydration mixture - for treatment of severe diarrhoea, this is particularly important if travelling with children. Lomotil is also useful.

6 Antiseptic such as povidone-iodine (eg Betadine) - for cuts and grazes.
7 Calamine lotion - to ease irritation from bites or stings.
8 Bandages and Band-aids - for minor injuries.
9 Scissors, tweezers and a thermometer (note that mercury thermometers are prohibited by airlines).
10 Insect repellent, sunscreen, Chapstick and water purification tablets.
11 Condoms

In the Philippines many medicines will generally be available over the counter and the price will be much cheaper than in the West, but they may be marketed under a different name. Some medicines are supposedly available only with a prescription form, but, it seems, it's not compulsory for every pharmacy to see one. Antibiotics are available in Philippine pharmacies without prescription. Manila is the best place to buy antibiotics.

As in other developing countries, be careful of buying drugs, particularly where the expiry date may have passed or correct storage conditions may not have been followed. It's possible that drugs which are no longer recommended, or have even been banned, in the West are still being dispensed. In the bigger cities you have a better chance of getting proper medicine at a clean, well-equipped and busy pharmacy rather than at a small store which sells cigarettes and Coca-Cola as well. In small towns choose a pharmacy connected to a hospital or recommended by a doctor.

Health Preparations Make sure you're healthy before you start travelling. If you are embarking on a long trip make sure your teeth are OK.

If you wear glasses take a spare pair and your prescription. Losing your glasses can be a real problem, although in many places you can get new spectacles made quickly, cheaply and competently.

If you require a particular medication take an adequate supply, as it may not be available locally. Take the prescription, with the generic rather than the brand name (which may not be locally available), as it will make getting replacements easier. It's a wise idea to have the prescription with you to show you legally use the medication.

Immunisations For the Philippines no immunisations are necessary, but the further off the beaten track you go the more necessary it is to take precautions. For the Philippines a yellow fever vaccination is necessary only if you're coming from an infected area. All vaccinations should be recorded on an International Health Certificate, available from your physician or government health department.

When organising your vaccinations make sure you plan ahead as some of them require an initial shot followed by a booster, while some vaccinations should not be given together.

The possible list of vaccinations includes:

Tetanus & Diphtheria After an initial course of injections, boosters are necessary every 10 years and protection is highly recommended.

Typhoid This is an important vaccination to have if you are travelling in areas where you think hygiene may be a problem. Available either as an injection or oral capsules.

Hepatitis A Havrix 1440 is a vaccination against this common travel-acquired illness. The vaccination provides long-term immunity (possibly more than 10 years) after an initial injection and a booster at six to 12 months. Gamma globulin is not a vaccination but a ready-made antibody. It which should be given as close as possible to departure as protection lasts for only two to six months.

Hepatitis B Travellers should consider the hepatitis B vaccine if you anticipate contact with blood or other bodily fluids, either as a health-care worker or through sexual contact with the local population. It involves three injections over three weeks and a booster at 12 months.

Basic Rules
Care in what you eat and drink is the most important health rule; stomach upsets are the most likely travel health problem but the majority of these upsets will be relatively minor. Don't become paranoid, trying the local food is part of the experience of travel after all.

Drinks Water in the cities should be safe to drink, but if you don't know for certain, always assume the worst. Ice from ice factories should be OK too, but sometimes it comes from tap water frozen in plastic bags, in which case you should be careful. Reputable brands of bottled water or soft drinks are generally fine. Take care with fruit juice, particularly if water may have been added. Milk should be treated with suspicion, as it is often unpasteurised. Boiled milk is fine if it is kept hygienically and yoghurt is always good. Tea or coffee should also be OK, since the water should have been boiled.

Water Purification The simplest way of purifying water is to boil it thoroughly. Technically this means boiling for 10 minutes, something which happens very rarely!

Simple filtering will not remove all dangerous organisms, so if you cannot boil water it should be treated chemically. Chlorine tablets (Puritabs, Steritabs or other brand names) will kill many but not all pathogens. Iodine is very effective in purifying water and is available in tablet form (such as Potable Aqua), but follow the directions carefully and remember that too much iodine can be harmful.

If you can't find tablets, tincture of iodine (2%) or iodine crystals can be used. Two drops of tincture of iodine per litre or quart of clear water is the recommended dosage; the treated water should be left to stand for 30 minutes before drinking.

Food Salads and fruit should be washed with purified water or peeled where possible. Ice cream is usually OK if the brand name is Magnolia, but beware of street vendors and of ice cream that has melted and been refrozen. Thoroughly cooked food is safest but not if it has been left to cool or been reheated. Take great care with shellfish and fish and avoid undercooked meat. In general, places that are packed with travellers or locals will be fine, while empty restaurants are dubious.

Nutrition If the food you are eating is of low nutritional value, if you're travelling hard and fast and therefore missing meals, or if you simply lose your appetite, you can soon start to lose weight and place your health at risk.

Make sure your diet is well balanced. Eggs, beans and nuts are all safe ways to obtain protein. Fruit you can peel (bananas, oranges or mandarins for example) is always safe and a good source of vitamins. Try to eat plenty of grains (eg, rice). Remember that although food is generally safer if it is cooked well, overcooked food loses much of its nutritional value. If your diet isn't well balanced or if your food intake is insufficient, it's a good idea to take vitamin and iron pills.

In hot climates make sure you drink enough - don't rely on feeling thirsty to indicate when you should drink. Not needing to urinate or very dark yellow urine is a danger sign. Always carry a water bottle with you on long trips to avoid dehydration. Excessive sweating can lead to loss of salt and therefore muscle cramping. Salt tablets are not a good idea as a means of preventing dehydration, but adding salt to food can help.

Medical Problems & Treatment

Self-diagnosis and treatment can be risky, so wherever possible seek qualified help. Although treatment dosages are given in this section, they are for emergency use only. Medical advice should be sought before administering any drugs.

An embassy or consulate can usually recommend a good place to go for such advice. So can five star hotels, although they often recommend doctors with five star prices. (This is when that medical insurance is really useful!) In some places standards of medical attention are so low that for some ailments the best advice is to get on a plane and go somewhere else.

Climatic & Geographical Considerations

Sunburn You can get sunburnt surprisingly quickly, even through cloud cover, use a sunscreen and take extra care to cover areas which don't normally see sun, eg, your feet.

A hat provides added protection, and you should also use zinc cream or some other barrier cream for your nose and lips. Calamine lotion is good for mild sunburn.

Prickly Heat Prickly heat is an itchy rash caused by excessive perspiration trapped under the skin. It usually strikes people who have just arrived in a hot climate and whose pores have not yet opened sufficiently to cope with greater sweating. Keeping cool but bathing often, using a mild talcum powder or even resorting to air-conditioning may help until you acclimatise.

Heat Exhaustion Dehydration or salt deficiency can cause heat exhaustion. Take time to acclimatise to high temperatures and make sure you get sufficient liquids. Salt deficiency is characterised by fatigue, lethargy, headaches, giddiness and muscle cramps, and in this case salt tablets may help. Vomiting or diarrhoea can deplete your liquid and salt levels. Anhydrotic heat exhaustion, caused by an inability to sweat, is quite rare.

Heat Stroke This serious, and sometimes fatal, condition can occur if the body's heat-regulating mechanism breaks down and the body temperature rises to dangerous levels. Long, continuous periods of exposure to high temperatures can leave you vulnerable to heat stroke. You should avoid excessive alcohol or strenuous activity when you first arrive in a hot climate.

The symptoms are feeling unwell, not sweating very much or at all and a high body temperature (39°C to 41°C or 102°F to 106°F). Where sweating has ceased, the skin becomes flushed and red. Severe, throbbing headaches and lack of co-ordination will also occur, and sufferers may become confused or aggressive. Eventually the victims will become delirious or convulse. Hospitalisation is essential, but meanwhile get patients out of the sun, remove their clothing, cover them with a wet sheet or towel and then fan them continually.

Fungal Infections Hot weather fungal infections are most likely to occur on the scalp, between the toes or fingers, in the groin and on the body (ringworm). You get ringworm (which is a fungal infection, not a worm) from infected animals or by walking on damp areas, like shower floors.

To prevent fungal infections wear loose, comfortable clothes, avoid artificial fibres, wash frequently and dry carefully. If you do get an infection, wash the infected area daily with a disinfectant or medicated soap and water, and rinse and dry well. Apply an anti-fungal powder like tolnifate (Tineaderm). Try to expose the infected area to air or sunlight as much as possible and wash all towels and underwear in hot water as well as changing them often.

Motion Sickness Eating lightly before and during a trip will reduce the chances of motion sickness. If you are prone to motion sickness try to find a place that minimises disturbance - near the wing on aircraft, close to midships on boats, near the centre on buses. Fresh air usually helps while reading, and cigarette smoke doesn't. Commercial antimotion-sickness preparations, which can cause drowsiness, have to be taken before the trip commences: when you're feeling sick it's too late. Ginger is a natural preventative and is available in capsule form.

Infectious Diseases

Diarrhoea A change of water, food or climate can all cause the runs; diarrhoea caused by contaminated food or water is more serious. Despite all your precautions you may still have a bout of mild travellers' diarrhoea, a few rushed toilet trips with no other symptoms is not indicative of a serious problem. Dehydration is the main danger with diarrhoea, particularly for children, so fluid replenishment is the number one treatment. Weak black tea with a little sugar, soda water, or soft drinks allowed to go flat and diluted 50% with water are all good. With severe diarrhoea a rehydrating solution is necessary to replace minerals and salts. You should stick to a bland diet as you recover.

Lomotil or Imodium can be used to bring relief from the symptoms, although they do not cure the problem. Only use these drugs if absolutely necessary - eg, if you *must* travel. For children Imodium is preferable, but do not use these drugs if the patient has a high fever or is severely dehydrated. Antibiotics, norfloxacin or ciprofloxacin, may be required for the treatment of severe diarrhoea but seek medical help as soon as possible.

Giardiasis The intestinal parasite (Giardia lamblia), is present in contaminated water. The symptoms are stomach cramps, nausea, a bloated stomach, watery, foul-smelling diarrhoea and frequent gas. Giardiasis can appear several weeks after you have been exposed to the parasite. The symptoms may disappear for a few days and then return; this can go on for several weeks. Tinidazole, known as Fasigyn or Metronidazole, known as Flagyl, are the recommended drugs.

Dysentery This extremely serious illness is caused by contaminated food or water and is characterised by severe diarrhoea, often with blood or mucus in the stool. There are two kinds of dysentery. Bacillary dysentery is characterised by a high fever and rapid development; headaches, vomiting and stomach pains are also symptoms. It generally does not last longer than a week, but it is highly contagious.

Amoebic dysentery is more gradual in developing, causes no fever or vomiting but is a more serious illness. It is not a self-limiting disease: it will persist until treated and can recur and cause long-term damage.

A stool test is necessary to diagnose which kind of dysentery you have, so you should seek medical help urgently. Where this is not possible the recommended drugs for dysentery are norfloxacin 400 mg twice daily for three days or ciprofloxacin 500 mg twice daily for five days. An alternative is co-trimoxazole 160/800 mg (Bactrim, Septrim, Resprim) twice daily for seven days. Do not use this drug if you have a sulpha allergy.

Cholera Outbreaks of cholera are often widely reported, so you can avoid such problem areas. The disease is characterised by a sudden onset of acute diarrhoea with 'rice water' stools, vomiting, muscular cramps and extreme weakness. You need medical help, but in the meantime, treat for dehydration (which can be extreme) and, if there is an appreciable delay in getting to hospital, begin taking tetracycline, 250 mg four times daily. It is not recommended for children under nine years nor for pregnant women.

Hepatitis Hepatitis A is the more common form of this disease and is spread by contaminated food or water. The first symptoms are fever, chills, headache, fatigue, feelings of weakness and aches and pains. This is followed by loss of appetite, nausea, vomiting, abdominal pain, dark urine, light-coloured faeces and jaundiced skin; the whites of the eyes may also turn yellow. In some cases there may just be a feeling of being unwell or tired, accompanied by loss of appetite, aches and pains and jaundiced skin. You should seek medical advice, but in general there is not much you can do apart from resting, drinking lots of fluids, eating lightly and avoiding fatty foods. People who have had hepatitis must forgo alcohol for six months after the illness, as hepatitis attacks the liver and it needs that amount of time to recover.

Hepatitis B is spread through sexual contact with an infected partner or through skin penetration. It could, for instance, be transmitted via dirty needles or blood transfusions. Avoid having your ears pierced, or tattoos or injections done in places where you have doubts about the sanitary conditions.

Typhoid Typhoid fever is a serious gut infection caused by contaminated water and food.

In its early stages typhoid resembles many other illnesses: sufferers may feel like they have a bad cold or flu on the way, as the early symptoms are headache, sore throat and a fever which rises a little each day until it is around 40°C (104°F) or more. The victim's pulse is often slow relative to the degree of fever present and gets slower as the fever rises, unlike a normal fever where the pulse increases. There may also be vomiting, diarrhoea or constipation.

In the second week the high fever and slow pulse continue and a few pink spots may appear on the body; trembling, delirium, weakness, weight loss and dehydration are other symptoms. If there are no further complications, the fever and other symptoms will slowly go during the third week. However, you must get medical help before this because pneumonia (acute infection of the lungs) or peritonitis (burst appendix) are common complications.

The fever should be treated by keeping the victim cool; dehydration should also be watched for. Chloramphenicol is the recommended antibiotic. The adult dosage is two 250 mg capsules, four times a day. Children aged between eight and 12 years should have half the adult dose; younger children should have one-third the adult dose.

Worms These parasites are most common in humid, tropical areas. They can live on unwashed vegetables or in undercooked meat or you can pick them up through your skin by walking barefoot. Infestations may not be obvious for some time, and, although they are generally not serious, they can cause severe health problems if left untreated. A stool test is necessary to pinpoint the problem and medication is often available over the counter. If you think you might have contracted worms sometime during your travels, it's not a bad idea to have a stool test when you get home.

Tetanus Tetanus occurs when a wound becomes infected by bacteria which live in the faeces of animals or people, so clean all cuts, punctures or animal bites. Tetanus is also known as lockjaw, and the first symptom may be discomfort in swallowing, or a stiffening of the jaw and neck; this is followed by painful convulsions of the jaw and whole body.

Rabies Any bite, scratch or even lick from an animal should be cleaned immediately and thoroughly. Scrub the area with soap and running water, and then clean with an alcohol solution. If there is any possibility that the animal is infected, medical help should be sought immediately.

Schistosomiasis Also known as bilharzia, this disease carried by minute worms is found in the southern Philippines. The larvae infect certain varieties of freshwater snails found in rivers, streams, lakes and particularly behind dams. The worms multiply and are eventually discharged into the water surrounding the snails.

They attach themselves to your intestines or bladder, where they produce large numbers of eggs. The worm enters through the skin, and the first symptom may be a tingling and sometimes a light rash around the area where it entered. Weeks later, when the worm is busy producing eggs, a high fever may develop. A general feeling of being unwell may be the first symptom; once the disease is established abdominal pain and blood in the urine are other signs. The infection often causes no symptoms until the disease is well established (several months to years after exposure) and damage to internal organs irreversible.

Avoiding swimming or bathing in fresh water where bilharzia is present is the main method of preventing the disease. Even deep water can be infected. If you do get wet, dry off quickly and dry your clothes as well. Seek medical attention if you think you have been exposed to the disease, a blood test is the most reliable means of determining whether you have contracted the disease.

Sexually Transmitted Diseases (STDs) Gonorrhoea and syphilis are the most common of these diseases; sores, blisters or rashes around the genitals, discharges or pain when urinating are common symptoms. Symptoms may be less marked or not observed at all in women. Syphilis symptoms eventually disappear completely, but the disease continues and can cause severe problems in later years.

The treatment of gonorrhoea and syphilis is by antibiotics.

There are numerous other STDs, for most of which effective treatment is available, though as yet there is no cure for herpes or HIV/AIDS. The latter is becoming more widespread in the Philippines, using condoms is the most effective means for preventing the transmission of the disease via sexual activity.

HIV/AIDS can also be spread through infected blood transfusions - note that most developing countries cannot afford to screen blood for transfusions. It can also be spread by dirty needles - vaccinations, acupuncture and tattooing can be as dangerous as intravenous drug use if the equipment is not clean. If you do need an injection, it may be a good idea to buy a new syringe from a pharmacy and ask the doctor to use it.

According to the Philippine Department of Health (DOH) there were 380 known AIDS cases in the country as of mid-1993. The number of HIV infected Filipinos at the time was estimated by the National AIDS Prevention Program to be 35,000 in all. Awareness of and knowledge about this illness are not yet widespread in the Philippines; the decision to use a condom is still mostly left up to the male partner.

Insect-Borne Diseases

Malaria This serious disease is spread by mosquito bites. Symptoms include headaches, fever, chills and sweating which may subside and recur. Without treatment malaria can develop more serious, potentially fatal effects.

If you are travelling on Palawan and Mindanao where malaria is more widespread than in other parts of the Philippines, it is extremely important to take malaria pills. These are available in various forms, so ask your doctor for advice.

Mosquitoes appear after dusk. Avoiding bites by covering bare skin and using an insect repellent will further reduce the risk of catching malaria. Insect screens on windows and mosquito nets on beds offer protection, as does burning a mosquito coil. Mosquitoes

may be attracted by perfume, aftershave or certain colours - light coloured clothes are generally better than dark. The risk of infection is higher in rural areas and during the wet season.

Dengue Fever There is no preventative drug available for this mosquito-spread disease; the main preventative measure is to avoid mosquito bites. A sudden onset of fever, headaches and severe joint and muscle pains are the first signs before a rash starts on the trunk of the body and spreads to the limbs and face. After a few more days, the fever will subside and recovery will begin. Serious complications are not common but recovery may be prolonged.

Cuts, Bites & Stings

Cuts & Scratches Skin punctures can easily become infected in hot climates and may be difficult to heal. Treat any cut with an antiseptic solution. Where possible avoid bandages and Band-aids, which can keep wounds wet. Coral cuts are notoriously slow to heal, as the coral injects a weak venom into the wound. Avoid coral cuts by wearing shoes when walking on reefs.

Bites & Stings Bee and wasp stings are usually painful rather than dangerous. Calamine lotion will give relief and ice packs will reduce the pain and swelling.

There are various fish and other sea creatures which have dangerous stings or bites or which are dangerous to eat. Again, local advice is the best suggestion.

Snakes To minimise your chances of being bitten, always wear boots, socks and long trousers when walking through undergrowth or rice paddies where snakes may be present. Don't put your hands into holes and crevices.

Snake bites do not cause instantaneous death and antivenins are usually available. Keep the victim calm and still, wrap the bitten limb tightly, as you would for a sprained ankle, and then attach a splint to immobilise it. Then seek medical help, if possible with the dead snake for identification. Don't attempt to catch the snake if there is even a remote possibility of being bitten again. Tourniquets and sucking out the poison are now comprehensively discredited.

Jellyfish Local advice is the best way of avoiding contact with these sea creatures with their stinging tentacles. Dousing in vinegar will deactivate any stingers which have not 'fired'. Calamine lotion, antihistamines and analgesics may reduce the reaction and relieve the pain.

Bedbugs & Lice Bedbugs live in various places, but particularly in dirty mattresses and bedding. Spots of blood on bedclothes or on the wall around the bed can be read as a suggestion to find another hotel. Bedbugs leave itchy bites in neat rows. Calamine lotion may help.

All lice cause itching and discomfort. They make themselves at home in your hair, your clothing, or in your pubic hair. You catch lice through direct contact with infected people or by sharing combs, clothing and the like. Powder or shampoo treatment will kill the lice and infected clothing should then be washed in very hot water.

Women's Health

Gynaecological Problems Poor diet, lowered resistance due to the use of antibiotics and even contraceptive pills can lead to vaginal infections when travelling in hot climates. Maintaining good hygiene and wearing skirts or loose-fitting trousers and cotton underwear will help to prevent infections.

Yeast infections, characterised by a rash, itch and discharge, can be treated with yoghurt, or a vinegar or lemon-juice douche. Nystatin, miconazole or clotrimazole pessaries are the usual medical prescription.

Pregnancy Most miscarriages occur during the first three months of pregnancy, so this is the riskiest time to travel. The last three months should be spent within reasonable distance of medical care, as serious problems can develop at this time. Pregnant women should avoid all unnecessary medication, but vaccinations and malarial prophylactics should still be taken where necessary. Additional care should be taken to prevent illness and attention should be paid to diet.

Contraceptive Pills & Tampons Contraceptive pills and tampons are available in the larger towns and in tourist areas, but it's still advisable to take some with you. Tampons are hard to come by, and indeed are hardly known of, so you need to give the pharmacy staff a good description of what it is you are after when you send them off to search the shelves!

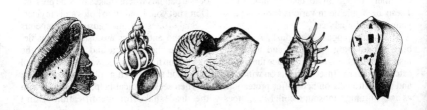

Index

MAPS

TEXT

LONELY PLANET PHRASEBOOKS

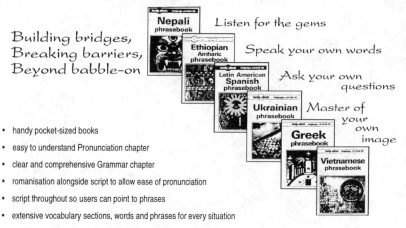

Building bridges,
Breaking barriers,
Beyond babble-on

Listen for the gems

Speak your own words

Ask your own questions

Master of your own image

- handy pocket-sized books
- easy to understand Pronunciation chapter
- clear and comprehensive Grammar chapter
- romanisation alongside script to allow ease of pronunciation
- script throughout so users can point to phrases
- extensive vocabulary sections, words and phrases for every situation
- full of cultural information and tips for the traveller

'...vital for a real DIY spirit and attitude in language learning' – Backpacker

'the phrasebooks have good cultural backgrounders and offer solid advice for challenging situations in remote locations' – San Francisco Examiner

'...they are unbeatable for their coverage of the world's more obscure languages' – The Geographical Magazine

---

Arabic (Egyptian)
Arabic (Moroccan)
Australia
  Australian English, Aboriginal and Torres Strait languages
Baltic States
  Estonian, Latvian, Lithuanian
Bengali
Brazilian
Burmese
Cantonese
Central Asia
Central Europe
  Czech, French, German, Hungarian, Italian and Slovak
Eastern Europe
  Bulgarian, Czech, Hungarian, Polish, Romanian and Slovak
Ethiopian (Amharic)
Fijian
French
German
Greek

Hindi/Urdu
Indonesian
Italian
Japanese
Korean
Lao
Latin American Spanish
Malay
Mandarin
Mediterranean Europe
  Albanian, Croatian, Greek, Italian, Macedonian, Maltese, Serbian and Slovene
Mongolian
Nepali
Papua New Guinea
Pilipino (Tagalog)
Quechua
Russian
Scandinavian Europe
  Danish, Finnish, Icelandic, Norwegian and Swedish

South-East Asia
  Burmese, Indonesian, Khmer, Lao, Malay, Tagalog (Pilipino), Thai and Vietnamese
Spanish (Castilian)
  Basque, Catalan and Galician
Sri Lanka
Swahili
Thai
Thai Hill Tribes
Tibetan
Turkish
Ukrainian
USA
  US English, Vernacular, Native American languages and Hawaiian
Vietnamese
Western Europe
  Basque, Catalan, Dutch, French, German, Irish, Italian, Portuguese, Scottish Gaelic, Spanish (Castilian) and Welsh

---

LONELY PLANET JOURNEYS

JOURNEYS is a unique collection of travel writing – published by the company that understands travel better than anyone else. It is a series for anyone who has ever experienced – or dreamed of – the magical moment when they encountered a strange culture or saw a place for the first time. They are tales to read while you're planning a trip, while you're on the road or while you're in an armchair, in front of a fire.

JOURNEYS books catch the spirit of a place, illuminate a culture, recount a crazy adventure, or introduce a fascinating way of life. They always entertain, and always enrich the experience of travel.

ISLANDS IN THE CLOUDS
Travels in the Highlands of New Guinea
Isabella Tree

Isabella Tree's remarkable journey takes us to the heart of the remote and beautiful Highlands of Papua New Guinea and Irian Jaya – one of the most extraordinary and dangerous regions on earth. Funny and tragic by turns, *Islands in the Clouds* is her moving story of the Highland people and the changes transforming their world.

Isabella Tree, who lives in England, has worked as a freelance journalist on a variety of newspapers and magazines, including a stint as senior travel correspondent for the *Evening Standard*. A fellow of the Royal Geographical Society, she has also written a biography of the Victorian ornithologist John Gould.

'One of the most accomplished travel writers to appear on the horizon for many years . . . the dialogue is brilliant' – **Eric Newby**

SEAN & DAVID'S LONG DRIVE
Sean Condon

Sean Condon is young, urban and a connoisseur of hair wax. He can't drive, and he doesn't really travel well. So when Sean and his friend David set out to explore Australia in a 1966 Ford Falcon, the result is a decidedly offbeat look at life on the road. Over 14,000 death-defying kilometres, our heroes check out the re-runs on tv, get fabulously drunk, listen to Neil Young cassettes and wonder why they ever left home.

Sean Condon lives in Melbourne. He played drums in several mediocre bands until he found his way into advertising and an above-average band called Boilersuit. *Sean & David's Long Drive* is his first book.

'Funny, pithy, kitsch and surreal . . . This book will do for Australia what Chernobyl did for Kiev, but hey you'll laugh as the stereotypes go boom'
– Time Out

LONELY PLANET TRAVEL ATLASES

Lonely Planet has long been famous for the number and quality of its guidebook maps. Now we've gone one step further and in conjunction with Steinhart Katzir Publishers produced a handy companion series: Lonely Planet travel atlases – maps of a country produced in book form.

Unlike other maps, which look good but lead travellers astray, our travel atlases have been researched on the road by Lonely Planet's experienced team of writers. All details are carefully checked to ensure the atlas corresponds with the equivalent Lonely Planet guidebook.

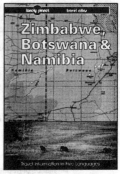

The handy atlas format means no holes, wrinkles, torn sections or constant folding and unfolding. These atlases can survive long periods on the road, unlike cumbersome fold-out maps. The comprehensive index ensures easy reference.

- full-colour throughout
- maps researched and checked by Lonely Planet authors
- place names correspond with Lonely Planet guidebooks
  – no confusing spelling differences
- legend and travelling information in English, French, German, Japanese and Spanish
- size: 230 x 160 mm

Available now:
Chile & Easter Island • Egypt • India & Bangladesh • Israel & the Palestinian Territories •Jordan, Syria & Lebanon • Kenya • Laos • Portugal • South Africa, Lesotho & Swaziland • Thailand • Turkey • Vietnam • Zimbabwe, Botswana & Namibia

---

LONELY PLANET TV SERIES & VIDEOS

Lonely Planet travel guides have been brought to life on television screens around the world. Like our guides, the programmes are based on the joy of independent travel, and look honestly at some of the most exciting, picturesque and frustrating places in the world. Each show is presented by one of three travellers from Australia, England or the USA and combines an innovative mixture of video, Super-8 film, atmospheric soundscapes and original music.

Videos of each episode – containing additional footage not shown on television – are available from good book and video shops, but the availability of individual videos varies with regional screening schedules.

Video destinations include: Alaska • American Rockies • Australia – The South-East • Baja California & the Copper Canyon • Brazil • Central Asia • Chile & Easter Island • Corsica, Sicily & Sardinia – The Mediterranean Islands • East Africa (Tanzania & Zanzibar) • Ecuador & the Galapagos Islands • Greenland & Iceland • Indonesia • Israel & the Sinai Desert • Jamaica • Japan • La Ruta Maya • Morocco • New York • North India • Pacific Islands (Fiji, Solomon Islands & Vanuatu) • South India • South West China • Turkey • Vietnam • West Africa • Zimbabwe, Botswana & Namibia

The Lonely Planet TV series is produced by:
Pilot Productions
The Old Studio
18 Middle Row
London W10 5AT UK

For video availability and ordering information contact your nearest Lonely Planet office.

Music from the TV series is available on CD & cassette.

PLANET TALK

Lonely Planet's FREE quarterly newsletter

We love hearing from you and think you'd like to hear from us.

When...is the right time to see reindeer in Finland?
Where...can you hear the best palm-wine music in Ghana?
How...do you get from Asunción to Areguá by steam train?
What...is the best way to see India?

For the answer to these and many other questions read PLANET TALK.

Every issue is packed with up-to-date travel news and advice including:

* a letter from Lonely Planet co-founders Tony and Maureen Wheeler
* go behind the scenes on the road with a Lonely Planet author
* feature article on an important and topical travel issue
* a selection of recent letters from travellers
* details on forthcoming Lonely Planet promotions
* complete list of Lonely Planet products

To join our mailing list contact any Lonely Planet office.

Also available: Lonely Planet T-shirts. 100% heavyweight cotton.

LONELY PLANET ONLINE

Get the latest travel information before you leave or while you're on the road

Whether you've just begun planning your next trip, or you're chasing down specific info on currency regulations or visa requirements, check out Lonely Planet Online for up-to-the minute travel information.

As well as travel profiles of your favourite destinations (including maps and photos), you'll find current reports from our researchers and other travellers, updates on health and visas, travel advisories, and discussion of the ecological and political issues you need to be aware of as you travel.

There's also an online travellers' forum where you can share your experience of life on the road, meet travel companions and ask other travellers for their recommendations and advice. We also have plenty of links to other online sites useful to independent travellers.

And of course we have a complete and up-to-date list of all Lonely Planet travel products including guides, phrasebooks, atlases, Journeys and videos and a simple online ordering facility if you can't find the book you want elsewhere.

www.lonelyplanet.com
or
AOL keyword: lp

LONELY PLANET PRODUCTS

Lonely Planet is known worldwide for publishing practical, reliable and no-nonsense travel information in our guides and on our web site. The Lonely Planet list covers just about every accessible part of the world. Currently there are nine series: *travel guides, shoestring guides, walking guides, city guides, phrasebooks, audio packs, travel atlases, Journeys – a unique collection of travel writing and Pisces Books - diving and snorkeling guides.*

EUROPE

Amsterdam • Austria • Baltic States phrasebook • Britain • Central Europe on a shoestring • Central Europe phrasebook • Czech & Slovak Republics • Denmark • Dublin • Eastern Europe on a shoestring • Eastern Europe phrasebook • Estonia, Latvia & Lithuania • Finland • France • French phrasebook • Germany • German phrasebook • Greece • Greek phrasebook • Hungary • Iceland, Greenland & the Faroe Islands • Ireland • Italian phrasebook • Italy • Lisbon • London • Mediterranean Europe on a shoestring • Mediterranean Europe phrasebook • Paris • Poland • Portugal • Portugal travel atlas • Prague • Romania & Moldova • Russia, Ukraine & Belarus • Russian phrasebook • Scandinavian & Baltic Europe on a shoestring • Scandinavian Europe phrasebook • Slovenia • Spain • Spanish phrasebook • St Petersburg • Switzerland • Trekking in Spain • Ukrainian phrasebook • Vienna • Walking in Britain • Walking in Italy • Walking in Switzerland • Western Europe on a shoestring • Western Europe phrasebook

Travel Literature: The Olive Grove: Travels in Greece

NORTH AMERICA

Alaska • Backpacking in Alaska • Baja California • California & Nevada • Canada • Chicago • Deep South • Florida • Hawaii • Honolulu • Los Angeles • Mexico • Mexico City • Miami • New England • New Orleans • New York City • New York, New Jersey & Pennsylvania • Pacific Northwest USA • Rocky Mountain States • San Francisco • Southwest USA • USA phrasebook • Washington, DC & the Capital Region

Travel Literature: Drive thru America

CENTRAL AMERICA & THE CARIBBEAN

•Bahamas and Turks & Caicos •Bermuda •Central America on a shoestring • Costa Rica • Cuba •Eastern Caribbean •Guatemala, Belize & Yucatán: La Ruta Maya • Jamaica

SOUTH AMERICA

Argentina, Uruguay & Paraguay • Bolivia • Brazil • Brazilian phrasebook • Buenos Aires • Chile & Easter Island • Chile & Easter Island travel atlas • Colombia • Ecuador & the Galápagos Islands • Latin American Spanish phrasebook • Peru • Quechua phrasebook • Rio de Janeiro • South America on a shoestring • Trekking in the Patagonian Andes • Venezuela

Travel Literature: Full Circle: A South American Journey

ISLANDS OF THE INDIAN OCEAN

Madagascar & Comoros • Maldives • Mauritius, Réunion & Seychelles

AFRICA

Africa - the South • Africa on a shoestring • Arabic (Moroccan) phrasebook • Cairo • Cape Town • Central Africa • East Africa • Egypt • Egypt travel atlas • Ethiopian (Amharic) phrasebook • Kenya • Kenya travel atlas • Malawi, Mozambique & Zambia • Morocco • North Africa • South Africa, Lesotho & Swaziland • South Africa, Lesotho & Swaziland travel atlas • Swahili phrasebook • Tunisia • Trekking in East Africa • West Africa • Zimbabwe, Botswana & Namibia • Zimbabwe, Botswana & Namibia travel atlas

Travel Literature: The Rainbird: A Central African Journey • Songs to an African Sunset: A Zimbabwean Story

MAIL ORDER

Lonely Planet products are distributed worldwide. They are also available by mail order from Lonely Planet, so if you have difficulty finding a title please write to us. North American and South American residents should write to 150 Linden St, Oakland CA 94607, USA; European and African residents should write to 10a Spring Place, London NW5 3BH; and residents of other countries to PO Box 617, Hawthorn, Victoria 3122, Australia.

NORTH-EAST ASIA

Beijing • Cantonese phrasebook • China • Hong Kong • Hong Kong, Macau & Guangzhou • Japan • Japanese phrasebook • Japanese audio pack • Korea • Korean phrasebook • Mandarin phrasebook • Mongolia • Mongolian phrasebook • North-East Asia on a shoestring • Seoul • Taiwan • Tibet • Tibet phrasebook • Tokyo

Travel Literature: Lost Japan

MIDDLE EAST & CENTRAL ASIA

Arab Gulf States • Arabic (Egyptian) phrasebook • Central Asia • Central Asia phrasebook • Iran • Israel & the Palestinian Territories • Israel & the Palestinian Territories travel atlas • Istanbul • Jerusalem • Jordan & Syria • Jordan, Syria & Lebanon travel atlas • Lebanon • Middle East • Turkey • Turkish phrasebook • Turkey travel atlas • Yemen

Travel Literature: The Gates of Damascus • Kingdom of the Film Stars: Journey into Jordan

ALSO AVAILABLE:

Brief Encounters • Travel with Children • Traveller's Tales

INDIAN SUBCONTINENT

Bangladesh • Bengali phrasebook • Delhi • Goa • Hindi/Urdu phrasebook • India • India & Bangladesh travel atlas • Indian Himalaya • Karakoram Highway • Nepal • Nepali phrasebook • Pakistan • Rajasthan • Sri Lanka • Sri Lanka phrasebook • Trekking in the Indian Himalaya • Trekking in the Karakoram & Hindukush • Trekking in the Nepal Himalaya

Travel Literature: In Rajasthan • Shopping for Buddhas

SOUTH-EAST ASIA

Bali & Lombok • Bangkok • Burmese phrasebook • Cambodia • Ho Chi Minh City • Indonesia • Indonesian phrasebook • Indonesian audio pack • Jakarta • Java • Laos • Lao phrasebook • Laos travel atlas • Malay phrasebook • Malaysia, Singapore & Brunei • Myanmar (Burma) • Philippines • Pilipino phrasebook • Singapore • South-East Asia on a shoestring • South-East Asia phrasebook • Thailand • Thailand's Islands & Beaches • Thailand travel atlas • Thai phrasebook • Thai audio pack • Thai Hill Tribes phrasebook • Vietnam • Vietnamese phrasebook • Vietnam travel atlas

AUSTRALIA & THE PACIFIC

Australia • Australian phrasebook • Bushwalking in Australia • Bushwalking in Papua New Guinea • Fiji • Fijian phrasebook • Islands of Australia's Great Barrier Reef • Melbourne • Micronesia • New Caledonia • New South Wales • New Zealand • Northern Territory • Outback Australia • Papua New Guinea • Papua New Guinea phrasebook • Queensland • Rarotonga & the Cook Islands • Samoa • Solomon Islands • South Australia • Sydney • Tahiti & French Polynesia • Tasmania • Tonga • Tramping in New Zealand • Vanuatu • Victoria • Western Australia

Travel Literature: Islands in the Clouds • Sean & David's Long Drive

ANTARCTICA

Antarctica

THE LONELY PLANET STORY

Lonely Planet published its first book in 1973 in response to the numerous 'How did you do it?' questions Maureen and Tony Wheeler were asked after driving, bussing, hitching, sailing and railing their way from England to Australia.

Written at a kitchen table and hand collated, trimmed and stapled, *Across Asia on the Cheap* became an instant local bestseller, inspiring thoughts of another book.

Eighteen months in South-East Asia resulted in their second guide, *South-East Asia on a shoestring*, which they put together in a backstreet Chinese hotel in Singapore in 1975. The 'yellow bible', as it quickly became known to backpackers around the world, soon became *the* guide to the region. It has sold well over half a million copies and is now in its 9th edition, still retaining its familiar yellow cover.

Today there are over 240 titles, including travel guides, walking guides, language kits & phrasebooks, travel atlases and travel literature. The company is the largest independent travel publisher in the world. Although Lonely Planet initially specialised in guides to Asia, today there are few corners of the globe that have not been covered.

The emphasis continues to be on travel for independent travellers. Tony and Maureen still travel for several months of each year and play an active part in the writing, updating and quality control of Lonely Planet's guides.

They have been joined by over 70 authors and 170 staff at our offices in Melbourne (Australia), Oakland (USA), London (UK) and Paris (France). Travellers themselves also make a valuable contribution to the guides through the feedback we receive in thousands of letters each year and on our web site.

The people at Lonely Planet strongly believe that travellers can make a positive contribution to the countries they visit, both through their appreciation of the countries' culture, wildlife and natural features, and through the money they spend. In addition, the company makes a direct contribution to the countries and regions it covers. Since 1986 a percentage of the income from each book has been donated to ventures such as famine relief in Africa; aid projects in India; agricultural projects in Central America; Greenpeace's efforts to halt French nuclear testing in the Pacific; and Amnesty International.

'I hope we send people out with the right attitude about travel. You realise when you travel that there are so many different perspectives about the world, so we hope these books will make people more interested in what they see. Guidebooks can't really guide people. All you can do is point them in the right direction.'

– Tony Wheeler

lonely planet

LONELY PLANET PUBLICATIONS

Australia
PO Box 617, Hawthorn 3122, Victoria
tel: (03) 9819 1877 fax: (03) 9819 6459
e-mail: talk2us@lonelyplanet.com.au

USA
150 Linden St
Oakland, CA 94607
tel: (510) 893 8555 TOLL FREE: 800 275-8555
fax: (510) 893 8563
e-mail: info@lonelyplanet.com

UK
10a Spring Place,
London NW5 3BH
tel: (0171) 428 4800 fax: (0171) 428 4828
e-mail: go@lonelyplanet.co.uk

France:
71 bis rue du Cardinal Lemoine, 75005 Paris
tel: 01 44 32 06 20 fax: 01 46 34 72 55
e-mail: bip@lonelyplanet.fr

World Wide Web: http://www.lonelyplanet.com
or *AOL keyword: lp*